Yard Life:
Exposé, Real Life
Inside of Prison

Sodo Austin

Cadmus Publishing
www.cadmuspublishing.com

Foreword

Change is good, but not easy

By Lonnie D. Perkins

Over the years, I have become known as "Hoover Lon" to most people aside from my family and childhood friends. That name is associated with being loyal to a fault! I have put my loyalties for un-worthy things and people before the very people whose D.N.A. matches my own. I was simply "Doing Me", selfishly to the fullest, because I was "Representing"! Looking back on my life inside these walls and electric fences, I now recognize that, I have not been caring or having a lack of regard as a coping mechanism, because I was quick to handle everything in the same physical fashion, which was like a universal language no matter where you were from on this planet!!!!

I sincerely called myself walking a straight line forward, because walking backwards wasn't an option, while in reality, looking on my past, I recognize that I was simply walking in circles. I was destined to repeat the same errors over and over again. The same as walking around the track on the yard, footprints over-lapping until they eventually line up perfectly, because with practice, we all got good at things, including errors, because we're walking that straight line, "In our minds"! It literally took the weight of reality to fall on my head for me to snap out of it. My mom has been telling me since I was young that "I was hard headed". Then, as an adult, I learned firsthand that I was "hard headed" when it proved hard enough to stop a bullet and then I thought that, "Mom was telling the truth."

The biggest wakeup call that shook me to my core happened when I understood that so much has changed right before my eyes! But, in all actuality, I now know that the change I was seeing was through my own eyes so I tried to rationalize what this all meant. After all, having a "lack of regard for things" meant looking past things. But suddenly, so many things that I had seen and heard now bother me in ways that it never once did! This was the moment that I recognized that I had changed and I cared. That's why I was agitated by some of the weirdest things. So, for the first time in a long time, I followed my first mind and disassociated myself from my sources of agitation. I now try not to so much as be in the same vicinity of those agitations and I'm committed to standing firm on that decision and it's a constant struggle, one that the "Me of old" never wasted one "iota" of energy giving half a thought on.

It's not easy to give up being judgmental of others, even though when I was in my 20's I was nothing like these characters. Now the more comfortable that I become, doing what's best for myself and the people who truly care about me and love me, regardless of my faults. I no longer see myself as being loyal to a fault because now investing time and energy towards changing the way that I think and the way that I act, I now think of my future that's beyond these facilities. There are so many things that I want to do and there are so many people that I want to show my new definition or love and loyalty, (my family). Hey, call me a late bloomer, I'll accept that title. But the fact of the matter is that, I'm really onto something with changing the way that I think. It's a challenge at times, but I'm motivated to give the new me a chance to live his best life!!!! No doubt that I am worth it and I embrace the challenge that I have issued to myself, "To be loyal to my loved ones and myself!!!!"

"Loyal Lon" 2020

Introduction

"Yard Life" are tales that derived from actual prison life experiences, events, and struggles as I've ventured through the maze in this unbalanced world, as I know it to be and have experience it this far 18 years into my life sentence. The different trials and tribulations I've been through walking on the different prison yards, the politics, the violence, and the mental and emotional roller coasters. It also gives you a look into my street life as an active gang banger, my childhood and the different relationships. By way of telling what we call "war stories" behind the wall, to the different cellmates and those I've met and have bonded with over the many years of my incarceration. This is the everyday yard life existence, politics, violence, mental and emotional roller coasters, and war stories.

"Yard Life" tales and stories start in reverse, from High Desert State Prison (my current facility and location) considered the most dangerous, violent, and deadliest 180 housing design prison in California right now. The very graphic tales and stories are uncut, raw, violent, edgy, vivid, and full of emotion. As I've made my journey through this prison maze on the various yards I've landed and walked on, I quickly learned they're no two yards the same as far as how they function or the individuals on them. Every yard has its own challenges and situations from politics to the economy. From Tehachapi's 180 Level 4 yard until now High Desert 180 Level 4 yard. I've made it a point to be aware and mindful of my surroundings and to never take things or situations for granted. To always remain vigilant and relentless in my walk and to make it a point to also not fuck with undesirables (dudes with no moral compass or values and who are genuinely bullshit) whom I've dubbed autobots. An autobot is also someone who's a follower. His following the next man comes natural. He doesn't think or speak for himself. I'm far from an autobot. You can't dictate my program or tell me how to think or talk. At the end of the day, I'm going to do and be me and stand on My beliefs, My morals, and My principles. Against all odds, I've also made it a point to only socialize with those who stand for something and are on the side of right, win, lose, or draw. Those who are willing to do what it takes to survive in this maze, against all odds and can be counted on, those who are thrust worthy and loyal, someone who knows how to be a friend, respecting and valuing the friendship. To fuck with those who let real things and real situations propel them in conjunction with motivation that fuels their desire to move the way they do. I'll be breaking down my over standing (understanding) of how I believed dirty politics and yard politicians worked.

From my belief, yard politicians engage in a lot of self made interest. It's generally about their interest and trying to remove anything or anyone they deem a threat to their cause at that particular time. They don't care if they knew you 30 years or 50, they would play ball on you (physically harm you) if the interest changed. They're in a mindset I couldn't get too. In a mode, I couldn't be in. They're not above being dirty or playing dirty which is something that's common with them and getting the next man to go along with whatever the objective is which is the autobot. If the autobot doesn't comply, the standard practice is to turn on them. You challenge a politician or go against them and you'll be brought up on manufactured charges and removed. One of two things will happen, one lie. It takes two people to lie, one to tell the lie and the other one to confirm it. That's a common one nowadays. The second one, they'll dig up a present issue that's been basically resolved years ago. Keep in mind, it has to be justified as to why you were removed, the narrative has to fit and make sense, that's a mindset, a mode, it's a culture, in prison. Love for you, loyalty to you, and respect for you is a mirage. It doesn't exist, as long as an interest exists.

I can't say all yard politicians are of bad intent and have bad intentions, but a lot are and do. You do leave the exception to the rule, there are those who have good intentions and do play fair. His basic push is to make sure mutha fuckas are playing by the rules and respecting them, not jeopardizing the tribe (homies) as a whole. He has no objectives or hidden agendas, he's not out to back door anyone or politic them, he has no political ambitions. He's the voice and enforces the rules, plain and simple. You can't knock a dude wanting order. Who wants chaos and his homies running amok with no rules? That's not in the best interest or good for anyone, that's a crash waiting to happen, that's simply liability, just a matter of time. All liabilities have to be removed. Even I overstand that, it's no getting around it. That's just common sense and practical.

That's just clean reasonable politics, nothing dirty or foul about that. If politics are in play, I rather it be productive than not (being bad or backwards). This politician you don't have to keep him in your peripheral vision. He's not looking to get fly on you (harm you). He doesn't have to check his moral program because his compass isn't off. I personally looked at all politicians the same, feeling as though they were all bullshit dudes and always on some dirty shit. My views changed once I was able to differentiate the types for myself. There are always two types, real dudes and bullshit dudes, and from all tribes, Crips, Bloods, etc. That's just one of life's realities, the good and the bad. It's designed that way. It's just up to the individual to be able to separate the two and distance himself without making himself a target of the bullshit. It's all in how you navigate, but always be mindful of your surroundings objectively. They're constantly playing chess. You may think I'm putting a 10 on it (exaggerating), but remember this, the root of it, is official.

Fucking with them, they'll leave you believing that the negative equals realistic and the positive equals unrealistic. Your whole thought process, values, and morals will be distorted, lost in an identity that isn't yours and finding yourself being led and misled, conforming and perpetuating the dirty shit. Contaminated, with no shame for their insidious conduct. For the most part, that's all that's about, all to most things and conduct, dirty, internal, and external. Knocking each other down and knocking those down around them that's not playing their game or in their mode. I can hear them now, "Don't watch me. Watch the T.V." Meaning, "Why are you watching my dirt shit. I have to watch you. You don't mean me any good my guy, or those I fuck with." I've always tried every conceivable alibi within the realm of reason to justify my thoughts, but they're justifiable and justifiably so.

I see the blows not matching the daps or the smiles, dudes are foul. Lulling those into a false sense of security, how can I not have a preconceived notion? I've seen you work and maneuver, I know your capabilities and your ability. My honesty in my words and thoughts are vividly expressed, which leave me exposed, as I go into my sometimes dark mental and deeply bruised psyche. My bitterness, pain, and frustrations keep me moving on raw emotion as I navigate my way, though I overstand what it imprisons (life, love and forgiveness). The contents of "Yard Life" are an intriguing bundle of my moods. Sometimes warm and funny, yet very reflective, offensive, challenging and defensive, depending on the subject matter I'm bringing forth. "Yard Life" is based on real things and real situations as it pertained to me and my journey. As I've walked in my boots on the yard, mine alone. Our walk on the yard could never be the same; our boots aren't the same size. As noted, any and everything spoken on though, throughout this journey has been stamped in the books already and is in ink (documented, and the incidents and persons involved were in the open for all to see).

It's all yard knowledge and has already taken place. I'm not exposing or speaking on anything that hasn't already been acknowledged or exposed with my incidences included that part! This ride you're taking with me is no doubt a rollercoaster and a high one at times (smoke in the air). You'll get to know, learn and overstand the journey. The maze and the man behind the pen as it is with me, through my visual lenses vicariously. Enjoy the ride. One more thing I'd like to make clear before you read further into my effort. I have reconstructed some dialogue based on my not remembering everything verbatim.

"SoDo"

"I believe Allah is a giver and a writer, and his gifts to humanity are our talents. When we nurture and cultivate these talents through time, they transcend into passions. We can begin to evolve into writers, and as writers with every new creation we re-create. We are complimenting the creator with creation, through creation . . . and the cycle continues."

ACKNOWLEDGEMENTS

First and foremost, I want to thank and acknowledge the All Knowing and All Giving Allah, My Lord and Savior, for blessing me with the know-how, determination and ability to compose my words and thoughts, putting them on paper. Without you, "Yard Life" wouldn't be possible at all. I want to acknowledge my uncle, Johnny Washington (RIP), no longer here on Earth, but will forever remain in my heart, who's always been an avid supporter and believer of me until his death win, lose, or draw. I will love you always, pop. I want to acknowledge my Aunt Martha, who's been more to me than an aunt. You've always been a second mother to me, and I've always been your black sheep child, also one of my biggest avid supporters and believer of me, right or wrong. I will forever love and appreciate you for being there for me and standing by me, you and Uncle Johnny. I want to acknowledge my giantest avid supporter and believer of me, my Mother Dorothy Ann Diggs.

Mama, I know I've put you through it emotionally and at times physically, with the running around you had to do due to my shenanigans and episodes over my life, going back and forth to LP (Los Padrinos Juvenile Hall), Central Juvenile Hall, Y.A. (Youth Authority), to the pen (prison). You've always been there for me. A gesture or one of the many thoughtful and selfless things you do or have done throughout this/that time. I wish there was so much more that I could do or say to show you my sincerest gratitude and appreciation for you and towards you. I wanted to take this opportunity though to put it on blast. To say that everything you do and have done is and has always been noticed, much appreciated, and never took/taken for granted.

I love you and appreciate you for the kindness and dedication you've show to me. Bullet proof love and bullet proof appreciation. I dedicate to you "Greetings Mama", the song off my "Bitterology" CD from '02. This verse: "Greetings Mama/It's a notation/From your son in jail/Apologizing for your tears, fears and constant hell/I put you through/Hanging out with my homies a lot/Keeping you spooked/Watching the news when guns rang on the block/Barely can take it/Stressing fearing I'm shot/On your knees praying/Hoping I make it back to the spot/Same page/Different days/Wishing it stop/Facing three/Plus a new beef/Eluding the cops . . ."

I love you Mama. I want to acknowledge my cuzzo Christopher L. Newton Sr., for becoming an avid supporter and not turning your back on me like the rest of the so-called family had and have fucked with me constantly over the years, on the level you have, its much much appreciation, respect, and love cuzzo. I will always have major love for you my guy, real niggah shit! I want to acknowledge my God Brother Lil Trey Deee (Darren Shanks), you already know what it is bro. I have nothing but major love and respect for you. Hands down you've always been a real one and a man of your word. We've walked on the yard together and endured the struggles as we know and know them to be on this side of the maze, yet, remained solid, relentless, and vigilant in our push as Long Beach Crips and men. I love you Niggah! I want to acknowledge my guy Hoova-Lon for contributing the forward, to this project and adding more insight to the mindset of the incarcerated and his ability to be aware and conscious. I also want to acknowledge the newly formed friendship bond and connection between us. A friend indeed, one you would want to have. A real solid and loyal guy who I deem plays fair and by the rules. Much love, respect, and loyalty.

I would also like to acknowledge the ones I've condoned who never fucked with me during my struggle and times of need. Basically wrote me off, leaving me for dead. So with that, fuck you, fuck the breaths you breathe, your values, morals and belief system. It took this incarceration to really realize and overstand what this we had wasn't real but merely a figment of my imagination, nor was your loyalty, smiles, concerns, laughter, or tears real, also a figment of my imagination which you've confirmed, there is no illusion. I appreciate you the most. Lastly, to my haters, keep the hate up and my name in your mouth. I need and enjoy the promo. Trust and believe I appreciate you.

"Allah, please keep watch over me, as I ready myself for yet another day behind these walls of uncertainty, for temptation and evil lurk constantly amongst unguided and lost men. Being dressed in your armor I'm protected and I know I will, with ease, defend against these dangers, unknown or otherwise, in battle, against each and every attack. In your name, I offer this prayer.

Amen."

ABOUT THE AUTHOR

Esteemed Greetings,

Hopefully these paragraphs greet you in the best of health as well as a strong positive mind frame, as I do my best to compose a brief combination of words to best describe myself. My pen pseudonym is SoDo Austin. I was born in 1971 to Dorothy Diggs and Tony McClinton on September 6th, in Dominguez Valley Hospital in Long Beach California (the hospital no longer exists), under the zodiac sign of Virgo where I was raised in the 70's and 80's as a native. It's where I began running in the streets and being involved in various criminal acts (gang banging, selling street pharmaceuticals from crack cocaine to marijuana, and robbery), starting at the age of 14, which ultimately led me to being incarcerated, it was a revolving door.

I started going to juvenile hall, L.P. (Los Padrinos) and Central, both Los Angeles County Juvenile Hall Facilities. Shortly after, I graduated to C.Y.A. (California Youth Authority), being charged as an adult at the age of 16. It wasn't long after that 3 year sentence I found my way into the California Department of Corrections (C.D.C.) doing my first prison number (E02459) in 1991 at the age of 20. A number I was initially given at the age of 16, when I was charged as an adult for a robbery spree, I went on and was sent to C.Y.A. I've never been to any Los Angeles County Youth Camps. I bypassed them. My activities continued after I was released from prison and having discharged my prison number, picking up a fresh one (V73507) after being struck out (three strikes) and given a lengthy life sentence, which I'm currently 18 years into. It's no one's fault but my own. I played with the game and this is the result of it (Mama tried).

I accept complete responsibility for my own actions. It was my walk to walk and my path to take. I knew the risk and yet shot my shot. I believe (my belief) some people's destinies are already destined and prewritten. It just has to be played out over the predetermined time. Sometimes it's just decided for you. As with fate having a way of changing the course of your life when you're stopped at a fork in the road, it's been decided. Allah knows all and it's him and him alone who'll decide how my chapter ends. It's in his hands. Whatever he has in store for me, beyond my 50 years on this earth, it will manifest itself in due times. Until then, I'll continue to do and be me and hopefully find love as I continue to walk and exist on these yards, in these lines, in this unbalanced maze we call prison. Amongst convicts and inmates I'll also continue to stand on what's right over wrong, staying vigilant and relentless in my pursuit of continued morality and values, compromising neither.

In advance, I would like to thank you for having an interest in me and a vast curiosity which was enough to have you interested in reading "Yard Life".

"SoDo"

TABLE OF CONTENTS

1

D amn, ain't this a bitch! C.D.C. has me way out of the way (far from southern California home), in this lost civilization where it snows. I haven't been in the snow since being in Tehachapi, the beginning of my time from '05 to '08. I'm sitting in High Desert State Prison in Lassen County, "No Man's Land". This is just what it is being from Long Beach, California (Los Angeles County). Shit, it's basically "No Man's Land" to anyone from down south (southern California), Especially L.A. County, regardless of your race or tribe (affiliation), no man's land is no man's land. If you were getting visits, it's pretty much a wrap for you now, except for those chosen few that are fortunate to still have someone in their life, holding them down, life sentence and all. I've heard a lot about this spot over the years, never anything good.

This was mainly at a time when this spot was considered to be a Wood spot (white inmate). Basically, their playing field with home court advantage. It wasn't a good spot to be in being black. The deck was stacked but as always, that was nothing new. Blacks have always been up against it with the deck being stacked, but always prevail. I've always heard how active High Desert was and is and here I am (as recent as 2019 being in San Quentin ADSEG Overflow). I would be lying in my bunk in my single man cell, listening to dudes that were in High Desert and was there because they were waiting to go back. They were just out for court and Quentin was the pit-stop. I would hear them talking over the tier about how bullshit High Desert was, how far it was and basically what was going on there. None of the individuals that were talking all expressed they didn't want to go back and wish they could be rerouted elsewhere. I'm lying there thinking, "I'm glad I'm not going to that mutha fucka."

They were like, "It's cold and depressing." Though it's changed over the years, it's still active. Super! When I first drove up, I was told High Desert wasn't as turned up (active) as it once was, but I can't tell. Looking back now, the dude who was telling me this, he was out of the way, wasn't running with a tribe, basically a civilian (non-affiliated). His only chance of getting into something is if something popped off racially and he happened to be on the yard. He didn't have any worries as far as political. I haven't really heard of or seen civilians being politicked. Don't get me wrong, it does and has happened. As far as some are concerned, prey is prey, especially if the interest is beneficial. My short time here, I've gotten a cold reality check of where it is that I actually am, a level 4-180. It's been a minute since I've been in this type of setting and environment. It's real in the field. It's nothing to lose your life if you don't watch it. Ball is being played (violence with weapons). After being in Solano for 5 years it's a culture shock, whole different vibe, environment and mood.

After being on some super laid back shit, it's too easy to lose your way. Based on falling into how relaxed and comfortable a level 3 is, and can be especially not having been on a level 4 in a long length of time, sometimes you do lose your way. Every now and then though, you'll get your shit woke up (reality check) by seeing something that'll have you like, "Oh, yeah, I am in prison" when it's all said and done. Some level 3s are just as active as a level 4, shit does go sideways, and will get ugly, don't be fooled. As for 50 Land, it does have its moments, especially with the other races, their line pushing (politics) works a lot differently from ours (Blacks), and their tolerance for certain shit is zero, when it comes to their politics and policies, it's no secret. They're for the most part pushing as one, on one accord.

As my guy was saying, no doubt, one of the biggest obstacles when dealing with a lot of tribes (gangs/sets) as far as Blacks are concerned, it leads and contributes to a lack of unity when some feel that they aren't properly being represented, and of course there's always that ole saying complex amongst us Blacks. "Niggahs can't speak for us." This is such and such, whether it's Long Beach, L.A., or wherever, nonsense that leads us as a whole back to square one. When it comes to issues of race, there is no such thing as that's on, that tribe, and it shouldn't be, my opinion. For the simple fact, it's a cop-out, the biggest cop-out there is since anything done that crosses racial lines will involve us all. Not to play on anyone's ego, but we're always quick to punch on our own, even though sometimes it's necessary, but yet hesitate when it comes to letting our nuts hang in another direction. It's always suggested that we unify and stand firm as one unit and tighten up without disunity of contradicting each other, because many voices talking at the same time drown each other out and the message gets lost in translation, real talk.

At the end of the day, you have to respect it for what it is and as it is. I'm a realist and strictly about real things and real situations. By no means am I a politician, though I follow the rules and guide lines set based on my representing a tribe. I represent my city and my homies, therefore I fall in where I fit in. All the dirty politics and faulty shit that comes along with this shit, I'm not with, for or about. That's just not my make-up. When you lie long enough and loud enough, dudes will tend to believe it, especially autobots. That's why bullshit dudes succeed in their shenanigans, most of the time, playing dirty and being with the antics, but it shows time and time again though that consequences of others, dong the same shit, don't deter them from continuing down that path, as if they have immunity, or just above being DP'ed (physically disciplined). I'm going to always stand and be for the right side of a situation. Right is right, wrong is wrong, and bullshit ain't nothing. Outside of that, dudes are horse playing (playing games). Like these dudes running around on these yards, always looking to throw their hands up when a serious situation comes about. Quick to say "we can get down" (fight), "we can catch that fade" (we can fight), "Niggah, you're horse playing" when the other side comes (other race). They're about that life, they're playing ball, its weapon play, period, make no mistake. Best believe they're not horse playing, which we as Blacks (fuck the gang aspect) have seen far too many and way too many examples of how the other side moves and naturally operates (second nature).

Moving a long, I've just finished doing a 17 month SHU program (Segregated housing unit AKA the hole or sandbox) only doing 9 months of it. Well, 9 months and some change, just a little over 9 months. I never actually made it to the SHU. I basically did it between two ADSEGs (Administrative Segregation Units, AKA also the hole or sandbox). I caught a battery with a weapon on an inmate, a whole other case in April of 2019. At first they were talking about I was being charged with an attempted murder, and then it was bumped down to just a battery with a weapon on an inmate. When I was in the cage, in the program office (sub-station) waiting to be interviewed and sent to the sandbox, a police (C/O, Correctional Officer) came to the cage I was in and read me my Miranda rights and went through the motion, followed by, "You want to make a statement?"

. . . "Nah-uh" (no) . . .

"Next!" The police went on to explain to me why the charge changed, doing his due diligence. It was due in part to where I stabbed my victim, in his neck, and the distance away from an artery. Then shot a joke, saying the change was the lesser of two evils. After being here a little over a week or so, I met a few heads on the yard, as I attempted to adjust to this environment and those around me. Trying to see who's who and what's what for myself, feel shit out. Survey the yard and the dynamics, off top though, I wasn't feeling a lot of these dudes, so with that, I know a distance must be kept though I'm respectful and cordial to all. As a man, you have that coming as a courtesy, but it don't mean, I fuck with you, or will fuck with you beyond a dap and a "what up". There's nothing to be read into that's all it is, a dap and a "what up", especially when my bullshit Niggah detector goes off, like a metal detector.

A couple of dudes that I've hollered at (talked to) pulled my coat to bits and pieces of the different shenanigans that goes on around here and who the main culprits are, autobots included, though too, I'm always mindful of the source and character of the individual doing the coat pulling, feel me. For all I know, he could be a salty actor or hater attempting to try to poison me, but I don't rock like that, I judge shit and situations for myself unless for certain, the source is solid and the character of that person is flawless as far as his push. I would have to know his intentions and his get-down (actions) as a good guy. Outside of that, I'll take it in and process it, for what and as it is. I don't allow the next man to dictate my "who I fuck with or choose to fuck with" program. That's all the way out!

Homie or no homie, I don't do the autobotism. When I first landed on the yard from R and R (receiving and release), I landed on D-Yard in building 6, in the cell with a young Crip from Hub and Dub (Compton and Watts). He was from Watts 99 (nine-nine) mafia named Ace. He appeared to be a solid and straight young homie, who himself had just gotten out of the sandbox for putting some work in (went on a DP) a day before I landed. I was in cell 226 with him in D6-C-section. Young homie wasn't on any funny shit with me, though. I was fresh off the bus and had no paper work (papers showing why I was incarcerated and how I landed in High Desert not coming from a reception yard).

He welcomed me with open arms and blessing me (giving me) with the necessities: soap, deodorant, and shower shoes, along with some toothpaste. He also got at the police working in the building tower for me about letting me take a shower because I had been on that hot ass bus for hours, which I was allowed to do. I could've took a bird bath (a wash up in the sink) hitting my vitals, ass and nuts, underarms, and feet. I had no problem with it had that been the case, but why, if you can hop in the water and do what you do. Either way though, I was touching some, be it a shower or bird bath smelling like hot dog water. We conversed for a while before calling it a warp for the night. He was kind of giving me a bar of how dudes operated around here. The first thing he said though was, "Ain't no secrets around here. Mutha fuckas know everything and everybody's business." I took that as dudes around here don't mind their business and have nothing else better to do.

He also let me know as well that I had a few Long Beach homies on the yard, but on the lower yard which consisted of buildings 1-4. I'm on the upper yard buildings 5-8. He told me about the homie Dirty Mike from 20's, and the homie Young Ace Capone from Insane (Young). He didn't mention another homie, besides those two. I met a few other Blacks in the section. It wasn't that many, as it never is, being outnumbered by Hispanics. It's always Hispanics with the numbers. I met a couple of cool Bay Area dudes that was straight (alright), Hersh and June, along with a few Damu's (Bloods), Mad Face and J. Smash from Swan Bloods and Baby Ghost from Ghost Town.

I also met Squeek from 60's. He was straight too. He was the first person to mention something about paper work. It was more or less, "Yeah homie, make sure when you get your shit (property) you show your 'work' (paperwork). Niggahs need to know how you got here and where you came from, because dudes be sliding through (getting by without showing anything)." I was like, off top, that's the first thing I do anywhere I land. I'm very in synch with the formality. No problem with it champ. I also met Snake from East Coast 1200 Block when he came to the cell looking for me cellie (cellmate) Ace who had moved a couple of days after I got in the cell with him. He had had that move in the works before I pulled up. Actually he was supposed to have moved before I got here but the prison had been on lock down due to some metal coming up missing, so High Desert shut everything down, all movement, so they could do their yard and building search using the metal detectors. Basically that episode fucked his move up temporarily. From what I gathered from Squeek, the next day after being in the cell, the homies didn't know I was in 6-building because he told me Dirty Mike should of already tapped in (came to check on me) being as though he has major access at moving from building to building, plus he has movement from the lower yard to the upper yard due to being some type of college clerk or something. He picks up and drops off college work and homework. Once word reached him and the homie Young Ace Capone, he pulled up and hollered at me (talked to me). He asked me, was I straight (did I need anything) because he knew I didn't have my property yet and wouldn't for at least a week, due to shit being backed up and delayed.

The day I arrived, that's when I found out that High Desert was on lockdown, as we were in the holding cells in R and R, waiting to be processed in. Seen by the nurse, put on clothes and talked to the Sgt., then given fish kits (a small brown cup, a spoon, a roll of toilet paper, a flimsy small plastic comb, a small toothbrush, and some tooth powder in a small gold envelope, a couple of wool blankets, sheets and a pillow case). The police working in R and R was saying High Deserts on lock down. Five to ten minutes later he's saying the lock down is over. Initially, I was like "Here we go. What the fuck did I walk in to?" However, whatever it was, it was. That's when we (people I came in with) found out later, about the metal coming up missing. One of the dudes I met knew Lil Sugar Bear from Insane (Long Beach Insane Crip) and asked me did I know him.

The last time I actually saw him was when we were in the L.A. County jail together briefly and had been cellies on the 4000 floor. We had to DP a homie; well he was claiming to be a homie. Anyway, this clown rolled up in super max when he got hit up (asked where he was from) and he was claiming Babyz saying he was Du'rocc from the set (gang). I was in super max with him in the same module as I was coming in from the county. He was sliding by me out of the door when I got completely into the module (it's really a dorm). I was hit up (asked where I was from). "Lil Tic Loc Insane Crip."

Then I heard, "That was your homie that just rolled it up (packed up his belongings and said he couldn't be there)." A few weeks later, after bumping into Lil Sugar Bear on the 4000 floor and moving into the cell with him and a couple of Hoova Homies, Snow (I forgot which Hoova) and someone else, forgot his name completely. Blame it on the PCP.

So, Ole Boy popped up in the module we were in, one of the porters came to our cell and told us we had a homie in the dayroom. He had the police pop our cell door (open it) so we could go see who it was. When I saw him I instantly remembered him. I'm like "Oh yeah, what's good homie, yeah we're in cell such and such (I forgot the cell)." We told the police it was cool, he could move in our cell. The police had looked at us funny, like he knew we were up to something. After we got in the cell the porter came and had called Lil Sugar Bear to the bars and whispered. The police said if ya'll do something to him let it be on the next shift.

After shift change, we whipped him with a shower shoe, one of those hard plastic Bob Barker ones. I held him and Lil Sugar Bear whipped him. Then he held him for me and I whipped him, pulled his pants down and whipped naked ass cheeks until they were purple. He was hollering too. Word got back to Baby Du'rocc from the set that me and Lil Sugar Bear had whipped Ole Boy with the shower shoe, so supposedly he was talking shit and had issues with that and put it out there when he sees us, either of us, it's on! I'm like, "I don't give a fuck, whatever. I'm not turning anything down (refusing the challenge)." About a week or so later, I was starting my trial and rain into Baby Du in the Long Beach court holding cells, him and a few other homies.

In my mind when he walked into the cell with them and saw me, it's on. It was as if everything was cool, we all spoke and dapped each other and they took a seat. The issue wasn't even brought up. Even if it was an issue he didn't speak on it. I didn't speak on it. The last time I saw Lil Sugar Bear before that was on the streets. I was with him and his female, Brandy, when he went to jail for a dope case, the one he was in the county jail for. He had already sold dope to an informant when I got in the car with him and Brandy. Long story short, we were blocked in by the police in the brown van, they hopped out pulling guns, had us get out and lay face down. We were cuffed and searched. He had marked money. She had a crack pipe, and was on parole. I wasn't on parole at that time, I had gotten off. I didn't have shit on me and was let go. He went to jail. After I'm walking up the street, I turn around and Brandy was walking behind me. Yeah, wow. How does that work?

Back to Mike though, he was in the cell with the homie Young Ace Capone from the Youngs. For those that don't know, Youngs, Babyz and Insane are all the same Insane Long Beach Crip set. That's when he told me about Tasha and Andre Brown's nephew Chumlee (not his real name, he just gets no play in my ride, no recognition). Like those who didn't support me, help me in no type of way, hated or snitched. The only reason an autobot would get play in my ride is for the purpose of exposure of his antics and shenanigans. You should already know if you left me for dead, you get no play. Anyway, he's from 20's and was also on the yard, but on the lower yard with him and Young Ace Capone.

Dirty Mike and Ace Capone were in 2-building and Chumlee was in 3-building, the orientation building. It's the building you would go to before being permanently housed in a regular building, either on the lower or upper. Mike, then was like "We're going to pull you to the lower yard with is in our building and you and Chumlee can be cellies, that way you're not the only homie on the upper yard by yourself." I gave him my info and he was going to make the move happen. He hollered at me for a few minutes but we didn't get into much, due to my being in the cell and him on the tier. Trust and believe, ears were open trying to hear something. The next day though he came back to the cell baring gifts, on some homie looking out shit. He slid me (gave me) some gloves, a beanie, an ink pen, a cup (little born one wasn't going to cut it), a bowl, shower shoes, soap, and 2 deodorants telling me to use one of them to swap for some toothpaste because he didn't have any extra ones. He was waiting for canteen (store). I had already told him what my cellie Ace had slid me. Before he left he was telling me I should be on the lower yard the following weekend. That they, the police, only done those type of moves from building to building on the weekends, but in house moves during the week. He had wanted to run something my me that had took place on the lower yard though, with the homies and the self proclaimed Crip Keepers (SMH) it turned out to be nothing serious. However, the move didn't happen as planned, a Damu ended up somehow moving in the cell me and Chumlee were supposed to occupy, that mike had put in motion for me and Chumlee.

A few days later, he police in the orientation building ended up kicking Chumlee out of their building to the upper yard, in this building with me. At first they were going to move him in 216 in B-section, which is the same cell we're in right now. I was in C-section still in 226 by myself. The night he was on his way to the building (this one), Squeek told me he was on his way and at the time he was the Mac-Rep for the building. The Mac-Rep is someone that supposed to help fix a situation you may have. Not really fix it, but see if it can get resolved, whether it's with an inmate or with the police. Most of the Mac-Reps these days only want the position to move around for self interest. He told the police it would be cool if Chumlee moved with me, since we had already had a cell move in with each other for the lower yard, plus we were homies from the same area. A female police, Rochella, who worked our building, was initially like, "I don't know, McClinton might not want him now." This is what she told Squeek when he came and got at me. I told him to tell her it was good and to make it happen.

Chumlee moved in that night. The next day he got a morning porter job so that pretty much and cancelled us out on the moving to the lower yard. So, it was Dirty Mike and Ace Capone on the lower yard, and me and Chumlee on the upper; two on that side and two on this side. Dirty Mike is about to go home though in about 60 days, though he should have been going home on the 3rd of this month, which is March, but due to some fuckery he's stuck and has to ride it out like a champ. Chumlees waiting for him to bounce (go home) so he can slide him the majority of his shit when he leaves. The rest of it is going to the homie Ace Capone. Mike already shot (gave) Chumlee his CD player and a few CDs. I'm trying to get that Smokey Robinson Ultimate Collection from Ace Capone, who mike promised it to. I'm going to see how that's going to play out.

See if he could see a BG with it (Baby Gangster). I didn't see Ace Capone's high yellow ass for at least a week or so later. I got the chance to see him when the building police in the tower called me to go to the patio to get my property. When I came out of our building, mike was on the yard and he ended up walking to the patio with me to get my property. Ace Capone was at the door of the yard, but he was on the patio side. Me and Mike pushed through once the door opened. Me and Ace embraced and started talking. He was basically filling me in on shit. It was also the first time and Mike was able to talk face to face. Everything was straight for the most part. I was telling them about my incident with how I got here and telling them about some so-called homies and autobots.

Turns out, both of them I was speaking on were known for shenanigans and being on some foul shit, especially S.T. (not his real name, you know the deal, he gets no play in my ride). I was told he was going to get hollered at (DP'ed, disciplined) for all the foul shit and stunts he'd been pulling with homies. It was like, homies can't wait to catch up to him on these 4 yards. Yeah, everything really all came together for me, with and about the dude S.T. and this is coming from another 20 how foul he is. A 20 and a Young like, "That dude ain't cool, he should've been voted off the island." I ran the whole situation down to them while I waited to be called for my property. It was basically like this, I had been in Solano already 5 years and for the last 4 to 5 months I was on the yard by myself, doing and being me. A few homies started pulling up on the yard. A couple of them went home. Mind you, before they pulled up, I was doing my shit (hustling) nothing major. Doing enough to keep my head above water and making it make sense. Me and my cellie, Loc from Front Hood, who had been my cellie the whole time I was there. At this time, I had a few dudes that were delinquent and owed me some bread (money). I was really only tripping (upset) off one dude in particular, a dude named Oppie (not his real name), a White Crip from Venice. We were straight for the most part and had done business a few times so I didn't think nothing of it, that he was good for it. I had some so-so product at the time, which I let him know. I liked keeping good business. He was straight with it, plus I gave him a player deal so he could at least feel good about the situation and I gave you the heads up (warning). I shot him something for "two dollars" (two hundred) that was worth "three dollars" (three hundred), fat too, a large amount. The face he was short (close) to the house (going home) I'm thinking he's going to get the business handled, like before, last thing on my mind. Dude is going to play games, running the risk of having a situation on his hands that would jeopardize his exit. Yet Oppie started bullshitting and horse playing, he's telling me he can't get no greenies (green dots), but I'm hearing later he's sliding (giving) greenies to the Northerners (Northern Hispanics). I'm like, "Hold up, what part of the game is this." We're having side bar after side bar (private conversations). He's constantly telling me he got me, but all the time, he's getting shorter and shorter. I'm starting to feel like it's the stall tactic, buying time.

During this time he's in the cell with a Long Beach homie from 20's named K (not his real name, it's disrespectful to my set), definitely no play in my ride. I'm even getting at him, like "What's up with your boy?" He told me, "My cellie saying he got you (going to pay me) but feel like he has to watch you because you're looking at him funny." It was being revealed in slow measures.

He also told me he told his cellie Oppie, "You need to pay Tic, before it (the situation) goes somewhere else."

He said Oppie was like, "I ain't trippin'. We can get down (fight)." Get down! Get down! Dude, you're horse playing. I'm about to poke your stupid ass (stab you)! Get Down! Yeah, ok, hold that thought though! A straight clown. What the fuck do I look like, getting down with you over my two dollars? Like we're prize fighters or something in Vegas fighting for the purse. No bueno, that's out! All the way out! When K told him it was a little more complex than that, Oppie took it for a joke . . . his bad!

Lauren Hill said it best, "It could all be so simple but you'd rather make it hard." My cellie, L Loc, even tried talking to Oppie, telling him he needed to handle that business before it goes somewhere else. Again, he took it for a joke, confusing my laidbackness. So, all this was going on while one of the Moons from Babyz was on the yard and his cellie Tray Bang from Babyz. Then S.T. pop up, B.D. from 20's pop up, another Baby name Tall (not his real name) pop up, then H.B. (Head Bustah) from Long Beach West Coast 80's pop up, then it was another homie from 20's that popped up, but he has some other shit going on 20s/BGF, real cool dude though. Anyway, I don't hit the yard on Sundays for nothing, not because of sports; it's just my fall back day, unless I'm running a play, conducting business, or handling some other business. It was rare to see me on the yard on Sunday, period. The whole time Tall is there, he's trying to make something happen (make money), S.T. too.

In fact, those two had gotten tight and were trying to put their heads together, working on something S.T. is in my ear the whole time, "Yeah homie, when this play (business) happen, I'm going to fuck with you. You're a real homie. You're not a set tripper. You and Tall are the only two who's straight." This that and the third, Bullshit Niggah the while time. All along he was not cool, him nor Tall.

Now mind you, Tall, being a homie from the set, a younger homie, I'm sliding him shit (giving him stuff) 60-60, here and there, like "Do you my Niggah" sliding him tree, knowing he's hitting his boy (giving his boy some). I didn't care either way. It was yours to do what you chose once it left my hands it was out of my control. I sent my Sony CD player to S.T. because he didn't have anything yet. Before I slid it to him, K had it for a couple of weeks. I wasn't tripping off it. I barely used it, plus, we, me and L Loc, had a radio hooked up to his CD player that played loud. So, being a homie, an older homie at that, it was an easy call. Saying all that to say I embraced them, like I've embraced any and all Long Beach homies, regardless if you're 20s, West coast 80s, Brick Boy, Blvd Mafia, or from my direct tribe (Insane, Youngz, Babyz). It's LBC, City by the Sea. I'm not ever on any funny shit with homies unless they're showing me funny shit or I see the autobot conduct then my lane change. So Boom, S.T. finally run his play. Not the one he'd been waiting on, but one to just jump in the mix for time being. Mind you, again, I'm already in the mix, doing shit myself, but you know, you can never have too much tree. I had tree and 60-60. He pulled up on me, "Look, at first I wanted to slide you something and you serve your people you're already fucking with (dealing with)."

I'm like, "Cool, its good."

He went on with his pitch, "Because you got access to bounce in this building and that building, because of your job."

At that time, I was an IDAP worker (Inmate Disability Assistant Program). I basically pushed inmates around in the wheel chair and assisted them in other matters if they were in need of assistance, including helping them write letters or fill out forms. This is the other reason he claimed he wanted to fuck with me, bullshit! He was forming a plan, I didn't see, I appreciate the lesson though. Good job. The reality though of the matter, I didn't have access to the buildings like that though. This was his reason for claiming he initially wanted to do business. He already had his justification for his narrative. You have to have that, doing foul shit. It's just a form of bullshit to sell to the autobots to get them to go along with it. Dumb ass autobots! The whole situation was premeditated. The only time I was allowed in any building was if the police were calling for me over the P.A. system on the yard if I was out there or my cell door would be popped (opened). "Aye, McClinton, you're needed." I was picking someone up or dropping them off from or to a doctor's visit, education, law library, or program office, the substation, when I had to go there, I would immediately drop whoever it is off and do it moving, I would let them handle their business and come back. I was allergic to that sop. That's the only time I was in any building, so we'll just debunk that lie, paying attention, autobot, other than that it was a no go. A negative on going in and out of buildings at will. Now, if I was one who fucked with the police, it would've been a different story.

That's not what I do though. I heard he told his autobots and his homies he only fucked with me for that reason. I had that movement, which was to justify his reason for giving me what he gave me. So, remember me saying I didn't come out to the yard on Sundays. Here was his play (his game). He'd given me something allegedly. I say allegedly because I couldn't see it. It was wrapped already. For all I know it was toilet paper. I didn't see you wrap it. I'm just taking you at your word, thinking you're a real dude and a homie. Especially treating you how I was treating you. I never opened it to verify its actual contents. To this day, I still don't know what it was, but now knowing the character, it was not what he was claiming it was. Bet that! But if I'm holding something, that's just what it is, I'm holding it. And you gave me something too, to hold it.

I'm not opening it. It's not mine to open, period. I'm not even that type of dude. I'm not built or wired that way. I'm straight all the way around the board, loyal as fuck, trust worthy and solid, and I'm not strung out on drugs (SMH). Up to that point, I'd been down 15 years plus. I've never done crafty, foul, or scandalous shit on these lines, nor am I known for this type of conduct, nor have I ever owed anyone for drugs, gambling or anything else. That would cause an issue or get me voted off the island. I don't have any habits. My name has never been tossed up (spoke on) for no bullshit behavior. I know how to jail (do time) and conduct myself accordingly. No where I've been, I've been involved in some bullshit. None of that, my records been clean. Amongst homies and other dudes I've come across and have dealt with. You don't just up and start having issues or a track record, this is your norm.

So for me, it's totally out of character and would be. It's not what I do. "Yeah, he gave me something for holding something." He also had a second claim which he was claiming he didn't want to keep nothing where he was, which was overstandable because he barely got there and didn't know dudes in his building like that.

Again, I'm like, "It's good." One, because he is a homie, and two, I didn't think he was a foul actor, I thought he was genuinely a straight young homie. All along it was a guise on the highest level, which is the type of characters you're dealing with today. I was recently told too by a dude, the rules for prison for the next 20 years are being set right now by the younger dudes and any and everything goes, especially the ones with all the time.

I had to agree, from seeing what I see and the mindset and what's considered the acceptable code of conduct. Anyway, I accept the bundle. The next day, S.T., the very next day, sent word to me in my building to shoot it to him. I get it to who he sent for it, he do with it what he do and send it back. Now, to me, and it's just me or am I crazy? That didn't make no type of sense I didn't see it at the time as suspect (suspicious). Why didn't you take out what you needed or was going to use before you slid it to me to avoid the back and forth shit? And risk exposing the biz (business) knowing the type of environment we're in. It's real bastards everywhere. The spot (Solano) is known for them. "A snitch anywhere is a threat to real Niggahs everywhere." Why? Because, he was setting his play up.

Shit wasn't moving like that at that particular time, it was flooded (too much of things). Not only that, but he was indulging himself and with other dudes and passing shit out (giving it away), basically fucking it off. Keeping it all the way real, the shit was low-key trash. A few people said it, he knew it. It got you there for a hot second, and then the ride was over. You probably got a 15 to 20 minute flight, and then you were right back regular. Straight garbage, boo boo! Basically everyone blew it, said it was trash. So, I'm assuming that's when he began to really concoct his bullshit. I still had my own shit, I was sitting on, personal and otherwise, that was gas. The day after he sent for it and got it back to me, he asked for it a second time, which as a Saturday. Someone came to my cell, talking about S.T. want you to shoot that, bring it to the yard. This isn't even the same individual. It's a different person entirely, so mind you, it's the very next day, and he wants it again. Do you see the bullshit yet?

2

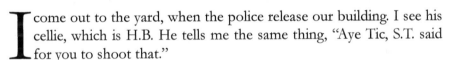

I come out to the yard, when the police release our building. I see his cellie, which is H.B. He tells me the same thing, "Aye Tic, S.T. said for you to shoot that."

"I brought it out and passed it off."

He doesn't shoot it back this time. Instead, the very next day which was Sunday, he sends word in my building for me to come outside. When I come out, it's him, his road dogs, Tall and the Homie Tray Bang. We all start walking. Tray Bang and Tall slowed up and me and S.T. walked ahead of them. First thing out of his mouth was, "Aye homie, I don't know what happened, but the 'sack' came up short, like way short."

I'm like "Whaaaaat! You have to be bullshitting, because I know for a fact I didn't fuck with it." I thought he was clowning at first and waited for the punch line. It never came.

Then he said it again, "Yeah, the sack was short." Giving me a specific number.

Now I see, he's for real and isn't letting this go. He's really going there. Now I'm like, "Dude, I don't know what happened. All I do know is I didn't fuck with it. I don't play with Niggahs like that." I've never done it, why would I do it now and start with him?

He kept saying it, then he said, "I can't take that kind of loss, but look, since you're a homie, I'll work with you. Just shoot me 'two dollars' and we're good."

I'm giving him the opportunity to abort the horse play, I'm like "Dude, I didn't fuck with the sack. That ain't me." So, being sarcastic, I'm like "You know what, yeah, for sure I got you. Two dollars is good." I saw it wasn't going anywhere and he was adamant in his pursuit, seeing he really had me confused from my relaxed and chill demeanor and my age. In my mind, I'm going to deal with the situation. In the face of a legitimate threat, a real Niggah ignores nothing. Everything isn't reparable. I'm not a grudge dude, but right is right and wrong is wrong. I'm a man first. The situation may've had me pistol hot and in my feelings, but it gave me some real context. I'm like, ok, I'll deal with this after I deal with this other situation. A real situation, because what he's talking about is manufactured and flat out some bullshit. I got you at ease. You're thinking you're getting something, and for free, no less. In your mind, you feel you have you one (a victim), it's good. In my mind, you have your people fucked up. If a dude goes in your shit (property), he's in violation, straight up! What's to talk about or negotiate? You're not trying to negotiate shit, for what, you've been disrespected. You're supposed to be on dude ass, like back pockets.

Dude got at you sideways, you're at him, period. Point blank, there's nothing to talk about, right? "Don't do me no favor, talking about since I'm a homie you're not tripping." If you haven't been giving dudes passes, homie or no homie, don't give me one and I'm legitimately in violation, do your shit! Because if the role was reversed and you went in my shit my boy, it's nothing to talk about, period. I'm playing ball or have ball played on me.

"You went in my shit, you disrespected me." Dude wasn't even mad, he was on, "Just slide me two dollars and we're good." Where do they do that at? Then later, come to find out he's on drugs, him and his crew, that explained a lot for me. I gave Dirty Mike and Young Ace Capone a short version. Mike's response was that sound like some bullshit he'll pull. That just confirmed what I had already suspected. Ace Capone whole shit was S.T. be on some bullshit with Insanes anyway, he's a low key set tripper and stay doing little shysty shit. Then, he went into some shit about I.T.F.

(not his real name), a homie at the time, from Youngs. He was telling me about the incident with him that happened and that it was him who tried playing ball on him. It was public knowledge prison to prison. I had heard something about it, but was getting bits and pieces my god bro, Lil Tray Deee was telling me about it too. Me, him, and I.T.F. use to correspond tough, through a 3rd party. After the incident, all communication ceased. It's not like getting it straight from the source play by play. My bits and pieces became a much clearer captured moment (picture) I personally too, read the black-n-white, the CDC 115 (Disciplinary Document) from the incident, when the homie sent his paper work to me to check out. (SMH) The homie got at him with the strap (knife) and I.T.F. done it moving (ran). That part was never mentioned to me. This is what I read. Once the property officer called me to snatch up my shit, me and Young Ace dapped and hugged and he went back to the lower yard.

Mike helped me with my property. I received all of my property except my T.V. When the property officer opened the box, my T.V. was broken. I'm like, "Fuck, here we go with the fuckery." The property officer asked me why was I here (High Desert). I told him, "A SHU kick out, for a battery."

He replied, "Oh, because from the looks of this I thought maybe a staff assault or something and that's why your T.V.s broken."

I was like, "Nah, not at all." But it just shows, that's one of the many ways they'll retaliate against you for doing something they feel was bad conduct on your part, or just your push in general, writing them up or whatever. So, he gave me the format to get the situation rectified with the 602 process (A 602 is an appeal you can file for an action you deem wrong against the police or administration) and he verified everything on paper and signed it. The next few hours a 602 was in flight. I wasted no time, had to get on it. I couldn't just take that L (loss).

Mike helped me carry my property all the way back to the building, to my cell. By the time I was done getting my stuff, the yard had already closed. Me and Chumlee been waiting to watch some T.V., all we've been doing was binge reading, reading book after book after book and playing fucking dominoes. Besides that, we would chop it up (talk) about the city and bitches, telling war stories. You can only do so much of that before you get burnt out on it. His mom is the home girl, Hop from the set. Before he became my cellie, he had popped up in the building at my cell door to holler at me and tap in (check on me). He wiggled (found a way) his way to the upper yard from the lower yard. When he came to the door, he was like, "What's up, cuz? Chumlee from 20's. I'm Tasha Brown's nephew." I remembered seeing him, but he was real young when I last saw him, looked different.

He grew up on 20th and Linden, looking like his uncle, Andre, one of my childhood associates who passed from the virus. BG Tic Loc, Insane Crip. He was like, "I wanted to come too, so you can have a face with the name, before we became cellies." The police let him hang out at my door before they ran him off and put him out of the building. As with mike, we couldn't get into much because of me being in the cell and him being on the tier. Ears but he wanted to tell me about how he got to High Desert. I told him we'll discuss LBC business (Long Beach Crip) once we become cellies. Once we did become cellies though, we chopped it up. He was telling me about how some homies, D Deuce from 20's and MoTray from Babyz jumped him at Corcoran State Prison, and how the tables were turned and it didn't go as planned for either of them, not that I didn't believe the incident, a South Sider was there and saw the get-down (situation), confirmed for the most part, of what he said. He lived in the section with us. Before we moved to B-section from C-section, the South Sider and Chumlee were speaking on the activities that happened on that yard. "I saw you fool, you got busy." The whole situation that led up to that day from what I gathered was a culmination of things that came to a head. He basically was pussying the fact the homie there on the yard didn't like him and was hating on him, wanting him removed. We moved from C-section to B-section because the young Crip homie from Watts, I moved in the cell with, fresh off the bus, wanted to move back to this building from 8-building with his homie Tic, for whatever reason. I didn't ask nor did I care. I wasn't tripping either way. It was good with me. Him and my younger homie Vamp 3, who I first met in '08 in Calipatria (Calipatria State Prison) from 9.2 Hoover (Nine-Deuce) came and got at me, asking could he get the cell back because he and his homie were trying to move together.

I told them it was good with me. He even offered an incentive. I wasn't tripping either way. Chumlee was reluctant. He didn't want to move. I got at the young homie the next day on the yard and told him it wasn't cool because Chumlee wasn't trying to bounce. He really wasn't trying to move because of the relationships he had with a few people. A few days later it was a go. It got worked out with the promise of that incentive for Chumlee (SMH). Though C-section was straight as far as the blacks but I wasn't feeling it like that personally. You had Bay-Areas, Damu's, Squeek, and a million Hispanics, none of whom I fucked with. I was cordial and respectful all the same. Moving to B-section though was a better look (reason) for two reasons. My boy Vamp, and Hoover-Lon from 7.4 Hoover (seven-foe) my work out partner. Me and the homie hit the yard every day, holler at a few people, give a few daps, and we're out, straight to the slab (a concrete slab we work out on) to bust down (workout). For the most part, we'll work out the whole yard. We'll wrap it up about 20 minutes before they announce equipment recall. After the announcement we head back to the Black Area and post up (lean up against the wall), talking until it's time to get patted down and go back in the building. The buildings work like this, for yard. Two buildings go out to yard at a time. The two even buildings go to yard together 8 and 6, and the two odd buildings go to yard together 5 and 7. The Black Area on D-upper works like this. All Blacks, no matter where you're from, your faction, your tribe, or affiliation, we share the Black Area. One common area as far as tables and bars (work out bars) in our area. We do share the basketball court and the slab with the Northerners. One of the slabs has a punching bag on a pole. We also share a bar area and handball court with them, but yeah, the Black Area is shared between Crips, Bloods, Civilians, and Bay Areas.

The lower yard is totally different, mainly because the yard is a lot bigger, real roomy. Everyone for the most part has their own area. Crips, Damus, Bay Areas, Hispanics, Others, Whites. I haven't really got all into the dynamics of that side of the yard. I just heard that part and the fact they're a little more political on that side of the yard as far as line pushing and structure. There's nothing wrong with order, as long as its order without hidden agendas (political ambitions), and dirty politics. They'll always be a stratus behind dirty prison politics because the dirty shit is the shit that's perpetuated by and practiced mainly by dirty Niggahs and autobots. I'll say this, power of any kind compels dudes to do whatever to obtain or sustain it. Power in the wrong hands is dangerous and it's simply a liability. To have the wrong hands possess power, nothing good can come from that situation, no more than putting a gun in their own damn mouth and pulling the trigger. . . Bloom! I'm all for order though because without it, shit is chaos and with chaos comes problems that get compounded, and then it's a matter of time before the violence follows.

With order, dudes know, it'll be consequences from choices or decision made out of haste or feeling like you're bigger than the car (your tribe/homies). You're horse playing, homie. You'll be dealt with accordingly! You'll look around and find yourself two on one'ed or three on one'ed (two people fighting one person or three people fighting one person), depending on what took place, but at the end of the day, your ass off the yard and in the sandbox with your stupid ass pending transfer. Talking about, "What I do, why this or why that." In some instances, you may come back to the yard, depending on if the infraction was a felony (serious) or misdemeanor (minor), but an infraction never the less. It can also depend on if marriage chrono's are signed. It's just a document you sign agreeing there won't be any more issues. It's just the police covering their asses.

The flip side, someone won't sign one and dudes are split up, sent to different yards. Usually it's the victim who leaves, but if that's an option and someone doesn't sign it, he just basically put himself in a fucked up position to be politic'ed by his homies. That's a situation that's clear and concise, it's a wrap. No matter what, you're supposed to sign the marriage chrono, if you're good with that choice, then don't just deal with what comes with that. If it's still an issue, so be it, it's what we signed up for when we started representing the set. It's not just about the set, but about everything that comes with it, good and bad. You still have to stand, even when it's hard to stand. The one down side of being in no man's land is there's no tree, its only wax, which is mostly miss than hit and miss. It gets you where you're trying to get though, most certainly, but I'd rather have the grass. Reason being there's no tree though is because it's too loud. With wax it's low-key as far as smell. I've had my fair share. Me and Chumlee be blowed sometimes. He would buss a move (work a deal) or one of his dudes he fuck with might slide through and bless him. A few times H.L. pulled up with a kite (note) "See what this do Tic." Needless to say it got twisted and blew! Me and Chumlee hit the day room blowed.

I saw H.L. and was right himself. He was like, "Did it work for you?"

I'm like, "Shit, you see me don't you?" We laughed. I had dumped (got rid of) some throw away CD's. Basically they're scratched CDs you're turning in for new ones. The limit is ten. If you have ten and want more, you buy throw-aways off the yard. Not literally off the yard, but from someone who has them for sale. You can pretty much find anything you want if you have the funds.

I also dumped some stamps another time. I don't really be clucking (selling stuff) off to smoke, that's out! Every now and then I'll fuck off something to smoke though, but it's really depending on what it is or how I got it. I'll rarely give up food. A dude likes to eat, especially when I'm blowed and have the munchies. I'm trying to knock something down. I'm all in my locker on myself, looking for something, and I'm hooking-up (preparing) and eating weird shit. Might be weird but taste good as fuck. Would I eat it on the natch (regular)? Nope. My cellie L Loc in Solano State Prison it's more of a medical facility, use to trip off of me. I'll put both peanut butter and jelly in my ramen. I'll put jelly on a salami sandwich, that's just an example. I'll sit there and eat a whole box of Swiss rolls, bag of chips, a pack of chocolate chip cookies, a soup (ramen), and some crackers, mind you, I've put peanut butter on my Swiss rolls and cookies. Bite the Swiss roll, eat a chip, but a cookie, eat a cracker, and eat some of the soup on some high shit. Just weird food and snack combinations, it gets real with the munchies. As for the liquor I've drunk a few times. I'm used to making it myself, so with a lack of sugar around here the whole dynamics has changed up. The only way you're making reggie (regular pruno) which I personally prefer over white-lightning (pruno with the sugar cooked off) is to use outside of the fruit, anything else that contains high sugar content. You can't use those sugar substitutes, blue, pink, or yellow boxes for reggie. It doesn't work and it's nasty as fuck. You know it was tried though. You get no syrup or jelly around here. They're serving us some watered down sugar free syrup in a pack, and sugar free jelly in a pack.

You can't get variety oatmeal, flavored creamer, hard candy, unless its sugar free. It's a lot of other things we can't have either, which is considered alcohol material. They've become restrictive with a lot of stuff, due in part because of dudes talking to them and giving up the game. "Oh, you know we can make drank with this, that, and the third." Basically giving up the sugar ingredients and its started getting gradually taken away (SMH). Shut the fuck up! Coming from the sandbox at San Quentin State Prison to here is a big change as far as being able to make it. I was able to go up (make it) every week and I was solo in my cell. They still give you real syrup, and real jelly in the packs there and you got jelly a lot more than any other place I've been. I was drunk every weekend. I got white boy smashed. Me and Chumlee made it a couple of times. He came to the cell with a large Folgers container full. He had just started cooking (process of it, sitting up fermenting). It still needed a few days. We ended up coming up (getting) on a wax stick though and ended up drinking the reggie before it was actually done. It was straight though, it got us there (head change). It's nothing like a stick and a drink. That's how I like to get it, when I take that ride. I like having both and just go there until I'm mentally levitating. If I have a cigarette on top of that, I'm just doing way three much. I'm going in! I made one and the same shit happened, got a wax stick and ended up drinking it before it was done, though it was cool. It wasn't nothing more than a short dog, two to three cups. Don't have the right shit to make a batch-batch (a big batch, eight to sixteen cups). Plus, I'm just getting here. I'm trying to adjust and figure this shit out, where and how I can get what I need, in general.

High Desert is truly an environment shock being way up here. My cuzzo, Nip, told me he looked it up and it's in the middle of no-where. My young dude Vamp though slide me and Chumlee a couple of cups every time he go-up (make it) and come down (strain it). It's always reggie, mixed with white lightning, straight gas. We're waiting on him right now to come down. It should be in a couple more days. Hopefully a wax stick will be on the menu. On some real shit, High Desert is a real depressing ass place. A dude trying to stay faded (intoxicated) as much as possible, real talk! Nothing is really going on here as far as being able to really make moves, to do and be you. Those claps are all but non-existing around here. Where I came from, Solano, all day you could get a touch for eight dollars a flip for five dollars. I got banged (caught) for three in three years and was A1-C/C status, where all of your property is taken for a period of time and you're housed in an area with inmates on the same status.

Each time I was banged, I was put on C-status. My first 115 for one was 90 days C-status, then twice for 60 days. Before I caught my SHU, I was in the process of buying another one. I told myself, after I got banged for the last one, I was straight on them, wasn't buying another one, but shit, you get too use to having one and being able to reach out and touch a mutha fucka (get in contact) and get shit done, like ASAP. I've walked a few people in Nic's (Nic's check cashing) to have them slide money on my cellies books (account) for me, was talking to them the whole time they were doing it. I even talked to a female while she rode her bike on the way to a Nic's in the rain. It was no more of the "Oh, I'm gonna do it!" Yeah, okay, fuck all of that. Let's handle that while we're on the phone. Now, if you tell me you're going to do something, I can stay on top of it. So you can't use, "Oh, I forgot." I'm at you. I'm going to hit you up, "Aye, you take care of that?"

Having one does serve its purpose indeed. Then, you know dudes are fucking with the porn sites and those dating sites (P.O.F. etc.) trying to crack something. That's a job you have to be dedicated to. It takes work, time, and energy to weed out the bullshit bitches on those sites. I've tried, but aborted. I don't have the patience to do it for hours on end. I'm straight. Now, as for the hustle around here, from what I'm hearing and seeing, it's a headache and drama. It seems every time I'm passing someone conversing, it appears heated. I'm hearing "these mutha fuckas over here owe such and such", "this mutha fucka owe me, him and him", "this person owe that person owe", I'm like damn, dudes not getting their money. Same type of shit, I just left.

I'm passing someone else. He's talking about he's ready to go-up (blow the yard up/kick off a racial riot) on some fuck this type of shit, frustrated about not getting paid. Sometimes it's the cost of doing business. I pass someone else. He's talking about turning on someone in to his people (basically, letting someone's people know he owe and has been owing. It's been too long). More than likely it's someone of another race or faction that owes him. I've already been forewarned though by several individuals about hustling around here, if I so choose to indulge in the activities. Like I've told them all, I'm straight . . . Suuuper! After hearing too, what the policy was, if you turned someone in (Hispanics/Southern) to their people and they owe you and is bullshitting about paying you . . . That's out! I'm suuuper straight!

Then I heard, if you' were to act and take off on another race behind your money and it goes up (a race riot), depending on how bad people are hurt and you were to come back to the yard, you'll be politic'ed and removed by your tribe from heavy outside (other tribes/blacks) influence. I'm like, "Whoa!" Basically, if he's not removed, everyone else will band together on a united front and remove you all (your tribe). It's a cold game. Yeah, they have some cold shit going on around here. "Yeah, I'm straight!" I'll pass on that one, that's a ride I won't be taking. I basically got re-routed here. I wasn't even supposed t come here, but it is what it is. I'm here now, fucking with CDC (California Department of Corrections) and their shenanigans. You just go with the flow and keep the line moving. A police came to my cell early in the A.M., waking me up out of my sleep, tapping on the bars, talking about get ready, you're leaving in 45 minutes. I had a small batch going that had been cooking for a few days. I got up and strained it real quick with a t-shirt, then after quickly cleaning up; I brushed my teeth and washed my face. After that, as I was packing my shit up and braking the cell down, I stared drinking. I couldn't see pouring that out . . . That was all the way out! Yeah, I would've been horse playing. It wasn't bad either, fairly decent. I had a head change.

By the time the police came back to the cell to snatch me up, I was feeling nice and toasty, and feeling myself indeed! When I got to R and R and a police asked me my name and CDC number, I gave him both. Then he asked me where I was going. I didn't know for certain, but either Kern Valley (New Delano), or CSATF-Corcoran (Corcoran State Prison). He looked on a paper and then said, "Nah, you're going to High Desert."

I'm like . . . "High Desert!" Yeah, typical CDC with the fuckery. So yeah, the fuckery happened. Technically though, I was endorsed to go to New Delano or CSATF Corcoran. I don't know if it was due to no intake at those spots. If I got caught up in Quentin's and High Desert 's traffic, or if there was enemy concern and it was a last minute re-route.

For the most part they don't and won't just move you to a spot based on the totality of circumstances. The administration can determine an enemy situation exists, thus separation alerts can be put in place as to your enemy list. To my knowledge none of the involved has stated there's lingering animosity. One can assume the administration felt it's an enemy concern and put the separation alerts in place for whatever reason. It basically means I can only go to certain prisons, prisons where my enemies aren't. To ensure it anytime I'm moved to another prison for disciplinary reasons or a level drop transfer the CSR board checks the prisons I'm being endorsed to, according to availability before endorsing me there, so there's no endangering the safety of anyone, nor jeopardizing the security of the institution from a potential threat. I was in the sandbox at San Quentin from Solano on an ADSEG to ADSEG overflow transfer. It's what the administration does when the ADSEG you're in is full and you're doing a SHU program. They'll ship you out to make room for the lesser offense dudes that'll be kicked back to the yard. If you're waiting to go to the SHU and you have your final copy (paperwork you receive after you've had your hearing from your 115). Yeah, you're up out of there, that's how Solano got down around there. You're stage exit left.

I never actually made it to the SHU, an actually segregated housing unit. I stayed in the sandbox in Solano from April 26th to my born day (birthday), September 6th, 2019. I left there, going to Quentin and I stayed there on the second tier in Carson (ADSEG unit) in cell 2C35 from my born day to January 5th or 6th, one of those days, making it here, I think it was the 6th. At this time, Quentin is a 50-50 prison (their yard has PC's, protective custody inmates programming there with their GP, general population). That's a no bueno, a no go. So, when I speak on my being at Quentin, knowing what type of spot it is, and how its viewed by general populations in general that aren't 50-50, I make it very clear how and why I was there to clear up any confusion or potential side eye off top, leaving no room for error on anybody's part, especially autobots. They love taking shit and running with it. Clear and concise, when you first pull up in the unit (it's 5 tiers with a front and back side, it's just like old Folsom when I was there in 1991). The first thing you hear is all of the different races hollering over the tiers, trying to see who came and who's active. It gets noisy and loud real quick.

"Is there any whites that came that's active?"

"Any blacks that came that's active?"

"Is there any South Siders that came that's active?"

"Any Northerners active that came?"

"Any others?" (Native, Asian, etc.)

Hispanics and whites immediately are having their people put a line (string or sheet strips with something with weight on it, so it can move up and down the tier or over the tier). Together, so they can fish with them to get their paperwork (lockup orders) before they embrace them, communicate with them any further than that initial intro or offer them anything, a care package, something to write with, paper, state envelopes, or stamp or two with the envelopes, pen, deodorant, soap, toothpaste and shower shoes to borrow and possibly a few soups and coffee. They need to see that work. It's a good policy though, I respect it.

That's policy though, in any sandbox, ADSEG or SHU. All of the ones I've been in, that's how it worked. If you didn't shoot it or didn't have one you were suspect and you got nothing until you produced it. It's a must have or its no bueno. It's just the way things operate, so dudes know who you are and why you're in the sandbox. It's on a need to know basis, because you want to know who's around you, who you're functioning with and talking to, whether he's your neighbor or down the tier from you, which is only fair and is to be expected. Due to the SNY shit, dudes that are SNY and have tapped out, locked it up feeling their life is in danger and they can't be on the yard. They normally have them in their own area in the sandbox, separated from GP inmates, but the administration will mix them in and you wouldn't know unless you see their work. They'll try to act like their regular when they're not. They've tapped out or told, straight horse played! And the games they'll play. You'll be fishing; they'll pull your line in, take whatever off, cut your line or smear shit on it. Then curse you out! You'll be all type of bitches and punks, suuuper disrespectful! My take on snitches most rules can be null and void, except one, snitching. As I've said, a snitch anywhere is a threat to real Niggahs everywhere. That's just period point blank. Nobody likes a snitch. Nobody likes a rat bastard around or wants that type of person around. There's no use for his/her presence. What they stand for goes against the code. You learn that at an early age from your mama, I know I did, as a kid. "Boy, stop running in here, telling me shit." You're getting popped (hit) and ran up out of there (kick rocks), especially with a hood mama growing up, she didn't play that telling shit. My mama wasn't having it . . . at all!

That was instilled in us early. That telling was a no-no and wasn't cool, no bueno. So there's no excuse for it or employing that you didn't know any better or that it was wrong to do. It's just not cool, period. That's why largely it isn't accepted and is frowned upon by most. I say most because you do have the exception to that rule, those that condone it by being complicity in it, regardless of their reason. In my book though, if you condone ratism, you're a rat too and can't be trusted as far as I'm concerned. Stick yourself Tony. Condoning shit you know its foul, you're complicit in the shenanigans. Now, stick yourself again Tony. It's complicity on their part. They've aided and abetted in the bullshit. Bottom line though, if you're not GP, dudes aren't fucking with you. You have nothing coming and that's conversation included, for the most part.

When I got on the tier and in the cell, I was called immediately "Aye Black, where you came from?"

"Solano!"

"Are you active?"

"Yup, I'm active, indeed!"

"I'm such and such, nice to meet you." (I forgot dudes name). After introducing himself he told me where he was from.

"I'm Lil Tic from Long Beach Insane. Nice to meet you!"

Then I was asked what cell I was. I'm like, "2C35." After that, random blacks started calling me and introducing themselves, telling me their names, where they were from and what cell they were in. Even the active Northerners, South Siders, others, and whites introduced themselves, but then the lines got blurred right, but quickly got back in focus, I was confused. You had dudes coming from off Quentin's main-line, talking about they're active. True, they are, but only to each other. They think it's good because they know who the SNYs are on the yard with them and they don't fuck with them. I was hearing them over the tier saying it

"Yeah, we don't fuck with the SNYs. They stay over there, we stay over here." Dude, you're programming with them. You're on the same yard.

Regardless of the distance, you're sharing the same space. I call a ball, a ball and a strike a strike. It's like you're taking stripes off a tiger, it's still a tiger, dude you're horse playing! But then have the audacity to be in their feelings. If you don't talk to them and start trying to justify the situation, like you're doing them wrong. The difference is you can't go where I'm able to go, big difference. I damn sure don't want to go where you're about to go. I'm good. So after being there a minute (a few weeks) I was seeing that the Blacks that were coming to the sandbox from other spots, like the Bay, Wasco, here, Solano and a few other spots, weren't fucking with those dudes who were claiming active but coming from off Quentin's main-line. I peeped that quick. What was crazy though and where the lines got blurred, you had a few Blacks that were active, GP programmers, from a few of those spots I've named that were fucking with them tough. Talking and laughing with them, sliding them shit, accepting shit from them, the whole shit. I'm saying to myself, "What's going on here."

It had gotten to the point that an active Wood named Big Block got at me, when we were at yard in the cages (dog kennels). His cage was next to mine. He called me to the fence before we started working out. He was like, "Aye, Tic, It's nothing personal or against you, but my people are going to have to kick back (stop) on fishing with your people, because some of them are fucking with these guys coming off the main-line and we're not with that." The South Siders followed suit form what was being heard over the tier. I don't know if the Northerners were on the same shit. I wasn't tripping either way because I wasn't on the tier fishing like that. I fished maybe like 3 times, sending my paperwork out. Outside of my neighbor Smiley, who was a South Sider from up North (northern California). He came to Quentin with me. I moved in 2C35 and he moved next door to me in 2C36. We both came to Quentin together from Solano.

We rarely had to fish with each other because the police passed from cell to cell for us, magazines, coffee, books and soups. So the fishing was dead in the water, not happening anymore, with the South Siders, Whites, and Others for sure. I'm assuming the Northerners was with it because after a while you didn't hear them fishing with the blacks, they were fishing with. It was kept respectful though, as to why the fishing ceased. It was just that simple. They weren't fucking with anyone coming off the main-line, Blacks included. With them, if for some reason, they (whites, others and Hispanics) and some Blacks, go to the main-line, they'll be back within 24 hours. When the other races get kicked out of the sandbox to that line and they're active, they're coming back, right back to the sandbox, attacking the first person they see. If they don't, it's ugly for them. U-G-L-Y ugly. Even if the tables were turned and they were attacked before they could attack, they were back, whupped out (beat up). I hate to say it, but if I had to keep it a thousand, which I will, nine out of ten when a Black got kicked out, to that line, he wasn't coming back. I've seen it multiple times happen. He's staying right there, like it's cool and he's still going to be active, like he's coming back to GP if his points for some reason go back up and he's a level 3 or 4 again. He's not exempt from whatever issue that's going to come his way from him making that choice, a conscious choice! A choice is only a choice because we make it so, based entirely on our own priorities, preferences, desires and values. All the choices we make throughout our life are only choices because we're composed of different parts, striving for different goals. There's no coming back from that ride, period, it's pretty much a wrap, real talk. Don't get me wrong, I've seen other races stay too. Even a wood I knew, that I was in Solano with, he was their low key guy, calling shots.

3

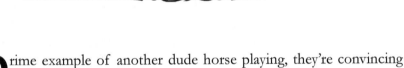

Prime example of another dude horse playing, they're convincing themselves its cool to be on a 50-50 yard and they can come back to these 3s and 4s if their points end up rising again. They're going to be in for a rude awakening. You basically tapped out and that's how dudes are looking at it. For every 1 person that's not tripping, 3 are. That's all it takes and its foot to ass, sucks to be you. But yeah, back to the script at hand. A Black named Trell from down our way (Southern California), a civilian, hollered down the tier and asked me, did I have a line (string with something heavy tied on it to slide from cell to cell and over the tier, a toothpaste tube with soap inside of it flattened, a flattened lotion bottle, they call a big body, or just a simple peanut butter pack with either soap or wet tissue inside of it attached to a hook, which is a staple to catch the line of the person you're fishing with so you can pull them inside your cell).

I told Trell to hold up, let me get situated and I would be back at him. He told me, "Cool." and to holler back when I was done. After I cleaned the cell, the metal bunk, the walls, the bars, the shelves, the locker, the sink, the toilet, and the floor. You have to, dudes be living like Vikings and vermin, straight foul! I made a sheet line to fish with, and then I made my bed. I made the line long enough to get at least 5 to 6 cells down the tier. He lived in 2C40, 5 cells down. My line may have been a bit longer. I just ripped a few pieces of sheet and tied them together. It ended up being long enough to reach him. An empty peanut butter pack was already in the cell and some soap. I used the staple from my paper work and put it together.

Once I was done, I called down the tier to him. "Excuse me on the tier. . . Aye . . . Trell!" When he responded, I let him know I was ready for him and to pull up (shoot his line).

He slid his line down the tier, a few cells past mine. I shot my line out of the cell over his and pulled back, letting my hook catch his. Then, I pulled him in the cell. I hollered down the tier, "Touch down." (I got you in the cell).

He responded, "Pull. It's a 'onetime' on there for you." A onetime could be anything. I pulled his "line" until I got his envelope that was attached to it. I opened it up. His lock up order for why he was in the sandbox was enclosed. I didn't trip off of where he came from. I just read the reason why he was in the sandbox. A female staff felt uncomfortable with him in her class and there he sat. She felt threatened and got him removed. Shit, that's all it takes is for any free staff (a person that's not a police) or the police to say you threatened them, or they don't feel safe around you and you're up out of there, see your ass in the sandbox pending transfer. It was implied. I sent mine as well, it's courtesy. If someone shoots you their lock up order you're supposed to send them yours. For me it's protocol. I'm going to do it anyway. Again, it's just to ensure you know who you're around. In your midst, you're fraternizing with the undesirables you wouldn't know unless you see that work.

I slide my paper work in his envelope and pushed it back outside of the cell. "Excuse me on the tier! Aye Trell, pull one time!" He pulled the line to his cell. After he hollered "touchdown" I game him enough time to read it. I then hollered down the tier to him and said it loud enough for whoever was listening that was active that if anyone wanted to see my work it was good and for him to shoot it to them.

Initially no one spoke up or asked to see it, but then another Black was like, "Shit Trell, you read it. You say it's good, it's good."

There it is right there. Trell hollered to whoever that was, "Yeah bro, he's good. He's back here for bussing on some shit (implying I stabbed someone). He got a battery on an inmate with a weapon." He slid his line back passed my cell and again I fished him back into my cell hollering, "Touchdown." Then after taking my lockup order out of the envelope I pushed his line back out of my cell on the tier. I told him to take off (pull it back) then told him to have a good night. He told me to do the same. I really wasn't into all that being on the tier shit all hours of the day, talking and doing all of that fishing. However, I would assist through, every now and then, based on my being active and functioning with the active dudes, all races. Dudes would fish and would do it from breakfast until after dinner, until it was time to shut it down for the night. Once the morning roll call ended and chow came and the trays were picked up, the fishing and talking began.

With the morning roll call, each race would say their good mornings to their people. They would call a homie's cell, saying good morning, calling every one of their active homies. Once one race is finished with their roll call, and then the next race goes. After each race does their own people, then they call a different race. Such and such, we send ours to you and the brothers. Such and such, we send ours to you and the South Siders. Such and such, we send ours to you and the Northerners, then the Woods, then the Others. They do the roll call again at night. After the night roll call, it's supposed to 86 (stop) the fishing, all of that resumes the next day.

I didn't participate in that roll call shit, though I know it was supposed to show solidarity amongst the active. I showed my solidarity with the group workouts in the cages. Only the active races participated, calling to each other. Basically, the message being sent is if you're being called and said good morning to or good night to, you're active. The building got the noisiest when a bunch of SNY's would pop up. They'll holler all day, some would be on some disrespectful shit. Then their stories of why there were SNY were hilarious. I would just lie back on my bunk with my back up against the wall and listen to them. I heard some wild shit boy! The cell next to me, 2C34 for some reason they (police) stayed rotating SNYs in and out of that particular cell. The last dude they put in these was a young bay cat. He hollered over, "Aye, cell 35!"

I'm like, "Yeah?"

"Aye, what's good with you bro, this is 'such and such' (I forgot dudes name)."

I'm like "What's good?" He asked me was I active. I told him yeah, I was active, an active Crip out of Long Beach from Insane. He told me he was from the Bay and he was active. I asked him where he came from and he said he was off of Quentin's mainline. I told him to have a good day. I didn't fuck with him no more, no convo, at all. Before him, it was three Northerners who were drop outs. When they would ask me if I was active and I told them I was, it was a wrap. They would stop talking, knowing I wouldn't talk to them. I was good with that though. Some will keep trying to talk to you until you have to get at them on some other shit.

"Look, I'm trying to be respectful about the situation. You're not active. I'm not fucking with you, period. Stop calling over here." They'll hear your name over the tier and will start trying to call you, like you're cool.

I shut down on them quick. You're getting no room to go nowhere else to be like, "I know Tic, we were fucking with each other at 'such and such' spot . . ." That's out! All the way out! Just before I left Quentin, I had got a kite from an NC (Northern Crip) named Yacc. He introduced himself and was like, he's trying to find a route to shoot his paperwork to me. He had just found out I was back there in the sandbox and had been trying to holler at me. A dude from Fresno named E.B. he said barely told him I was an active Crip. It was E.B., Yacc, and a dude from Harlem, but from listening over the tier he was fucking with dudes off the mainline or was from the mainline himself, so I immediately dismissed him, never spoke to him. E.B. was in Solano with me so I knew what was up with him. The kite was sent to me from a Damu named J80 out of San Diego. If I can recall, he was from Skyline Piru, it might've been Lincoln Park. Me and him hollered a few times in the cages and over the tier. He stayed on the tier underneath me. He would holler at those dudes off the mainline. So, I had to back up off homie. Anyway, Yacc was like, "That was crazy how E.B. didn't tell him I was back there until a day before he transferred. (SMH) He was also on, trying to establish a line of communication, which was cool. But, I told him I'm cool with talking on the yard or with shooting kites, I'm not on the tier like that, I'm out of the way. He was asking about what the deal was with dudes talking with dudes from off the mainline.

My response, "I have no clue what's up with these dues. I don't fuck with them like that." Then he went into some shit about him and a Kumi cat had been talking and they're trying to do this and that and the third. I'm like, "Look, I'm straight on all that, but you can check my shit out (paperwork)." His kite ended with "As soon as I find a safe route, I'll send my work." I struck (wrote) him a short kite in return and sent my lockup order, which I got back the next day along with his. E.B., I knew from Solano, he was in my building on the mainline when I was in 12-building. I didn't interact with him, but knew who he was.

When him and his cellie (autobots) popped up in the sandbox, these two characters let some Northerners tell them, since I've been in the sandbox, I was in the cell with a Wood. It was their Neighbors who said it, but trip the only way I could've been in the cell with a Wood was if I was a PC and we know that couldn't have been true. I didn't leave the yard a victim nor did I tap out. Those Northerners got me confused with someone else. I've never had a cellie the whole time I had been back there, until I moved from 214 to 230, with King from 4-7 Neighborhood (Foe-Seven). Before I was in 214 I was in 114 in 9-building, the overflow building and I was solo. I even received a 115 for refusing a cellie while I was in 9-building. I didn't want to move because I had gotten comfortable. They were trying to move me back to 10-building, which was the actual sandbox, 9-building was a main-line building with a taped off area for dudes in the sandbox. They fed you better because you were getting CTQ trays. This is a tray you would get if you weren't mobile medically or if you were on some type of quarantine. The main reason though I didn't want to move was the fact you could interact and get shit from homies off the mainline, those that lived in 9-building.

You had action too, at telling them to get at other homies to send you shit, pass kites, etc. To get whatever was sent to you all you had to do was have it put on a table in front of the row of cells. There were a few alright police that would assist you. They would snatch it up for you and give it to you at dinnertime or at breakfast time when they picked up the trash, having to open your tray slot on your cell door. Hell nah! I wasn't trying to shake (leave) 9-building, too much access to shit and to homies (those that I considered homies outside of the city and my tribe). Dudes that I had been programming with for years on the yard and knew I'm straight and solid. Not those so-called homies that had just drove up, that I didn't know from a can of paint.

Those weren't homies. Those dues were on some other shit. For me though, there's a difference between liking someone and tolerating someone which is how most relationships are on the yard. A lot of dudes are tolerated, but not liked. It's a lot of dudes I don't like, but I tolerate them. Really though, we weren't homies, just shared a common interest, LBC.

Those you shouldn't trust:

1) Those who say, "You can trust me."
2) Those with easy answers to complicated problems.
3) Bullshit politicians.
4) Those who aren't capable of truth or reason.
5) Those who can't stand when standing is hard.
6) Those who are complicit.
7) Those who aren't loyal.
8) Autobot.

Things you never do: Never underestimate and never over trust. I didn't just see the yard, I noticed the yard.

But yeah, the Sgt got at me and gave me a little wiggle room (allowed me to stay) telling me though the next time they came for me to move I had to vacate the spot. I'm like, "Cool!"

Prior to that though, he had sent a police at me on some aggressive and sideways shit. We were on the concrete yard in the cages. A police pushed up to my cage and was trying to push a cell move slip through. "Just sign this. You're moving in the cell with 'such and such'." Then he was like "If you don't you're getting a 115."

I immediately go on the bullshit. I tell him straight up, "Do what you have to do, because I'm not moving no mutha fucking where!"

"So you're not moving?"

"Read my lips. I'll take a 115. Add it with my other one." I walked away from the gate and he was still standing there trying to persuade me, but I stuck to my guns, "Write it up!" He did just that. The reality, he could've come smoother than he did. I still wouldn't have moved, not at that point. That was a 115 that was predestined. I had that one coming.

So, at no point had I had a cellie before I moved with King. These autobots didn't have enough sense to look into it before just running with it and taking the word of another race over your own (SMH). You don't have to be a prophet to see what's going on, the writings on the wall. I made sure I had it all sorted out before we parted ways, autobots are real characters. Some of them will go off the deep end without a life jacket and will frontline some bullshit. Going off the deep end without a life jacket and front-lining bullshit is young dudes mentally nowadays. I didn't need them going anywhere, spreading bullshit that wasn't true, talking about "Tic was in the sandbox with a Wood They were cellies". Not what they saw for themselves, but what they were allegedly told.

Knowing the mentality though, it would've been flipped around and put as if they saw me in the cell with the wood with their own eyes, horse playing! Made me reflect on a Surah in the Quran, I believe Albaqara 42, "And do not mix the truth with falsehood and hide not the truth when you are in the know" the whole situation was pseudo. I had a boy back there from Fresno named Green Eyes who I fucked with on the main-line kind of tough. He was back there for catching a staff assault on a couple of police he squabbled up (fought) with them in front of the chow hall area. You can assume at the end of the day, No Eyes got another issue though, he did his shit. It comes with the territory. Retaliation goes along with it. His cell was by the shower in what would be considered A-section. I was in what would be considered C-section. So, when shower time would come, I'd try to get to that side of the building. He was in cell 242 I believe. I ran the situation down to him about what was said.

He immediately got defensive, "That's bullshit Tic, I've been back here the whole time and I know you weren't in the cell with no Wood, plus I can see straight across the dayroom to your cell and see the cell the dude lived in that they were speaking on. I don't know how they got that confused." The dude I got confused with was taller. I'm only 5'6", dude was like 5'9", 5'10" with a bald head, like me. He had no facial hair. How the fuck you confuse me with that dude and he's light completed, much lighter than me.

I don't know why, the Northerners tried to put that out there on me like that. That shit was straight manufactured. I wouldn't have even heard it had not E.B.'s cellie brought it to my attention on the yard in the cages. I knew who he was by sight, but that was it. Him and E.B. were cellies in 12-building with me. Me and him happened to be across from each other in the cages. We made eye contact. I'm like, "What's up homie, I'm Lil Tic from Long Beach Insane. I'm an active Crip!"

He was like "I know who you are." Then he went on to say how he wasn't going to talk to me because he heard, key word heard, I was in the cell with a Wood. That was out! I let him know that that was some bullshit and wherever he got it form they were bullshit too. I've never been in a cell with any mutha fucking Wood. I was pistol hot. He wouldn't tell me where he got it from but I knew because I could see right into his and E.B.'s cell and their neighbor's cell from my cell. I play the door (be on the door when I hear keys, loud talking, excessive movement or doors opening). I could see them talking to each other through the cracks in their wall by the door of the cell. Sometimes it would be E.B. talking to them or his cellie. Him or E.B. wasn't even in the sandbox yet. When that dude was in the cell with the Wood and the dude was in the cell with the Wood maybe two days and then he transferred out. It wasn't that many blacks in the sandbox at that time and wasn't coming. It was only two other Crips in the building other than myself, King from 4-7 and another neighborhood Crip that came off the yard King was on, A-yard. Something had happened with him on the yard. Later, when I moved in with King, he was explaining Ole Boy's deal. I wasn't there to see it and its second had so I won't speak on it.

Dude stayed in the cell, he only came out for showers. He never hit the yard or talked to anyone. King did say though he was in his feelings. I assumed he was bad, based on his conduct, but the reality was he just wasn't fucking with people (no socialization). He was in his feelings about whatever happened. There had been another Crip back there come to find out, but he was on the low and didn't socialize. King didn't even know he was back there. He was one of my Yong homies from Babyz. He was super quiet and out of the way. He had come off of the level 2 yard that was pretty much it as far as being back there. So, I don't see where else E.B. and his cellie got that bullshit from. Other blacks weren't near them and I've never once saw them fishing on the tier with anyone. So most definitely they got it from their neighbor and that's just crazy. What's crazier, Northerners could clearly see my cell and see cell 216, which is where the Black was with the wood. How can you confuse the cells, especially when every time a cell door opens near or around us you're on your door, playing it as well? Not only that, but I know they could see me fishing with my neighbors who were Northerners in 215, Chevo and L.T. on a regular basis, and fishing with my other neighbor who's also Northerner in 213, Young Buick. Therefore, you have to know I'm active if they're fucking with me on any level. Just like I know they saw me fishing with both neighbors, E.B. and his cellie saw the same shit. Just like they had to hear us, me, Buick, Chevo, and L.T. sometimes, talking on the tier. These autobots nowadays hear shit and run with it. They're dangerous. They don't look into shit for themselves, incapable and lost, just take what they hear at and for face value, fuck the truth.

"Oh, I want to be down with the majority ass Niggah", whether it's right or wrong. If I wasn't there or I didn't hear it with my own ears, I'm not speaking on it because it's helping turn a false into a true, get a bar (pay attention). When shits constantly repeated and repeated enough it becomes true, even when it's not. Just like when the fake politics come into play. All it takes is for two bullshit dudes to set the tone. It only takes two to confirm a lie. One to speak at it and the other one to confirm it, and then the bullshit is in motion. Compound that with the drug use and there you have it, disaster! Green Eyes though ended up getting at E.B. when E.B. ended up showering on that side of the building. I could see them talking from my cell and the body language. They're both Fresno dudes, Green Eyes is older, around my age, 50 or maybe a couple of years older. E.B. is young, you know, that lost misguided and impressionable age, susceptible to autobotism.

The next time I got around to that side to shower Green Eyes told me he got at E.B. and put him up on my get down (the type of dude I am and how I push). He also told me he got at E.B. about the whole wood situation, telling me to not be spreading bullshit because he was opening himself for a wreck. Basically, let him know too not to be biting off into that because it wasn't true. He (meaning me) been back here the whole time and never had a cellie, let alone a Wood! I got at both of my neighbors too, L.T. and Chevo in 215 and Buick in 213, asking them if they had heard that. All three were clueless to the situation but just like Green Eyes, they said the same shit, "We've been right here the whole time. In fact, we're the ones who told you the Black dude was in the cell with the Wood." then went on to say, "If that was true, you know we couldn't fuck with you, Tic." My point exactly. Get a bar.

I asked them to get at their people so we can clear the matter up and put it to bed. As all of this was transpiring, K had popped up in the sandbox, but we hadn't spoken about the situation yet. I had planned on getting at him my next trip to the shower by his cell. We're on the same tier. He was back there already by the time I heard this, because he fucked with both E.B. and his cellie on the yard (main-line). I knew he would holler at them on his way to the shower, or if one of them showered by his cell. I would also hear them hollering at each other over the tier, naturally assuming one of them got at him about the wood shit, but to my surprise, come to find out they hadn't, especially based on K being from Long Beach. By the time I had gotten back to the shower by K's cell, E.B.'s cellie had moved out with him and into the cell with K. Him and E.B. had a discrepancy with their situation. He wasn't feeling it and bounced on E.B. It wasn't no telling going on or nothing. He did run their whole situation down to me though and I gave my opinion. E.B. didn't even know his cellie was moving. I knew before he did.

"I'm bouncing, I can't fuck with E.B.!" His whole thing was he was about to go home, E.B. got life, "Gone and take that, let me scoot and I got you." What in the Renege-aration is going on?

So once I get to the shower, after Ole Boy moved in with K, I hit the wall to get K's attention. Once he responded and we got passed the pleasantries, I'm like, "Aye K, these dudes around here is burnt the fuck out."

"Why you say that?"

"Mutha fuckas around here talking reckless, saying I was in the cell with a Wood."

He was like, "What!"

I'm like, "Yeah!"

"That's crazy homie, and some bullshit."

I'm like, "Tell me about it."

I asked him did his cellie mention it to him. He was like, "Nah, he didn't say nothing to me about it." To me that within itself was suspect. Why wouldn't you mention a situation to a Long Beach dude about a Long Beach dude if it was out there and you're now in the cell with him? I don't get the punch line. When I bumped into E.B. in Quentin walking to the cages he came to the fence closest to me and we spoke about the Wood shit and he spoke on his and his old cellie's situation. Who knows which one was the real one. I got two versions. It's always two sides to every story and three when the truth gets told. But, whichever way it went, it came from their mouth to my ears and it wasn't second hand. E.B. left a couple of weeks before I got to High Desert. I think he went to Corcoran. So far, since I've been here, I've heard about multiple incidents where dudes had been chipped (murdered). Death is a constant companion in prison on a level 4-180. Especially 4s in general though. It's crazy to be able to normalize it, but how can you not though? When it's a part of your reality to the point of being immune to it and it has no affect on your psyche. You're feelings grow numb, pushed to another realm. It's no different than being on the streets and witnessing death. You grow numb to it. It's a part of your environment. You can't trip off the candle melting. Yard life and life in general goes on.

"In prison/Picture me having visions/Nightmares of my death/On the yard bleeding/I breathed my last breath/Call me crazy/This drama done made me/It's shrewd/I'm only playing by the rules/Handle or die homie/I could never be broke/Full of that spray and bomb smoke/Recognotice the scope/It's bitter child on my throat/I took a oath . . ."

As of right now it's said that High Desert is the most dangerous prison in the state of California, hands down. It's not hard to imagine it's that active and clear to see. We were on the yard last month, I think it was February. Me, my guy Hoova Lon, and I think my cellie, Chumlee, but I'm not sure if he was with us or not. We had just finished working out on the slab and had just made it back to the Black area. We were standing near the tables watching two older Crip homies, D Mac from Compton and L.J., I didn't know but figure he's a Crip homie; it's all I've seen him with.

Anyway, we were watching them play chess. As soon as Lon walked away from the table he heard the yard tower police yell "GEEETTT DOOOOWWWN!" He yelled more than once, as he ran on the cat walk towards the incident. Us around the table didn't get down immediately, we looked around first to see where the threat was and who the threat was, assessing the situation quickly. You can't get down. You have to know what's up. Once we saw we weren't the target, we got down.

Police started running from all four of the buildings towards the situation. The police also came running through the door on the main yard from the other yard and the lower yard. The alarm was still going off. They started throwing smoke bombs, with block guns being fired. "Bloom, Bloom, Bloom!" Two Northerners were on one of their people, relentlessly doing him in. The shit being used (big ass knives had length). There was no chance of survival, especially how they were putting work in. He was getting hit (stabbed) in his head, face, chest, and neck with all metal, even through the thick smoke they were determined. When it was all over and the situation got under control, dude was moving around then rolling over on his stomach, then up on his elbows. While he was on his stomach he put his head down. He was bleeding like a mutha fucka!

I'm like, to myself, "My man's over there hurting all over, he can't keep still." He rolled back over on his back, both arms go up in the air and come down. One of his legs goes up in the air and comes down. One of his legs goes up in the air bent at the knee. It looked like he was trying to work out a cramp. His body was shutting down. Then his leg went back down. After that, he wasn't moving. The whole yard just sat on our pockets, watched, and waited for the yard to be recalled. The van came on the yard and got dude. Then about twenty or so minutes later we heard, then saw the helicopter coming from a short distance. It reminded me of a night I was in my turf (neighborhood) trying to evade the police on foot with a pistol on me and on parole. I managed to get away but it was a close call. I would've gotten caught, I would've been struck out (three strikes) I stayed throwing rocks at prison (taking chances).

Later that night we found at that dude died a day or so later, it was in the news paper. He was hit like forty plus times. "Deeezam!"

The next situation came about with my guy. We were on the slab as always, working out and talking with Chumlee and Get Drunk (not his real name, you know the deal. What is it? Yup! No play in my ride). But, he's from 20's, he just hit D-yard from C-yard, from getting into a squabble with someone over there. Both of his eyes were black and swollen from being shot in the face by the Block Gun. They will fuck you up. My back was to the yard, Lon is in front of me so he can see behind me. Get Drunk and Chumlee were facing in the same direction as Lon. So all three homies were walking up, Grove Mack, T-Bone and B. I see Lon's facial expression and turn around and that was when I see them. They all had weird looks on their faces.

Lon was like, "Hold up Tic, let me holler."

I stepped to where Chumlee and Get Drunk were standing. We watched as the drama was unfolding. T-Bone and Lon exchanged words, then B and Lon exchanged words, then Lon told B to beat it. "Get on." It was something to that effect. Then they started to fight. They were both aiming for the face. B caught a stunner. It rocked him. He landed some though. Without being biased, they both had done their shit.

The police came running from their buildings as the alarm was going off and a couple smoke bombs were thrown, "Bloom, Bloom!" They both had gotten in a few hits before the tower caught the motion and yelled "GEEETTT DOOOWWWN!" After the police cuffed them and took them off the yard. They were back from the sub-station before the yard was recalled. Program had resumed and I resumed my workout, after we switched from the slab with the South Siders to the other area where bars were another slag and a punching bag.

Lon and B had to go directly back to the building. I guess their program was over for the day. Both of their names were being called over the P.A. "Perkins and such and such, take it back to your building" (don't remember his name). Before Lon went in the building, he was able to spin (walk) a lap around the track with Vamp. He needed to calm down. It looked like that's what Vamp was trying to do, calm the homie down.

You could see it all in Lon's face, he was in his feelings. The homie was beyond pistol hot. He was AK-47 hot. Everybody knows the reputation and knows the guy. He's a relic and an 80's throw back. He wasn't feeling that whole get down (situation) that's from mere observation, without a word being spoken on it. Get Drunk was like, "Man, what do ya'll have going on over here?" For a few days, the yard had been smooth, then another episode occurred, a few days ago, the hub and dub had a two on one situation going on which was about to be a three on one, but the third party didn't make it. He didn't get to throw one punch. It was over as he got there. The yard felt kind of weird when we came outside. It didn't feel right. Couldn't put my finger on it, but I was with who I fuck with and can see the other one. I keep my eyes on my young dude Vamp though. I scan the yard for him until I can see him. As me and my cellie come out of the building we holler at a few dudes and dap them as always.

We dapped the Crip homie from Compton who turns out to be the one on the other end of that two on one, about to be three on one. He was working out by the homie Capone from 7th St Watts who we also dapped and hollered at. Another Compton Crip homie was on the ground doing push-ups. Once he had finished his set and rose up I dapped him. By this time Lon just came out of the building and went to the table area as usual. He hollered at a couple of dudes, gave them some dap, and had me grab the blanket he uses on the slab for his crunches. I don't do those, but I do everything else, oh, and I don't do the T-Bars, though I need to. We (me and Lon) head for the slab. Just as we were finishing up our first 20 reps of burpies, "GEEETTT DOOOWWWN!" The alarm started going off. The police started running from buildings and the yard door comes open, police run through, coming from C-yard and the lower yard. You already know dudes are not getting down until we see where the festivities are, who it is, and where it is.

Just so happens these festivities were directly by us, maybe 20 to 25 feet away from the concrete slab we were on. My young cellie I was first in the cell with from Watts, Ace and Blue Devil from Compton were on, the homie from Compton who I had first dapped when I came out of the building, they were two on one-ing him. Ace's cellie Tic came to help but it was basically a wrap (over) by the time he got close. The smoke bombs were tossed, "Bloom, Bloom!" They were still at him, but finally stopped. Me and Lon were down wind of the smoke. That shit had us choking and coughing. After they got them off the yard, the program resumed. Me, Chumlee, Lon, Calbo from 11-8 East Coast (Eleven Eight), an Other (Asian), and his cellie were on the slab. Chumlee, Calbo, and the Asian had barely walked up, at different times. After everything resumed, Chumlee and the Asians dipped off (walked off), leaving me, Lon, and Calbo on the slab. Calbo then left the slab and began walking and talking with his homie, Scooby from his street (Eleven-Eight), who lived on the lower yard.

Looking for Vamp, Me and Lon spotted him and his boy, Snake from 1200 block East Coast. They were in front of our building. Me and Lon started back doing our burpies. Vamp popped up to the slab asking were we straight? We told him we were good. He left, heading back to the Black area, walking across the yard and then the alarm is going off for a second time, "GEEETTT DOOOWWWN!" Again, police are running from the buildings and back on the yard from the other yards, busy morning. We're looking for the activities; we spot it, and then got down on our pockets.

It was in front of our own building. It was Snake and Scooby on Calbo. By the time we spotted it, Snake had just slammed Calbo on the ground and he was being socked on (hit). When the smoke bomb got thrown and exploded, Snake got down, and Scooby got a few more punches in before getting down. Yard resumed, but for recall. That was two incidents back to back. By the time everyone made it to their areas, Blacks, Whites, Northerners, South Siders, and Others, "GEEETT DOOOWWWN!" We're all looking around for it, but don't see anything except for the police running from their buildings again, for the third time. Some of them barely made it back inside and off the yard. The alarms going off and we hear multiple shots going off from the block gun, "Bloom, Bloom, Bloom, Bloom!" The lower yard had activities going on. The smoke was coming on our side of the yard. The wind was catching it since our area is closest to the wall that separates the lower and upper yards. From the position we were in (Blacks and Northerners) we were coughing up lungs to the point of tears being in our eyes.

After being down for about 10 to 20 minutes, it could've been longer, could've been short, but it seemed forever, The police called A-section of my building to take it in. As soon as dudes started to get up and were moving towards the building another alarm, back down they go. "GEEETTT DOOOWWWN!" Look around again to see nothing except the police running for the opening of the main yard door. Something was going on in C-yard because they were running in that direction. I'm like, "Damn, this day got real active with the activities and it's not even summer yet!"

I can only imagine what that's going to look like and be like. I know I'll be around here for at least three years, unless at some point I have to get my hands dirty. It is what it is though. As long as I'm able, I'm willing, but you know, the mindset being older, the reaction to a situation is a lot different. I'm not trying to be rolling and tussing around on the ground with no mutha fucka. If I have to go there it has to make sense. I place and maintain value on my life, especially nowadays, with the disrespectful conduct of some young homies who weren't taught right. They don't give a damn about respect or about the fact that you've earned yours and still remain a presence on the main-line and wasn't one of those who took that walk of shame (going PC/SNY). I'm always mindful of the fact, with any incident that gets physical there's a risk. You have to always be mindful of the risk of being shot by police in the tower, whether it's a yard tower or building tower, outside or inside.

The shots could come from any direction, meant for you or not. Come from in front of you, or behind you, you'll never see it coming, "Bloom!" You're dead as fuck. Sometimes you could be the victim and still get it, "Bloom!" That mini isn't a joke, get a bar. You always have to be mindful of the risk you're taking and always have to feel an issue is worth it based on the risk factor. If it's worth it, so be it, do what you do. I will say this, spontaneous shit is spontaneous shit, and it can't be helped. It's just the risk you run stepping out of your cell.

Premeditated shit though, you know what it is going in, so if it's worth getting shot for its worth playing ball for. Even those that aren't involved in the festivities are at risk at times, and having nothing to do with nothing could catch one of those hot ass rounds. The incident is way away from you and "Bloom!" You catch one (SMH). Anytime something is going on and the yard is put down with shots being fired (live rounds) I'm being watchful of where the tower police are and what direction they're shooting in. Me personally, I'm not trying to be an accidental victim or casualty with my people (family) getting that fucked up call, "Oh, we're sorry to have to inform you, your son was an accidental victim of circumstance." Yeah, your people might get that loot (money), but yo ass dead! As you get older you don't heal as easily and as quickly as you once did when you were in your teens and twenties. Trust me, and the pain kind of lingers.

My last actual physical alteration was a minute ago, before my battery with the weapon. It was with a youngster from the city (Long Beach) from Babyz. Yeah, I still had a step or two left, despite my physical ailments, Type 2 Diabetes, Valley Fever's lasting effects, and asthma. Technically, I shouldn't have had to because it was a few homies younger than me and my older homie from the set Big Ant Dog that could've and should've stepped up. However, no bueno. It was not the case. Me and the older homie handled the biz! We weren't suffering from any type of ism that keeps you from getting your hands dirty. This was in Solano.

So, a young homie from Babyz named Ray III or L.R., he went by both, pulled up. He appeared to be straight, a little extra (touch demeanor), but straight none the less. I liked him and I had remembered him from off the north side of Long Beach, just a kid trying to hang out. About a month or so of him being on the yard, it came out that he'd done some Sammy the Bull (telling). The matter was looked into ASAP and it was confirmed automatic, that's a vote off the island. You have to go. The big homie Ant Dog saw the work as well as other homies. Also, some outside of the tribe, his cellie Ace Rocc, Pomona or Altadena, one of the two cities he's from had knew the whole script from communicating with Ole Boy's mom. Later, he was like, he wasn't trying to get involved. From what I gather, he liked him and didn't want to expose him, but exposed everything afterwards. Tattle-tale moms even called Ace Rocc wanting to know why her son got jumped on when he got told on too by his co-defendants. (SMH) Whole lot of rat-ism went on. Basically, he snitched because he was snitched on! No excuse homie, you were horse playing. That's no bueno! I ended up getting the work on my clap. It was a screen shot from someone posting it on Facebook. So, I'm like, ok, the homies know what the deal is, it was discussed, he's out of here! Me personally, I felt the punishment should fit the crime, snitches don't get whupped off the yard but that is another day and time. Certain measures should be taken for certain situations.

However, majority rule. The vote was to just whup cuz off the yard and send him on his way. I'm not bigger than the vote though, so whatever. Then, I thought about where I was because when I first got there I mentioned a knife and mutha fuckas thought I was speaking in Chinese (bok bok bok). "It's not like that around here Tic."

The longer I was there, I saw exactly what they meant to an extent. "Hey, I wasn't knocking the program. I just came from Kern Valley." You still had your shenanigans going on but mutha fuckas was just horse playing, running around trying to resolve everything fighting. Dude will owe you and if you ask about your money he feels you're sweating him, looking for a reason basically not to pay you. "We can get down!"

"Dude, if you don't knock it off!" A lot of bullshit went on in Solano.

So, we had the pow-wow but didn't include Nino from Long Beach, West Coast 80's, another young homie from the city, due in part because he fucked with Tattle-Tale. We didn't want him to expose the situation and task at hand. So, we left him in the dark, leaving no room for error, whether directly or indirectly. Not saying for sure he would've exposed it, we mainly didn't want him to act differently.

4

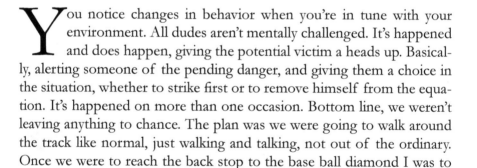

You notice changes in behavior when you're in tune with your environment. All dudes aren't mentally challenged. It's happened and does happen, giving the potential victim a heads up. Basically, alerting someone of the pending danger, and giving them a choice in the situation, whether to strike first or to remove himself from the equation. It's happened on more than one occasion. Bottom line, we weren't leaving anything to chance. The plan was we were going to walk around the track like normal, just walking and talking, not out of the ordinary. Once we were to reach the back stop to the base ball diamond I was to bend down as if to tie my shoe, stopping all of the homies, not out of the ordinary.

Any time someone stops to bend down to tie his shoe, whoever he's with stops too because he's vulnerable with his head being down. So, while I was down supposed to be tying my shoe, that was the signal for Lil Kelly Boy from the set to take flight and attack. I'm bent down fucking with my shoe for a cool minute and nothing happened. I rose back up and we started walking again. I'm thinking, okay, It's about to go down when we walk another lap. It didn't. I even bent down again a second time. Tattle-tale was clueless. Nino was clueless too, though he mentioned something to the effect of "Damn Tic, you need some different shoe strings." We all started laughing.

As we walked another lap I'm like, "Fuck it, we're about to pull over to the Crip table. Fuck all this walking." The table was empty so we posted up. Everyone knew something was amiss with the Long Beach car. There were a lot of eyes on us. We're all standing around, me, Tattle-tale, Big Ant Dog, Dip Dog, Lil Kelly Boy, and Y.F. (Young Foolio). Nino sat on top of the table on the edge of it. Still, nothing was happening. I started talking to Nino. I stepped closer to him. He'd been doing little shit anyway that needed to be addressed to get his mind right. No one had said anything to young homie, but his program wasn't being felt. First thing, he had been on the yard 30 days and no one knew he was on the yard. I know for a fact I didn't. He was in the cell with Snake from 30's (Harlem). Second thing, he was running with the young Neighborhoods like he's doing an O thing (40s, 60s, etc). He was not fucking with homies (Long Beach) like that. Ok, granted, its dudes (not homies) feel a certain way about me fucking with the Hoovers as I do.

Not as much as them speaking on it, but by their actions (acting funny towards me). At the end of the day, I know where I'm from and I know I'm a Crip. Like, dudes know, that's a relationship that goes back to Hoosane. To this day it's not a thing. It's more of individual relationships and bonds. It's going to always be a history and love there, especially with homies my age and older. Though me, being from that era, I'm going to always have that love though they're no longer Crips, but criminals (crims). After I finished talking to the homie Nino, basically telling him how that looked suspect, him being on the yard that long and not tapping in with the homies, "Who does that?" At the time it wasn't any other homies in that building (11-building). As a matter of fact, Big Ant Dog was in that building, just didn't know he was in there. He didn't make his presence known. I basically told him, "Snakes not your older homie, your homie period. You're not from Harlem, you're from Long Beach. He can't dictate your program. You're not coming to the yard because he's not. What the fuck!"

We didn't know what that was about with that situation. I addressed the elephant in the room with him running around with the neighborhoods. It was to the point, his loyalty had been questioned. Homies didn't know for certain which way he was going. "Cuz, you're with them or are you with us?"

"I'm with the homies."

"With that being said, when they get into something, make sure you don't involve yourself. You're LBC!" He was low key spooked, thinking he was going to get flighted. He started looking around, feeling a certain type of way. Shit, we had to know where he stood, checking isn't cheating.

Then that's when Big Ant Dog turned to Tattle-tale, "Cuz, we heard some fucked up shit about you and saw some fucked up shit!"

Tattle-tale was like, "What?" No one moved as Ant was talking and he was trying to explain his side of the situation. I'm like, fuck it! I fired his shit up (hit him). Before he could recover I scoop slammed him and got on top of him. He covered up and went into his shell like a turtle. He was tucked in so I couldn't get a good one in. I busted his lip though. Ant Dog started hitting him too, getting those ribs.

We were on him for a cool minute before the police were on to us. The alarm goes off. The tower spots us finally and we were right in front of the tower. Crip table sat right there, literally ten feet away. The tower police yells from his window, "GEEETTT DOOOWWWN!" Before the police ran to us we had scattered like roaches when the lights come on. Me, Ant, and the rest, we went ahead and stopped hitting him because we weren't getting him that good, wasted energy. We were just getting the top of his head, arms, and legs. He was curled up the whole time. The police didn't really know who to get. The tower police kept pointing and saying "Him over there! Him! Him!" The police were like, fuck it, take them all right here! Me, Ant Dog, YF, Dip and Tattle-tale. They didn't fuck with Nino or Lil Kelly Boy. We all came back to the yard except Tattle-tale. We were kept in the sub-station in the cages for a few hours. Ant Dog and Dip got wrote up. That was crazy Dip got wrote up though. He didn't do anything. He was just a victim of circumstances. Shit happens. Initially I didn't know if they got Nino because he was well away from the incident. He was all the way by the pisser when I first looked around after being cuffed and stood up.

That next day when I got up, I was sore as fuck and kind of stiff. I've been sorer though. Other Crip homies were saying they were disappointed in the younger homies from the city (younger than me and Big Ant). They felt it was crazy to have us, me and him, on a younger dude when it was younger ones who could've handled it. The initiative had to be taken.

Somebody had to step it up. I more or less took it upon myself to go because what little rep I have I wanted to keep it in tact, regardless. I've been down 16 years thus far and haven't had no bullshit on my handle (name) in regards to my conduct and push. Me being on the yard with a Sammy the Bull and its known he's snitching, I can't have that on my record. That's a stain. I can't be complicit in that behavior, no bueno! "Tic was on the line with such and such knowing he was telling."

Nah, I wasn't about to have that on me. Ant pretty much felt that same way by stepping in. Even though he shouldn't have had to, he's like 50 plus years old, but he did. When it comes out and who was present, questions will be asked. For the most part though, I concern myself with issues that concern me and my general well being. I'm not trying to have no bullshit of sorts on my name, getting no mud on it. Bullshit has a tendency of following you. I'm going to push and move accordingly! I can't be passionate about something unless it's one-hundred. It has to be authentic to who I am. I'm pro whatever, as long as it makes sense. In truth though, there will always be massive overlap with dudes trying to have a foot in and a foot out, but going nowhere fast. Seems like the only way to travel for some dudes. It's a fast life we're living in this busy prison world. Here it is Monday since those incidents I spoke of on the yard that happened Friday.

Chumlee pushed out to work. He's a morning porter. He wasn't out there that long before he was coming back into the cell telling me the yard was down and the police were locking all the porters up. It went up again with Calbo, Flux, an older East Coast and another Crip who just drove up on the lower yard. I don't know who he was or where he came from but him and Flux got on Calbo on the patio. From my overstanding, Calbo had been going through that everywhere he land. Whatever it is, that took place with him, and his homies are tripping, super! I give it to him though. He's remaining strong and didn't tap out (go SNY). Dudes have been known to tap out for less than. Hold up, the jury is still out on that, to be continued.

But just in general, we all have to look at our short comings and failures and own our side of the street when it's all said and done, noise needs volume to matter. Situations, something I've come to learn and overstand is, it don't matter what's against you when you know what's within you. Just like with the moral compass. The moral compass can only point you in the right direction, not take you to it. I've had many conversations with dudes whose morals I've questioned, due to their demonstrations and conduct in general, picking and choosing what's right and wrong. When it's wrong, from jump (from the start), there is no right and wrong, it's wrong! Stop horse playing! When it's regarding immoral shit, according to the code we push by, as street dudes, gang members, or bangers. We know the difference between what's foul and what isn't, what's acceptable and what isn't. A ball is a ball and a strike is a strike, all day. I don't have to tell you that, or explain that to you. Tell you, just because dude has the sack on the yard and he told, he still can't stay. But you have dudes that are with that.

The right thing to do is remove him. The wrong thing to do is allow him to stay. That's when dudes thirst and morals come into play, he's for sell. As I'm always saying, a snitch anywhere is a threat to real Niggahs everywhere. We're supposed to be held to a certain standard being who we are, pushing what we're pushing and when we don't, we're held accountable, period. It was a lot of that talk around Solano about who was telling or who was suspect from this tribe or that tribe, but nothing was being done to these dudes. Either they had a sack or access at something dudes needed. All it was was talk and dudes talking about, "I'm not fucking with him because he's telling." What! I'm not talking to him because he's suspect, but yet you're allowing them to stay around (SMH). The world around a man has a way of becoming too loud at times. It was a Bay Cat, I forgot his name. He was on the yard crew at this particular time. Someone produced some paperwork on him. The whole yard heard about it, so it's out there that his homies were going to get at him. You think? He heard it too and was ready, stayed coming to the yard, doing him. When nothing happened, word got around that the paper work wasn't even real. What! Got jokes! Not only didn't anything happen to dude who the paperwork was produced on, but nothing happened to the dude who allegedly produced the alleged manufactured paperwork. What in the hocus-pocus is going on? I was like, wow! Really! That's how that was sold huh? In truth, it was a lot of telling around Solano. You had to really be careful with who you fucked with, real talk, and who you were around. You had to pretty much keep shit to yourself. Once you let your business get out there, it's out there. You tell a mutha fucka keep this just between you and me, yeah, he's going to agree of course he is, but you might as well have not said it. Can't hold water.

A secret best kept is a kept secret! Once incident I can recall real vividly. My cellie had come up on a small piece of product, somebody owed him a few dollars and paid him with that, double up. Who's going to turn that down? He hollered at a few dudes. They all wanted it, but didn't have the loot. He didn't tell them it was him he just knows who has it. He got at this one Sac Cat (Sacramento). Told him the biz and told him keep it between them. When we were on the yard we saw him talking to a few of his Zilla homies, or dudes he just fucked with. I was standing next to my cellie when Ole Boy looked in our direction. Then who he was with looked in our direction. Nine out of ten, here's how that convo went. "Yeah bro, he got some of that shit, but want his bread first." and it had been dryer than the Sahara Desert. I'm sure those other dudes he got at were not dumb and figured it out and spread it to whoever they dealt with. My cellie had the goods. He didn't have no sack, nor were he serving (selling) anything. He just happened to come up on that one small piece he was trying to dump by the time yard was over and we were back in our cell, maybe 20 to 25 minutes later, after count and before chow, the cell was raided.

The police came deep. They pulled us out, escorted us to the showers, and strip searched us. "Get naked!" We undressed, handing the police one piece of clothing at a time. Then, "Open your mouth, stick out your tongue, hands in the air, lift up your nuts, turn around, lift up your left foot, right foot, bend over and spread your cheeks." Hold it, flag on the play, that's not happening. I'll squat and cough, but that's all you're getting!

"Well, how about we take you to potty watch?" That's when they take you to the sandbox and put you in a cell with no running water, no toilet, you have to use a medical toilet which is just the seat with a bucket lined with a plastic bag.

"Let's go. I'm not tripping." The Sgt that was with him told the police to just have me squat and cough. After they finished tearing up our cell, we were allowed to go back to our cell. We couldn't clean up until after we came back from chow. They called it, maybe 5 minutes later. They searched the cell and had stripped us out, but didn't find shit. We didn't have shit. They had bad intel. Tell your snitch to stick himself, Tony. There was no need to ask what that search was about. It wasn't a secret. It was someone in the building leaning in his cell door way with his hat on pulled down low, talking about, yeah, I dropped a dime on yo ass while eating a banana. It wasn't a need to ask because we already knew. The police in Solano stayed getting intel, that's the only way they were able to bust dudes, their sources. Most of the time, their info would be accurate. When they would usually hit a cell they came out with something. If it was anything other than a phone you were going to the sandbox and they wouldn't come unless it was sandbox worthy. They have some cold sources. If a mutha fucka know your business or it got out, trust and believe, those boys (goon squad) are coming. Those aren't regular police. Those are police that police the police. They also deal with prison gangs, drugs, certain types of investigations, etc.

You really don't want those dudes fucking around with you. Once your name came across their desk you have problems. They could just pop up at your cell and take all of your paper work, phone book, paper period, and keep it for weeks, saying you'll get it back after we're finished with it, in the name of an investigation. I was pretty much low key and out of the way. I personally only fucked with 2 dudes who were much older than me. They both were from the Bay Area. Simes was 82 or 83. I adopted him. He was Grandpa. My other guy was from Oakland and L was from Berkley. Ray, Sims, and Larry Lovely, my guys right there. We fucked with each other daily. My boy Rame from Oakland, who look dead on Ole Boy from the show Empire (I can't think of his name at this moment. Fuck!) Wow, Terrence Howard. He's just a fat version of him. Anyway, he would see us and would say, "There's Tic and his broken spokes." That was the name of our crew that he gave us, Tic and the broken spokes. But yeah, we walked to chow together, ate together, were on the yard together hanging out sitting somewhere or walking laps. We would hang out or walk laps after I worked out with my boy Merch from Nutty Block Compton Crip. Sometimes with just him or with my boy Tray from the Bay. He was from Vallejo. When I wasn't working out with both of them or either of them, I worked out by myself near the handball court. I stayed away from all the bullshit for the most part, the autobotism, the back biting, the hating, and the opportunist, though sometimes it found its way to me in spite of my best efforts to avoid it. Dudes just like bullshit and conflict. They feed off of that shit. Without it they don't exist. Get a bar. Like the shit with Tattle-tale. That's a given, granted. A young dude ends up popping up from the city (Long Beach) in the building I was in, which was the building I was in the whole 5 years I was there. Mind you, 5 years, same building, same cellie, L Loc, Front

Hood Compton Crip. Good ass homie right there, good dude. We had a couple of bumps in the road starting out, but it got smooth and we clicked and bonded, we jailed.

So anyway, someone came to the cell (202) and said, "Aye Tic, you have a young homie from Long Beach Babyz who just came last night. He's in cell such and such." (When I don't remember something or a name, I'll use 'such and such' as a point of reference). I didn't see him though until the next morning at breakfast. He introduced himself. The name he introduced himself to me with I don't recall, but I could tell by his demeanor and disposition it wasn't that of a young homie. He wasn't a homie like that. I embraced him though, based on. Then as I saw how he moved, he didn't move like a homie. Later, it came out and from his own mouth, he wasn't actually from Babyz, but had been running around in the county (L.A. County Jail) with some homies and was put under the wing. They didn't put him on (initiate him), he just ran with them and hung out like an honorary member. None of the names he mentioned I was familiar with, granted you're not going to know every homies name, especially with a set like mine. Two-ones (21st Streets), three to four generations. G homies, Big homies, and two generations of BGs. I'm second generation. Then you have one-sixes (16th Streets) that's two generations at least, if not three. Then you have the two-threes (23rd Streets) and their generations.

They were just really coming into their own before I came to jail. They had been out a couple of y ears at that point at least. I hung out with quite a few on the north side. Some had been converts from a gang called Young Murder Squad (YMS), but a few were East Siders. Most were North Siders, like my little homie Baby Tic. He's an original North Side Kid. Well, he's not my homie any longer. I don't fuck with dude or the Big One, Big Tic. The only reason I've kept the name is because I feel the names were mine. I put in work for the name and made the name, not them. I kept the smoking pistol, my generation of BG known the biz, they know how active I was. My homie I fucked with when I was out, Lil Spit, Budda, Hog Dog, Big Ace Capone, Bubba, Gangsta Ace, Baldie, BG Rocc, Tiny Kool Aid (Ice Cream), Ed Dig, Baby Meech, T Mac, to name a few. I had my few Youngz I fucked with as well and put work in with. I had my few Big Homies and G Homies I fucked with. Back to Ole Boy though, he started running with the Muslims, which is cool, but if that's your thing don't straddle the fence. Do one or the other. For me, Islam is my preferred religion.

I'm just not a practicing Muslim right now, though I still pray and read my Quran. The praying is here and there, but I read daily, every morning before I start my day. I'm just more so into being spiritual and having that belief in a higher power. I took my Shahada (declaration of faith) in Salina's Valley State Prison my first prison term in 1998. I took the name Sahir Asad. I forgot the meaning. Anyway, a homie at the time I had been cool with and had been writing raps with from Youngz took issue with it. He was like, "Technically, you ain't supposed to just be able to walk off the set like that, but I'm not tripping if that's what you're doing and you're serious about it. Do you." He went onto say there's no back and forth, it's one or the other. I chose to do my Islamic thing. I had been down (incarcerated) like 9 years and I was months from the house. I planned on doing something with myself differently when I got out, which was truly my intentions, which is every dude's intentions when they're attempting to do their religion thing.

Though, some do find religion for the wrong reasons, or they're trying to hide under religion to escape the activities and obligations of being a gang member/banger in this maze known as prison, feeling as though it's an easier route to take and safer route to take. I've seen it time and time again, dudes 18, 19, 20, gang members turning Christian or Muslim. In my case, that wasn't the case. The whole time I was active and functioned with the homies, participating in all activities, representing the set. I was constantly catching more time. It had gotten to the point my Mama was like, "Damn, you must like it in there. You're not trying to come home?"

First week in Salinas Valley from Calipat, we (Blacks) got into a riot in our section in the day room, during day room time, with the South Siders. One of them took it upon himself to stab a Black named Folsom. He was a Damu out of Pasadena from Denver Lane Bloods, without trying to communicate to resolve whatever the issue was, through proper channels. So, it went up! Riot ensued. Home team came out on top. It was only that one knife used and it apparently was gotten rid of because no one else was stabbed. It was all hand to hand combat after that. What was used wasn't even all that hot. We'd just gotten there, had nothing.

My religion path didn't last too long, but I gave it an honest try. I even went to the Masque a few times and stayed praying, but events happening got me off my deen (religion). It's a known fact that the set beefs (feuds) with the East Side Longo Hispanic street gang. It's a long going feud that exists on the streets to this day. It's more of a racial thing than a gang thing, though it started being gang related. I kept having run-ins with them to the point I'm like, fuck it, it's on! You want to keep trying to get at me, now you got me. But you know what's crazy? 20 plus years later, the dude took issue with my turning Muslim in 1998. Still has an issue with that. He's still tripping off of that. We've never had an issue or beef prior to that. We were cool. Dude, fall back and take a breath. Too much energy on some bullshit. The result of Longo's trying to press; I fell back into the life, full throttle, all gas. Back at meetings and renewing my hand with the BG homies. Renewed my hand on that ass! Back to dude. He was trying to do both. He's around certain people, "It's cuz this, cuz that!" Then he would be having issues with dudes from other tribes and would be like "On the dead homies!" That's when I took offense and had an issue with him.

Dude, you're not from Insane, you're not from Babyz, so whose dead homies? Not mine, you're not even from the set, stop horse playing! What dead homies are you speaking about? It was blasphemy! You didn't even know any of the dead homies. I can run off a list before my time, during my time, and after my time. Such as Baby, Meech, Big Meech, Tag Along, Big Earnest, Big Cass, Big Fred Dog, Big Kook Aid, Baby Kook Aid, Ippy (Infant Black), Lil Man, Big Ruck, Big Slep Rocc, Big Bouncer, Lil Loc, Will Sane, Deaf Tony, Big Poncho, Blue, and I.I.P. (Insane in Peace). I told dude to kick back on all that, on the dead homies, it's going to be an issue.

Dudes would come to me talking about he's getting at other dudes foul and he's claiming the Beach. Basically saying he could really get into it with someone and we (homies on the yard) wouldn't know what was up and got took off on behind his foolishness. That part we weren't worried about. If it happened, it happened, but while you're talking off on us, what do you think we're going to be doing? Hassan is his Muslim name. He was talked to and was told to get his shit right. A few days after the talking to, he got into it with a dude from the Bay and turned it down (refused to challenge). A no-no! Not only did he turn it down, but he aggressively turned it down. The aggressive turn down being animated with the hand gestures but saying you're not trying to fight and don't want to. I just told homie, check me out, keep Long Beach out of your mouth, Babyz out of your mouth, and Insane out of your mouth or we can get down right now. I though he would've taken that route, he's younger and bigger. No bueno!

Well what if Long Beach got into something? Don't even let that bother you champ! He goes to the Law Library and calls himself telling my Big Homie, Big Duck from the set on me. Big Duck asked him, "What did you do when he get at you like that?"

"Nothin!"

Then he told him, "Since you didn't fire Tic's shit up, keep Long Beach out of your mouth, period." For the simple fact that if this is what you're representing, how are you going to let the next man tell you to stop without resistance. Me and Big Duck had started meeting up in the library every Friday and tap in with each other to keep each other up on what was going on, on our side of the yard. I was basically grand fathered into a position as far as the yard. Dudes would come to me with issues and not any other homie, even the ones that had been there before I got there. I really wasn't trying to be in that position because that's not what I do. I'm not a front man or shot caller. I guess though since they knew I would handle an issue as far as homies, they came to me and being older. But nah, that wasn't my lane. Hassan ended up being moved to A-yard where Big Duck was because he had gotten into it with a retired homosexual, who turned Muslim, in the Law Library. Some were saying it was a lovers' quarrel. Ask me, something was fishy about those two. Hassan had grabbed someone's cane in the Law Library and whacked Allen over the head with it, sending wooden shrapnel everywhere. "Whaaack!" It broke in a lot of pieces. That shit was crazy. I had an incident. It really wasn't an incident. It was merely a few words with a Pomona homie named Trip, from 3-5-7 (Tray-Five-Seven, Pomona Crip). He's R.I.P. now though, good homie.

The homie Trip had got into it with some dude whose Baby Mama Trip met on Facebook. The homie passed the same day he left Solano. Damn! Dudes were fucked up behind it. A few homies saw it on the internet. A police had heard it first and looked it up and told someone on the yard, that's how it got put in the air. Our words took place a week before he was to go home and a day before dumb ass Hassan got into it with Allen. He was supposed to have told Hassan he couldn't be on the Crip work out area. I took offense to it and asked him about it. I was on some shit like, can't no-one tell nobody from Long Beach where they can or can't be, especially in a neutral area. It didn't go anywhere. He said though that that didn't happen. Someone's lying and he wanted to know who said it so he could confront them and let them know to keep his name out of their mouth. Rightfully so! It wasn't any big ole deal, I told him and that was that. But yeah, the homie was feeling some type of way about the whole situation. You could tell by his posturing. The Devil was working. The next morning after breakfast I get into it with a young dude who was supposed to be from East Coast named Melly. I don't even think dude was official. He didn't even stay in L.A., never even lived in L.A. he stayed in some city. Some East Coast Crips fucked with him, some didn't. You know how that goes. Dudes get funny like that if you're not official (really from L.A. they don't see you the same). Anyway, I had a little tobacco. I sold a few cigarettes here and there. Someone told him I had some. See, I told you mutha fuckas talk.

He wanted to buy one. I had no problem with it but told my cellie to tell him to shoot my loot first and I got him (would sell it to him). Normally I'm selective and funny with who I deal with. I was funny like that and didn't care who you were or what you had. I wasn't dealing with you under any circumstances; your money might as well have been counterfeit, Pesos, Chinese, Rubles, or any other currency. It didn't spend with me. As a matter of fact, I didn't have nothing, fuck what you heard, if I didn't invite you. He asked me, basically, could he give it to me later. Um, that would be a no! You want to smoke now, I want to eat now. Fair exchange, no robbery. Dude catches an attitude and is in his feelings. So what, you're not going to do shit!

Prior to our run in after breakfast, during morning day room, he was in the Crip area where my cellie is, with a few other Crip homies. They're all working out, except him. He's just over there, holding the bars up (leaning on them) being a loud mouth. He tells my cellie, "And yeah, you're bullshit ass Bay Area cellie ain't shit, tripping off of a punk ass cigarette."

L Loc corrected him, "He's not from the Bay." Then he looked around until he spotted me. I was sitting on some cement steps, meant to be worked out on, with my guys Sims and L. We were talking. L Loc pointed in my direction and told him, "There he goes over there. I bet you won't go over there talking that shit to him."

I didn't hear about it until we were back in the cell. First chance I got I approached him, "Check it homie, I'm not from the Bay. I'm from Insane Crip. If you didn't know, now you do!" I waited to see if he was trying to go there or something, but I didn't see any signs of posturing or gesturing, so I walked away.

He ended up being alright though, after the fact, though a little reckless with that mouth. I liked him actually. I started fucking with and talking to him. I sold him a stick or two, here and there, and cigarettes. As far as homies, they came and left Solano. The only incident I've had with a homie outside of Tattle-tale was with Y.F. It was just words, but it got heated. Dip got in between us, "Ya'll tripping." Big Nana was in his feelings, feeling like I owed him something because I had something going on and in the lane.

"Cuz Trip, you stay in and out of this mutha fucka, I don't know of anyone or heard of anyone you sent anything to, or done any type of looking out, no one."

"You're not privileged, nobody owes you shit!"

He asked me for some trees. I gave him a stick. "Aww Niggah, that's all I'm good for?"

"You're lucky you got that and that was a struggle, real talk!" Not only that, but you're on your way home again and in a few months. If you don't knock it off and stop with the horse play.

He was married. I don't have a bitch. I'm eating off the land. My situationship that I had three kids with stopped fucking with me long ago. When he asked me for some soups, I guess he was looking for a case or something, I don't know, but I slid him 4 or 5 soups. He had something else to say about that too. (SMH) I don't recall what me and Y.F. had words about, I just know I flashed on him (went off on him). Indeed, it was close to being ugly. It's my boy though, Habibi. I was pressing like, "Dude, I don't give a fuck about none of that noise coming out of your mouth." He had me pistol hot. I told him to leave me alone and to stay the fuck away from me.

He was like, "Leave you alone. Leave you alone? Oh you're not fucking with me no more? Leave you alone!"

I was over the situation and walked away from him and Dip. Me and the homie didn't speak for a minute. We were straight after that. This was prior to all of them horse playing. After the shenanigans with Tattle-tale I wasn't really feeling that crew of homies like that no longer, questioning what type of homies I was really around. I told them already anyway that if I ended up going (on that mission) I was cool on dudes. When nothing is going on it'll be a different story. "I'll do this, I'll do that." As soon as an issue comes up, its excuses or reluctance to step up. (SMH) I asked them who can go in the cell and come back out with some work, showing they've been getting active, done anything! I can! It's not a spot I haven't landed on that I didn't get my hands dirty. I've always stepped up. Didn't nobody have shit to say. Oh, after the fact though, I was going to do such and such, but you and Ant handled it. Cuz, stop playing!

At the end of the day, dudes just stood and watched two older homies do something they should've stepped up and did. I'm just keeping it a thousand, that's what happened. I'm not putting any 10s on 2s. My cellie and the yard can verify that reality. One thing I won't do is lie on a dude. Second thing is I'm not going to do, lie on nobody, or lie on my dick. Bullshit kept coming. YF and Dip had a boy they fucked with, kind of tough. It was brought to my attention, dude was solid. He's not with the bullshit. He handle his business, he get his money. Normally I wouldn't have fucked with him. I fucked with very few, especially with loot. Since he was Dip's and YF's boy, I went against my better judgement and fucked with him (SMH).

He shot his shot, "I'm a real one, I don't play games, this that and the third." Those you shouldn't trust: those who say, "You can trust me." He was a bullshit dude too. He gave me some greenies, one wasn't right, it came back invalid.

When I get at him he was like, "I'm going to get at dude and fix it."

A few days pass, I'm telling L Loc I need that loot. When I see Dip I asked him, what was up with his and YF's boy? "Is cuz going to come up with those funds?"

This is Dip, "We can get at him if he's playing games. We can get on him."

Nothing ended up happening. It was straightened out a few days after that. I stopped fucking with him, just for the whole situation. Once it was an issue with you on any business, it was a wrap. I'm not fucking with you again. I had to stop fucking with YF on that page too, he messed it up for everybody else, being a homie. No more business with homies. If I had something to slide a homie, I slid it, outside of that, no bueno. I tried working with homies, but as we all know, business with homies never really works.

Homies are always trying to get over because you're a homie. No homies though couldn't say I acted funny with them or I wasn't trying to look out because I did. They couldn't say I was on some funny shit. It's not in my nature to act funny with homies or those I fuck with. I gave

YF a "Look cuz, dump these for me and you keep these four for me, 2 for you."

He was like, "I got you." A couple of days later, he brings me the four back, but not the two, talking about its slow and this, that, and the other.

Ok, I'm looking at him like, "Where's the other two?" You didn't complete your end of it, to keep two. Instead of tripping out, I just told him, "That's you, don't trip. It's good."

You know though, you tore your draws with me. I'm not fucking with you on anything. You can't get anything or buy anything. He basically fucked himself. I kept it and he felt it. I was dealing with his boys from other tribes around him, but not him. He couldn't get a stick almost a year later. I had started messing with him again, only though because he was loading greenies for me. Every time he done it for me, I slid him one stick. So, let's just say he stayed blowed when that started. I wanted to trip, but I knew where I was willing to go with it. Plus, he was half ass cool guy. So, I just cut off his water and hurt him that way. Since I've been here at High Desert I ran into a couple of heads I was in Solano with. Abu from 3-5-7 was on one (acting up) in Solano. Everyone called him Super Crip, even the police. He'd have his flag (grey bandana) tied around his head like Pac and would be belling (walking) like a mutha fucka. 3 Pac. He push the same way around here. He's an older, turned up Crip homie with the business. He was down there, dong his shit. He got on Ace Rocc from Altadena with a couple of his Pomona homies. Yeah, Ace Rocc I was speaking on earlier, that I said was in the cell with Tattle-tale, me and Ant got on. I said he was from Pomona, but when I actually thought about it, it hit me, Altadena. Abu got on this other clown named John John from I.E. behind my cellie L Loc. He knocked John John out. He was out cold, standing on his feet. He had told me about Trip, but I knew already. I saw young Frost too, from Park Village Compton Crip. I didn't get to holler at him though because I was at medical and saw him passing by the window on the patio. Abu's on the yard with me, Frost is on the lower yard.

Someone was telling me since he's been up here he's changed. He's not the same Frost. Yet to be determined. I ran into another dude from the Bay named Bud from Pittsburg. He lives on the lower yard too. We were in the sandbox too in Solano together. He saw me on the patio a few days after I got here. He was on his way to New Folsom. We also worked together in Solano on the line (main-line). He was on the yard crew and I was the IDAP worker. I would be out there third watch with the yard crew, hanging out on the hand ball court wall during chow and after chow until a little after 5 P.M. Before night yard was run. I would post up on the wall or would be walking around the yard. Sometimes, I would walk in the chow hall with different buildings. My building and mainly YF's and Dip's building. You know, running plays and such. Me and him were cool for the most part, until we bumped heads.

5

 One day at work, when he was on his way into the kitchen through the back door with his water jug (big Folgers's jar) to get ice water, I had asked him to snatch mine too and grab me some. He shot some slick verbal at me (said something smart). I was like, Damn! Because this is what we did out there, look out for each other. So, I was like, "You're on some funny shit, huh? If I was a Northerner you would've got it!"

A few more words were exchanged and we stopped fucking with each other, period. He disappeared. I thought he transferred, but come to find out he was in the sandbox and had been for a minute. He saw me before I saw him. I was walking from the shower one day and happened to see him coming from the yard.

We didn't get to go to yard together, but we weren't fucking with each other anyway. One day though we ended up on the yard together, in the cages. We spoke and started talking. We talked about why we were in the sandbox. He was like, "Damn, I wouldn't have thought you were on that type of shit. You were layed back and out of the way."

Perception will get you for the most part. People though only see the person you allow them to see, thus controlling the perception of you. That's with anyone. You'll see who they want you to see, never judge. Yeah, I fooled a lot of individuals with that one. Just because I didn't, it didn't mean I wouldn't. I was just in chill mode, trying to do and be me without all the extra shit. I'm a layed back person. Even my IDAP co-worker Tae, who's a Northerner, was like, "Damn Tic, that was the last thing I thought you would've been back here for." He was back there for an attempted murder. From what he was saying, he just got swept up in the process. Same shit with my old neighbor I was on the line with Mousey, a Northerner from Loma Lind. We were neighbors for a long time. He was in 201, I was in 202. He was my boy. We dealt with each other tough. He had a few cellies, but I liked his cellie he had named Bang Bang of all his cellies. Mousey kept it a thousand with me, good dude. When he saw me in the sandbox, he asked me why I was back there. When I told him, he had the same reaction and response, "Of all people, not you Tic. You were out of the way." He thought though, it was a Bay Area named Dave I was in the sandbox for named him Wavy Davey. Dave was alright. He just had a tendency to overextend his hand, putting himself into binds and situations.

I told him, "Nah, it wasn't Dave, it was Green Eyes." He knew who Green Eyes was, though he assumed it was Dave because he knew Dave had owed me a couple of dollars when he left the yard. He actually was snatched up like four or five in the morning by the Goon Squad, him and his cellie.

He was again like, "Damn Tic!" He let me know that if I needed something I know where he is (his cell). So far, that's been it. I haven't run into anyone else from Solano that I knew or knew of. When I first got to Solano, I moved in the cell with L Loc. He was straight as fuck. He's a good homie, around my age. I'm a year older than he is though. We gelled. We lived together for 5 years, sharing that small space, and he's no little dude. We've only had a couple of little disagreements, but we were good and got past them quickly. I used to think, boy, my hands are going to be full fighting this big mutha fucka!

For the most part, we just jailed and clowned a lot. We ate a lot to-gether too. My guys a jail house cook. He's a chef of jail's fine dining. He knows how to blend spices and put it all together. Nothing ever tasted the same. I was gaining a lot of weight, we ate so well, and without using a fryer (a hot put broken down and the plate is used). He done all of the cooking and I had started making pies. You know, with the bananas, syrup, peanut butter, jelly, oatmeal cookies, chocolate chip cookies, and two types of candy bars. I also was his prep guy. I would cut up the bell peppers, onions, cheese, and all of the meats we would use. We had a cool system, always a team effort.

He would bring back milks from work. If they weren't cold he had ice. He would also bring back food from work in the kitchen at night, sometimes I would ask for certain stuff, but for the most part he would bring shit back for me, mostly the good stuff. He would also slide other homies food, or dudes he messed with when he came back from work. He never tripped off of passing out state food. A lot of dudes that work in the kitchen would sell it to you. I get it, if that's their hustle. L didn't do drugs, no type of drugs, nor did he smoke cigarettes. All he indulged in was alcohol. He loved to drink, him and me both. There it was mostly reggie we drunk. We really only drunk white lightning on our born days or on occasion. For years though we've made it. I'm talking about four or five gallons at a time. We would be in the cell white boy smashed, drunk as fuck.

Sometimes we would both pass out, wake up, and start drinking again. Sometimes we would have my tree so I would be over the top. One time, I got so smashed I was in the day room and had been drinking, and was still drinking in the day room. It went bad. I was walking from one side of the day room to the other side. This is where it got tricky. How it got tricky? As I was turning the corner it went black, lights out. It was as if I went into a dreaming state. I was no longer in prison, I was on the streets and I was arguing with my situationship (female I had three kids with). So yeah, I blacked out. When I opened my eyes a bunch of eyes were looking down at me. I guess they assumed it was a medical issue, mind you, it was a medical facility.

"You aight?" Still kind of out of it I stayed on the floor for a minute. I kept hearing someone say, "Didn't nobody do nothing to him, L. He just fell out, right there." Surprisingly, the police didn't see anything. My cellie and some other Crip homies came around the corner, ready to trip. I guess someone had went back to the other side of the dayroom and told him I was on the floor and out. I got up off the floor, my mouth was bleeding, and I had chipped my front left tooth. I was walked to the cell by my cellie. He got our door open and I went into the cell. I was done. Still drunk as fuck, and moving around in the cell, I had managed to make a butt naked (plain with no extras) soup. I ate a few bites, left it on my locker, and climbed on my top bunk, almost falling off it twice. I was out as soon as my head hit my bed.

I was just drinking though. I had been blowing trees earlier, for most of the day pretty much. I did blow a stick right after chow, which was when I cranked up my drinking. I got like that one other time, but I didn't pass out. It was on my born day in 2017. I was fucked up though. Me and the homies were drinking on the yard. Me, Dip, and a citizen (non affiliate) from the city named Quese. We all thought he was really a 20 Crip because of a few stores he told. It all related to them in some fashion, shape, or form. I don't know why he didn't just bang 20 Crip. He grew up with them, hung out with them, all the shit.

I think YF was drinking and the homie T from Long Beach O'Hood as well. I was hugging the pole on the basket ball court, trying to hold myself up. The next thing I remember, I was in the cell, like how did I get in here? The homies had walked me to the building and to my cell, making sure I went inside and didn't walk away from the cell until the door had closed. That was the end of that. I stopped getting drunk like that on the yard. The homies didn't have to tell me, I don't it on my own, because I know I was a liability. Being out of the cell like that is never cool, or a good look, because if something were to happen, who am I good to? No one! I'm not good to anyone, myself included, jeopardizing myself and those around me. I couldn't protect myself and would've had to be helped. I know for a fact I couldn't have gotten away with that anywhere else, especially on a level 4. Homies would've DP'ed me. Definitely I would've been two on one'ed for that violation. I knew better. I just got loose. But yeah, we stayed faded (drunk) around that spot. The homie stayed bringing the stuff we needed to make the mind go round. We would have so much material, we had to stash it in other cells and gradually get it back as we went up (put a batch together). The same way a fat person would stash candy bars and cupcakes all over the place. Even after the period where we had to stop cooking wine, we would still get the material and let other wine makers make it and break us off our issue, we kept drink. I kept trees, a consumer of the leaf! No doubt, I'm a PH. L use to roil over sometimes two, three, or four in the morning and smell the incense burning and see me blowing. He would rise up and look at me. I would be over by the sink, going in, smokes everywhere.

One time h e was asleep, and I was getting it in. Incense burning, the music's playing, and I'm in the middle of the floor 2-stepping to some old shit. My backs to the door, the music is down low, enough for me to hear keys or something, I'm in mid puff, smoke in my mouth. Ms. H, a 4 foot something older red haired police, cool as fuck normally unless you rub her the wrong way, she was in stealth mode. She popped up on the door. She does have a super foul moth on her. She's real reckless with it, but she only got at certain dudes foul, real disrespectful. She'd call a mutha fucka a bitch real quick. "Biiitch!" She's an old school white lady though. She would wear her hair the same way, the style never changed, a bun that sat on the top of her head. A little hung down in the back and in the front, a little hung down on the sides of her face. Damn, I can hear her now, "Biiitch!" The way she said it was like a shot gun blast. You just wanted to run over to her and take her down, like "Biiitch! You better watch that shit!" You could talk shit to her and she'll talk shit back. She wouldn't write you up either. According to her and in her mind, she got the best of you. She talked the most shit. You just really had to do some bullshit for her to write you up or hit your cell (search it). Everyone been to Solano knows about the older, short, red headed, white police named Ms. H.

She did get at me once, sideways and I cursed her out. She was like, "Fuck you, McClinton and lock it up, Bastard."

I was like, "Yeah, yeah, yeah, old ass broad." Never called me a bitch though, not once, and we've had a couple verbal shoot outs, but yeah, bitch was her favorite word. On some real shit, she was an acquired taste. She didn't like you and there was an issue to her, you were fair game. Stand back, here it comes ya'll, "Biiitch!" I just knew though, one day someone wasn't going to have it and knock her old ass out!

So yeah, my backs to the door, but I could hear some light tapping on the cell door window. I turn around and she's motioning with her finger for me to come here. My back is still to her, I put the stick out with my fingers. I let the smoke slide from my lips in a light stream and walk to the door, "Oh, what's up Ms. H?"

"What are you doing in there, young man?" (Her favorite word outside of bitch)

"I'm not doing anything. Just listening to music and about to clean up the cell."

"What's that burning in there?" She already knew it was trees. I played the game with her though.

"Oh, I don't know. That's why I was burning incense, it was a funny smell."

She laughed, "Alright, it was a funny smell, young man. I'm tired of getting high coming up the stairs right here. Keep it down and burn something stronger. That shit's weak."

I just said, "My bad, Ms. H. I got you." She was on her way, mumbling something. My cell was right there at the stair case. I was in 202. Anytime someone came up right there, they're going to catch a whiff of trees burning, at times, regardless of the incense. The majority of the time, if it wasn't me, it was a neighbor on the tier. Our area stayed lit up. I waited for her to go down the stairs on the other end. After I watched her go across the day room floor, I lit it back up and resumed what I was doing.

L had woken up, well, got up rather, because he had heard the situation with Ms. H play out. He just shook his head and laughed, like you're crazy a hell. He called me a hype on a few occasions, because I smoked the stick until it was singing my fingers. As Lon would say, they were burning and smelling like pork rinds. Trip, police piss tested me thirteen times, talking about the tests were random tests. Bullshit! How are the tests random when you're testing me monthly around the same time, random my ass! Nothing was random about those tests. There's no way you're going through thousands of inmates in a 30 day period. It's impossible. How am I on testing anyway to this extent, I'm not on mandatory testing.

I've never had any possession cases, or drug use write-ups, nothing, nor do I have anything in my c-file (institutional records). I wrote them up, telling them they're targeting me, but for what though, what's the reason? I don't hang with druggies, nor do I do drugs. Ok, I get the environment, but still. Solano had a drug problem. The piss testing stopped. The thing though, anytime and every time they popped up talking about a test, I took one, no problem. I never refused. I talked shit, but never refused and I never gave them a dirty of all the tests I've taken. My shit came back clean every time, which shocked even me. I was Smokey the Bear! I don't know how I never got a dirty when they would test me. It probably would've been only a couple of days without smoking. All I was doing was drinking a lot of water, but then too they probably got on me, because one of those rat bastards had me in their mouth, "He smokes." It's a lot of telling around Solano. I didn't think that much telling was possible. We lost three phones fucking with those rat bastards (stick yourself Tony for being a rat). The times we've lost them, there were always some type of group going on (N.A./A.A., Gogi, something). At the bottom of our stair case, when the police came through the side door, which is right there where the group is being held. We couldn't even get the police siren sound (alert, letting us know the police were in the building and about to blitz a cell).

Normally it was the yard police coming in from them getting information from a source or several sources (SMH). The alert is usually done as a courtesy for all, letting everyone know, "Aye, get right. The police are on the move, or they're entering the building." It's a heads up. We didn't know shit until it was too late and they were already at the door. I know one thing: 12-building had some cold rats in it, the coldest. The last phone we had, I was in the cell and had just got off of the phone with my ex-situationship, Lois. She was on some bullshit as always. She was telling me, my daughter with her, Kaemaijay whom I called Tweet, said she hated me. I got in my feelings quick. I told her I didn't give a fuck what she said and so what if she hated me, she wasn't the only one. If she did, she'd been poisoned against me by her people, her mama included. Me and her were straight. We had begun to build a relationship and bond when she was a lot younger. Her people (Aunt Maxine and Uncle James) would allow her to communicate with me. They were raising her. My situationship didn't have custody of her or my other two kids I had with her. They were in the system in Colorado. Me and my daughter would write each other and I would call her. My situationship wasn't in her life. I tried to be, as only I could.

The two that were being raised in Colorado by a white family, as I was told, my oldest by her (situationship), Christian who's 19 now, and my daughter by her, Solie who's 18, has aged out. As for them, I'm sure there's a lot of questions and confusion, and rightfully so. I'm sure it wouldn't be easy for them to talk to me, or even see me, or even if they wanted to, dealing with all of the feelings and emotions. Being that, I am their father, but a father they don't know and a father who loved them only from a distance. I know a lot is weighing heavy on them. I feel, probably deep down, they had harbored resentment and anger towards me for the whole situation, with my not being there for their growing up, and for them having to grow up with strangers, in the system, only having each other during their adolescence and childhood. There is a fourth kid, Elijah, but there's a cloud of major doubt about him.

Though he has my last name, he's a possible suspect at best. I saw he's a possible, because she was fucking her ex-deceased husband's homeboy the whole time. I would of questioned the other three, Christian, Solie, and Kaemaijay, if they didn't look so much like me and my other three kids by two other baby mamas. My Jr., my son Brandon, and my other son, Craig. I couldn't deny them at all. Not even if I wanted to. I caught her ass too, dead bang. I caught her with him (dude she was fucking), at a motel called the Aloha, on Columbia and Long Beach Blvd., behind Long Beach Memorial Hospital, where my kids were born (Christian, Solie, and Kaemaijay). Elijah was born there too. The Aloha was a short distance from her sister, Debora's house, on Esther, on the East Side. Her baby sister, Lee Lee, had an apartment over there too. Both apartments sat behind a house. You had to drive up a drive way to the back. I was already at the motel. Me and my side piece, one of them anyway, had been serving (selling dope) out of that motel for about 4 or 5 months. Had it booming!

My side piece (Young Squeeze), Miko, was my Big homie's niece, who I'm named after, but I call him Lil Sugar Bear now. Anyway, she had left to go handle some biz for us. We only had a little work left, so her home girl, Cynthia, who smoked came and scooped her up, taking her to Ghost Town. So I'm at the room by myself, sipping on some alcohol and smoking weed, waiting to dump what little work is left. I'm not going to lie, I wanted to fuck Cynthia's thick ass. She was short, chocolate, big titties, big hips, and a big ass (SMH). Thick! Mind you, I'm a self proclaimed Strawberry King (Strawberries or Berries are women who have sex for dope). If they were right, they got it. I didn't fuck with the Dirty Birds (dirty crack heads, always dirty looking and not taking baths, and keeping their self up). I only messed with the clean ones, clean clothes, looked decent, smelled good, and had something going on. Mando (Mandatory), I strapped up! One time a condom broke on me and had me shook, but that's another story. So yeah, I had caught Cynthia by herself one day and got at her, on the low. I was like, so when are you going to let me fuck Cynt? She was like, "Nah Niggah, unh-unh. You're not about to have me strung out on your ass, having me and Miko fighting." I left it alone though, but I still wanted to, and she had some nice DSL's (dick sucking lips). Cynthia would ride us around sometimes, running errands or just picking me up or dropping me off somewhere when I wasn't trying to drive. She was Uber before there was Uber. I'm at the room, Miko and Cynthia in traffic. I have the porno cracking, grease out, and I'm sitting in the chair smoking a blunt.

All of a sudden I hear this familiar sound. You know cars, you know fords and their transmissions. I knew this sound for certain. I've been driving the car for months. Technically it wasn't mine, because I didn't buy it. I came to the house one day and it was parked in our driveway. Where it came from I couldn't tell you, even to this present day. Came home, it was there. She had the keys, so I'm assuming it was hers, which means since we're in a situationship and you're my situationship, it makes it mine too, plus she didn't drive. I'm sitting there and I'm thinking my minds playing tricks on me. So I'm like, "Nah, it can't be. . . It wouldn't be." I pushed pause on the DVD player and had to investigate. It got real all of a sudden. I got up and went and looked out of the window. We're on the second floor, so we could see down into the parking lot from our room, how I wanted it. Security purposes, etc. But sure enough, it was the Taurus. I could clearly see her and see the driver. It's as long as they'd been having sex, under the guise of brother and sister. That's how I was introduced to him, "My Brother."

When I was introduced to him, by all of them, her sister Debora, her sister Lee Lee (who I also wanted to fuck and was attracted to, Lee Lee was a sexy ass, slim goody), and her told me the same, this is our brother. I got at Lee Lee too, like, "What's up?"

She was pretty much like, "If you weren't in a situationship with my sister, I would let you fuck." She never told on me, so the door was open. I figured, it just had to be the right opportunity or situation and it was all systems go. I would've done some nasty stuff to her. But yeah, this dude was in my house and around me. I'm not knowing or thinking nothing. I'm taking all of these people for their word. I watch them from the window for a minute to be sure they're there, for a reason other than for me.

Then I'm thinking, they wouldn't know I'm here. They're here for one thing, to get a room. When he left her by herself in the car, he walked into the back entrance into the courtyard. I gave him time enough to go to the office, and then I came out of the room and walked down stairs. When I walked into the office, he was just getting his key, when he looked and saw me, it was like he saw a ghost. Before he could say anything, I'm like, "Cuz, on Insane Crip, you have two point one seconds to get that bitch the fuck up out of here. I don't care where you take her, but bounce from here."

He started trying to tell me they came there to serve some dope. She's not into that, the dude was lying. I'm like, "No, ya'll didn't. You don't have to lie to kick it." I left the office and headed for the parking lot. I caught her getting out of the car and grabbing their stuff for the night. No doubt she had a whore bag, an overnight bag with fresh panties, bra, tooth brush, deodorant, soap, change of clothes and hair gel. I lean around her, nudging her out of the way, snatching the keys out of the ignition and threw them across the parking lot on a roof. I took their bottle of alcohol, opened it, and took a sip or two, throwing it on the ground, shattering the bottle. They had some food. I took that shit out of the bag and started eating it. I did have the munchies and it was still warm. I dumped the rest on the ground. Then I went in her purse, took every dollar she had and slapped her up. Hell yeah. It got real domesticated. I pushed her in the car and was choking her. She's trying to grab my hands and breathe. I eased up, only to slap her some more. Stupid ass, not for cheating with him, but for getting caught.

Before I had pushed her, she tried to get at me like a simpleton, telling me that her and him followed me to the motel. Total opposite of what he just told me, clearly it was a lie, from both of them. They were horse playing. What ya'll were bringing me some drink and some food? If you don't knock it off! The car doors open. Now I'm squatted down talked to her. He can't see me, but he's walking towards the car, telling her, "Man, look what you got me in to." So this was her doing.

As he got closer I jumped up and put my dukes up, "Cuz, we have to get down." Stage left, he was out. He just left her.

The next day, being so close to her sister's street, I knew where they would be. So, me and the homie T'ken from the set Youngs went on Esther with the bangers (pistols). We pulled up in the drive way and got out of my car. I believe we were in my brown Seville, on Daytons, or my Coupe. As we're walking up the driveway the rest of the way, I see Ole Boy, her dude, under the hood of the Taurus. He looks up and sees me and the homie. He started moving around the car, putting more distance between us. I'm trying to holler at him, but when I look around, I see Lee Lee and her baby daddy in the door way of her apartment. At the end of the day, it's her, (Lee Lee's baby daddy homie), Lee Lee, her older sister

Debora, and her husband, Perry, who had just opened their door and were standing there with one of their kids. They were all just looking at us. I'm asking dude, what's up? I already had had my pistol out. I wanted to just burn his ass, but I knew if I did, they all would've told on me. Lee Lee, her baby daddy, her oldest sister, her husband, the kid, and situationship. I'm an outsider, they're all family.

No doubt in my mind they would've come to court. I didn't trust any of them like that. I put the banger up and me and the homie left. "We'll holler!" While she was creeping with dude, I had crept with her brother in laws sister, Mary. Me and her got a room at the Sand Piper hotel on PCH, going towards the traffic circle. One of my spots I used, to duck off, that's kind of out of the way. Of all places to creep, they thought they were out of the way. Thinking they were in a low key spot, in the cut, and wouldn't get caught. Never in their wildest dreams did they think they would run into me there. A spot apparently they felt was secure and I wouldn't be nowhere in that area. Come on now, I'm a Long Beach dude, I'm all over Long Beach, and in some of the oddest areas I normally wouldn't be in. Sucks for you. . . Busted!

I'm subjected to be anywhere though and in some of the darkest corners. I'm an East Sider with East Side ways. So yeah, me and Mary fucked and sucked on each other. When I talked to her last, she had the nerve to question me about having sex with her sister in law, Ida. I told her the real though, I didn't fuck Ida, which was true, I didn't. It was Ida's sister, Mary. Now you know. I was also sexing this other female named Chardon who stayed in the set on the block known as The Ave (Martin Luther King Avenue). She stayed across the street from Mary, Ida, their mother Betsy, their little sister Didi, and the homie from the set, Ray (their brother) who was the original Baby Tic, before he was Ray Mansin. He's a good homie and a solid homie, he just wasn't feeling "Big Tic" so he aborted and got his own name.

I was also messing with this female named Latrice/Trice, who stayed across the street from the Aloha (see, I'm everywhere). She stayed on 29th street, directly across the street from the Aloha. I met her before I met my situationship. She was a hook up, my second day out of Salina's Valley in 1998. Miko was my road dog. We hustled together, stayed together, slept together and fought sometimes, the whole nine yards. We were together every day.

So, as I was saying, me and situationship had been in a heated conversation before the police hit my cell, took me to the shower, and stripped me out. The phone was in my boot. L was at work and hadn't come back yet. When he did come into the building, they immediately snatch him up and escort him to a shower, stripping him out too. I could hear him asking, "What's going on?" He hadn't seen me yet, in the upstairs middle shower.

I'm asked, "Who phone?"

I'm like, "Who you got it from!"

I'm like, "Man, that's another eight dollars down the drain, messing with these rat bastards." I'm about to go right back in A1-C. It's about to be the 3rd time. At that point, I was straight on the gadgets, at least for a while, so I fell back, done. Me and situationship hadn't spoken in a while before that. I should've just left it alone. Fuck it. It wasn't like she was a factor in my life and she damn sure didn't do shit for me the whole time I've been down. Legally, it's a situationship still, but only on paper. Out of sight, out of mind. But I should've known from get go, she wasn't loyal, the loyal type, or wife material. If I had a do-over, I would've just fucked and kept it moving. Suuuper regret! Had my grandmother been alive, I don't think I would've messed with her. Granny would've seen her for what and who she was.

Biggest regret, marrying her and having kids with her. I can admit I loved her at one point, but that evaporated long before I came to jail. On some real shit, I've never met a more delusional person in my life, and she's a habitual liar. She will lie straight to your face. Cold thing about it, she believes her own lies. I never believed shit that came out of her mouth, but the physical that went into it and came back out if it continuously until I bussed my nut! I got caught up in the illusion, the pussy and head was good. Basically, I wanted some house pussy, somebody that was home waiting for me that I could have sex with. I had been locked up a minute and I was trying to lock something down.

I messed up and married her (SMH). Didn't even know her like that. I met her after I got out of Salino's Valley in '98. I met her over at the home girl Samantha's house, the home girl Trouble from my set. Fine, thick, and yellow, she's a breed (biracial black and white). Suuuper ass too! I actually met situationship's little sister Lee Lee first, with her sexy ass. Me and my kin went to Samantha's house because he messed with her, they had a little situation going on. Lee Lee was doing her hair when we walked into the room. Initially, we though Lee Lee was who I was supposed to be talking to, but she wasn't. It was her sister.

I had already sized Lee Lee up. I'm like, "Hell yeah, I'll fuck. I'll beat it up, sexy slim goody!" So when she finally showed up later, she was like, she was debating about coming, because basically the home girls a ratchet and she knows the type of dudes she mess with. Lee Lee leaves, me and her make a pallet on the floor and just talk. The next time I saw her, her, my kin, and Samantha came to Cat City (Cathedral City), scooped me up from mom's house (picked me up). We went to my female kin's house, who stayed in DHS (Desert Hot Springs). She wasn't there. She was in traffic, more than likely with a dude. That's where me and situationship had sex for the first time. Shortly after that encounter, I ended up catching a violation of my parole and going back to the pen. Trip this, for terrorist threats and possession of a fire arm. News to me!

My foul ass baby mama, Jackie, lied on me! Mad because I didn't want her. She called the parole people saying I threatened to kill her and I showed my kids a gun. Plain and simple, bitch lied! I'd done no such thing. It was all because I didn't want her. I went to see my son's by her and she kept trying to show me her ass. She wanted me and saw I had no interest and it fucked her up. I was long over her, no feelings at all, or attraction. I was a grown ass man at that point and not the young kid she was used to dealing with. She was used to my going in and out of jail, coming home messing with her, but that was the kid me. When I got out we would dip somewhere and have sex. Those were my juvenile hall days (LP/Central). She was used to that, but I was what, 13, 14, 15? You're horse playing, even when I went to Y.A. and got out, we had sex. She felt rejected by me and couldn't handle it.

She had me locked up for 10 months for that little stunt she pulled, which I did in Ironwood (level 3). Situationship initially though I just got the pussy and shook (hit it and quit it). She found out later I was in fact incarcerated. I guess she felt better about the situation. We communicated the whole time and before I got out she moved to Cat City with my moms. We got married in mom's living room when I got out. Then, within a month, Riverside County made me leave their county and go back to L.A. County. I had to go back to L.A. County where I moved with my Uncle Johnny and Aunt Martha in Lynwood, California. They embraced me with open arms. My cuzzo (cousin) Nip helped me get a job where he'd worked for years in Torrance, California, at the Mobile Oil Factory.

It wasn't long before situationship moved from moms spot in Cat City back to Long Beach. I was no longer there. She moved with her older sister, Debora, who at the time stayed on Atlantic in some yellow apartments off of New York St. Her little sister Lee Lee lived in those same apartments. I would go and stay the whole weekend with her and her kids there (her older sister's place). On my off days, my uncle and aunt would drop me off and pick me up. Me, her, and her four kids, John, Camille, Craig, and Nicholas, moved on the north side of Long Beach. At the beginning, the situationship was cool, but then she started pulling stunts. I came home from work and she wasn't home. The house wasn't cleaned. I didn't have any food cooked. I had to go up the street to Louie Burgers and get something to eat. I got off work around 5 P.M. She called me and told me she couldn't get home because the buses stopped running. "If you don't knock it off!"

When she called me, my boy at the time, I.C. (not his real name) were standing out front by the hair salon. We stayed in the back, behind it. Me and him were leaning up against the building, talking and drinking a beer. As we stood there, we watched busses pass by, coming from the East Side and going to the East Side. (SMH) Bitch got jokes. I didn't know it at the time, but the kids were a couple of blocks away at her uncle and aunts house. The ones who would years later have my daughter Kaemai-jay. Basically, she was free to get loose and hang out, east side bound. Yet, she didn't want to live on the East Side, just hang on it. She has plenty to say bad about the East Side, though. It was this that and the third. My boy asked me if I wanted to go scoop her up. At first, I was like I'm cool, but then was like, fuck it!

So we go to the East Side where she was at, her sister's spot. When we get there, music's playing loud, you could hear loud talking. Oh, it was going down. When I walked through the gate, there were a lot of heads, male and female, with drinks in their hands, laughing and talking. I look and see situation, dancing and shaking her ass with some dude with a cup in her hand. You could hear someone telling her, "Aye, Lois, your husband is right there by the gate. He just walked in it."

"No he ain't. You trippin. He at home." She'd been drinking. I called her, she was still kind of dancing when she turns around and sees me. She starts walking towards me. I'm pistol hot.

When she got close to me, I'm like, "Check this out. I don't know what type of games you're playing, but go get your shit and come on!"

She tried to act like she wasn't trying to leave. I just told her if she didn't come and when she did her shit was going to be outside, every one of those green trash bags.

Somebody told her, "Girl, you better take your ass home with your husband. It ain't shit going on down here." Me and I.C. left and went and got into the car. She walked her ass through that gate and brought her ass to that car and got in. He dropped us off at her people's house and we got the kids and went home. After they got baths and ate, they were in the room, we went to ours. After we talked, I got some pussy and went to sleep. She rode me until I blew up, "BOOM!" Her reverse cowgirl. Oh. . . My. . . God! Doggy style, no joke, and her head skills were like no other. I can say she took pride in sucking the dick . . . and she swallow! We had sex a lot too. She got pregnant fast with my first baby with her, Christian. Then came Solie, and then came Kaemaijay. The possible, he came shortly after Kaemaijay. He's between me and Ole Boy, I caught her with. Her brother! (SMH) He could be Juju's too; a bullshit homie from the set who she claimed she never had sex with. Liar, liar, pants on fire! She said they never had sex, but I don't know who she tough she was telling that lie to. She was flat-out horse playing with that one. He no doubt got the pussy, but she wanted to talk him down and bad mouth him, talking about I wouldn't fuck him, he's dirty. Yeah, ok! I didn't care either way, so what if you did. You had a past before you met me, except for that past you kept in your present. You kept having sex with that past. Yeah, so, me and my daughter's relationship went sideways. I know she was turned against me, but I'm cool with it. I don't lose sleep over it. I didn't do shit to her for her to hate me, so she can sit on it!

It messed with me at first, but I got over it. I've technically been emotionally turned off for years. I've turned that volume off and pulled the button off. I'm numb to the emotional shit or responses, especially with those I have no connection or bond with. Technically, I only have my mother, my aunt, and my cousin. I had my uncle (R.I.P.). Everyone else is mere strangers. I feel nothing for a stranger. Pac said it best, "How can you feel for a stranger?" Real talk, out of sight, out of mind. I've been down for 16 years and so called family left me for dead. They don't mess with me. I don't hear from them. I can't call them. They don't do shit for me, nothing. Couldn't see me with nothing, but they love me and care about me. You know what? You can sit on it too! Fuck your care about me, and fuck your love! But the crazy part, if I had a date and were getting out, the story would be different. They would all be messing with me, but let me bounce back.

6

It shows you how your family really isn't family, how they really feel about you, and what they think about you, especially catching a life sentence. How easy it comes to them to say, "Fuck you." You're in there, we're out here and you know what's crazy about that? I could've just as easily been in here with a life sentence behind them, going to bat for them and putting mine on the line, because I'm loyal. I was for, with, and about family. You had issues with them, you had one with me. It was nothing to talk about. I would've killed behind them and would've lost my life behind them. This is how I see I would've been treated. Though, it really gives you context. It also gives you something to think about, conditional versus unconditional. Sometimes, when I'm lost in thought, when the cell lights out and my T.V.s off, I reflect on what was, what is, and what will be and I like my chances of a brighter day. Cancel culture is nothing new to the incarcerated.

Me and my cellie had this conversation one day about family or people in general with writing letters. He was like how people on the streets don't write letters, some have never even written a letter, wouldn't know how to write a letter. Don't have a pen or pencil, let alone paper or stamp.

He was telling me how someone on the streets told him they have to buy paper, stamps, and envelopes and find something to write with. He was also saying how it's just something not done out there basically and not practiced. We, in prison might be the last letter writers that exist, like the dead poet's society, or a lost breed. He was like, "In reality homie, we have to think. It's people on the streets that grew up without having written a letter or even knowing how to address an envelope, because the art of letter writing has become truncated, abbreviated, and high tech (the emails and the shit that's in the electrical clouds that exist)." Ok homie, so to that extent, I get it and can see your point and you giving them passes. Those though, before the high tech shit came into play (the truncations and abbreviations) you're just flat out not fucking with us on some outta sight outta mind type shit. So to that I say, "Holler if you got me, fuck you if you had me." Trust and believe, I'm always going to do me. I'm never going to be without or do without. I'm from the gutter. I'm going to get my blessings. I find ways to make it make sense, just like I'll find a way to publish this book.

What I did learn was this, can't no one hold you down, but you and your supportive unit. If don't no one ever in life fuck with me, I know four who do and it would've been a fifth if my uncle, Johnny, would've still been alive. He just passed a few years ago. It truly had me in my feelings when I found out he passed. I love my guy. He was a good person and a god fearing person who loved people and life. Two things he loved doing were cooking and eating ice cream. "Kate, I got some cream!" I cried for a couple of days and numbed myself with pruno and sticks until I finally passed out, leaning up against the wall on my bunk. I remember getting the letter my aunt wrote that had me stuck, sitting in the same position, reading those words over and over again.

"I'm sorry to have to send you bad news about pop, but he has gone on to be with the Lord. The family is doing ok. I have my kids, my grandkids, and great grandkids to help keep me going. I have sent you a copy of pops obituary to have for yourself. PJ Sullivan showed up to the funeral also. It was good to see him. Keep us in your prayers, as we will keep you in ours. We will send pictures when we can. Call us, if you get a chance.

Love,

Aunt Martha Washington"

A couple of other family members have passed as well since I've been down. Neither affected me. I felt nothing at all. I don't know them. We didn't interact or function together in no type of way. I've been in prison for 16 years. Again, how can you feel for a stranger? Everyone out there that's considered family are strangers, except those I've mentioned. I'm more than sure they feel the same way about me.

So, neither of us can't miss a relationship that doesn't exist. But yeah, me and situationship would talk and she sees the conversations not going her way, she's in her feelings. The first conversation we had after 10 years went cool until she starts lying immediately off the dribble (beginning). "I've always loved you. . . No, I'm not messing with nobody." (SMH) Then she starts asking me all these questions, looking for closure. "Did you leave any kids out here other than ours I should know about? Did you fuck Ida (Mary's sister)? Were you fucking Chardon? I heard you were fucking Blackie's daughter, Miko. Were you?"

"No. . . No (her sister). . . Yup and yup." I admitted to everything I've done and was doing. At this point, who cares? So I kept it all the way a thousand with her.

She couldn't though to save her life. She's taking her lies to her grave. "No, I wasn't fucking nobody else. I would never have cheated on you. You were my husband."

"What did that have to do with the price of tea in China?"

"What does that mean?"

"Exactly!"

"I've never cheated!" Then she played the victim role. Wow! It was all about what I've done, how I treated her, what I've done to her. She had done nothing. It was all me.

I was like, "I can admit, I fucked over you and cheated on you. I did that. Yeah, I was fucking."

You stopped fucking me. I guess you wanted to be exclusive with Ole Boy. I had to get it somewhere. What was I supposed to do? Just like you said, I wasn't fucking you. So, somebody was getting that pussy and that head. I wasn't. We had our kids back to back. They're all a year apart, actually months. If she would've been breast feeding, she would've been walking around with National Geographic titties (those island women that are in those National Geographic books with those long ass titties hanging to their stomach). As much as you liked having sex and sucking dick, you didn't turn into a nun.

She started making bullshit ass promises she never had intentions of keeping as far as keeping in touch and stepping up. "Papa this. . . Blackman that." That's how that last conversation went bad. She called me "Blackman", a name she called me (one of them anyway, papa was the other one) when she so-called loved me and cared about me. I told her flag on the play basically.

"Don't call me that name or any other name as an endearment ever again. You don't give a fuck about me or my well being." I basically let her know that I was over her, mentally and emotionally checked out, just done. The realization really just sat in. True to her nature and who she was, she immediately got defensive and even disrespectful. You know the deal, hurt people hurt people. Her emotions go up and down like a seesaw. She goes into why did I call her? You don't even ask about the kids, those in the system in Colorado. Then she starts telling me about her man who she initially lied about having.

She goes into how long they've been together, what they have, what they're doing. So why did you lie? It was no need. You weren't going to hurt my feelings or affect me. I told her though, you know what, "Aye, you're right, my bad. I don't know why I called you, but don't trip. I swear to God it won't ever happen again." That's been years ago.

When I told her it wasn't going to happen again, "What you're not calling no more?" Ding ding ding! What did she win? That's exactly what that meant. If it wasn't for the few memories, she would've been forgotten. Not the good memories, the bad ones. The only good ones, which don't count, are the sexual ones. Now though, I feel completely nothing for her or towards her, not even as a situationship. She's just someone I've had a few kids with and was a part of my past, and I have two more of them (women I have kids with). Being locked up, you learn a lot about those who were around you and how much they really messed with you when you're up against it (as far as what they felt about you). Now, it's no longer a guise. They're exposed. You see where the relationship really stood. When you first hit the sandbox, things slow down. Like on the streets when you're first locked up. You're in that cell by yourself until you go to committee, left with and to your thoughts.

Your mind is everywhere. Luckily for me, though, I would be alright. I had trees and gadgets. I basically smoked for a few weeks to keep my mind off shit for a hot second. I gave a few sticks away and blew the rest. I was blowed as fuck in that cell. I couldn't do any thinking in the first cell I was moved into. It was too much moving around and walking. They called that section Front Street. I had to wait until they moved me to the over flow building, which was 9-building. That's where I refused to move from. It's the main-line. It's activity. I'm hollering at dudes from my cell when they come to the water fountain to get water.

My boy Tray from Vallejo, I worked out with occasionally on the yard, was in his cell, 115. A Damu named Snow was in cell 118. Dude I poked was in 117. I was in 112 I believe. Fish from 5-2 Hoover (Five-Deuce) looked out and shot me some stamps to get at my folks. Rome, a civilian from Long Beach who lived in the building was on some funny shit (autobotism) messing with those dudes. A dude named Juju from Compton Farm Dog acted funny towards me too and we were straight, but all of a sudden, he allowed dudes to poison him and taint him and we were tight way before any of those dudes popped up. (SMH) But you know that's how yard life goes. Dudes can be influenced against you when you're character has been nothing but solid. As for Rome, I could care less. He's not my homie, nor a homie from the set. So, he could keep his funny shit. My Damu boy, Dee from VNG, looked out too, shot me some soups and told me as soon as he made it to canteen he'll hook me up. He kept it a thousand with a Crip on some real guy shit. He didn't change or switch up, "What up Dee!" "I'm in my zone. I've finished that second line three, you've read one and two and it's a four (blood of my enemies), stay you home boy!"

My other Bay boy, Keetay, kept it solid with me. He was in the building. He didn't switch up. My boy Merch from Nutty Block Compton Crip didn't switch up. They knew the business and my character. You can't taint or poison real dudes. Yeah, that dude S.T. had been shooting his poison and trying to taint dudes, true to autobotism, dudes jumped on board. At the end of the day, some can recognize bullshit when they hear it. As for me, I'm going to always stand on the side of right and going to always be in the right, on the right side of it. You can say what you want about me, but you can't say I haven't been handling my business, or keeping it a thousand. I'm pushing on the line, still active, and I'll be fifty next year. I'm not Big Homie, I'm just Older Homie. Knowing the code and where the lines are, respecting them for what and as they are. I'm never going to let bullshit dudes change me, taint me, or poison me. Keep me from being me. I'm not even sour at dudes. It was just another teachable moment. I'm still going to keep pressing. 20 Dee (not his real name) from 20's had moved in 9-building. Him and Akeeli, his homie, had had a fight on the yard, so they moved him from 11-building to 9. I was doing something, more than likely in my cell, with my ear buds in, watching T.V. because I didn't hear Tray Calling me, trying to tell me the Long Beaches were in the building helping 20 Dee move in.

He said he was calling me and called a couple of times. He told me he was hearing S.T. saying all types of shit, how he was going to do this, that, and the third to me. If I came back to the line, he's going to rush me. I was like, "Yeah?"

"... For sure!" Oh, you wanted to rush me for stabbing someone, but not because I supposedly went into your sack. (SMH)

Tray was like, "Wasn't nobody else saying nothing. It was all him. 20 Dee wasn't saying nothing, K wasn't saying nothing."

He also told me he could hear Oppie trying to whisper (pointing basically), "He's down there." Meaning me. Trying to tell them what cell I was in. Suuuper mark! Wouldn't even come to the cages on the yard. Every time I would walk passed his cell going to the yard, he would just stand on his door, looking at me. Hell yeah, I'm going to the yard any time the cell door opens. The Damu thought it was a joke as to the situation, but he has room to talk. He was worked out of five dollars by one of the young Compton Crip homies and didn't do shit. A mutha fucka thought he was going to horse play with me over my two dollars and got his stupid ass stuck... Playing!

Me and Tray heard that the Damu had a kite speaking on me and him. Allegedly, I done what I done (stabbed dude), because I was trying to leave the yard, so it was a stunt (committing an act to leave the yard). Leave the yard, for what? Who was I scared of and I wasn't in fear of nothing. I've been on that same yard (B-yard), same building (12-building), same cell (202), same cellie (L Loc) for 5 years. Leave for what? My program was straight and I was doing me. Why would I want to fuck mine off? Because you claimed I owed you. I ain't owed nobody shit. Never had no debts and I don't do drugs. Dude, S.T. was on some bullshit. He knows like I know, I didn't owe him and he was trying to pull a stunt. Then, I heard from K that S.T. said, "At least I got his C.D. player. I got something."

Technically you stole. You could've got it to me after I left the yard but you didn't. I let you use it, being a homie, because you didn't have nothing in your cell as far as entertainment, just like I let K use it, being a homie.

Like a real homie would and did. I didn't have to. Then you come with the shenanigans, because I was cool and laid back, feeling as though you had a victim. It wasn't going to work out how you envisioned it in your head. I've been in prison half of your life. It's not the first time I've come across your kind. A few days after the Long Beaches were in the building (9-building) helping 20 Dee, I had talked to him briefly before he moved out of the building, going back to the other end of the yard.

He was moving to my old building. He gave me a few messages from my cellie L, we never talked about the situation. I knew what was up though. I know how dudes operate. Tray also mentioned too that while 20 Dee was talking to me, he was facing Oppie, making facial gestures and head motions, as if to say whatever, basically trying to keep me off guard, as if all was cool (SMH). Kids! All that did was let me know, as I've already knew, that he supported his 20 homies shenanigans. After all he is from 20's and that is his home boy. I've been hearing about 20 Dee's antics and shenanigans long before I set eyes on him. Low key set tripper and Insane hater!

Him and his homie S.T., I was schooled to them. It all checked out and made sense after I assessed everything for what and as it was. Those dudes are bullshit, period. I'm a firm believer in karma. When you do shit to people, dirty shit comes back to you and not always in the same way. I don't have dudes talking about I was foul or scandalous and I better not be caught on a level 4 yard. I've been on that 3 yard, the only 3 yard I've been on in my 16 years. Otherwise, I've been on a 4 and High Desert is my 3rd 180. I just came from committee. I've had 45 points and was on my way to a level 2 (lower level). Why would I fuck that off? Leave for what! Really, I was trying to lean back and kick my feet up, and work on going home. It's a lot easier to go home from a level 2 because the administration sees you're programming and not fucking up. Like I've said though, I can hit 4's, no worries. I haven't done no bullshit on no yard I've been on. My prison record has been solid. I haven't been caught up in shit! When it's been time to step up, I've stepped up. Dudes aren't running around on these prison yards with my name in their mouth, saying I'm bullshit, foul, or on dope. If they are, it's an autobot supporting the fake and manufactured propaganda perpetuated by the bullshit dude. I do recognize bullshit dudes (autobots) do follow and support other bullshit dudes, which I finally get and overstand. I don't trip off of those types of dudes, for the simple fact they'll always exist in this world. My boy Tray, someone owed him some loot. He decided to press (get aggressive) a little harder on who owed him. He went to meet up with some of his homies in the Law Library. Once he left and went back to the yard, he was being called to the sub-station. It went from that to, "You're not going back to the yard!"

They had a 1030 (which was a kite saying his life was in danger). A 1030 is an anonymous kite or note sent to the police. They put him in the sandbox for his safety, pending transfer. Now, when all of this initially took place, I was on the main-line still. Word was going around, he dropped the 1030 on himself and he was trying to leave the yard because his homies were plotting to get on him (attack him). Wow! That's like when it comes to dudes tapping out (giving up because they can't deal with the politics no longer, or they feel they're in danger), you have to take it with a grain of salt, especially when you don't know. Dudes could be on a smear campaign, trying to smut a dude up (put dirt on someone's name), which nowadays plays a role in yard life, dealing with crooked politicians or just foul dudes in general. It's a million of them.

As far as someone saying a dude has tapped out, you have to be mindful of the fact, it doesn't always be the case. Dudes are quick to say, "such and such tapped out" or "did you hear such and such tapped out", then a year or two later you'll run into that same dude, like damn, I thought he tapped out! (SMH) That's why half of the time when you hear it, I pay it no mind. All it took was two, one to spread it and another bullshit dude to confirm it. The shit was being said so much it became true according to dudes. That easy to smut you up! No proof, just the word of some bullshit clowns. Nowadays, in this climate, dudes don't work off proof or facts, just word of mouth.

Me personally, I didn't feed off into the rumors and bullshit, nor did I speak on it or spread the poison, though I did tell him I heard it. Like the shit Snow did, he spoke on me and Tray. He wasn't even on the yard. Then when Tray didn't come to the yard (the cages), he spoke on him (his situation) just as I'm sure he spoke on me which I've heard he done and I believe it, because of his character. We've never had any issues. I used to push him around in the wheel chair when he had his surgery on his foot, even when I didn't want to and having to hear him and his homies talking while they walked along side of the wheelchair. "Blood, Blood, Blood, Blood this, Blood that." I'm like come on now, a Crip is pushing you.

As I've said, I've seen it many times before, what these dudes do and are capable of is nothing new. It's a rerun of the same ole show. Then it got back to me. I should've stuck Oppie, because I knew he was going home. What did that have to do with the price of tea in China? Not a damn thing! He played with my loot, wasn't trying to pay me, so I handled my business, period. All that I snaked him, or he was a Crip, or I didn't tell anyone or let anyone know I was going to take off. Dudes knew the potential of it. Being an issue, it should've came as a surprise, as long as it been. My cellie knew it was an issue, K knew it was an issue, his boy knew it was an issue (his boy he messed with on the daily), an older dude named T Brown from Pomona. All three of them hollered at Oppie. Do you think it stopped there? My so-called homies on the yard knew, because I'd been speaking on it for weeks. Dude needs to pay me my loot. He's been holding me up from running a play (handling business). I had other loot, loot in the streets, and a few dollars on my cellies books (account). I was just trying to run a few different plays at once.

So all that, dudes didn't know it was an issue or the potential of it going somewhere else. They can knock it off, they're horse playing! Trust and believe, behind the scenes amongst each other, it was spoke on. A few outside of who I shared it with shared it with whoever they deal with. "You know Ole Boy owe Tic. He's tripping." As far as actually telling someone flat out I was going to play ball on dude, only two knew who I won't reveal. They knew. One probably doubted it, that I would take it there, how laxed I was and cool, didn't see it in me.

The other one told Oppie, "He's not going to come at you playing, and I don't think he's doing any fighting." He got a front row seat due to my needing his cover to get my banger, which he gave me. Outside of those two, I wouldn't have told anyone else. You just can't be speaking on shit around Solano, or giving heads up.

The potential of it getting to the sub-station or back to Oppie or to dudes in general, chances are high and I wasn't willing to take that ride. In any tight situation weigh the odds. If you stand to lose more than you stand to gain, go with the odds. Besides that, you don't just trust anyone with that type of sensitive information. Trust by definition responsibility resulting from confidence placed in someone. Get a bar. Who I felt mattered, felt counted, knew. I also knew they would be the voice of the real. Without tainting the true version of events when speaking on it as it pertained to the facts of the matter, once it was being addressed.

However, and to my surprise, when I first talked to K, when we were in the sandbox on the yard, he was like, "Yeah cuz, S.T. and dudes (autobots) were spreading you left because you owed him." Then he went on to say how he told S.T. I wasn't like that and since he'd been on the line he hadn't heard nothing foul or scandalous about me. But S.T. wasn't trying to hear it, he was intent on smutting my name up. It was mainly the three who were on the foul shit, S.T., Tall, and 20 Dee. Campaign, put smut on Tic! He was like Tray Bang and HB from 80's weren't saying anything.

But any rational thinking really tripping off of everything at surface level, it doesn't add up. The math is way off, but has a common thread: the mathematicians doing the adding. He was like, "They weren't trying to hear me. I'm just one voice in the car, so its majority rules." I'm listening to him like wow! If I know something is foul and that's my strong belief, because it's wrong, I'm going to stand adamantly on it. For no other reason but it being the right thing to do.

I saw Richy Rich from 4-3 Hoover (Foe-Tray) that morning as he was walking back to our building, "Leave that dude alone, he's a buster (coward)!" I don't think he knew what was going on as far as the situation (me being owed two dollars). K Rocc and his little homie from 40's saw me that morning. Didn't speak, they just nodded as they were passing me, indicating they saw the move. Me and Joker, I forgot which East Coast he was from, talked briefly in the sub-station. In the cages, they brought him in there, putting him in a cage next to me to sit for a couple of hours or something, a cool out period. He had told me my banger was still in the grass after they took me and Oppie off the yard, but didn't no one grab it and get rid of it!

I'm like, "Damn, why didn't anyone get it and dispose of it cuz?" He was like, he didn't know, but he saw what had happened and I could've got him a lot better than I did, but I did get him. I gave him a verbal (a message) for my cellie before they took me to the sandbox, right before a police named Sunderland came to my cage, telling me my cellie L was getting my shit together. I can only imagine what was going through L's head when the bullshit reached his ears about me owing S.T. and that's why I did x-y-z knowing me. He lived with me for 5 years, knows me very well, and knows my get down (actions/character). He knows I'm not the type to owe or do foul shit. Shit, in fact, my trees I was blowing in the sandbox, most of it came from him. I had some too, from someone else who had owed me. I also had go-go. I wrote him a kite though, explaining the situation to the best of my ability without giving my away as it pertained to dudes on the smut campaign. I did get to see him briefly when I passed him and the homie T.O. from Nutty Block, sitting outside by the gate while they were at work. He asked me was I alright? I let him know I got the loot he sent my people for me off of his books. Shit, I needed those two dollars. Basically, it was my last dollar fifty, plus that two dollars Ole Boy owed me. Outside of that, I had a few dollars though in the streets. Twenty five here, ten there, fifteen there, shit like that, crumbs off the land type shit.

I didn't tell anyone to collect it or who owed it to me. I let them live (have it). I just left those crumbs alone, debt paid at my expense. You owe me nothing. Once I left the yard, the debt was cancelled. That's how I got down, but that's how it supposed to work and should work. Not see a dude 5 years later, "Aye homie, you still owe me 3 dollars." Literally 3 dollars, 10, 15, or whatever. It's small and should've been dead. Shit come and go when it's all said and done. The yard just went down right now on the lower. Everyone already knew the business from what I heard. I heard it was too yesterday, the Bay Areas were going to get on one of their people.

You can pretty much imagine who else heard it and knew it was going to happen. It's not too much they don't know before it happens. Thus far, High Desert has been active indeed! Me and L got along well for the most part. I'm a year older though, but he's bigger. Big Lil Bro, me, and the homie jailed and gelled. There wasn't any funny shit going on. He wasn't a funny dude. He kept it one way and all the time real. We clowned a lot in the cell and have talked about a lot of shit over the years, knew each other well.

I like having cellies that aren't homies for the most part. Homies feel privileged and entitled. You have to take critical pauses at times. It's not where you're from, but how you come. We can jail and we can gel. I prefer cellies though really that aren't homies from the city, or from the set. As homies, dudes feel not only privileged or entitled, but feel they can do and say just anything without a filter. Out of these 16 years I've only been in the cell with two Long Beach homies by design. Hypothetically, this due, when you come back from hard, he's sitting on your bunk, eating an oyster and rice bowl, your shit mind you, have the whole cell smelling good and he's sucking on his fingers and wiggling his toes, watching the Simpsons, talking about, "What's cracking (going on) on the yard cuz?"

At the same time, laughing at some shit Homer or Bart done. Damn dude, if you opened my shit I better at least have me a rice and oyster bowl too. Lil Tray Deee was my first cellie that was actually a homie from the set (Daren Shanks). We were cellies for three years. We were also cellies in the sandbox after leaving the line for the melee in Calipat. Then, once he left for Delano, I was in the cell with G Boy, a young homie from Blvd Mafia Crip, another Long Beach homie, and that was only for a couple of weeks or so and then I left for Delano. I thought Lil Tray Dee and me were going to land on the same yard so we could link back up. That was the plan. I landed on B-yard and he landed on A-yard. I forgot where the homie Ray Dog from Youngs went, Chew from O'Hood, or G Boy. They were endorsed somewhere, I forgot.

We were all split up, me and Lil Tray Deee were the only ones endorsed to New Delano. I think the dudes we got into it with from Dodge City landed at Salinas, don't quote though. That incident had happened in 2010 in Calipat. I can pretty much recall all of my cellies in the 16 years I've been down, because it wasn't that many. I'm a good cellie. I know how to jail, I'm clean and neat, and I clean up, and also clean up behind myself. I shower, I'm not loud, I don't bring heat to the cell, and I don't fuck with the police! I don't have the police in the cell because I'm on the yard doing some bullshit or getting into it with them.

I'm always mindful of the fact my cellie could be dirty or doing something. I'm not trying to bring attention to the door and have him caught up. I don't argue with the police or play with them. I keep it strictly convict, however I'm respectful and mindful. No cellie I've had ever had anything to say bad about me nor have any moved out on me. Most importantly, I keep cell business cell business. What's done or discussed in the cell is supposed to stay in the cell. It shouldn't reach the yard. That's how I rock (how I do it). Chumlee though is my actual second cellie from Long Beach on the main-line. I was just on the yard earlier, talking to Cavi from Pomona 3-5-7 (Tray Five Seven).

We were just talking about this very topic. He was on some shit like, "I like Bay Area's for cellies because they talk different from us down south (southern California) as far as their slang and how they talk, they dress, and move different from us." He was like, "I'm trying to be around something other than I'm used to." I get that and it makes a lot of sense. I've had a couple of Bay Area cellies. We even discussed that all homies aren't going to be compatible, just because they're homies or just dudes from the same city. The shit don't work all the time and just because you get along on the yard don't mean you'll make good cellies. It's a whole different thing. Once you live with a dude, you'll start seeing and noticing characteristics or little shit you hadn't seen. For the most part though, you'll know off top if you can live with a dude or not, or if we're going to be able to jail or gel, or if he's a certain type of dude and it's not going to work.

I personally don't have issues or hang ups, especially being older. I blow my trees, sip my reggie, and I write my scripts. Thus far, I've written a few scripts, "Outta Sight-Outta Mind", "Rim Shop", "Been a Long Road Back", "16 Bars", "Ponds", and a mafia series called "2nd Line". It's three, but I'm working on the fourth one, "Blood of My Enemies". I've also written two street lit books I need to re-work at some point, "Feeling Some Type of Way", and "Ah Bitterchild State Ah Mind". I've never let anyone read either of them. I've let several people read the scripts who've become instant fans of my writing. The first thing they wanted to know though was why I hadn't turned them into Urban Novels (even here). They were also like, its crazy how I'm sitting on all this talent and not utilizing it. I let my Damu boy Dee from V.N.G. (Vaness Gangsters) read my shit, instant fan. "Homie, you don't know what you're working with do you. You're talented as fuck. You should be rich!" I'm average I feel. I just know how to put stories together.

I don't feed off into the hype, or into my own hype, but I do realize I possess the talent and the gift to write. Everyone can't do it and I do it even better blowed. I feel I write better blowed. To me, that's when I do my best writing. I'll put one in the air and I'm in my zone, out of the way and doing me, that's pretty much my program. I'm blowed right now. I'll watch T.V. but a lot of times it's watching me. I do music, not often though. I'll have to be in the mood to do music. I'm writing a letter to a female. If I have one or interacting with one if I'm drinking and blowed or just on my chill shit. Now I'm writing this "Yard Life" knowing the different points of view and the different things I'm speaking on will no doubt make for interesting conversations.

Right after I was talking to Cavi, I started talking to Hersh, my Bay Area dude. I was telling him the foundation and premise of "Yard Life" and how that everything that goes on with us at this point in this maze is basically "Yard Life". It evolves around it however you want to see it or view it. We're on a yard and we're going through all the trials and tribulations that come with it.

Whatever it is, we're going through personal or otherwise and we deal with as we deal with it. We're dealing with a lot of different shit, different personalities included, on a daily. We all have different coping mechanisms. We're dealing with police, other races, rat bastards, other tribes, as well as dealing with the outside. It can be a bit much. I gave him a bar of where I was going with it, as far as the integrity and how I wasn't exposing any violence that occurred that wasn't on the books already (documented). If it wasn't yard knowledge and already known to all, no bueno! It had to have happened on the yard, in the open. The incidents I'm writing on happened in front of everyone on the yard, thus it's not a secret and I'm not exposing anything I shouldn't be. It's public record/yard knowledge/115's have already been issued and dudes have already been booked. The victim has gone wherever, the suspect has gone wherever, and programs resumed. He was telling me he hadn't come across dudes that had written books and had really spoke on my city or my homies. I told him I've read several books written by dudes in prison (which I would never mention by name) from other factions, who speak on their movements and their contributions as to helping pave the way for generations coming after them. I also told him it's rare to have Long Beach Crips spoke of in regards to contributions.

Especially if it's a dude from L.A. writing it. We're not L.A., we're L.A. County, a big difference and a lot of dudes called us Rich Crips, like we weren't just as grimy or just as easty as any other East Side, or West, or North Side. We've never been liked by many, even to this day, but I know for a fact, my homies represented the city and the set, and we're active as well in the 70's and 80's, making it possible for other Long Beach homies to talk these lines. For the record, we existed on the map, believe that.

Didn't shit happen on the yard today while we were out there, not on our yard or the lower yard. They had us get down though once, just before yard was over. Something happened on C-yard. That's where the police were running to. Most of them are out of shape and its funny seeing them try to run across the yard. They're out of breath before they're off the dirt. I don't know how in the hell they pass their physicals. Some of them look like they're about to pull a hammie. You can tell they're out of breath and tired as fuck. Not in shape at all. Me and Hersh chopped it up about some other shit as well. Something he said made a lot of sense about how dudes have different definitions of solid and most times its self serving, their specific use of it, the actual representation.

7

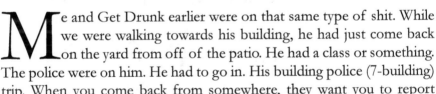

Me and Get Drunk earlier were on that same type of shit. While we were walking towards his building, he had just come back on the yard from off of the patio. He had a class or something. The police were on him. He had to go in. His building police (7-building) trip. When you come back from somewhere, they want you to report back to your building. If you're taking too long getting back, they're calling for you over the P.A. "Such and such report back to your building." We were speaking though in general on how these dudes on these drugs are trying to get real Niggahs removed from off these yards. It's like if you're not on drugs and a part of that culture, you're an outsider.

You don't function how they function, or move how they move. You're not with the scandalous shit that they're on or with. So, it's a matter of time before right and wrong clash, because the two can't co-exist. It's impossible and where a lot of fuckery and dirty politics stem from and come into play. Dudes on these drugs. Those that can't get them or just trying to get high. They're taking meds they shouldn't be, just to get high. They're killing off a part of their brain that actually worked. (SMH)

His whole thing was, you can't trust dudes on drugs and you shouldn't. They're unpredictable.

It's just crazy how dudes have the nerve and audacity to be mad at you and feeling some type of way because you're right and standing on it. You're weird because you're not doing drugs or on drugs. Mad and upset because you have morals and values. What the fuck! Another conversation I was having with someone, he was telling me how he was cool on this banging shit, well being a member, none of us are banging because we all have enemies on the line we beef with (feud with) on the streets. He was like, if he tells his homies he's cool, they'll trip. That's not the first time I've heard that from dudes. They know what it's coming to and know what it is.

That conversation had me thinking back to when I was in Solano and Tiny or Baby Pep from 20's got at me like, "I'm letting you know Tic, I'm cool on this shit. I'm on another page and trying to go home. I'm not that same dude I was. I'm good." He was like, "From now on, don't address me as Pep. Call me by my government name, Ricky, or Hodge."

I was like, "For sure. You got that!" Who am I to tell another grown ass man he can't stop claiming his set. If that's not him, it's not him. That's not my call to make. We all have our own shoes to walk in (get a bar). Dudes kill me with that. Survival on this yard, it's hard to shake some. I've been despised so many times, but that don't change none.

Me and homie were chopping it up about how these dudes will talk to you but at the same time have one of their hands in their pants, like they're clutching a hold of something of some kid. That's not cool. We both were on the same page. Shit, we're trying to see both of your hands in plain sight when you're talking to us. Blacks have that bad up here in High Desert with that shit, the younger ones especially. It doesn't matter who they're talking to. You even have Hispanics doing it, not a lot, but a few. That shit ain't cool at all! Then the topic changed to the current state of prison and where it'll be in the next 10 years with the mind state of this younger generation and with some of the older ones my age trying to conform to the ways of these younger ones. It's crazy. Trying to stay or be relevant (SMH). It's all good until they turn on you. Add that with the drugs. As soon as you speak on it, dudes start looking at you, like you're the crazy one or the weird one all because you're speaking truth and fact.

That's why for me I'm always mindful of what I speak on, how I speak on it, and more importantly who I'm speaking to or are around.

Dudes look for a reason when it's not serving their interest. They're opportunists too. If they see an opportunity other than what they had in mind, they're going to take it. I'll say this though to that, karma comes quicker for the dudes on the other side of the gun though. The yard is noisy, but you can still stay sane.

Today, while me and Lon were on the slab doing our burpies, Snake was standing near us doing what he do, taking a head count on the yard, but to no surprise, it was more South Siders than anyone else combined, which is the norm though. Everywhere you go, it's the same script. It's going to always be more of them and for the most part they're going to be on the yard and be counted for. There's no staying in the cell or going in the building at in-line. They have mandatory yard. You better be sick or half dead and can't move. As does Northerners, Others and Whites. Do they like it? Probably, but it's their policy. Blacks are renegades for the most part.

We're the only ones who don't push that policy and wonder why it's ten to one or seven to one when shit happens. A lot of dudes are trying to dodge the what if. Won't come out or make excuses about why they didn't or couldn't. That's the guilty conscience, "Oh, don't let it be tension in the air, you're going to see who's going to show up for the dance with their dancing shoes on!" Faces you would normally see, you wouldn't see until after the tension passes and everything's back to normal (SMH). "Cuz this, cuz that! On God, I was ready!" Straight horse playing! If you don't knock it off, pick it back up and knock it off again!

Snake counted a hundred plus South Siders, twenty something Northerners, thirty Blacks, us three included, a hand full of Whites, and a hand full of Others. I don't know who's the shortest as far as the number count, the Whites or the Others. In our section (B), there are only five Blacks on the top tier. Me, Chumlee, Vamp, Lon and Silent from 9-2 Hoover (Nine-Deuce). On the bottom tier it's two Damu's, VRU is out of Compton, he's a Piru, and you have P.F. from Bop out of Lancaster. The other Black is a tall weirdo that came from New Folsom. He told us he came here because he got into it with some Damu's there. Yeah, I think that's where he said he came from. Whatever happened, he's salty as fuck about it.

"I don't fuck with Bloods!"

"I could care less."

Fuck! This cell is cold right now. I still haven't gotten my T.V. yet. This shit is crazy.

I put the 602's in (grievance form). It does get granted, right? So they acknowledge they were at fault, which they were. When I left my cell, my shit was in working order and it wasn't broken. My T.V. being broken sure wasn't on my inventory sheet. When I got here (High Desert), the property officer at the time, Wilkes, opened my property box. The stand on my T.V. was broken, which had to be a deliberate act. You can't drop the box and the stand just breaks off. It was other property in the box with it, not only that. I wrapped my thermal shirt around it.

If I had to guess what happened though, it was the bullshit clerk. When San Quentin's clerk came around, he was calling dudes by their last names and passing out property sheets (inventory sheets), pushing them under the cell door. He was telling dudes to just sign them, without going over them, and push them back underneath the cell door. If he don't know it off! When the weirdo got to my cell door and pushed the sheet under it, I read it, but I didn't see my T.V. listed on the sheet. I'm not signing that, that's out!

When I address it, he's telling me what's on the sheet is all I have. You have me fucked all the way up. I'm not signing that. I have a T.V. If my T.V.'s not on there, I'm not signing it. It's no bueno. "You have a T.V.?" Didn't I just tell you that? I was in ADSEG and I had my T.V. Now he wants to play games. "You can't have T.V.'s in ADSEG. You had a T.V.?" You mean to tell me you're in this prison and on the main-line and you're working in R and R, and you don't know T.V.s are allowed in ADSEG? Stop playing! I slid him the paper back (actually kicked it back). I kicked it under the door with the pen and told him to get that shit up out of here. I'm not signing it. "Don't get mad at me. I'm not the police!" Either the police, one of them, caught an attitude because I wouldn't sign the paper and broke my shit, or that clown did, trying to steal.

He's back 10 or 20 minutes later with my T.V. added on the sheet. Then I signed it and told him, "Good looking out (thank you)." As I've seen though, some bullshit was put in play. Wilkes, the police, told me to write a 602, and assisted me, telling me what to put on it. He wrote on the back of a new inventory sheet that when he opened the box, my T.V. stand was broken off of my T.V., verifying it.

He left with the paper, making a copy for me and giving it to me. He gave me two options. They can keep my T.V. and I file the 602, or they can give it to me and I can have someone on the yard fix it for me. That would be a hard pass. The homie Dirty Mike was like, "Nah cuz, just file the 602. They're with the bullshit up here. If the wrong police go in your cell, they're going to take it." The police Wilkes was like, listen to your partner. I filed it, and it was granted.

But the police at Quentin were sending a replacement stand to repair my shit. I haven't heard anything back for a minute from it, so I wrote a form 22 (request for interview form) to the R and R Sgt. He was talking about Quentin haven't sent my replacement T.V., but I wasn't inquiring about no T.V., my T.V.'s already here.

I was inquiring about the replacement stand and High Desert repairing my T.V. It was said that no replacement stand was ever received by R and R, even if it had, they wouldn't be able to repair my T.V. because they're not a repair shop. I had an invoice from Quentin saying they had sent the stand and it was received here on the 7th of February. A police named Cena came to my cell before breakfast a few days ago. He had basically told me to re-do my 602 and have Quentin replace my T.V. with a new one and have it sent here.

He was telling me, being real, they don't really have anything to do with my T.V. being broken and they can't give me a broken appliance. He also told me he looked for a T.V. he could give me until I got situated, but there were none at the moment. So now I'm waiting for me other form 22 to come back with a response. That I sent to the L.T. (Lieutenant) after the R and R Sgt (Sergeant) got at me, so I can send a fresh 602 to them with the old one. This shit is crazy as fuck. I just received a few dots and dashes (letter) from my moms the other day telling me that Chardon just told her she was pregnant again by her baby daddy.

Chardon was with me when I came to jail on this case in '04. I was pretty much on the run. I first met her at my situationship's in-law's house the night I picked her and the kids up on the Ave in the set. When I went into the house, I saw her young ass. She was 18 or 19 at the time. I think I was about to be 30 or was 30. We made eye contact. I knew given the opportunity, I would be fucking her.

That opportunity came two or three weeks after that. My boy at the time, I.C., was taking her home girl Meme's fine ass out, which is a young home girl from the set. Meme asked Chardon if she wanted to go. If she did, she could kick it with me. We ended up getting a room after we chilled at the beach, smoking and drinking. I fucked. The pussy was snug (that snuggy). The next day, I was at the spot (dope house) serving. I sent one of my boys to her house, telling him to tell her I wanted her to slide (come) through. She came 10 minutes later. She already knew what I wanted with her. I closed the spot down and we got it in (had sex). Me and her young ass fucked a lot.

I recall another time, we were on the Ave in an abandoned apartment that my G home girl, Sugar Mama moved into. Situationship's in-law's stayed in the front apartment and she lived across the street. Me and Chardon were in there blowing a blunt of some cool struggle (low grade marijuana). It had us high as fuck though. I asked her what was up with the pussy.

She was like, "What's up with it?"

"Can I fuck?"

She nodded her head yeah. It wasn't anything covering the windows, so we had to go in a small hallway in the cut. She took her jacket off and laid it down. She had a shirt on. She pulled her panties off and spread her legs. I ate that pussy first, had her young ass going crazy. She started shaking and trembling, trying to close her legs, telling me she can't take it. I made her cum.

Then, I put my dick in her and fucked. I made her cum a second time, then nutted, "UNGH."

Keeping it a thousand though, she couldn't suck no dick. She tried though. I give her an "E" for effort. We would get motel rooms a lot. We'd kick it (hang out), smoke, and fuck. That's what we did. She caught feelings. Another time, on Halloween, we had her mama's swoop (car). We went to the top of Signal Hill where you can look out over cliffs and see the city and lights below. Cool spot. I used to go there as a teen with my oldest kid's mother and have sex with her.

Me and Chardon blew a blunt, plus I was drinking. I had her drink some with me. She wasn't a drinker. In fact, before then I never saw her with a drink. She just liked blowing (smoking). We ended up in the back seat and her on top, riding my dick while I held her hips and pulled her down. Then she laid down on top of me, working her ass and hips until she started cumming, Shortly after making me cum. I use to spend the night at her sister, Michelle's house with her in Compton in Mona Park's turf (neighborhood), off of Willowbrook, by the rail road tracks. She stayed nights with me at mom's spot. When she has a spot with her home girl, Sheila, I stayed over there a night or two. The same apartments where Trice lived. In fact, Trice still lived upstairs and I was still fucking her off and on. Me and Chardon were sex buddies, but then I started having feelings for her.

We never had a baby because at the time she didn't want any kids, so she was taking precautions. We messed around for like 4 years. I can say there was shit, but it was all good. When I was gaffled (locked up by the police), we were together in a motel room in Palm Springs, California, off the 10 Freeway West. It was early in the morning, around maybe 5:00, or 5:30. We had just finished having sex and were about to blow a blunt. Someone came to the door and was knocking. It was an older white dude, asking about if our smoke detector worked. I never opened the door. I just pulled the curtain slightly back and looked out at him. I could hear him clearly though. "Do your smoke detectors work?" After he walked away from the window, it dawned on me. "Hold up, that was either the ones, police, or the ones sent him to see if I was there." Either way, it was ugly.

I told Chardon that was the police and I was about to go to jail. She started tearing up, saying it wasn't the police and for me to stop saying that. I started to chain smoke. I knew the deal. The phone starts ringing and she answers it. "Hello . . . yeah . . . yeah . . . yeah . . . uh-huh . . . Oh." By this time, she was already looking at me. I knew then for sure. "Baby, it's the police. They want you to come out with your hands up." I grabbed the blunt and fired it up. When I came out of the room with my hands up I looked around, to the left and to the right. It was police everywhere. They were behind cans, on the roof, behind fences. It was crazy. It was like they were coming to get Osama bin Laden. She was the last pussy I had and that was 16 years ago. She rode it out with me for awhile. She didn't just shake (leave) like most bitches would have. That's why today I have all the love and respect in the world for her.

She done what no other bitch in my past ever done, kid's mothers included. She thugged it out, stayed by me. All while I was in the county jail she came on the weekends and put money on my books. She came to Wayside, another L.A. county jail facility, with my homie T-Meech's girl, Hot Sauce who's from the set, Youngs. His baby mama's actually Chardon. Rode it out with me through my time at Tehachapi's reception yard. Until I hit Tehachapi's 180 yard, up the hill 4b. After I was there a few months I told her I loved her, will always love her, but she could go live her life. I had a life. Then she told me she wouldn't have any kids for at least 5 years.

Her son just recently turned 10 years old. Mind you, he was 4 when I left. Before she left though, she sent me a nice package and bought me a CD player that kick start. Good looking out lil mama. I just reconnected with her in 2016 and she came to visit me way up north, northern California, a few times 8 hours away from the city. Her people were like, "That bitch much love that Niggah." Yeah still! She brought moms, my mother, too with her for me. I haven't seen moms in 16 years, but we talked throughout the years. That meant a lot. She scored a lot of brownie points with me for that, lifelong. That was a good look, it went a long ways. Also when I needed something or wanted it done, she handled it.

When I hit her sister, who I consider a sister, Shadena on Facebook, I left my phone number in her inbox. We started from there. It was like she never left, the transition was smooth, fell right back in. She fell in because she still loved me. Still do, fact. We used to have mental and emotional phone sex when she got off work. I would talk to her while she drove home every morning. Sometimes she would take her shower as soon as she got home. I would watch her take her shower, she would prop her phone on the sink and would be talking to me. I had full view of the shower with the curtain pulled back. She would proceed to give me a show. She would start rubbing between her legs, rubbing on her pussy, and between the lips. Then she start finger banging herself, fast then slow. Fast again, and then slow. She'd move to her pearl tongue, rubbing on it. Before I knew it her body is shaking and trembling like she was catching the Holy Ghost. She let out a moan and was screaming on her fingers, which she put into her mouth after I asked her to. She does it!

She wasn't finished. She started a second time and put her foot on the side of the tub and go in, starts doing it. She's rubbing on her pearl tongue then pushes her fingers back inside of her. She had my "dick" hand as fuck. I started pulling on my shit (jacking off) and going in with her while I watched her until I nutted in the toilet. "Unghh!" L worked the mornings in the kitchen too, so I usually had the cell to myself. Me and Chardon would have our morning sessions. It became routine. One time she was showering and Shadena had to pee, she was pregnant around this time with her son.

Chardon had to get out of the shower to let her in and she was right about to orgasm. When Shadena had to use the bathroom I know I was about to nut, she fucked my groove up! When she came in the bathroom and sat on the toilet to do her business, I could hear her peeing. She saw the phone and how it was propped up, how it was positioned. "Bitch, what you in here doing? You got Tic on the phone, ole nasty ass! . . . You nasty Tic!"

I was already busted, "Ayyee Shadena!"

"Ooh bitch, ya'll nasty, let me hurry up and get up out of here!"

If she wasn't in the shower, she would be in her room in the bed with her sex toy, a pink rabbit. I would watch her play with herself with it, listening to her moaning and seeing her shake, telling me she's about to cum while I got my pull on. I had her get doggy style on the bed working the toy from the back. I even had her sucking on it. She would put the toy down and use her fingers.

We done us (phone sex) for awhile before her baby daddy, who is a homie from the set, came back into the picture. He's one of the No-Good's I hear. They met through Meme. I guess one of those same situations. Meme was messing with another homie and they went and kicked it (hung out). Meme stayed, hooking her up with somebody. The same way she was going out with I.C. and asked Chardon if she wanted to come, so she could come fuck with me. But you know, she ended up going back to him, I saw it coming though. She started changing and I could tell because I've seen the episode. It's a re-run. I've seen it before. I just told her, "Check it out, I know what's up. I can respect it. You could've told me the business."

She got quiet. I was like, "It's cool. Your boy's not tripping, just don't be a stranger." Then I'm like, "You know where I'm at. When you feel like tapping in with me the door's always open." That was the last time me and her spoke, that was late 2017. It's 2020 now, a lot has happened since then.

Moms stay talking to her though, off and on. She would hit moms' phone every now and then, tapping in with her, which is what she did. That's when she told moms about being pregnant, during one of those calls. I just tatted her name on my right upper arm, in 2016. I'll never cover it up for the simple fact, at the end of the day she's loyal, a rare breed. She's shown her loyalty to me time and time again. I'm big on loyalty! She'll always have my love, respect, and loyalty. McNeal (get a bar) she's done something none of my baby mamas or my situationship have done, love me or showed loyalty. For certain, I can say she loved me and will always love me. If I was out, no doubt, she would fuck with me.

I have a skit on my music page *Reverbnation.com/roughchild7* where you can hear the chemistry we have. Even after all of the years we've been away from each other or been around each other, it's me and her. It's called "She Love Me (Box Love)". I messed with the music tough for a minute on the streets and had a producer named B.J. from Acacia Block, Compton Crip, recording under his street scholar imprint. I've recorded numerous songs with him. I have a few projects on *Datpiff.com* as well. I let this dude I met on Facebook put my vocals to tracks, a lot of them came out straight. I was just pretty much having fun. It's nothing like being in the booth in front of the mic, blunt burning in one hand and a cup of alcohol in the other, headphones on, beats playing in your ears and you're going (rapping).

I loved that shit! I kept my music authentic, I didn't rap about shit I didn't do or have. I sung some as well, under my other alter ego "Eddie Kane Jr." I've done a project with my people, way different production, which is called "Inside out". I was supposed to release it in 2017 but it was put on hold, had the C.D. covers done and everything. It should be on my Reverbnation page, the cover. It's only two songs off the project on Reverbnation. My singing can be heard on "Lay You Down" and "The Streets Don't Love Nobody". If I normally have singing on my hooks, I do it myself. But yeah, music is a passion of mine. I'm done with it now, but I'll pick up a pen and write a song. The rapping is over.

My cellie, L, got on a few songs. He only wanted to do it when we were drinking and getting right (drunk). I would be drinking and blowing. We would be in the cell on one (getting loose) we pretty much stayed on one though, we were drinking every week and I kept my trees. I'm not going to lie, I'll be going through some shit some times and I need that head change; needing to take that cheat off. This shit gets real mentally. You'll be on a cold emotional rollercoaster, dealing with so much shit and having to stay mindful of a lot.

You're dealing with autobots, multiple personalities, bullshit ass dude, family shit. It gets hectic. So at times I need to let my hair down and I'm bald headed, by choice. Just need that escape from the current reality for a while, letting my mental evade the present. Going back to the streets, I'm thinking about the different bitches I've been with. Those I've had sex with, who had the best sex, who sucked the best, who was a beast in the bed, the different places I've had sex with them, which one rode the best; the scenes playing out in my head. I start thinking about the many different sexcapades with Chardon, situationship, Trice, Miko, even Mary; how they done a certain thing, moved a certain way or moaned. This was my regular line-up , though I messed with other ones outside of them. I would think about the situation with my kids, especially my daughters Solie and Kaemaijay, how I left them out there in the cruel world to fend for themselves without me. I never anticipated that one. I never wanted to have daughters and not be in their lives, to be there for them, to be an example of what type of dude not to mess with. It wasn't in the cards though, nobody's fault but mine. It's spilt milk now.

It's nothing I could do to change the situation though I wish I could rewind the tape. So when situationship told me my daughter Kaemaijay said she hated me just the other day, I came to the realization maybe it's because she felt abandoned, because I'm not out there with her. Then I quickly shook that notion. She's her foul ass mother's daughter with her characteristics, values and morals, with no respect or loyalty. That realization I came to. She's 17 now. I haven't talked to her since 2016. I'm done with all of the reaching out and bending backwards, that's done. You're not messing with me, I'm good with that, damn sure not going to lose any sleep. In general though, it's just crazy how when you're out there it's all good. Soon as you come to jail you see the real!

It's like you never existed, or never mattered while you're out there. It's I love you this, I love you that. I fuck with you! You hear it all, everything in the book, from friends to family and especially a bitch. It's on to the next dick. It comes easy as breathing to them. Just like with so-called family. You would think because they're family, it would be different. It's no different. They'll leave your ass for dead quick. I've been taught family isn't family, it' just a title and a label that means nothing. Outside of those I consider my family, fuck the rest! I've been here before though, it was the same shit as when I was down all that time in the 90's, no baby mama, no family except for my usual supporting cast.

Moms, my Uncle Johnny (R.I.P.), and my Aunt Martha, no matter what I've always had them. When I was out though, I had the love and being messed with, all fake though. Really, I should've seen it coming and shouldn't have expected it to be any different. No matter how much I messed with them. It's a rerun of the same ole picture, the only difference now is moms is a lot older, my aunt is a lot older with her situation, health-wise. My uncle and I now have my cuzzo, Nip, my aunt's baby boy. He looks out for me when it matters. He doesn't write as much but he does tap in and holler at me from time to time. When I had my gadget, we tapped in every morning with each other. I would hit his phone around 5ish, "Top of the A.M. cuzzo, have a good day sir."

He'll hit me back, "You too!" If it was something I needed to mention, needed him to do, I would ask then, or mention it then.

On if it was me speaking on whatever it was I needed to. It would always be before we went to work, most of the time. I get up early, 4:30 every morning, wash up, make my coffee, turn my TV on and ready my Quran. Same with cuzzo if he had something to mention, he would get at me then. We've spoken on the phone, but we mostly just texted. Him and moms were the only ones I mainly communicated with. My Aunt Martha could no longer speak or write, but when she was able to, we communicated often. She wrote and sent me cards during holidays and born days.

She's been my second mother. I look at her more like a mother than my aunt. I don't remember there being a time her and my uncle weren't in my life or running to my aide like as if I was one of their kids. They've always been a constant presence, right or wrong. Moms too, we've always been close. She's always been a presence and a constant one, she'll always come running to my aide too. Cuzzo is older than me, but I remember when I was younger he would tolerate me. We weren't as close when I was coming up, because of the age difference and him doing him.

We interacted with each other when I was out. We didn't hang out or nothing. I would see him at work and I would see him at Aunt Martha's, his mother's house, from time to time. So yeah, me and L would always chop it up about many different things. We talked about venturing into other sets. He'd even told me he hung out in my set. One of his homies were messing with one of my homie's girls, Baby Insane. I'm like I didn't venture like that but I had been in the Avalon Gardens, because I was messing with this female over there named Kim but they called her Snoop. Her brother was evil. I met a few of them and they were cool, Freddy Kruger, Big Cisco, Popeye and Big Shug. I met a few others but can't remember, blame it on the sherm. I've also ventured into the Wilmington Arms, Park Village Compton Crip's set, with my boy Robbie Rob who was from over there. I met a couple of him homies. I don't remember any of their names. I was high and had been drinking. Robbie Rob's cousin was my producer, B.J.

We got into our top 10 rap artist, my top 10:

1. 2Pac/Makaveli
2. Ice Cube
3. Kendrick Lamar
4. The Game
5. Nipsey, Hustle
6. Dr. Dre
7. Nas
8. Jay Z
9. 50 Cent
10. Biggie

I remember his top one was Ice Cube. We've gotten into this very topic on a few different occasions. As far as having daughters, he's has two he communicates with and two twins he'd been trying to know. Amber and Evie he communicated with very different and complex relationships from where I sat observing. I can say he, no doubt, loves his daughters. I just didn't agree with how they would act towards him, with all of his effort and energy he was putting forth. I use to voice my opinion but you know, he's like, "They're my daughters regardless." I feel you homie. Like I would tell him I'm not having it. You treat me a certain way, it's fuck you too, that simple. We're not white, that's white people shit. Plead with kids that are not trying to deal with you or you're buying their love and doing things so they'll accept you or like you. Fuck that! You don't want to deal with me, cool. That's where I'm at, with or without my life sentence.

He would call and talk to them when he could, if and when they felt like responding. He stayed going the extra mile. He stayed reaching out and trying to be in their life. He would send loot to them. He has a life that should be the other way around. He sent them cards, sent gifts and gift baskets, just to be slapped in the face. I felt bad for the homie because it wasn't right, but that's just how much of a good dude he is. Evie would switch up when she would be with her dude and wouldn't call. However, he felt more connected to Evie because she was more down to earth and street. Amber, from what I gathered, she's the one that breaks his heart the most though because he felt they should've been able to be a lot closer than they were.

He was around her and done stuff with her when she was younger. I remember when Amber told him she was coming up to Solano to see him. He waited and waited and waited on the visit. She was a no show. You could see in his face the hurt. I used to tell him all of the time how he was a better man than me and how I couldn't do it (take the treatment). As soon as I see the disregard, I'm done. You won't have to worry about it no longer because now I'm cool on you. He would tell me he couldn't be that cold. I've had someone tell me I had a heart like Hitler. Wow! That was deep, King. King was my cellie in the sandbox in Solano. I had barely started talking to him before we ended up being cellies. The move was a compact move, a move where the police needs the cell and you're by yourself and are able to take a cellmate.

I wasn't tripping though, I was cool with it. I could cell up with just about anyone and can get along, as long as you're not dirty or a weirdo. I would see him in the cages at the yard, here and there nodding my head at him in passing, "Alright then Black." One day, we were in cages close to each other and were able to have a chance to talk. He was in the sandbox for a battery on an inmate with a weapon. Him and some of his homies got on a dude, fucked him over. The dude had been raping old ladies and sodomizing them. His homies were able to evade the scene, he was the one caught up and riding it. Dude they got on got sliced up pretty bad with a razor gizmo (razor melted into some sort of plastic). They gave him, King, 20 something months on a SHU program. He'd been postponing his hearing and had already been in the sandbox a year.

He should've left there, long ago, but rather postponed the 115 hearing. I did too initially, but every one's situation is different. I was in 214 for a cool minute by myself, wasn't many Crips coming off the yard back there like that. Blacks would trickle in sporadically, mostly victims. Me and King played the door. Dude would be coming in, in wheelchairs, limping on crutches, in casts, in neck braces. We would be like, "Damn, what happen to him!" One dude had bandages on his legs. It seemed like dude were being literally kicked off the yard. What are they doing, kicking dude in their ankles and knees? We were at the door looking and shaking our heads. It's some bullshit going on, out there on the line! The police put Crips in the cells with Crips, Damus in the cells with Damus, Others with Others, South Siders with South Siders, Northerners with Northerners. They don't mix the races or factions. They normally wouldn't mix civilians with gang members. They tried, for the most part, to keep them celled together which was fine with them. I haven't run into many civilians. They wanted to be in the ell with someone affiliated, in the sandbox or the main line. Now the only exception to this in the sandbox is if you're SNY, then in that case it is what it is, anything goes. I've seen Black and Hispanic, white and Black, other and white, being a SNY. It doesn't matter. The last time I saw the Black and the White was when I was mistaken for being the Black in the cell with the White. I still don't see how that blooper was made when I had been functioning with my neighbors on both sides of me who happened to be Northerners, my boys Chevo and L.T. to my right, and Buick to my left.

You best believe their homies inquired as to who I was and why I was back there and did I check out, had they seen my lock up order. One thing about them, if they haven't seen your work they're not fucking with you and will tell you quick too. No disrespect but I can't fuck with you. If you're not active, dude just want to know who they're around and who's around them. L.T. and Chevo sent me their work and I sent them mine. All good, everything checked out. Then I sent mine to Buick and his cellie, all good, everything checked out. I was good with all of the Northerners because my work has been seen and the word was out. They share info.

Which still baffles me, as to how that mistake was made coming from one of them. Clearly, it wasn't me. Mind you, I had refused a cellie and hadn't had one. Come to find out, after the fact though, the dude I had refused was the quiet young homie from the set. The one who came off of the 2 yard. A short female police name Ramirez came to my cell door, "Are you taking a cellie , McClinton?" I just told her I wasn't refusing a cellie, I just wasn't trying to move to 10 -building right then but I'll take one if it's an issue. I'm not moving though. She left only to come back to tell me, "Nevermind, you're already been written up from refusing this person previously." Well get gone then! She was cool though.

They ended up moving him in the cell with K, before EB's cellie moved in with him. Initially K refused the young homie too, not even knowing who he was. He didn't want no cellie. He took the write up too, but that was the second time they'd gotten at him about taking a cellie and he at that time went ahead and accepted him. They were only cellies for about a week before the young homie was shipped out.

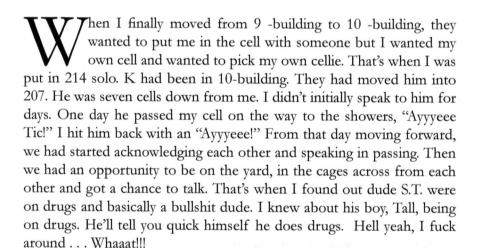

8

When I finally moved from 9-building to 10-building, they wanted to put me in the cell with someone but I wanted my own cell and wanted to pick my own cellie. That's when I was put in 214 solo. K had been in 10-building. They had moved him into 207. He was seven cells down from me. I didn't initially speak to him for days. One day he passed my cell on the way to the showers, "Ayyyeee Tic!" I hit him back with an "Ayyyeee!" From that day moving forward, we had started acknowledging each other and speaking in passing. Then we had an opportunity to be on the yard, in the cages across from each other and got a chance to talk. That's when I found out dude S.T. were on drugs and basically a bullshit dude. I knew about his boy, Tall, being on drugs. He'll tell you quick himself he does drugs. Hell yeah, I fuck around . . . Whaaat!!!

He was telling me he was talking to his homie, 20 Dee, about the situation with S.T. 20 Dee supposedly asked K, "Well if he didn't do it, why did he agree to pay S.T.?" The real question should've been, "Why didn't your homie take off on me from going in his shit instead of saying just pay me this and it's good?" Flag on the play right there! That's that autobotism and homie-ism, a lot of ism's play a part of yard life; yard-ism, street-ism, individualism, snitch-ism, self-ism, tribe-ism, and coward-ism. K told him he couldn't answer why I agreed to it, but was like, "I don't think Tic done that, it don't make sense. He was doing his own thing, he had shit and been looking out." Sarcasm is a mutha fucka! Yeah, how much I owe? You got that! Two dollars you say, that's what's up. I was never going to allow myself to be worked, that's wasn't acceptable and I'm a lifer.

This is where I have to live, until it's time for those doors to open for me and if I can't live safe, I'm going to live dangerous. It's just that simple. K was like, "But now that I'm able to talk to you, the shit he was saying don't add up and when I get back to the yard I'm going to talk to 20 Dee again." K was also like, "He asked S.T. why did he give me the shit to hold and not him, and we're in the same building?" He told K because I was able to move in and out of the buildings, which is a lie. Everyone around there knows my job didn't work that way, and for one I was holding it not moving it for you.

You didn't want K with it because one, he didn't have shit, two, he wasn't in traffic, and three, you knew what you were planning. I'm sure you already discussed it with Tall, my so-called homie and your cellie. Ya'll were too tight for you to not have him in on it. That's just crazy. I fucked with both of them and looked out! It doesn't pay, kindness gets misconstrued for weakness. Just as you being laxed, you have to be soft because your chest isn't poked out or you're not talking loud. Nowadays, you have to have habits that navigate those balances just based on the type of individuals you're dealing with in these 2000's. K was telling me how S.T. was telling other Crips, "Yeah, he went in my shit. That's why he done what he done, because he owed me and wanted to get off the yard." Two dollars, which was nothing to me. I gave that away passing shit out constantly. While I was still in 9-building I had gotten at one of my other bay cats I messed with and told him to see if he could run a play for me, but holler at my cellie, since I had that dollar-fifty on his books.

He gets back to me, saying he got at my cellie and guess S.T. was near or in ear shot. I don't know dude be so nosey. They dial in to what's being said around them. Anyway, S.T. tells him to tell me I owe. I told him, "Good looking out." It was good. I know Keetay was like, "What the fuck", thinking to himself. Knowing me, it had to be more to it than that. That's not Tic's get down, which everyone knew around there. But I had been a recent yard flip too. A lot of new heads, but for certain my name never came up in anything foul or scandalous. All of a sudden though, these dudes pop up and those like them bullshits in play. Truthfully, I don't see how I didn't see they weren't cool. I'm normally a good judge of character. I saw and heard shit they would do and say on the yard. I don't see how I would be any different. Where I fucked up and I see it now, is where I was being just too cool. You can't be too cool with those types and looking out (giving them shit).

They simply took my kindness for weakness. I think back to when I think I was first tested, but I let it go because he put it on his set. He doesn't know how it happened. I think from that lack of responses on my part he felt he had one. At the same time, you didn't say you don't it purposely, or just said, "I did that!" You would've certainly gotten a different response and reaction. What I'm referring to is when I let him use my C.D. Sony player. I had the number "3" waxed on the center of it. When he brought my C.D. Player on the yard and I saw it didn't have the 3 on it no more. I'm like, "What's up with my 3?" He was like, "I don't know, on the set I didn't see no 3 on it." I let it go at that, wrong thing to have done. Now he's a shark in the water circling.

I couldn't prove though he did get it with it on there because it went through several hands before reaching him. That was my main reason for not making it an issue. Come on now, you're from 20's, you're a Deuce, it's a 3, and I'm a Tray. Just for the record I haven't been on these lines, 16 years being a bitch! I'm a solid homie, a righteous homie with a moral compass, nor do I prey on people. Not what I do or what I'm about. You can't run into anyone, that's been on the line with me that'll tell you I've owed, I'm foul, I'm on dope, or I'm a bitch! One thing for sure, we know bitches don't last on the yard. What else can't be said about me, I'm not a functioning homie, or I haven't gotten my hands dirty? I have plenty of 115's that beg to differ and I've moved on some shit.

I won't speak on that because it's not on the books (in black and white). I was only caught up the time that ultimately has me sitting in High Desert because I had to double back. I was free and clear of being caught. In my mind, we can't co-exist. How can we? I would've been horse playing thinking otherwise. I just moved on you and woke your game up (stabbed you in the neck). I wasn't about to let dudes or autobots get in your ear and pump you up to try and creep on me. That's all the way out! Do I look like I have fucking "Stupid" tattooed on my forehead?

But yeah, I gotten away initially and was heading back to my building. That's when I ran into Richie Rich and he hit me with, "Leave Dude alone, he's a buster!" Just passing K'Rocc and Fo-Up when I passed the Woods area. They intentionally made eye contact nodding at me. I basically done what they wanted to do but couldn't, knowing it would've went live. It's heavily frowned upon when a White is running with the Blacks representing Crip or Blood, many melee's and riots occurred behind it. Because the Whites feel if they're White they should run with them, and if not it's an issue.

It's been cases where the Whites would be like, "Dude has a certain amount of time to get off the line or it's going up." Some of the white Crips and Bloods buckle to the pressure and leave on their own thinking it'll prevent a crash (riot) not wanting blood on their hands, in my mind. But at the end of the day they have the support, they stand firm. We're with them 100% because they're considered one of us. Lead the push, we're behind you. In some cases the Hispanics (South Siders) be on that same shit, making it an issue if a Hispanic is running Black.

Here it is, if a Black is running with them we care less. It's not an issue. It that's what he's doing, then that's what he's doing. For all we know that's who he grew up with and been around. I knew though what those Woods were thinking when they made eye contact and nodded at me. Nah, I didn't do ya'll dirty work. I still had my banger in my jacket pocket and I turned back around. He was just standing there in the field wiping at his neck. I knew then I was going to the sandbox. I was prepared mentally. Cuz played with my loot, period, point blank. All that other noise Niggahs was making, they can miss me with. I'm moving through a different frequency.

Apparently the sentiment was felt, because Dude had come to that same conclusion knowing me and knowing my get down. That and my cellie getting at Dude with the un-cut (real) version. K told me too that that shit had been talked about for a week or so after we were gone off the yard. It didn't go up with anyone behind my actions in regards to the situation with the so-called homies. Shit, when it's all said and done I didn't know who he rain with. As far as Neighborhoods, Gangsters, etc. However, I heard later that Sho-Lines (Venice Shore Line Crips) ran West L.A., never knew that.

As for Oppie though, I never knew how he ran with. He only hung out with T-Brown. When he wasn't with T-Brown he was in his cell.

He didn't program like that, especially the yard. Have seen him though holler at a few other dudes, but I'm assuming he's running a play. When he did pop up, he would stop at the Crip table and keep moving. All of that hanging out, no bueno! I was told though, it was felt T-Brown was on some bullshit trying to get back in the building to get a banger. But he was on it. I had you homie! I personally didn't feel T-Brown being on the bullshit, especially having firsthand knowledge of everything. Come to find out, though latter, he was invested. Oppie owed him five dollars, sucked to be him! He even went to wake Oppie up, "Why ain't you in the dayroom right now trying to get on the phone, trying to get Tic out of the way?"

"I'm Sleeping."

So yeah, I told the police Ramirez a second time when she came to my cell asking me was I taking a cellie. I told her I was tripping, it was good, to bring whoever it was.

Since E.B.'s cellie had moved in with K, they wanted to move E.B. in with me. He had to move in. I was there longer, I wasn't moving. She figured it was good we were broth Crips. I had even signed the paper saying I was cool with the move. He signed it as well, it's a go. For some reason though, in the middle of the play he called an audible and switched up (changed his mind) when it was time to move. Ramirez was pistol hot. Her face was red as fuck. She called him a fucking weirdo. She also told him he better not ask for shit because he had shit coming. I stayed in the cell solo after that for another week before the police that wrote me up for the first and only cell refusal came to my cell. "Aye McClinton are you taking a cellie?" He thought this guy King over here in 230, he's a Crip too. He's quiet and don't fuck with anyone. I'm like, "What, he's moving over here?"

"No, He's been back here longer. You have to move over there."

I saw the relief in his eyes when I agreed to move. I wasn't tripping the first time. I just didn't want to move at that time. I still had to shoot my shot though, with staying in my cell and having him move.

His cellie was gone, only two days before they were on king to get a cellie. He didn't get any cell (alone) time. He had told me he was only without a cellie for three days and that was the longest. Sucks to have been him. A dude need that solo time for as long as he can get it, when he can get it. His precious cellie had been an Up North dude that didn't bang. However King felt he was an undercover Damu or affiliated with them at best, because he would B's on words that had C's. If you didn't bang, what was that about? "Bracking" (cracking), "bookies" (cookies), "boffee" (coffee), so at best, yeah, he was a sympathizer and supporter.

He had came off of the 2-yard and was sent to the 3-yard, went from dorm living to cell living, a major change. Soon as I got into the cell, I dug into my bags finding my work so he could read it. He slid me his, though we had spoken already on the yard about the reason we were in the sandbox. The work just confirmed the story and situation and it could be verified as the real. If anyone asked, yeah I've read his shit, he's straight. We tripped off. A lot of Blacks that were back there they weren't going to the yard and they remained single-cell status and dudes couldn't verify why they were even back there. Me personally, I didn't mess with dudes. If you weren't active and I hadn't seen your work and you weren't trying to reach out and you were Black, fuck yah! I wouldn't speak, would walk right pass your cell door. I had unpacked my shit. Being an older Crip homie, he gave me the bottom bunk. I wasn't tripping either way. I was still more than capable of hopping up and down off the top bunk.

I felt his get down. He respected older active Crip homies. It's not that many left. King was straight. I found out he was into the same shit I was into writing. He was working on a book when I moved in. I started working on a script called "Ponds". I found out that the same thing with Lon, we have writing in common. He's published several short stories. He's actually the reason and driving inspiration that drove me to write this book. I was inspired by his book he'd written about his journey on the streets and in prison.

I was like, damn my guy's been getting it in (going through things and withstood it). Some of the things I had read I've heard about it over the years. The name Hoova Lon rang like a school bell. He's known all through the penal system, especially CDC by friend and foe alike. He goes back to back in the day. The rep supersedes the guy for sure. A good guy though, no doubt. But yeah, his book from the portion of it I've read is a good read and it's a page turner, so much activity and drama. His description and accounts will have you there with him. When he gets around to putting it out, it's a must; you get a bar of it.

I had given him the beginning pages of this one to get his input and feedback. He told me to keep pressing and keep it authentic. No doubt homie! I just finished reading a story Lon wrote called "Never a Dull Moment" about his wife Lisa working in a crazy house. That shit had me laughing like crazy! He really had me laughing reading another story about his grandma called "Big Mae" that's her name, Big Mae. Shiiit! Big Mae wasn't no joke and she had jokes.

I was really laughing at how he described how she was talking to him and whupping his little fire-starting ass at the same time. We had that in common as well, being kids and fire bugs. I loved setting shit on fire. I had set these two palm trees on fire in some apartments and got a whupping. 39 minutes later, I went to Church's Chicken with my mother and set a trash can on fire right in front of it. Two ass whuppings 30 minutes apart. Big Mae gave little Lonnie a pass the first time he burned some shit up. His passes were dunzo, she tightened him up (spanked him) oh that shit was funny.

Me and King chopped it up a lot too about shit, made reggie, and wrote. He was a young Crip homie around my oldest son's age. He had his head on right. He had morals, values and ethics. Whoever laced him, they laced young homie right. He was on his shit, as far as the do's and don'ts and how to function in prison. I saw through his conversations, we've had a many, that his lines weren't blurred nor did he do drugs. His thing was drinking. He didn't even blow. He too didn't like speaking on things he wasn't there for or didn't hear from the source. He was telling me about A-yard and things that were going on over there with bullshit dudes and autobots, with the shenanigans, can't escape them.

He was like, basically, he was out of the way, but would tap in at the Crip table. Then he told me he would go work out and then pay basketball. Even when you're not feeling dudes like that it's still good to go tap in then bounce. Because I'm over though, we spoke on my situation with my so-called homies and once I ran it down he immediately saw through the shenanigans and was like, "Niggahs are foul!" He was like, "If it was me and I knew you and your get down, I would've been speaking on your behalf, this, that and the third." He felt it was some suuuper bullshit on K's behalf because he should've been on my side of everything. Because he knew what was true and what was manufactured which came out of his own mouth, "They wasn't trying to hear me." Though you knew the real. He even told me, K, they'd asked him why he let me do it. Dudes were really horse playing with that question. Why did he let me do it? Because I couldn't stop him, his mind was made up.

They were allegedly pistol hot with him. He was back there in the sandbox, because he went to R and R. They found contraband in his package, unbeknownst to him. When they found it, it was in the big Folgers jars. The phones were spotted first, the rest was exposed. They allowed him to leave because, initially, they just found the phones and tobacco. He never signed for it though. By the time he had made it back to the yard he was called to the substation and was put in a cage. They had found the drugs. He didn't know about the drugs until they told him they found drugs, "Once the toxicology test comes back we'll see what the extent of your charges will be." It came back, they found drugs.

So he was booked for that too. He was like he had no knowledge. It just got sent in his name, though he suspected a culprit. Later though, he's talking about how when he catch up to S.T. he was going to slap him. For all I know, that was cap (bullshit, just conversation) because him and his cellie ended up going back to the main line. A few dudes popped up back there from our side of the yard. I didn't hear anything about him and S.T. getting into anything, they didn't pop up back there. Even when he was leaving the sandbox, "I'm about to go slap me a Niggah." That made me think when he got back on the line did he tell them he was fucking with me back there or he lied? Fact is you were, talked to me on the yard in the cages, and on the tier when I had showered by your cell and you looked out with rice and soups when I was waiting to get to the store myself. You could've been doing it to keep up appearances. Either way I wouldn't trust you, no way now knowing your position of complicity, compliancy is compliancy. Which basically mean you're on the side of wrong, when you know wrong is wrong.

As far as I'm concerned, you're not my homies. Not mine anyway, clearly! I'm a righteous homie on the side of righteousness. I stand for real things and real situations. Again I don't prey on dudes or try to fuck over them. That's not who I am or what I'm about, even if they're weak or a buster. To me, that makes you weak as an individual with a serious character flaw. Let people be, everyone's not built Ford tough. In all of my years of doing time in prison, I've never once had my name mixed up in no fuckery. I was like, "Whoa!" Dudes really went there with it, but you know karma's a bitch. I'm a firm believer, look where I sit, it didn't come back the same way I dished it. An Other named Cyco from Long Beach T4L (Tongan For Life) came back there. He was in 12-building with me. I messed with him here and there until he showed me his true colors.

He got whupped off the yard for outstanding debts. I saw it coming. He was doing the most cold thing. He had loot and kept shit. I hollered at him briefly on the vent, he was in the cell below me and King either in cell 130 or 131. That was it I didn't holler down there no more. Then some Blacks who were running Other popped up that were in 12-building with me. They were running again. Tito was from somewhere up north. His cellie too, I forgot his name though. They were booth cool. They moved to 232 a couple of doors down from me and King. When we had the chance to holler on the yard Tito filled me in on what the word was on me on the yard.

"Oh, Niggahs know the real. Your cellie let Niggahs down what was up. Trust me Tic, Niggahs know the real." Which re-affirmed what I believed. Dude and his autobots were spreading falsehood that a real dude's going to see through and a bullshit one is going to roll with, because they're on the same page. You know minds that think alike. I would really trip off of that shit in the cell at night when I would lay it out. It fucked with my head because I'd never experience such foul behavior. That was over the top, lesson learned certainly. I'll never deal with anyone like that ever again. Call myself looking out, no bueno! Though Crips weren't really landing in the sandbox like that. That's how I was able to be by myself for as long as I was. A few started popping up much later.

Ant from East Coast, I forgot which one, he was back for court. My boy was burnt out, smooth kid though. He had got caught up with some work and a banger. I think he had said he came from Delano. I was on the yard with him before he left. Lefty from Harlem, a young kid, popped up too. He got two on one'd. The two little Crip homies who got on him were back there as well. They were over the tier clowning about it with Ant and laughing. You know how young homies do. They were also clowning across the entire dayroom from one section to the other with another young East Coast name G Bone. I forgot which one of the young homies who had got on. Left was from Main Street, forgot his name as well I never saw the other one just heard him. I guess they were clowning too hard because you could hear Lefty say, "Ya'll didn't knock nobody out!" They were big clowning, we knocked cuz out, we put feet on him, G Bone egging it on and laughing. I didn't care for G Bone when I met him. I felt he was kind of extra.

I ended up having a confrontation with him about the building phone. The phone wasn't hanging down like it normally is. Dudes would hang the phone down so they could get on it first at dayroom, same dudes every day. Then they would line up their homies behind them. Fights almost happened behind the phone. Phone bandits, dudes that has to be on the phone 24/7, I got on the phone here comes G Bone sliding up, "That's me." I'm like, "It wasn't hanging down." I called it first though. One of my boys I messed with told me he did call the phone first so I dropped it, "You Niggahs play too many games!" I walked off, he started mumbling some shit. I turned around, "Cuz, I don't give a fuck about none of that you're talking." Come on my dude, I know how you're built, I've been around you. In that short period of time you didn't fool me. You're a young, young Niggah, my youngest son's age.

I wasn't going to touch you but at the same time you weren't going to touch me either. He turned out to be alright to an extent, still too extra (acting tougher than you actually are). He's just one of those dudes that is easy to rub you the wrong way, even when he don't mean to. Solano out of nowhere just got an influx of young L.A. Crips on the yard for that Y.O.P (Youth Offender Program). It was chaotic when they hit the yard; we had gotten a few in our building. It was mad. They were off the hook (unruly) and turned up (hyper aggressive). A few of them washed out putting too much on it being extra, which was expected. Got voted off the island. See yah, wouldn't want to be yah! He's out of here coach.

Then you had some that were catching back to back 115's from fighting to delaying program. It didn't take long before the administration started shipping their young asses up out of there to 4-yard. Of the places they had to get sent to was Solano. They in my opinion should've been sent to the 4-yard first to get their feet wet. Solano isn't that place, it's a medical facility where young dudes can easily be misled and misdirected with the wrong idea of prison; thinking it's ok to do certain things and not being held accountable. So in their minds this type of behavior is acceptable. No bueno! The reality is you're being pumped up for a failure. The only thing you'll learn from Solano is how to be a victim.

They're learning bad habits and not being properly laced. They're just running around doing what the fuck ever. Let them do them! Once they saw that Solano was starting to ship their young ass up out of there now they want to start asking questions. "Big homie, what the 4-yard like?" Oh you can't tell me shit this that and the third, now it's "Big homie, what the 4-yard like?"

You weren't trying to listen then, now you want to hear what we were trying to tell you. Now it's how can I stay? You didn't realize just how good you had it at Solano, now you're about to go get a real bar of what prison is with structure and discipline. Solano had neither. Young Frost from Park Village was a casualty of not realizing how good he had it, wishing he was back at nice ass Solano. But a lot of shit that went on in Solano with dudes. They're going to have to answer for their actions at some point, especially being dirty and doing dirty shit hitting these 4's and 180's. Bullshit always tends to track you down! It's been many instances of it. It was coming back, such and such went to Delano and got whupped out, such and such went to Corcoran and got whupped out, such and such went to High Desert and went S.N.Y. It went on and on.

As far as my homies coming to Solano, as an older homie I would tell them, "Look, It's really not like that up here." It's not an active spot. It's not prison first off, it's a medical facility. Damn near everyone here has medical issues. I might as well have said its buster central, everyone's a victim. I was only a Solano because I really had an issue medically. I came from Delano with Valley Fever. Me and a dude from 60's on a yard were the only two at that spot to catch it. Crazy huh? It had me going through it.

I lost a lot of weight rapidly. I thought I had a cold then the flu, turned out to be Valley Fever. I laid in the cell for a couple of weeks. I couldn't eat, I was sweating, and my breathing was fucked up. I went to medical, they told me, "Just drink some water". I was given some cough drops and ibuprofen then sent on my way. I went from 215 to 190. I went back to medical, I was down to 160. I was sent to CTC (Correctional Treatment Center) this is where all of the major medical care is done. The medical on the yard is basically a triage. They didn't know why I was losing all of my weight in a matter of weeks. It spooked me and it spooked them. They didn't know what was wrong with me. They couldn't diagnose me. A doctor saw me and he ran some x-rays. Once he saw my x-rays, that's when black spots could be seen on my lungs. "Get him the fuck out of here!" I was then changing out of my blues into a red paper jumpsuit.

I was put into a car and driven to San Joaquin Hospital on the outside. I was hooked up to an I.V. and cuffed to a gurney. I stayed parked in a hallway with both of my escorts, police from Delano. I was eventually taken upstairs and a battery of tests were done on me. My results: Valley Fever, also known as "Cocci". I was admitted to the hospital there. It was serious. I didn't know what the hell it was or what was going on. I was then taken to a floor that was designated for prison inmates. I put on my ass-less gown and got on my bed where they cuffed one arm and foot to the bed rails. I was given a container to piss in, which I had to turn on my side to use and then I was hooked up to a second I.V. Every few hours someone came in and gave me a breathing treatment. They kept taking blood.

They told me had I stayed there another week I would've been dead. I stayed in the hospital for five or six days. It could've been seven. The food was straight. I watched cable with a remote. It was so much shit to choose from. One day I fell asleep, one of the police that was watching me for the night was watching something. I just know it was some bullshit. I rose up like a mummy like, "Why'd you turn from what I was watching?"

"You were asleep."

"Don't you have a phone and a laptop? Turn that shit back!"

He was pistol hot. He put the remote on the bed and I turned it, tucking the remote. He was horse playing. The T.V.'s for my entertainment. He has a phone and a laptop. We can sway though, I won't say nothing. The police just sat in the room with me 24/7. It would mostly be male officers but I've had a couple of females too watch me, the mountain hillbilly type. Trip the bathroom didn't have a door on it so the police could see you and smell you. They were that close, sat just outside of the door.

I went in there and blew the joint up, the gas was vicious. The police watching me that night ran her ass out of there. Stage exit left! I was in there getting it in. Sucked to be her. I laughed, it was funny as hell. She was like, "Oooh, what the hell did you eat!" I hit her with a few silent but deadlys. She came back with some air freshener. Oh that shit was funny. No shame! I would be chopping it up with another white Crip named Whitey Bone from California Gardens. He was straight, he was a cool dude. He just lied a lot. He was starting to get into shit that was unnecessary, I like him though. Dude thought he was a coward but nowadays dudes' definition isn't the same. Personally, I thought a coward was anyone that has all the tools to handle a situation at that time in their space and then choose to do nothing about it. I would get at him though, "Homie you need to slow your roll." He had a crimie (co defendant) on the yard. The homie GQ from his set, California Gardens, he was straight too; a young Crip as well, with his head on straight.

He would talk to Bone too, telling him to fall back on the bullshit. Then when Bone was officially told he was being transferred I told him, "You fucked up now. You should've kicked your ass back."

"I'm not tripping, it's good, it's whatever." Talking that tough talk nephew, you're about to be tested now let's see if you withstand it! I get there, High Desert, his homie June Bug I meet from his set tells me Whitey Bone just left here a while ago (his last main line as GP). Whitey Bone had tapped out and ended up going S.N.Y off of this very yard. Wow, that's crazy! This was Mr. I'm-not-tripping, Mr. it's-good, and Mr. it's-whatever. Now it's Mr. S.N.Y. June Bug didn't really go into the specifics as to why he went S.N.Y. He was like, "some shit happened." I had heard that very same thing from his crimie though, before I left Solano's main line.

But here it is. I'm hearing it again from his homie who was here when it happened. How I first met June Bug, he was walking towards me on the yard. I'm a new face. I'm standing by myself with my green laundry bag in my hand. I was standing by the slab where South Siders were working out. One, it was a security issue. Due in part because I was by myself and no other Blacks were near the area. If something were to have happened, it would've been curtains for me before anyone could get to me to help me. Not only that, I didn't have no banger to at least fend off the attack. I would've had no action.

Two, It kind of looked funny; a lone Black away from all of the other Blacks and a few feet from the police who were sitting on a bench under the gun tower. Looking back on it, it did look kind of suspect and weird as fuck. I was on my way to the patio to get what I thought was a package, but turns out to be my Quran I had requested while I was in the sand-box. In San Quentin . . . no doubt! The police had told me I had to stand where I was standing, behind the yellow line waiting to get on the patio; which is where you stand when you're going on the patio for packages or for laundry.

June Bug approaches me, "Aye OG! You straight, I see you're down here by yourself. What's good? Why are you down here?"

"The police told me I had to stand right here." I'm knowing nothing, I'm new to the yard, I'm not knowing the business so I'm just standing there. I'm thinking its how they do it. June Bug was like, "Nah homie, you don't have to just stand here, the police playing games. Come to the tables and when you start seeing people come off of the patio push back over here." We started walking towards the Black area, where the tables were. That's when I saw Abu, Suuuper Crip, walking towards us. Some-one had told him it was another Crip on the yard so he was coming to see who I was and to greet me.

As I got closer to him I knew who he was. We gave each other the what-up-brody hug and some dap. June bug was like, "Yeah homie, I didn't know whether or not you were Black, I just saw you were down here by yourself and had to see what was up." Me and Abu posted up against the wall by the tables. June Bug spent off (walked away). Abu started telling me about Trip, his homie that rest in peace from his set that was in Solano. He had also begun telling me about shit on this yard, about the cluelessness and lack of awareness that was going on, and how dudes weren't security conscious or concerned about their safety.

Telling me about how lost dudes were and about the autobotism going on, on the yard; how dudes were on that bring-a-fist-to-the-knife-fight mentality. With that mentality and knowing what we know of the other races and how they like playing ball, it's a battle rarely won but they do get won sometimes. A scared man will do some amazing shit, almost matrix like.

I don't care who you are, if someone's coming at you with a banger and you don't have one you're spooked and two senses will kick in, your fight or flight. Either will happen, there's no in between. You go into survival mode or get dead mode. You're going to fight and shoot your shot or you're going to flight, using your rationale you're choosing to live to fight another day. We all know that flight route is going to play out. All someone saw were you running, that's all computed and registered. You trying to get somewhere. Makes you think too, hold up, how is this dude giving out play by play of what happened during a riot. Those are the ones that kill me. You giving out play by play, but what were you doing during all of this?

You couldn't have been participating thus leaving your own security at risk. Someone could walk right up to you and put your beans (brains) on the concrete or dope fiend you (sucker punch you from your blind side), because you're horse playing. Oh you're the I'm-going-to-hold –the-phone-camera ass dude. Hopefully though, these dudes will figure it out. It's either that or they just don't care. Here it is though, on the streets you're quick to pick a gun up and shoot! In here though, you won't pick up a knife when it could possibly save your life. I don't overstand. This is the logic I was given. You're not real with yourself, how can you be real with me? Groups and numbers don't mean shit if the math doesn't make sense.

That's a false sense of security because out of that group or those numbers how many are going to get active? How many will run? The majority of the time it's just me and Lon together, kicking it and working out. Some times Chumlee will be with us, for the most part it's just us two. We stay away from the crowds and are pretty much to ourselves. Just two older homies and I is a G-homie (big homie). It really only took me a few weeks to really assess dudes and figure them out. Paying attention tells you everything you need to know and listening. I've told you about my bullshit Niggah detector (BND). It goes off, "Stay away . . . stay away . . . stay away". He's not cool, they're not cool. I'm not trying to meet you, greet you or talk to you. I'm straight, off the dribble. So what if I'm closing myself off? I'm good with that because it's going to keep me away from the suckering and the bullshit. I'm dealing with enough shit as it is. I don't need to unnecessary drama or baggage, or the luggage that comes with a lot of dudes, homies or not. I've gotten I'm "antisocial", it's not so much as that I'm just anti bullshit dude, anti autobot, me personally. I don't need to know everyone on the yard or need to mess with them. They don't need to know me or mess with me. That's my version and it's singular.

As for what a dude feel about me or how he thinks about me, it's not my business and really I could care less. Just give me my allotted distance of ten feet if you're not a friend or someone I mess with. But yeah being in prison, it's nothing to dive into serious depths. It gets real, real fast. It's by far a playground where children play or an amusement park where children go on rides. You can easily lose your life. This environment is not a game or mere child's play. This is not a reality to be taken lightly or an evading reality. It should always be treated as such and never taken for granted. It'll cost you more than you're willing to pay.

A lot of time I'm with the shit I've seen or see, it's just mind blowing. I can't be the only one who can see this shit. Just when you think you've seen it and heard it all, here comes another version of it, a 2.0 version. You never stop learning, that's for sure. That is if you're trying to stay in tuned and focused. Just the other day I was tripping off of something with the South Siders, as far as them being real security conscious. I realized that they don't really shower like that, they bird bath. Every now and then with the exception of those, of them with jobs, they'll get in. Outside of having a job, a few would shower in our section. For the most part, no. I thought it was just in my section or my building. A homie said the same about the South Siders in his building. He just said they don't get in because of security reasons. It kind of made sense, it came up

+ 122 +

though because for the past few days we've been fucked out of dayroom per the SGT, but it's showers and phones. The homie was like, "Shit, we'll be able to get in because the South Siders don't hop in, they bird bath." I paid closer attention and that what it is. In my section a few Blacks and a few Northerners hop in at dayroom. One of our showers though, it's broken and has been for a while.

If everyone did shower at dayroom outside of those who was jobs it would be hard getting in. You would fuck around and had to bird bath. There's a lot more South Siders in our section than Blacks and Northerners combined. It's only a handful of us in the section and we share a table and a phone with a small area. We also share the one bench in front of the T.V. You have to think, all of the South Siders have cellies. A few more has moved into the section. The Northerners has cellies except maybe one and that won't last long. As for us, Blacks, me and Chumlee are the only cellies. The other one's Slient, P.F., Vru, Vamp and the weirdo doesn't have cellies. Lon is single-cell status. Which puts us as Blacks at even more of a disadvantage, we're already out numbered from observation.

9

I know though, if it were to go up we'll compensate for those extra feet and hands we don't have in this small space because it'll get ugly. Outside is one thing but being in a confined space is another. Which I've been in before, in Salinas Valley in 96 with those South Siders. The only person was hit (stabbed) was Folsom from Pasadena, which was how everything kicked off. That was my first experience in a confined space. The initial push, I hesitated but instincts took over and I got my licks and kicks in. I had a target I wanted to put hands and feet to, but he was too far away deep in the fray. He was smothered by homies, they were on him. He was the one who hit Folsom, which wasn't as bad as it seemed. He was also a street enemy, off of the West Side. I'm sure I was his target at some point. The police didn't attempt to breech the day-room. They stood outside of the section in the hallway looking in from the window. It was going down! They watching from the hallway for a minute, the tower police is out of his window aiming his gun hollering, "GEEETTT DOOOWWWN!" The Alarms going off, it was chaotic. No one was severely hurt.

Folsom was aright too, he was only poked in his stomach. No vital organs were hit, nor was he bleeding a lot. It couldn't have been any type of meal banger. We only been there a few days to a week and we hadn't been on the yard yet. The cells were brand new with welding dust everywhere. But then again, I don't put anything pass those dudes. They're very MacGyver-like, with gizmos and gadgets and weaponry. They're very knowledgeable with crafts I'll give them that, very skillful. I'm a bit more knowledgeable on my surroundings now and of the program around here beginning to adjust accordingly but will never be comfortable or get comfortable. That's how you conform and become laxed and that's not a good luck because you become vulnerable.

Before I close my eyes, after my nightly prayer, I rewind my whole day. Every conversation and every interaction I've had during the day around the yard and with whom. My rewinds were premeditated; I play everything back and dissect it. In moving forward, I have to make sense of any and everything, I embrace my choice or by force. Me and Lon just yesterday were speaking on embracing dudes. How from now on, we would have to know who we're embracing before we embrace them. Everyone's not who they claim to be. Dudes turn out to be weirdos or just bullshit, with hidden agendas or with baggage. BND is going off, "Stay away . . . stay away . . . stay away!" We share a lot of the same views, see a lot of the same shit and are on the same page. My other nick name I was given by younger homies was "Old Grumpy Cuz". It was said that the older I got the grumpier I got, "The older you get the grumpier you get. Wow! Really! You don't like nobody! You're always talking about you don't like this person or that person, or don't like this or that! Just grumpy!" It was King from 4-7 (Foe-Seven) I was in the cell with in the sandbox who hit me with the I have a heart like Hitler. At the end of the day though, I stand on my truth and my reality.

We were talking about an issue with one of my sons, Brandon. I was telling him how I went to Bakers Field to visit with my son and ended up telling his bullshit- ass mama I wanted to take him for a year, so I could connect and bond with him since I had been in the pen when he was born. I just wanted to bond and connect with him. I tell her to just give me his paper work, social security card and birth certificate, and I'll handle the rest out of earshot because I had walked down a hallway with her. I had my girl Miko with me and my kin. She gets at me like, "Why did you bring them with you, why couldn't come by yourself?" I couldn't believe this silly rabbit! I was in a situationship with her when I went to the pen, leaving the streets in '90 barely out of Y.A.

She fucked my homie Lil Hucc-A-Bucc from the set thinking I didn't know or wouldn't find out. You dirty bird! I ran into Hucc later and got the whole script when we became cellies in Calipat on C-yard, before I went to Salinas Valley. The homie told me everything. We weren't just homies but childhood friends since elementary. I knew him as Phillip too and his last name. So yeah, he spills the beans and even if by accident it's a small world. I had known he fucked though.

The one and only time she came and saw me in the county jail, she brought my kin with her. The same one I had with me, with my girl. As they were leaving the window in the visiting area on the way out, I'm still sitting at my window. Lil Hucc-A-Bucc had a visit too. He was a couple of rows away. I guess she saw him and stopped at his window and they chummed it up, they were real friendly. My kin came back to my row and go my attention, he pointed and I looked where he was pointing and saw them. I just nod and he left. As he's telling me, I'm like, "Keep talking my Niggah!" She didn't do shit for me while I was locked up, zero, zilch, nada. She laid down on me the whole time, mind you she had kids and we were still in a situationship legally. Keeping it a thousand, we're legally in a situationship now.

But nah, she didn't do shit for me period; no letters, no loot, no visits, no pictures, nothing! But you wanted me to stick my dick in you, silly rabbit! She was truly horse playing. I take my son with me, instead of taking him to the house with my situationship, my son Chucky and situationship's kids John, Camille, Craig and Duck (Nicholas). I took him to my mom's house on the East Side. I stayed on the North Side. Long story short, I geared him up, brought him some clothes and shoes, got him toys, a Play Station and some other shit so he'd be comfortable. Me and him were headed to the North to the house so he could be with the kids and bond with his baby bro. He could go there; I just didn't want him living there. I'd rather he stayed with moms. So as we're on our way he blurts out, "I miss my mama and my daddy!" The record started skipping.

"Huh? Say that again!"

"I miss my mama and my daddy!" That's what I thought you said. I told him not a problem. I will get him back to them ASAP.

I turned the swoop around and headed back to moms' house. I got his paper work and took him to my aunt's house in Lynwood. I asked my Aunt Martha and my Uncle Johnny would they send him back to Bakersfield for me to his mama and daddy, on the Greyhound bus. Call and let his mama know he's in route. I gave them the money for the ticket, thanked them and I bounced, got back in traffic headed back for the city. To this day, I don't know if he got back by bus, plane, train or car. I could've cared less at that point and I never checked to see if he'd made it.

He was like ten or eleven I believe. King was like, "Damn, you cold!" How? He wanted his mama and his daddy! So I sent him back to them. He didn't want me so I sent him. He's grown now and acts like he's working with feelings. I don't give a fuck about dudes in their feelings. You don't have a pussy, you're not a female. Your name isn't Solie or Kaemaijay. If I cared about feelings it'll be these. Miss me with the daddy issues, dude! You can sit on those! I tried messing with him, he pushed me away so that's his issue not mine. I've done my due diligence, I reached out. I've been in the pen since '05. He never reached out to me or tried to tap in so that's where it stands. My two oldest, same shit. They haven't reached out to me or tried to mess with me. Then my daughter, she just switched up, basically turned on me. Then my two in Colorado if they don't reach out, it is what it is. The last one I'm not really tripping off of him because I don't' believe he's mine anyway. Cold thing about it all, I have three granddaughters and I've never gotten pictures. I don't even know their names. I just know they exist. They're by my two oldest sons. I heard my situationship's daughter had a baby, don't know the name or if it's a girl or a boy, nor have I seen any pictures but you know what, she's not my daughter nor is that grandchild so really it doesn't matter. None of her kids ever messed with me or liked me anyway. I never got close to them or allowed myself to have feelings for them like that. Secretly, I knew they didn't like me. I didn't care though, I had my own kids. I may have been around you as kids but as adults don't know you; don't care to, feel nothing for you either way. So you're not messing with me, doesn't affect me or my energy. I was beginning to get close with my son Brandon's sister, Tina (Christina). We were building a bond and connecting. I had begun having feelings for her as a father figure.

She started calling me "pops". We talked a lot about different things and I'd given her a lot of sound advice; relationship type stuff and about life in general. We tapped in with each other every morning, every day basically. "Top of the morning, young lady" was my text. She hit me back

"Morning pops!" Her mama took issue with me and her daughter getting close. She had a real problem with it. She has her own father, she needs to get close to him and have a relationship with him. By no means was I trying to take his place, I just see as a daughter figure and if I could pass knowledge to her, why not? She's my son's blood at the end of the day. She basically got at Tina and told her she needed to stop fucking with me because I wasn't her pops! I'm like wow, really? I would give Tina a lot of fatherly attention and advice. I even offered her money to feed her kids when someone stole her purse.

I offered but she turned me down. She lost rent money and her money to feed the kids. I couldn't pay her rent but it wasn't a problem to slide her something to get groceries for her kids. Those are my son's nieces and nephews. She was upset and crying, I felt for her. I was hustling so I was like, "Look, if you have a card I could send you 60 or 70 dollars to it so you can feed the babies until you figure your next move."

"Nah, we'll be ok." Her mama was like, she's too proud. I told her mama though, because I didn't want her feeling some type of way or reading into it; me offering Tina money to feed her kids.

People's minds are wired fucked up and they try and see something that isn't there, that's my son's little sister, period. Me and her would talk for a good 30 minutes. We would text off and on during the day and night. I was still at Solano. I stopped talking to my baby mama though. I wasn't feeling the hate so I just stopped calling her or my son's sister. I didn't want to cause no static (problems) between them. I was giving her advice about her dude and his situation. He had got locked up and was facing life and someone was telling, damn rat bastard, typical episode. She was keeping me in the loop so I could tell her how things were working. She was new to it and seemed like she wanted to stay down, unlike her mother. I encouraged it because you don't find many who would even want to. I could tell it was messing with her head, emotionally and mentally, weighing heavy on her.

She had a new baby too, he was her baby daddy. She genuinely loved dude but the situation was taking a toll on her, plus she's a young mother, she has other kids. It's a rerun too, I've seen the episode. I heard. Confused, lost and conflicted she was, she was fighting with herself internally.

Top it off, he's doing something that's a no-no. I did the same thing with her mama 20 plus years prior. He's like, "Aye, you cheating on me? You fucking around on me? Are you going to stay down and be here for me?" He was basically defeating his cause by putting that added pressure on her. She would go to court with his moms. When his mother went to visit she would go too. I saw her intentions and what motivated her, she was trying to stay strong. I told her though to be honest with herself and with him, but with herself first. Therefore, she could be real with herself, him and the situation. Whether it was my place or not, I felt as a Niggah locked up it was my duty to get at her with some real shit. I'm on this side of it, I know the effects.

I told her like this, "Don't tell him you're going to be down and will be there if you're not! Don't lie to him and tell him you are and don't. Let him know the real, let him know the real and don't lead him on or string him along." Kill the horse playing. It's just as simple as "I'm young, I'm too young for this. I'm not ready to deal with it. I do love you though, I'll be there for you as only I can be no promises and I'll send pictures when I'm able to of me and the baby." Aye, dude can respect that a thousand percent, and can accept it for what and as it is whether he's feeling it nor not. It's better than being closed off, like with my BMs. The whole time I was down I've never received captured moments, nor had I had any communication with my kids. Ok cool, you weren't messing with me but you couldn't allow me to connect and bond with my kids. You were that wrapped up in your new dick?

Especially when they were older and could overstand what was going on and able to write with your help. In your mind though, "He's locked up, fuck him. He doesn't need to bond with no kids. They have somebody out here." Yeah, every new or different dude running in and out of your house, doing what you do best. I'm sure though, Tina took need to some of my fatherly advice, processed it in her own way, coming to her decision, her reality. As to what's best for her and her kids, at the end of the day that's what it's about; her and her kids' mental health, well being and happiness! Me personally, I can respect it and accept it for what it is, as it is as long as she's a female keeping it a thousand.

My overstanding is never zero, nor is my willingness to adapt and adjust. I don't need to the games and roller coasters mentally or emotionally. I knew enough though about the dynamics between them and with the situation to give her the advice I gave her. Plus I gave her something to work in her mind. I've been on the other side of that loaded pistol with one in the chamber, dealing with her mother and my other baby mother to my situationship. Unloyal, dead beat bitches! I know first-hand what it is to be in dude's shoes and feel what he's feeling or felt. As for the questions, I've been that dude asking those very questions. That's not the dude you want to be.

You'll come to learn not to ask certain questions and let shit play out as it's going to play out. The reality will present itself by one's actions. A thing you don't and won't have control over is who she's with, who she's having sex with, what she's doing, how she's doing it or where she does. I'm telling King in a conversation, "I don't have to answer to nobody or defend my actions or beliefs to nobody but Allah, and Niggahs ain't him when it comes to my safety or my well being.

The topic had come up about how other dudes always has something to say, about how you're doing and being you. Why are you watching me watch the T.V.? Mind your business. It really doesn't cost you a dime, my dude! I'm not messing with your movement, your flow, your lane, your loot or your survival. I shouldn't concern you, period, point blank. What, you're mad because the enemy of my enemy is my friend? What, I have hustle and you don't? What, I've gained weight, I'm eating too much? What, I'm not fucking with you? Why am I your concern? Why do what I do matter to you if it's not effecting you or your program? We were talking about the L.A. County, telling stories about shit that went on while we were there.

We talked about the Tuna's, dudes that were civilians but active with the activities, fighting etc; who were being used for gang members and bangers amusement on the weekends Friday, Saturday, and Sunday nights. They were being made to fight each other and members and bangers would bet on the fights "I got 10 on my tuna! . . .Bet!" "I got 15 on mine! . . . Bet!" We were in dorms the bunks are moved to form a ring. If we're in the county in a module we're in a cell and they're in the middle of the floor. They'd go a few rounds, Tunas are turned up non-affiliates; T (Tuna), u (up), n (non), a (affiliates). He got a kick out of a story about when I came from Wayside and I landed in 2100, county jail module. Big Tray Dee the big homie from the set was a trustee, a worker who cleaned up and pass out meals. We hollered briefly and him and Lil Sugar Bear were tight. After a couple of days of being on my tier a dude from PBG (Play Boy Gangster Crip) got pulled off of the tier by the deputies. We, the tier, didn't know it but he was in his cell. A single-man cell mind you, working out as ass naked with a head band and wrist bands on he made from the elastic from the socks. Anyway, it was count time. A female deputy was on the bottom tier doing her count. We on the upper tier could hear her down there. You could hear her keys rattling, could hear her speaking here and there to someone as she passed cells making her way down the tier. She makes it finally to the upper tier. You could hear the door at the end of the tier open and close. You know she's now on the tier. All of a sudden we hear, "You nasty muther fucker." then something to the effect of, "You wouldn't do that to your mother."

Everyone tried to get focused, trying to hear. A few words could be slightly heard afterwards coming from the cell down the tier. The female deputy finished her count and left the tier. We knew that wasn't over. Seconds later, all you could hear was "Who was that!" Who was she talking to? Then Ole Boy from Play Boys spoke up, "Aye ya'll, that was me."

I forgot his name, I just remember him being short and light complected. This was like '04. About ten minutes after the incident and him briefly explaining what he said had happened, 20 deputies hit the tier marching. All you could hear was in synced boots hitting the floor. She was leading the pack. They had on their riot gear, they told him to turn around and back up to the bars. Basically no bueno on his part. We heard some slight verbal exchange but not much.

Then we heard deputies saying it's a lot of soapy water on the floor and what was that on him. We thought it was boo boo, thinking he put in on himself so they wouldn't want to touch him. It was grease or baby oil, one of the two. We didn't know what it was. They told him again to turn around and back up to the bars. He refused and was saying all types of shit to them. The cell door open and all could be heard was slipping and sliding after a few deputes went in. Then we heard a lot of hollering and "Okaaaay!!! I give! I give!" Minutes later his butt-naked greasy body was being dragged down the tier pass our cells with his hands cuffed behind his back. After he and the deputies were vacated it was like, "What the fuck!!!" Then the laughing and clowning ensued. King was laughing at that one. I'm in the building one day, me and my boy Rame, no bullshit this dude really look like Terrance Howard, just a fat version of him. Fucking with him, I'd call him Lucious Lyon. Real good cat though, we were messed with each other pretty much. We were talking about how clowns were running around passing bad greenies to dudes and their homies weren't getting on them (disciplining them). Basically letting them run around building debts and not paying, instead of keeping it clean. A lot of this was going on. He even had a few dollars in the air for his tattooing he'd been trying to collect. Every week, he's ready to fight someone, "Bruh, these Niggahs just don't know!"

Damn near half the population was on some form of something. I remember back in the days, No bueno! Homies didn't play that drug shit. Weed and drinking's cool, that hard shit no bueno. They didn't play that or homosexuals. DP'able offenses, felonies! I was a handful of dudes not on nothing. I'm strictly tree and drinking. I don't do druggies, not my crowd. If they don't do trees or drink they do nothing at all, sober all the way around, don't do shit I've never seen so many homies using hard drugs. I was used to seeing them on trees exclusively, it's crazy. This is where a lot of the bullshit and nonsense is stemming from, these fucking drugs. Dudes are losing their minds, morals, values, and self respect. Dude will owe you knowing he can't get anything else from you until he pays, so what does he do? He goes to the next dude who got it.

The first business is going straight, you're going to get paid. Then second time he comes back bullshit is in play. He's on to the next dude, leaving a debt with you. Dudes played again, horse playing with little to no regard for repercussion. No one was holding dudes accountable for their behavior. Me and Rame stayed having in depth conversations about dudes running around Solano. One dude I missed with, Dave, I called him Wavy Davey, he was out of Richmond. He was a cold piece of work. He's always over extended himself when he knew he shouldn't. That was his main issue. The same time Oppie owed me, he owed me two dollars too. Normally, I didn't fuck with anything that would get your door kicked in. I did thought at this point it went cool but only because I only fucked with him.

I'm like, "Aight." That was a quick flip. I did it again against my better judgment. He kept shooting people to my cell, "It's the last time." He promised me he had me, and then when it was time to pay the man here come the shenanigans. So much to the point I wrote him a kite, which I normally didn't do, as a courtesy. I did though. I told him needed to get his hand right with me or I'd have to take it to his folks. I respect protocol, but if protocol's not respecting the process then fuck it. I'm doing the next best thing and I know you're still running around doing and being you. Tear mine off! Handle it or it'll get handled. I ended up getting my loot, except 25. Someone owed him 25 so he pushed them on me, "Look, you owe me and I owe Tic." Handle that for me. Being that it was someone who owed him was from the city (Long Beach) and someone I messed with, I agreed and that person agreed so it was good.

He started playing games with the 25, "Soon as I get on the phone, I got you." Days pass.

"What's up homie, you got that?"

"Oh I got you tonight. As soon as my girl gets off work I'll have those greenies for you in the morning."

The next day I get hat him, "You know what, I'm not about to do this to you!" I went to Wavy,"You still owe me, your boy playing games and I need it by Monday!"

It was Friday, that was the last straw. I stopped fucking with Cyc, he showed his true colors. Came Monday 25 was sitting in front of my door. Give me, me! He was trying to get at L-Loc, to get at me, telling me to calm down and to kick back. He got me! L Loc told him "you need to pay the man, you're already know how Tic is". I wouldn't sweat dudes, I gave them that room. I didn't have sweat suit on but if you told me something I expect you to keep your word. All we have is our word as men. Anything outside of that is a misoverstanding. Dudes would have the homie pistol hot behind his loot, he really had patience though. Though he would vent to me, he still had patience. I don't recall really when he said he wanted to get on a dude about his loot. The homie was like, "It's always a situation with you."

He used to be tripping off of me. A few times I just fell back because I was getting tired of chasing these dudes about my loot. I knew eventually it would go bad for someone. Whether it was coffee balls or a card I was selling you it was a hand to hand policy, from mine to yours, from yours to mine. It worked for a minute then I fell back into old habits of doing business. When I was putting the coffee balls together or drawing my cards I'm not trying to sit on them. It started off smooth as always then shit falls back into that old pattern of having to chase dudes around, even when I was doing my two for one's with my pork skins and chili. I give you one chili, you give me two back. Everything though I've done I've always ran it by my cellie. I trusted him, I always wanted him to know the biz incase he needed to let it be known as to what really happened, what it was about, or what the deal was. Everyone and everything was a breaking point. Real talk! The last deep conversation we've had was about representing our sets at our age.

Which sends your mind back to how that homie or something in the set that we've took notice of aspired to achieve, or to be had us jumping off the porch heading into traffic (the streets) head first at that young age feeling like once I'm in it, I'm in it until death do me part; different time, different climate. But he's really at that point of being like, "Fuck it!" His thing though is tripping off of what homies will think or how they'll feel about it. When is it enough though? Dudes are grand fathers! He has two, I have three, "Cuz, I'm really cool on this shit. I'm tired of these bullshit dudes too." Every time an issue came up it's "What L Loc think" or "What L Loc's going to do?" You dudes can't think for yourself or handle it?

Like with me, I wasn't trying to be "big homie" on the yard. I don't care about none of that; my position is of an older homie. I voice my opinions or concerns when need be. I'm not trying to be the voice, but a voice someone else can always assume that role or title. That's not what I do. However, I've had to step in when there wasn't anyone with rationale or an ability to think without caving to the pressure of outside forces. Issues were constantly brought to me not anyone else "Get at Tic! . . . Get at Tic! . . . Get at Tic! He'll handle it or get it handled". I wasn't looking for that position. I don't aspire to be a big man on campus. At the end of the day I'm for and about community and doing what's right by the community (LBC) East, West, and North.

It was known that I was keeping it clean and pushing right, wasn't with the shenanigans, so dudes felt comfortable and confident in my ability to keep shit not only clean but fair. That's why me and Big Duck started tapping in every week. He's filling me in on the A-yard shit and I'm filling him in on the B-yard shit. His exact words "You got it over there, keeping pushing". "Aye Tic, such and such owe and he's bullshitting on paying" . . . Debt paid! It was taken care of.

"Aye Tic, one of ya'll homies (LBC) came from Salinas Valley he kicked off some bullshit with the Hispanics and didn't tell anyone shit." Homies from that end were tapping in with homies on the line via gadget saying cuz need to be DP'ed. I forgot his name. I just knew he was a young 20 homie. He was in 9-building but he was moved to A-yard. He never landed on our yard. He went straight from 9 to A-yard in less than a day. Big Duck looked into it and he was trying to get some young homies from the city to handle it. No bueno! No one wanted to step up so his cellie, a Long Beach civilian, Jaquese handled it. My cellie came in the cell from the yard and told me it was an issue and I might want to go out and check into it. At this time it wasn't but me and the home GP from 20's we discussed it, that we'll look into it if he came on the yard. Before we gotten to see him or talk to him he was sent to the other side. Outside forces were really trying to make sure that got handled. They kept blowing up certain dudes, "Make sure that happen!"

"Ok, cool, but how we see fit! However he's on A-yard, holler at them over there. Send word to Big Duck." I shot to the law library and hollered at Big Duck. He told me the situation was handled, though disappointed in the young homie Bud from the set Babyz. I guess he was doing him and didn't want to sacrifice what he had going on. I thought though, this is what dudes signed up for and he was called on. I told the homie Duck, "It won't be the last time you'll be disappointed." I saw Bud too, a few days later of talking to Duck, walking pass him and didn't speak. He knew who I was. We'd met before he moved on that side of the yard. Duck was pistol hot though because a non-affiliated had to handle homie business. He volunteered to, "I got you big homie, even though I don't bang but I'm from The Beach (Long Beach)." You think about it, that should be embarrassing. That's the type of dudes we're dealing with on the line.

Not wanting to do shit, just slide right through without having to get their feet wet or their hands dirty. Usually when a dude turns down tending to business, he has an issue coming and in some cases voted off the island. When I was in Delano on our side of the yard we took turns and everyone got one, wasn't no volunteers. It was next man up, everyone's keeping it shitty. We had an older homie, Ed Dog from BLVD's, he was pretty much layed back. I was in my late 30's everyone else were in their 20's except for the homie T Capone from 20's, he was older. I think Motto from 20's was in his early 30's. I believe Baby Webb, C Dog (Junay), Smoke from Dodge City, and I think Tray Rag were in their 20's. Oh and a tall young homie from West Coast 80's, KC 80. He ended up tapping out.

Junay had gotten on him behind an issue. I never got the scoop, Oh Tone from 20's was in his late 20's I believe. Baby Webb and Smoke ended up getting on another homie. He had came off of A-yard because he didn't sign a marriage chrono; a paper saying you can be on the yard together with the person you had an altercation with. He had dope fiend another homie and didn't want to be on that yard any longer so he didn't sign the paper, thus landing on our yard. The homies inquired as to the situation. He told us, flat out, he didn't sign the marriage chrono because he didn't know he had to.

How do you not know? That's like, turning down a fade (refusing to fight). You know not to do that. We know the repercussions of that with the homies. It's an issue! All day I rather take a fade with one dude than be DP'ed by two for turning down the fade. That's just no bueno! I don't get dudes. They'd rather get DP'ed then to take the one on one fade, that's just crazy. If you don't get two on one'd it'll be three on one'd to get you off of the yard. See yah! You've been removed. Sometimes it'll go bad. It can cease at the DP or it can keep going everywhere you land until he goes SNY or just tapping out.

That can depend on the type of program is going on, on that yard, and who's on it and what they're on. You can land one spot. Dudes will feel like you've been DP'ed, it's done, go somewhere else. It's "Fuck that, get up out of here!" A cold piece of legislation, turning it down is a lot worse than it's worth. It's a lot that comes with that act. But like I've said, it could all depend on the yard you land on and what dudes are on with the marriage chrono situation. How shit is today, it varies. Some homies may feel you got the message and dead it. They homies whupped him off of the yard and went to the sandbox, coming back a couple of months later.

Smoke was like, "Damn homie, you acted like I wasn't going to handle my business the way you looked at me and were looking."

I was like, "Nah homie, I was just looking but I did think I was going to have to step in. Ya'll were taking a minute." Right after that Junay got on KC80, it was like two or three days later. They both came back to the yard, but then another issue came about in his building, he was in five. Something happened and then he went to the sandbox and had tapped out. S Bone, my boy from 5-2 (Five-Deuce) Broadway, tried hollering at him in the sandbox. He told S Bone he wasn't good anymore (went SNY). Damn, that was crazy. This dude's 6'11 or something, tall as fuck.

About a week or two after that situation me and Tone from 20's had to get on Shorty Mac from 20's. He could've come back to the yard but wouldn't sign the marriage chrono. Me and Tone signed one while we were in cages in the substation. The police told us he refused which helped us no to go to the sandbox where we were headed. They felt since he wasn't coming back to the yard they kicked us back to the yard.

They'd hit us with smoke bombs and I got hit in my lower back by a block gun round and was sprayed in the face and head with mace. That block gun got me and broke skin, had my back on fire. It was stinging and my eyes were burning. Close range getting hit with the block gun hurt like fuck. That was the second time that shit happened; shot in the back and sustained broken skin. A few issues had followed him from a few spots. Everything was discussed and at the end of the day it was on me and Tone. I messed with Shorty Mac, he was cool but you know how shit goes when you're in traffic. There are still rules and regulations to this shit. A dude can love you like a rock but he'll throw your ass.

We've all signed up for something, though the code doesn't mean the same thing no more to some as it once did. It took on a whole different meaning for me as long as I'm pushing and representing my city and the homies. It's insane first then LBC and I'm going to move accordingly, all rules apply as long as they're in accordance and on the side of right. Everything has to be justified and not just fitting some narrative. None of that dirty shit, dirty politics, or hidden agendas. That's a pet peeve. If a dude has an issue coming let the reason be legit and not back handed. If he deserves it, he deserves it. It is what it is. Got my vote! I don't harbor dudes under no circumstances because I would be condoning bad behavior. How would that make me look? It is crazy though, what dudes are condoning and contributing to . . . wow!

Nowadays dudes are not trying to do nothing but when there's no drama or no issues in the air it's all good. That when dudes start popping it (talking tough) like they're with it. As soon as there's an issue it's all types of excuses and buck passing, "I can't do this because of that, I can't do this because of this, I would but this and that and the third." If you don't knock it off! It's not that the homie didn't know that he just allowed his expectations to get clouded. All bullshit aside, Ole Boy should've gotten an issue. The homie know it too, that's why he's venting. He even said as much saying, "I wish it was other lil homies here." The homie was feeling some type of way in his emotions. The homie was on his way to a transitional house. He did end up leaving though a month later. I haven't heard anything from him as of yet. You know how that goes, out of sight out of mind. C.G. was on the yard too, he went home. He was a good young homie. He got out and immediately started doing his music, real tough. He sent me, my cellie L Loc, and Y.F. captured moments. I saw a few of his videos; he was doing his shit, handling his business.

When he was leaving he shot a couple of the homies his info and number, keeping it a thousand. I initially didn't want it; you know how dudes are talking that talk. They have no intentions of keeping in touch or looking out (doing monetary things). It's just something to say on their way out of the door. I'm going to do this, that or the other, or I'm a real one I'm not like the rest of the dudes. If I fuck with you I fuck you with. I heard it all before, that rerun is a repeat! I normally ever take dudes info or number. They're just taking to make conversation. It took me two months to even call him. He kept telling Y.F. to tell me to hit him. I finally did, "Sup cuz? . . . Nothing, same ole shit. . . Yup yup!" I talked to him a couple more time, after that it was a wrap. You know dudes be faking! As I suspected from the get go, another bullshit dude. Every dude I've fucked with that was going home sung that same song "Blah blah blah!"

Homie just go home. Why do dudes do that? It's not necessary then it turns out you were bullshit. C.G. was still on the yard when that shit had happened with Tattle-Tale. I told the homie, "Go home you're short, it's good." He only had a couple of weeks or so. For a minute he was acting like he wanted to get active still, knowing he was short. Kick back, lil Niggah, go home! When I first got there T.J. from BLVD was on the yard. I had been wanting to holler at him for a minute behind some shit I felt he was out of pocket on.

When I saw him he was going into eleven building, I was on my way in twelve building. I called his name it, it was him, I wasn't sure at first. I just told him we had to holler. I told my cellie me and the homie have to get down, I told him why. The next morning I saw him at the breakfast I was sitting with my cellie and a couple of his Compton homies. When we all left the chow hall I called T.J., "Aye cuz, we gotta get down!"

Dudes started looking. He kept pushing and was like, "Whaaat!"

"We got to get down!"

He was like, "Hold up, let me go to my building and drop something off."

My cellie was like "Snake from Harlem" was shaking his head. I waited, he never came back out so I pushed in my building.

My cellie ended up going to a Ducat, an ID size piece of paper telling you you're on an appointment schedule going somewhere at what time and where. While we were at dayroom I just happened to look out of the window. I saw T.J. and my cellie in the field talking. When my cellie came back in he was telling me T.J. was like, "That lil Niggah better not get at me like that again or it's on!" Lil Niggah, I was 40 something, what the fuck! I was told to leave that situation alone. We didn't after that for a month.

We gradually started talking. This shit is crazy. We just ate breakfast. High Dessert food is trash. Not only is it trash, it's suuuper short. It's cold as fuck in this cell right now. It's also snowing right now too. I'm looking out of my window at the snow falling. My view is cool. I can see mountains, big trees, a road, and smaller trees. The only thing messing up the view is the fence with the barb wire along the top of it going in both directions to my left and to my right. I'm sitting here with boots on, two pairs of socks, thermal pats, thermal shirt, t-shirt, shorts, and a big ass orange jacket on with fake material indie of it that look like ship skin. It doesn't do much, just what it can.

It looks like the old school bomber jacket without the hoodie. I also have my beanie on. I'm in the cell like this, it's Sunday it's going to be ugly outside tomorrow. I'm going out, I won't be working out, I'll work out in the ell which I had been doing anyway the first few weeks of being here (High Dessert) trying to start a program. Then I would still go out and work out with Lon but yeah we'll be posted up for the most part. I will be bundled up whenever they open the cell door for yard a dude's up out of here. I just don't stay in the cell on the cell arrest (don't come to the yard). I'm on the yard daily, rain, sleet, sun or snow, and security conscious. Feel me? Once I'm out, I'm out pretty much. A lot of dudes aren't, as soon as in-line is announced, dudes kick rocks and leave the yard

In-line is where you can go inside of the building early, not having to wait until the end of yard. If it's morning yard, recall is like 11:45 AM. If it's the afternoon recall is like 3:45 PM, the in-lines at 2:30 PM. Dudes would go in 10:30 AM in-line, or 2:30 PM in-line. The yards damn near a ghost town both in-lines. The yard's already short on heads as far as the Blacks, and then more go in. Again the numbers don't matter, but damn! If something happen it just happen, because I'm out there regardless. I don't do the staying in the building or the in-lines. It has to be necessary or an important thing that has to be taken care of. Outside of that, when I come out I'm out until recall, period. Besides, if anything were to happen I'd rather be on that first wave. After that those who weren't prepared will become that second wave.

The chances of getting hurt elevates on a second wave. Then it can go to a trickle situation to where it'll go tit for tat, like back and forth until it fizzles out. That's on some racial shit. The Black on Black crime, it's going to play out how it's going to play out depending on the players and the situation. You never know with the variables at play. What I can avoid, I do. I'm not on no fake turnt up shit, tough guy shit. For the most part, I try to stay out of the way and in my lane. If it comes to me though, I'm not turning it down. I'll deal with it accordingly. I'm older now, so I'm a bit more reserved and laxed. I'm not as quick tempered as I once was. I have more of a tolerance.

I'll try the diplomacy route and talk matters out, especially with my race, if it can be. It doesn't always have to go straight to violence even if that's all dudes respect or recognize. However, don't confuse that with softness or something therefore acting as if you're trying to press your will or you weight over here. I'm still a man at the end of the day and still have to walk these lines. I'm going to get it how I live. I know my lane and I stay in it. Homies know though I can be counted on, no doubt! . . . It's LBC! Love my city!

10

If it's some bullshit that's addressable and it needs to be addressed, lets address it and move forward. Otherwise, dead it (leave it alone). I don't do the crowds. It's never been my thing or the grouping up. In reality, it only takes a couple of heads (people) to figure it out and come to a consensus. I really rather hear about it, if it's go time. I'm good on all of the extra shit, all the back and forth and who wants to be the voice in charge, who's this, who's that. Too much noise, getting nowhere, pure nonsense. Too many Chiefs, not enough Indians! At the end of the day, we're not doing anything but alerting the police that there's an issue or potential issue. At best, putting the potential target(s) on notice, "We're planning on coming." We're trying to figure it out but hold on. . . Horse playing! Why? Because dudes are going to get uncomfortable and become standoffish, thus creating a problem before it actually is one.

To the point of making someone spooked to where the gun is jumped (reacting before an act is acted out) and it's on! The turn up! I've always been taught, it's not what you do but how you go about what you do. . . "On Crip!" Some dudes are not feeling that because they're in denial. Denial is a funny thing though I've come to overstand and appreciate.

Like I've said, I'm no prison politician, nor am I political. I'm just on the side of right and what it stands for. I know the lines and I know where they are. I know too when you cross them enough you don't know where they are. I respect the code and I push by it. I also overstand we have to deal with the world as it is. The one we're in (prison) and not as we wish it to be. Think about the question, How come your distant perception is more valid than your present truth?

Mind you, being where we are and the state of the environment, along with the type of individuals you've dealt with and are dealing with. Me personally, I stay critical thinking and assessing things. You have to. Someone has to. The one thing that I continue to learn is that I don't know shit! It's much more to learn and be learned, especially with yard life! One thing though about critical thinking, you learn how to ask questions. Not just questions, but the right questions and when to ask them, can rely on autobots. It's not just what you ask, but how you ask it, when you're hearing shit. You can't be a dude just talking and accepting shit at face value when it's about the next dude. Me, I'm asking questions.

I'm not passing judgement. I'm not giving my input or a view until I'm satisfied with my questions being answered. Dudes play too many games and stay horse playing when they're not eating half of your back out (back biting you, talking about you behind your back). When dudes aren't fully engaged with the situation around them, they can easily fall into lostness and become lost in the madness of the yard. I'm not one to be poisoned, so I assess it all. You can't poison Tic. I'm fully vaccinated. Whatever issue you have with a dude, that's your issue. I'm not getting sucked into it. That's not my drama. I don't take sides. I'm neutral. Nor do I harbor, especially if it's between homies on some internal shit. I don't get involved in homie shit at all!

Don't think you're going to come to me about another homie and I'm going to just jump on your side. That's now and in the past. That's not how I operate. Now, if the homie done some bullshit, that's a different story. A personal issue is a personal issue amongst homies. Leave me out of that shit. Homies stay doing that will get into it with another homie or has an agenda and will try to suck another homie into it. "Cuz, it's this that and the third. The homie said or done this. He's foul." Not only try to suck you into it, but have you roll with it.

You don't know if the homies on some bullshit or not. You don't know what's true or what isn't, but because the homie you mess with said it or a homie you've known longer, it must be true. If that isn't autobotism, I don't know what is. That type of activity though will catch up to a guy, in some form or another. Especially if someone had hands put on them. You moved in the blind, you had no proof or facts! That's not what homies do, or supposed to do. That's dirty pool! Where's smoke, there's fire. It's already hot! That goes back to the bullshit dude being too concerned with liking dudes or with being liked himself. I wasn't born to give a fuck about if a dude liked me or not, or concern myself with being liked because when it's all said and done, I'm going to do and be me.

I don't concern myself with who likes me or who doesn't, or for what reasons. It's not my issue. These very things I'm saying, me and L Loc have had these very conversations. Me and the homie really chopped it up in the cell and vibed on some shit. We challenged each other too. You know the adage, "Iron sharpens iron." We broke it down like a Garcia Vega, sitting on my mama's steps. We touched on various issues and topics about life in general, homies, family, and a lack there of. We talked about set shit, bullshit with homies around the yard, bitches, and getting loot. We had more in common than we realized, besides growing up in the 70's. We both smoked water (sherm/pcp) on the streets. We would laugh at the stories that we heard about ourselves from other people. I couldn't remember half of the shit I've done unless I was coming down off the high, otherwise it was a blank. Two incidents I could remember though, vividly. One, me and the homie Juju from the set caught that fade (fought) in the set. We were on 21st and Olive in the back of the home boy Big Ant Dog's baby mama, G.G.'s apartment building, in a little grassy area. I was just hitting the set, getting off the bus, so I'm on foot. As I'm walking up the block I can see some young homies behind the homies baby mama's apartments and asked them if they wanted to smoke. What young Niggah going to turn down some weed? I told them to go get some blunts. I have the tree and I gave them three dollars. Two of them hopped on bikes and went up the block towards Atlantic Ave. I still have my backpack on. I hear, "There go cuz, right here!" I turned around. I'm thinking it's two homies at least, but it was just Big Mouth! Mr. Turn Up.

"Cuz, we got to get down!" This is what he says to me.

I'm like, "Whaaat!"

"You heard me!"

"On Insane Crip cuz you ain't saying nothing!" I tell one of the other Young homies to hold my backpack and don't let cuz get it.

"Don't worry about nothing homie. I have it." I had my pistol in it. I'm wet (high off pcp), but had started coming down some. Me and him started squabbling up (fighting). He couldn't do anything with me high. We were a round in when the young homie from Youngs, T Dur Dur, came and broke us up. He heard the commotion when we had apparently fell up against an old raggedy wooden gate. . . "Bloom!"

He runs to the back of the apartment and sees us. "Juju, what the fuck cuz!" Juju said something and bounced (left).

My thoughts then went to "Fuck cuz, I'm about to heat his ass up!" He's a bully type dude anyway, a low-key mad-dog. The type you euthanize. I let it go though, but what I was thinking, "He got one more time to cross my line on some bullshit, then we're going to really see what's up." We got into it in the first place because he told my BM bullshit ass he fucked my wife. You probably did. I don't put nothing passed a bitch, especially that one. Basically, "So what!" What type of dude is that though? Of course she denied it. That's what she does. "He's this that and the 3rd. He's dusty. He's a dirty dick type Niggah. He just watched my kids. He gave me his GR (general relief) check and his food stamps!" She was saying all types of shit about him, trying to convince me he didn't fuck. In reality, all she did was confirmed it by trying to down play it, by trying so hard to justify their dealings. "Guilty!" He fucked, period.

Either way, I didn't care. That was her pussy. If she chose to fuck dirty dick or dusty cuz, that was her business. It happened before me as far as I know. I'm sure he wasn't the only Insane she let fuck before I started messing with her. She was a whore all along and fucking out of both pant legs. Ms. "I don't fuck nobody from Long Beach, you're the first!" (SMH)

"Yeah . . . and weed don't get you high. What the fuck ever!" So yeah, he tells my BM Jackie he fucked my wife. Why though? For what reason? That's shit broads do, so what, you fucked her and your point was?

Cold thing about it, I've never had an issue with dude, got at him foul, nor had a run-in. We were always cordial when we saw each other in the set or in traffic. Here it is though, you're speaking on me and how you fucked my wife. Big whup. You want a cookie? You weren't the first, you weren't the last. It's just pussy my dude. You didn't get anything special or sacred, you got what everyone else got, whore pussy. She must have had you sprung (in your feelings). An ole tender dick Niggah huh? I had it for 5 years and got my dick sucked on a regular. So, big whup (not a big deal)! I told Loc too about the incident I had when I went to jail (in my boxers, running down the street in them on the North Side). The homies said when I saw the ones (police), I started running up the block. I don't even remember taking my pants off. The ones catch up with me. I'm kicking and flopping around like a fish. Then they tied me up in some leg restraints, cuffing me. The next thing I knew, I was in the Long Beach City Jail. After that, I ended up in the County Jail.

I was put on Summary Probation for that shit. Loc was laughing because I was animated, telling him the story. Imagining myself doing the shit they said I was doing. I had another incident I was told happened, but I remember slightly the incident, because I just finished smoking a stick (pcp cigarette) with my baby mama and her dude. I had been coming around as of late, messing with my two sons by her. Her dude lived there had nothing to do with me. I spent nights with my sons, sleeping in their room with them. At this time they were teenagers. I ironed my clothes there and took a couple of baths there, here and there. Me and her were cordial and we talked. Dude for some reason was threatened by my presence. I saw how he started to move and act. Me and him had to talk and air shit out.

I'm like, "Aye Phillip . . . Aye homie, let me holler at you dude!" Then I'm like, "Trip (listen), I don't want your bitch. She's just my baby mama. I'm cool on her (I don't want her). You don't have to worry about me." Even though we had had sex, but it was before him and a few months after I was out, which was actually the first and only time since I was grown. Yeah and after that stunt she pulled and had me locked up on those bogo (bogus) charges. I wasn't trying to hit (have sex) again. One and done. I was passed the "what it would be like now phase" as a grown man to have sex with her, or the "how it would be phase". I was a teenager when I last had sex with her, before then and surprisingly it was still decent. Her pussy was still decent and she was a cool fuck. Like I said, it was just the once and I didn't press to hit it again. The thrill was gone. We (her, me, and her dude) were smoking a stick. She had hit it (took a puff), one last time, leaving me and him there to kill it (smoke the rest). We were standing between the front house on a paved walkway that led to a back duplex, separated by a wooden fence. They (him, her and the kids) stayed in the back. She went through the fence, which was actually a rod iron gate and it closed behind her. I hit it again and passed it. After hitting it again, I was cool (had enough). I told him to go ahead and finish it.

As soon as I turned around with my back to him, walking to the fence and opening it, this clown ass Niggah comes up behind me, tries to pull me backwards, and then bites me in the middle of my back. I remember doing the chicken wing. After that, I was told, I had somehow worked my body around and started to jab him with some quick punches. They knew they were slow, you don't move too fast high on sherm. So, he grabs me and we fell. The last thing I remember, he was running through the fence. I'm about to murder this dude! He just doesn't know. I left, my BM had my sons give her my number because she didn't have it. She calls me, "Can you leave him and that situation alone please. I have to live here with my kids and yours too." I told her I lost my Bitter Child chain, my Raider earrings, and some loot and my two way (two way pager/side kick) was broken. She was like, "He'll pay for it and replace the other shit."

"Cool!" I wasn't going to tell her rat ass shit. She would be the last person to know anything. Her and situation were neck and neck on that status. Couldn't trust them. But that's what I had planned on doing. I was missing in action for a week, hadn't been around to their block (23rd and Earl) at all. When I did though, I was waiting for him underneath his car with my strap (gun) at my side, cocked and loaded, waiting for him to come out to go somewhere. It never happened that night. The next night I was in their alley behind the duplex with the strap, waiting for him to bring out the trash. That didn't happen. My sons had brought the trash out. They never saw me though. I was ducked off (concealed). A couple of nights later, I came back and had gotten on their roof above their door. I could lean over the edge and shoot down. He never came out. BM did, the kids did, never him. Mind you, I was doing this at night.

He'd been taking the trash out, he'd been coming out of the house at night going somewhere. All of a sudden though he switches up. BM's mama gotten at me and was like, "Leave that alone. He's not worth it." She knew the business, knew I wasn't leaving it alone. This Niggah bit me, broke my shit, and had me losing shit. I wasn't leaving shit alone. That was out! All the way out! Whaaat! No Bueno!

L was like, "Damn, that was some crazy shit!" He was like, "Under the car? On the roof? In the alley?" Hell yeah, I was on a cold stake out! Allah was with that dude and had him covered and me.

He was about to be 86'ed (gone) and didn't know it. Horse playing will get your subscription canceled, real talk! It was a couple heads given the right opportunity, I would've blew their beans out (brains). He told me about a few of his sherm episodes that had me laughing like crazy. With that whole situation with me, it was my ego in conjunction with working with feelings that fueled my desire to move the way that I did. Life on the yard is a funny thing, but a dude embraces all that's thrown at him and refuses to fold or falter. It will have you shaking your head though.

Seeing what's seen and hearing what's heard. . . Whoa, and compounded by the many different personalities and autobots. Truth over bullshit. I respect the blatant shit! If we're supposed to be real dudes, let's be real dudes. You have a lot of weirdo's running around. They think they're normal though. For homies, older ones, I big up you (give you your ultimate respect) and salute you for still pushing (main-line programming, 6-p). In this prison matrix and not falling to the wayside and influences knowing the opposition we're facing, as older homies on the line, yet remaining and doing you. Sometimes I've engaged myself in a mental tug of war. I've pulled and tugged until things have come to me, trying to figure stuff out that I was having a hard time overstanding. That's why I rewind my days at night, when it's quiet, before I go to sleep. So much noise, so much volume.

The program around High Desert had been fucked up. The police were feeling some type of way (in their feelings) because of an incident that took place on the patio with Calbo, the second time, which ultimately got him removed all together from the yard. They were only allowing four people at a time on the patio to get packages or go to medical or something, and yard got cancelled. As of now, shit's calmed down, or appeared to have. You still have dudes grouping up and politicking about something or another. That's a daily occurrence with everyone, some harder than others. That's a normal captured moment. Nine out of ten, it's because someone owes someone. A day hasn't gone by that I haven't heard about someone owing someone. "Such and such better stop playing with my loot before I get on him." The coldest thing I was privy to and didn't care about it either way was when someone told me (someone of another race) that he'd given someone else of another race a dollar to handle something for him. That dude took his dollar and paid an outstanding debt he had (SMH). He told me the dude brought his greenies back with a number off (switching the last number) telling him, "Here's your greenies." No bueno! Personally I think it was cap (bullshit) from get-go. I don't think it was ever a play in motion. At the end of the day, he shot his shot and came up on some greenies to pay his debt. That was the play, conning him(SMH) real live horse playing! The greenies were run and they were no good. They'd been used. Wow! If that wasn't a felony, I don't know what was! "Yeah Tic, I just got out from a life sentence. I don't need the bad karma."

How's that bad karma? Dude took your loot and paid off his debt he'd owed for a while at your expense. How's that bad karma? Because if you turn him in (let his people know what he'd done) they'll do something to him and that's your problem or fault how exactly? You're the one who was fucked over in the scenario, so you should feel bad if they smash him? Wow! They do have some weird ass policies around High Desert certainly, but he could've turned him in. It wasn't a debt. Dude flat out stole. "So how does that supposed to work?" He should've walked the plank!

From my overstanding, if someone is turned in for a debt, they'll have to pay x-y-z just for being in debt with someone. Once that's paid and their work out is completed, your debt is paid he owes you nothing, that's the risk you run. It's the cost of doing business. That whole get down is crazy as fuck! You get my shit, whatever it is if you decide not to pay me and I turn you in, I'm not getting my loot. . . What the! I don't know who came up with that policy, I guess checking isn't cheating, but whatever. I'm not having those worries because I'm not putting myself in that type of situation. I'm cool on the shenanigans.

It's straight up bullshit. I won't be having any part in the activity on any level. I don't need the headaches that come along with it. It's just too much. Too much horse playing. L was on the gadget with his homies. He had just found out his G homie, K.T. (not his real name) a reputable front hood Compton Crip, had just been killed in their set. His homies were tapping in, telling him about the incident. He told me many stories about K.T. who reminded me a lot of my G homie, B.L. (not his real name) from the set. No nonsense type of homie that's still active. Dudes know if you rub him the wrong way you better stay out of his way, giving him that distance, he'll holler at you!

The broad Cynthia, yeah, her thick chocolate ass that used to give me and Miko rides, she was mad at me once because I stopped messing with her. I had her slanging for me (selling dope). I took my phone from her and what work (dope) she had left because she was dipping and spending my loot like we were having sex or something. I'm like, "Bitch, I gave you yours to do with what you chose to. Smoke it or sell it. Why are you fucking with my work?" Dipping in my sack and spending my loot. You're not giving Tic no pussy or no head. If you don't knock it the fuck off with the horse play. She's trying to get in with B.L., so she tells him I said he was serving (selling) some bullshit work. I've never said this. It was flat out a lie.

True though, I had bought work from him once. She didn't know that though. He came to the International (a hotel) to a room I was in with five or six smokers (crack heads) waiting to serve them. My normal plug (connect) had me on hold, so until he was ready, I just copped a quarter of an ounce from B.L. I paid him and he bounced. As soon as I served them, they were putting some in their new pipes to smoke. As soon as they put flames to their pipes taking hits, that shit turned their pipes black, like they'd been smoking on them for weeks or months. Needless to say, they were all pistol hot and looking at me for closure. "I don't know what you're looking at me for. That's out! I got nothing for you!" Ya'll saw I just bought that. I'm not taking the loss. I left. Sucks to be you! I never even talked to Cynthia. A few days later, my big homie, Big Half Head, came to the Aloha where me and Miko were serving as usual. He was like what's up with you and B.L.? As far as I know, nothing. Why, what's up with us? He said he's hot at you about something you had supposedly said.

I told Big Half to call the homie so I can see what's good. He called him and handed me the phone, "Cuz, what's up. It's Tic." I basically let him know the homie Big Half let me know he felt I said something about something. I asked him where he was. He told me in the set on 2-1 and Lemon. I know exactly where he was. I went over there and talked to him. Apparently it was a mis-overstanding. We straightened it out though. L was like, "Damn, I just talked to the homie. That's crazy." Then we had started talking about how that type of shit could happen and how dudes have to be careful when he's out there in traffic when he get out.

A month or so after that, a childhood homie from the set, Baby Bullet, was killed in Bakersfield, California. I heard behind a bitch. His cousin, Lil Bullet, had gotten killed, just before he did in the city. Dudes are out there dying off over bullshit! I had messed with Baby Bullet when I was on the streets and I hung out with him on occasion in Bakersfield. We blew blunts, smoked water and some K.J. K.J. is something the Bakers-field dudes smoke on the regular, what water is to Long Beach, Compton, Watts, and L.A., K.J. is to Bakersfield. It's like a powder version of water. The last time I saw him, before we hung out as adults, we were in SRCC (I think it stands for Southern Reception California Center, not sure). SRCC is basically where you go before you land where it is you'll be serving your time in Y.A. There's two. One for Southern California, and one for Northern California, NRCC. I was waiting to go to YTS (Youth Training School). He was on his way to Fred C-nelli's. We weren't as close as we'd once been. You could've considered us like brothers at some point. We were straight though. We grew up together. Me, him, and his brother Coo Coo from 20's.

When I was hanging out with Bullet, Coo Coo was doing time in the Feds. I hadn't seen him since we were like 14 or 15 years old. "What up, Ashy-Bash!" A name I sometimes called him when we were young. The name stayed. Between their house and ours, we lived next door to each other. Oh trust he didn't like being called that, but you know kids. You see another kid don't like something, you keep doing it until you fight about it. I know losing his only blood brother weighed heavy on him. He had two steps though (step brothers), Dee Dee and Tony. I know their sister, Tawana, was feeling it as well.

I saw Tawana's thick ass once when I was in traffic with a homie. She was wearing some Daisy Duke shorts. I was like, "Damn!" She had a Niggah's dick hard as fuck. I had a little crush on her when we were younger, but she was a few years younger than me. I think when I was 13 she was like 10. She could've been 11. I just know she was too young for me. I still liked her though. Around that time I had started having sex with Jackie who lived across the street from us, who would later become my BM, but I'm not going to lie, seeing Tawana grown and thick as she was, I did want to fuck. I didn't pursue her though. I could've, just didn't. Yup, indeed, I could've seen myself behind all of that big, round, yellow ass, hollering at her doggy style, gripping her hips, straight up! I think I had action at it.

She told me she had given one of her son's my middle name (Kae-funn). "Uh-huh." I must've been on her mind. Just thinking about her now though got me like, "Wow!" I wish I would've pursued it and at least ate it and fucked on it a few times. I wasn't trying to be her dude (her significant other), I was in a situationship. I just wanted to lay up (have sex). I horse played! Off top though, after assessing everything, L came to the conclusion it had to be some really elaborate on his thoughts. I can imagine though where his mental went.

I'm on the same shit. It's much bigger than the captured moment, presented. It was other forces at play, not my place though to speculate or give an opinion as to what I may have thought at the time. I was just privy to his vent. A lot of shit will remain and always remains in cell shit. Even though we're no longer cellies, especially the just between us conversations. We've had more than a few of those just between us conversations. Those automatically stayed in cell. The only time I would speak on in cell shit is about food he'd made, some clowning around we'd done, about some drink we'd made or about some pies I've made.

It would be, with my Broken Spokes, L, and Sims, or with my Oakland guy Rame (sup Lucious Lyon), or possibly with my fat Damu boy Tee from Pasadena, or my neighbors Mousey and Bang Bang. It was a few homies who had popped up on the yard, beyond the fist I'd mentioned. Tiny Pep, I think he was Tiny Pep from 20's, he was there for a while before I'd gotten there. He fell back (stopped being affiliated) and had became full fledge program facilitator, working on going home and generally tired of all of the fuckery that came with being affiliated. Before he went to the 2 yard, he'd stopped being a gang member. He's just Hodge or Ricky.

He was like, "I'm finished with this shit." I think it was 2017, or 2018, but could've been 2016. We had talked previously and got some shit off our chest. We weren't feeling each other since Calipat. When I first saw him at Solano, I didn't mess with him. I would just see him in passing, but come to find out it was just a miscommunication, Q and A misoverstanding. I'm like, "I was on some fuck you shit!"

He was like, "I was on some fuck you too type shit!" I told him I felt he was acting funny (standoffish/non-communicative) and on some funny shit. He didn't mess with me. He messed with Lil Tray Deee. They were boys. He told me though that I was the one acting funny and on some funny shit.

For some reason he felt the incident in2010 in Calipat on the B-yard that had happened with the Long Beach homies, and the Dodge City Crips happened because me, Lil Tray Deee, Ray Dog, G Boy, and Chewy were drunk and tripping. Fact is, none of us had been drinking at all. I don't know where he pulled that form. Who does that? But dudes who can't hold their liquor or get brave when they're on it, trying to turn up, only get tough with that liquid courage, saying and doing things they otherwise wouldn't do. In his mind though we were drunk. Even after I told him we weren't, he still insisted we were. Ok Hodge! C Bone from 20's was out on the yard when the incident happened. Pep was out there too. He was coming from work in the kitchen. He headed for his building to go inside after he hollered at a few heads.

He spoke on that too, saying he went in because he saw we were drunk and tripping, but then said, "I saw ya'll, shit looked normal. You know how ya'll were. I didn't think nothing was up." C Bone, when all the dust had settled and everything was over and the yard was down, he was laying inside of the yellow crime scene tape perimeter as a participant in the festivities.

He hollers out, "I'm from 20's, I ain't had nothing to do with that!" Wow! What did 20's have to do with it? At the end of the day, we're LBC. We're a collaboration effort. One for all and all for one. I know in my mind, Pep assessed the scene and felt or knew something was up. He had too. He fucked with Lil Tray Dee on a daily. This day though he goes right into the building without a dap to no homie. I wasn't tripping. We didn't fuck with each other. I was on some fuck your dap anyway. He was like, "I wasn't fucking with you drunk Niggahs on that drunk bullshit."

I told him we weren't drunk. "Yeah ya'll were!"

"Ok, Hodge!"

We became cool though. He was actually a cool dude. Lil Henderson Blue popped up on the yard. He was short timing. He's under his uncle from the set, Big Henderson Blue, one of the Dan Dogs. It's a bunch of them. I can't remember which one he was, but a homie told me he changed his name to Gray Feather from Babyz. Him and Broaham, from 60's, kept bumping heads. It was ongoing. They were working together in a shop on The Hill (all of the vocational classes and shops located on a hill). They had hit each other with PVC pipes and fought. They were boys though on some real goof ball shit. That was it as far as homies popping up. Motto from 20's was on A-yard for a minute. He ended up going to the 2 yard too.

Big Ant Dog was over there. Boy Blue (what up, Cat Fish?), Lil Kelly Boy was over there. He left Solano and went to another spot, came back to the 2 yard. A couple of other homies were over there as well. Big C was on A-yard for a minute. I don't know where he went. Beenie Boy from 20's was on A-yard. He went into Delancy Street on that yard. Face Nitti from Babyz was on A-yard too. B-yard for the most part was alright. You could get your loot, you just had to really k now who to fuck with and who not to, because dudes were always with the shenanigans. A lot of the shit going on, on the yard, was behind dudes horse playing with the loot. Wasn't anyone being played ball on. They were barely being punched on.

Dudes would be as bold to get your shit and be like, "I'm not paying you, but we can get down." (SMH) Whaaat! If you don't knock it the fuck off, pick it up and knock it off again! The couple of major incidents that went on was between the IE's (Inland Empire's) and the Neighborhoods. They had a cool scrimmage (melee) on the yard.

My cellie L, Fudge from Grape (Grape Street Watts), and a few other Hub and Dub had a quick little scrimmage with some Damus. It went up and it was over, no one got caught. It was like, "Bam Bam Bam Bam Bam", it was done. How that happened, I couldn't say. No one went to the sandbox. I didn't go to the yard that day, so I didn't participate, but it was over and done with. L came back in the cell all muddy from where he fell, breathing hard and pumped up. "We just got down with the Damus!" He was telling me now he was on this one Damu named Zeek from Oak Park in Sacramento, California, had him by his dreads, putting the pound on him. L isn't a little dude, that's a big ass dude, literally!

He looks like one of those dudes you would see in the pen in the 80's Green Mile looking ass Niggah. Illa from Zilla who was in it, he's another Damu. He was telling me who all got active as far as Hub and Dub. They did their do! Old ass L Loc still getting in the field represented for the old heads. It isn't too many of us walking around on these yards. Dudes are trying to get rid of us with the shenanigans. Outside of that, some Kumi dudes had a cool scrimmage with each other. Dust was flying everywhere. As far as Crip homies getting it in that I can recall, Nuttso from 60's got down with HB from Compton in the dayroom in our building (12-building). Trip, 6 Bone got it in with Lefty in our building. It was a few others. It was active though. Every new wave of young dudes, shit went haywire.

The last homie I got to holler at before I left 9-building was Baby J Smash from Compton Nutty Block. I called him when I saw him in the 9-building. He was like, "Who's that?"

"It's Tic!"

"Cuz, you burnt out!"

I'm assuming he was referring to my incident with Oppie. He was straight though. Him and L worked out a lot together. I hollered at him a few times on the yard in passing. He just told me to stay up. I just met his big homie, Big J Smash the other day on the yard. He was saying Baby Smash was on his way up here to High Desert from Cantilena State Prison. I'm looking out of the window right now. It's snowing, like fuck, it looks like a white Christmas. The trees in the mountains and brush are covered in snow. Even though I'm out there in it this morning. We have yard, so it's a workout day in the cell, but I'm going to wait until after yard so I can bird bath right after, then kick back and shower tonight at dayroom.

I will be bundled up out there, two beanies, 2 pairs of socks, my boots, thermal pants, thermal shirt, two t-shirts, and my jeans, plus my puffy wool jacket and gloves. It's cold too. Me and Lon probably go catch a wall and get snowed on, if he even goes out. It's coming down right now too, thick. He's coming out. I just asked him when the doors just opened up for the trays and trash. In Solano I didn't do the rain, though sometimes I would. Sundays and rain, I wasn't fucking with (staying inside). Here though, it's a much different environment. I'll do rain, sleet, or snow. My boots and hands can be accounted for.

Can't anyone say Tic don't be on the yard, or he's dodging it. I'm out every yard on deck. I'm damn sure not going to be sitting in the cell. For what? I don't even stay in the cell to work on this book, knowing I'm try-ing to get it finished. Right now, I'm A2B (no job), or A2-Bum. You have nothing coming. No weekend yard and phone calls once a month. So I'm just out there on the yard Monday through Friday. When I finally get one and get my A1A status again, meaning I'm back working, I'll be back out on the weekends, both days. I just had to do a form 22 so I can turn it in tonight. I'm asking the R and R Sgt if I could get a loaner T.V. which I'll return upon the dissolution of my granted appeal, my T.V. is repaired as granted, or I get another T.V. This shit is crazy as fuck. I'm going through all of this bullshit! My T.V. was broken, which was proven and verified, clearly, but they're not trying to do the right thing, still horse playing! It's simple. Replace my shit, or repair it. It's not complicated. One thing they like to do is play games and try to wait you out until you abort the appeal (602). They purposely take you through the ringer and hope you will abandon the process, giving up. They bank on it. That's out though! I'm not hustling and I don't have anyone to replace my shit.

Moms would. She would save up for me and do it, but I don't want her to, because they're going to figure it out. There's so called family out there, but they haven't fucked with me since I've been down, so I know for sure they won't do it. I wouldn't ask anyway, I know they don't fuck with me like that. They left a Niggah for dead, as soon as they heard I was locked up. Since the word gone, but I'll hear "Oh, such and such said hi." I would hear, "Such and such sends their love." Not trying to send no energy though (loot). Straight up, fuck your high and your bullshit ass love and sit on it! Your hi and your love is faker than blue dollar bills, get that shit up out of here! Just words with no substance behind it.

And to think, I would've laid my life on the line for you (SMH). In death or life in prison, to protect you, if need be. All you had to do was call and I was coming to your aid and assistance, doing what family do. Assist you or handle it! I see though, my definition of family is different. I wasn't looked at the same way I looked at them! Oh, it's a wrap now. You were cool on me, now I'm cool on you. I've come to learn and over-stand just because you're related by blood, it doesn't mean you're family. There are more people that are not blood related to me that have love for me than my actual blood and treat me like one of their own. You share DNA, but that's it. It means nothing. It's just a common thread that joins you. I'm stronger for it though, mentally, emotionally, though detached. Now I'm mentally and emotionally unavailable. I only have love and re-spect and an unwavering loyalty to my moms, my aunt, my uncle (R.I.P.), and my cuzzo Nip, no doubt, my son Dre.

Moms, my aunt, uncle, and cuzzo, they've played a part in my space (life) and continue to as only they can. It's not based on what they can do for me or about what they've done, it's the presence. I know they're there. They have a presence I'm constantly though tapping in. They've always kept it a thousand with me as well, never lied to me. I respect that part the most. They never felt the need to lie if they couldn't do something they just straight up tell me, "Can't do it now but give me some time and I got you." It'll happen, just not right now. I can respect that. I can respect them saying I can't do it because such and such is going on. I haven't wrote because of this that and the third, but what's going on? I'll get at you later. For the record, I've never been a needy dude since I've been in prison, due in part, I'm one of those types that'll make it happen and make it make sense. That's why when I did ask for something, or needed anything, I was able to get it. God respects the child who has his own and can get his own.

They figured (my supporting cast) if he's asking, he must really need it, because he doesn't ask often. It's far in between and it doesn't be much. I've also never burned bridges. You never know when you may have to cross over it again. It's dumb to have a fire behind you while you're crossing it. What I've also come to learn is how people will ask you, are you straight (alright) or if you need something, when in reality, they're just asking because they feel they should, but it's not genuine and really they're hoping you say that you're good or you don't need anything, feeling as though at least they've done their due diligence of asking. If you're truly that concerned, I'm not hard to find. If you're trying to find me and you're trying to send me some energy, shoot it, tap in!

Yet, you'll hit a dude on the thirty third (just an expression of a much later time, or on the flip side) with, you never asked or I didn't have your information, how could I write? How could I do this that or the other? This is the text book answer given or the shit they tell other people, as if my information is hard to get or I'm hard to find. There's such a thing called Inmate Locater. You know dudes names, it's no excuse. When I would be asked if I was straight or if I needed something I would say, "No, I'm good." In my mind, you were looking for that response anyway. You were just making conversation and feeling obligated to at least ask.

11

There was no intention of looking out (giving a guy energy) or messing with him like that. I was told by an older homie that if someone was genuine about wanting to do something for you, wanted to see you with something, or genuine about being in your space, their actions would reflect that, it would be natural. If their intentions were genuine, they wouldn't have to ask you are you straight, because they took the initiative and proactive steps to ensure you were, which would be appreciated. But when they ask you that question, "Are you straight?"/"Do you need anything?" either of them, it's no real substance or intention behind it, just more words and they hope you tell them no. They're really not trying to mess with you like that. That's like if they wanted to talk to you, they would have loot on the phone for you to call, even if it's only twice a month, which I feel is cool. If you can't call them and it's not an option, they're not trying to talk to you. It's just that simple. Some dudes don't get that and brake their necks to try and get a homie to make a three way call (a third party) for them.

"Can you have your girl call my girl for me?"

"Can you have your homie call my brother?"

"Can you have your sister call my cousin?"

If these people wanted to talk to you, you would be able to call them. Quit horse playing!

I'm very mindful. Me and L Loc would have these type of conversations too. We would go in (talk about something in depth) about how mutha fuckas leave you for dead, as if you never existed and you never co-existed. Wow, yard just got cancelled. I was looking forward to going out in the snow too. The police claimed it's because it's a staff shortage and they can't run yard and they were running packages (passing them out). It's still snowing. I'm looking out of my back window. We just find out shit was halted because the Damu's just fought on the patio and the police aren't feeling it and in their feelings, so they're tripping. It's one of their pet-peeves. They don't like activity at all on the patio, mainly because that's where the sub-station is located.

The last incident in Solano was in the dayroom with Tray whupping on this Damu affiliate (he didn't represent Damu, just hung with them or used to be one), named K.P. I'm assuming K.P. was out of my boy Dee's area (VNG). I guess Tray was tired of K.P.'s shenanigans with his loot. K.P. was a real slickster. One of those old school, light complexioned, long ponytail wearing, jive ass dudes, always trying to work you from an angle. He was cool for the most part, but bad business. It's not his fault. To him, it's checking ain't cheating. His philosophy was this, if he owes you and you ask about your loot, as far as when are you going to get paid, it's once or twice, as soon as he gets his hands on some greenies, he's going elsewhere to spend them, putting you further on the back burner. You're not a priority. You'll get it when you get it!

Everyone isn't going to accept that shit and feel it's unacceptable. If he's sick, you're really not getting your loot. He even told me, "Tic, if I owe a mutha fucka 50, he's only getting 25. That other 25 is going to the man." Yeah, he's telling me this, but I'm soaking it up like a sponge, good data. While I'm taking it all in, I'm saying to myself, you'll never owe me shit because if you owed me 50 and you just told me how you got down and you shot me 25, It's going to be an issue, because I know you're horse playing! I'm not allowing it. Give me me (give me what you owe me, or what you have for me). That's all I ask when time comes, give me me.

"Oh, we can get down!" Who gave you that route as an option? You don't dictate what's going to happen or how it's going to play out. You're horse playing again, get a bar. I guess Tray had been on hold a bit too long for his liking, or his taste and was frustrated with him. This I Know for a fact, he was on some fuck this dude type of shit. I know his method to his madness. He doesn't care about fighting you. Fighting you, the debt is paid, it's cancelled. He would've been shocked bucking with my loot. Sometimes caution has to be thrown to the wind and let shit play out as it's going to. Someone's going to be butt hurt (in their feelings) about the situation. That's how the cookie crumbles sometimes. You're not going to please everyone with actions you take, at times, even when you're in the right. Someone isn't going to be a fan, that's just prison and how the ball rotates. But am I a bullshit dude for the pride, I feel in the strength of my own decisions that weren't influenced by my consciousness? The last time that I checked, the answer was no! In here I lust for my moral compass to remain intact, my will and determination to keep pressing forward with some good smut captured moments to jack my dick off to. Even though I have a memory rolodex full of sexcapades, I was out there on the streets having sex with all types of bitches, including my strawberries. Whaaaat!

My favorite memory though is when I came home one day after being in traffic for a couple of days. My ex-situation had company over. I walked into the house. It was her sister, Lee Lee, the one I wanted to fuck on, just once. Her sister-in-law, Mary, who I already had sex with and ate the pussy, and their home girl Misty, who lived in the Carmelito's (large apartments on the North Side). I spoke to everyone, "Sup ya'll?"

I went into the bedroom. Situation was like, "Blackman!" She followed me into the bedroom, closing the door behind her. "Blackman, are you here to stay or are you in and out?" I'm here to stay. That's what I do, stay home, after being tired of running the streets constantly needing some shut down time, food, pussy, at the house, blow, and relax, which she liked. She sat on the edge of the bed and told me to come to her, step between her legs, which I did. Her legs were spread open and I stepped between them. She undone my pants, pulled my dick out, and started licking it up and down, down and up, real slow. When she came back up, she sucked me deep and hard into her mouth. "Ungh!" I'm like, "Ooooh Shiiiiit!" She went to work, like a young calf on a cow's titty. She sucked vigilantly and continuously at a slow pace, deep throating me. You felt every muscle in her mouth and tongue, work! I had my hands on my waist, looking down at her and watching my dick slide in and out of her mouth, work! As she sucked, her eyes were closed and she was moaning.

I lasted as long as I could. The next thing I know, "Unghhh-unghh!" I was cumming in her mouth and down her throat. She continued sucking and swallowing me, relentlessly. After I was done, she pulled and jerked on my dick, making sure she got it all, had me on my tippy toes.

While she was in the room sucking on my dick, I could hear her sisters and friend in the living room talking and laughing. (SMH) On the streets, I lusted for four things. Good weed, loot, good pussy, and good head. Another rolodex memory I have is of me and Trice who stayed across the street from the Aloha Motel on 29th St. Me and her were in her bedroom getting it in (having sex). We had come from the movies in Lakewood, in the back of the Lakewood Mall. That whole night was crazy. We were sitting in her red Chevy Cavalier blowing on a blunt, getting high.

We were high as hell needless to say. We ended up locking the keys in the car on some high shit (SMH), not realizing it until after the movie was over. I forgot what it was we went and saw. We came out of the theater and headed to the car. She was looking for her keys and couldn't find them. Initially, she thought she lost them inside of the movie theater. I just so happen to look inside of the car and there the keys were, hanging from the ignition. (SMH) "Damn!" I was about to shatter her window. "No, Tic!" We ended up calling a tow truck service, costing me 50 bones. I took it out on that pussy though. She served the dick all night. She rode me, I had her doggy style, I got it from the side, I had her face down ass up, I had her flat on her stomach, getting it from the back, and she sucked on the dick. Trice was the first pussy I got fresh out of the pen in '98. Situation was the second. I pretty much had sex with Trice the whole time I was in my situationship with situation, Trice, Chardon, and Miko. Me and Miko stopped messing around like '03, in the beginning. Me and Trice stopped a little before that, growing apart. Me and Chardon though, we never stopped. It was ongoing with us. I had sex with her hours before coming to jail on this case in '04. I think I was addicted to pussy. One was never enough for me. I had to have multiple bitches to fuck. I was a real live horn dog, real talk!

I can say though, I didn't leave any more kids out there without me. I didn't have any outside of the ones with me and situation has. We have the three that I know for sure are mine, the fourth one is suspect and will always be suspect in my eyes until there's a DNA test done. I don't believe, or am I convinced, he's my son. The last name doesn't mean shit. Females put last names on kids all of the time of dudes they don't belong to, it's common practice. I'm not having it. I don't know, so I'm not claiming shit. What's in a name? She has too many skeletons in her closet and bones started falling out of that mutha fucka! A lot of shit she was doing or had done, she didn't think I knew about, thinking she was that tight with her shenanigans. She was foolish in her thinking. I'm never a simpleton. I don't fall for fried ice cream or boiled cookies.

I knew what was up. I just never brought it to her attention. What use would've been, she would've denied, denied, denied. I get it. You're not supposed to tell on yourself. I didn't waste my time, effort, or energy with it, I just rather let her think she was just that damn tight with her shit. No bueno! Weak! She was going to do what I'd expect her to do and nothing less. She lies so much, she believes her own lies. You're delusional and detached from reality. If you're not shit, own it! She's not capable of truth or reason and is very un-loyal. I was always told people that had nothing to hide, hide nothing. No this isn't weed philosophy, me being high thinking I'm being deep. It's me just being in tuned and seeing shit as it is, for what it is. My keeping it a thousand, raw and uncut, leaving myself exposed, based on real activities, events and situations as they pertain to me. Going into my sometimes dark and deep bruised psyche with a bundle of moods, warm, funny, reflective, challenging, proud, and defensive, depending on the subject matter.

The honesty in my words leaves me too exposed, but I'm standing on my truth. If I can't, then why even bother putting my dots and dashes to paper. Being concerned with who may be butt hurt isn't a concern of mine. I wanted to come as politically correct, vivid, and raw as Lon's book, "Addicted to Drama – The Memoir of a Menace" and as honest, anything less would be a misoverstanding. So much shit has taken place in my life, my memory isn't what it once was, but what I can remember, I'll paint the picture to the best of my ability. I did smoke water. Speaking of water, I was a late bloomer. I hadn't been smoking it that long before I came to jail in '04. That shit just took over. I was addicted. I had to smoke it every day, though I still smoked my tree every day, water became priority one. My homie, Big Half Pint from the Youngs set got me started on it. Prior to then, I never had an interest in smoking water. I was cool with my tree and some alcohol. The alcohol started when I was thirteen. It was Old English Malt Liquor, 40 oz., and Bump Face Gin (Seagram's Gin) with juice, either orange juice or Super Socco (a sports drink). I got into the Hennessey around fifteen or sixteen. I love my Yac (Cognac).

Me and Pint were with the big homie from the set, Big Cyco Mike and his brother.

We rode in the big homie's swoop to the BG homie's spot on the North Side, a few blocks from where me and Pint stayed and actually Cyco Mike too. He stayed across the street from me in some apartments. So, we get to BG Ruck's spot and he was on (had it). We were close to his spot and had to walk the rest of the way for some reason. The swoop just died and wouldn't start back up. It could have been a dead battery, who knows. I just remember getting out of the swoop and pushing the rest of the way on foot. When we got there, all three of them snatched something up. From there, we ended up going our separate ways. Me and Half pint went one way, and Cyco Mike and his brother went another.

Me and Half Pint hit a back street. He fired it up, hitting the stick a few times. "Cuz, hit this shit, tray times for the set!"

"Nah cuz, I'm straight!"

"Just tray times!"

"I don't fuck around. You go ahead though. Enjoy you."

"Come on cuz!"

I fell to the pressure. "Aight cuz, shoot it!" I hit it three times. It was a wrap. The love affair began that day. He'd been smoking it and was used to it. I was a rookie, first time on the field of play. My first trip, I was stuck holding a tree. It was like I was glued to it. I couldn't pull my hands off of it (SMH). We ended up from that back street. How, I couldn't tell you. I don't know where Pint was, but I was at a Young homies spot (house) on the North Side. I don't know how I got there, at all.

I remember the homie saying, "Aye Tic, where you came from? How'd you get here?" I didn't know. I was out of it. I didn't even know where Pint was. His uncle from 120 Raymond (One-Twenty) had called him. He had gotten killed in L.A. somewhere, caught slipping. "Aye ya'll, isn't this ya'll homie out here?"

Next thing I remember after that, I was at home in my bed. Couldn't tell you how I got there. I guess situation smelled it on me and tripped out. When I woke up finally, after being out, she went in (talking shit) on me. "Nah mutha fucka, I'm not going through this shit no more. Fuck that! You're not about to be up in here, beating my ass off of that shit and around here tripping. You have me fucked up." Guess she was having flash backs. She went on and on and on. I just laid in the bed looking up at her dumb ass, like, "Bitch, shut the fuck up!" I didn't say it. I just thought it in my mind.

Her ex-husband, a dude named Craig from Santana (Santana Compton Crip), went by Cowboy if I'm not mistaken. I'm not sure, but what I am sure of is he used to be high off water and beat her boney ass. Hence, "I'm not going through this shit no more, fuck that!"

She told me how he would be off that water (high on it) and would be on one (acting up). So basically, she was traumatized from that whole experience and seeing me on it brought back memories. Somehow, I don't think that was the only reason he was whupping her ass. He ended up dying. Her story though, her version of it anyway, he came home from somewhere and he was tripping. He was wet and had started going in on her (being loud and aggressive towards her), allegedly she grabbed a knife and backed up into a corner, holding it straight out in front of her and he charged her, running into it.

The reason he succumbed to his stab wounds was because he bled out in route. The ambo (ambulance) took too long getting to its destination (hospital). She went to jail though and got out. Can you believe though, she hit me with this shit, right before I was about to fuck for the first time. My pants down, rubbers on my duck, her pants off, panties off, her legs spread and cocked, talking about, "Hold up, I want to tell you something first." Really! The record skipped. Did you really just stop me? This is what I'm thinking. My hands on my dick, I'm about to go in the pussy, the heads literally on her lips, about to rub in between them and push in. You put your hand on my chest as I was about to lower myself down on you. "Wait, I want to talk to you!"

Now, in my mind, I'm thinking she's about to tell me she's hot (got something). She began running it down (the situation with her and her deceased ex-husband). I'm listening and nodding my head, "Yeah, yeah, yeah, that it? I feel you, I feel you." and all that shit. "Can we run that now (have sex)?" That shit was crazy.

Me and Half Pint had become water buddies. Every morning we would walk to a liquor store on the North Side. All the way to it from the cover of the alleys we would travel, as to not be seen by enemies or the police while we smoked our stick. The alleys shielded us as we smoked. It took us a couple of hours to and from and it was a ten minute to fifteen minute walking distance. That shit had us horse playing! I didn't blow but with a few homies. I blew with the homie Tumac from the set. We smoked in his garage. Him and Half Pint stayed in the same apartment complex on Linden, on the North, on a corner. He also went by a half head, or was one. I forgot which one. I called him Tumac, or just Mac, as I did other homies around.

I smoked with another BG homie from the set, the homie Evil, or Dre. I called him Evil though, he's related to my two oldest kids. They're cousins on their mama's side. I also blew with my boy Blvd Dre from Blvds (Blvd Mafia). He was Marc's and Henderson Blue's boy, both homies from the set. They hung out on Henderson, off of 19th street. I knew of Henderson Blue and Marv, but hadn't met them. Plus, I never got around on that end of the city and hadn't been around that area since I'd lived over there on Magnolia off of 19th as a kid going to Washington Jr. High, in the 7th grade. I met Henderson Blue the day I had just finished shooting at a dude from Compton who had gotten into it with my G home girl, Sugar Mama, but was fighting with my BG homie, BG Rocc. He was like, "Cuz, you should've just walked up closer and leaned over them and ganged him (shot him) while he was fighting with the homie on the ground." Uh, that was no bueno!

I wasn't trying to accidentally shoot the homie I had just skinned a homie about ten minutes later shooting at my man (my target). I ended up meeting Marv though before I met Blue. I also smoked with my boy Dearsay from Compton Neighborhood Crip. He's the young homie CJ from the set (Babyz), mom's Tina, baby daddy. They stayed on the North too, on Linden, but on the other end of it. Me and him went to Atlantic Drive (Atlantic Drive Compton Crip) to get water. I've been to the 7th Street Watts too, getting my issue. My homie Lil Dirty Red, BM used to have gas. I had been to their spot on Lime in the set a few times when I was messing with Dirty Red, getting work.

So, she had been familiar with my face and who I was. She knew the homie knew me and I was in fact from the set. It had been a minute since I'd been over there, fucking with Dirty. I go over there and I knock on the door. She opens it and sees me standing there, but doesn't appear to remember me. I asked her could I get some water. She dummy up on me, "Huh. . . water. I don't slang water, but who are you again?"

I'm like, "Wow, this shit is crazy. I'm Lil Tic from Insane." I saw her facial expression trying to compute my name and face. She drew a blank. Blvd Dre was with me, but he stayed downstairs and waited for me out front of the apartments.

"Oh, nah, I ain't got nothing!" Me and Blvd Dre done it moving (left). She was leaving as well. She went and got into her swoop and pulled off. Before me and Dre could leave the area and had been walking up 2-1 towards the King (Martin Luther King Jr. Ave), she spots us and pulls up on us.

"Aye, come on. Meet me at the house!" Once we get back to her block to the apartments, I go back upstairs and Dre waits for me out front. She was like, "What did you want?"

"A 50 pour!"

"I just had to go hit a corner to check and see who you were. I didn't remember you." I told her I didn't know how she didn't, even though it's been a while, because I would come to the house with Dirty to get work on more than a few occasions. It finally registered in her mind who I was exactly. It was only right that she went and ran the handle (name). It was going to come back exactly who I was. I was in the set every day, all day, jumping around the blocks. You might catch me on 20th and Olive, 21st and Olive, the Ave, 21st and Lemon, Lewis and Rhea, 20th and Myrtle, or several other spots. I wasn't mad at her and she was by herself, so precaution was necessary. I respected it. Could never be too safe being a female in the lane. Dudes can be weirdos. They're weirdos with dudes, so you know. She wasn't about to let no dude in the house alone with her if she didn't know who he was. I don't know where she went or who she asked about me, but wherever she went in the set, they told her exactly who I was.

Damn! The snow is really coming down now. I've been watching it off and on for a couple of hours. Yesterday I didn't get out. We had morning yard too. Today we have it this afternoon. Hopefully it doesn't get cancelled for some reason. The police are saying states are being put on quarantine. It's been on the news a lot too. The Corona Virus is what they're calling it, or Covid-19. It's no joke. People all over are getting real sick. Some have died.

They're cancelling visits up here for a minute. Don't know when they'll resume. They're saying it's bad out there with that virus going on. They were also saying something about packages will be backed up because there won't be drivers to bring them to the prison. However, whoever has one on the grounds, they're good. Oh, clarification, a Bay Area dude named Drake who's the building Mac-rep just pulled up on me, telling me the package companies aren't taking orders until they figure out what's going on.

He was also telling me about the visits being cancelled and that his sister was telling him now people are out there on the streets, getting into fights over supplies, toilet paper, cleanser, paper towels, etc. There's a shortage of stuff out there. Stores are running out of shit. He was like, "It's all over the news." I had been seeing it, but not really paying that much attention to it. I still don't have my shit yet. This shit is crazy. The T.V. situation is cut and dry. Nothing is just that simple with CDC. Everything has to be complicated.

If it's not complicated, it's not right. I just got my 602 back and I re-sent it last night, back to San Quentin. Hopefully it gets straight now. I'm tired of being without my shit. I came close to going on a hunger strike to get the administration's attention, but Lon was like, "Nah homie, that's a little extreme. Your shit is granted, just ride it out!" That was going to be my go to, because I know hunger strikes work. I've stunted on the police twice already doing them. Ok, ya'll want to play games, this is what I have going! I wouldn't take any trays and would cover my cell door window. I didn't argue and fight with them or call them names, for what, it wasn't going to solve my issue.

The first time I stunted (committed an act) I was in Kern Valley, or New Delano, it's called either. I was up for a medical transfer and was supposed to go to Solano, a medical facility, for having caught Valley Fever, a serious condition. For some reason, it was taking them forever to move me. They kept putting it off and the transfer was a high risk emergency transfer. It had been almost a year since I was up for transfer. What was the hold up? They couldn't provide the medical care I needed, having Valley Fever. I'm still affected by it to this day, breathing complications and aching bones.

They don't like hunger strikes because it has to not only be document-ed, but after 72 hours the medical staff has to be notified so they can start weighing you for weight loss. Then, the administration starts getting involved. Sgts, Lts, Cpts, assistant warden, then the warden, then eventu-ally to Sacramento, CDC head quarters. "What's the problem? Why aren't you eating?" The first day I told them I was putting them on notice. "I'm not eating. I'm on a hunger strike." I didn't take food for three days. By the fourth day I was talking to a Sgt. The fifth day I was getting plastic bags to pack my shit. I was leaving for Solano. You can't say what won't work until you demo (put a demonstration in motion).

The second hunger strike was when I was in the sandbox in Solano in 9-building. A female police came to my cell. She was the property officer for the sandbox. She tells me I was being moved to Vacaville on an AD-SEG to ADSEG transfer and to pack my property, she would be back to get it. She gives me a few plastic bags and leaves.

After I'd finished packing my stuff, she comes to my cell and takes it. I'm supposed to leave the following morning. Plus, Vacaville is only across the street, no more than a five to seven minute drive. I was to leave with a couple of other people. When the time came to leave, everyone left but me. At the end of the day, I really wasn't tripping. Cool, I'm staying. I was still like, "Damn, what the fucks going on!" I hollered at an alright police named Lu, old school police who tried working with you on issues instead of dismissing it, especially if you weren't disruptive or an ass. I asked him what was going on with my move. I didn't ask until at least two or three hours had passed. He left my cell and went and talked with someone.

The property officer finally comes, but only after I inquired, "Oh, you're not leaving now. Your move was cancelled."

You would've thought though that was something she would've come and mentioned ASAP. That was too much. Like right though, I'm like, "Ok, so where's my shit at?" She tried telling me it's going to be a few days, she has other property to do.

Now she has me in my feelings. I'm saying to myself like, "Bitch, where's my shit at?" It's only been a couple of hours. You didn't put my stuff away yet. She tells me the 10 day process of property has to start over. "You have me fucked all the way up! That's out!"

Then she say, "Get the Sgt, he's going to tell you the same thing!" I didn't ask you that though! I never mentioned the Sgt. She figured he was going to side with her anyway over me. Police shit!

So I'm like, "What do you mean my process has to start over? You came to my cell and got my shit, the move was cancelled which you know. You should've brought my shit back to my cell, period. You got it from my cell. It already been processed. Wait my ass!"

I ended up moving to 10 building which as I've said is the actual sandbox. I put in a form 22, trying to respect the process. I wasn't getting my just due. I'm talking to other police, I'm getting the run around and bullshit after bullshit. That's it, it's on! I'm about to walk their game up (fuck with their program). See how they respond to this hunger strike! I'm on a hunger strike. I put a sign on my window, completely covering my window up. The sign read, "No food here. Get the fuck away from my door. I'm on a hunger strike!" They read my sign and kept moving. I could hear them on their tier, talking amongst themselves, "What's going on with him?"

Before the medical process could even get started the Sgt made an appearance. "Look, you haven't given me any problems back here, so I'm going to talk to her and see that you get your shit. Now will you eat?"

"No!"

I wasn't falling for the shenanigans. Comply and then they renege. No bueno! I tell him, "I'm not eating until after my shit is in my cell and not before."

He kept it solid and stuck to his word. The next day, the bullshit broad came to my cell and was opening up my tray slot, talking about, "Come over here and sign your property slip!"

"You tell your dog to come over here. I'm not no fucking dog!" She was in her feelings. I didn't care about none of that. I've been respectful. You wanted to horse play!

"Weirdo!" She started trying to talk shit as she was giving me my property. "Oh, you think you're special? You have to have your shit before everyone else. You don't have to wait, not you, not Mr. Special!"

I'm like, "Check this out, you weirdo bitch! For one, you took my shit from my cell. For two, you knew the move was cancelled. All you had to do was walk my s hit back to my cell, period!"

"No, no, it's all about you, Mr. Special!"

"You're right. It is!"

"Do you want your shit or not?"

"You're the one talking still!" I signed the paper. As she put my stuff on the tray slot I started raking my stuff into the cell on the floor. She saw me doing it and felt it was a green light for her to do it. Hold up, flag on the play princess! "What the fuck is wrong with you? Don't be raking my shit on the floor!"

"You're doing it!"

"Bitch! It's my shit!"

Then she left, slamming the tray slot behind her, "Bitch!" Yeah, she was about 5 or 6 bitches! After going through my shit I see she left stuff out that I previously had in my cell already (SMH). Games! I put in another form 22 asking for it back. By the time it was answered, it was another property officer assigned to the spot. The bitch quit, dizzy ass! Just up and quit. Couldn't hack it. Too much for her. She wasn't trying to do that job. She has other issues going on and we heard about other police weren't fucking with her. She was a rat bastard, she was telling on them. Basically she was being shunned and ostracized by her coworkers. Even the police don't like snitches. They'll use a snitch though. Can't stand them, but will use them for an interest (end game).

I asked this Black police named Martin, young Black police around my second oldest son's age, to holler at her initially. He was like, "Man, I don't fuck with her. Nobody do!" After going to the sandbox initially, I was already mentally and physically preparing myself for the next odyssey, as far as where I'll end up landing. In my mind, if dudes were going to try and get at me, behind me being in the right, behind a dude playing games with my loot, and behind a bullshit dude and his autobots putting false shit in the air, so be it. It is what it is. It's about to get real dangerous! You don't want to respect the real or accept the real, so you're going to respect my violence! That simple.

Because at that point, it's now personal. You don't care about what's right, only what's being said, which isn't true. So therefore, you're just on some dirty shit, out to fuck over a Niggah for no rhyme or reason other than being dirty and perpetuating dirty shit. Not concerned with facts or looking into the situation for what and as it is. When I landed here, I immediately got at what homies were on the line here and temperature checked. "Cuz, x-y-z is what happened with me, which had nothing to do with a-b-c, and these are the players and characters, but this is a-b-c." I checked temps. Ok, these are thinkers and not autobots, given the explanation. The real of the matter was saw and the bullshit of the matter was weeded out. Then I learned x-y-z about the same characters.

All heard was believable based on the stunt S.T. pulled with me. He's just a dirty dude. Homie, I'm not really that dude I was that you met. That was the laid back me, the chill mode me. You took that and ran with it and judged me, but you were going to meet the real me from Insane Crip! The one not on drugs (water). I'm a LBC homie, a solid homie who's been walking on these lines without issues, drama, dirt, or scandal on my name that could get me voted off the island. Never snitched, never ran off a yard, never DP'ed, or can be tied to bullshit on no line. I've been to

Tehachapi, Calipat, Delano, Solano and now here. Three 180's, one 270, and one 3 yard. Not a smudge of bullshit! But all of a sudden I'm going to be with some foul shit, dudes are horse playing! Not my character, not how I rock or who I am! My tail stays wagging. I don't tuck my shit! I'm still tripping off of that shit and it's almost a year ago. It was in April 2019, now it's March 2020. I just got a Valentine's Day card, a late one from my childhood sweetheart. We've always had a thing for each other from kids.

Sharon Rene Moore. A couple of weeks ago I had written to her to tap in with her when I first got here. I had to let her know I had been out of circulation due in part because I was in the sandbox without having her address. I would've written a lot sooner. The last time we were in contact before we reconnected, we were 16 years old. She was my girlfriend them, but our history goes a lot further back to the 70's. It goes back to our adolescence, 4 or 5 years old. Shirley Mo (I'm sure derives from Shirley Moore), her mother, and my mom Dorothy were like besties. She was my god mother and my mother was Sharon's. Sharon also had a brother named Poot Butt and a sister named Carolyn. They were both younger than us. Me and her started liking each other way back then and playing games that kids play at that age, which is ironic because we hadn't has sex until we were like 15.

We had been messing around as boyfriend and girlfriend over the years on some puppy love type shit. She was a bit more advanced than I was. She had had a baby already. I think she had her around 14 or 15. It was around there, had to be 14 because she already had the baby when we started hanging out. She was always a hot ass, even when we were kids. She didn't like clothes. She would run around with no shirt on and in her panties. Yeah, she was way more advanced than me.

By the time we did have sex for the first time, I was like yeah, pussy good! She knew how to do it back, how to wind and roll her ass and hips. I wasn't surprised though, she did have a baby. I only had been having sex for about two years when we did it. I was already a full fledge horn dog. A walking sex machine, trying to put my dick in every hole I could. I didn't even discriminate. I would've put a bag on a bitch head. I was still learning my craft, so I didn't get it-get it with all the other shit. The having her on top, her being doggy style, her being bent over, you know, all of that other level shit. But shit, her being on her back with her legs spread open was cool too.

My baby mama was the first one who rode me though. My baby mama, Jacki, I think my oldest son was made like that. "Ungh. . . shit!" My first doggy style was an older home girl from the set named SM (not her real name). At the time, she was smoking dope (crack). She had a big ass. I had her doggy style on a couch in a garage. I just held her big ass hips and watched her ass pushing back into me, into my stomach, over and over and over again while she winded and rolled her ass and hips. They were continuous and in a slow circular motion until she had my young ass going crazy, "Ungh! Ooh shit!" Baby mama would ride me until I was soft and she would still be trying to grind on it. As time went on and I got older, I leveled up (upped my sex game). Sharon though had communicated with me for a few months or so before I got caught up (caught my case) and went to the sandbox. She had seemed like she was about to hang out for a minute and do some of this time with me, no bueno. She fell off like they all do. She'd written a few letters, sent a couple of packages and it was a wrap. We would talk on gadget, she even sent me a few titty captured moments and a few panty ones. Of course, I sent her a few dick pics. She never sent me any pictures from the streets through the mail though she kept promising to. I still haven't gotten any from her, whatever that's about. I just recently sent her the pelipost hook up. Maybe that'll give her incentive to shoot me some, we'll see. We had kind of fell off though, prior to me getting caught up. I see, she's really not a writer like that. I'm cool with that, just tap in and h it me up every now and then. In her card she was explaining she had been going through shit, but she still loved me and she apologized for not really applying herself. She was like, "Look, I have a life. My bills are steady coming, but every now and then I could do shit for you, but I really would like for us to write and talk to each other, if you want to."

I hit her back (wrote her back), "Indeed, it's good! Let's move forward." Like I've told her, "We'll always be good. I'll always love you and mess with you." Oh, and she's married, living with her husband.

Back to home girls I hit. A few, only a couple though, leveled up and were stand outs. Mya and Checc-a-hoe. Checc-a-hoe hollered at me one night when she stopped by the spot (dope house). She was like, "When are me and you gon go fuck and kick it?"

I told her whenever she wanted to and, "As a matter of fact, you can come back a little later tonight and we can go get a room." When she came back, we went and snatched up some trees, blunts, and some drink from the Highway Center, that was the Liquor store everyone went to, in the set.

We ended up at the Sandpiper in Signal Hill. We got the room and chilled. We were talking, blowing and sipping. I had already gotten comfortable. I was in my socks, my boxers, and wife beater (t-shirt) on the bed, with my back up against the head board. It wasn't long before she got naked and I came out of my wife beater and boxers. I had her bend over on the edge of the bed first. Her pussy was dripping wet. I slid right in. I was beating her pussy up from the back, like Ali in his prime.

I had her moaning, like she was telling me to slow it down. Ass cheeks were jumping, shaking, wiggling, and jiggling. I'm watching them move as she started pushing back into me, "Ungh, ungh!" After she started cumming I was right behind her, following suit. "Aaaaahhh!" Pussy was fairly decent. I didn't fuck a second time. As for Mya, me and her got it in like we were in a relationship. It happened a few times. She's thick as fuck too, and her head game (oral sex) is on point, plus she swallows. The last time we done something, it was a quickie. We were outside on a cut (somewhere you can't be seen). I just bent her over and pulled her shorts down, then her panties to the side and got inside her.

Her pussy stayed wet and warm. "Aaaahhhh!" Damn bitch! She was like, "Come on cuz, hurry up!" "Unghh-unghh!"

The last time I saw Mya's fine ass, she was in the room at the American Inn. It's a motel in the set on PCH (Pacific Coast Highway) and Lemon, next to IHOP, with the homie Joe Cool from the set. When I went into the room, he was working on Snoop Dogg's last meal CD artwork. He laid it out on the bed so I could see the whole thing. He was doing his shit. She was walking around the room in her wife beater and panties. I slapped her on the ass, "When are you gon let me fuck again cuz?"

"Whenever, you know how we do."

"Bet (ok)!" Joe Cool just shook his head.

I got a chance to talk to Mya when I was in Solano. I was talking to Lil Sugar Bear and he was like, "Guess who I'm with." She was trying to reminisce. Before I could say who, Mya was already on the phone, "Ayyeee Niggah! When you coming home? What's up with it?" She started talking about how we kicked it. I heard she lost her leg in a car accident. She didn't mention it and I didn't say anything about it, but I'm sure she knows I know. At least thinks I know. She just went passed it. "What's up! Remember when we used to have fun?"

"Hell yeah, I remember." He didn't even give me a heads up that he was putting her on. I could've been saying anything and she could've had her ears busted (hearing something disrespectful towards her). I could've been like, "I don't want to talk to that one legged bitch!" or I could've just been like, "Fuck her. I'm not trying to talk to her."

"Yeah Niggah, we got it in, didn't we?" I hear Lil Sugar Bear in the background saying something with his bullshit ass, my boys burnt out for that one (SMH).

Me and L Loc were talking about berries we had nailed in the set. The coldest berry I had was Donna. Donna was shaped like a coke bottle. She stayed on 2-1 (two-one). She was right. Thick in all of the right places, small titties, flat stomach, and a big ass. The first time I messed with her, I was serving by her house. I had been seeing her, but never got at her.

12

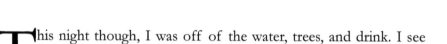

This night though, I was off of the water, trees, and drink. I see her, "What's good?"

"You tell me!"

"Can a Niggah get some head?"

"I got you!" I slid her some work (dope) and we were in her front yard. I pulled my dick out. She had squatted down in front of me and sucked me hard and deep into her mouth, "Ungh!" She told me to let her know before coming in her mouth. You could tell the way she sucked dick she enjoyed it. She was all into it and was moaning. She sucked and slurped loud. Her head was wet, sloppy, and noisy.

She almost didn't get told shit! She felt it coming and took it out of her mouth and started jacking me off. A couple of days later I was back by her house and she asked me what was up. I'm like, "Shit, you know me, I'm game for whatever." We went into the abandoned house across the alley from hers. The sliding door was open and we go inside. Yeah, she's been using this spot to smoke in, fuck, and suck dick in. When we go inside, she tells me to put my back up against the wall. She bent down in front of me and I pulled my pants and my boxers down to my ankles.

After I took my rubber out of my sock and opened it, putting it on my dick.

She already had pulled her pants and panties down and had begun backing up closer to me. I put my head in and she pushed and scooted all the way back into me, bragger her ankles. She really started pushing back into me, I grabbed her hips and let her go to work. She just continued to push back into me, winding and rolling her ass and hips in a wide slow circular motion. She was doing it like I was her man. After she nutted, I nutted right after her. I pulled the rubber off my dick after I pulled it out, then she squatted down in front of me, sucking my dick into her mouth. I told L too about the last time I fucked her. I was pushing (walking) up Myrtle when I saw her on Myrtle and Damon on the corner, talking to one of her home girls. Just as I was approaching them, she was like, "Girl, I'll holler at you later. Let me holler at him right quick." She asked me what was going on with me.

I'm like, "Shit, same ole shit, just trying to make it add up!"

She hit me with, "You trying to get it in or something?"

I'm like, "It's good!"

We hit the alley behind the Highway Center. She was wearing a snug fitting black and white stretch dress with no panties on. Her ass jiggled and shook when she walked in it. I'm high as hell and I'm on liquor. I got behind her as she pulled her dress all the way up over her shapely ass, bending over and grabbing a hold of the pole. I opened my pants, pulled my dick out, grabbed my rubber and put it on. I'm looking like, "Damn, look at all of that ass." I slid right up inside her, "Ungh!" She was wet quick. After we finished, I bounced off (left).

L started asking all types of questions. I started laughing. L likes details. You can't tell him a story without details, talking about bitches, so I'm usually animated with my stores. The last time I saw Donna, I was with situationship and we were in a check cashing spot on Long Beach Blvd and Anaheim. She was in line right in front of us. I didn't know it was her at first. I was just stealing looks at a big ass in front of me in some snug fitting jeans. Situation saw her, but only if she knew she was looking at a bitch I'd fucked and got my dick sucked by on several occasions, saw her butt ass naked and gripped her hops. Donna saw me with her and acted like she was supposed to, like she didn't know me. She didn't speak. She knew too that we were behind her with her slick ass.

She started shifting from left to right. She knew what she was doing. Loc started laughing. He was a lot of berry stories about missions he's been on with them. I think every homie that's from a set has those certain berries he's locked in with and always go back because that pussy fire (good sex), and her head is bomb (good oral sex). One had me spooked though. A bitch named Charmaine. The rubber had broke and I was fucking her raw and nutted in the pussy! I didn't realize it until I pulled out and saw the ring of the rubber was around my dick. I should've known something. That pussy was just too good, too warm, and too wet. Extra warm and extra wet. I'm like, I better not be burned (I better not have caught anything)! She was like, "You got me fucked up Tic!" I'm just saying. L Loc really started to laugh. Charmaine had body, suuuper!

So I'm still on rewind, telling my story. I go to Delano in 2010 from Calipat. From R and R I go on the yard to a cell with a dude from Harlem 30's. He was cool. We were cellies for about two weeks. Then he transferred, going somewhere. I stayed in the cell by myself after he left for a cool minute. I had met Set Trip from West Coast 80's. He was in another building. My boy Young Boo Dog, from Youngs, was on the yard. He was in 5-building and worked in the kitchen.

I hadn't seen my boy since Tehachapi and we were in the sandbox, in the cell together, before I was kicked back out to the main-line for that incident with Sugar Tank, aka Cat Eyes, aka C Dog, Changa. Allegedly I had said something about Boo Dog and the incident we were back there for. If that was the case, how was it that I was on the yard with him well after the incident? That's just bullshit dudes for you, running off at the mouth about nothing. It wasn't worldwide news because it was nothing as far as getting beyond Tehachapi on our yard, it was in-house, but that's a bullshit dude for you, and an autobot. First chance I was able to holler at Boo Dog about the shit, he found it funny, but at the same time, disturbing because he knows how serious bullshit can be, all based on lies and lies being spread, which dudes easily do to fit some sort of narrative.

He was like, "Wow cuz, really? That shits crazy right there, but that's Niggahs for you, but you know that!"

"Homies asked you about it?"

"Hell yeah, Niggahs asked me about it!"

"Didn't they know, me and Treach were communicating the whole time?"

"I don't know what they knew homie."

"You know me and Treach were boomeranging kites back and forth. I'm sure they knew. It was easy for them to ask him, 'Aye, what's going on with the situation.'" Treach is no longer Treach, he's Jack Dog now. What up homie!

Boo Dog could've easily sent word back to the yard after I left the cell. "Aye, Tic ain't cool!"

He was like, "Plus, my brother in law, Lil Styme from 7-4 (Seven-Foe) Hoover was on the line. I could've sent word to him."

"My point exactly!"

I even mentioned that very fact to the homies, which I should've even had to do in the first place, but whatever. All dudes had to do was pause and use common sense and stop suffering from autobotism. Think. A mind is a terrible thing to waste. I told Boo Dog about how the homies called me to the chapel to holler at me, as if I wouldn't go. "Why wouldn't I? I'm straight!"

When I walked into the chapel, the homies were already there waiting for me. Big Saddle Head, Boy Blue (Cat Fish), Breeze (Don't know which Breeze he is, I only knew one and that's Big Breeze), Treach, I want to say Ray Bone too, but I can't remember. Boy Blue off the dribble came to my defense. "I know cuz. That's not his get down." He was basically like, "Nah, not cuz!" Boo Dog kept saying how crazy it was, as I was telling him the story.

Then I told him about the dude from No Love (some little San Bernardino or Riverside gang) named Foe-Tay, something to that effect his name was. He was in the cell with my boy, Big Lerch/Lurch from 5-2 (Five-Deuce) Hoover. It was said this dude, Foe-Tay, was being reckless with his mouth! I told Boo Dog this clown had been saying I spoke on you when I left the cell and landed in BMU (Behavioral Management Unit), where him and Twin from Q102 East Coast Crip were cellies (get a bar). Prior to me running into them on the tier, a few doors down, Sugar Tank was on the tier with them. He was their neighbor. He apparently asked them for something and they asked to see his work, or they just asked him to see his work. However it went, work played a part in the equation. It boiled down to, "We got you, but let us see your lock up order!" Sugar Tank went in to, "See, what happened was, Tic told on Boo Dog that he beat me up!" These two dudes never saw Sugar Tank's paper work and just ran with what he said. Him not showing them his paper work should've been suspect off the dribble, you would think, but you have to look at the type of dudes you're dealing with. Already in their minds, "Ooooh, can't wait to get back to the line and tell Niggahs this!" I didn't find none of this out until after this Foe-Tay character went home (SMH).

I was on the line for damn near a month and nothing was said or brought up to me about anything. Treach hadn't got at me, Styme never said anything to me, no one did, not even Lurch and he was in the cell with the No Love dude. I immediately go into my investigative mode. I'm going to get to the bottom of this shit ASAP and going to trip. Niggahs have me fucked up! I can't sit on that or keep silent. That's something you don't do. You have to meet those types of accusations head on and go balls out if necessary. I'm always hearing these types of situations and dudes not addressing them.

They're content with the situation. "I'm not tripping on that, dudes can say what they want!" On that, "It's not true mentality, so I'm not worried about it". That's the wrong way to think. Fuck you mean? You're horse playing. Dudes are looking at you funny and talking about you, "This Niggah here!" Cold thing about it, they suspect you're hearing the talk, yet waiting to see if you're going to address it, or just let it linger in the air. Even if you don't catch the talk initially, at some point you will, because it's being spoke on so much.

If someone just doesn't pull up on you (walk up to you), "Aye homie, such and such is being said." With me, I didn't hear shit, and dudes walked around me daily, even those of them I messed with. You know what they told me later though?

"We didn't say anything because we knew it wasn't true."

Wow! I couldn't believe my ears, and they knew the game. I rather you get at me so I can address it, but by you not saying anything denies me that opportunity to do so. You mess with me daily, so what gave you that right to keep me in the blind for so long with something you knew about a situation that could possibly affect me? What gives you the right to cover up skeletons with fresh dirt! We're supposed to be cool.

After the chapel thing, I went and hollered at Treach. He was telling me to go holler at Twin and his homie, Dog from East Coast. I locate Twin on the yard first and pushed off (walked away) heading in Twins direction, pulling up on him. "Cuz, you saying I told on my homie young Boo Dog?"

He was like, "Nah cuz, not me. I don't get down like that. That was that dude Foe-Tay. I didn't say shit. It wasn't East Coast business for me to speak on."

"Your name came up so I'm hollering at you about it."

"On East Coast, I wasn't speaking on you!"

I move on to see where his homie Dog is. I spot him and pull up on him. "You said I spoke on my homie, Boo Dog?"

"Nah cuz, not me, I don't even know you like that!"

"I'm just hollering because your name and Twins name came up!"

"On Coast, I didn't say shit!" Ok, consider it addressed. I went and hollered at the dudes, they said it wasn't them. Twin said it was Ole Boy Foe-Tay and he's gone to the house (went home).

I got at the homie Big Lurch, "Homie, that was bullshit, you knew and didn't tell me and we mess with each other every day. That's how my groove Niggah getting down with me? I thought we were better than that homie!"

"I didn't say anything because I knew it wasn't true." Me and Boo Dog finished talking about the situation, then he slid me some tree, which he had already said he would have for me the previous yard. Big La La, the big homie from East Coast, I guess saw me talking to Twin and Dog and inquired as I was leaving Dog. He heard what was said to him in regards to me and why I was getting at them.

I personally had talked to La La about the situation in the Law Library. He told me basically he got at both Twin and Dog, telling them, "True or not, that's Long Beach business. They'll handle it. It has nothing to do with you, East Coast, or East Coast Business."

Big La La is a cool homie. I like the homie. He's solid, no nonsense, and fair. He's not for or with the dirty shit. Stand up guy! Besides Boo Dog at Delano, Big Angel from the set was there on the yard. Him and Ghost Face were cellies. That was it at the time. I hadn't seen Ghost Face or Angel. Dudes were telling me though Angel worked in the sub-station and that I would see him at some point. When I finally did see him, he was on some weird shit, "I'm straight!" I wasn't feeling the greet or him. He acted as if he didn't know me or remember me from our old Folsom days and I was a young kid in '91. I felt his vibe, not a problem on my end, because I'm cool.

I never had the opportunity to see Ghost face. He heard I was on the yard and sent word to me. He sent his (his love and respect). He also sent word he was going to send something my way, hold on. Before I actually had the chance to see and talk with him, him and Angel got rushed (attacked) by some Woods in their building on their tier. They ended up leaving, going to the sandbox, and then landed on A-yard. Before I arrived to Delano, the Woods and the Blacks went up (had a riot) and it was supposed to have been over with.

Little incidents kept occurring and the Long Beach homies went up with the Neighborhoods on A-yard. That's how Set Trip ended up on B-yard, the homie from 80's. He had just landed on the yard right before I got there. Our first conversation was about the A-yard incident. He gave me a heads up to be on alert, just in case dudes were tripping. There were a few Neighborhoods that came from A-yard with him too. I had to get security conscious immediately. I don't know what I've just walked in to, plus I'm seeing the wood situation still has embers well after the fire. I heard Angel and Ghost Face landed on A-yard and the homies tripped on Ghost Face about a situation with Big Half Pint.

Here's the thing, he'd been on B-yard for a minute, didn't anything happen with him. I talked to Set Trip about the situation, which he knew about and was like, "I wasn't doing anything. I ain't seen no paper work!" I can respect that for what that is. I assumed that was the consensus of everyone. "I hadn't seen no work, I'm not doing anything." Which, in my opinion, is a good policy to have. No fuckery involved, no dirty shit at play.

How can you though act on hearsay alone, moving without fact or proof? Yet it continues to happen. I can see there being an exception to the rule, being it's just common knowledge amongst the Set, or the Car as a whole (LBC, or wherever). It's known, it's out there, and it's fact! It's crazy because it's like a lot of dudes are conflicted about the situation. Some are saying he did, some saying he didn't. Some have no opinion, some don't give a fuck. I knew him from the streets, from off of the North where I met him and a bunch of other Young homies. He had been to camp. When he came home, the same day he came home, him and a few Young homies stopped by my spot to holler at me. I told them, I'll holler at them later. "See you back!" That was the last time I saw him. He was snatched up by the detectives about a little situation. They'd been on him since he was released from camp. I wasn't messing with none of the dudes as far as around where I lived. I was introduced to them by Big Half Pint. I really kept all my dealings East Bound (the East Side). I didn't do the North like that, or the dudes. A lot of them around the area were YMS (Young Murder Squad). I'm not sure if Ghost Face was YMS. As far as I recall he pushed Youngs. He was an East Sider. The YMS though ended up turning YFC (Young Foundation Crew). Youngs, if you will. They were going to the East Side, getting put on (initiated). One of the Young homies with Ghost Face when he came by my spot was Baby C.J., who was no doubt from Youngs and an East Side kid, I.I.P. (Insane In Peace) homie.

Baby C.J. was killed after I left the streets in '04. He was a good Young homie, I fucked with him a lot. He fucked with those YMS dudes a lot. Pretty much because he stayed around them and they were homies. He stayed with his uncle, Big C.J. from the set. I fucked with the big homie almost every morning on the Ave in the set. He would smoke a blunt and kick it on a brick wall. I remember when I first met Baby C.J., when he was running around on the set, hiding from Big C.J. The big homie used to be on his bumper (would be on him about fucking up).

"Aye Tic, you seen my unc?"

"Nope!"

He'll take off running in another direction. Wild Child, another one that was with Ghost Face, when he came by my spot, was one of the ones in Ghost Face's circle who told on him, making a statement, getting Ghost Face snatched up. Then I guess when all of the accusations were flying, that's when the dark cloud began to hover.

Wild Child went into obscurity. He was moved to Lancaster with his folks and was ducked off (tucked away), but occasionally reappeared back to the North, under the cover of darkness, staying inside and out of view. Certain homies that didn't stay on the North would be on the North, posting up, near or by his house, hoping to holler at him. Stop talking Niggah, it never happened though. First off though, if you knew and saw him, he's the pretty boy, soft looking type that will crack under pressure. He looks the type, literally. "I'm telling!" The question is, why would you even have him involved or around some felony type shit? His whole disposition should scream suspect, don't do shit with this dude.

I'm pushing, that's what it is. Me and him conversated, but we kept it general. We basically talked about life and how to stay out of the way. I respected the fact he never tried to shoot his shot or engage me in his talk. Just as he kept his dealings with us to a minimum, I kept mine with him to a minimum. A lot of dudes though won't tell you they're cut. Usually if you hear it, it'll be from someone that knows them that's been around. Some will tell you, but not directly. You just have to pay attention to shit they say and how they say it, or how they use certain words. It's there for you to know if you're really paying attention to what's being said and how it's being said. With him I was told, and not by homies, that he was cut. Personally though, I could care less if you're cut or not.

If you're straight, I'll fuck with you, but to an extent. We know where that line is, as far as where the exceptions are. Me and PF too were speaking on how you have to know when to stand down and when to push play in certain situations and how it's sometimes bigger than any 1 man. We talked about how it doesn't make you a punk or soft or less than. What it does do is make you smart. You have to know when to act, when not to, and when it's not to your advantage. We overstand how easy it is for shit to go bad, sideways, or crooked. You have to recognize it and accept reality for what it is.

You have to put ego and pride to the side or be a victim of them. It's your conscious choice to make, fuck horseplaying. Some things aren't in our best interest and aren't meant to be pressed, real talk. He was telling me how he should've went a different route with his situation. Not only did it go bad, but he was security conscious. Sometimes we can be and you never get to it. That was the same thing that happened with Dev when him and TC had that situation. He was security conscious but never was able to push play. Sometimes you have no choice in the matter, shit just happens or will happen regardless and it's out of your control.

With him, or around him, keep shit misdemeanor, because if it's felony type shit, you might as well walk your own ass to the detectives and confess because he's telling. Not dry snitching (telling bits and pieces of the truth indirectly), flat out telling! Sammy the Bull! I didn't hear anything as far as talk about Face until I hit the county jail. It went in one ear and out of the other. "Nah, not lil cuz. He's solid and he was with that play!" I had been hearing homies had been getting at him, trying to chop the paint, homies that has seen his work. It's been said copies exist and is circulating. I really didn't know what to make of it. I just know he's been dealing with the situation and hadn't took that walk of shame as of yet.

Before Boo Dog went home, we never discussed the Face situation. We just kicked it and hung out a few times on the yard. It was hard really catching up with him, because he was in another building and he worked in the kitchen (a satellite kitchen). I was in 8-building. Yeah, he really tripped off of what I was telling him about the homies, how they had got at me. After he went home, a few other homies had started popping up on the yard. Junay (C Dog) from Youngs, Baby Webb from Babyz, T Capone from 20 Crip, Ed Dog from Blvd Mafia, Motto from 20 Crip, was already there, in another building. Shorty Mac from 20 Crip, KC80 from West Coast 80s, and Smoke from Dodge City Crip popped up. I wasn't feeling Smoke right off, due to what had just happened with the homies and a couple of his homies at Calipat. I wouldn't speak to him for a month or so, then gradually we started talking. Tone from 20 Crip ended up popping up on the yard, who I ended up going on a DP with on Short Mac. It had almost been an issue with Motto. He had a few things going on, but the most pressing was behind fumbling at the goal line with the ball when he shouldn't have been in the situation in the first place. He put himself there.

It was an issue that had been on going, but kept under wraps between the homie and the individual. That fumble was a costly one, one you're not trying to lose on. The individual knew if he brought the issue to the homies what would happen, how he would get paid. When the situation did come out, K.O., a homie from 8-3 Gangster (Eight-Tray) was like, "I like cuz, he's the homie so I wasn't trying to get him fucked over. Plus, I just wanted my loot!" He was like, "I've been patient and I've been working with him. I'm not turning him in now. I just need my loot!" The homie was doing K.O. a favor, so he was going to look out for him for doing the favor. K.O. is a really cool homie. I fucked with him at Calipat where I first met him.

So I know he was going to look out for the homie decent. The homie goes and secures the situation, but then decides to do some flossing (high signing) like it's his situation. Boom, Goon Squad push into the kitchen where he worked. It hadn't started yet, panic mode set in and the fumble happened. That's what the Goon Squad does. They pop up on some random shit. You look up, there they are. Once the situation was secured, it should stay secured. Your bad! That issue got resolved, they figured it out though. Shortly after that, him and a Damu/Muslim from San Diego named Beat Em Up, squabbled up in the freezer at work. He told the homie afterwards if he wasn't straight he could get that (fight again)! It should've went up (Crip and Blood riot), but it didn't. It was left at that, which wasn't felt by all. Some felt it should've been the bell, ding-ding! That was unheard of, Crip and Blood squabbling up and it didn't turn into something on the spot. That would've turned into something, like it did when some Damus said something came up missing and it was the Crips who were involved, well a couple of specific Crips.

The Damus called themselves, rushing them and other Crips jumped in it, based on they are Crips and you are Bloods! One of my young homies from my set jumped in it, Tray Rag, because he was nearby and got there. The shit went up behind something that wasn't even factual. It was pure speculation as to who the actual dirt bag was. Stealing is a no bueno! Dudes do not like jail house thieves, period. They're looked down upon as a dirt bag. Picking up shit you know isn't yours, not cool dude! Don't even pick it up, it's not yours, doesn't belong to you.

Anyway, the Damus acted on speculation and nothing more. That's not cool either, acting on something because you think something or though something. After that issue with Beat Em Up, the homie get hit on the dice, for more than he could handle. Basically, chased burnt money. Stop chasing it, that gets you deeper in the hole, let it go. The homie Project Steve from PJs was like, "Look Motto, I'll work with you, but I need my loot and rightfully so! If you knew you didn't have it like that, you should've cut your losses long ago." It becomes you're gambling on your ass. You don't have the money, you're hoping you'll win. That usually goes bad.

Yeah, homie makes bomb cards (good cards), but what dude you know will accept five dollars in cards? No bueno! He managed to get himself clear of the situation, but we (homies, me included) told the homie to knock off the gambling, especially if he didn't have it, because that could become a potential situation with another faction behind his gambling and ability to handle it. What do he do? He goes and gets hit again, only this time he ended up being transferred and going to Solano, which is where I bumped into him, where we hollered at services during Ramadan. Before he bounced, he was able to tap in with Ole Boy and slide him something to ease his pain, which was better than losing all the way around the board.

The homie was on the bubble (about to catch a DP). It had been a premeditated conversation. Dudes been hollering at you, you kept having issue after issue after issue, love you though.

Fuck, it's cold as a bitch! We just came in from yard and it's snowing. It's going to be a minute before it warms up some in the cell. It's been snowing since five this morning. It'll slow down but not stop. Shit, it's cold! While we were out there on the yard, it went down. Something was going on, on C-yard. "GEEETTT DOOOWWWN!" The alarm was going off and police were running from their buildings.

Me, Lon, and Chumlee were chilling. We were talking and getting snowed on. We were down for about a good 20 minutes. An Insane, a Hoover, and a 20, two older dudes and one younger, hanging out on the regular. Shit, we're on the yard, out there rain, sleet, or snow. Yesterday when we were out on the yard, it was snowing. We didn't know what we were going to do as far as working out. Yeah, we work out in the snow too! We decided to do pyramid push-ups, 25 down. 25, 24, 23, etc, when a snowball beef broke out with me and Chumlee. He hit me with a big ass snowball while I was down doing my set "pooofff!" He dropped it on my head. Some got inside of my coat. After I finished my set and was trying to get the snow out from under my coat, Lon went down to do his set. "Pooofff!" He got Lon too, talking about guilty by association. After Lon's set, it was Chumlee's set. While Chumlee was down, I got some snow, "pooofff!" I got his ass back, then he got me again, then Lon got him. When we left the slab, it was fucked up with a lot of snow.

We had a little fun. A mood lightener is good for mental health, especially around these types of yards and climates. Those are rare moments on a very active 180 yard. By the time we made it to the Black area, the Damus had just started a full fledge snowball fight. . . "Pooofff! Pooofff! Pooofff!" Everywhere! Me, Lon, and Chumlee were standing near the wall, away from the activities. The next thing we know, Chumlee gotten himself engaged in the massive snow war. It was mayhem. He got one of the Damus and they (all of them) bombarded his ass with snowballs from various angles. "Pooofff, pooofff, pooofff!" From Everywhere! He had gotten creamed. He had snow everywhere.

Me and Lon just watched the chaos and laughed, especially at Chumlee (SMH). The Damus kept the gas on. Chumlee stopped. He was good after being massively assaulted with snowballs by the Damus. They didn't stop bombarding each other though. They kept it going until yard was over and recall was called. Dudes started moving towards their buildings. They had a little bit too much fun. Me and Lon and Chumlee threw or dropped a few and it was a wrap (over).

But yeah, Big Half Pint finally hit the B-yard. He had been there already at Delano. I didn't even know he was up there or even on A-yard. He had told me that's where he was. He was telling me about what had went on, on A-yard with the homies and the Neighborhoods. He was also telling me how it was being said that him and Lil Half Pint didn't come to the yard when it was supposed to go up with the Neighborhoods. From what the homie was telling me, it sounded valid and appeared plausible. Basically, it was like shit jumped off before him and the homies section was released for yard. They were cellies. Whatever happened, happened before they could make it to the yard. Either the homies took off (attacked) or the Neighborhoods took off.

All he knows is him and Lil Half Pint never made it to the yard. Then the issue with Face came up. He was disappointed and upset with homies behind not getting on Face. He even brought the work out, "Cuz, read this!" I read the police report. What stood out to me mainly was the part where he was saying, "Yeah, Pint could've done it, he's crazy like that." Basically using Pint's name. Some homies say police reports don't count or shouldn't count. It's just a report. He didn't get on the stand. Plus, police can put whatever they want to on the reports. Totally plausible!

He asked me had I seen him. I'm like, "Nah, I hadn't seen cuz." As far as that goes with that situation and keeping it a thousand, a ball is a ball and a strike is a strike. If cuz is in violation, it's because he made a statement which you're not supposed to make at all, no type of statement. You're supposed to exercise your right to remain silent. So, remain silent! This is according to the code and lines, or are we that far removed from what we should or shouldn't do? We know what we signed up for. We also ventured into the discussion about the homie's big bro. It's out there and it's the same situation with Face as far as the issue. Same instance, the only difference is it's his bro. Same accusations and black and white. His position, "Fuck that. Niggahs bet not (better not) put their hands or nothing else on bro." I mean, who wouldn't feel that way about their flesh and blood? That's family.

We know the reality of it without having to play devil's advocate. Right is right, wrong is wrong. An instance where you got on a homie at King's Park with a lot of homies and home girls there, because he made a statement in the back seat of the police car and got spit on by the homie, the statement was made against. Basically, on some "I didn't do it, it was him" type shit.

Pint and me were on the handball court working out when someone walks up to me and hands me a kite. "Aye Tic, this came from such and such." The kite has my name on it, BG Tic, LBC." This came from your homie Slow Poke on the lower yard. Now mind you, Pints right here. He hears and sees the whole play. I open the kite and start reading it. I wasn't tripping off Pint reading the kite. It came from a homie, he's a homie.

Pint walks up behind me as I'm reading the kite, "What Slow Poke's talking about?" I guess he gets to the part that catches me off guard too.

"Get Pint. Cuz left the homies for dead on A-yard!"

Pint was like, "WHAAAT! Get Pint! Awww cuz! I know Niggahs bet not try to snake me."

I'm like, "Cuz, Niggahs over heres not tripping off of you and that A-yard shit. The issues been discussed already. You're not in the wrong. You didn't do shit. That wasn't your fault. Niggahs didn't wait. They knew what section you and the homie were in, if in fact it was them who took off first." If it was the Neighborhoods who took off first, it really was no control over that situation, but that's just me in my rational thinking. I survey the whole field. At the end of the day, the whole situation played out by design. It played out that way because it was meant to.

Pint immediately wanted to slide to the lower yard and holler at Slow Poke about the situation at hand. He asked me to go with him. Cool, let's go! We couldn't make it though. We were stopped at customs and turned around. The police knew we weren't on the lower yard and wouldn't let us walk through the gate going onto the lower yard. Knowing Pint as I did, I knew he was going to get over there at some point in the near future. He was pistol hot! I've known Pint since he was about 8 or 9 years old, so we go back to karate shoes and bomber jackets. I knew his bro too, from back in the day. He's my age or closer to it. Yeah, we go back pretty far.

We lived on the same street as kids, 19th and Lewis, across the street from each other. They stayed in the brown apartments, we stayed in the lighter brown ones, or were their apartments gray? Damn, that's crazy. I can't remember! Blame it on the sherm! On our block, all the kids hung out and played. The homies had a no nonsense moms named Pat. She wasn't for no games. She would really tear Pint's little bad ass up! He was a bad lil fella! Both of them though, him and his bro, stayed on punishment. After we moved off of 19th and Lewis, we moved to 20th and Cerritos and we didn't see or mess with each other as much. Shortly after moving on 20th and Cerritos, moms wanted to move again. When I was a lot younger, moms didn't like staying put in one spot too long. She should've been a gypsy. She loved moving around. She slowed down a lot, started to settle in one spot in the 2000's. 5 years, 7 years, those are records that wouldn't of never happened when I was a kid. It was "Go, go, go!"

Once we moved from 20th and Cerritos out of the set to 63rd and Orange, I would catch the bus on Orange back to the set and hang out with the homies every day. I hadn't seen my boy Pint in years. I'd been to Y.A. and to the pen. When I ran into him in Chino on the Violators yard, he was doing a parole violation too. We instantly knew each other's face. When I walked through the chow line, he was serving food. It took me but a minute to remember homies name, Nakia. We started talking and were like we'll link up first chance we get. We stayed in the same building, only he stayed upstairs and above me. I only had been there about a couple of weeks for some reason. I was missing him in the kitchen because I hadn't seen him before then.

Big Smokey from 20's with his bullshit ass was there too. Bullshit Niggah! Still the homie, but bullshit! Can't help but to love him. His brother, Big Fruity, was from the set (I.I.P.). Me, Smokey, and Half Pint would walk around the yard on the track, chopping it up (talking). We talked about the Enemigos and putting in work on them when we got out, cold combo! It was actually with him I renewed my hand (recommitted myself to the set). We got it in! Trays! Confirmed and confirmed. He was a homie I was most comfortable with and didn't have to worry about the bullshit, or him not being solid and vice versa. Pint ended up leaving B-yard, going to the sandbox for getting caught with a banger (knife). The police hit his cell and it was a wrap. That was in late 2013. I haven't seen him since. He should be back on the concrete though (streets). I'm sure he is. 20 Dollars from 20's (Lil 20 Dee), I just met him, I didn't know him. Basically I wouldn't. He's a lot younger than I am. He's my kids age.

He's a young homie who came off the lower yard from getting into something with the homies over there. He didn't really go into detail, nor did the homies send a kite to our side (upper yard). He wasn't voted off the island, so we assumed whatever it was, it was dead (no longer an issue). He did stress though that the homies locked up on his gadget (kept it/took it). He was like, he let them use it and they wouldn't shoot it back. He asked my opinion on whether or not that was stealing. My thing was this, if it happened that way, it was considered stealing, but if they done it and told you they were locking up, that's a different story, because you were told you weren't getting it back, hence, we took that! He talked about it daily, trying to get clarity. It was what it was.

I ended up getting another cellie. The cellie I ended up with after the homie from Harlem left was a dude from the Bay Area. The police asked me could he move in because they needed the medical cell he was in. He would only be in my cell for a couple of weeks. He was up for transfer and on his way back up to Northern California. The homies Trey from Santana Compton Crip and Snoop from Mona Park Compton Crip were cellies and stayed upstairs. They were like, "Nah Tic, fuck that fool!" I ended up letting him come to the cell though. He taught me how to make white lightening, teaching me his way. Everyone has their own method, but the premise is the same. I started making it and getting my loot. I used to mess with my Damu boy, Gangsta from Pacoima Piru (2p's). I had got him white boy wasted on his born day. He was layed out on his back and had thrown up. It was reggie too, with kick, like Bruce Lee. It took him down, boom, bam! He was like, "Yeah, I was fucked up. You did that!"

I met a dude named Two Guns from Inland Empire. He hollered at me, asking me could his little homie, Shady 80 move in with me. He's a straight youngster. He's solid. This that and the third. Shady was getting into it with his cellie, another older Crip homie. They weren't really gelling, plus he was one of those older dudes that's set in his ways and likes shit done a certain way and is easily agitated. So, it was like, he was on young homie about everything and anything. So to avoid them physically clashing or blowing up the yard (their homies having an altercation) his older homie wanted to remove him from that situation.

I let Shady move in with me. Shady 80, aka Tutu. He was a straight youngster from Colton City Crip. We got along, vibed, and gelled. I laced him on a lot of shit and I showed him how to make alcohol and make cards. Just things to do if you didn't have anyone on the streets looking out for you, you could look out for yourself. I even laced him on how to hustle as far as the game. Basically, showing him how to feed himself so he wouldn't have to run around asking anyone for anything. Feed yourself! We remained cellies for the whole time I remained in that prison. Same cell. He didn't have any habits and he didn't do drugs. He didn't even blow trees. He just drank and smoked cigarettes. Lil Tray Deee was the only cellie I've had that blew trees other than Chumlee and Sugar Tank. Chumlee got it going right now, as I'm sitting at this desk. What I liked most about Shady, he was very receptive to shit and he listened. He saw that I wasn't a bullshit older homie still pushing Crip that genuinely fucked with him, even though he wasn't a young homie from my set, but a young Crip homie. He had homies in the building. His homie Low Down from the PJ's and Two Guns stayed tapping in with him. I started messing with Low Down though. He was straight. He had life and went home on that nonviolent third striker shit before that window closed, which it did and fast.

A few people got out of the window. I think the older Crip homie, Studder Box from Santana Block Compton Crip got out on it, or was in the process. He could be home. Low Down left in 2013. Studder Box left the yard, him and another one of his homies had to DP a homie. I really didn't mess with too many dudes in Delano either. I did mess with my boy J.C. (J Capone) from Gateway Posse Crip in Palm Springs. Him and his bro, Lil Bro, Lil JC. Big JC was initially on the lower yard and moved to the upper yard. We both worked in the main kitchen together, but we go back to 94-96, when he was a young homie. I met him when he hit the yard at Calipat. Him and his locs (dark glasses). His homie, Nuttso, who's a Muslim now, was in the cell with my homie, Big Ant Dog. When he first drove up, I didn't like him. I was feeling some type of way because my kin had just got shot up by some of their homies in Palm Springs. He was shot like six times, a couple of times in the face, in his chest, his arm and somewhere else. I saw it too, on the news. Calipat got all of the news. Their local news, news of the cities that were close by, even Arizona's news. When I went to Ant Dog's and Nuttso's cell, I'm talking to them, Nuttso was like, "My homies laid some shit down last night!" I was like, "I saw that." Not knowing it was my kind. I had kin out there, but they stayed in DHS (Desert Hot Springs) and Cathedral City (Cat City). Oh, and Palm Springs too. A week later I get a few dots and dashes from moms, telling me about my kin being shot in Palm Springs, and he was in the hospital fucked over (in bad shape).

Then, I got on the phone and was able to get bits and pieces. My Aunt Martha and Uncle Johnny had written too, telling me about him being shot up and didn't know if he'd make it. He ended up pulling through. He was heavily prayed up (prayed for a lot). I sent him a card and a long letter, telling him in my dots and dashes not to tell on nobody and to keep his mouth closed. He don't know who shot him, he didn't see the shooters, or knew them, he knows nothing, it was too dark. My thing was this, you're out there in the streets trying to live and be about that life, then be with what comes with it too. Keep your mouth closed, move by the code, and accept it for what it is. Get a bar. If you're in your feelings, get your run back (retaliate). Do not involve the white man in this shit. Keep it 100.

If dudes get caught, let them get caught, but not by you cooperating or assisting the law. No bueno! If you do, remember this, you're dead to me. I'll never fuck with you, ever in life. I don't do snitches. Kin or no kin, nor do I condone snitching. Don't matter who you are, that goes against my ethics and compromises my moral compass. That's out! I don't do that type of horse playing, period. I know though, the female family members felt differently about the situation, feeling I was wrong for telling him what I told him, but so what! He's in the streets. That's the cost sometimes. Shit happens to street dudes. They go to jail, they get shot, they get killed. Involving the police don't fit nowhere in that equation, nowhere at all!

13

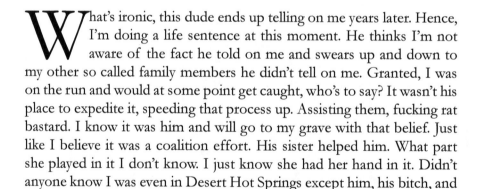

W hat's ironic, this dude ends up telling on me years later. Hence, I'm doing a life sentence at this moment. He thinks I'm not aware of the fact he told on me and swears up and down to my other so called family members he didn't tell on me. Granted, I was on the run and would at some point get caught, who's to say? It wasn't his place to expedite it, speeding that process up. Assisting them, fucking rat bastard. I know it was him and will go to my grave with that belief. Just like I believe it was a coalition effort. His sister helped him. What part she played in it I don't know. I just know she had her hand in it. Didn't anyone know I was even in Desert Hot Springs except him, his bitch, and his sister, and my other kin who lived with him and his bitch.

He had no reason to tell on me, his bitch or his sister either. With her, she's suspect at best, which him, he's a rat for sure. So, it went down like this. It was a cold play. Me and my young piece (female) Chardon was out there. Me, being on the run, I moved around constantly and would only stay somewhere no more than three days and I'm pushing (leaving). My route was from Long Beach to Bakersfield to Moreno Valley to DHS to Compton. Then I would reverse my route and change it back. It worked.

Chardon was moving me around for the most part and I was always on the passenger side. I wouldn't drive, she drove. At no time could I be pin pointed as far as where I would be or when. I switched up my movements. Not moms, not my aunt, not my uncle, and I had communicated with them daily until I felt they were on some other shit with me. I had stopped communicating with them and hadn't again until I was locked up and a year or so had passed. So me and Chardon were in DHS, messing with rat bastard and had posted up at his house for a day, messing with him, his bitch, and my other kin. After leaving his house, me, him, and Chardon went with him to his side piece's spot, some whore bag named Mo (Monique). She had a booming body, but her face was a butter face (everything was straight but her face). Chardon just had a born day so she just wanted to hang out with me and wanted to get a room.

We go and get a room at the Motel 6 off of the 10 Freeway. Rat bastard wanted to use my truck, telling me he'll come and pick me and Chardon up at check out time the next morning. I was like, "Cool." I'll go get him, he'll bring me back to the room and drop me off. He's the only one that knows me and Chardon's whereabouts. The only one. We hadn't told anyone, period. After he brings me back to the room and leaves, me and Chardon walk through the parking lot to Denny's to get us some breakfast, even though it was late in the evening. Pancakes, over easy eggs, toast, you know.

Then we walked to the Mini Mart, getting some blunts and cigarettes. I think I got beer for me too. We go back to the room. Then we eat some of our food. She starts breaking down the trees. I start to break down the blunts. We're about to blow. I had opened my beer and was sipping on it. We had been took off our clothes and gotten comfortable. She's in her panties and bra and I'm in my boxers with no shirt on. We smoked after she rolled the blunts. Then I laid her back on the bed, pulling her panties off and parting her legs and started eating her pussy. As always, I had her going crazy, sucking and licking on her pearl tongue and working my tongue in and out of her. Then, I went up, starting to lick and suck on her boobies while I Fingered her wetness. She moved her hips and ass slowly on my fingers as I worked them, continuously in and out of her wet pussy until I made her cum. She moaned and shook, "Aaaaahhhh!" After I got up and pulled my boxers off, she waited with her legs spread. I got between them with my dick in my hand, pushing deep inside of her, "Unghh!" I started slow, stroking that pussy. Her eyes were closed, her head moved from side to side as she moaned, moving her pussy, her ass, and her hips. She wind and rolled up and down, down and up, around and around, up and around, down and up, down and around.

We had sex twice, blew another blunt and went to sleep. Around 2 in the morning or 3, we woke up for some reason, but we ended up smoking another blunt, only half of it, then smoked a cigarette. We lay in the bed talking, then I grabbed her, pulling her on top of me, letting her ride me. After making her cum and I shot inside of her, we kicked back for a minute and got another round. That was the last time my dick would invade those walls. I did put my dick in her mouth. She tried sucking it. That wasn't her skill set she had though, but she did get an E for effort. So, while me and Chardon are doing this, at some point this dude gets pulled over in my truck, unbeknownst to me or her. He has two guns in the truck. I guess he's pulled over, the first things out of his mouth is, "If you let me go I know where someone is that the Long Beach police are looking for."

My thing though, playing everything back like I do before I go to sleep at night, how did the police even know I was in DHS, well Palm Springs too? Long Beach police at that. No way Long Beach police should've been in the Desert. They're Long Beach police! They should've been nowhere in the Desert looking for me from the jump (from the beginning). Secondly, how did they know to come to the Motel 6 and specifically to that door? Can someone explain that to me? No one knew that but him, no one. He was the only person to know where we were. Can't say we were followed because as we drove, no swoops were behind us and we were on a desolate road, a long one at that. Any swoops behind us, we would've saw the lights, so that's out! Thirdly, how did they know to drive me directly from the Motel 6 to his house without any directions from me? They drove me straight to his house. They even joked, "Do we turn left or right, right here at this corner?"

I didn't say shit. Didn't have to, they knew exactly where they were going. He lived to the left. They turned left. We pulled right up to his house. Was that a coincidence? Nah uh, absolutely not! I mean, I call a ball a ball and a strike a strike. I may've been born at night, but it wasn't last night. He flat out told on a dude (SMH). He's a rat! Stick yourself, Tony. Then the police asked me could they go inside of the residence and get my belongings. What belongings? I have no belongings there! "The belongings in the residence." They were adamant about me having belongings in the house. How would they even know I had stuff in the house? They wouldn't, unless they were told I had shit in there. He gave it up!

Trip off of this shit though, this is the crazy shit, mind you. At this point, dude never had a case or done no time. His record was basically clean. The police find two guns in the truck, neither of them are mine. I was charged with them though. We know what happened there. "See Mr. Officer, what had happened was. . ." He wouldn't have gotten any time. If anything he would've been put on probation, at best. Scary ass dude but claim you're a real one, yeah, real snitch! To this day he believes in his mind I don't know he's the one who told on me. He rather see me with life than him on probation. That's a bitch Niggah!

He actually believes that I believed the explanation that was told about the events surrounding my capture. No bueno! You're a rat, you know you're a rat! So what, you didn't get on the stand or made any statements on paper (police report). You didn't have to. You gave them me. You basically made your statement on scene of the stop. That brought you in contact with them and you gave me up, period. Rat bastard! I should've known something was up with you while I was out there and should've left the Desert. When the dope spot was raided and you somehow got away but was in the spot along with everyone else and didn't go to jail but they did, I knew it was something funny going on with you. How does that happen, everyone to go jail, but you? How does that happen?

"I'm still scratching my head!" Then a few years prior to me getting out of the pen this dude, Baby Bullet and his brother, the homie Coo Coo, do something. I think it was a robbery or something. They go to jail and he don't. I'm just saying! I don't think it started with me. He been had telling in him, but you see, that's why one of his kids passed, in my opinion. Karma! Karma don't always come back the same way, even though you don't care about your kids, you're a dead beat anyway.

I got at Ant Dog about getting on Nuttso. He was like, "Stand down on that. Cuz don't have anything to do with that." I was on some bullshit and working with feelings. Me and J.C. though messed with each other tough in Delano and he had been communicating with my folks baby mama for years. I think they had a thing once upon a time. This is the same bitch who's house it was the police went to. She was from the North End, which is gateway Crips neighborhood. She never lost ties with them dudes and had been writing and communicating with J.C. while messing with my kin.

To this day her and J.C. tap in with each other, that's my boy though (Sup Niggah)! I also messed with the homie Stitches from IVC. Good homie. Me and Shady were in the cell watching TMZ when we saw his big homie from his set, 40 Glock, who'd been writing and communicating with him and sending him shit, getting beat up by the game. He was like, "Hell nah, and this Niggah games talking shit to the homie!" 40 was trying to get somewhere. We got our hands on a gadget that night. Shady called 40's wife, getting at her about what we saw on TMZ and told her he wanted to holler at 40. He didn't catch up to 40 that night, but when he did, which was a few days later, "Cuz, what the fuck was that? Me and my cellie was watching TMZ and saw game on you. I know that wasn't you doing no running?"

He was telling Shady, "Nah, what was going on was, it was a situation going on, off camera mutha fuckas couldn't see, with his homies. I couldn't do shit!"

I'm in the background laughing. The gadget had to be on speaker. Wouldn't work otherwise.

"Who's your cellie?"

"Oh, Lil Tic Loc from Long Beach Insane. It's Big Tray Deee's homie." 40 Glock and Big Tray Deee messed around with each other, doing music. Tray Deee would hang out in Shady and 40 Glock's set in Colton with them. Shady told me he met Big Tray Deee and Nate Dog through 40 Glock and they both would hang out. He was telling me how Nate Dog would be messing with his home girls, pulling up in limos, picking them up. He was also telling me how 40 had practically raised him and a few other of their homies (zoo babies), so they were close, more like family than homies. To them (his homies and 40 Glock), he's Tutu, not Shady 80. His young ass kept me laughing, talking about his family, his brothers, his pops, Big Rose, a player type cat who got loot and messed with a gang, a lot of females.

Oh, and he kept fly swoops. His stories about his BM had me laughing like crazy. My sides used to hurt from all of the laughing. He's animated too, like me telling his stories. Some funny shit! Me and Shady would talk about a lot of shit too. I would tell young homie what type of shenanigans to look out for as far as dirty pool (games dudes play to politic you). I told him he had to have habits that navigate ups and downs. I told him about how rhetorical fires will burn him, playing with them. I told him about the autobots. I also told him to watch who he eats with because dudes are like bitches, get vindictive when you stop eating with them. What I really wanted him to get though was there aren't true allies, just common interest. It was mando. I had to let him know, don't get the game twisted just because a dude says he's a homie, doesn't mean he is or his intentions are in your best interest. It was his first time in the pen and I felt I had to do my due diligence as an older Crip homie to share what I could to at least get him focused in this unbalanced maze.

He would tell me he's learning shit on his own, as it comes, no one has been getting at him. So, as an older homie and an older Crip, I would lace young homie and school him. I also told him too, never be scared to ask questions. If you don't know something, ask. What I liked most about lil homie, he was willing to learn and he was receptive. My main thing was letting him know that he always have to be mindful of who he surrounded himself with. Never allow the next dude to influence your thoughts or your decisions. Always be your own man and never be a yes boy. Always be on the side of right, therefore nothing will or can follow you. Let your actions be about what you're about. Never compromise your values or morals. Question any and everything you feel is questionable. I also told him, "Homie, never let anyone else's movements dictate yours." As I talked, he listened. He was interested in what I was saying. My words weren't falling on deaf ears. He was processing my thoughts. Also let him know if I didn't like him I wouldn't waste my breath trying to give him proper guidance.

I didn't want to see him tainted or being corrupted by getting the wrong schooling, because the effects were long lasting. That could end his career. Being set up for failure is an option when it serves a purpose. I've constantly seen young homies fall under the wrong teachings, then find themselves on that other side of the fence (SNY yard). Not only finding themselves on the other side of the fence, but wondering how they got there, or took that walk of shame. All behind thinking that what they were taught they were being taught right, when in actuality they weren't. They were taught to fit the next dudes narrative and interest. I was telling him too you need a hustle, because of x y z. You're young right now. All of this shit is new to you. You're still in contact with everyone, homies, bitches, and family. It's new to them, then reality sets in and you start seeing the dynamics change.

It's going to get old at some point to those on the streets. Just like how that new car smell fades you're your new car, dissipating. Out of sight, out of mind is going to become your reality. Then it's about fending for yourself, making sure you're straight. Your homies on the yard aren't going to take care of you. They'll look out for you here and there though with things you need, but not want. Soups, coffee, a little beans here and a little rice there, some chips. Yeah, you can get that a couple times, then it's like, "This dudes heavy. He better get some type of hustle going. A Niggah's not about to be taking care of no Niggah." You most definitely don't want to be that guy that homies stay talking about, "This Niggahs always wanting something or needing something." That's not a good look, not at all.

Be a man of your word. All you have is your word. Stand by it. Don't be one of those dudes being labeled as bullshit! If you tell someone something, follow through. It plays a major role in your navigation when it comes to this yard life shit. Once you're labeled bullshit or a liar, that's your label. "Here comes this ole bullshit ass Niggah" or "This bullshit lying ass Niggah" (SMH). Those dudes can't be counted on or trusted and will always be looked at in a certain way. Believe it or not, everything you do, you're being judged on and judged by. How you move, how you react or respond to things or situations, you're being watched and critiqued, especially in this vote a Niggah off the island culture, just as dudes back bite each other. Me and Shady are like this (twining 2 of my fingers). I talked to my dude Shady a couple of years ago. The young homie C.G. gave Shady my digits and he texted me. First he texted me then he called. I didn't recognize the number, so he almost didn't get answered. I rarely answered numbers that were blocked or I didn't recognize. It was no bueno! He was tapping in from another spot. The homie T Loc tapped in with me within hours of each other. Come to find out, they were in the same spot, just different buildings. Mr. Alcoholic, he's the homie, but he's a bullshit dude. Love bro though, but he's bullshit.

Me and Shady hollered for a cool minute, catching up with the latest. It was good hearing from him and seeing he was still doing and being him, appearing to have his head on straight. That's a good kid right there. I'm sure we'll bump into each other again, landing on A-yard together. He's a lifer, so it's probable. We're FB buddies too, though I haven't been active for a couple of years. Me and the homie T Loc hollered a few times. He was telling me he'd gotten married and got a good girl. Shit, about time. It took him a minute. I'm not mad at him. He made Baby

Webb, hooked him up with his girls moms. Me and T Loc go back too, from back in the day.

I met him in Old Folsom in '92. Angel was there too then. That's when I first met him. Me and T Loc worked in the main kitchen together in Delano. When he started, I had worked in the Bakery. When I first started I was working sanitation, then I got a job change, going to the bakery. Don't get me wrong, the sanitation gig was better and allowed me wiggle room (room to maneuver) in other areas of the kitchen. I was able to get access without being questioned, but the bakery served my purpose, to make it make sense. T Loc started off in the scullery on pans, trays, and pots. I would go to the scullery and tap in with him and hang out. Sometimes I would help their crew. We used to get blowed as fuck in the scullery. We would blow trees and blow the smoke into the machine where the steam and water were. A lot of times we would blow in the bathroom, 4 or 5 deep sometimes. Me, my boy Greedy from Bounty Hunters, T Loc, S Bone from 5-2 Broadway (Five Deuce), Squirrel from San Diego, I think he was from 30's, sometimes T.C. from Compton would be in there with us, or K.O. from Eight Tray Gangster. We used to have blow sessions in that mutha fucka (bathroom)! Oh, Toons from Santana too would sometimes be in there with us.

We would sometimes blow in the large freezers. Police started cracking down on our smoking so me and the homies would have a wic (a long piece of twisted toilet paper) being the first few through the metal detector and getting searched, so we could go to the back door before the police finished with everyone, giving us time to blow. We would light the wic outside on the water heater so we could blow. We had to switch up. By the time everyone else, including the police, made it to the dock area, we were already blowed, just waiting to be let into the kitchen so we could do what we do, get our munchies on. A daily event, beat the traffic (beat everyone else), blow, then go inside of the kitchen and eat up every fucking thing in sight. Chips, cookies, trail mix, almonds, cereal and milk, whatever. I was gaining weight fast. We smoked a lot so we ate a lot. T Loc ended up getting a job change and coming to the bakery working with me.

We ended up falling out with each other before he got the job change behind my reggie. We were making reggie when opportunity presented itself. I had some going (cooking) already, him and his boy from San Diego had put a batch together. My batch would be ready by the time I was to be back at work that following Monday. Theirs wouldn't be done until that following Wednesday or Thursday. They decide to drink my shit Sunday, a day before I got back.

When I got back to work, I went to get my shit. It wasn't there. "Cuz, where's my shit?" I knew the police or the free staff didn't mess with it, because of where I had it tucked (hidden).

Someone was like, "T Loc was drinking Sunday." Him and his boy, I forgot who it was, but I was pistol hot.

I look for the homie in the kitchen. He's smiling when he sees me like it's a game or something. "Cuz, you got me?"

He was like, "It was ready, so what I put together, that's yours when it's done." Who told you it was cool to do? How do you know I didn't have nothing going on? You just took it upon yourself to help yourself to my shit. "Damn cuz, you tripping?" Then he was like, "That's small shit!"

"Small or not, it wasn't yours to fuck with!"

After walking away from him, we hadn't spoken in a few days and I intentionally stayed away from him. He had me hot! He was walking around the kitchen and saying stuff, making comments, though it wasn't about him or what he was talking about, wasn't worried either. If he would've shown any signs of aggression towards me, like it was going to another place, then we would've had to get that out of the way (fight). Some homies don't know where lines are. They feel they're privileged or they can do shit based on being homies. No, that shit don't work like that. It's still a thing called personal space. I'm not a broad, you can't just get at me all sideways and just do whatever with the exception of being my childhood in the mud Niggah, or my day one. What was crazy, the homie had the nerve to be mad and in his feelings when he was the one who was out of pocket. How do you call yourself mad? I told Shady about the situation when he got back to the cell. "Man, that homie shit!"

He was like, "He was mad and he got you for your shit."

"Ain't that some shit though? He mad and got me."

Loc likes drinking. My cellie was in The Bay (Pelican Bay State Prison) with Loc. He would tell me a story or two about Loc and his episodes. He was like, "Loc would have it and when he did, he couldn't be seen or found. Let someone else have it. There he was, with his cup and the small talk (SMH). If he knows it's about to be ready and some drinking is about to go on, he's hanging around." That sounds about right.

I just talked to moms yesterday. The phone company's giving out free calls where you can call straight through due to this Corona Virus shit. Either the phone company or CDC wants you to be able to tap in with loved ones. That was the 19th. We get free calls again on the 26th. I'll tap in with my Aunt Mart. If I get a second call I'll tap in with my cuzzo, Nip. Fuck everyone else!

Those three are the only family I have. Moms was telling me she was told it was best for her to stay in the house, especially being her age and being more vulnerable. I asked her had she talked with my aunt Mart. She was like, Nah, it's some funny acting ass shit going on, on Lyndora at her house. Gwynn, my aunt's caregiver, stopped bringing my aunt around to visit moms and stopped taking moms calls, whatever that's about. Though my aunt can't speak, she can mumble certain things. She overstands you and will laugh if you say something funny. I'm not going to lie, it was weird and awkward to me and for me the first time I called the house and wanted to talk to her. She wasn't talking and laughing with me as she had just been doing months prior to her having a stroke.

My uncle, Johnny, her husband, had just passed and she took it hard. I think that's what triggered her stroke, putting it in motion. She has been with Unc for as long as I could remember. They were never without each other. They went everywhere together and done a lot together, practically everything. The third anniversary of his death was just on the 8th. I can imagine where heart and emotions were, thinking about her best friend. She really loves that guy, w hole heartedly. I now aspire to love and be loved, like what they've shared over the years, over the course of their life with each other. What they'd shared was special, sincere, and deep. At the end it was death that separated them. Those two were like peanut butter and jelly, they went together. I tap in with her often, though she doesn't write, she's still able to read, so I write her once a month for sure, but I try to tap in twice. I know she worries about me, so I do it to let her know her nephews aight. I don't tell her about stuff that goes on with me when and if I've gotten into trouble, or if I'm in the sandbox for something serious, especially now.

I tell my cuzzo Nip though what's going on so he'll know what's going on. I'm selective with what I tell moms. I tell her shit, but not everything, because I don't want to have her worrying or stressing. I had her doing that growing up as a teen. I kept a lot to myself, just like with my situation that got me in High Desert at this moment. I was selective with what I told her. She just got bits and pieces and a watered down version. I was just speaking on this subject with my cuzzo Nip when I wrote him yesterday. I was telling him how I never told my aunt about what happened with me recently, but was saying I knew she knew something was going on because I had moved from Solano to San Quentin to High Desert, switching spots within a matter of 9 months.

She's far from a simpleton. She knows I don't move like that, so I'm sure she knew something was going on or went on. I was at Tehachapi from '05 to '08, then went to Calipat and was there from '08 to 2010, then I went to Kern Valley from 2010 to 2014, left there and went to Solano. I was at Solano from 2014 to 2019. Now I'm here at High Desert in 2020. I got here January 6th. I still haven't gotten used to the change with my aunt. I'm used to her being a lively person and full of energy and always in an upbeat mood. I would call and talk to her a lot before and after my uncle passed. We would talk and laugh for at least an hour or so. "Oh boy, let me go, Johnny's going to be back and I'm not even dressed yet, running my mouth on this phone" or "Oh Kate, I'm running late for church, let me go. I let time get away from me. Call me later, hear?" We'd always lost time talking. We'd talk a lot. Me and my uncle Johnny would talk, but not like me and Aunt Mart, because Uncle Johnny would be in traffic, running an errand or getting some loot. He done a million things. Unc was a hustle man and a jack of all trades. "Aaayyyeee Kate!"

Me and Unc were close. We spent a lot of time together when I was out, as with me at an early age. I would cut his hair every week. He would always come where I was for me to cut his hair. I would run a lot of errands with him also, do odd jobs with him. He'd done a lot of odd jobs, landscaping, janitorial stuff, hauling things and helping people move or moving them himself. He loved cooking and loved eating ice cream. I took it hard too when I got the news he had passed. I had just talked to him like a week or two prior to his passing. It just hit me, Boom! They're like my second parents. They've always been in my life, since I could remember and have always been there for me, right or wrong. I was their bad kid, always into something.

Regardless of that fact, they were always there for me and could be counted on when I needed them most. As a juvenile coming up and really getting off of the porch and into trouble, they'd always come to visit me from the halls (juvenile hall), to Y.A. and they would always bring me things I needed and wanted when they came to visit me. They've never came to prison to see me, but they've always communicated with me and have done things for me, sent loot, packages, pictures and reading material. I don't recall a time every I'd been denied anything. When it came to me, they've always been there for me. Unc passed in 2017. It still feels funny not having him around, not hearing his voice or his infectious laughter. As it feels funny not having conversations with Aunt Mart, the way we had been all of those years. The dynamics have changed. Having one sided conversations takes a bit to get used to. I would hear her mumbling and laughing like crazy. She's still her old self though, in a lot of ways. I love them both dearly and miss them. I'm looking forward to calling though. It's been a minute. I just hope I'm able to get through. After I got off the phone with moms and went back to my cell, my cellie brought me the consent letter from Lon, giving me consent to use a story he'd written called "Change is Good, but not Easy" for my forward.

Once I had it and read it, I was like, "Yeah, this needs to be my forward. It represents Yard Life." I asked Lon if I could use it. He didn't have a problem with it. He gave me a go. I had told him what I was writing about and had shot him a few pages to view. I had initially asked him to write me a forward for this book, Yard Life. He told me he got me and in fact he had just written something just for what I was doing. I'm like, "Cool!" It was called "What the Fuck" (WTF) basically speaking on dudes actions and moral compass, speaking on how the shit they do is questionable, hence, what the fuck!

We have a lot of those conversations on the yard (SMH). We're really on how drugs are fucking these dudes up and crashing them and causing them to go out backwards. "Aye, psst! I know you hear me calling you. You're coming down. You know you need to go back up. Stop playing with the game. You're walking around with an attitude and mad at the world. Why be mad when you don't have to be. So what if you don't have the greenies for me right now. Tell this fool whatever he wants to hear. Once you have me, fuck him, what is he going to do? We'll go up on his stupid ass or kick it off! (It's the drugs talking still) Look, I'm right here tucked between his cheeks in the bundle. Me and my boys, we're all fat ass 50's too. What are you waiting for? Get at this dude! See, you're horse playing. You're not trying to get right. You know you need me right now. You know you want me. Just tell him you have him in a few days and it's good. Just slide me to you. Tell him on yo mama you got him (drugs still talking). Once you get me, figure it out later, but right now it's me and you baby! What's a debt though? If he wants a fade (fight), it's good. He can get what he's looking for. You're not a bitch!

A squabble ain't shit if he's tripping. He's not playing with a knife, trust me. He's not built like that. Ain't shit going to happen if you don't have his loot when you told him you would. You know what he's going to do? He's going to work with you! See, I told you. Closed mouths don't get fed. See how easy that was? Dudes that got me ain't trying to sit on me. Know why? Because I'm not good to them after so long I'll go bad and be weak. I have no shelf life (drugs still talking). Now, let's get to the cell so you can go up. Yeah, yeah, yeah! That's him right there, break me all the way down. Crush me up some more. Don't leave no shards. There you go! Ok, I'm good to go now. I'm ready to take that ride down that passage! Yeah, line me up. Ok, make the straw right quick. One sniff, two sniffs, I'm in now! Yeah!

You know the drill (drugs still talking). I'm about to start running. Go ahead and tilt your head back for a minute. Enjoy the rush. Ain't I'm fire? Sniff a couple of times. Yeah, you feel me now? I got you on huh? Your body sped up, your hearts beating fast, now you're looking for shit to do. Yeah, go ahead and put the straight stunting bitches on the wall. You've been putting off. Now you're noodle grooving (working your jaw from left to right). Look at you! You're grinding your teeth.

(Drugs still talking) Go ahead and look out of the door to make sure no one walks up on the door, you know what time it is? Better yet, cover up the windows. You know you got to pull on the dick for a few hours. Unghh! (Hours later) No, what are you doing? Don't stop, keep going. We can bust one more time! Yeah, nope! We're not taking a break. (Hour and a half later) Don't even think about food. We're straight on all of that. We're not eating shit. Fuck some food! As a matter of a fact, let's go up again! Go get at ole boy and get some more, worry about it later. Fuck the debt, that's small shit! Besides, you're on (high), your lies are leveled up. He can't see through them. None of these clown ass dudes can, especially the homies.

(Drugs still talking) You lie better when you're off of me you're move convincing on me, more manipulative, conniving and more turnt up (aggressive). You're better at the dirty politics when you put them in motion and when you plot on homies with other homies that don't fuck with me. They're always trying to tell you me and you can't fuck around. Who are they to tell you we can't fuck with each other? You're a grown ass man, telling you I'm bad for you, telling you I have influence over you, telling you I have dudes not trusting you. Can you believe that shit? You shouldn't be fucking with me? I'm down with you, I'm for you!

(Drugs still talking) Fuck these dudes! Nah, you don't hear nothing. Kick back, that's just me. There's nobody out there on the tier, but you know what? They have been watching you lately. They could be plotting on you. You know how dudes already hating on you and don't like you. Yeah, your homies could be on some bullshit. It might just be a DP, I don't know. Me, I wouldn't be feeling it. You might want to write a kite and say you're not safe, but look, I'm not going to be with you though, I can't take that ride with you homie. You're on your own. I'm just crystal meth!"

This is the mindset though, the thought process. It's the drugs talking to them which is the very reason why a lot of shit is going on, on the yard. A lot of good dudes have took that walk of shame behind drugs. The drugs start talking to them. The next thing you know, they're tapping out (locking up, going SNY). Nowadays you have the dudes on drugs, trying to get rid of the homies that don't do drugs. The druggies band together, scheme and plot together, and if you're not on that page, you're in the way because what they're with, you're against. Therefore you're opposition. I've seen it go down time and time again, bullshit at a high tech level. It's like, wow! (SMH) all rationale is out of the window. Moral compass is messed up, can't be trusted. You're differentiation meter is off. You can't separate between what's real or what's bullshit. Nothing out of your mouth can be believed.

You're a liar! Words come easily and dudes distrust them. Yeah, you claim I'm putting a ten on a two, but the root of it is official. By all means though, do you. Just don't impose your bullshit on me or involve me in what you have going on to the point where it's affecting me. Do you know the difference between reality and fiction? Fiction has to be credible. I'm going to leave it at that for the moment, but yeah, me keeping at a thousand, win, lose, or draw validates me. I came to realize we all have the power to re-write our story, to re-cast the drama of our lives and to re-direct the actions of the main characters (ourselves). The outcomes of our lives are determined, mainly by our responses to each event as trials, temptations, and disappointments test our characters and strengthen them.

Know too, somewhere between, supposed to and want to exist (get a bar). You're supposed to do the right thing and want to do the right thing, based on. Check this out! Even a garbage can get a steak. A man that doesn't stand for something will fall for anything. Real talk! I used to tell young Shady that, also telling him to take all of his stumbling blocks and turn them into stepping stones, learn and grow from your mistakes, therefore you won't repeat them. What you know is different from what you know. The later comes only from lessons, painful or otherwise. As with High Desert, when I first got to Delano I had to feel out the environment and temperature, not knowing what I was walking into coming from Calipat. I didn't know whether or not it was going to be dudes feeling some type of way (in their feelings), about the Calipat incident with the Dodge Citys, but as with every situation or incident for the most part someone may be butt hurt about what went down or how it went down. That's just yard shit for you and a serious account of yard life. At the end of the day though it happened and can't take it back.

As for me though with the Calipat incident personally, what the fuck would I look like being present for a situation and just stand around watching when my homies are getting down? That's all the way out! That was never going to happen. I was in there. I'm not ever going to just stand and watch homies get cracking and I don't participate. My conscience wouldn't permit it. Everything will get figured out later once the dust settles. That's like the older homies would tell me "when in doubt take off (attack) and figure it out later". It's nothing ever personal. It's not only something I'm supposed to do but something I want to do. It's what I've signed up for, being from where I'm from, and representing what I represent.

I'm from Long Beach, no doubt, but I'm from Insane Crip first! I had two homies from my immediate set cracking, so I crack! No hesitation. That situation seems to always find itself being brought up or it just comes up as to why it happened, the reason, or my name being heard, "Oh, you were a part of that situation." I don't want to keep talking about that, especially with their homies. As far as I'm concerned, it's a dead issue. It happened, it's over with, Niggahs know how this shit goes. We clash and have clashes. We move on. As far as grudges, I don't hold them for those that do, it is what it is.

The last person to ask me about it was Twenty Dee when I was in Solano. "Yeah, I heard about what happened with the homies and the Dodge Citys. What led to it?" I guess because we're supposed to be pushing An Harbor Area alliance due to being both Harbor Area Crips. However, we Blacks don't push Harbor Area, that's what the South Siders push. We push what we push, we just happen to be in the Harbor Area, but nah, that's now what we represent.

So, there was an alliance from my overstanding between us (LBC) and the Dodge Cities, due to the Harbor Area connection, but with any alliance there's going to be issues and complications because someone is going to have an issue with the structure. "Oh Niggahs can't tell us how to do us, Niggahs can't dictate that, on and on and on" to where it's like, you're not pushing how we're supposed to push as an alliance, so what's the purpose? If you're feeling like you're not falling under the same script (rules and regulations) why are we even in an alliance, because at the end of the day, Long Beach can stand alone as we've been doing. Truthfully, it kind of fucked me up when I was told the Dodge Cities and Harbor Cities push with the homies. It was a first. It was news to me, but I'm like, fuck it, and embraced it. Ok, this is what we're doing.

Don't get me wrong, I knew though, we've had a history in the pen with both Dodge City and Harbor City and on the streets, but never really cliqued up, not that I'm aware of. Though, I'm aware of us fucking with each other based on where we're from and how close we are to each other. The only thing that separates us is a big ass bridge that looks like the San Francisco Bay Bridge. I remember back in the 90's, the Dodge Cities and Harbor Cities were doing them. They didn't push (move) with Long Beach, though certain dudes messed with certain dudes on a personal level, having their own connections and bonds as men. I've had several Harbor Citys I was cool with and still am cool with, Pookie and Dallas, and the homie Ant, but some spots (prisons) you land at both Dodge City and Harbor City don't fuck with Long Beach like that, but we're cool based on the Harbor connection. Going back to the alliance thing with the Dodge Citys, it's whatever's clever. If that's what homies are doing, that's what it is. I'm not bigger than the car, I fall in with the flow of things and the natural order and way of them.

I play my position and do my part. If I agree or not it's bigger than me, but at the same time, it doesn't mean though on a personal level I have to like you or even fuck with you. We're just sharing and having a common interest as a whole. Us, being Harbor Area Crips, that's it. Outside of that we don't have to be friends or homies. Back to young Shady. I told him too not to worry about what dudes had to say, especially when it was different from the truth. He'll come across a lot of that and autobots. Dudes will manufacture shit if you're not being felt or pushing in the same manner as the collective, especially if they're on some dirt bag shit. It doesn't have to be a reason, nor do you have to give dudes a reason, just be mindful. As with being mindful of the fact, twenty percent are things that happen to us and eighty percent of them is how we respond to them (get a bar).

Know too, certain things you can't bounce back from or can't repair. It's dunzo. Once shit's bad, it's bad. There's no delete button or start over button. I'll say this, don't turn over rocks you can't put back and always think before you act or respond. It's never just about you, but the collective. You're already aware of the culture (vote a Niggah off the island). Value and cultivate relationships with good dudes regardless of the tribe or race. Never close yourself off. There's a lot of good dudes still exist, Crip, Blood, civilian, enemy, etc. I basically told the young homie shit that I would want someone to tell my son, had he ended up locked up, any of them. You want to know what's crazy though? It's possible to do the right things, all of them, and still end up with bad results. Crazy huh? That's prison for you. That's yard life for you.

14

Something the big homie Lon had told me today on the yard that made a lot of sense and it was something I'd never gave much thought to. You can't dictate how individuals from other tribes or factions choose to DP their homies behind a debt not being paid, if you were owed but wasn't getting your loot. We were talking about a policy that's applied here. I'm like, "It's bullshit how it's implemented." It started with me and Capone talking about the hustle and him telling me the rules of fucking around. We had already spoken on it before, he just went a bit further as far as perspective. He was telling me too how he had to struggle with himself internally when shit didn't play out accordingly, having him pace his cell floor back and forth.

He knew he couldn't respond how he wanted to, not being satisfied with the policy and having to accept tied hands or take his chances. He was like, "If you take off dudes are going to ride with it, not really having a choice because it's racial, but you will get got if you come back from the sandbox and land back on this yard." Then he was like, "If your homies don't get at you, then dudes will push up on your whole car." It's like if ya'll don't remove him then your whole car will be removed. That's really how their pressing around here.

I'm like, "Whoa!" Basically, you took off because you didn't like how the situation was handled by the other faction or race, which you can't do or allowed to do. However they choose to DP their homie, that's what it is, hence Lon making the statement he made about dudes not being able to dictate how dudes DP their homies.

Cap was like "I sat back and saw what was meant, saw it for what it was, an adjusted." Me and Chumlee were talking about a bitch holding a dude down while he's doing his time, basically being there for him and giving him the energy he needs physically, financially, emotionally, and spiritually. It's always though someone wants to know how a bitch can do time with a dude. Not 'how you do it?' but 'how you do it!', there's a difference.

The one that's asking is really saying, "I don't know how you can do it. He's locked up!" You know how? Loyalty! I've had several females ask me that question, usually it was from someone that had no comprehension or concept of the word loyalty (faithful and showing faithfulness) to the situation. They've never been loyal to anything or anyone, let alone a situation, couldn't even tell you what it mean nor could they show you or give you a demo. It's never been them or about them. Loyalty is foreign to them. Talking loyalty you might as well be speaking Chinese. It's like this, if you're with the right dude and you're the right bitch, even if it's just your homie or a homie, lover, friend, then you can do the time with a Niggah if you want to, life sentence and all! I'm not ever saying it's easy, however it does require self control on your part. The real though, even the busiest bitch can make time for the right dude locked down, regardless of his time, real talk.

If it's truly something you want to do, it's in you and you're fucking with him like that, you're going to handle your wax (business). For most of them, it just come easy to walk away and move on to the next situation, with the next dude. Being loyal is not an option, yet they claimed to love you and give a fuck about you. It proves how they really feel or where you really stand with them. The real is being exposed for what and as it is, for what it is. No more hiding behind mere words. Now you're in a position to where you have to prove them and what you're about. I've had these conversations with damn near every cellie I've had, past and present ones. It's always going to be a conversation when it comes to a real bitch and a bullshit bitch!

The real bitch is keeping it loyal to the soil (the situation) regardless of how shit played out between them. She's going to do him, but do her (live her life as only she does and can). He's going to get his energy, but she's going to do her. I can respect it! The bullshit bitch, she's just out. It's no bueno, dead in the water! But at the end of the day, dudes know the type of bitch he's fucking with. There are some out there that's with the get down (being loyal). As I've come to really overstand, it takes a certain type of bitch that's mentally and emotionally built do deal with the life style. Not only the life style, but what it comes with.

A lot of them aren't built or equipped for it. It's just it is what it is. Can't really knock them for being who they are or being about what they're about. Can't blame them for their lack of loyalty or incapability. It's just who they are. It's in their DNA, which I've come to accept over time. Though, I overstand this, I would never mess with no bitch in my past if I got out today, with the one exception. Baby mamas or situation, no bueno! You fall into the bullshit bitch category, just out! Dead in the water! You didn't let me breathe or couldn't see me breathing! That chapter in my space is over and done with, no repeat. Especially a baby mama or situation, suuuper!

I wouldn't piss on any of them if they needed me to, or put them out if they were on fire. Delano had its moments while I was there. It got better for me though, when I started messing with my Bay boy, Rock from Oakland. He worked with me in the main kitchen. We started hanging out and talking. He basically took a liking to me and saw how I moved, felt my program. The main thing he saw and recognized was I didn't talk and could be trusted. I was worthy of a blessing, so he pulled me into the fold. The fact that I knew another well known Bay dude, that was loved and well respected, didn't hurt either. As far as he was concerned, if I was messing with that guy and on a daily in Calipat back in the day, I must've been not only a solid, but a good dude. I met M.L. in Calipat in the early 90's on my first term.

Mike and my big homie, Big Tic Loc (AKA Lil Sugar Bear) were tight and dealt with each other daily. So, through their relationship we got cool too and had started messing around tough, real solid dude and he was about his loot. Eventually allowing me to eat off his plate, like I was one of his fellas. He was indeed about his loot. He had a life sentence back then and got out from under it.. I heard he came back for the same felony. He's dunzo now. He's that dude on the streets (well known and feared), of Oakland. Known for getting loot and parking shit (crime scene tape)! My buy Rock let me eat too and laced me. What he liked though about me, I always kept it a thousand (kept it business and kept it real) with him, and he never lost fucking with me. It was a plus all the way around. It was never any bullshit or shenanigans.

If something ever went sideways or came back crooked with a greenie, I back tracked and found my guy I needed to, making sure the homie was always taken care of and straight on his end. Always showing my appreciation for the love extended to a Crip! From what I saw, he didn't fuck with many dudes, nor did he just fuck with any dude. He was selective with who he allowed in his circle, so it was a real privilege. He laced me on the game and how to do me and how to be safe while doing me. Showed and taught me what I needed to know to make it add up and make sense. I'll always have much love for my dude and respect for his get down, good dude. He didn't have to pull me in his world, especially my being a Crip and not a Bay dude. It went beyond that. It was on some trust and real recognize real shit. In turn, it was mando I kept it all the way solid with him. One thing you don't do is fuck over good dudes or people in general. You cultivate those types of relationships and respect them. You build and exert your loyalty, sanetaining (maintaining) the bond.

He who loses loot, loses much. He who loses a friend, loses much more! I had just got situation's number. I had been in Delano at this point about two years. Her aunt, Maxine, gave me her father, David's number. I hit him and asked him to ask his daughter was it cool for me to get her number. Honestly, I didn't think it would be a problem, based on, which it wasn't. When I hit him back he gave it to me. I'm not going to lie. I was trying to check the temperature to see where the call would go and to see where her headspace was. We talked. The conversation was going cool, then the questions started coming.

She started lying off the dribble. She didn't even have to go that route. We could've started from a clean slate, but she chose to lie and get at me like I was a gofer (go fer anything). She started telling me she wasn't messing with anyone at the moment. At the moment, mind you though, we're still in a situationship. Then as time progressed with our communication, it was, "Oh, I didn't know we were still in a situationship, damn! I've been committing adultery." In my mind she knew we were. Wasn't no divorce papers, but at the end of the day it wouldn't have mattered.

She's out there and I have life. No doubt she's going to fuck and suck. That's who she is. Just like the next bitch that shares that DNA and code.

This is her, "I thought you hated me and didn't want to talk to me again."

"Nah sweetheart, I can never hate you. I would have to care about you to hate you."

I see and overstand clearly now. The whole captured moment. I hate the fact I allowed you to blind me. I may not be shit, but I own mine. You're really not shit. I'm locked up, but you're the loser! The only thing you have going on, the fact that you're free. You kept hollering, "I'm a woman! A woman!" You weren't even a woman enough to have and raise your kids. How can you call yourself a woman when you lost them behind alcohol, then tried to blame someone else? You and I know what's going on! Your older ones don't even respect you, yet you have the nerve to turn my daughter against me. It's cool though, no loss. Your other kids you turned against me long ago. Didn't really matter because I don't feel for a stranger anyway. The cold thing about you, you're in denial and a fucking liar who believes her own lies. The worst.

On some fucking real shit, I wish I would've just fucked you that night in DHS and done it moving (never saw you again). You're my greatest regret in life and breeding with you. I wish I wouldn't have had kids with you. A mistake in my life I can't recover from, because of there being kids and there being that constant reminder you existed. We existed at one point, though they don't fuck with me. They only carry my name, even the possible. In all honesty, if they chose to change it, I wouldn't be mad about it. Real talk, erasing any existence of you as if we never exited, as if we never met at Samantha's house that night, laying on that pallet with you talking, my bad.

As with anything though, you learn and you move on. You learn from choices and decisions made. Though sometimes I don't take my own advice and will be the first to admit that about myself in this maze of unbalanced madness we call yard life. I consider myself to be a fairly reasonable dude who's ambitious to a fault. I also have an adventurous side which tends to get me into trouble and have gotten me into trouble. I'm extremely loyal and dedicated to those I deem worthy. I also consider myself to be a brutally honest person which tents to get me into trouble also. If I wasn't in prison, I would've still been out there caught up in my Crip life style, missing the chance to find myself. My present situation though has given me more than enough time to do some soul searching and heavy reflecting. I overstand a lot of things I hadn't about myself and people, including so called family. I now build the framework to things, beginning it from a nonjudgmental state of mind as it pertains to me. I now do what's essential to growth and overstanding how you handle feelings and emotions can have an impact on the outcome of circumstance.

I realize being realistic, friendship with a woman is the only thing I'm emotionally equipped to handle, due to my current situation of confinement at this present time. Sometimes in this situation it's better to have a friend than to be in a relationship, thus alleviating all of the drama that comes with being in one. I think the friendship will go a lot further in the end. You can miss the emotional rollercoaster rides and there are no expectations. To me, friendship is when two people go through things, good and bad, knowing that that person is always there, trooping with you (doing time with you), no matter what. You make a mistake, they'll still be there. They're not going anywhere. They're there for the long haul.

They're always there for you and you can trust in them. Trust is hard to find these days. I was one of those dudes that didn't trust females with anything about myself for fear she might use whatever she knows about me against me. Trust no bitch! Though I was in a situationship, I never trusted situation, nor did I trust my BM's ever. I learned at an early age that every female speaks on their previous dude with their present one, or a dude she's around. Situation told me about her turbulent relationship with her deceased husband. It was toxic, like ours was. She would tell me how he would get high on water and put hands on her. How he cheated on her. How he got his loot. She even tried giving me his swoop. His people wasn't having it, none of it. "Bitch, you're not getting his car!" Mind you, she's the reason he's gone. What possessed her to think his people were handing her some keys? Done a few days in jail, got a fine and probation, they were in their feelings and rightfully so. The shit we as men speak on about an ex-situation is different from what they as women speak on about an ex-situation and the reason is sex.

When I talked to situation a few years ago, that subject came up. I'm like, "Just like I know you spoke on me to that dude you're in a relationship with."

"No, I don't. Why would I speak on you. For what? Why would I do that? You never came up and you don't."

"Really? Am I supposed to believe that? When you gave me the whole script on your deceased husband, the night we fucked. Not only that, you spoke on me and on us to a dude who claimed to be your friend. He knew a lot about me and us and I didn't know him. He couldn't got it from no one but your bullshit ass, Me. I don't speak on you! Yeah, ok! If you've never stopped speaking on me, move on. I'm not that fascinating or interesting. I don't know why I didn't see it. You're really foul!"

This dude she's speaking on me to is an oppie (white dude). He's telling me shit that went on between me and you in our house. The thing is, he never mentioned anything you told him you'd done. It was about what I'd done to you. How I mistreated you. The whole shit, nothing about you, isn't that ironic? That dude didn't know me from Adam. I never met him. He was connected to you, you alone. Yet he know a lot about me and my business. You know what? I don't even know why I would've thought anything different from you. You are who you are. It wasn't like I didn't know you weren't to be trusted. That's why you never knew certain shit about me, just for that reason. Wasn't trustworthy. You only knew what I allowed you to know and wanted you to know, like I knew you weren't trustworthy. I figured out you weren't loyal. Again, it shouldn't have surprised me. At the end of the day, I shouldn't be mad. How could I be? I didn't even know you like that! I rushed into shit with you without really getting to know you. My bad! I did get to know your sex though. We did have a good sex life, I'll give you that. I can't even front (downplay) on your sex game, leveled up.

I've at times thought about the last time we had sex, which was at Debora and Perry's house in Watts. We were in the living room and Perry was in his bedroom. I don't know where Debora was. How I whipped out and you sat on me backwards on the couch and rode me while I held your hips. You moaned as you wind and rolled your ass and hips in a slow and nasty circular motion until I busted in you. If I can recall, the last time you sucked on the dick we were at Misty's, in the washroom. You told me to lean up against the washing machine, then you unzipped my pants, unbuckling them. After you locked the door you squatted down, taking my dick in your hand, started licking it, getting it wet, up and down, down and up. Then you sucked me into your mouth and into your throat, "Unghh!" Putting your hand on my stomach.

I just looked down at you, watching your braids moving around as you sucked me in and out of your mouth. I'm seeing your eyes closed and listening to the sucking wet sounds coming from your mouth. Thinking about that one I jacked off a few times in the cell. I use a lot of memories with you sexually to jack off. Sometimes still do! Shit, Chumlee is gone now! He's running around on the yard. Just thinking about it as I'm writing it wants to make me whip out and jack off. You do serve a purpose at times, mentally. Then it's over. I've really learned the true essence of what it means when they say, "If you're easily had you can't be worth that much." I agree. Being incarcerated and dealing with the things we're dealing with on a daily becomes draining and frustrating. It's a world where everything is controlled and manufactured. You have to know when to humble yourself and be humbled. We have to learn to listen to ourselves in order to learn how others might be receiving our words as well. One thing you never want to do, you never want to alienate yourself, even if you're not feeling the dudes around you. The main thing, never let dudes see you wearing your thoughts or your feelings. You never let a dude know what you're feeling or thinking.

It's too much power for the next dude to have. Ask yourself this question, "What aspects of a situation do you have control over?" Then let go of the shit you don't. Walking on a line (a prison yard) and being on a yard isn't as complicated as dudes make it out to be. For the most part, dudes put themselves in the predicaments they find themselves in, but not always, because you do have a lot of bullshit dudes on some fuck shit! They don't play by the rules and generally are on bullshit, love to keep bullshit going and stirred up! Those types of individuals never last long. It doesn't take long for someone to get fly on them.

One thing too I've come to overstand is when you do bullshit, bullshit will catch back up with you. For instance, how I've been hearing about the activities going on in the L.A. County Jail, particularly with the 20's and 80's pushing with the Neighborhoods. Those type of activities could come back to bite you in the worst way. Dudes are not in the county for the duration, you're prison bound, shit can get real sticky for you. Trust, I've seen it play out. Yeah, sometimes shit will stay where it's at, but depending on the circumstances and severity of a situation, dudes are in their feelings. It's just a lot of variables. Back to what I was saying before I let myself drift off, bullshit will always catch back up with you. You might be on a yard doing shit you know you wouldn't get away with somewhere else, figuring it's all gravity (good). Then you leave that prison, landing where dudes are that have been hearing about you and your shenanigans. Now you have an issue. Don't be surprised. Homies are going to want to know what your malfunction was on that line.

Homies want answers. You know, all of the stunts you'd been pulling, the dirty politics you'd been playing. You know, all the bullshit you kept stirred up. Okaying shit that was bigger than you, that you had no consent to ok, yet you did! That should've been off limits, better yet a no bueno! Not only did you put yourself in a fucked up position, but every autobot that was dumb enough to follow your lead blindly. They followed you blindly because they were on the same goofball shit you were on. Either way, they'll have to answer for their participation at some point. Oh, it's a snitch on the line. This is known knowledge, but you run with, "I didn't see the work, I'm not fucking with it."

Dude, it's common knowledge. It's not a secret he's telling. Everywhere he lands, homies are on him. It's not speculation, it's stamped! You're horse playing! You and your autobots are under that same act. That's that bullshit I was just speaking on that will catch back up to you! So, you were with such and such on the line and you didn't get on him? Homies aren't trying to hear about what anyone else didn't do. They're not there being questioned about it, you are. You're under the gun. You have to explain and answer as to why you didn't step up to the plate. Fuck them! What effort did you make? What did you do? Did you at least try to throw a rock at him? How about throw some dirt in his eyes? No? (SMH) Dudes can say what the fuck ever they want about me, but I'm going to always be on the right side of a situation, walking on these yards, being on these lines. I'm not going to be a victim of a fucked up decision or choice I've made. I've always been told, never make a dollar decision for a penny reason. A lot of shit I've seen and been around played a part of the way I think, feel, and assess shit. How I do it in prison on these yards and how I deal with the streets (females, kids, etc). It's for that reason I move the way that I do. You'll never find your place until you find your purpose.

We know we have our flaws, our sins, and our weaknesses. We know that at times we're hypocrites. Knowing often enough, we try to seem different from what we are. As we also know, that we're no one to judge the next dude, even when we criticize, dislike, or hate. We know we shouldn't judge other people because if we were judged by some of the standards or the same standards we use, we would find ourselves condemned (get a bar). Most though I feel are justified. How can you not judge when you're seeing a person's character and actions are just blatantly bullshit? Everything he stands for is everything you're against. From the shit that comes out of his mouth, to his thoughts, to the way he moves, bullshit!

Check this out though, you can't hide behind a mask forever, but for so long and it's one thing about masks, it's always one thing that's going to give you away. Dudes are already on you (aware of your bullshit) champ! You've already been exposed. That time and place will present itself and the play button will be pushed. At that point you've already lost your way. The spotlight weighs a ton, pressure weighs even more. I'm pretty picky and choosey when it comes to all areas of my life. I'm a Virgo, so I have a very strong personality. I like what I like. I hate what I don't like, as crazy as that sounds. My views and opinions are vast. When I'm by myself, my moments are very reflective. I'm constantly trying to figure out what I could do better, or what my next move is or should be. I'm obsessed with making things count or add up. I've shed many tears over the years and they've been salty as fuck! No matter who we are, we've all been through it, dealing with relationships, mental and emotional, especially in here. We've all been hurt and took through the bullshit. Damn sure been wounded. Some of the wounds run deep, some may be superficial. A loss is a loss though, regardless of the nature, the pain and hurt comes in many forms. By no means though would I ever shed a tear over a bullshit ass bitch! Mainly because I'm never that invested, no matter how good the pussy and head was, no bueno!

Yesterday, on the yard, I was talking to a Crip homie about common sense. Like, I was trying to tell the homie, "Common sense isn't so common with these dudes. They're so caught up in autobotism, it isn't funny. They're just remotely walking around most of the yards." You would think though common sense generally accept simple explanations, it appears though they can't grasp that concept. It's not complicated. I get it though, autobotism is a mutha fucka! Their tunnel vision is stuck on stupid, focused on the wrong shit. Really, common sense isn't hard to use. The mind is a terrible thing to waste (SMH). Either something happened a certain way or it didn't, it's as simple as that, really!

Anything other than that is clearly a misoverstanding. You know what though? If a dude's heart isn't right, there's no telling what he'll do, or how he'll think. Luckily for me though, I know how to read hints, indirections, and evasiveness, for the most part, along with common sense. Hence, I pay attention to all details, considering the environment, you have to. It's a safety mechanism. No matter what though, however hard shit gets, you have to keep your head up and keep pushing forward! Me, I'm just trying to sanetain (maintain) in a dirty game. I know what I'm up against and who I'm up against. The line couldn't be more clear, realizing everything's good until it goes bad. By paying close attention to individuals traits, actions, and patterns, you'll be able to effectively break them down and see what they're about. It's ok if you throw dirt in a dudes eye, just give a Niggah a good reason for doing it. Feel me? One of the Crip homies I was talking to on the yard brought up politics. I'm like look, I don't do politics. That's not my get down., but I'll load the gun! I'll leave that shit to dudes that's in that mode and interested in it. I'm good! Show me a politician's friends though and I'll show you your future choices and consequences. I'm into community (LBC) above politics. Though it's not me, I don't knock it though, due in part, because without order, you're stuck with chaos and renegade-ism. Like, I'd stressed to my guy H.L., I'm just on the side of right following protocol.

We're all aware of the fact that whatever effects one directly affects all indirectly, so the need exists. Just because a dude is in prison doesn't mean he's lost his sense of reasoning. About myself, there are no preconceived notions or great illusions. I know what I am, who I am, and where I fall in. I know what I'm good at and what I'm not good at. As I know my strengths and weaknesses, I'm never confused. I'm familiar with my lane and comfortable in it, all day every day. I'm a firm believer with the belief of getting in front of any and all situations, leaving anything to chance or get out of hand. If it's my issue, I'll dictate the outcome. I won't let it be dictated. There is the curve and then there's ahead of the curve. Problems are deep rooted, but there's always a solution that lies to any and all problems. You just have to find them, as long as you're mindful. It's not I who does what I do, but He (Allah) who allows it. My truths are my truths and although you may not agree, there are a lot of dudes who can relate, but can't express what they feel for whatever reason.

From time to time, you're going to encounter dudes you like and have fun for and who believe as you do, but will disagree with you over a particular approach, decision making protocol, methodology, or movement. You're individuals. You mess with each other though. You may have to come to the realization that he may have been right, even though it's often hard for us to admit. On occasion, we're dead ass wrong. We're all wrong from time to time. The key is acknowledging that, and then being able to accept it for what and as it is. With fucked up situations, I believe they're just an advancement on a dudes learning. You're constantly learning and walking on prison lines (yards), especially on the 4 yards, having to be aware of your surroundings. I tell these young dudes all the time, this prison shit is not a game, it gets real, real quick!

You can die in this mutha fucka! Not only just die, but can get caught up in this unbalanced maze we call prison. It's seriously some bad and evil people amongst us that look like us, act like us, talk and walk like us. My push (prison movement) represents me having the strength to move on from anything or anyone not worth my energy or time, real talk! The shit these dudes are talking about don't affect my day, my month, or my year. When I left Tehachapi, going to Calipat, I landed on C-yard. Me and Lil Pooley (P) from 60's were put in the cell together, both coming from Tehachapi. I hadn't really seen him before, because in Tehachapi we were in different buildings. We were cellies for a few weeks, then he moved to his B-yard. Then after P, I got a dude named No Good from 5-5 Neighborhood (five-five).

While me and No Good were cellies, the homie Boy Blue and another homie named Dre from the set drove up (moved into the building). We were all on the same tier together. The homie T Scrap (Tiny Scrappy) from Youngs, and the homie 51/50 from Youngs, were cellies and in the building too with us. They were on the bottom tier, we were on the top tier. I found out Breeze who was in Tehachapi with me and Boy Blue was there, but in another building. Bullshit dude, come to find out. Funny acting. Von from Blvd was in the building with Breeze. My cuzzo Nip used to be married to Von's sister Cookie, and had a son with her. My cuzzo Jackie used to be married to this weirdo. My Aunt Mart told me he was there and I reached out to him based on the family ties. Come to find out, this Niggah's a weirdo and he's bullshit with the funny shit. I wasn't tripping though. I never met him, but had heard his name from being spoke on in the family, growing up I knew my Aunt Mart knew him and my cuzzo was married to his sister and at one time he was married to my cuzzo Jackie. I also would hear his name pop up here and there by homies who called him a weirdo and called him a bullshit Niggah. He was also in Solano with me, but he was on A-yard.

The homies on A-yard were talking about getting on him behind something, that and the fact he's a weirdo. I didn't intervene or speak on the issue, fuck that weird ass Niggah! Once he was on some funny shit with me, my attitude went straight to fuck him, he gets no love or support from me, it's no bueno! So what, he's my little cuzzo's uncle or has ties to my folks, I don't have you or your back. I don't care where I land and he's there, "I don't know you, I don't!" As for this dude Breeze, he knew I had just gotten there from Tehachapi and I hadn't gotten my property yet. I asked him to send me some basics until I got my property. This Niggah was on some funny shit. It was cool though, I just know what type of dude you are. I was never without and I had a lot of property, food, clothes, all of my appliances, T.V., C.D. player, C.D.s, fan, hot pot, hair clippers, a lot of hygiene (soap, tooth paste, lotion, shampoo, deodorant, body wash, etc.) for the most part during that time. Moms, my Aunt Mart, and Uncle Johnny kept me straight. I didn't want for anything. For me, it was like good to know what you're on with me. I don't forget that type of shit. I just hope for your sake you're never in need of assistance. Straight up, I got nothing for you. You know what it is off of the dribble. I treat Niggahs how Niggahs treat me, whatever the next Niggah is on, I'm on, fuck a Niggah mean! Boy Blue and the homie Dre stayed on C-yard. I went to B-yard and was moved into 5-building which was temporary. I met Beenie Boy from 20's, Pep from 20's, (I had met another Pep from 20's in Tehachapi, the slim, light skinned one), a dude named Osama from some North Side set in the City. I forgot where he was from and I met M.D. from Mac Mafia, another North Side set. I ran into one of my old guys from back in the 90's in my early Calipat days, Demon from 4-3 Gangster (Foe-Tray). He pulled up on me while I was in my cell and he looked out.

"What you need cuz I got you on Foe Tray!" He left my cell and came back, dropping off a bag on the floor in front of my cell. Real homie shit and he wasn't from my tribe. He left and came back a second time and blew some trees with me. Them dudes as far as homies in that building, after Demon done what he'd done as far as looking out for me and blowing with me, not being from the city, just a good dude knowing a good dude, I was cool on them. I saw the bullshit they were on instantly. Two 20's, two North Side Niggahs! It didn't take a rocket scientists to know what they were on. I'm not a set tripper (not liking you because of where you're from or what you represent and act a certain way towards you), nor have I never been in prison. I'm a Long Beach Niggah period!

I don't do the funny or the weird shit. I'm straight up Long Beach, yet I still have to ride with you (stick by you win, lose, or draw). If it's an issue with Long Beach external off top. What was crazy, when I was in the sandbox, I'd gotten an ear full about how this dude Osama, M.D., Pep, and Beenie Boy would be dissing the set. I saw through all of that shit. I knew all along what type of dudes they were. It wasn't any secret, sneak dissers! Know the kind, know the type, but yeah, their actions towards me set the tone with how I interacted with them. I kept it cordial though, based on. As a matter of a fact, Osama was from 858 (Eight-Five-Eight). Him and M.D. were cellies and Pep and Beenie Boy were cellies in 5 block (5 building). I stayed in 5 building for three days and was moved to 3 building in the cell with Lil Football from 8-3 Gangster (Eight-Tray). When I heard I was going to the cell with him, dudes were saying, "He's a Muslim" and "He stays tripping on some bullshit". When I moved in the cell with him, he was straight as fuck, real cool homie. I ran into another one of my guys from there in the 90's, Big Sin Sin from 8-3 Gangsters, Q-Ball, Mad Face, and K.O. when they came to the cell to holler at Football.

We know they didn't just come to holler at Football. They wanted to see who his cellie was and where he was from. It's what we do. When I moved in, he was on C-status (where you lose your appliances for 30-90 days). He didn't have a T.V., but he had a C.D. player. I guess he'd borrowed from one of his homies which he let me bang (listen to). "Go ahead and do you homie. You heard of Raheem Devahn?"

I'm like, "Nah!" Right before I had moved in he had a cellie, but had got on him (attacked him). That very same morning I moved in. His previous cellie had went into Football's personal property and took an address, writing someone or just had the address or something to that affect. Either way, Football fired his shit up (hit him)! Football was telling me about the situation. I'm like, "Dayum!"

The thing is, you have a lot of bullshit dudes like that straight dirt bag! I was supposed to move to 2-building with the homie Tutu from Youngs. I had saw Lil Tray Deee in the kitchen where he worked. He wanted me in the building with him. Willie G (Willie Gaither) was also in the building, but had just went to the sandbox. That's how I was going in the cell with Tutu. Willie G ended up coming back to the building and back in the cell with Tutu, so that basically cancelled my move. C Bone from 20's was on the yard too. G Boy from Blvd Mafia came to the yard later, as did Big Sac from 20's. It was a few Dodge Citys on the yard, Goon, Baby Crip, T Loc and two others, I forgot their names, really could care less. I didn't fuck with them anyway, none of them. Chewy from 4 Corner Block popped up on the yard, then Cartoon from Mac Mafia and Ray Dog from Youngs popped up. 51/50 had popped up on the yard from

C-yard, Real Bitter homie right there. He wasn't feeling the homies. He didn't really mess with me. That was Lil Tray Deee's boy, which I was cool with.

I ended up moving in the cell with Lil Tray Deee. We last saw each other in the L.A. county jail. His cellie ended up going to the sandbox. Coast Boy from 80's and Tiny Snoop from 80's were on the yard and were cellies. Tiny Snoops Bro told me he went SNY (SMH). Wow! Chewy ended up going SNY too (SMH). Don't know why, but it's public knowledge as to his walk of shame. Me and Lil Tray Deee ran into the homie Young Dirty Boy from Youngs in the sandbox once we left the yard for the melee, when Willie G moved to the C-status building which was 5-building. 5-building was a regular functioning building, but that's where they were sending dudes on C-status.

Cartoon had popped up and off all cells to pop up at. He ended up at Willie G's cell to move with him. The Mac's had banged (killed) his lil bro, Chris, so off top that was bad blood. On some yard, the Youngs were tripping on the Macs. A Mac Mafia couldn't be on the line with the homies. The homies were tripping. Chris was one of those guys, well loved, well respected, and with the business. When Cartoon pulled up to the cell, Willie G asked Cartoon where he was from.

That's something dudes do when someone pull up to their cell, talking about moving in. "Where you from homie? I'm such and such from such and such." Willie G waited until the cell door was open after Cartoon told him where he was from and rushed (attacked) Cartoon. They fought. The homie didn't fair too well, but he struck first. That was Willie's second incident. The day I landed on the yard from C-yard, the homies were telling me three homies had just left the yard. M.C. from 20's, Motto from 20's, and Willie G. Motto and Willie G. tried getting on M.C. That's how it was said, "Tried getting on M.C." The only one came back to the yard was Willie G. Motto and M.C., I didn't get to see or meet either one.

Motto though, I hadn't seen since we were young, him or his big bro, White Boy Jason. M.C. I've never met though. The homies were also telling me Lil Low Down had just left there (Calipat) going home. There was another older homie around Willie G.'s age named Wash from the City. I don't recall if he was claiming the set or not, but he told us that he had a couple of kids from the set, which I knew of by name only. He was running around there, doing the most. The homies was starting not to feel him. He would bogus beg from homies (have stuff but would still ask for stuff), and he would be caught up in shady deals or in the middle of one.

The homies were fed up and tired of the shenanigans and decided he had to be voted off the island. A young homie from Reefer Mob named Flash, and T Loc from Dodge City were sent to handle that wax. They tried to get on Wash, but it went crooked (the tables were turned). Wash whupped both of them on the yard.

Wash had T Loc at the back door of 5-building on the cement step, balled up, punching him out. Homies told Reefer Mob what was he waiting for, get in there. Reefer Mob kept horse playing, pump faking (acting like he was going to attack, but kept pausing). Wash turned around and saw him behind him, seeing him hesitant, and left T Loc and got on him (Flash), on his bumper! "GEEETTT DOOOWWWN!" The yard go down, the alarms going off, police are running from buildings. It went on for a cool minute before the police were even aware of what was going on. I was in education, at the door, on the window, looking out into the yard. I saw the whole thing play out (SMH).

It played out the way it had because they were hesitant and spooked from the get go. You could tell they were spooked because they didn't approach the situation like hyenas. They were hesitant and pump faking instead of just going at him full throttle. The tables turned on them. They had the element of surprise and fumbled. He didn't know it was coming. They lost the advantage and it went crooked for them. None of them came back to the yard. Me and Lil Tray Deee were chilling and catching up. The first day I was in the cell with the homie, he had got us some reggie and we leaned back.

We were chopping it up about the County Jail, about the set, about bitches, about homies, and about what was going on, on the yard, before I pulled up. Another one of my old guys from the Calipat days in the 90's was on the tier with us, a couple of doors down. Dallas Carter was from Harbor City, good homie, quiet, and always to himself. He's never really messed with a lot of dudes, always selective with who he messed with and loved gambling. I hadn't seen Dallas in years. I knew though, he was still around, because he had all day (life). When he saw me, he smiled and shook his head, hitting me with my government. I hit him back, "Dallas Carter!" Then I'm like, "Sup Niggah!" Last night we were at day room. I had hopped in the shower. My cellie was in the cut (out of view of the tower), getting tatted by an Other named Spider. The homie Lon was talking to his neighbor, a Northerner named Gordo. Vamps was at the table as always, gambling with the Damu, V'ru, playing pinochle. P.F. from Bop was standing at the table watching them. From the shower I could see the whole dayroom and most of the inmates, except my cellie. As I'm showering and I'm on the bottom tier, three Sgt.s walked into the dayroom through the door, followed by two regular building police, which were our building officers. They're heading straight in my direction. I don't panic though. I remain cool as a fan.

I keep showering, though security conscious. They stepped directly in front of the shower and started looking down at the drain. It had been clogged or something. It wasn't functioning properly, so there were flooding issues. I finished showering and come out after I was dressed. They were still looking at the drain. Then they vacated. When I walk by the table, P.F. was telling Vamp and V'ru how he was in spook mode, thinking they were coming for him. He was like, the police stay fucking with him on some random shit, because of his past and his activeness with staff assaults and stickings. He was like, they would just pull up on him, wanting to search on him.

So, when he saw them coming in the door into the section, he was on shook mode, being security conscious. Vamp was saying the same shit, but how P.F. had him on shook mode by how he was moving around. Vamp was like, "You were about to give yourself away and me, moving how you were moving." I didn't budge or panic, I just kept doing what I was doing. The gig was about to be up. The main thing though is not to panic because when you panic you fumble at the goal-line. At the end of the day, where are you going? We're in a box. There's nowhere to go. You just have to ride it out. You can only juke them for so long (dodge them). Every Black in the section is in the dayroom, shit, it's only Silent, me, Vamp, V'ru, Lon, my cellie, and the weirdo dude in 115. Groove Mack moved to A-section a couple of weeks ago. It's not like you can dip to a cell, or put anything in the pisser. I know a few of us are security conscious. You have to be, due to the uneven balance that exists. As far as that goes though, you have to be security conscious here. It's high octane (serious), no horse playing, sir! Anything less than being security conscious, you're horse playing, straight up!

This is High Desert. You better knock it off and you better enact a single minded approach to your priorities and your safety. I'm not just involved, I'm thoroughly involved. Your courage, intelligence, and resilience allow you to push the way you need to. Learning from other dudes past, you minimize your growing and learning pains, which keeps you conscious and keeps you safe. It's safety first, bullshit isn't about anything, though for some it takes pain to get focused.

15

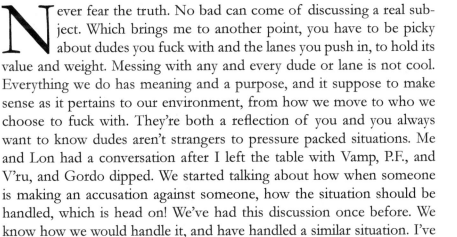

Never fear the truth. No bad can come of discussing a real sub-ject. Which brings me to another point, you have to be picky about dudes you fuck with and the lanes you push in, to hold its value and weight. Messing with any and every dude or lane is not cool. Everything we do has meaning and a purpose, and it suppose to make sense as it pertains to our environment, from how we move to who we choose to fuck with. They're both a reflection of you and you always want to know dudes aren't strangers to pressure packed situations. Me and Lon had a conversation after I left the table with Vamp, P.F., and V'ru, and Gordo dipped. We started talking about how when someone is making an accusation against someone, how the situation should be handled, which is head on! We've had this discussion once before. We know how we would handle it, and have handled a similar situation. I've only had the one situation of that nature in the 16 years I've been down, which was early on in the beginning of my time. That was the situation with Sugar Tank when I was in Tehachapi. It was when he told that Foe Tay Clown and Twin from East Coast I spoke on Boo Dog, because he couldn't produce his paperwork to show them when apparently he asked for something and they wanted to see it. Before anyone gives you anything in the sandbox, you have to show your paperwork or you get nothing. Simple protocol, there's nothing confusing about the process.

It's a show or it's no bueno on everything, conversation and all. When I returned back to the line I didn't hear it right off, but as soon as I did I pulled up on dudes, ready to trip. I couldn't have that. I had to address that immediately. I didn't hesitate to address the situation. I met it head on. You can't have that attitude, like it's not true so I'm not tripping. That's out! Just walking around and accepting the accusations as they are is unacceptable. That's just something you don't do and can't do. Dudes will look at you funny and speak on you behind your back. You're cool with that? I'm not!

At some point, if you don't address it, your homies will address you, "Cuz, you're just letting that go. You're not going to address it?" If you don't address it, they'll be feeling some type of way and will get on you, as they should. The mathematics are simple. On some real shit though, how can you be cool with accusations being made about you and just walk around the yard like it's nothing, don't even attempt to address it? I don't see how dudes do it. It's not acceptable behavior. You can't be turnt down (non-aggressive) on that issue, especially if it's involving some telling type shit, you laying down, or claims of something that happened that hadn't. If you know something isn't true, you're supposed to address it, especially in those instances. If you don't address it, it'll make you look guilty and the situation true, even if you are innocent and the accusations aren't true, it can affect you moving forward. You're not trying to have that type of issue lingering over your head in that dark cloud, especially in our environment. You're just not, nor should you want to. It's basically career ending when you look at what's being said and it's not being responded to. The worst mistake is trying to avoid the situation altogether, for what and as it is.

Stop coming around, stop coming to the yard and being distant. That's no bueno! A no go! Dudes are going to read into that, then it's an issue. You just can't leave that situation as is. That's just reality and what it is. In parting with that discussion, Lon was like, "Shit, a dude would have to take the initiative, but based on if I fuck with a dude, I'm going to move with him if dudes want drama with him, but I'm not going to address the situation for you though, not my issue." I felt the sentiment a thousand percent. A dude would have to take the initiative, period. IGYG (I got your back) straight up! Initiative is universal. You don't have to overstand it. You just have to take it, especially when it's necessary and a must.

Just like struggle is universal, you don't have to literally be living it to overstand it. We all struggle with many things. It's how we deal with them/it that matters. I can explain it for you, but I can't overstand it for you. Know this though, each situation constitutes a different set of possibilities, negative or positive, that'll work for you, or against you. Know this as well, we live in an environment that's dominated by all kinds of options from dudes on the yard and judgement, shits put under a microscope. Most certainly, dudes will continue to cross paths with each other like an intersection. Dudes are bound to run into each other, being on the main-line. Unfortunately, we don't always see ahead with such clarity. Sometimes, the implications of our choices are hard to anticipate and sometimes we're thinking only in the moment. In all actuality, you can't afford not to be able to navigate your way through the maze. Me and Lon got on some lighter shit and started clowning around, laughing. He's still in limbo, not knowing if he's going to be moved to the C-status building on the lower yard. He is a prime candidate for building 4. He had gotten a second write-up within a 6 month period. When or if he goes though, I'm going to move into his cell to hold it down (keep it for him until he comes back). For him, that's the plan anyway. Chumlee will be posted in 216, I'll be in 214. He was telling me he hope he could get a package sent before he's snatched up.

I told him though, if that happens and he's unable to get one, he can get one in my name so he'll be straight while he's on the lower yard. I'm not getting one until 3rd quarter. Me and Dallas caught up with each other and were clowning about the old days in Calipat. He ended up hitting me with some trees. Me and Lil Tray Deee still had some sippy sip (drink) and got right. Me and Lil Tray Deee got along and we clicked off the bat. He was teaching me how to play chess. Though I knew how to move the pieces, I didn't have a strategy, still don't to this day. I'll take a few pieces though. I still suck. He was also trying to teach me how to play Pinochle. I never was interested in it. I never really grasped it. Still can't play. I was on, it was too many cards, and too much counting. I can play spades and bones (dominos) though. I was kind of catching on though to Pinochle, but when we separated, I didn't follow through with playing. I pretty much aborted playing and stuck with dominos, which I've been playing since I was 5. I don't play spades at all anymore.

I had only been in 2-building with him, for like only a couple of weeks when I was told by the building police I couldn't be in 2-building. It was a workers building or something. I don't recall the exact reason, but I was up out of there, being sent back to 3-building. Lil Tray Deee told the police if the homie have to move I'm bouncing too. He moved out of 2-building to 3-building with me. Not long after we moved to 3-building, he ended up going C-status, moving to 5-building. He had got a 115 for possession of marijuana. We were drinking and blowing trees that day. It was on a Saturday. They called workers yard and he went outside, mind you we still had reggie and a little trees left, but he wanted to snatch up something from one of the homies. On the way back into the building on the in-line, an older white female police spotted what he had when it fell out of his glove when she searched him. He got booked and took to the sub-station.

He came back to the cell, but most of the reggie was drunk. I didn't know if the police were coming to hit the cell. They didn't come though. I was good and toasty! We finished what was left of the trees and reggie and just chilled out, doing what we do. We started talking, then kicked off a rap session. I'll do the beats and he'll start free styling. I'll beat on my chest or on the bunk. Sometimes I'll just ad-lib being his hype man while I'm doing the beats. I would repeat his words as he rapped and I would sing hooks for him. We stayed having our sessions. If smoking and drinking were going on, rapping was going on. But yeah, we could've waited for what the homie had for him.

A few weeks after that, Tutu had an issue follow him from somewhere else, which they always do. Sometimes it takes a minute to catch up, sometimes it's quick. Rest assure though, if it was foul play, it's going to catch up to you, no doubt. To think, otherwise you're walking around with your head in the clouds. You're fooling yourself. Not only fooling yourself, but really walking around lost. If you ran out, told, or done some buster shit and go somewhere else, dudes are going to tap in and shoot word. It's going to stay in dudes mouth. It will not be let go of. They want you touched. Niggah's really do cross paths, like intersections, real shit! Word travels, bad shit travels much quicker than good shit! Everybody knew what the deal was. I don't know if Tutu felt the tension, but he was kind of low key staying away from the homies. He was bouncing around the yard, messing with other Crip homies, going from group to group or individual to individual. No one outside of the car knew the business. He'd done that damn near until it was in-line. He stayed moving around the yard, we just watched him.

As soon as in-line was announced, he started heading for the building to go in. Lil Tray Deee started moving in his direction and calling him. Tutu kept walking towards his building. "I have a phone call. I'm going in. I'll holler at ya'll later." Lil Tray Deee was like, "Nah, hold up. Let me holler at you real quick!" Still moving in Tutu's direction. The building door was starting to close. Tutu shot (ran inside). Lil Tray Deee shot through the door behind him through a narrow opening, then it closed. We were all looking, like what the fuck! After about two or three minutes, we could hear a cacophony of block gun shots inside of the building, "Bloom! Bloom! Bloom! GEEETTT DOOOWWWN!"

They put the yard down, police started running from the other buildings to 5. A few minutes after that, Tutu and Lil Tray Deee came out of the building, escorted and cuffed. Tutu first, then Lil Tray Deee. You could see where Lil Tray Deee had been shot by the block gun, on or near his elbow, depending on where you were sitting. Some of his hair had came out of his pony tail and they were sprayed up (had been sprayed with pepper spray). Tutu didn't come back to the yard, assuming he hadn't signed a marriage chrono, certain he didn't, he checked out (went SNY), which was confirmed later. Another career ended. Lil Tray Deee came back to the yard a few hours later. The incident was the talk on the yard for a minute. No one before that had been chased into a building, chased down to be whupped on. Even the police were talking about it, "Shanks, fucking ran into the building after that fucker! Fucking shanks, running in buildings after guys!"

They would constantly make comments when they saw him, "No more running in other buildings, Shanks." Later that night, we were talking about the incident and he was telling me how Tutu had started running around inside of the building and he had to catch him. He was like, Tutu had ran near the tower and was close enough for the police to shoot him with the block gun while he was on top of him. I myself would be shot with a block gun months later, in front of that same building. It was my first time being shot by the block gun. That shit hurt like a bitch!

Over the years, I've seen dudes get fucked up by them, including the victims, while they were on the ground being whupped on. Heads busted open, busted noses, eyes put out, teeth knocked out, busted lips, etc. That block gun will indeed fuck you over, make no mistake. One time,

I saw a dude get knocked out. It may not be lethal, but it'll do a number on you, real talk! You will bleed. It doesn't just leave marks and bruises. White meat will show! I know from experience. Still have scars and discoloration on my back. That incident had pretty much been it for Lil Tray Deee. He was 5-building bound. The trees and now the incident with Tutu, he's out of here!

I ended up getting another cellie, which was C Bone from 20's, after Lil Tray Deee had gotten moved to 5-building. It went pretty quick (Lil Tray Deee being in 5). Me and C Bone was cool for the most part. We fucked with each other and he had gotten comfortable with me. He didn't really want me to move after Lil Tray Deee came back to the building. I move though, no doubt, back with Brody on the other side of the building, where Lil Tray Deee was moved after leaving 5. It didn't last long and was short lived. They moved Lil Tray Deee back out of the building, back to 5, saying he was kicked out too early. He still owes them a few weeks and back he went.

On his way back to 5, a dude from 60's was being let off of C-status and was coming to the cell on a swap, taking Lil Tray Deee's spot. That was out! All the way out. I didn't let him in. I was like, "Nah, that's not happening."

Tray Deee had told him in passing when he asked him where he was going and told Tray Deee to the cell he just came from, "My homie ain't going to take you!" A dude named Camouflage from Bakersfield ended up being my cellie. He was a Crip. I forgot which set, I remember though his set wore turquoise flags. He was cool as fuck and had a cool bitch too. She was thick as fuck with some big ass boobies. She reminded me of my bitch, Trice. She had some big ass boobies too. I used to like watching them bounce when she would be on top, riding the dick. I would have her bend down over me so I could lick and suck on them. Big ass titties would be all over my face while she moved on top of me. Big warm ass titties, my ex-situation's sister in law, Mary, had some big ass titties too. Not as big as Trice's but they were B-I-G! I still liked how they moved though when I fucked! Trice's titties would move, shake, and jiggle like a mutha fucka! When I had her doggy style on her back or when she rode me. Miko, Chardon, and ex-situation had some decent mouth full size titties, maybe a little more. Theirs bounced and moved when I fucked though. Camouflage showed me some cool lingerie captured moments of his girl. I had some cool bra and panty captured moments of Chardon I showed him.

We were smoking and drinking one day and he was telling me about how he used to fuck his girl in the ass. I'm like, "Shit, none of my bitches I was messing with wasn't having it."

Me and ex-situation tried though, as soon as I got the head in and started to push in, she scooted forwards, "Nah uh" my dick slid out, "No Blackman, that hurts." Then was like, "I don't want to do it."

I wiped the grease off my dick and had her get on top of me, reverse cow girl. While she rode my dick I fingered her ass. She had dick in her pussy and a finger in her butt. I can't front though, she had a nice little ass. It was small, but fat and round. Hell yeah. I wanted to get my dick up in it and fuck. I did fuck a few thick ass strawberries in the ass though. They let me get it in too and they threw the ass back, looking back at me while I fucked and gripped their hips, pulling them back into my strokes. Ex-situation was acting funny with the ass, at least with me, but knowing what I know now, another Niggah got it. Never the less, I got it else-where. What she wouldn't do, the next bitch would.

Me and Camouflage kicked it and chilled until Lil Tray Deee got back from 5-building, then Camouflage moved a few cells down from us. 50 (51/50) ended up moving into the building. I think he came from C-yard. He didn't really holler at me when he came to the cell. He came to mess with Lil Tray Deee. I wasn't tripping though, not at all. The homie was bitter at homies, due to them not getting at dudes that had got down on him (told on him). Basically, it was homies and their pops. I gather that much from him talking. I'd be salty and bitter too at the homies. I didn't take it personal. I never do, which my actions proved when he had got into it with a dude from ABK (Anybody Killer), a gang somewhere in Riverside. He stayed upstairs above me and Lil Tray Deee. The homie had gotten into it with dude earlier in the day. The homie was in the day-room getting his hair braided as he sat in the chair facing the cells. Me and Lil Tray Deee could hear Ole Boy upstairs, trying to get his cell open for some water, which he never does. It was a dead giveaway he was up to some fuckery. "Tower! Tower! 1-0-4, we want some water too!" After Ole Boy was down the stairs and at the water fountain, a few feet from the homie, the tower police had opened our cell and me and Lil Tray Deee had slid to the benches where 50 was sitting in the chair.

The move was so smooth, by the time he turned around to look in the homies direction, me and Lil Tray Deee were just a couple of feet from him. "What's cracking cuz?" He didn't respond. He just looked at us with a stupid ass look on his face and walked his tall ass back up the stairs, shaking his head. What did he think was going to happen? Fuck a Niggah mean! Though 50 was security conscious, Ole Boy was about to have a bad day, what was left of it. He wasn't going to get it easy. He was about to get maxed out! All the way out! Just for horse playing.

A South Sider we messed with that stayed a couple of doors away from us peeped how we had gotten out of the cell and had posted up next to the benches. He was like, "Yeah homes, I peeped the move, me and my cellie. Ya'll had fool boxed in. He didn't even see what was going on until it was too late. You guys were up on him." Me and the homie Tray Deee didn't know what type of shit Ole Boy was on. Whatever it was, it wasn't going to turn out how he thought. I don't think he thought it through. I know for a fact he wasn't ready to go with it where we were going to take it. Every violent act is pregnant with new evil. Question, do you recognize when you made an error in judgement? In spite of 50's bitterness towards the homies, he's still a homie, whether he fucks with me or not. I'm still obligated to assist him. I'm still that person in terms of how I'm wired. Fuck the differences, I'm with you regardless and I'm going to ride with you, win, lose, or draw. That's how I rock. We just came back from dayroom top tier and I was telling Lon about Vamp giving my cellie, Chumlee, a 602 to put into the box earlier.

Chumlee walked the 602 downstairs and went into the hallway where the designated box is for 602's. Instead of him putting the 602 in the box, he asked the Mac-rep, Drake, to put it in there, because he don't put stuff in boxes. He didn't even read it. Drake opened it and read it, making sure there were no shenanigans going on, then he put it in the box and rightfully so. Protocol is you're supposed to read anything put in the boxes for someone, whether it's a medical form or a 602. Regardless of what it is, you read it first. You don't just drop it in the box, to be sure it ain't no horse playing going on. No matter who it is, read it.

If you're putting something in the box, any of the let someone read it first, so that it could be verified that it wasn't any horse play going on. It's a measure snitches use to tell or how dudes would drop kites on themselves to get off of the yard. Oh, it's a production. Yeah, you let someone read what you drip in a box to avoid the bullshit, the insinuation, or speculations. Avoid a label being put on you, putting you in a position where you have to respond or fall victim. Dudes stay with the shenanigans and will drop shit in those boxes without anyone reading them. No bueno!

It's a known fact it's a practice used (SMH). Me, personally, I don't or won't put anything in a box without having someone read it first, period. I don't play those types of games. I'm avoiding all areas of stagnation. That's just one of those things you don't do and should be conscious of. You have to be aware and conscious of everything yard life. You can't afford not to. Shit can get ugly fast and go bad even faster. Every action causes a reaction. Don't like the reaction? Stop the action. The homie was also saying he's not just going off of dudes word about another homie being good. From now on, I'm checking paper work no more taking homies word for it. I need to see it and they can see mine. This is based on a situation he's presently not feeling. No more just giving dude the benefit of the doubt.

Whether a homie asks for mine or not, I offer my s hit. "Here cuz, check me out!" Even with my cellies. "Here goes my work and here's where I came from." No horse play over here. Even though I've been gone 16 years and have been on various lines, dudes automatically figure I'm straight. How can I not be? I'm still on the line. I'm pushing and I'm active. It's Crip here! A lot of homies that been around a long time and on the line, homies aren't really tripping off of. It's the young homies that's popping up who need their tags rain. Don't just see the yard, notice the yard! I don't have to be a prophet to see what's to come, the writings on the wall. The subject of sacrifice came up in conversation, which a lot of dudes have no concept of, especially these younger ones.

They don't get or overstand sacrifices have to be made for a bigger cause. It's always a bigger captured moment behind sacrifice. Realistically, this is what you signed up for, but when the time comes to make it, it's excuses why you can't make it. "I just got a gadget. I'm not trying to lose it." "I got a visit coming." "I have shit in the mix right now, this that and the third." Sacrifices are essential in yard life. It'll come a time when we all have to make them, whether we'll feel it or not, it is what it is. I've made sacrifices without hesitation, because this is what I'm supposed to do as a homie representing homies and the city. Fuck what I have going on, fuck what I have or don't have, it wasn't a thought. You're in a mind-set, I can't move too. I know what it is to make a sacrifice. What sacrifices have you made on these lines? The real code in these 2000's is every Niggah for themselves. Selfishness plague, a lot of these dudes, real talk!

Strictly about myself, that's what it boils down to. Sacrifice is not in the equation. These are the dudes we go to bat with and for, mainly for. I'm willing to sacrifice for you, but you're not willing to sacrifice for me. What's wrong with that captured moment? This subject matter will constantly be a conversation due in part because you will constantly see the bullshit. An issue comes up, the buck start being passed (SMH). It's just simply a reality that exists. Another definition of horse play! All you can do is shake your head in disgust and disappointment and be like, "Damn!"

The unifying element you'll constantly hear is I'm always myself. That's why I'm well liked and well received by those I engage. I don't try to be someone I'm not. I'm content with being and doing just me, as I'm content with my vast overstanding of what it is and how it is to walk on yards and not be caught up in the nonsense. There's always a reason for any and everything I do or engage in. It's never without reason. I cultivate personal bonds with those I mess with and continue to cultivate them. I learn from all of my missteps, view them as diamonds in the rough, because they form. They let you know what to do and what to do better. I'm somewhat reclusive and I internalize a lot of things, like the complex of characteristics that distinguishes an individual.

These characteristics affect the way you think, the way you feel, and the way you act. Your personality characteristics influence your life from decision making to dealing with change, from solving problems to resolving conflict. I'm not a fan of overanalyzing shit. I believe purpose does reveal itself and when it's a point, it's active. I'm not with playing games. I'm with playing my part, playing my position, and being counted for when it matters. With my overstanding and knowledge I can't claim ignorance, for my visual is clear, as with my consciousness. I'm conscious of the things I need to be conscious of. Here's another random question. What's the best way to catch a snitch? This one I'll answer, you use another snitch. It takes a snitch to know a snitch. He knows the lifestyle, the customs, and the habits of snitches, simply because he is one himself. Does it make sense?

It's so much fucking snitching going on, it's not funny. It's crazy (SMH). But what's crazier, dudes can know a dudes snitching, but since he has a sack (drugs) and is feeding dudes, letting them eat off of his plate, it's a non issue as far as they're concerned. Any way you look at it though, you're condoning the behavior and you're harboring a snitch. You're complicit to the snitchism, fuck the reason. It's foul. We know that a snitch anywhere is a threat to real Niggahs everywhere. A snitch has no place amongst the solid. Technically, those that condone them shouldn't be either. That "Oh, he didn't tell on me" syndrome is no justification. Just because he didn't tell on you today don't mean he won't tell on you tomorrow, but when he does, now you have a problem with him.

No, the problem lies with him being around and existing where he shouldn't. He's a threat. I think every cellie I've had, we've had this conversation about a snitch and dudes condoning it. It usually stems from a situation just occurring. This dude or that dude just got whupped off the yard for snitching. Such and such just tapped out because he was exposed for being a rat and was able to dip before he got his issue he had coming. What gets me is how dudes play with the game, like it's cool and they won't be found out. Straight horse playing! It don't matter what type of snitching, snitching is snitching. So what, you told on the police because a situation went bad. You told, period. Point blank. When you got in bed with them, you knew the risk. Why tell on them? Let the next man eat so the economy can still boom. You constantly see free staff and police being walked off yards because of these rat bastards. Dudes get caught up and give the gig up! Tell the whole script, the whole play.

Who took part, what it was, how much it was, really (SMH)! "Oh, I told on the police. That's not telling!" Whaaaat! "I told on free staff, that's not telling!" Whaaaat! How do you figure that's not telling? That's telling and you're a snitch! Key word, I told. The last time I checked, told was telling. Told of tell/telling – to reveal: disclose. Telling is snitching. A ball is a ball and a strike is a strike. It's no getting around what it is. This is one of those subjects that'll never be removed from the equation due to the existence of the element and character. I'll stay pushing the policy, because of the threat you impose and because it's the right thing to do. I don't want you around me or near me. We can't co-exist. It's like on another case in point, with how dudes would call homies busters. Why are they able to co-exist? Why aren't they off of the yard?

Why are busters around? He's a buster, but he's around and co-existing. That part! It's just something I've always pondered on. I've heard it numerous times. "Cuz a buster. I don't fuck with him!" "Cuz done this that or the third, he's a buster." I try not to call dudes bitches or busters. I overstand dudes aren't built the same and don't move the same. Aye, as long as your actions don't affect me or those around me and you're content with yourself, who you are, who am I not to be? I'm not Allah. You're not telling, really, I could care less. You have to walk your own walk. I don't believe in pressing my way of doing things on the next dude, or my beliefs, views, or practices. They are who they are. That's a good way to be told on too. Me and Lil Tray Deee have had this conversation as well too. It was one of the last conversations we've had in the cell together in the sandbox. We use to talk a lot about the set, homies, and about the home girls. My, personally, I didn't really mess with home girls like that, particularly those I was around. I wasn't trying to sex on them. However, I was cool with a few of them though. Lil Tray Deee though was knocking them down (having sex with them).

I did though, have sex with the home girl Checc-a-hoe, but that was it. I really didn't look at the home girls like that and a lot of them were on pussy, having sex with each other. Don't get me wrong, I did have action at some. I was straight though. The home girl Mya don't count. She claimed the set, but wasn't from the set. It was a couple though I would've sexed. Lil Tray Deee was bitter too, like 50, about shit with a few homies, which I overstood and felt. Brody felt dudes wronged him and let him down. How he conveyed it to me, I wouldn't have felt the same way. I fuck with you tough, and we were close.

Homies loyalties were at question. I'm loyal to you, but you're not loyal to me. How does that work though? We supposed to have had a bond and a mutual respect for each other on some real Niggah shit! Which apparently meant nothing. I think though we're all feeling some type of way about a situation with a homie or two. I was telling Lil Tray Deee about an incident I had with the homie Gangster Ace. How I messed with him on some business shit. The homie was supposed to be going O.T. (out of town) at the time. I didn't have no goods at this particular time and my people I dealt with was M.I.A., so I was out of commission and the spot was booming 24/7. I was in need of goods. My hours at the spot were from 6 in the morning until 6 at night. I.C. hours at the spot were from 6 at night until 6 in the morning. Me and I.C. were boys and shared the spot and were eating together until we went bad. You know how that goes. If I ain't eating with you, I'm probably beefing with you. I quickly learned dudes are like bitches, get vindictive when you stop eating with them. I ended up getting goods from the homie Ace. Like 9 zips. I moved maybe 2 zips. Smokers (crack heads) were crying, so I stopped serving it.

I slide the homie back like 7 zips and some loot, telling him mutha fuckas were tripping. They were crying. He was like, "Aight." So, he takes the goods back, went and rewhooped it. It came back minus 2. He tells me I owe him. Niggah, you're horse playing! I told the homie that was out! I see him a few days later on the block 2-1 and Lemon. He brings it up, but in a joking type manner, but then laughs. Don't make me kill you! I'm looking at the homie like, really? I didn't take him serious, or as a threat. I just let it go. He knows what I was out there doing and how I was doing it. However, I did feel some type of way, just based on him getting at me like that.

Lil Tray Deee had asked me who were the homies I was fucking with. I told him mostly BG homies, Baldie and Ace (they're brothers), Big Ace Capone, Big Treach, Big Ace (Bay Bay), Baby Meech, Baby Bullet, Lil Bullet, T Dog, Hobo, Gangster Ace, T Mac (Tally), I.C., Tumac, Bubba, Budda, Hog Dog, Lil Spit, Lil Goodie, Tiny Laid (Ice Cream). As far as Youngs, Infant Stan, Big Half Pint, Lil Half Pint, Big Croft, Big Monster Rab, T Meech, Big Dan Dog, T Ken, Big Joe Dog, I3, Lil Bam, and a few others. As far as big homies, Big Half Head, Ivory Joe, Bird Man, Shawn, Earl, Big Tic Toc, Big Crazy John, Big Ant Dog (Anthony Bumphus), Dirty Red, Bit Scrappy, Big Junior Boy, Big K.R., Lil Kool-Aid, Big Touche, Big Lowdown, Lil Dirty Red, and a couple of others. I had met G Big Cass when he came home, after doing all of that time he had dreads that went passed his ass. It was an honor to meet the G homie I had heard so much about over the years as a teen. Though I knew B.L., Big June Bug, Gangster Blue, and Shaw Dog, and a few others, we didn't fuck with each other like that, but I was around. I was also telling Lil Tray Deee about an incident that had happened at Yankee Doodles Sports Bar with the Longos (Hispanic gang). Me, Ace, Baldie, their other brother Red, he wasn't from the set but he hung with the homies, and functioned as a homie. Big Croft, I.C., Gangster Ace, Hobo, Baby Meech and a few other homies were there.

Big Crazy John and a handful of other Big homies were there. I think B.L. and Gangster Blue were there. Can't remember. So, we (BG and Youngs) were told to dress casual and we weren't going to Yankee Doodles to do no tripping, just out to enjoy the Raiders game and chill with a few drinks. Nothing is going on, just watching the game that was it. Red throws a bottle, hitting a Mexican in the head. It goes up which spilled outside. Homies were running to their cars to get pistols allegedly. Some got in their cars and pushed. A few shots were fired. The police were called.

Me, I.C., Baldie, Red, and Ace ended up in I think the Jack 'n the Box parking lot down the street, away from the scene as we heard the sirens. Somehow, Big Crazy John and another big homie ended up in the same parking lot with us. Big C.J. was walking towards us like, "Cuz, I thought we said it wasn't going to be none of that!" We didn't know where the big homies came from. Red started bumping his gums and got smooth the fuck knocked out! He was horse playing, getting at the big homie like that. Talking big shit too! Ace and Baldie picked Red up from off of the ground, doing it moving (leaving).

That shit was like some comedy hour shit. He fell up against a parked car and slid off of it to the ground. They watched the big homie melt (knock out) their brother. Me and I.C. just looked at them and then looked at Red on the ground. Big Crazy John looked at Baldie and Ace like, "Whaaat! Ya'll need that?" When we got back to the set, Red had woken up. The homies weren't feeling how the big homie ha got at their brother and were talking shit. "My Niggah, ya'll could've dealt with that on the spot. We were in the parking lot. C.J. were standing there looking at ya'll waiting to see if it was an issue. Ya'll were the ones who just scooped Red up and bounced, now ya'll talking shit." It was a few of us at the spot on 20th and Myrtle. Somehow, the talk ended up getting back to C.J. Next thing you know, he was calling a meeting with BG's and Youngs, those who were present.

Those who were at Yankee Doodles. He made it a point to make sure Red, Baldie, and Ace were there and for no one to bring any pistols. Really, don't bring no pistols, we're going inside of a secluded auto shop at damn near midnight. No one knows we're here and the fact we don't know what we're walking into or who'll be inside waiting, that's out! No bueno! A few of us had them anyway on some cautious shit. Even on the streets, you had to be security conscious. So, we get there, we went to the big homie Dirty Red's garage where he worked on cars at the shop. We go inside, me, Gangster Ace, Ace Capone, Big Croft, I.C., Ace, Baldie, Red, Budda, Baby Meech, and a couple more homies.

Once we're inside and the doors close, walking into the garage part of the shop, we see Big Crazy John, Dirty Red, Shawn Earl, Big Saw Dog, Gangster Blue, Big June Bug, and Big Loddie. I think K.R. was there too. They weren't standing together, they were kind of spread out which didn't look cool and looked shady. Big Crazy John and Dirty Red were standing in the middle of the garage. Big Shaw Dog, Shawn Earl,

Gangster Blue, Big June Bug and Big Loddie were standing behind them, not directly, but kind of fanned out. The whole scene looked like an old school gangster flick.

The big homies were standing near something. A stack of tires, a work bench, a car, a rolling tool box, something. I was very observant of the surroundings. These are big homies and G homies, can't sleep on them. All I'm thinking though is, "Damn, this shit can get ugly in this bitch." I know for a fact, homies are heated (have pistols) on both sides. If you thought otherwise, you're stupid as fuck. It's guns up in here, all it'll take is a wrong move and it's a wrap. It's going to be a bunch of dead ass Niggahs up in the garage and no one knows we're there and wont until the next morning when the other people who worked there came to work. Bullet casings and pistols, it would've been ugly.

Dirty Red had the floor and was talking, "We're trying to resolve this issue between the homies and it's going to end here." That statement alone had homies uncomfortable. Red had to be spooked. So, Big Crazy John started talking, goes in, "Cuz, check this out. I'm hearing Niggah's got issues behind the Yankee Doodle shit. It's like this though, we can turn it into a BG, Young and Big Homie thang, or it can just be a family thang. Between me and them (pointing at Red, Baldie, and Ace)." Everyone's looking around at them, then back at C.J. and Dirty Red, who's standing next to C.J. as he's talking.

"However ya'll want to do it, when we leave up out of here, that can be the bell." Niggah's are quiet, Red, Ace, and Baldie didn't say anything. I'm like, "Damn, nobody have nothing to say (SMH)!" Lil Tray Deee was telling me he didn't really mess with a lot of the homies I messed with. He really only messed with his crew, Big Dirty Boy, the other Dirty Boys, and the homie Big Loddie. They pretty much only fucked with each other. I tell him about the incident with me and Big Ivory Joe when we were on Lime off of PCH (Pacific Coast Highway), across the street from the P.A.'s (Poly Apartments). A young 20 Crip had just been shot across the street next to the P.A.'s. Me and Ivory Joe were standing in a yard, talking next to some apartments that sat on the corner on Lime. A young 20 Crip just turned the corner, coming from off of PCH on his bike. I'm smoking a blunt and talking to big homie as the young 20 Crip were passing us as he rode in the street, he hollers out "20 Crip!" I holler back at him "Insane Crip!" He keep riding his bike down the street and passed a few cars, then decides he wants to turn around on his bike towards us, but still in the street. I never took my eyes off of him, me or the homie. I tell the homie, "You see this young Niggah buss a U (u-turn)?" "Hell yeah I see him."

Then I'm like, "Don't trip, I got it!" I reach for the 40 Glock, I pulled it, lowering it on the side of my leg, ready to go. It's off safety and it's one in the brain (chamber). As the young 20 Crip get 3 cars away, approaching us, I stepped out of the yard, "Sup cuz?" He turned his bike back around and went about his business. We watched him ride to 19th and Lime, making a right. That was the best choice in the world for him to make. He was about to get his young ass dead. The homie was like, "Damn homie, I didn't know you were strapped. I'm out here gang banging." My attitude was I rather the police catch me with it than the enemy without it. I've been caught slipping on more than one occasion.

The big homie was low-key kind of shell shocked. He had gotten shot up by some Enemigos (Hispanics). Tray Deee had told me he heard about the homie being shot up. We started talking about putting in work. He was telling me about him and his boy, Infant Tray Fingers, putting in work and about a few solo missions he'd went on, no deets (details). I told him about a few of my solos and some shit me and Big Half Pint bent a corner on.

I'm not going to lie, a lot of shit was going on early 2000's. BG's and Youngs were doing what they do, Whaaat! It was so bad, the Gang Unit pulled up on me, Hobo, and Infant Kool-Aid. Another homie was with us, but I forgot who it was. Cambell and Hunt were on some shit like, "We know what's going on. It's over. Stall that shit out." Then they pulled off. My second run in with them. The first time I was coming out of the yard at the spot on 20th and Myrtle. They pulled up just as I came out of the yard onto the sidewalk. They jump out of their car, leaving the doors open, moving towards me. "Don't run!" I didn't run. Run for what? "What's up?" "We haven't seen you around here before. Who are you?"

I'm just looking at them. "We're not familiar with the face. Are you on paper (parole)? Where are you from, 20's, 19th street, Insane, Youngs?" Before I could answer they were hitting me with another question. "Yeah, I'm on parole and I don't bang!" "Yeah right, lift your shirt up and spin around. Now roll your sleeves up." They saw the ICG on my right arm, the ESC on my left arm, and in big letters the ICG in old English style letters on my back. "What did they call you?" "Khaki suit!" Of course I lied. I wasn't about to give them my handle. That was no bueno! I couldn't see Tweedle Dee and Tweedle Dumb with it. They searched me and didn't find shit on me. Then Cambell was like, "Technically, you aren't supposed to be in an active gang area."

They let me go and as I was walking away, Cambell called me. They tried hitting me with the oldest trick in the book. "Aye, Khaki Suit!" I kept walking at first, then I turned around. He just wanted to see if I would respond. They finally get back in their car and as they were passing me they hit me with "Stay up, Khaki Suit!"

I went to the Ave (Martin Luther King Ave) where homies and home girls sometimes hung. It was basically one of our blocks we would be on. It's in the heart of the set. Lil Tray Deee was laughing at the name Khaki Suite, shit I came up with on the fly. I don't know where it came from. Cambell and Hunt pulled up on me and Hobo. We had just came from the Dairy and had crossed the street. They pulled up and jumped out on us. This was the 3rd time I had contact with Tweedle Dee and Tweedle Dumb. "Aye Khaki Suite, you and Hobo come over here and get on this car." They searched us. Hobo didn't have anything. Me neither, except about 100 plus captured moments in my pockets, which they confiscated.

I had on sweats with big pockets on them. Two on top and two on the side of the legs. Hunt pulled them out and began looking through the small stacks. He started calling homies by their set names, pointing at them. "Oh this is Half Pint here, this looks like Ace Capone. Oh, Joe Dog too. What has he been up to? Here's you, right here Hobo. Isn't this Big Half Head?" He keeps flipping through the stacks. "Ok, I see you Khaki Suit, you I.C. and Ace Capone. Is this Dur Dur?" Me and Hobo never respond.

16

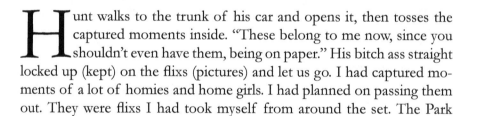

Hunt walks to the trunk of his car and opens it, then tosses the captured moments inside. "These belong to me now, since you shouldn't even have them, being on paper." His bitch ass straight locked up (kept) on the flixs (pictures) and let us go. I had captured moments of a lot of homies and home girls. I had planned on passing them out. They were flixs I had took myself from around the set. The Park (King's Park) and from the football game that was played at Eldorado Park between the Big Homies versus the Youngs and BG's.

The Big Homie, Big Loc (Herbie) and me had words at the game. He was basically feeling some type of way because BG's had started side line popping (tackling players on the side line that aren't in the game), and running on the field, jumping on the pile. He was like, "The next Niggah do it, it's on!" Me, being on my tip (my bullshit), the next play, I run on the field and jump on the pile that was on top of the Big Homie, Big Crazy John. He was quarterbacking for the Big Homies. Big Loc was like, "See, you Young Niggah's play too much." He just looked at me, mad dogging me. It was a few big homies there if I can remember. Big Half

Head, Big June Bug, Ray Bone, Big Dirty Red, and a few others. Between them, and us, we were deep (a lot of us) at Eldorado Park.

Lil Tray Deee was like, "Damn cuz, they took the flixs?"

I'm like, "Hell yeah, they took a Niggah shit!" Cambell and Hunt also had a few gray flags (bandanas) they took from homies. I saw a Raider fitted (football cap) and a Yankee fitted (baseball cap) in their trunk. They even had a Raiders Jacket in the trunk and now my captured moments are in their collection of shit they took from a homie. Somehow, we got on the subject of homies out on the streets fucking homie's girls on the low. I told the homie I didn't get down, but to each is on. Especially homies I fuck with and am around on a daily. I couldn't do it personally. That's just foul shit to me. You're kicking it with the homie every day. Ya'll hanging out, smoking trees, and drinking. This is your boy and on the low you're fucking his bitch (SMH)!

Nah, I couldn't do it. I wasn't built like that nor am I wired that way. There are lines you just don't cross, on some real Niggah shit! I don't care how good she looks or how she's made up (built). She could have one of the biggest asses I've ever seen, the fattest titties, or the prettiest lips, I'm straight. That's suuuper no bueno! I knew of a couple of homies that were fucking homie's girls. He did too. We talked about them and was like, "Niggah's are bullshit!" I was telling the homie about the homie Baby Ruck, how I ran into him on the County Jail Bus on our way to Long Beach Court. The homie had been off of the streets already damn near a year or a little less. We were having a conversation. He basically was tripping, talking about he knew homies were fucking on his baby mama, the young home girl Lil Mama. He was pretty much saying he wanted to get down with homies.

I tell the homie Ruck like this, "I don't fuck homies' girls or baby mamas. That's not what I do nor is it my demonstration."

Yeah, she was fucking. That's what she was doing. Not just homies, but a Compton Ducky Hood Niggah and a Damu Niggah too, off of the north side. I pull up in front of her apartments where she lived on the block (61st and Linden). The homie Big Half Pint and the homie Tumac stayed in them as well. Pint though was in jail too. He left after Ruck. There were a few Young homies out front, her, and a couple of IDKs (I don't knows). As soon as I park the swoop and get out, she looks in my direction. The homie Ruck's Little Brody is out front too. She was deeply engaged in conversation with one of the IDKs.

I pulled out a blunt, already twisted up, putting fire to it, sending a smoke cloud into the air. I'm sitting on the hood of my Seville. I had just came from the car wash, suns beaming off of the 100 spokes (Dayton Wire Rims). A couple of the Young homies walked to the swoop and I passed the blunt. She kept looking in my direction. I gave her the "Hell yeah I see yo ass all in a Niggah's face" look. Guilt is a mutha fucka. She walked away from IDK, walking up to me. "Aye Tic, can I holler at you over here!"

I get off of my swoop and walk away from the homies and we step off to the side. Eyes are on us. "Sup with it Lil Mama?"

"I miss Ruck. I don't know what to do without him out here. He's my heart! This that and the third." She hit me with the tears (SMH).

Aight, all that's cool. When have you wrote the homie last? You sent him flix of his daughter? You sent him some loot? Have you been to see the homie?

"No, no, no." It was like, "It's hard out here. I'm going through some shit and I cry every day. I just miss him."

I just looked at her and walked away shaking my head. I see how she's moving and what she's up to. All I said was, "I feel you!"

"Are you going to tell Ruck?" I didn't respond. She was no doubt doing and being her. The homie had mentioned Niggahs picking up his daughter or something to that effect. I personally have never saw any homie or anyone else for that matter picking the homie daughter up or playing with her, not while I was around.

I wouldn't have allowed it and would've spoke on it, especially if it was someone she was laying up with. That was out! The homies locked up and that's his baby! I wouldn't have allowed it being around, based on she's a little girl, but first off, she's the homies daughter. I didn't allow anyone to play with mine or pick her up. She has legs and feet, let her stand on them. Don't pick her up. Another thing, she's not yours to be playing with. But nah homie, I wasn't that guy. Lil Mama was the home girl. I didn't like her like that anyway, no disrespect. She wasn't my type.

Me, Lil Tray Deee and Chewy would work out on the yard together. A couple of other Crip homies from elsewhere would work out with us on the concrete slab. Me and Lil Tray Deee didn't fuck with a lot of dudes. It was a very few. We kept a small circle. We hollered at a few though outside of our circle, but weren't close to none, keeping it cordial though. We pretty much stayed to ourselves. We're still the same way to this day. A

Young civilian from Compton up in High Desert named K.C. was telling me he knew Lil Tray Deee and had met him at CMC. K.C. was telling me Brody was the same way and hadn't changed. Tray Deee stayed with a serious look on his face. He was quiet and he pushed around the yard, not messing with dudes outside of a few he embraced. K.C. happened to be one he messed with. K.C.s cool, he's a cool youngster. I mess with K.C. He has to be straight if Lil Tray Deee messes with you. He doesn't fuck with dudes like that. Most off the dribble would consider him antisocial. I'm the same way for the most part. Especially in jail. Here, all I fuck with is Vamp, my kid, my cellie Chumlee, and my guy Lon. Everyone else, I'm just straight with on some being cordial type shit.

I draw lines immediately separating myself, but if I fuck with you, I fuck with you! The only thing I don't do is get involved in homie shit. That's homie business. It has nothing to do with me, with Insane, or with Long Beach. My hands are tied on that. However, if I fuck with you and we're together and dudes try to step to you, I'm going to get involved. For one, I fuck with you, for two, they involved me, stepping to you, knowing I'm with you. Basically, I was put in it. Don't holler later though, that I involved myself in something that had nothing to do with me, because you involved me. Like with Lon and Vamp being from Hoover. I can't get involved in Hoover business. I fucks with you outside of Hoover business though and I'm with you, I'm in it. Just like if it's a homie from the set, internal, I'm not getting involved, external. It is what it is. Dudes pushing up on some turned up shit, live, camera, action! First and foremost, you're involving me and I don't know what you're up to, or what you're out to do. You brought your issue where I was. If you had an issue with either, you could've saw them elsewhere. By coming where I am, you're involving me. Fuck all of that "He shouldn't have got involved" when you came where I was to get at a Niggah or a Niggah I fuck with. You involved me! It's right and a wrong time for everything. That just can't happen. You didn't want me involved, you should have handled your business somewhere else, other than where I was, because you're putting me in a position whether I wanted to be in it or not. Basically, taking away my choice. For all I know, you're planning on doing something to me too. We'll figure it out later. If you didn't know or didn't overstand, you do now. Right is right, wrong is wrong. This is my mindset and my position on it. My boy Keetay from the Bay told me the same thing about Lil Tray Deee as K.C. had spoke highly of Brody from when he met him at Corcoran.

Keetay had his points go up to level 4 points and Solano was of course a level 3, so they shot him up out of there. Although there were dudes there with far more points than him, they just wanted him gone basically. He ended up at Corcoran. I could've swore though, the homie went to Tracy, but shit, Niggah's get audible in the middle of the play all of the time. Once Lil Tray Deee told him where he was from, Long Beach Insane Youngs, he told the homie he knew me and spoke highly of me and Tray Deee told him I was his Brody.

Tray Deee also told him once he got back to Solano to give me a hug for him and to let me know he sends his love and respect. He'd done just that. When he got back to Solano on the yard and saw me, he walked over to me and gave me a hug. "That's from your brother and he sends his love and respect." Keetay was like, "I just left your brother, Lil Tray Deee!"

I was like, "Yeah, that's Brody right there." A couple of weeks after that, I ended up in the sandbox for the sticking. The next time I saw Keetay was when I was in 9-building, which was the sandbox overflow building.

Me and Brody stay communicating through moms, who adopted him as her god son. She's been fucking with Brody since 08-09. They write each other and he calls her and they talk on the phone. She's always telling me, "Darren wrote me" or "Darren called me and he sends his Love and Respect". I send mine back his way. We were writing each other through her, but the police got up on it and I guess told moms to 86 (stop) the three way communication, so she stopped it and just started passing verbals. That or she'll tell me something he wanted me to know in her dots and dashes to me.

I'm always aware of his location and what he's up to and vice versa. Me and Brody were talking about the homie Deaf Tony (RIP) one day in the cell and I had told him about Lil Goodie, the homie from the set. How we were at the BG homie Budda's house on the north side off of Tehachapi and Orange at the meeting. We've had a few BG meetings at the homie's spot. At Vet's Park, King's Park, in a vacant apartment where the homie Bubba was a manager on 23rd and Locust, across the street from where my BM lived with my kids. So we're at the meeting, Ace Capone, Budda, Tiny Laid, Baldie, Ace, Lil Spit, T Mac, Tumac, T Dog,

I.C., Hobo, Lil Goodie, and Big Croft. I think Hog Dog was there as well, along with Bay Bay and Baby Meech.

I'm looking at Lil Goodie kind of sideways. Ace Capone caught it. The homie stayed instigating some shit, "Sup Tic cuz, you tripping?"

"Yeah, I'm not feeling the situation with Deaf Tony. How cuz just leave the homie when the Enemigos came through bussing and the homie got smoked?"

Homies that didn't know started looking around, "Who?"

I'm like, "This Niggah, Lil Goodie!"

"You got a problem with cuz?" This is Big Ace Capone asking me this.

"Hell Yeah I got a problem with cuz!"

Lil Goodie stated explaining how the homie got left, then here goes Ace Capone, "Cuz, if you're tripping and got an issue with cuz, we can take it to the statue!" The statue of Martin Luther King Jr. is in Kings Park in the set.

I'm like, "Bet (let's go)!"

Lil Spit was like, "Anything else we need to holler about?"

Everyone looks around at eachother and shakes their heads. "Aight. We're at the statue then." The meeting was a wrap. We head for our swoops, leaving the garage. Once everyone pulled up in the parking lot and had gotten out of their swoops, we post up, blowing blunts, talking, and waiting for Goodie to pull up and waiting and waiting and waiting and waiting and waiting!

We ended up waiting for a couple of hours, then ended up going to the Highway Center Liquor Store, getting some drink and more blunts. We just posted up at the statue, talking, blowing, and drinking. Goodie never showed up, nor did he pop up at another BG meeting and we've had several after that night. I was telling Tray Deee too about a meeting we had at the park in the day light hours. Normally though we just had night meetings and mostly at Budda's. I'm on my way one day to a meeting up at King's Park, leaving the Ave. I see the homie Ray Bone and tell him the homies are up at the park, and it's a meeting. I don't know why I just assumed he was a BG at the time but I did. Apparently not though.

Me and the homie together push to the park. We're kind of deep too. As we get into the park where the BG homies were, a few were like, "What's cuz doing here BG?"

Talking to me, another homie was like, "Cuz ain't a BG. He fuck with Big Homies! He's one of them!"

I'm like, "My bad, cuz!" Ray Bone turned around and bounced.

When I saw the homie in the County, he brought it up, "Cuz, that was fucked up that day you had me come to ya'll meeting and homies were tripping."

I'm like, "Shit Niggah, I thought you were BG all the time!" but then again, I should've though when have Ray Bone ever been to a BG meeting. Duh (SMH)!

He spoke on it again when I saw him a second time in Tehachapi, "This Niggah Tic is burnt the fuck out. Had me coming to a BG meeting at the park!"

Tray Dee started laughing, "Yeah, that was some crazy ass shit Tic. You set him up for that."

I started laughing, "Shit, I didn't know. I just assumed!" He asked me was Ray Bone in his feelings about the situation. I was like, "Nah, he didn't act like he was. We were clowning about it."

I asked the homie if he knew or have met T Bone from Santa Block or Skillet from 4 Corner Block (Foe Corner). I think he knew who T Bone was because T Bone ran with and fucked with homies tough, as if he was a homie, from my overstanding. I never knew of him. I was told he was from Santa. His name was T Bone and he fucked with homies tough, though he was from Santana. Skillet, the homie didn't know, period. Skillet dipped in and out of the set. He was messing with some bitch off of 19th Street and Olive, or Lime, I can't remember. I met both T Bone and Skillet through I.C.

T Bone and I.C. were Road Dogs. Before I started fucking with I.C>, when I got out of the pen, T Bone had went to the pen and had popped back up and had been coming around. I instantly saw the switch up with I.C. I wasn't tripping though. I severed ties and done it moving, "Fuck you Niggahs!" I wasn't feeling him, nor did I like him. Wasn't my type of dude. What me and I.C> had going business wise was a wrap. We just went our separate ways. I didn't really like T Bone or Skillet, but based on them being I.C.'s boys, I fucked with them, keeping it respectful and on some cordial shit, since they were around, but nah, I wasn't feeling them like that. Backing up off of I.C. was an easy call. I was cool and I couldn't do the company he kept. I didn't trust T Bone or Skillet. I.C. ended up going to jail, catching a dope case. The spot on 20th and Myrtle ended up getting the back and front door kicked in. The police raided, but not before Niggahs ate good. Us being tight by that time was dunzo and we were tight. Since I've been gone though, I've heard he'd had my name in his mouth, speaking on some shit he knows nothing about. He is speaking on me, but the homies had a lot to say about him. That should've been his concern, what he had going on, not me. We weren't even fucking with eachother when I left the streets in '04.

Why was I even in your mouth? You damn sure wasn't in mine. I didn't fuck with you. So what would be the reason? Truth be told, I was the reason homies didn't get at you long ago. Out of respect for me and out of love for me they didn't run you (go in your pockets). Most of the homies felt you were arrogant, too arrogant and funny acting. Then, to top it off, you're not even a Long Beach Niggah! It makes sense. I'd often wondered why I never saw you anywhere. School, park, around the set, I'm talking about as a kid, you're around my age. I never ran across you as a teen, never bumped into you in Juvenile Hall, nowhere, you just popped up.

When I got locked up, the homies got at him an few years later. When I talked to the homie Gangster Ace, he gave me the scoop. He told me the homies jacked him and robbed his clothing store he had gotten after I left the streets and he was ran up out of the set, on the streets, and voted off the island (SMH).

Worried about me though, don't concern yourself with me, champ. The homie talked about, "This dude bad. Now when I holler at homies, it's a clown session. Yah boy this, Yah boy that!"

"He's not my boy!"

"Cuz not official. He was never official." This is what I'm hearing and have heard. I was told him and his cousin are Orange County Niggahs. I never tripped. I fucked with him because he fucked with my folks (a family member) and had kids with her. Even if I didn't know you or mess with you, I should've or would've ran across you at some point, somewhere, coming up. I've been in The Beach all my life. Never laid eyes on him. I ran nothing but Long Beach Streets, especially the East Side! I've lived on Anaheim and Walnut coming up, Anaheim and Warren, California and Salt Lake. Before it was Martin Luther King it was California.

I've lived on 19th and Lewis, New York and Lewis, 9th and Olive, 10th and Cerritos, Hill and Lewis, Magnolia and 20th, 20th and Cerritos, and PCH and Pine. Growing up, I went to King's Park, Cal Rec Park, and Mac Arthur Park. I've been to Vets Park as a kid only a hand full of times. As for elementary schools, I attended Whittier Elementary, Lincoln Elementary, Signal Hill Elementary, and Cubberly Elementary. I've never been to C.I.S. (College Intermediate School) or Stevenson Elementary. I went to Washington Jr. High, Bancroft Jr. High, Franklin Jr. High, and Jefferson Jr. High. Then I was kicked out of regular Jr. Highs and had to like probation school. I went to the Learning Center on Pacific and 20th, then I went to another one another time, downtown Long Beach on Broadway in an old ass building on the 4th floor.

I didn't really do High School because I was constantly in and out of the Halls, L.P. and Central. Then, I finally landed in Y.A. I never laid eyes on him. I though all along he was a homie-homie (a real homie) though never questioned it. It's funny though how a Niggah can speak on me, but not on the shit he had going on. The fucked up thing is I've never spoke foul or nothing about this dude because we had been straight. Our difference was small. We fucked with eachother. I still wasn't tripping off of him, knowing too he knew Situation was fucking with the dude I caught her at the motel with and he was hanging out with them both in the Carmelitos. The dude I caught her with and his boy, T Bone, are both from Santana. They're homies. He don't think I know this though. She don't either. I knew the whole time, just never spoke on it until now. So, it was never a secret, at least not from me. What's crazy about that, I.C. hung out with her deceased husband and knew him. Knew her too back when they were together. His boy T Bone, her husband, and Ole Boy she was fucking after he died, hung out. I.C. and Situation never let on they knew eachother or had been around eachother. The joke was on me. It's good though, I'm not tripping it at all. I don't fuck with either of them.

You can be peace in my ear, or someone in my past. It is what it is. I asked Lil Tray Deee do he empty his banger when he's on a mission. I can't remember what his response was, but I think he said he does, can't say for certain. I know I told him I didn't. I've always left 2 bullets (get off me bullets) at least in my pistol just in case shit get tricky. You never know or think someone will pop out of nowhere until unexpectedly, getting off on you, Bloom! Bloom! Bloom! As you're trying to leave the area on foot, trying to clear a block. I know from experience, shit can get tricky. I've shot all 17 rounds, emptying my shit, and was leaving the scene on foot, running and damn near out of breath, when a mutha fuc-ka came from behind a van.

I didn't even see him. He got off like three or four shots. Damn near got me. "TIIIIC, WAAATCH OUUUT!" From that day forward, I never emptied shit. I kept my "get off mes" (bullets). That shit had me shook up. At least I can send something back, "Bloom Bloom Bloom! Back your ass up! Get off me!" I was still tripping off of being back in Cali-pat. It's been years since I'd been there. I was there on my first term on D-yard. I was a E number back then, E02459. That was when I caught my case with the homie Big Dan Dog in 1990. I went to the pen and he was sent to Y.A. I forgot how much time he'd done or got, but I had 14 years and 8 months, only supposed to do half.

7 years and 4 months, but you know how that goes. You're going to catch more time, especially back then. There were a lot of time bomb situations. It was the 90's. Me and the homie were jackers (robbers). We stayed on jacking sprees. We were out there jacking like a mutha fucka! I was on the same shit when I went to Y.A. and had gotten locked up in 88. Back then I was messing with my boy, Jackpot from Grape Street, Terry from Hard Time Hustlers, my boy Mike from Palmer Block, and John John from Mona Park. We were on our spree shit.

Me, Mike, Jackpot, and Terry was caught up. Terry didn't do any time. It doesn't take a rocket scientists to know what happened. He talked! He was pressured up (SMH)! Me and Mike went to Y.A. being that we were minors. Jackpot was grown so he was sent to the pen, but yeah, Terry horse played! Jackpot was given 4 years, me and Mike took 3 years. we had to take the 3 in order for Jackpot to get the 4. It was a package deal. Jackpot couldn't get that deal unless me and Mike went along with the script and we were charged as adults, hence I got my prison number E02459 in '88 at 16 years old.

If we didn't take the deal, it was a wrap for Jackpot. They were trying to jam him up. Me and Mike were like, "Fuck it!" and took the deal so Jackpot wouldn't get fucked over. They were on his head. His attorney came to talk to Me and Mike, "We need you guys to do x, y, z to help him out."

"No problem!"

My boy Dallas came out of the cell. We were on our way to Chow Hall. When he came out, he pulled up on me and slid me something to blow, then went back to this cell. He didn't go to Chow Hall. He rarely ate in there. Certain times he would though.

As soon as me and Brody came back from breakfast, we blew, then kicked back and waited for yard. As always, when we went to the yard, we dapped a few hands, spoke to a few dudes, and headed for the slab to workout. The same way me and H.L. do here, me and Brody's daily routine never change. It remained consistent the whole time. The 20's were on the yard. We hollered at them, Pep, Beenie Boy, C Bone, and Big Sag. There was another one but I forgot homie's name. I heard though he had gotten out and was smoked a few weeks later. That happened to the homie Sinbad from the set too. He wasn't out that long and had gotten smoked. I don't know the dynamics behind homies from 20's, but I know Sinbad was smoked behind a bitch. Just before I heard about homie from 20's being smoked, I heard the homie Big Cass had gotten smoked, then the homie Big Tic Toc. Both homies (I.I.P.).

The last time I saw Big Tic Toc was when I sold him a copy of my Bitterology C.D. at the 76 gas station on Stanley and Anaheim. I saw Big Cass last on the Ave before I was gaffled (locked up). The Dodge Citys were on the yard. This was before T Loc and Flash left for the incident with Wash. T Loc was basically the catalyst to the bullshit between us and them. He stayed getting into conflicts with dudes because he has no filter on his mouth, talking shit and being disrespectful. That's no bueno! It started on C-yard. When he was over there, I was over there too, on the yard. Dudes would come to the homies like, "Look, we know cuz push with Long Beach, so we're coming to ya'll. He's doing x, y, z and he's loose with his mouth, talking real reckless!"

The homies tried talking to T Loc, but then he got on some bullshit like, "I'm from Dodge City! Ya'll can't tell me shit. I'm not from Long Beach. Ya'll aren't my homies!"

"True that. We aren't your homies, but at the same time you're pushing with the car. You're pushing with the homies. If you feel you don't have to abide by the same guide lines, beat it! Do you!" Thinking you don't have to fall under the same script, that's out. If it applies to us as a collective, it applies to you as well, period, especially if you're pushing with us. If you don't want to listen, fuck you, you're on your own and don't come looking for support from the homies when your mouth gets you in a wreck. He had a couple of incidents on C-yard and then one of B-yard. With the incident on B-yard, he runs to his homies and tells them whatever he tells them, rightfully so.

It gets back to us and mind you, we're supposed to be pushing to-gether as a car. Dodge Citys basically told him "Fuck them Niggahs. You don't have to listen to them. You're from Dodge City. They're not your homies. We are and you can keep playing basket ball if you want to. You don't have to stay off of the court!" The line was drawn in the mud. Now we're feeling some type of way, but cool, do ya'll. Me and the homies Lil Tray Deee, Ray Dog, and Chewy are straight. Took a position. We basically told T Loc to stay off of the basketball court, because that's where he kept having issues and being reckless with his mouth. We basically felt we had that right to get at him, because they were pushing with us. Him and his homies felt differently. Cool!

When we got and really overstood what they were on, we were like, "Cool, fuck all of you Niggahs on this yard!" The 20's and the rest of the Beach remained messing with them, except me, Lil Tray Deee, Ray Dog, and Chewy. We drew the line in the mud after they took it there. The other homies embraced them and were cool with whatever they had going on and dapped them. We would keep moving. We had nothing to say to them dudes, didn't even acknowledge them. We kept our distance. I can only imagine what was being said behind our backs between the Dodge Citys, Osama, M.D., C Bone, Pep, and Beenie Boy. I don't think G Boy was on no shit like that. You never know though. When it's all said and done, yeah, we're LBC in here, but on the streets, we're all enemies and we beef.

The north side dudes, mainly Osama and M.D., were tripping off of Chewy not wanting to move to 5-building with them so they could do their North Side thing. He was cool with staying in 3-building with me, and Lil Tray Deee. We were chilling and staying out of the way and he saw how cool we were. We embraced him and pulled him into our little circle. He ate with us, blew with us, and drunk with us. They tried telling the homie Chewy, Me, and Lil Tray Deee would turn on him, because we were from Insane and aren't his homies. "You know how those Insanes get down. They're scandalous!" He told them me and Lil Tray Deee are straight and he fuck with us. We've shown him nothing but LBC love. They were feeling some type of way, but Chewy didn't leave 3-building, he stayed posted with us. What could they do though?

He was cool where he was, which was in 3 with us. What's crazy though, Chewy went S.N.Y. some years later. I don't know what happened. I just know that's where he is. Me, Tray Deee, and Chewy were on the yard every day with eachother and then when Ray Dog hit the yard, he was with us. That was our crew, Tray Deee, Chewy, Ray Dog, and me.

One day we were on the yard, the Hub Bub (Comptons) and Neighborhoods got into it on the yard, on the basketball court. I can't remember who got on who first, if the Comptons got on a Neighborhood or if the Neighborhoods got on a Compton. What I do remember though, they were able to line it up (fight head up, two at a time). Two go in the small hallway, do their thing, and two come out. Two more go in, two come out, until everyone got their issue. One thing about Calipat, certain police would let you get your issue. If you had a problem or if it was a problem, it can get handled without all of the extras and everyone kept it G (gangster).

A certain building would let you get in the upper middle shower, because it was bigger and had a lot of room to move around in. You go in there with your guy and squabble up. The doors closed and locked behind you. After you finish, it's opened and you go your way, early in the A.M. That kept shit suuuper respectful. Dudes knew if it was an issue you could get that out of the way. One morning me and Brody were up early, blowing on some trees, when our older Damu boy, Esto from Bounty Hunger, slid through. He was a porter (What up though, Esto). We let him hit it a few times. While he was at our door talking to us, we hear a couple of doors pop open. He was like, "What the fuck!" He quickly turns around to look and see what the deal was.

We look too and see two Crip homies heading upstairs to the middle shower, which we could see clearly from our cell.

They go in the shower, closing the door behind them and squabble up. After they were done, the door popped back open, they came out and went back to their cell. Esto would come through every morning with his grumpy old ass, fucking with me and Brody. Esto would come and lean up against the door with his broom. He didn't drink or smoke cigarettes.

I ended up running into Esto again at Solano six years later. He left Solano shortly after seeing him. He was there for a few months. He would clown me and Brody, because he said we drank a lot. He would pull up to the cell and be like, "What's up with you and that drunk Tic?" or "What's up with ya'll drunk ass Niggahs?" He had gotten into his feelings with us one time, because he had had a young homie in the cell with him who drank and we got him white boy wasted. It's not our fault he couldn't hang with the big dogs and went into the cell and tore Esto's shelves he had made down off the wall, falling into shit and he threw up everywhere. He had Esto pistol hot! Then he hit me and Brody with "Ya'll mutha fuckas ain't shit!" He was already talking about putting him out with his grump ass self!

He didn't like his cell program. Anyway, he was looking for a reason to give him the boot. Keeping it a thousand, Esto didn't like nobody's cell program but his own. His old ass went through a lot of cellies. "Nah uh, you gotta go!"

My boy Esto was a cold piece of work and would fire your shit up quick (hit you). He slapped one of his Damu homies hard as fuck in the face on the yard. Young homie didn't want no smoke (no problem) with Esto, and he came with the aggressive turn down, a way of saying I don't want to fight, but without saying the words (SMH). "Niggah, you slapped me, that's out!" He accepted that and went on about his way. He didn't want no problem after that, at all! I thought I was grump old cuz! I have nothing on Grumpy Old Blood! Oh yeah, Esto, I'm still making pies too, from when you showed me.

G Boy was running around on the yard on some funny shit. Me and Brody were tripping off of him. He was acting standoffish towards us and being distant. We wanted to know what he was on, so we pulled up on him, "Cuz, what are you on? You tripping or something?"

He was like, "Nah, it's nothing like that. I'm just doing me. I'll tap in. I'm doing me."

He would mess with other dudes, but wouldn't really mess with the homies. We weren't so much as tripping off of that. Do what you do, tap in though. Even if we weren't feeling a homie or homies, we'd still tap in and then push. It just makes for good relations. We weren't fucking with the Dodge Citys, period. It was no bueno! They were already on the funny shit, so it was an easy call. The main thing we heard was, "Insanes think the run shit. This Dodge City!" Ok, cool. We don't and didn't have a problem with that, none of that. We were tripping off of T Loc running around, getting into it with Niggahs and felt it was cool. Dudes were coming to us with the bullshit. On some real Niggah shit, it wasn't like he was going up, what he was doing was a lot of pump faking, acting like he wanted problems but really didn't. He didn't want no smoke, just talking, involving us.

At the end of the day, he was pushing with Long Beach, therefore we had that right to say something to him, due in part because if something would've happened we had to go with him, based on we were trying to prevent the bullshit before the bullshit came into play. Niggahs took it somewhere else though. The tension stayed kind of high on the yard between us. They weren't feeling us, we weren't feeling them. If we were with the other homies and they stopped to dap and holler at the, we kept going. If we saw the homies at the fence hollering at them, we'd stay on the slab, letting them finish before we went to greet the homies. It remained that way for weeks. We would pass each other on some "Fuck you" type shit.

Me and Brody had been talking about the whole little situation between us and them dudes. As I said, it all stemmed from T Loc and his shenanigans, and them feeling like we were trying to run something. Far from the case, homie. If it had been one of ours, he would've been hollered at the same way. If he would've kept it up, he would've been DP'ed. The mathematics are just that simple. You're not about to be running around on the yard horse playing and getting homies caught up, that's out! Oh for certain the business will get handled, if that's the case, but after the fact, the homie has an issue coming to him for putting us in that situation. We know how this shit supposed to go. As we know how it's going to end. In order to keep it real, you have to be real. This shits been brewing for weeks. It was bound to come to a boiling point. It wouldn't take too much more pressure. There was no type of communication whatsoever. There was no dialogue or nothing. No one was trying to talk or resolve the tension. Those other dudes, as far as we were concerned, wanted us to clash with the Dodge Citys so they could get rid of me and Brody, especially the Northside dudes.

The difference between them and us, they downplayed shit and we didn't. We reacted to shit they weren't comfortable with. A lot of shit that went on was kept form us and was handled without us ever knowing until it was settled. According to some, I was the trouble maker and had Brody pressing shit. Nah, that wasn't how it was. The truth of the matter, if it was an issue, our approach was to deal with it head on. Me and the homie pressed and Niggahs didn't like it. Dudes in 5-building would have shit going on and me and Brody wouldn't hear shit until it got resolved or it was swept under the rug. "Oh, you know, such and such happened, but it got token care of."

We're hearing it for the first time, like, "Whaaaat? When did that happen?"

"Oh, weeks ago!"

"Wow!"

We were in the blind, like when Coast Boy and Tiny Snoop had something going on. We get wind after bloodshed and they were gone off the yard to the sandbox. They would literally keep shit from us. They didn't want us taking it where we were going to take it. I guess they felt we would've fucked up what they had going on, but we played how we were supposed to. If it's an issue, lets address it. There's only so much diplomacy or compromise. What couldn't be said was we were on some bullshit. We kept it clean at all times. They really weren't liking the fact we were a bit too aggressive, feeling as though we would rock the boat, and dudes might go overboard and have to swim. Now I get it. They didn't want us messing up what they had going on and didn't want to lose shit.

So that was why we were kept in the dark and shit was kept from us. One some real shit, if shit would've happened, it would've been behind them and what they had going on. Me, Brody, and Chewy were out of the way. We stayed to ourselves. We didn't have no type of issues or drama. Ray Dog had barely gotten there. He wasn't there long enough to have issues or drama going on. Besides, he was out of the way too. Dudes didn't want to be held accountable either for shit, hence shit was simply swept under the carpet. "It's good. We took care of it" or "It's straight!" because we wanted to keep it a thousand, we were the problem, the trouble makers, and the bad guys.

That's what dudes do when you're pushing how you're supposed to. Look for a person to say, "You're on some bullshit" or "You're on some extra shit!" I've never been an extra Niggah, nor have I ever been a bully. I don't fuck over people if I can. I don't press dudes that I know or feel I can press. That's not who I am or what I'm about. If we got into it and I see you're not trying to take it there, I'm going to leave it alone. What do I look like, trying to press the situation when clearly that's not where you're trying to go (SMH)?

I don't take advantage if I see a dudes weak and I'm stronger than he is. It's just not my demonstration. That's like, if I got something from you and I owe you and I told you I'll have it for you when I come out of my cell, I'm going to have that for you, period. Even if you're weak, considered soft, or called a buster. I'm going to pay you because I gave you my word, whereas other dudes would be like, "You shouldn't have paid him. I wouldn't have. He's a bitch. He's a buster. He wasn't going to do shit if you didn't pay him." That's not me though, who I am or what I'm about. Plus, I'm a firm believer in karma. You don't just fuck over people because you can, just for the fuck of it.

Though I overstand where they are as I overstand the predator and the prey mentality. Predators do what they do. They're just being predators, preying on the weak. They're doing what they're allowed to do. That's still not my get down. If we're supposed to be some real Niggahs, let's be real Niggahs. You have your version, I have my version of it. I'm the same me though, wherever I go. I don't switch up, or change up, because I'm certain dudes or around a certain dude. I'm the same me as I'm never going to be who I'm not. I wouldn't be me acting like the next dude. I can't walk in your boots. We don't wear the same boot size. I'm only an 8. My views, thoughts, and opinions are my own, as my values and morals are. When you're in tuned, it brings a different kind of energy and awareness. Most of the problems in our world (yard life) are because of two reasons. We act without thinking, or we keep thinking without acting. A dudes character is essentially the sum of a dudes habits.

For those though with a lot of faces, pick one and stick with it. On these yards, perception is often very skewed by self justification, selfish desires, or the influence of those around us, which I've come to overstand. We simply don't know and will never know the true motivation of a dude, the real truth about a circumstance, or facts of a situation based on all you can do is do and be you, staying on top of your shit. Be accountable for how you push and how you navigate your way. Analyze what needs to be analyzed, consider everything thoroughly, and seek to fully overstand it before responding. Remain vigilant with being security conscious. Stay toned down. You have to be a part of the shadow, moving like a cat. You don't have to stand out or be heard. Personally, I'd rather be felt than heard or seen.

I weigh all odds. If I stand to lose more than I stand to gain, I'm going with the odds. You can't burn down a house to kill one single roach. I'm always mindful. You have to be in this life, especially when you can overstand and see shit for what and as it is. You open up to a different way of thinking. It's all about being structured and having structure. I've come to overstand, no one can become strong without things like adversity, drama, resistance, and problems. These are all struggles that make our inner selves grown stronger. In addition to that overstanding, I've come to overstand it's never good to show your emotions so strong, especially when the answers are uncertain. You could make an enemy that wasn't there before.

It's not like making an enemy is hard to do though. You can have an enemy having never had an interaction with him. He can only hurt you though by the shit you allow him to know. I've always had this, speak how

I feel, do how I feel mentality and at the same time, I'm still conscious of the consequences. Even though I'm walking around on yards, I'm still focused on my vision, making my challenges, temporary, but my vision permanent. A man that's not prepared for anything can only be prepared for failure.

17

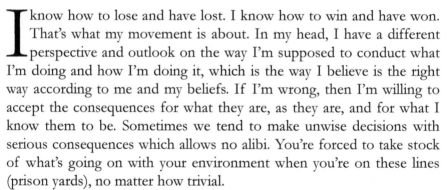

I know how to lose and have lost. I know how to win and have won. That's what my movement is about. In my head, I have a different perspective and outlook on the way I'm supposed to conduct what I'm doing and how I'm doing it, which is the way I believe is the right way according to me and my beliefs. If I'm wrong, then I'm willing to accept the consequences for what they are, as they are, and for what I know them to be. Sometimes we tend to make unwise decisions with serious consequences which allows no alibi. You're forced to take stock of what's going on with your environment when you're on these lines (prison yards), no matter how trivial.

Anything less is a misoverstanding and you're horse playing. The day it went up with the Dodge Citys, Me, Lil Tray Deee, Chewy, and Ray Dog were all together. We were walking around the track on the yard. I don't recall us working out that day. We were just basically walking in circles around the yard. Wasn't much of anything going on. We weren't high, nor had we drunk anything. We were sober as fuck. We had tapped in with the homies as soon as we hit the yard, as always, before we got into doing what we do. C Bone was out there, Pep was at work in the kitchen, G Boy was out on the yard, I believe Beenie Boy was on the yard too.

I don't remember seeing Big Sag, Coast Boy, or Tiny Snoop out there. They could've been. Thinking back though, Tiny Snoop and Coast Boy could've been gone off of the yard already. They had gotten into their issue a week or so before, behind a gadget we find out they went half on with two outsiders who they fought with at breakfast time. Me and Brody saw the blood on the ground and a beanie in front of 5-building walking to chow hall that very morning it happened. Me and Brody tried getting to the bottom of the situation with the homies Coast Boy and Tiny Snoop, but it was handled, wink-wink. As Brody, Me, Chewy, and Ray Dog walked around the yard, we'd pass Goon and Baby Crip from Dodge City a few times. You can feel the tension was up. Each time we passed eachother we just stared at eachother. Nothing was said. The mean mugging that went on said enough. At some point we stopped walking around the track and were smoking up against the curb. I was standing on it. We were clowning and chopping it up, having a few laughs. Goon and Baby Crip passed us a couple of times. When they made a third pass, they were walking at bit slower and just as they were passing, Baby Crip turned around. The homie Ray Dog was standing closest to him. Lil Tray Deee was standing next to Ray Dog, then Chewy. They were all standing on the track, up against the curb. I'm next to Chewy, standing on the curb.

The look on Boon's face, he wasn't feeling what was apparently about to happen. I saw it. He wasn't feeling it at all. At the end of the day, however it was going to play out, he had to ride with his homie, right or wrong, regardless. I think we all felt the conversation coming. It was premeditated.

Ray Dog spoke first, "Sup cuz?"

Baby Crip responded, "Sup with it cuz?"

Then Ray Dog was like, "What you Niggahs on?"

Baby Crip responded back aggressively, "Whatever you Niggahs on!"

Goon never spoke a word, nor did he show any signs of aggression. He just stood next to Baby Crip as he talked. I didn't doubt where the situation was going and it was going somewhere fast.

All I knew though was if it was cracking, I was cracking. The homies was like, "Insane Crip!"

Baby Crip responded, "Dodge City Crip!"

It went from zero to go real quick after Ray Dog hollered out, "Fuck Dodge City!" and fired on Baby Crip. They immediately started squabbling up. Somehow me and Brody ended up on Baby Crip, and Ray Dog and Chewy ended up on Goon. We were getting it in, in front of 5-building. The alarm started going off. You can hear it and know the police are running from the buildings. We never stopped.

"GEEETTT DOOOWWWN!" We still didn't stop.

"GEEETTT DOOOWWWN!" Still going.

"GEEETTT DOOOWWWN!" Still didn't stop.

"GET THE FUCK DOWN! Bloom! Bloom!" I'm shot in the back by the police with the block gun. I go down and get back up. Brody and Baby Crip continued fighting. I get sprayed in the face with mace along with Brody and Baby Crip.

"GET THE FUCK DOWN! Bloom!" I hear another shot, then another one, then the smoke grenade. The thick white smoke instantly started choking us. I go down again and the second time I stay down. The smoke and chemicals took its toll on me and was fucking with my breathing. Mind you, I'm asthmatic. As Brody and Baby Crip continued to fight, another smoke grenade was thrown and had landed next to me as I was on the ground, coughing up my lungs. I have white powder all over me, all in my face, on my head, and on my clothes, plus I'm sprayed the fuck up! I'm on the ground, gagging, coughing, snot running from my nose, and that mace has me on fire!

I can hear a lot of gagging and coughing around me, but can't see. My eyes are closed because they're burning from the mace and smoke. I think Chewy and Ray Dog were already down too. Tray Deee and Baby Crip were finally down. They were the last ones to get down. We were all powdered and sprayed up. I know my back was hurting and stinging. I was hit in the back at close range with the block gun. The goon squad finally descends on the scene, putting up their yellow tape, cones, and numbers. They made their perimeter as they started their processing and investigation, which surprised me, because no weapons were used. Normally they don't come for melees unless there were weapons involved.

At the time, we didn't know G Boy got in it. He wasn't even near us or with us. We don't know where G Boy came from. We just saw he was there and had been cuffed along with us. Somehow C Bone got cuffed too and was in the perimeter with us. We didn't know where he came from or how he ended up where he was. He started yelling at the goon squad, "Why ya'll got me? I didn't have nothing to do with that. I'm from Long Beach 20's (SMH)!"

I heard it like the whole yard heard it. He was like 15 feet away from me and I know what I heard, even if I have one bad ear. Yeah, as a kid I'd done some dumb shit, putting a pencil in my ear and lead broke off, fucking up my ear drum. I can hear out of it, not as good though. According to my mama, I have selective hearing.

As for C Bone though, he ended up taking that walk of shame on some unrelated event that occurred at another spot. In my mind, dudes were supposed to be coming to the sandbox behind us for getting on C Bone for that outburst! It wasn't like it wasn't heard. The whole yard heard it. I ran into someone years later that was there who asked me, "What was that about with C Bone?" As for anyone else though except for those dudes, C Bone would've been DP'ed as soon as the yard resumed. Off of the dribble, he would've been voted off the island.

"Where do they do that at?" he kept saying, "I didn't have nothing to do with it. I'm from 20's!" He wouldn't stop saying it.

I'm saying to myself, "Niggah, shut the fuck up!" As I'm sure everyone else was saying to themselves (SMH). They heard you! Everyone heard you! I'm still gagging and coughing, laying on my stomach. A medical technician that had just walked on the yard saw me and knew me, heard me coughing and gagging, seeing snot running from my nose, as well as all of the powder and spray on me, yelled at the police, "He has asthma. Get him to medical now!"

The goon squad wasn't trying to have it. They were like, "Fuck that. Leave him right there. He's a part of our scene. We're taking photos, this, that, and the third." I was immediately picked up off the ground and we're being walked to medical. My I.D. and a paper the police wrote on were put in my place on the ground next to a cone with a number on it which they took pictures of. After I was inside of medical and had gotten decontaminated, I was put inside of a holding cell/waiting cell, being locked in. Tray Deee, Chewy, and Ray Dog were still outside on the ground.

I still didn't know G Boy was involved until he came inside of medical with Tray Deee, Chewy, and Ray Dog. After t hey were decontaminated too, they were put in the cell with me and locked in. At first it was a lot of confusion with the police, as to them trying to figure out was it cool for them to put the homies in the cell with me.

"Nah, they can come in here with me. They're homies."

"You sure?"

"Hell yeah!"

Since I hadn't took captured moments outside with everyone else, the goon squad came into medical and took a few of me, mainly my gang tats. After they left medical, we started talking. First thing out of my mouth though was "Did ya'll hear this Niggah C Bone?"

Chewy and Ray Dog said they heard him. "Hell yeah we heard that Niggah!" Yeah, because I knew I wasn't hearing shit and my ears weren't deceiving me.

I don't recall if Tray Deee said he heard it or not. I'm sure he had though. The incident happened at morning yard and we got to the sandbox later in the day. We were stripped out in the shower, then gave our sandbox issue shoes, clothes, and a bed roll with a fish kit (spoon, plastic comb, pen filler, toilet paper, blank paper, and soap). Then, we were put in orientation cells. Me and Brody were cellies and Ray Dog and Chewy were cellies. G Boy was in the cell by himself. After a few days, we were put into regular cells. We stayed in that second cell about two weeks and then moved upstairs on the top tier. We moved next door to Bear from Gear Gang and Capone from U.G. Rolling 100's. Biscuit from Neighborhood 40's was on the other side of us, next door to our left. When we were downstairs we were next door to May May and K.O. from 60's. A South Sider was on the other side of us.

G Boy was upstairs with us on the same tier, a few doors down, with an old Crip homie, 8 Ball from Watts. I think he was from Grape Street, not sure. I do know he's from Watts though. The homie Young Dirty Boy from the set was on the tier with us too, a couple of doors down from G Boy and 8 Ball. Goon and Baby Crip were on the tier too, a little further down the tier. When me and Brody would pass their cell going to the shower, they would be on their cell door, mean mugging us. A few times we had passed, Baby Crip would be on some disrespectful shit. we never responded to him. We just kept it moving. Respond for what? He was taking it personal. We weren't. They were acting cool with G Boy though, telling him he was keeping bad company and we weren't cool. They weren't tripping off of him. It's us. Then they turn around and ask him could they see his incident report. When he sent it to them, they locked up in it (kept it). We could hear him asking for it. He never got it back from them and had to get another one from the counselor (SMH). We stayed in the sandbox for three months and some change, then we were sent to our next destination, Kern Valley. Ray Dog and Chewy were sent to Corcoran.

I think G Boy too was sent to Corcoran. Baby Crip and Goon were sent to Salinas Valley. Initially, me and Brody were supposed to go there, but they endorsed them there, so we couldn't and were keep aways. Brody left the sandbox before me, going to Delano (Kern Valley), so I ended up in the cell with G Boy on some compact shit. 8 Ball had left. It was good. I wasn't tripping and felt comfortable. I didn't have a problem moving with the young homie. Me and G Boy would chop it up a lot too, about all types of shit. He was filling me in on a lot of what was going on in 5-building and what was being said. A lot of it though, me and Brody had figured out, putting it together like a puzzle. He confirmed what we'd suspected.

What me and Brody had suspected all along about those dudes, we knew they weren't feeling us. It wasn't a big ole deal! Either way, I know I didn't give a damn about who didn't like me or feel me. I'm not one of those dudes that needs to be liked or felt. A Niggah don't have to fuck with me. I fuck with me! I'm cool with me and I like me. I like who's staring back at me in the mirror too, solid Niggah! You know what? Dudes can feel or say what they want, because like a G homie once told me, "A Niggahs going to always respect your violence." Dudes will say fuck you, but telling everyone but you. The heart carries the feet homie! But then when you get to the essence of who the characters and auto-bots are, you can overstand the mindset. You shouldn't expect anything less. Keep giving me promo though, I don't exist without you. Yeah, and since good deeds don't go unpunished, I'm not cool with dudes as I once was. G Boy turned out to be straight, a real cool dude. We've never really kicked it or talked on the yard, nothing outside of a dap and a "Sup with it". He would have me in the cell laughing like crazy. He had jokes. We've had a lot of deep conversations too. The first day I moved in with him I brought some reggie with me. Me and Brody had it going before he left, but it wasn't near done, it was still cooking.

G Boy didn't drink any. I got faded by myself. It came out straight. Me and Brody made a few batches before he left, in the sandbox. We had a cool program back there. We would go to the yard in the cages, work out, come back inside and bird bath, then we would fill our milk cartons up with a mixture of refried beans, ramen noodles, and rice and then eat our bologna sandwiches. After we ate, we would kick back, and read or write letters. I had just started writing this female named Karen who was locked up in C.I.W. That would be the morning yard program, when we went to the morning yard. Then the afternoon yard, we would go out and work out, then come back in and bird bath, then kick back, because chow wouldn't be far off.

Usually we'd just chill and talk. That's pretty much all sandbox's program. If for some reason though we don't have hard, we'll just work out in the cell, doing burpies, pushups, navy seals, squats, rocking chairs, calf raises, step ups on the toilet, and incline pushups off of the table stool, we may do leg lifts, when we're working out with all of the races, those that are active (Blacks, Hispanics, Whites, and Others). It's different up in Northern California.

The Southern Hispanics, Whites, and Others wouldn't do the group work out. They worked out together. That's how it was in Solano's sandbox. The Whites sometimes did their Wood thing. Most definitely didn't do the group thing. When they did, it was strictly with the South Siders and Others. Just the Blacks and Northerners would work out together, but then when I done the sandbox to sandbox transfer to San Quentin from Solano, it was different. The Whites and South Siders with the Others worked out with the Blacks and the Northerners. Inside of the building, if we didn't get yard, some would do cell to cell work outs and would be calling it out over the tier. You would have two or three cells working out together.

Two cells might be working out and they're on the second tier, two might be on the first tier and one might be on the third tier. All you would hear is, "Ok, today's cell routine will consist of (whatever it is they're doing) 50 burpies." Then you'd hear "Begin!" Then you'll hear, "Down! Up! Down! Up!" When we had no yard, I would do me on my solo shit. I wouldn't work out over the tier. I done all of the group yard work outs though. San Quentin were single cells which I liked better, because you had your peace and quiet and could hear yourself think. It's cool to have cellies, but you want your quiet time.

You would have cellies that talked too much, always had something to talk about and always moving around. The older I've gotten, I'm more into quiet, because a lot of shit agitates me. I talk, but it's a time for all of that war story type shit. Once you've told them all, you're repeating them differently and in different ways. Most stories consist of bitches we've sexed, bitches we've messed with and cheated on, bitches we've wanted to sex, how this bitch looked, how that bitch looked, who had a fat ass or a fat pussy, how this bitch sexed a certain way, how that bitch sucked a dick, who'd gotten beat up on the yard, who gotten called a bitch, a buster and didn't do anything, who turned down a fight, who'd gotten whupped off the yard, what you were doing on the streets, how you were getting loot, what you were driving, who you were messing with in the set, what homies and home girls you messed with, who you'd gotten into it with, shit like that. I've never spoke on unsolved mysteries. That's how cases are solved, so that's out! We would comment on a lot of women on T.V. shows and news shows.

"She looks good."

"She's thick."

"Her ass fat."

"Damn, she got some big ass titties."

"Look at her sexy ass lips."

"Hell yeah, I'll hit."

There'd be a lot of serious and deep conversations. Dudes get real emotional and passionate about the content, especially talking about how family, bitches, and homies lay down on you. So called family and homies, the bitches you can expect the laying down with them. These hoes aren't loyal. You're out there messing with them and doing what you do, but as soon as you go to jail, they're hitting the exit, like you've never existed.

You don't hear from none of them, but what I do overstand about family, blood makes you related, loyalty makes you family. Yet, they all claim to love you and have love for you, but you can't get a captured moment, dots and dashes, a stamp, no type of energy. You don't exist. Basically, fuck you, you're not out here. Family I was around, Moms, my Aunt Mart, my Uncle Johnny, and a host of others I'd interacted with. For the most part, me and moms have always had a good relationship. We were always straight. We've butted heads and have had our differences, but we've been good. It did go funny on my last month on the streets though, and our relationship became strained, but I overstand now, but then I was in my feelings about it.

She had heard I had started smoking sherm (pcp) and told me I couldn't come to her house no longer. I was like, "Ok, whatever!"

My Aunt Martha and Uncle Johnny had gotten at me the same way. I called their house one day and it was like, "You can't come here anymore." I'm like, damn, what have I done to them? I'm trying to figure it out, because I know smoking sherm can have you doing or saying some bullshit and not remembering it. I kept coming up empty. I was drawing a blank in my mind. I've never done anything to them. I've never stole anything from them. I've never disrespected them, nor had I ever done any physical harm to them, so it really had me in my head. I'm like, "Ok, cool!" I hung up the phone. It is what it is. I still loved them. I didn't go too deep in my feelings to where it was like, "Fuck moms, fuck my aunt, and fuck my uncle!" Nah. I just gave them their space and respected their wishes. I hadn't spoken to them though, after that exchange, for about a year. I wouldn't try to contact them. My attitude after I was incarcerated was like, "We're going to keep it the same. Ok, they weren't messing with me while I was still on the streets. I'm good. I'm not contacting neither of them." and I didn't.

With my cousins, my Aunt Martha's kids, I've never really had a relationship with them, I guess because I was a lot younger than they were. So, they really just tolerated me. Did they have love for me? Absolutely not. The one though I've had more interaction with was my cuzzo Chris (Nippy). We've always been good and have been cordial, never have had any issues or drama. We would se eachother at functions at my aunts holidays mainly and stuff like that. Sometimes I would be at my aunts and he would come through. I saw him though a lot more when I stayed at my aunt's house when I had gotten out of Ironwood State Prison after doing a ten month violation. I would also see him at work when I worked at the mobile oil refinery in Torrance where he was an operator and I was a scaffold builder, working for Brand Scaffolding. He helped me get that job.

He helped me through his boy Clyde who worked for Brand Scaffolding at the refinery. Though short lived I appreciated him helping me. I probably worked there a little under a year before I was drawn back into the streets full fledge. Out there in the thick of it, gang banging, hustling, hanging with homies and having sex with multiple bitches, drinking heavy, smoking blunts and smoking sherm. By this time, I had been gone from my aunt's and had moved on the north side with my Situation. Sometimes cuzzo would pick me up for work, a time or two from my aunt's, if my uncle couldn't take me. He normally took me to work, every morning, even when I had moved. Cuzzo had took me to work a time or two from my spot when my uncle couldn't. My cousin only by blood, and her daughter Donisha. Neither of us never really had a relationship.

They were always funny acting towards me. We've talked here and there, but you wouldn't think we were related.

We would occasionally see eachother too at my aunt's. For the most part they didn't fuck with me. Our interactions were minimal at best. Our interactions were really forced. It wasn't because we were family. I see you, you see me, and that was the extent of it. I will say though, Donisha did holler at me a couple of times since I've been down and had sent me a book of stamps. That was back in '08. Me and Brody were cellies in Calipat then. Out of sight, out of mind. But her and her mama, Jackie, would write and fuck with this dude, Von from BLVDs regularly, yet I'm blood related. He was written and visited and was done for and he'd gotten captured moments. Me , I might as well have been a stranger. Apparently I was. I'm good though and been over it. I just know and overstand, family is just a word, and blood makes us related by blood only. I'm on some "fuck everybody" shit, outside of moms, my aunt, my uncle, my cuzzo, and my kids. Everybody else can sit on it!

My aunt's son, Greg, we're cool, but I overstand the situation with him. We've actually chilled and hung out on some "street Niggah" shit when I was younger. He had some fire (good weed) one time and we were drinking Old English. Maaan, he had me white boy wasted! He stayed with us a couple of times when I was younger too. He was pretty much in and out. He would be gone a lot. I've seen him once or twice as an adult in the early 2000's. My aunt's oldest daughter, Vicci, she really didn't fuck with me, but would speak if she saw me. Overall, she's always been funny acting and white washed, thinking she's better than everyone else. I didn't have other family members in a close demographic other than my aunt, uncle, and those cousins. They were in other cities, an hour or so away. I didn't really know them that well or interacted with them.

They were just people as far as I was concerned, strangers. No ties or connections outside of shared D.N.A. As for those I actually grew up with, we don't fuck with eachother, period, have no relationship, nor do I have relationships with their kids. We're on "fuck you" terms. Fuck me and its fuck you. They're strangers anyway, so it's no loss. My Brody, Tray Deee, that's my guy, my family! He's always remained loyal and that's what family is, loyalty. He'll be home in a couple of more years though, then I'll have him, moms, my aunt, my cuzzo, and my son, Dre. The rest of my kids are on their bullshit right now, but at some point they'll come around. They're working with issues and being in their feelings.

The rest of my so called family can not only sit on it, but can fuck themselves and the air they breathe. The line is drawn in the mud, been drawn. How you felt about me, I feel about you. There's no love either! I feel nothing for you. The thing though, thinking back, when I was around these people, the interactions were fake. The laughing, the talking, the act of concern, the smiles and the hugs, all pseudo! Basically, I was just something to interact with since I was in your presence, because you felt you had to and didn't want to be or seem rude. I'd rather you'd kept it a thousand and not fucked with me, and let it be known you weren't fucking with me than to fake it, because the whole dynamics of our existence would've been much different and played out differently, believe it!

I definitely would've treated you like a common street Niggah or Bitch! I recall an incident while I was staying with my uncle and aunt at their house. I had been living with them at that point for about a month. My cousin, Gloria Jean, and her daughter, Ebony, who is mentally challenged, had come over to visit Aunt Martha and Uncle Johnny. Whether she knew I lived there or not was irrelevant. You weren't there to visit me, you were there to visit them. I'm in the den, watching T.V., minding my own business. First, her daughter comes in, then goes back out of the room. Right after that, here comes Gloria Jean. She walks in the room, sees me sitting in the chair and speaks. This bitch must have been out of her rabbit ass mind, thinking I would speak to her.

You weren't trying to talk to me when I was in prison, not a peep out of you. I was gone for nine years. I haven't heard shit from you, but you want to speak. What you can do is get out of my fucking face, silly ass bitch! I was trying to keep it respectful in my aunt's house, but I really wanted to curse her out and tell her about herself, but I didn't out of respect for my aunt and uncle. Now she's dead though, I still feel the same way. "Fuck yeah!" when I heard she passed, I'm like, "Oh, well!" I felt nothing for her or her situation. Fair exchange is not a robbery. I could be on the same shit with my other cousins, but we know what it is at the end of the day. They don't fuck with me, I don't fuck with then. We're only related by blood.

Truthfully though, I don't know why I expected anything different, or even wasted energy tripping off of it. It's the same episode, just a different channel. What made me really think it would be different and we were really family? That was my bad! So yeah, Gloria Jean went in the living room and told my aunt and uncle I wouldn't talk to her or wouldn't respond when she spoke. Why wasn't I speaking" My Uncle Johnny told her not to worry about it and to leave me alone. I didn't have to speak or talk to her if I didn't want to, and I didn't. When she spoke, I just looked at her dumb ass like she had piss in her face. Plus, I didn't forget how she got at me when I was younger and lived with her. I ain't forgot that shit! Suuuper bullshit! I guess she saw the tear drops on my face and were tripping off of them as far as what they represent. Mine don't represent that, mine represent my shedding tears for my Uncle George (Deek Boy), which I'd gotten in1990 in the county jail by Big Stagger Lee from 8-3 Gangster (Eight-Tray). She was in there with them like, "He's a killer. You didn't see those tear drops on his face?"

My aunt told her like this, "We're not worried about Kaefunn doing anything to us."

What the fuck did she mean, "You let him stay in ya'll house with ya'll. He has tear drops on his face. He's a killer." Whaaat! Bitch, so what if I was. I've never done anything to family, nothing at all! Can't no one in the family say I've done anything physically to them, or I was a threat to them, in no type of way. If t hey do, they're a mutha fucking lie, and the truth isn't in them. Yeah, F.Y.I., what the hell do I look like, shedding a tear for someone I allegedly killed? You've been watching too much damn T.V. (SMH).

Though a lot of war stories have been told, a lot of deep shit is spoke on as an outlet. Being able to vent and get shit out that's been bottled up helps. It helps to have a sound board and someone to talk to, especially someone who can identify with the struggles and having the same type of issues. They know it, they overstand it. Every cellie I've had, we've engaged in deep conversations. Some would talk about how they were out there with BM and they were doing this that and the third, but BM would shake (leave) and do them (live their life) as soon as a dude would hit the county. Block on the phone, no visits, no letters, no loot, and no captured moments.

I was just out there with you though. We were doing and being us. What happened to you loving me and shit was straight! What happened to our history, the shit we've been through? All of that became null and void, as if it never existed. Then, here comes the bullshit. You start hearing she's out there doing this that and the third, and being a ratchet (whore) with the next dude playing daddy to your kids. Soon as you get out and you're back on the bricks, here she comes, trying to fuck with you. Like that's an automatic and she has that coming. Bitch, that's out! All the way out! I'm not fucking with you! You weren't fucking with me while I was down, period. Then you want to hit a Niggah with "I didn't tell you to go to jail. You left me out here with these kids." What was I supposed to do?

Bitch, how about remain loyal! It's not about you doing and being you. Live your life. DO what you do. All I ask is you do me, keep it loyal. I know you're going to fuck. So what? That doesn't concern me, but you getting your dick shouldn't stop you from being there or stop you from letting my kids be in my life. It's not what you do, but how you do what you do. Do you, but do me, do us! Don't just lay down and stay down on a dude. Be there still, regardless, and remain a presence. Have a presence as only you can and do. Send a dude some energy. Hit a dude on special days with some captured moments of you and the kids, born days, father's day, Christmases. Tap in every now and then with a few dots and dashes. It can be a note with the captured moments.

Nowadays, it's way easier for you than it used to be back in the day with all of this new technology and sites that sends captured moments directly to us. You can send captured moments directly from your instagram, FB, or your phone to certain sites and they'll send the captured moments for you, for a small fee. The same with sending a dude some energy (money). Log in, tap in, they've made it easy for you. There's no excuses. If it's something you want to do and you're trying to be involved or get involved, it's there for you to do it. I'm not going to do the foot work for you, or give you the sites, but they're out there (no free promo). A dude shouldn't have to tell you he's in need. He's locked up. You know he's in need. Send a dude some panty and bra shots. Let him know he's thought about, even if he's not missed, just thought about. Get to clocking when something remind you of him and go crazy with that gadget!

Get a home girl you mess with to take some for you. Shit, a Niggah you mess with can take them too! Give a dude one in your favorite position. Do it for a dude, what he can't do for himself. It's simple. Get creative, be creative. If it's something he didn't ask you to do and you feel it something he'll like and it'll go a long way, just do it. Handle that shit! Basically, you're that link for a dude to the streets. Hit a dude with a few dots and dashes, even if it's once a month. Let a dude communicate with his kids. Send those captured moments of them. Help them write, at least once a month. It's basic shit though.

For the most part, we bash them bullshit ass bitches on how it's all good when we're out there with them but as soon as we're locked up, it's fuck us and on to the next Niggah, no matter how good we were to them. Regardless if we cheated on them or not, it didn't take from the fact a Niggah was there and doing what he was supposed to, doing his part. Not only that, but there with you and for you. So what, we went through shit and had issues. Who don't? So what, I cheated. I still loved you. We were still together. We still fucked with eachother. I was still about you, still down for you, still had a presence. I can't get that. Don't that count for something? Didn't I mean something? Didn't we mean something? Where is the loyalty?

I really could just go in on them, but my point is to try and get them to see it for what it is, as it is, for how we're looking at it and how we feel shit should be and how it should go, regardless. Yeah, Niggahs did do them out there, no doubt, but still done us (me and you). I'm not saying not to be in your feelings or trying to discount your feelings or yours aren't valid. I'm saying, don't let them be the reason or be a reason not to be loyal. Loyalty is everything. BM's, wives, or just bitches we're out there playing house with, all get bashed for being disloyal or committing acts of disloyalty all the time. I know I haven't come across no loyal one in my 40 plus years of living on this earth. Oh, they're loyal as fuck when you're out there though, you'll never know otherwise until or unless a situation presents itself to see where it lies.

They're down with you, for you, and all about you, as long as you're out there, but realistically what bitch is going to tell you if you go to jail it's a wrap? I'm quite sure if they did, the dynamics of the relationship wouldn't be the same. With me, my bad was with situationships. I've had two. With Situation, my last three kid's mama, deep down I knew what type of bitch she was, but I still chose to get in that situation. I can't blame anyone but myself on that look, and it was a bad look. A regretful look on all fronts, from the kids, the relationship overall, and especially the situationship. All bad! We can never co-exist or be friends. If I had it to undo, I would. I wish that part of my life never existed.

My cellie, King, said I had a heart like Hitler. "You're brutal bro!" He would always tell me that when I'm speaking on certain situations. It's not that I have a dark heart, I just get frustrated with the bullshit and I see shit for what and as it really is. Why is it though, a dude have to filter through all of the bullshit in order to get to the heart of the matter?

Like dealing with bullshit dudes we have to deal with on the yard, when an issue comes up even with that when you're silent, when you know something is wrong, you're basically condoning it by being complicit. Which took me back to K and the Solano situation with S.T. and Tall. You're silence when you know something isn't right and is in fact wrong, you're condoning it, saying you're with it. Your silence spoke volume. Me and Lon were speaking on this at yard this morning, speaking on how a homie could allow something to be said without correcting something that for a fact isn't true. Nothing foul, just speaking on you as to why you're acting a certain way towards an individual.

"Oh, this that and the third happened, because the homie just don't like him." When you know why the homie don't like him, real reason he doesn't like him, instead of correcting the situation with dudes, you allow what's being said to be said, knowing what's being said isn't true. You know why shit played out the way that it did, the real reason. Not because I have something against him personally or I just didn't like him, or I'm just tripping and on some bullshit. By you being silent, you're condoning it, period. Really, you're horse playing and contributing to autobotism. It was cold as hell too this morning. We're only getting an hour yard a day because of this Corona Virus shit that's going on.

For dayroom at night we're only getting an hour and a half to limit the people being out at the same time. They'll do dayroom release, releasing all three sections a, b, and c, all lower tiers. Then, once dayroom is completed and the lower tiers are back in their cells, all three sections a, b, and c top tiers will be released for dayroom. Once dayroom is completed, it's a wrap. It's over for the night. On the yard, whether we have morning yard or afternoon yard, is only an hour and only your building is out. Normally it would be two buildings out at a time.

I'm in 6-building, so it would be 6-building and 8-building together on the yard, morning or afternoon yard. If we have morning yard, then 5-building and 7-building would have the afternoon yard. The next day it would switch up. 5 and 7 in the morning and then 6 and 9 in the afternoon. Right now it's just one building per hour, per yard, morning or afternoon. Me and Lon dap the dudes we dap and we head straight for the slab, getting our money (workout in). We're consistent with it too. It's every day, rain, sleet, or snow. We get our money and always security conscious. Speaking of being security conscious, a lot of dudes aren't trying to be, nor are they interested in being. They would rather run around putting up their dukes. That's cool if that's the only option or it's spon-taneous, but just running around consciously putting them up, you're horse playing! My conclusion, dudes are afraid of going to the sandbox or afraid to possess one.

Don't want one, won't make one, or won't ask for one. They're cool, period. I'll fight, no doubt, if it came to that, but it wouldn't be by de-sign. I'm not going to sit in the cell and be like, "I can't wait for the next yard so I can get down with such and such!" That's a premeditated fight. That's out! If I'm in the cell on some premeditated shit, it's not going to be about a premeditated fight, that's for certain. I don't do the horse play! I've had conversations as it relates to the relationship we Blacks have with the Northerners. In no way is it the same as it once was back in the 90's. We used to be tight back then, really fucked with eachother. I now really overstand the origin of the relationship as far as it pertained to the Blacks and how they became allies. It really wasn't what I had believed initially.

Over the years though the relationship has deteriorated, we've start-ed to bump heads and clash. To my knowledge, there's been a few riots and scrimmages, though you still have personal relationships with some, but overall the relationship isn't what it once was. I know the difference because I'd functioned with them heavily in the 90's. It was full support both ways. I don't know where and when it went bad or went wrong. If I were to guess, it stemmed from the Bay dudes, which soured the rela-tionship. It's an educated guess. However, as a collective, we're all Black, so it strained the relationship collectively. It doesn't just become a Bay problem, it becomes a Black problem. I've been cool with several over the years and have had close relationships with them. For the most part, they're cool dudes. One thing I do know about them, if they fuck with you, they fuck with you, whether you're on the line or in the sandbox, especially if you're solid and you're active.

On some business type shit, they'll mess with you much quicker than your own. They'll also be on some player shit with you. Good business, as long as you keep it a thousand and don't burn that bridge. As for the Southerners, that's a relationship in prison that's always been at odds. It's always been a volatile one. That bad blood is deeply rooted and etched in stone from Old Folsom to San Quentin. Don't get me wrong, you have your chosen few you're cool with and can fuck with, but as a while, it is what it is. It goes deeper than prison. Shit, nowadays when you get down to it, it's more racial, more so on their part because Blacks in general have never been racist towards other races.

I know my distance and know not to ever get comfortable because at the end of the day I know what it is. Today we're cool, but tomorrow you'll be the one trying to stab me. We Blacks, when it comes to interacting and dealing with the Northerners, we only have contact and interactions with them if we're in Northern Cali doing time. I'm speaking on Blacks from Los Angeles County, Riverside County, San Bernardino County, and Orange County. That's really the only time we're in contact or are interacting with them.

There are not too many prisons they can go to down in Southern California. The closest I was aware of was Delano, where I was, and they had been on the lower yard. They were separated from the South Siders. They weren't programming together. The South Siders were on the upper yard. The police made sure they didn't come into contact with eachother. That was 2013-2014, when administration tried to integrate them and have them program together. It went up! It was ugly and got uglier. The Northerners moved first. Everyone else, Blacks, Whites, and Others got out of the way so they could handle their business. The South Siders we interact with in some form on the norm, because we're on the southern end of California. They're the predominant race in all California (southern mostly) prisons. The Blacks are outnumbered, maybe five to one, could be more, just a guess.

What I do know, it's more of them than us, but yeah, Lon was like, "Did you hear Smash (J Smash from Swann) was speaking on how consistent we were with our workouts every day?"

"Yup, I heard him."

I told Chumlee, "See, that's what I was talking about, how dudes watch us." The thing is, when you think a mutha fuckas not paying attention to you, he is. Someone's always watching you, friend and foe. Don't ever think you're not being watched, especially by the Hispanics, Northerners, and Southerners. They watch everything. Trust and believe, they know who'll give them a run and who wouldn't.

They can just about figure who's security conscious and who isn't. It's their position to watch, learn, and study adversaries. They listen as well. That's how they know who's who and know names, which was confirmed when I had a South Sider call me by name and I'd never had a conversation with him. That happened a few times. "What's up Tic" or "Aye Long

Beach" which translated to me, "I know you're from Long Beach." If he knows, they all know. It's their job to know. My mind work the same way. I watch, I learn, and I study. I damn sure listen.

My mind works that way just based on. It was a teachable moment for Chumlee. That's why you have to be mindful of who you mess with or associate with. Someone's always watching and paying attention to your surroundings and moves being made. Everyone on this line knows me and Lon are together on a daily and workout together. When Chumlee wasn't around, it was still me and Lon. Our program doesn't change. We dap those few hands and it's off to the slab to get that money and we're always keeping our eyes out for Vamp, making sure he's in our sight or line of sight, always positioning ourselves to cover the yard visually from two angles. You're spotted before you're close enough to bring harm and we're cocked and loaded, there's no horse playing around here.

The homie is 50 plus, and I'll be 50 next year. Chumlee will be 33 in fifteen days. He's still wet though to a lot. We're trying to wake his game up to the most common sense shit so he can avoid most areas of stagnation. It's important you stay vigilant and never relent. I stay telling him though, when you use emotions over intellect, you make fucked up choices and decisions. Me and Lon both be on him, trying to have him structured and on his shit, just being on some homie shit, with concern for his well being. Plus we fucked with him, genuinely. You can tell no one took the time to lace or school the homie, or tried to guide him to avoid self destruction. That, or he wasn't receptive. I could see that with his attitude. "I don't give a fuck (SMH)!"

It's easy to wreck and end your career on a yard or as a gang member. I've seen it happen too many times. We can't always direct what happens in life. Much is left to chance, but it's inevitable that both good and bad come our way. If you can take preventative measures to avoid the bad, why not? What can it hurt? You have to be productive in your growth, where you're lacking, and be receptive to it. It's going to help your push and your awareness, keeping you focused and moving in the right direction. Me and Chumlee were talking about lies. I broke down lies to him like this, "Lies are the product of fear, malice, and envy. They can drive dudes to acts of desperation."

18

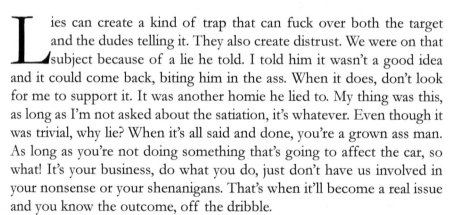

Lies can create a kind of trap that can fuck over both the target and the dudes telling it. They also create distrust. We were on that subject because of a lie he told. I told him it wasn't a good idea and it could come back, biting him in the ass. When it does, don't look for me to support it. It was another homie he lied to. My thing was this, as long as I'm not asked about the satiation, it's whatever. Even though it was trivial, why lie? When it's all said and done, you're a grown ass man. As long as you're not doing something that's going to affect the car, so what! It's your business, do what you do, just don't have us involved in your nonsense or your shenanigans. That's when it'll become a real issue and you know the outcome, off the dribble.

That's your ass, Mr. Postman! On some real shit, you don't want to be labeled a liar or a bullshit Niggah. Your credibility will get lost in that shuffle and your word won't mean shit. That's all we have on these yards is our word and our balls. A dude won't and can't trust anything that comes out of your mouth. You always want your word to carry weight and mean something. What is the word without the weight? Not a damn thing! Nothing! It's meaningless! That's not ever a good look. The difference between reality and fiction is fiction has to be credible. The thing about trust, if you don't have it, you can't overstand it. If you do, no explanation is necessary.

The things I talk to him about I have to really go into detail and explain it to him, breaking it down so that he fully overstands why I'm saying what I'm saying to him. It doesn't matter what it is I'm speaking on. I try to break it down to his level of overstanding so that he grasps it and can process it for himself. I just left dayroom right now and I just finished talking to moms. She told me Brody had called her the other day, I think on the 24th. Today is the 26th. March is almost over. Damn, this month went by fast and tomorrow is Friday already!

We have afternoon yard. It's been kind of calm on this yard as of late. C-yard though has been acting up. They've put our yard down once this week, twice last week, to run over there. When it goes up, it goes up on this yard though. The politicians stay at work. All you have to do is just observe your surroundings and you can see them at work, if you know what you're looking at. A blind man can't see it though. He's blind to everything and everything around him. Somebody is always grouping up or pairing up in discussion about yard issues or issues within their collective, even when you don't visually see anything going on. Something's always going on. Since I've been on the yard I've come to overstand what was said about nothing is secret. If it's something going on with someone, Blacks mainly, it'll more than likely hit your ears, none out of ten times, which technically shouldn't happen.

In house business or issues should remain in house, especially if it's on some violence. You're not trying to alert your target or whoever it is you're trying to holler at, which will make it harder to carry out to your advantage. If something is anticipated, you've lost the advantage and the element of surprise, because now they're prepared and awake, no longer asleep. It can work against you, because now they have options, which you had total control over, where as there were none. It's just some shit shouldn't get out. Like in Solano, you really didn't know who messed with who like that.

You could be speaking on something to someone you mess with, he repeats it to someone else that he messes with, and that person could mess with the dude you might be trying to get on, or he might mess with a dude that messes with him directly. There you have it. You've alerted your target, giving him the option to strike first or get off of the yard, either way, it's a bad look. He shouldn't have had that option. I've told Chumlee this a lot because he has a tendency to just blurt out shit without thinking, like he has fucking Tourette Syndrome and has no filter. You have to be mindful of what comes out of your mouth and who you're speaking to. Dudes are messy like bitches. They run their mouth and can hold water. "Oh, Chumlee said he was going to do this that or the other to such and such. Chumlee said fuck such and such." There you go, some bullshit is in the air, just that quick, because you don't have a filter and you don't care who you say shit to. That very person you just said some bullshit to about the next dude, you don't know if he mess with that dude or mess with someone else that mess with him. He's going to repeat it. Basically, you have to be mindful or you'll find yourself caught up. Now you're caught up in some bullshit, because you had no filter on your mouth and wasn't mindful of who you were talking to, but why? In your mind, you didn't do anything wrong. The reality is totally different. You've done everything wrong. It could go bad.

Me personally, I see stuff for what and as it is. If you're out of pocket (in the wrong) you're out of pocket, period. All of that you don't care, you'll do such and such, save the tough Niggah shit! No one is above being touched. You'll get an issue. Never forget that! To believe otherwise or that you're untouchable, you're living with a false sense of security. Homies will bring it to your tough ass! Play ball on you or pound you out for the simple fact that your actions are affecting more than you and jeopardizing more than you. No one is above being touched. We can all be touched, me included. It's bigger than just one dude who can be easily voted off of the island. If dudes get hurt behind your horse playing or stupidity, you have a serious issue to deal with and answer to, real talk!

I'm not going to tell a dude anything is wrong, or steer a dude in the wrong direction. My homie-ism is realism. I'm not going to sugar coat it or water it down, especially if I mess with you. I've been schooled and laced by good, real, and solid older G homies. G homies that have always played fair and have always kept it clean from everywhere (different sets), not just from Insane. I've met a lot of G homies from all over that were straight and always willing to lace a young homie correctly, from 40's, East Coast, Hoover, Watts, Gangsters, Raymond, Bounty Hunters, Oakland, SAC, Berkley, much of what I know I credit to them. Apparently I've soaked it up and was receptive to it, because I'm still pushing on these lines. Even now I'm still soaking it up and am still receptive to it.

You're never too old to keep it current. I know what I'm about and what I stand for. I'm good with me. I've leveled up. Part of defining who you are is making decisions about what you won't be.

I overstand every lane isn't the passing lane. I'm going to stay mindful of where it is I'm walking, and of the dangers that lurk, taking nothing or no one for granted. As I would never over estimate or underestimate a situation or person, neither are to be played down. Both are capable and able of anything at any time. Unpredictability is a mutha fucka! I just got my other book, "Feelin Some Type ah Way" back from Lon. I wanted his input on it. It was written several years ago, which I'll update. He told me the contents were spot on, due to the subject matter. His only real critique was to lose all of the Ebonics. Minimize it to where it'll appeal to a broader audience and can appeal to them.

Being who he is and pushing how he pushes with his vast knowledge as it pertains to the content and context of "Feelin Some Type ah Way" spoke volumes. His advice is considered taken. I have another one I had written called "Ah Bitterchild State ah Mind" which is basically the part one of "Feelin Some Type ah Way". "Feelin Some Type ah Way" is an extension. The only difference is the titles and chapters. The context are the same. "Ah Bitterchild State ah Mind" isn't in my possession at the moment. I had sent it out, because at the time I had what I thought would be help with it, as far as assisting me with the self publishing.

She basically went back to her baby daddy, since he was ready to be a daddy to his son, which I didn't knock and respected. So, I told her to just shoot my book to moms for me and wished her luck with her family thing, which she'd done. I haven't heard nothing from her or about her since, so moms has it. As a matter of a fact, the last time me and moms talked, I asked her about it, telling her not to let it get away from her and to sit on it until I tell her otherwise. Both "Ah Bitterchild State ah Mind" and "Feelin Some Type ah Way" are street lits. I view "Yard Life" as prison lit, because it's about prison life as it pertains to the yard. "Ah Bitterchild State ah Mind" and "Feelin Some Type ah Way" are about the streets and the code of the streets. I'm speaking on various topics, from snitching to hustling.

Basically like what I'm doing now, but on the streets with it. I'm on strictly real things and real situations with what I write. I've written several scripts which I'm constantly told I need to turn them into urban novels. At some point I will. As of now, I'm focused on "Yard Life" and it's fruition, then I'll double back and revisit "Ah Bitterchild State ah Mind" and "Feelin Some Type ah Way", switching things up. Last night, when I was talking to moms, she was telling me about the Corona Virus and how Long Beach had a curfew. Damn, it's ugly out there (SMH). I'll bet you smokers (crack heads) are running around dipping, dodging, and creeping around. You won't stop them from getting that hit!

I tapped in with Aunt Marty Lou this morning and wrote my cuzzo, Nip. They're the only ones I tap in with and who matter to me. Once I no longer have them, my connection to the streets will end there, other than my son Dre. Unless I come across a friend, which is all I'm looking for. I'm cool on relationships. I'm only equipped to handle a friendship. No labels, because my expectations I feel can't be met, and if that doesn't happen that would be the extent of my world as I once knew it, as it pertains to family. I don't have any other family. This essentially will become my whole world until I resurrect. Having a relationship with so called family with me is done. I'm over it. I'm accepting no olive branches from anyone, or communication at this point, 16 years in. Keep me buried!

Lon just sent word through Chumlee that he just lost yard for 30 days for his last 115, which was for the fight he had with B on the yard. He still doesn't know yet what's going on with him going on c-status and moving to the c-status building. The fight made him a candidate, so now it'll be just me and Chumlee on the slabs. Once it's known that Lon is on 30 day loss of yard, eyes will be watching to see if we'll fall off. Don't hold your breath! The program doesn't stop. I'm fully committed to my health and well being, especially at my age. Plus, I'm representing for us old dudes. I'm going to keep getting my money.

My consistence is consistent, believe it! It's a little cold outside too, so I'll definitely have my jacket. I was out this morning before breakfast. I had lab. They wanted to draw some blood to test my AIC. Every time I look around it seems like they want to draw blood for something, damn vampires. I started to refuse though. I'm like, "In my mind, why so much blood and why so often? What are they really doing with it?" Vampires I tell you! "We need blood for this, we need blood for that." They have those big, thick ass needles. I'm not tripping off of the needles, but damn! That shit looks like some shit they tranquilize horses with. "If you don't knock it off!"

The yard was straight. It wasn't anything going on out there, just cold as usual. Me and Chumlee made our rounds, dapping a couple of people, then hit the slab and got it in. The name Chumlee came from the show Pawn Stars. Chumlee is one of the workers that works there. He's the fat, heavy set, white dude with the long, straggly hair and funny as hell. Lon just started calling him Chumlee, so it stuck. That's what we call him. He's fat and always disheveled. It fits him. I just received some dots and dashes from my cuzzo at chow times, which is for the most part when mail is passed out in our building. You pick it up when you grab your tray, if you have any. You'll know though if you have any as soon as your cell door opens for chow. They call your name as you're walking out of your cell, "Such and such, you have mail!" Cuzzo was just tapping in with me, letting me know all was well with him and Aunt Mart. He mentioned my daughter, Kaemaijay. I let him know though I basically don't fuck with her. When I wrote him back I informed him of the situation with her and I. I love her, will always love her, but I'm good on her. She's messy, disrespectful, she's also turned on me as well, allowing her mother's side of the family and her mother to get in her head, and she also had the audacity to say she hated me. I haven't done anything to her for her to take that position towards me.

I'm cool with it though, because at the end of the day, she is her mother's daughter. What's crazy though, when her mother didn't want anything to do with her and wasn't fucking with, I was the one tapping in, writing her, calling her, and trying to get involved and be involved. When I would come up on loot I would break bread with her, bought her shit, bought her her first cell phone, but you hate me! I've turned the volume down to zero on that whole situation, emotionally and mentally. I'm just over it. Keep me buried! I went on to tell cuzzo, anyone outside of him, his moms, my moms, and my oldest son, they're to me what I am to them. No love, no feelings, simply strangers. I had commented too on my daughter's Aunt Maxine who had passed last year and her Uncle James.

They had custody of her and was raising her when she was took from her mother (Situation). As I was telling him, they were okay for the most part, to an extent, but they were on some funny shit with me too, which I recognized long ago. I never cared for them either, so the feeling was mutual on my part. Based on my trying to be involved and get involved with my daughter, and trying to communicate with her as only I could, I knew I had to hold my tongue. I knew I had to keep things cordial with them, because they held the power over the situation, so I couldn't voice my opinion or my true feelings about anything, and let it go. I knew though, a lot was going on behind the scenes, like someone listening to my calls when I would talk to her, which was obvious. I would ask her something, she was pausing like someone was telling her something and she was listening to them, then she would respond. Though I was frustrated with all of the weirdo shit going on, it was a bigger captured moment. At the end of the day, fuck them too. I didn't tell cuzzo my true feelings, but those are my sentiments. They had a lot of fuckery going on in regards to me and having a relationship with my daughter. They could've done more to encourage and help cultivate the relationship between me and her.

The same shit with her mother's bullshit ass. She'd been on the same shit, not encouraging or helping to cultivate a relationship with my daughter. She didn't because she didn't want me in her life. I honestly though think she didn't care about none of the kids she had with me. It was too easy for her to disregard and dismiss them. After I was locked up I was hearing a lot of foul shit about her and shit she was doing, which didn't come as a shock or a surprise. My kids with her had been took from her twice and put into the system. She didn't raise any of my kids, or had been in their life. The only kids she kept were the four kids she had before me, by her three other kids' fathers. She never pulled the wool over my eyes. I knew it was three.

Her Aunt Maxine, the one who'd passed, and her Uncle James had my daughter, Kaemaijay and she shipped my other kids to Denver, Colorado, allegedly until she got back on her feet. I felt she was getting rid of them because she never kept in touch with them, because if she had, how was it she allowed them to be put in the system a second time? I felt once she sent them out there with her friend, she washed her hands and walked away. They were out of her hair. Clearly she wasn't in constant communication with the friend, because my kids wouldn't have been in the system. My thing was this, why were they even sent out of California? My mother or my side of the family would've took them, but being the vindictive person she is, she chose the route she took, and now she's telling any and everyone who'll listen to her bullshit that my mothers the reason my kids were sent to Denver and ended up in the system, which is clearly a lie perpetrated by her. She's been telling it so long she believes it and has other people believing it. It's all bullshit though. My mother had nothing to do with my kids being sent to Denver, or being put in the system. That was a conscious decision on her part to sent them out there and neglect them. It was her lack of communication that ultimately led them to be put into the system a second time. It was all on her.

Yet she's pushing the blame elsewhere. We know what's really going on! Stop saying it was my mother. That wasn't the case. You sent them to Denver. They ended up being neglected by your friend. Your friend's daughter who's actually your niece called child services and told them to come and get the kids, because her mother was neglecting them and she was too young to take care of them and they were put into the system. But you think she tried to get involved and get them back? Fuck no! What she did do was keep it pushing with her life, as if they didn't exist or didn't come out of her, which I didn't overstand how a mother could just leave her kids or just disregard them so easily, then to justify it by blaming the next person for her deed. Kaemaijay was in Long Beach and on the North Side. You think she went and fucked with her or tried to get involved or be involved? Fuck no! She was in Long Beach too. I know this because my daughter would be crying for her and asking me about her.

I didn't have the answers for her, but I didn't bash her mother or talk down on her to my daughter. It was obvious she loved the bullshit bitch and was in her feelings. I wasn't going to tell her her mother wasn't shit and she didn't give a fuck about her, though I wanted to so she could stop crying over her or wanting her when she wasn't wanted or loved by her. Once I was locked up, my kids were no longer a tool or leverage that could be used as far as I was concerned, so they were of no use to her. Why were her kids kept and mine weren't? The people around her know the real, but they suffer from what these dudes in here suffer from, auto-botism and complicity. My daughter's heart was broken already. I wasn't about to crush her.

Maxine and James would tell me all of the time how my daughter would be asking them about her, or would be crying for her (SMH), so though I'm incarcerated, I tried as only I could to get involved and be involved, even more so attempting to fill that void and empty space in her heart and in her life. Not only me, but my Aunt Marty Lou and my Uncle Johnny got involved and would be involved. They were allowed by Maxine and James to go pick my daughter up, basically letting her know she did have other family on her father's side that did give a fuck about her and wanted to be involved and got involved. They would take her to church on Sundays and would have her on the weekends. They would do stuff with her and for her, like they've done with and for me all of my life.

Somewhere her attitude changed towards them and changed for them. I don't know if it were her actions or her people actions. I just know all of a sudden it was a 180 degree turn and she started acting funny with them and stopped wanting to go to church with them, or wanting to be at their house spending time with them, stopped being appreciative of them or of their time, effort, or energy, which I wasn't feeling at all. Here it is, they care and they're showing you they care and you spit on their gesture, which I took as a major disrespect and disloyalty! Yet your mother doesn't give a fuck about you. You just up and stop going to church with them, stop going to their house, and stopped calling them, ungrateful ass!

I took that shit very personal, because they done it not only because you were their family, but because you were my daughter. They've always been good people, loving people, and caring people, and for you to act that way wasn't cool! So what if you were a kid, you were old enough to know and overstand what you were doing. You weren't that young. I'm not letting you off the hook so easy. They might've, because that's who they are. I'm much different. Moms got involved as well and would be involved. My mother would start getting my daughter on weekends. She would get Tweet on Fridays. Moms would do stuff with her, take her places, and buy her stuff, spend time with her.

I have a lot of captured moments of them together doing things and of them out in traffic somewhere in my photo albums. Doing different things and going different places. Moms really enjoyed spending time with her and doing stuff with her. Really getting involved and really being involved as a grandmother, as her grandmother. Clearly she loves Tweet and showed her this. All things changed. Not the love as far as with moms, because moms will forever love her granddaughter, but the relationship changed. The relationship took a turn for the worse and was 86'ed. There were no more going to moms house, hanging out, or going places and doing things.

Basically, my daughter lied on moms and moms wasn't having any of it. She doesn't horse play! She's the type that'll separate herself from shenanigans real quick. She's simply not with or for the bullshit and will cancel you! Moms is definitely with the cancel culture and don't care who you are if you're on some disrespectful shit, or on some disloyal shit. Consider that ass cancelled! She'll cut off all communication and will change her phone number, "See yah!" That's just her. She don't play no type of games and could care less about your feelings. You can sit on them, that's where I got it from. "Fuck your feelings, sit on them!" So anyway, my daughter goes back home after being with moms the whole weekend and tells her aunt and uncle a bunch of off the wall shit that moms supposedly had said. First off, moms has no problem telling a mutha fucka how she feels and will read you (tell you about yourself) in your face! Have her all the way fucked up and she damn sure wouldn't use a kid to do it. I know for a fact she wouldn't put a child into any grown people shit. Who does that? What was said was moms supposedly told my daughter that Maxine and James didn't give a fuck about her and they only wanted custody of her because of the check they received for fostering her.

Why would moms say that to her? Better yet, how would she know what financial dealings are going on in that house hold? The reality was, she would tell moms all type of stuff when she would be with moms. "My aunt said this, my uncle said that, this is going on, that is going on." She was the one telling moms they didn't care about her and that they were getting money for her, but weren't spending it on her, telling moms how they were buying her cheap stuff and she would have to wear it over and over. However moms had told me how my daughter would come to the house. Her shoes would be too big and her clothes would be too small, and her hair would never be done, how she had started buying my daughter stuff and doing her hair.

Now, to this day that relationship is fucked up and she's 17 now. Moms refuses to have anything to do with her and won't talk to her, called her messy and bullshit! Why would you mess over someone that was for you and about you? It really didn't make sense to me, but then again, being who you are (a product of your mother) it's overstandable. You are your mother's daughter. She's messy, bullshit, and disloyal (SMH).

Chumlee said I have a heart like Hitler too! Cold dude! I mean, it is what it is though. I'm sure my cuzzo in his mind was like damn, he's harsh, "shh" shaking his head. I can imagine him "shh" when he get the full bar of my venom towards all parties concerned. The thing is so called family are getting at me, like I've done something to them harmful or disrespectful, which isn't the case or have never been the case. I would tell Brody this same shit. In turn, he would say the same shit about his BM and his folks. Trust and believe, there are a lot of bitter dudes in prison, bitter dudes period.

"You're the one who went to jail. You're the one who got himself caught up." Where was that same attitude when I was doing shit for you or when I was messing with you or when you needed me and I was there for you? We were cool then, but we're no longer cool when I come to jail. I was good when I served a purpose or had a purpose. For what it is, I see our dealings came with limitations. Our relationship came with limitations. Family came with limitations. Feelings towards me and for me came with limitations, limited too! Limited to me getting locked up and I'm no longer useful to you or what you have going on or your cause, whatever it may've been. Actions speak volumes.

Tray Deee asked me, "What if down the line they want to fuck with you?" This was '09-2010. At that point in time I may've been open to it and may've even reached out, but as of 2016, it's a wrap. I'm over it! I had told my cellie, King in the sandbox in Solano, I wouldn't give a fuck if it was 20 years from now and that was 2019, I'm not fucking with them. Continue to act like I don't exist or have never existed, I'm good with that and stand on it too! I'm good!

I'm strictly dealing with those I'm dealing with, those I have a relationship with, and with the world I'm in. Outside of that, I'm unavailable mentally, spiritually, or emotionally. I've checked out. I have no effort or energy for it or to put in it. I'm still somewhat adjusting to this environment. There's no lane for me to really slide into. High Desert is one of those spots that you have to just really sit back and gauge, letting the lane develop. I just came back in from yard. It's the weekend. The police let all of the A2B's, dudes with no jobs, out too, along with the workers, A1A's. I didn't do shit today, which I normally don't do anyway on the weekend.

Anytime though my cell door is open, I'm up out of that bitch! I'm always going to be accounted for, even on the off chance of something happening. I'm there. Another set of feet and hands, and I'm security conscious. I hung out with Vamp for most of the yard. We hung out on the basketball court, chopping it up. Me and Snake chopped it up for the first 20 or something minutes by the tables, talking about "2nd Line" and making another part to it (part 4), and he was talking about I needed to make another part to "Outtah Sight Outtah Mind" too. Right now he's reading "16 Bars". He's read all of the "2nd Lines" and "Outtah Sight Outtah Mind".

We've had long dialogue about the characters. He's really invested in them. "16 Bars" though he said he's really not into. I think because the "2nd Lines" and "Outtah Sight Outtah Mind" had turned him bias because they're violent and active. "16 Bars" is about music, minimal violence, and activity. Once he's done, I'm going to slide him "Ponds", then "Ah Long Road Back" and "Rim Shop". He also wants to read this, "Yard Life", and "Feelin Some Type Ah Way". I've made yet another jail fan of my work. That was crazy though. South Siders and Northerners were playing basketball today with eachother and with bats. It fucked me up. I've never seen any bats on the 4-yard being played with since I've been down this go round. We Blacks were watching and looking like, "What the fuck!"

The homie Vamp went to ask the South Siders if we could play. Basically, to see what the response would be. We wouldn't have played, but wanted to see if we could had we wanted to. He was told he didn't think so. It was just them and the Northerners. So that'll be a conversation for certain for those who's tripping off of it. Ok, so, now what's good? What's really going on? They were doing their thing with eachother too in Solano, playing handball. Me personally, I could care less, as long as it's not breaching our security. At the end of the day, they're Hispanic. It's bound to happen, plus times are changing. Within the next 10 to 20 years I wouldn't doubt if they came together as one. It wouldn't surprise or shock me.

You can believe though, it'll come to be it's inevitable. It was a similar situation and there was a discussion. The Northerners wanted to South Siders in Solano to come on our end of the yard, which we shared with them, so they could play handball together. That was no bueno! That was where we programmed together. It was told to the Northerners that it would be breaching our security. "If ya'll want to play handball with the cool, it's your prerogative, but play with them in their area, on their handball court." We didn't want South Siders down on our end of the yard like that. Come on now, that's breaching our security. We Blacks already wasn't feeling that Blacks and Northerners were supposed to be fucking with eachother, but yet they were always standoffish. "We don't want you guys walking through here (their area we shared). We don't want this that and the third!"

It was as if we were Enemigos too, yet we were co-existing and fucking with eachother, which came with stipulations, limits, and boundaries in common areas we share. I didn't get it or overstand it. We're fucking with eachother or we aren't. They could be getting water at the water fountain and it's just us and them present. They'll put security on each other as if we're going to attack them (SMH). Whatever. Their words and actions didn't align. It'll get figured out, once a discussion is had as to what's going on, on this side of the yard. Comments were being heard, "What's up with that? Oh, that's the new thing!" I think the homie Snake asked too to play, just to see what the response would be. Truthfully, I don't think any blacks that were on the yard really cared about playing with them. I know I didn't. I don't do jail house sports. I'm strictly spectator. I'll watch, but that's it. I have a bad attitude and a temper. That doesn't mix with sports. It's just some bullshit waiting to happen. You hit me wrong, I'm having an issue with it. You foul me too hard, I'm having an issue with it. You hit me in the face with a ball, I'm having an issue with it.

I just simply avoid all physical sports. I've played though in the past. I wouldn't play them now though. Anyway, I'm much older. I'm good! I can't be spraining, fracturing, or breaking anything. I don't heal as quick as I once did and shit hurts a lot longer too. Both times I was shot with the block gun, it took a minute to get over the pain and to heal, plus I was sore as hell too with those few incidents. My back, my head, my face, my arms, and my legs, from doing all of that movement that hadn't been done in a minute. The next morning I would get up and could barely move from the stiffness and soreness. I'm like, "Man, fuck this. The next situation I have, I'm playing ball." Especially these young dudes, running around and thinking they're going to punch an old Niggah. That's out! All the way out!

What the hell do I look like around here, a 50 plus rolling around on the ground with a 25, 26, 27, 28 year old, or younger? You're horse playing! I would be too. It's not going to happen, champ! One night, me and L Loc were in the cell talking and he was telling me about his BM and how she had spit on him and he lost his mind. He was telling me how he had got on her and had her on the ground, straddling her, hawking loogies on her face. Not just once, but continuously, over and over again. I told him about the time when I had spit into Situation's face.

We were in the Carmelitos and as usual she was on her stupid shit, and I hawked a loogie, spitting in her face. It was slimy as fuck and had slid down her face and down to her chin, pausing and suspending off of her chin. She started trying to hawk one to spit back on me. She hawked up something and spit, only she didn't get me, she got her sister Lee Lee. "Biiitch!" They started having words and started fighting. I was up out of there.

A week or so before that, I was at my boy Nu Nu's spot from 20's. We were smoking a blunt and sitting on the stairs outside when my boy C.C.

from Park Village bent the corner, coming to the back of the apartments where we were. He was all orange. At first we didn't know what the fuck it was. He has been sprayed up with mace. His head, his white t-shirt, his gray sweat pants, and his shoes were soaked. C.C. was blinking his eyes and wiping at them. I'm like, "What the fuck happened to you cuz?" Nu Nu started laughing and clowning, "What happened Niggah?"

"This Niggah's wife sprayed me, and she sprayed Marie!" Marie was his girl and the home girl from the set. Come to find out the homie Lil Treach (Jack Dog) is her baby daddy. He has twins with her. When I find out, I'm like, what? She's whupped, skinny as fuck and ugly as hell. So anyway, C.C. tells me him and Marie got into it with Situation and she sprayed them up.

First she sprayed Marie, but then when C.C. tried to ask Situation what happened she sprayed him too. I hit the blunt again and bounced. I left C.C. and Nu Nu behind the apartments to go home to see what the biz was. When I get to the house, Annie (her mother) tells me Situation and her sister Lee Lee had just left and were on their way to the Carmelitos. Long story short, I tracked them down and came up behind them. As I put my hand on her shoulder, she spent around with her mace in hand and caught me in the face. "Biiitch!" My eyes are on fire and are burning like crazy. All I'm thinking is I'm about to beat this bitch ass, but that was out. I couldn't see shit. I'm trying to wipe at my eyes and my face, making it worse. Out of nowhere I'm getting hit, "You not going to be putting your fucking hands on me because I sprayed them. Fuck them!" I hadn't even said shit. Not one word. Then bam! I'm sprayed, then I'm getting hit. Then "Get em biiitch! Kick em in the nuts!" Then poof, right in the nuts! Unghh! Down goes Frasier! I fell on the ground and balled up, then I was being hit again. I knew Lee Lee probably got her some licks in. I couldn't see, but I don't think Situation was hitting me that fast. Then I almost was hit by a bus trying to get away from them. I was blind, nuts hurting, and I couldn't see. Her hits weren't shit or her premeditated kick after the pain subsided. L and Tray Deee both found that story amusing.

Chumlee just got his laugh in too. I told him that story. Me and Brody stayed drunk in the sandbox as we did on the line. When Silent from 4-3 Gangster (Foe Tray) came to the sandbox a couple of weeks later, he told us he came up on our four gallons of reggie we had in our cell. That's how you know the situation with us and the Dodge Citys was spare of the moment. It wasn't premeditated, it just happened. If it had been premeditated and much more serious it wouldn't been no fighting. Ball would've been played for certain. To be truthful about the situation was really all that serious because we basically stayed away from them.

They weren't in our space and we weren't in theirs. The line had already been drawn in the mud and dudes knew what it was. We're not fucking with you Niggahs! While me and Brody were in the sandbox we had been boomeranging dots and dashes to the homie Smurf from Youngs. He told us he had gotten on the Dodge City that was in his building. Still no C Bone. He was still on the line out there chilling (SMH). The other side (homies) remained neutral on the Dodge Citys. It was crazy though how Pep just came to that conclusion we were drunk being the reason why shit had happened. All of this time, 6 years later, that's what he had though and had been spreading, which wasn't the case. Dudes were sober as fuck. Actually, we were trying to find some trees. We already had the reggie, 4 gallons of it. We were trying to get white boy wasted like we had on our born days. The homie had threw up. We were wasted on his day and on mine. We would pass out on his bottom bunk, wake up, and do it all over again. Me and L would do the same shit, get wasted. I've never fell out on his bunk though, though I could've. A dude stay trying to take the cheat off this shit, get real hectic mentally and emotionally at times, even spiritually. You need that temporary mental escape just to go somewhere else for a few hours to another space. This shit will drive you insane! My escape is trees and alcohol. Some chose much harder shit. I'm cool on all of that though.

They're choosing psych meds trying to escape, not realizing they're really going somewhere else. Over time, it's gradually taking over their mental state in a real way, causing another whole set of issues and problems. For others, it's hard drugs like crystal and black (heroin) for that mental escape, and alcohol. You have to figure everyone is doing something to escape. We deal with a lot, though it may not seem like it. A dude needs that escape somehow, someway, or he'll be overwhelmed and consumed by all of the rhetoric and bullshit around him on a daily. You're dealing with the police and their bullshit, you're doing with these dudes and their bullshit, and whatever you're dealing with on the streets, that part!

Me and Brody would make three and four batches or reggie every week, only losing maybe two in a six month period. We constantly went up. Me and L too. He worked in the kitchen, so we always had material. The most we've made were five and a half gallon batches. We would go up every week too. The whole time we've made it, we'd probably lost maybe three batches. We had a police who had told us he wasn't tripping off of us drinking, because he saw we weren't causing problems in his building as a result of it and for the most part we've stayed in our cell with it, never bothered anyone or caused drama. Cool! He gave us a pass. He just told us to keep the smell down and burn something.

Initially though me and him clashed. Me and L were on the yard one day and when we came back inside, a porter, I think it was my boy Rame or my boy Tee. Tee worked second watch, but was still out bullshitting. I just remember he was still out. As I came inside of the building, one of them was like, "The police been in your cell." I'm immediately hot, pistol hot. We had four gallons going. The police sees me talking to the porter and calls me over to where he's standing with that "I gotcha" look on his face (SMH). I just knew the shit was gone. What the fuck I want to talk to him for? I'm not trying to talk to him! "Aye McClinton, let me have a talk with you!"

I'm like, "What the fuck you want to talk to me for? I'm tired of you fucking with my cell. You're always going in my cell!" I'm going off, fuck this, fuck that. His female co-worker came over and stood next to him.

"Biiitch! What the fuck you come over here for? Your stupid looking ass ain't going to do shit. Fuck you too! Fuck you and your spray!" I was bluffing about the spray. I was not trying to get sprayed. I was just on a roll and it sounded good. "Fuck your spray Biiitch!" I flipped out on them. She pulled her spray and just stood there, but had scooted behind him. She was spooked.

My cellie just came into the building from work. They went to him, "Can we talk to you? McClinton isn't being reasonable and he's being confrontational and belligerent with us." I walked away, leaving them talking to L.

L came to the other side of the dayroom where I was and got at me, "Aye Tic, they were like 'Gant, why is your cellie tripping and carrying on? We didn't even take anything from your cell. He just went off on us and we were trying to talk to him. I was just going to tell him to keep the smell down.'" I ended up apologizing to him. I wasn't told to or asked to, just felt I should've, though based on. I knew I was on some bullshit. That's something I normally didn't do. I wasn't into that. I don't flash on the police or argue with them, because if it's that serious why do all that? They're human and a man just like me. If it's an issue and it's that serious, it's serious enough to handle or deal with. Though, it would be a losing battle, but fuck it.

Trust and believe it'll be a losing battle, because they're going to royally fuck over you once you're cuffed and removed from plain view and cameras. You might win the fight, but I guarantee you won't win the battle, absolutely not. My thing is this, if I'm not going to take off on them, why even get argumentative or confrontational? That's just wasted energy really, so I don't do it. When they get slick with their mouth or do bullshit I don't even respond or give them a response. I'll just keep it moving. They're trained to try an agitate you and get you riled up. Their tactics are weak once you figure out their game. You're not going to get me to bite or feed off into your shenanigans. They hate when you don't. Once you bit they figure they have one and will keep fucking with you to get that reaction they want from you so they can write you up or send you to the sandbox.

I've had a couple of incidents with them on some standoff type shit. One time we were walking to chow at Calipat and the police had pulled over K.O. and Mad Face from 8-3 Gangster (Eight Tray). Me, Brody, and Chewy stopped. The police tell us to keep walking. That's out! "We're not going nowhere. We're standing right here until ya'll finish with the homies!"

"You guys take off or you'll be in cuffs!"

"Get to cuffing. What are you waiting on? We're not moving!"

Mad Face and K.O. told us it was cool and to go ahead and push. Then and only then did we move and walk towards the chow hall. Later though, they were like, "Good looking out 3rds and Long Beach!"

It happened again at Solano when a Crip homie had gotten jacked up and being patted down. Me and a few homies I was with stopped and were watching the police and waiting for the homie they had jacked up so we could all walk back to the building. The police told us to keep walking. "We're not going anywhere. What's next?"

"If you don't walk, we'll put the yard down!"

The homie they had jacked up, I can't remember who it was, he was like, "I'm good homie. Ya'll can go!" We initially had hesitated for a second, then started walking away slowly. He finally caught up to us just as we were off of the dirt, making it to the sidewalk.

A few days before that we were in the chow hall, Me, Tee, and Wavy Davey sat at a table, but there was an empty seat at the next table. The white female police comes to our table and tries telling one of us to fill in the empty space. Now we watched her racist ass the whole time we were in line, seeing and watching Hispanics and Whites not fill in spaces, because they didn't want to sit with Blacks, or they were trying to sit with their homies. She didn't say a fucking word with her racist ass! As soon as she see a Black doing the very thing she saw them doing, here she come with her issue.

"Can one of you fill in that empty space?" Biiitch, that's out! Neither one of us moved. We ignored her stupid ass. Biiitch, get up out of here! We kept eating and talking as if she wasn't standing there. We weren't going to be on no dry snitching type of shit like, "You didn't tell those Mexicans and Whites to move, so we're not moving." We just ignored her. She knew though what it was and what was really being said without it being verbalized.

19

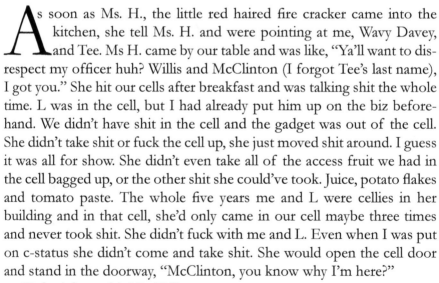

As soon as Ms. H., the little red haired fire cracker came into the kitchen, she tell Ms. H. and were pointing at me, Wavy Davey, and Tee. Ms H. came by our table and was like, "Ya'll want to disrespect my officer huh? Willis and McClinton (I forgot Tee's last name), I got you." She hit our cells after breakfast and was talking shit the whole time. L was in the cell, but I had already put him up on the biz beforehand. We didn't have shit in the cell and the gadget was out of the cell. She didn't take shit or fuck the cell up, she just moved shit around. I guess it was all for show. She didn't even take all of the access fruit we had in the cell bagged up, or the other shit she could've took. Juice, potato flakes and tomato paste. The whole five years me and L were cellies in her building and in that cell, she'd only came in our cell maybe three times and never took shit. She didn't fuck with me and L. Even when I was put on c-status she didn't come and take shit. She would open the cell door and stand in the doorway, "McClinton, you know why I'm here?"

"I don't have shit Ms. H.!"

"Ok, I don't have to come in, do I?"

"Come on in!"

"That's alright."

She would leave and our door would close. She knew I had a T.V. and a C.D. player which they're supposed to take normally while you're on c-status. Every time I've went on c-status I've pretty much kept all of my shit and have never sent it out to hide or tuck. None of the police in our building fucked with me and L because we were out of the way and didn't fuck with them or their program. Easy call.

Every now and then you'd have a non-regular come in our building and try pulling some bullshit, but usually they would sit the fuck down somewhere. This isn't even your building dude. You're just here on some overtime shit. Sit the fuck down somewhere. Do your 8 and hit the gate. Why make your job hard and complicated when it doesn't have to be? Some police would come in and would be on some extra'ed out bullshit! They would be in cells with their flash lights, looking behind lockers the building had, under them too, looking in trash cans and picking them up. They would look under the stair case with their flash lights. We're watching them, shaking our heads. They need to sit they mutha fucking ass down somewhere! Sit the fuck down! This is what we think to ourselves, sometimes we verbalize it.

Then you have those police who wanted to come right in the building, hitting cells. Ole be all I can be ass mutha fuckas! Sit your ass down too, Barney Phife! Damn! A lot of dudes lost gadgets like that, fucking with non-regulars, always moving around, lurking, and looking in cells. They even hold keys when they would walk. Shit the regular police weren't doing. The non-regular police stayed trying to make a bust. Shit got dangerous when a non-regular worked, because they were unpredictable. Unpredictability is never a good look. Dudes would constantly stay getting stumbled up on fucking with non-regulars. Non-regulars walking up on them, catching them with shit. They're too unpredictable and they move around too much. They create work and situations for themselves instead of falling back and leaving things as they are. The regulars don't even push like that. They do their jobs and rightfully so. They're doing what they're supposed to. What they're paid to do, not a problem, but they're not on no high powered and extra'ed out shit like the non-regulars who are just there for 8 hours then up out of there. They're with us five days a week and dealing with us. It's not a hit and run situation, not by a long shot.

They're not on no extra'ed out shit and when they are, they're fucking with their main targets who they target. Most of the regulars didn't fuck with us, but they did have their pets, dudes that gave them a reason. Not all police had pets, though certain ones. Their pets are the ones who got their cell hit and would have stuff token that they shouldn't have, for constantly having their named called for running around the building, delaying lock up, hanging out on the yard before it's opened, having the yard police call the building on them. Basically, being on the radar you become a pet, though really when the police see they can get you to react to them.

I personally found it funny because dudes would bring that shit on themselves, never locking up on time, always out of bounds, always hanging on doors, always doing dumb shit, always bringing heat on themselves and the police to their cell door, "Step out!" I've never done either. I lock up, I don't run around, I'm not out of bounds and I damn sure don't do dumb shit to bring heat to myself or the police to my door. I'm cool on all of that shit! I know how to stay out of the way and do me without all of the extra shit. I'm mindful. Some police play the game. They'll fuck with your cellie shit, playing games to have ya'll clashing. I'm well aware of the tactic. They're hoping to get you and your cellie to fight, using him to get at you, doing what they can't do but want to do. They know it'll mess with their job, so they go about things using other means and methods. Some idiots fall right into their traps, not seeing the bullshit. Dude, you've just done the police dirty work for them. How do you feel, stupid? The mind is a terrible thing to waste (SMH).

In general though, you have to be really mindful of the police. They're playing serious games. You always have to be mindful, especially during racial incidents. Some of the police, you really have to watch because of their racist mindset and the kit they're working out of. I've noticed on several occasions in our building how when a racial incident occurs and there's still lingering tension, and they're testing the water, they're quick to test it at your expense (Blacks).

For instance, there's a police in our building who works three watch in the tower. When he releases for chow, he'll release me with four South Siders and won't release Lon, or he'll release Lon with four South Siders. It's clear me and the homie are the only two Blacks on our tier with four South Siders in between us. You would think the police would let us out together to give us a chance if something did happen. Instead of being four on one it would be four on two, a fair fight. That's just one of many games that's being played. They'll accidentally open your cell door during tension. Yeah, accidental my ass. Everything the police do is premeditated and they're mindful of everything that they do towards us Blacks. I never take my shoes off in the cell until the bar is locked, locking all of the cells at 9 P.M. You never know when your door will accidentally just open up, especially during an incident. You won't catch me slipping like that.

Chumlee just left the cell, telling me about a potential issue with the Woods. Apparently a Wood had gotten mad at a Black and called him a Niggah. Not Niggah, but Nigger! Neither way from them is cool though, period. So, I'm assuming I'll be addressed and the Wood will be DP'ed. Fuck the reason it was said, you took it there. We'll see how it'll play out. What I don't like though is only a select few knew about it and not letting the rest of the building know as it pertains to the collective (Blacks). Yet we have a Black mac-rep who supposed to be representing us. That's his job as mac-rep, to keep us Blacks aware of anything that affects the collective. That's what he signed up for, to ensure that if and when an issue arises, he informs every Black in the building of whatever is in the air, especially if it's racial. Not run to your homies and tell them and tell a select few other Blacks in hopes they'll tell everyone in their circle. That's not how that works. For this reason, you never trust the next man with your safety or your security. Dudes are weirdos. No one should be in the dark when it's a racial issue. My cellie isn't a mac-rep. He shouldn't have had to come and tell me shit. This is the kicker though, the incident happened a couple of days ago (SMH)!

Though he's a porter I'll still catch shit. He'll hear shit anyway and will bring it to me and Lon so we're not in the dark. The mac-rep was just at my cell door talking to me about any and everything, never mentioning the Wood calling a Black Niggah! I'd asked my cellie why didn't the mac-rep tell him. He's out there with him, but he didn't get it from him. He got it in passing from someone else. He tells me the mac-rep told him. He though he knew (SMH). Ain't that a bitch! He though you knew! He was supposed to know you knew. You're out there with him and two, it's not even a lot of Blacks in our building.

Every Black face you see you should've told. These dudes are lame and game goofy, suffering from me-ism and only being concerned with what they have going on and their homies. That's why shits always going bad for Blacks. Always with that selective shit. "Oh, I'm only going to tell my homies and a couple of other Blacks." They had that weird shit bad too in Solano. You can have an issue going on, but won't hear about it until dudes are like, "Make sure you're out there!" Out where? For what? What happened? You're just now hearing about it after the fact (SMH).

Dudes are walking around you, walking past you, and not saying anything. At some point, sometimes you'll get a dude like, "Aye, such and such happened, you heard?" but well after the fact. "Nah, I ain't heard shit!" Then it's like when you're on the yard you can see a bunch of grouping up and could feel the tension. What the fucks going on? Then out of the blue it's like, "Oh, such and such happened earlier." Like, what? Then you'll get told about whatever the incident was. Dudes have this behavior and mindset bad. You'll be walking around the yard unaware of an issue and not know it, being in harm's way and clueless.

You can be in or near the area of the race that the issues with and potentially become a victim not even knowing, because you're in the blind. If you depend on the next dude to keep you safe, or up on things, you're going to be in bad shape. A lot of these dudes don't care about their own safety and security. You'll be a fool to entrust them with yours. For the most part your safety and awareness is on you. Who's better to ensure it than yourself? That whole situation of selectiveness is just crazy to me, but this is what it is. It's a Black issue, but you're only telling a selective few Blacks, but as a whole it affects me too, and my wellbeing. Oh, but you'll come to me when you want me to get involved with my support! Now the thing is I'm going to move and be involved regardless, when it's involving anything racial, that's mando, but damn, can I get the heads up? Can I have a choice of how I'm going to do me? All I'm saying is give me my option.

You're taking dudes choice from him when it's all said and done. That's just keeping it a thousand, but I've remedied that, trust me. You stay security conscious, you don't have to get security conscious. If I don't mention the Wood situation again, it was deaded (nothing happened) and wasn't pressed.

Well, I finally got a bar of what actually went on. So the word was a homie was getting out of the shower and a Wood was trying to get in the shower and had asked the police from his cell could he get in. The Wood was told no or he was ignored. Then the Wood hollers out from his cell, "What, I have to be a Nigger to get a shower?" Then the Wood wrote kites to the homie, basically apologizing, which was crazy, because he killed any chance of denial or deniability. He knew he was wrong. That's why he wrote the kite, also a bad move on his part. You've just admitted to it and you put it on paper. The Woods are aware of the situation. We'll see how it all plays out.

What was crazy though, someone we fucked with knew and didn't mention it to me and Lon. You were supposed to tell us (SMH). I take note to everything, everyone, and keep score. It was cold as hell today on the yard too. Snow was still on the ground and the wind was blowing. So while the Corona Virus program is in effect, we'll get yard every day, because we're only getting an hour. I'm good with that, we're getting yard. I just go out and chill. I don't work out on the weekend. I'm only 5 days a week. You do have to let your muscles rest. When I caught Valley Fever and almost died I was shut down afterwards for a while. I didn't work out for a cool minute. I wasn't feeling it and my body wasn't having it.

I had no energy and my bones ached, plus I was suuuper weak. My bones still ache, but I'm able to get it in. I don't work out as hard as I once did, but I get enough in to make a difference, health wise. I'll do a 100, 8 count burpies. I'll do a 100, 6 count burpies, 100 squats, 100 rocking chairs, 25 downs (25 pushups, 24 pushups, 23 pushups, so on and so forth down to zero), 1000 navy seals, 100 josheries, 100 pushups on the bars, 50 on the high bar, and 50 on the low bar. We'll mix it up though, working on different things. We'll also do 100 calf raises. Lon and Chumlee would do sets on the T Bars and do jack knives. I wouldn't. I would just do extra pushups on the top and lower bar. With the time limit we have now, by the time we do our five different routines, it's yard recall.

We do each workout by sets. That's with us, with this hot hour, we have to work with. When we're on our regular schedule we'll do five to six routines. If we hadn't finished and they call in-line, that's letting us know Blacks and Northerners have to switch work out areas with the South Siders, and we would finish up in the next area. Tomorrow is Monday. Back to the routine.

Fuck it's cold in this cell right now. I'm sure it'll be cold outside tomorrow too and we have morning yard too. I'll be wearing a whole lot of clothes and bundled up for sure. I think I'm anemic too. I haven't been diagnosed, but I'm always cold. When it's cold, I'm freezing. When it's freezing, I'm passed that.

I was thinking about my daughter, Tweet, earlier (SMH). Damn shame! I hadn't thought about her in any type of way before I had gotten that letter from cuzzo speaking on her. I found myself saying, "So what!" when he was saying she was a Jr. and went to Jordan High on the

North Side of Long Beach. Honestly, I could've cared less about what was going on with her or in her life. Once you've turned on me, it's a wrap. There is no fucking with me again. You don't get another chance to turn on me. Your character spoke volumes. The only way to fix us is to go back in time. You've lost my trust. I was telling Chumlee and the homie Lon about how if someone get at me a certain way and I've done nothing to them, all bets off. At that point though, I was talking about homies, but the same premise applies to whoever! With homies I was more or less saying if a homie tried to get at me on some false or fake shit, then that means I'm no longer a homie.

Thus, if I'm not a homie, then with you, no homie rules apply. We're not homies, we can't be if you get at me like that. In my mind, for every action there's a reaction. Cause and effect. I see things for what it is and as it is, especially when reality is clear and there's no misconception. Me and a homie spoke on bussin on homies or putting feet on them. Technically we're not supposed to play ball on homies or put feet on them. It's frowned upon, because if you're a homie how can you be treated like an enemy? You play ball on enemies and kick them. In any physical confrontation the objective is to fuck them over. It's a DP-able offense if you do it. It goes back to if you're getting at me like an enemy, like I'm not a homie, and on some bullshit, all bets off, because you're on some other shit! At that point, you're just trying to fuck over me for whatever reason you've conjured up in your mind. Now I'm an enemy. Self preservation is one of the strongest motivations we have, believe it!

I had a crazy ass dream last night and of all the people to dream about I had a dream about my ex-sister-in-law, Lee Lee. Usually when you have those type of dreams you're thinking about that person before going to sleep. I found it kind of strange though. I was riding a bike somewhere in Long Beach and when I turned a corner all of a sudden I had Lee Lee on the handle bars. Then we ended up in the bed. She was naked and on top of me, riding me reverse cowgirl. I was doing her the same way I would Situation. I would stick my finger in her butt while she rode me. Yeah, that was a crazy ass dream. I woke up but then feel back asleep and the dream picked up.

Now I had her bent over a dresser, her panties down to her ankles. I'm gripping her hips and pulling her back into my strokes. She's moaning and pushing back. Just as she's cumming, she knocks all of the stuff off of the dresser, "Ahhhhh!" When I buss I wake up, "Unghh!" I've had some crazy ass dreams over the years. I have had a dream about Situation having sex with the dude who told on me too. I probably dreamed about it because it was in the back of my mind. I've heard from a few people that they've had sex. I don't put anything passed her. If she did, so be it. Really, I could care less. It's what whores do, they have sex.

Though I've wanted to sex Lee Lee, I've never pressed it. The door was open and was never closed. She's never told on me. I believe it could've happened given the right time and circumstances. If I was asked do I believe she had sex with dude, yup, pretty much! With everything that I know about her, "Yup!" That's why I say the last baby with her is suspect. I honestly don't think or feel he's mine and I've told her that when I talked to her a few years ago. What bitch you know though that's going to keep it a thousand and tell you if it's the next dude's baby, let alone tell you she don't think it's yours? She's going to take that to her grave with the rest of her lies and secrets. You see this shit every day on Maury.

"You are not not not not the father!" It's always daddy maybe, mama's baby! As soon as I said it though, "He is yours. This that and the third!" As expected. I wouldn't think anything different from her. I expected her to say that. The thing is, I don't believe nothing that comes out of her mouth. She's an habitual liar! Fact! I use to have a lot of dreams about her when I first was locked up. All of the sex we used to have. We've had sex in bathrooms, cars, outside in the back yard, a wash room, and motels. We've had it cracking! I've had dreams about Mary, Chardon, Trice, and Miko. Me, Chardon, Trice, and Miko had sex a lot too. Me and Mary had sex twice.

I've even had dreams about a few berries that I've had sex with. That was suuuper feeling my sex game. Charmaine, Donna, Baby Face, and G.G. I've also had a dream about one of my BM's home girl I had sex with named Odea. I don't know why I had that dream. Her pussy was trash. Straight garbage. Her sex was garbage. She did not know how to fuck! That was a waste of loot on a motel room. At least her head game was gang related! She had porn star head!

I've also had nightmares and I didn't like going to sleep. Just from what I've seen, been around, or have done. It would fuck with me. I would wake up out of a dead sleep and sit up like, "What the fuck!" It all seemed so real. The visuals were like whoa! Sometimes I would wake up sweating and breathing hard and my hearts beating fast. I'm like damn. I would look around the cell and wipe my face after sitting up. My cellie would be asleep. That went on for about six or seven months off and on, then it just stopped. I would be shot up and bleeding too, trying to wake up but couldn't. Something would be literally keeping me from waking up. I don't know what that would be about. It's like you know you're having a nightmare and trying to wake yourself up, but you can't. Something is keeping you asleep. I would be spooked and I'm not easily spooked at all.

That took me back to spirituality and beliefs. You know our people, Black people are from the South and mostly came from Texas, Arkansas, Alabama, Mississippi, the Carolinas, Georgia, Tennessee, etc, so they have a lot of beliefs when it comes to spirituality and believing in spirits and haints (demons). Deeply rooted in their beliefs and spirituality.

Me and a homie were taking about how when he had woken up and couldn't move, like he was paralyzed or suffering from some sort of paralysis. He was telling me how his eyes were moving, but his limbs weren't and it spooked him. He was saying too how his moms and granny had told him that he was being held down by a demon sitting on his body. I told him about my granny telling me that very thing before. What the homie told me happened to me as a child multiple times and it happened to me as an adult on multiple occasions. Spooked me every time. I didn't know what the fuck was going on or what to think! All I know is it spooked me. I couldn't move and I was conscious. Nothing worked but my eyes. When I told my granny about it, she told me the same thing. That was, "A demon sitting on you!"

The conversation switched up to dreams and what I was told about dreams, specifically about having dreams about falling off of a building, a tall building. If you're falling off of a building, wake yourself up. You're not supposed to stay asleep because you could die. It means your hearts beating too fast and it can explode. You're never supposed to let yourself make it to the ground. Wake up. I've always woken myself up and never allowed myself to hit the ground, "Splat!"

I've had dreams about prison riots between us Blacks and the South Siders. I've had dreams about the Whites aiding them. Both sides having major casualties! Blood everywhere, bodies sprawled out on the yard, dudes on the ground being kicked and stomped out. One time I had a dream about being dragged to safety after being stabbed and I had blood all over my shirt. That shit woke a Niggah up, real quick! Another time I was playing ball on a South Sider and didn't see one coming up behind me and he got me in the back with 14 to 15 inches of metal, dropping me to my knee, waking me right up out of my sleep.

I had that dream the same day I saw the Northerners on the yard putting that work in on their people. That dream was out of the blue. All of them be. I hadn't had a dream about a prison riot in years, or about me being stabbed. I guess seeing that up here triggered something. I hadn't seen that to that extreme since my Old Folsom, Calipat, and Salinas Valley days. Snake was telling me too, right before I got here, the Woods had flat-lined a couple of their people. One thing I can say for certain, they do not horse play up here in High Desert when it comes to their people. The Hispanics up here don't horse play either. A mutha fucka will get a helicopter ride up out of here! Real ass talk!

I saw that firsthand how serious it is up here and can get. It's real in the field in High Desert. You better toe the line or it'll go ugly for you around these parts of Lasser County. All I can say is you better be on the right side of a situation. The wrong side isn't healthy. I hollered at Hersh about his homie Drake last night because he's from the bay and because Drakes the mac-rep and a Niggah's trying to get an overstanding as it pertains to communication and a lack thereof. Hersh pulled up on my door and was telling me he was going to have Drake come and holler at me. I saw Drake on the tier, but he didn't stop. I'll more than likely see him on this morning's yard, if we have it. I'm still trying to holler at him. Everyone is trying to figure out though how the situation is going to play out with the Woods. Will it be an "ah ha" moment (SMH)? We'll see. So yeah, one of the last conversations me and Brody had before he left me in Calipat in the sandbox was us clowning a lot of hood rats in the set. We got on Brandy, a young slut a lot of homies ran through in the set. Brody told me he hit (had sex with her) too. I know a few homies personally that've had sex with her (SMH). She was ran down early.

I heard a couple of years ago, Situation's oldest son, John, married her. Wow! Really! Her! Not on your life! I don't know what possessed such an act on his part to marry her (SMH). Her name was ringing like a gang bangers hot pistol hand.

Even to this day, "You know Brandy?"

"Yeah, I know that hoe (SMH)!" I don't even know how that came to be or how he missed her rep, but that wasn't a good look. Everyone knows about Brandy on the East Side. You can't bring her name up without her being called a hoe, slut, or ratchet. I call bitches whore bags and she's definitely one. The last I heard, he was still married to her. No kids, says a lot. If he has kids they wouldn't be by her. Her internal organs are fucked up (SMH)!

That had me thinking about some shit Situations oldest sister told me one time. She was like, "You know what? You're my favorite brother-in-law. You're the only one who never tried to fuck me." You know what I told her? "You're safe with me!" I couldn't do it. Wasn't anything about her physically attractive to me. No ass, no titties, and just whupped, but knowing how she used to get down, that was out anyway. No bueno! She was out there in the streets. As a person though she was cool as fuck. Really cool people. I didn't really know her like that and was rarely around her. A few times though I had spent the night at her house with Situation when Situation stayed at her house briefly. While I was staying at my aunts and would go there on the weekends.

Then she stayed the night at my house the first New Years Eve we had there. Me and Situation only lived there at that time about five or four months. Her and Lee Lee stayed the night. That night was crazy as fuck too. We were drinking a lot of Christian Brothers, hence how my oldest son by Situation got his name, Christian. He was probably made that night. Me and Lee Lee smoked blunts. Situation and Debra didn't smoke trees. Lee Lee ended up getting white girl wasted. Debra had gotten so white girl wasted she had pulled down my shelf unit that had cabinets on the bottom and all of the crystal glass and other glass that were sitting on it. She basically pulled it on top of her and when some of the glass broke, she cut her ankle or leg and was bleeding bad.

Situation and Lee Lee tried tending to her. They managed to stop the bleeding. A couple of hours after that, me and Situation were in the room in the bed getting it in. We were both wasted. I bussed a lot of nuts that night in that pussy. She sucked the dick, but I wouldn't buss in her mouth. I made her stop and I got back in the pussy. I got her doggy style, flat on her stomach, she rode me both ways, regular and reverse cowgirl. I got her on her side from the back, I held her legs up and got it while she layed on her back. She does know how to work her hips, ass, and pussy from any position you have her in.

Another dream I had was when me and L had just gotten our second gadget. I dreamt the police hit our cell and had me and L strip out in the shower, then found it in the cell. The same night we got it, I had that dream. We had a cool run with it though before they ended up actually hitting us (SMH). Bullshit ass dudes! At the bottom of the staircase having group. They couldn't give the warning sound. Hating ass dudes! Solano had a lot of haters. Dudes see you getting your loot, they'll huddle up and try to run a play. Between the snitches and haters, you had to level up and be on you're a game. B wasn't working. I played the back field on them suckers for the most part, so I passed with minimal flags on the play. That part! Me and Brody were talking about crazy ass bitches and how they would do retarded shit. I told him about Big Tic's bitch Nikki, how they were driving up Orange, about to come up the small hill to Hill St. Nikki had grabbed the steering wheel while he was driving and they drove into the tall grass from the street, making him crash into a wall. He smacked the wall, messing up his fresh paint (SMH).

I also was telling the homie about Situation and how I stayed out all night one night and came home. Me and I.C. passed my driveway. You could see my swoop. A island separated us though. We couldn't just pull into my driveway. We had to go all the way to the light on 60th and Atlantic and pull into the small parking lot of the Mexican market to turn around. It's early when we pass. I see my swoop. Something stood out. I couldn't put my finger on it right away. I'm telling him my windows looked frosted or something. They didn't look right. He was like, "You're tripping homie. It's just dew on the windows. Ain't nothing wrong with your shit!" I'm looking around, but I don't see anyone windows looking like mine. As soon as we pull into my driveway, I saw instantly, my tires were on flat. We got out of the homies swoop and as we're approaching mine, we see the flag on the play! I'm about to kill this bitch!

My paint, freshly done, was scratched the fuck up! My vinyl freshly done was cut up. I had sugar, flour, and cornmeal in my gas talk. All I'm thinking was I'm about to catch my third strike on this silly ass bitch! I'm fucking her ass up! All four of my tires were flat. A few spokes on my Daytons were bent like someone beat my spokes a hammer or metal, a pole or something. She pushed chicken bones and other stuff in my dash radio. She put a street cone inside of my swoop with a bike frame with no handle bars seat or wheels. My windows were smeared with cooking grease and corn meal. She had it on my seats as well. She also dumped the trash can from out of the house inside too.

I'm standing there in the driveway stunned, like did this bitch really get at me like this? Yeah, she did! I.C.'s laughing. I turn towards the house. The front window curtains are opened all the way and the blinds are raised. I could see her pacing back and forth in the house. It's bars on on the window. First I'm thinking like she had to have had help and she was pregnant. She didn't do all of this by herself. She couldn't have. If it wasn't her kids, it was her sister Lee Lee, or one of her bullshit ass friends. She didn't do it by herself. That's out! I go to the window. They're open too. "Aye Bay, what's going on? Come open the door!" She looked at me, "You got me fucked up!" I'm just looking at her.

"I'm not opening shit. You're not about to beat my ass!"

"Bay. . . Bay. . . let me in. I ain't tripping. It's cool. You know I'm not going to do nothing to you."

"I know you ain't. I'm not even worried about it!"

"Bay!" I went ahead and left with I.C. It wasn't happening. She was not opening that door. Me and I.C. went back to his spot. She done right though. Had she opened that door, I was beating that ass. She was many things, but stupid wasn't one. I ended up giving her a pass though. Brody was laughing. We got a lot of laughs out of situations we talked about. Some side and stomach hurting laughs with tears. Jokes stayed coming too. You have to know how to light the way in dark times. We had a couple of issues, but gotten passed them, nothing major or serious. That's Brody!

He should've been my blood. He's real family. I'll go to the end with him. We've shedded blood together in battle against a threat and we rode together. Fuck with him, you're fucking with me and vice versa. I didn't have to guess where we stood. Our bonds solid. He's a loyal homie and friend, real Niggah! One thing I do know, he's going to reach back. He's not even in that category of dudes that just say shit just to say it to hear themselves talk. He stands by his word. He's always kept his word with me. Anything he's told me he was going to do, it got done. We were speaking on the big homie K.R. one day and I was telling him I fucked with the homie a little bit. He's a good homie. I'd met him through Lil Sugar Bear. Me and the homie had done a lick together before, which is one of the first I'm down for. I saw him in the county about three months after I left the streets. In passing he was like, "Cuz homie!" He didn't have to worry about being implicated. I'm solid as they come. That was all me.

I don't do no statements. I take my issue and keep it moving. I've only had a few co-defendants, Big Dan Dog in 1990, and Jackpot, Mike and that dude Terry who never done no time in 1988. I could've had a co-defendant a couple, but I'm the one who was caught, so I rode it out like the champ I am. I rode it out solo and was struck out. I was struck out for each count of robbery I was booked for. They offered me 25 to life and that was supposed to be a deal. If you (them) don't knock it the fuck off! It was no way in the hell I was going to take no 25 to life. Whaaat! I took it to the box, twelve jurors, and was whupped over the head. I was stretched out like Gumby and Pokey.

My attitude was this, if you're going to serve me, come with it. I need that twelve in the box. I couldn't see myself accepting 25 to life all willy-nilly. I knew what I was getting into as I knew if I lost it was going to be ugly, and it was. I took it well for getting all the time I received. I got my issue and done it moving. What else was I going to do, break down? Cry? Kill myself? Those weren't options. Homies would say, "That shit just haven't hit you yet, Tic." I'm still waiting. It hasn't happened yet. I seriously doubt if it ever will. Meeting me, you would never think I have 335 years to life. I have more time than a serial killer and I hadn't killed anything.

I know I was broke off, more so from my history of being a known jacker, which has been my M.O. since I was a teenager. That's basically all I've ever done time for, robberies. I'd caught a couple of pistol cases and one dope case in the 80's as a juvenile, but I know with this situation Karma played a factor for all of the dirt I've done and have gotten away with. I feel too, they've cleared their books with some cases, basically added cases that fit my M.O. whether I'd done them or not. I was in the area and I was jacking establishments and people. "He could've. Let's put it on him. Its case solved!" They can clear it. It's done all of the time. It's common practice, especially with Blacks. Yeah, for sure, I'm guilty of some, but not all of the cases I was charged with.

With walking these lines, survival is the first law of nature, in the land of the beast, next to self preservation. Then comes the preservation in the face of a legitimate threat. A real Niggah ignores nothing though. You have to always be mindful of that fact. Survival first and foremost. Overstand your position on the field. I went to the yard this morning. It was cold as usual, but I was good. Chumlee had to stay in the building to work, so I hit the slab solo. Vamp ended up coming to the slab and we done some burpies. Snake came to the slab with us and posted up. He didn't work out. He just watched us and talked.

I talked to Drake before we went to yard. He pulled up on the door. He was telling me that that incident with the Wood actually happened Saturday afternoon and only a certain few people know what had happened. I told him though how crazy that was and how crazy that actually sounded, that everyone didn't know the biz. I also told him that he was the mac-rep and he should've made sure everyone knew. He tells me I assumed everyone knew. Wow, really homie (SMH)? At the end of the day it's a Black issue. You're the mac-rep. You should've made sure everyone knew. Another dude actually told me asking about it was starting trouble. Whaaat! Are you serious? Then he hit me with, "That's just looking for trouble and problems. That was a small issue. Didn't no one say anything to the South Siders when they use it amongst themselves. We need to stop picking and choosing who it's cool for and who it isn't cool for." Yeah, I'm out! I just walked away from dude. I knew his kind of people just from his statements (SMH). He's that aggressive turn down dude. He's trying to play it safe and not rattle no bushes, don't want any rattled either. The outcome with the Wood situation ended up dude having to do a work out, issues deaded.

Though dudes were in their feelings, can't tell another race how to DP their own. That's how they chose to handle it. That's what it is, even though they could've cared less about dude using the word. Trust and believe they're all using it amongst themselves. We're all type of names in private, Sambo, Porch Monkey, Spook, Darky, just to name a few. IF anything, they probably told him not to be so vocal to where he can be heard. If they had any type of feelings about it, it was that, being vocal. It could've potentially been a situation that could've blown up the yard, so that was the word. He had to work out, me and Vamp saw him though.

I was tripping off of it, like damn! That's crazy! When the facts changed, my opinion changed. It wasn't my situation, but I would've been more vocal about it just based on I knew he was referring his words to me and though he was talking to the police, he was talking to me, he knew he was talking to me, and referring it to me which he confirmed by writing me a kit apologizing. In general though, I trip off of dudes when it's another race an issue is with. It's no animation or aggression. It's whatever. I'm really not tripping, but let it be an issue with another Black or a homie. It's no communicating, no overstanding, no anything. It's, "I'm on him! We're on him!" (SMH) It's the guillotine, off with his head! Dudes are trying to press and are vocal as fuck! We're going up, fuck that! Fuck this, this, that, and the third! With all of the extras and animations (SMH). All I'm saying is this, be the same way, regardless as to who it is. Have that same fire and passion about the situation. Don't be turned up on your own, but turn down when another race is involved. That's all I'm saying. Yet, there's a question mark as to why the other races, including the police, don't respect us Blacks as a whole, but individuals get theirs. I don't give a damn who you are. You're going to respect a dudes violence if nothing else. I'll call a ball a ball and a strike a strike. I've had this conversation with homies and with cellies. They've all agreed with my assessment.

My assessment, which is real shit, you want to go balls out on your own, but when it comes to the next race, his panics mainly, "That turned up shit is out of the window. It's no bueno!" You've turned humbled and civilized. Now you know how to talk and communicate and have overstanding. Whaaat! Who is this person? Who are these people (SMH)? Real shit! But whatever floats your boat though. When I get to Tehacha-pi, level 4, 180 yard, I had just left Tehachapi's reception yard where I stayed for three months, after leaving 6, the L.A. County Jail. I was glad to have left the county. It was crazy and too much shuffling around and carrying your whole existence in a green mesh bag. Everywhere you went you took that bag with you. Your food, cosmetics, mail, captured moments, court documents, etc.

You're constantly on the move. You can never get comfortable, module after module, dorm after dorm, bus ride after bus ride. Tehachapi's reception yard is like most reception yards. For the most part not a whole lot going on, but a lot of cell time and reading. Oh, and plenty of war stories. You have no entertainment but books. No T.V. or C.D. player/radio. You're doing time. You're also a step closer to your final destination. That's all reception is, no music, no T.V., just you and your cellie in the cell telling war stories and talking about the streets. You may come across a few good books. Outside of working out, you're writing letters. At the time I only had Chardon tapping in with me. I also tapped in with Darla who'd I've been communicating with for years while I was locked up. I met her in '92, on my first term and we've been connected ever since. We've had a cool relationship which was never a physical one. Back in the days though, in earlier years, '92, '93, '94, she would suck on the dick at visiting. It was a lot looser way back then and much easier to do things and get away with them as long as you weren't doing too too much. It's always been it's not what you do, but how you do what you do. I use to finger bang her. She would wear sun dresses.

I would sit next to her, side by side, and would put my hand under her dress, in between her legs, which she slightly opened so I could penetrate her with my fingers. After she would cum I would have her suck on my fingers. Once though, we had went on the patio and she had squatted down in front of me while I faced the window looking inside of the visiting room and sucked on it a few good times. I used to go under her shirt too and play with her big ass titties. A few times she would sit next to me, side by side, unzip my pats, pull my dick out and stroke it until I was nutting on her hand and in it. A few times she gotten away with sucking on it at the table, but the deed was never finished. Came close though.

That was the extent of our physical activity sexually. Shit, under the circumstances, I was good with it. When Chardon came to Solano, the only thing happened outside of us doing a lot of kissing was me going under her shirt, playing with her titties. As she called it, I was feeling her up. I was trying to get my hands in her pants, though it wasn't happening. Her pants were fitting, snug on her, and she had a belt on. It was not happening at all. Whaaat! She only came a few times, twice by herself, twice she brought moms. Once she brought moms, she brought my daughter. They wouldn't let my daughter in though. She had to stay in a friends outside trailer until visiting was over. Something with her birth certificate or the notarized note. The times moms did come, we didn't do too much. I kept my cool. We still kissed though. By herself though, without moms, I kept her ass pressed up against me. At the microwave or by the vending machines, pulling her back into me. "Stop, Tic!" I knew I was getting her hot and bothered. "Stop Tic, you're making me wet!" I kept doing it. She really didn't want me to stop. No doubt, I felt lil mama up, felt on her ass and between her legs. Whaaat! I had her rubbing on me for sure. Reception wasn't anything much going on around there, really.

The side of the yard I was on, which was separated by a chain link fence, had a couple of buildings which were considered level 3, mainline buildings. We had a few Long Beach homies in those buildings. Ten Speed from 20's, and Fumbie from 20's. In the building I was in, as far as homies, it was the homie Reese (Tiny Sadiki). It was another young homie I didn't know and never heard of and he was a white boy claiming the set. Though we have a few, I didn't have a problem with homie, I just didn't know him. The homie Reese knew him though. I ended up taking off (attacking) on him. He ran his mouth and I took flight! I just fired his shit up and he was cool. The police didn't catch it. He just went his way.

He came at me on some goof ball shit. "Aye cuz, you said I wasn't from the set?"

Whaaat! If you don't miss me with that stupid ass shit! I'm looking at his dumb ass, "If I did say it, I would've said it to your face, straight up!"

"Fuck you mean?"

"Well, if you di-!" (bing. . . bing) Whaaat! I didn't let him finish the sentence. I lit his shit up!

He was already on my shit list, talking about he whupped on Big Tray Deee. I'm like dude, if you don't knock it off! You ain't done shit to Big Deee. He was like, "Me and Tray Deee got into it and I shot out his back window in his car when he pulled off." Me and Tiny Sadiki looked at eachother and shook our heads, like this clown is lying his ass off. Dude, you know you're lying. Why are you saying this shit? Then I just told him, "Aye homie, you need to kill that and stop lying. None of that happened."

"Yeah it did. On Insane it happened!"

"Aight, but kill that noise though. Niggahs ain't feeling it and not trying to hear it!" He changed the subject and conversation all together.

Sadiki ended up going back to court, back to the county jail, a couple of weeks later. Infant Stan was on the yard too. He was on the other side of the yard. The chain link fence separated the yard. It was three buildings on one side and two on the other. I was just trying to remember the white boy homie name. I just remember him being chubby with green eyes.

20

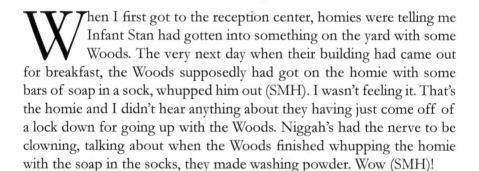

When I first got to the reception center, homies were telling me Infant Stan had gotten into something on the yard with some Woods. The very next day when their building had came out for breakfast, the Woods supposedly had got on the homie with some bars of soap in a sock, whupped him out (SMH). I wasn't feeling it. That's the homie and I didn't hear anything about they having just come off of a lock down for going up with the Woods. Niggah's had the nerve to be clowning, talking about when the Woods finished whupping the homie with the soap in the socks, they made washing powder. Wow (SMH)!

The last time I saw Infant Stan, we were in the set at the Highway Center at night. He was squabbling up with three Hispanics. I didn't even know it was the homie though. I just saw three Mexicans fighting with a Niggah. I pulled over, threw my shit in park, and got cracking with the homie. More Blacks had started coming and the Mexicans got on, ran for safety. Me and him though were handling our biz on them before more help came. They knew it was about to be a wrap. That was really an odd scene. Three Mexicans fighting with one Niggah and in the set. I'm looking around though, like where were Niggahs at?

What was really odd, I didn't have my 40 on me or in the swoop. That night, of all nights, not to have it. As far as I was concerned, that would've been a freebie. I had talked to my guy in Delano on the gadget and we laughed about that incident. He was like, "Damn cuz, where in the fuck did you come from?" Then I was like, "Where ever you came from. That was good looking out!" Even then, I was like, I didn't remember why I didn't have my banger. All I remember though was I didn't have it that night and if I had I would've sparked on them. What I was more surprised of was didn't any other homies pop up before I did.

Normally, homies are always up and down King, and up and down PCH. I forgot to ask him what the deal was with that shit that had happened with the Woods in Tehachapi on the reception yard. I never ran into him while I was there. I fucked with the homie a lot on the streets. I had a cellie from Gardena, Payback Crip. I forgot his name. He was cool though, except he stayed getting into it with the police about some sunflower seeds. He asked her for some, playing with her I guess. I don't know what he had going on. All I know is I don't fuck with the police. The shit went from zero to eighty. She was like, "Don't be asking me for my shit!"

"Fuck you then, you raggedy ass bitch!" He though she was cool and played himself. The next thing you know, she came back with her partner. Here we go.

We were pulled out of the cell and had to sit at the tables while they searched it. He's cursing her out the whole time, "Boot mouth bitch! Bucket head bitch! Ugly ass bitch!" She was a thousand different bitches. When they finished, they came out with some stuff in a bag. They fucked my shit up too. I knew the game they were trying to play. "We'll fuck with his cellies shit too and have them getting into it." All I did was move. He fucked with the police too much for me. I do not do the police. I do not need that smoke! It's no bueno! I ended up getting a cell by myself.

The first cellie I ended up getting was straight. He had been there already a minute. Him and his cellie weren't getting along, so I let him move in with me. He was only with me a week, then he was transferred somewhere. When you're in reception, dudes are constantly leaving, going somewhere. The next cellie I had was Lil Dev (Devil) from 4-6 Neighborhood (Foe-Six). He was straight too. We would stay up late talking about the streets. He would tell me about his homies, about him getting loot, and about all of the females he was messing with. We were talking about the county jail too. He was telling me about his neighborhood homies and the Hoovers. I already knew what was going on down there. I'd only been gone for a little over three weeks. He was basically talking about the beef they had going on in the county.

The neighborhoods had the 2000 floor and the Hoovers had the 4000. The shit they had going on was crazy as fuck! It was '04 when I was in the county getting a glimpse of the activity. It was like if the Hoovers caught the Neighborhoods on the 4000 floor, it was ugly for them, and vice versa. Neighborhoods caught the Hoovers on the 2000 floor. It was ugly. They were packing eachother out (jumping eachother), playing ball on eachother. They were ramming dudes in the butt with objects. It got real ugly. The deputies would work with them.

You would be lined up on the wall outside in the hallway, outside of a module, waiting to go inside. As soon as you got inside and into the dayroom, here comes eight or nine dudes, pushing inside of the dayroom. Where did they come from though? This was the 2000 floor.

"Where you from my Niggah?" Push right up all in your space.

"Long Beach Insane!"

"Yeah, yeah, we're not fucking with you. You fuck with the Hoovers. Don't ask for no runs, no passing, none of that. You got nothing coming!" That was the Neighborhoods when I went to 2600-2800.

"Whatever!" Ali Bob from 60's was the main one talking.

About a week after I was there in that module, I had went to court and when I came back, it was like four Neighborhoods by the door on the inside of the module, when me and another dude walked in. "Aye homie, where you from?" I kept walking. I knew he wasn't talking to me. They already hit me up. I'm thinking they're talking to dude, not me. I hit the stairs and began walking up them. Just as I get to the top of the stairs, I hear running behind me. I spin around quick and put my dukes up. I'm like, "Sup cuz?"

"Aye homie, where you from?"

"I told you Niggahs where I was from. I'm from Insane!"

"Oh, oh yeah, I forgot you did." He turned around and went on his way.

I was telling Dev about the incident. He was like, "Yeah, homies were on one." After I'd left the county and went back to wayside I had went to Super Max to a dorm. It was like six or seven Hoovers in there.

One of them spotted a Neighborhood they knew from the county. I guess tripping on him with a few of his homies. "We about to groove this Niggah!" They let him get all the way inside of the dorm, go up the stairs to the bed area, and pick a bed. Dude made his bed up and then got in the bed. The Hoovers had started migrating at the bottom of the stair case, but looking up towards the top banister, talking. Dude actually got into his bed and underneath his blankets (SMH). Horse playing! He knew they were coming. One by one they made their way upstairs, one behind the other and had surrounded the bed. Dude was on the top bunk, "Aye Groove, where you from?" At first he didn't answer. When he was asked a second time he raised up like the wrestler Undertaker. He looks around and sees he's surrounded.

"Huh?"

"Where you from Groove?"

"Oh, I ain't from nowhere homie. I don't bang!"

"Groove lying. Get Groove!"

He was snatched off of the bunk by his ankles, smack! To the floor he went, then a loud thud. They got on him and was on him like back pockets, front pockets, and side pockets. Somehow though, he managed to get away from them, making it to the stairs. He catches a foot to the back and was sent tumbling down the stairs. He got to the bottom and met some foot work (SMH). He went to the bars and got up out of there, leaving his possessions behind. "HOOOVAAA!" That's all you heard for a minute or so. When I made it back to the county, someone told me Big Tic was in the module, after I was hit up and told dudes my name, who were Hoovers. Big Tic, who's also Lil Sugar Bear, named after his big Brody Mitchell from the set, Big Sugar Bear. Somewhere along the line they weren't seeing eye to eye, so he stopped going by Lil Sugar Bear and went back to his original name, Tic Loc (True Insane Crip: Tic).

However, he was more known as Lil Sugar Bear, even to this day. A lot of homies from everywhere, from back in the days, will call him Lil Sugar Bear when they see him. I've known him since I was like eight or nine. Met him when I stayed on Walnut. I hadn't seen him since I was a kid and had bumped into him in Old Folsom in '91. He had came from Soledad with a broken jaw. At this time I was going by Dre Boy. I ended up taking his name, becoming Lil Tic Loc in Old Folsom. He was like, "I want you to push the name homie. I'm not fucking with my brother. I'm doing my own thing." At first, I was hesitant. I liked my name and it was original and I wanted to make my own name. The other homies really weren't feeling me changing my name to Lil Tic because they weren't a fan of Lil Sugar Bear, which became my driving factor and a catalyst to change it.

I've been pushing the name and have been representing him and the name ever since. So much so, it really became my name. I'm the most known by it, for putting in work on Enemigos and for being a shooter on the streets. Homies consider me really as Big Tic. On some real shit, I was going to stop pushing Tic Loc and start pushing Tic Eastwood, because I stop feeling his get down and he doesn't act or push as a big homies should. I've been down all of this that dude hasn't written me, sent me any captured moments, sent me a phone number, or sent me a dime, but yet I'm his lil homie and still pushed the name. He's just out there living his life (SMH). In reality, he's not a homie. He knows what it is though. Bullshit Niggah! So anyway, he was told I landed in the module and I was pulled to the cell with him. "Aye Lil Tic, your big homie is going to have you pulled. Get ready." When I get to the cell, he's in the cell with two Hoovers and a civilian. We were on the 4000 floor. I can't remember one of the Hoovers. Blame it on the sherm. The other one I do remember was Snow, older homie who was cool as fuck and layed back. Both of them were cool.

Me and Lil Sugar Bear were kind of catching up and he was telling me about what had been going on on the streets on some TMZ shit. I hadn't seen him since he went to jail on 19th and Magnolia. He had sold that dope to an undercover and was given that marked loot. I think he was in there or something else though at the time. I was with him when he went to jail. Me, him, and his whore Brandy were in his swoop, sitting there on the block, about to pull off from the curb when the van pulled up next to us. A few other police vehicles too, all under covers. Didn't know it at the time. Niggahs didn't know what the fuck was going on. They'd hopped out on us with their weapons drawn and pointing at us. "Get your fucking hands up now!"

We were told to get out of the swoop. We get out and were layed on the ground, cuffed, and searched. I didn't have shit on me. Brandy had a pipe on her. I wasn't on parole anymore, so I was let go. Brandy was on paper, Lil Sugar Bear too. They let Brandy go though, which I thought was crazy. On parole, have a pipe, that's for sure a one way flight to jail. I don't know what that was about. I had just hit the corner of Magnolia when he sees me. "Cuz, I need to holler at you!" He wanted to get at me because apparently homies had been getting at him about me. Talking about he better talk to me before something happen to me. I had gotten into it with a few homies and a couple of them were spooked which is never a good thing. A spooked Niggah is a dangerous one. The ones who were spooked went to other homies about the situation in my BG circle and with a few Youngs I was known for being Suuuper active with that banger, I tell no tale. I don't know what homie or homies pulled up on him about me. We hadn't got to talk. He was like, "Homies said you need to calm down. You're tripping!" Had I not came to jail when I did, I would've been dead probably. Dead or in jail for murder and not robberies, which ultimately didn't matter because I got time like I murdered some shit. At the end of the day, I was facing three strikes anyway, robbery or murder, didn't make a difference. I had a life sentence coming regardless.

That was the extent of our conversation. "Homies said you need to calm down. You're tripping!" That first shit though he said, telling me they told him he better talk to me before something happen to me didn't sit too well with me. I'm smoking sherm, so my mind already have me on noid (paranoid). Now I'm really in my head. "Niggahs are out to kill you. Get them before they get you!" He didn't tell me who it was that pulled up on him with this or who actually got at him. I started to look at him some type of way. I still don't know to this day and that was in late '03. It's 2020 now.

We're all in the cell one day, chilling. Me, Lil Sugar Bear, the Hoover homies and the citizen. The cell door com open and a dude I recognized from the 2000 floor who were with the Neighborhoods walk in. He recognizes me. I don't know for certain if he was in fact a Neighborhood, I just know he was with them. I didn't see him or hear him pressing dudes or hitting them up, but nine out of ten, if you're fucking with them, you're ducking with them. He walks in and gets hit up, "Where you from Groove?"

"I, I, I don't bang!" I'm like, to myself, aight, I'm not tripping, whatever. I wasn't going to say anything. I was leaving it alone. He started saying he know who I am. He knows I wasn't with none of that shit.

Looking at me, "Groove, you know him?"

"Nah, I don't know him, but I was on the 2000 floor with him."

"He bang?"

"Nah, not to my knowledge and I didn't see him on no bullshit."

He got a pass, but keeping it a thousand, had he been with the fuckery, yup, I would've gave him up. He could've been with the bullshit, but that was a demonstration. I didn't see or hear. Had they packed me out, I would've been on some bullshit whether he was or weren't, just the fact he was with them would've been enough. "Get that Niggah, hell yeah he's one!" Maaan look dude was spooked.

Snow and his homie were cool, but at the same time, dude was as good as got. I was telling Lil Devil about that whole situation. Two days later, Ali Bob ended up popping up at Tehachapi. He saw me in the chow hall and was looking at me, trying to place my face, like I was a face he'd remember for doing something to. I just nodded at him, nah homie, you didn't do anything to me. He nodded back at me, the look on his face finally confirmed, he'd placed me. When I did holler at him, he was asking me questions about the pen and how shit worked. A totally different person than the one I'd encountered in the county jail. I didn't recognize this guy. This was another person standing next to me talking, asking how this worked, how that worked, this that and the third.

Had I not knew who he was or what he'd been about or represented, I would've thought he was a cool dude just trying to navigate his way through the maze, but nah, this is a wolf in sheep's clothing. I saw you at work. The very shit he would say he wasn't with, he was orchestrating (SMH). Dudes had no win. Devil was like, "That sounds about right!" Dev was telling me how he was out there getting his weight up, getting loot, and how he had hating ass homies plotting on his downfall.

He use to have me laughing too, talking about his boys, one in particular, Pudgy or something like that. One thing about Dev, he was a tight dude with his stuff. I would give him stuff before he got his canteen, because that's just I do with cellies, especially if they don't have anything. I don't believe in eating in dudes faces without sharing or offering something. That's just not how I rock. I have no problem sharing or looking out and without looking for anything in return. I give from the heart. If I give you something, I'm not looking for anything back, and it's small shit to me. But when he got his shit, he wouldn't offer a Niggah a chip, though I wasn't tripping. I was super straight, my lil mama made sure I was good.

I'm like to myself though, "Oh, you're one of those guys!" Got you! Trust I was good though, and my pops, Tony, had popped up and was looking out for me. For the most part, they had me straight and I wanted for nothing. McNeal would come to the county and she would put loot on my books. I wouldn't spend much. I just bought what I needed, a few snacks here and there, writing material, phone card, and cosmetics. Pops would put loot on my books.

I knew too I was going to need all I could get loot wise, so I could get right once I hit the reception center. So, I wasn't messing off loot like that. When pops hit me, he would hit me with a dollar (hundred). Between the two, I was good. I had been fucking with my pops before I had gotten locked up. I hadn't grown up with him in my life. We kind of began our relationship when I was a teenager, around fourteen or fifteen. I spent a couple of days with him in the Nickerson Gardens where him and his wife and her kids lived. I stayed in his step son, Jerry's room. I think he was Nightmare or Night Owl from bounty hunter, something like that. He was locked up at the time. I never met him. He was from that KS they had going on back then in the projects. Though I never met him, I had heard of him being a joint from over there. Me and pops had lost contact after that for years. Had no contact whatsoever.

I had gotten locked up and stayed getting locked up. I ran into him with Situation in '02-'03, after being out of the pen for a cool minute. He had gotten the opportunity to meet two of my kids by Situation, Solie and Christian. She was pregnant at the time with Kaemaijay. Shortly after that we hadn't communicated again for a hot minute. He had somehow found out I was in the county and hit me up. By the time I'd hit the reception center and was there a month, he went down. We ended up doing inmate correspondence forms (CDCR 1074) and started communicating via mail. He was still sending me loot incarcerated. He would have his nephew Irison shoot it to me.

McNeal was still hanging and playing her supporting role, though I thought she would've vacated long before she had and I had to tell her to go live her life. She was being a real trooper and being loyal, being as young as she was and still being in traffic. But yeah, I was the one who told her to go due to my life sentence. Plus, it would've been selfish of me to expect her to put her life on hold for me. She had a lot of living to do. She had a life to live, life to learn, and life to experience. She stayed though until I made it to Tehachapi, 180 yard. She sent me my first clothes, shoes, C.D. player, etc, leaving me straight. Her parting words, "I won't have no kids for at least five years. I'll wait that long." Her sons now like ten or eleven. I've been gone sixteen.

She sent captured moments and wrote me more than I can say about any of my BMs or Situations ever doing. I'll always have a lot of love and admiration for her, even though she vacated on me in 2016. I'll never hold that against her, going back to baby daddy and having another baby. Congratulations, McNeal. I had her name tattooed on me in 2017. I won't cover it up. She earned that based on her having been in the trenches with me and held me down. Even more so after she popped back up and after all of those years of us not having contact or communicating.

It's a badge of honor and she soldiered it out, really trooping with me when I was on the run. That tat, its staying! Besides McNeal's name, I have my grandmother's name, Solie, and I have my daughter Solie's name. Hers and my daughter Kaemaijay's names are together. I also have my Aunt Mart's name on me, hers and my mom's name I'm going to have redone. I still have to get my Uncle Johnny's name put on me. The last thing I'll do is have my Uncle George's name redone. I should've been covered up Situation's name, but it's so light now I wasn't in a rush to do it. As soon as the opportunity presents itself though, it's out of here like a baby mama when a Niggah go to jail.

Darla had started writing me and I had her sending me magazines and stamps. She came and visited me in wayside. She came to L.A. with one of her friends and decided to pull up on me, tapping in since she was in the area. It was a surprise. I thought it was McNeal pulling up on me. It turned out to be Darla. When I was called for the visit, the last person I thought it would be was Darla. "Let me see those big ass titties!" Whaaat! She pulled them out and let me see them. Then she scooted back in her seat and pulled her dress up, opening her legs so I could see in between them as she pulled her panties to the side for me. "Stick your fingers in it and put them in your mouth!" Throughout this 16 she's been in and out, but present. She's always had a presence.

I finally leave the reception center and is driven right up the hill to the 4 yard. It had been snowing and it was cold as fuck. Snow was still visible on the ground. I stayed in the orientation cell for a day. G Rocc Head and his cellie, Breeze, just moved in the building together, upstairs from me. Rocc Head is a G from the set. I've known him for years. Breeze was claiming Youngs at the time, it was another homie upstairs named C Dog from the set and allegedly a BG, age wise. I didn't know him. Rocc Head had me moved upstairs in the cell with him. A few days later, Rocc Head and Breeze moved to another building and had me and C Dog pulled to that building.

We were pulled to the building and moved on the same tier with them. As me and C Dog would talk, I'm finding more and more out about him. One of the things I come to learn was him having kids by my childhood homie's little sister, Trina. Punkin (Deangelo), and Baby Kelly Boy (William) who goes by Rocc now lived on 19th and Lewis in the same apartments as me as kids. I think Trina was under Arsean, one of the homies other little brothers, and Anthony was the baby boy. I believe they have another little sister too, Theena. Their pops was Happy and their moms was Barbra. They have an older brother who stayed in San Bernardino somewhere. He would just pop up every now and then. His name was Antwuan, but went by Ant Dog from the set. Punkin and Rocc are from the set, Arsean is as well, but don't know what they call him. Their sister, Lacosta, is under Rocc, also a childhood friend.

Trina was young when C Dog was messing with her from what he was telling me, but when I thought back to who she was, she was young. I remember her being real young. When I was like 14 or 15 she had to be around 5 or 6. I just know she was a little girl. He was telling me how he didn't know how old she was when he started messing with her which made me think someone had to have an issue with that. "Her brothers, or their pops wasn't tripping on you?" I think he said Happy was at first but finally accepted it.

I bumped into Rocc in the county, well in wayside. I hadn't saw his fat ass since we were kids, running around on the block with Tyrone and Anthony (Baby Bullet and Coo Coo), who also lived in the same apartments. Shit wasn't really adding up with C Dog the more we chopped it up. He was cool as fuck though, but something wasn't right from who he claimed to have hung out with, to where he grew up and went to school. A lot of shit he should've known about the set, he didn't know. Like key spots for example, The Hutch or The Infinity. You're my age, you definitely should know about them or about free lunch at Cal-Rec, or at Mac Arthur's park. He was telling me he came from Salina's Valley, but went by another name. He told me he went by Cat Eyes. Why would you change your name when you get to a different location? That was just suspect to me. It didn't add up. It was most definitely smoke. You know what they say about smoke, where there's smoke there's fire. I know for a fact I've never heard of a Cat Eyes from the set, not around my age, and you were supposed to be a BG, nah! He didn't even know any of the BG's I would speak on, and these are known and reputable homies. Then you're telling me about homies I ran with, but you didn't know me. I took that as him being a dude that hears stories and put himself in them.

That's why I'm always mindful of what and who I speak on, because you have dudes who do that. Speaking on incidents or functions they were never involved with or at, just heard about them. Those he would speak on for the most part I've never heard of any of them. A lot of what I would talk about he wouldn't know, period, homies, blocks, or events. When I'm talking he would nod and make comments.

"Damn, that's right!"

"Whaaat, that's crazy!"

"The homies are burnt out!"

"I think I heard of him!"

"I think I heard about that!"

Text book shit. When I asked him where did he go to school, because he would always say, "I'm born and raised in this city"

Couldn't doubt it, he probably was, but he couldn't have been out there like he was claiming he was. I've never ran into him anywhere growing up as kids, or teens. I've never done Juvenile Hall time with him, never saw him at any of the schools I've attended or parks I've played at or went to. Where did you grow up or play at? What park did you go to? I'm a stop down born and raised East Side Bay Bay kid! I can answer every question I asked and with ease. I can answer them because I'm East Side. I'm a Long Beach dude, period. I can tell you every street I've lived on, what kids I've played with, who all lived on the block, what parks I've went to, what schools I've went to, the whole nine. I'm day one.

I started playing an old game we would play with dudes in Y.A. and in the Halls when we thought they were suspect (not really homies like that). "Cuz, you know Baby Kick Stand?" He started looking as if he knew Baby Kick Stand or have heard of him. You know that look you have when you're thinking it sound familiar? "How about the homie Big Loose Change?"

"Oh yeah, I think I know cuz. Did he hang out with John and them?"

I'm like, "Yeah!" This Niggah's bullshit. There is no Big Loose Change from Insane, Youngs, or Babyz (SMH). Dumb ass Niggah! "I guess you know Tiny Barb Wire too, huh? If you know them you have to know Infant Bumper Jack." I asked him what C Dog he was named after. This is where the real bullshit come into play.

You're from Insane? Get a bar. The only C Dogs I know from the set were Chris Gaither (I.I.P) and Junay (Wallace Vaughn), both Youngs, and Junay went under Chris. I'm like, "You're under Chris and Junay?" He looked like he was going to lie but said nah. He didn't even know them or heard of them. Then he tells me, "Nah, I'm under Chris Sanders."

Wait, wait, wait, flag on the play. Chris Sanders? "How is that? Cuz is from 20 Crip!"

Then he back peddles, seeing I wasn't going for that one. "Nah, nah, nah, not him!"

Then I threw him a life line, "You're pushing C Dog because your first name starts with a C."

Then he was like, "Yeah, yeah, yeah." Imposter (SMH), couldn't even tell me who put him on.

One day we were all on the tier, talking, laughing, and clowning. Me, Rocc Head, Sugar Tank (the name he changed it to and told me himself it was), this due Breeze, Boo Dog, and Treach. Me, Lil Treach (Jack Dog), Boo Dog, and Rocc Head were really talking about homies and home girls, the only ones basically. Breeze and Sugar Tank were clueless as to either the homies or the home girls. Neither of them knew any of the people we were talking about or clowning, but would laugh at something they found funny.

"Sane, you crazy. You were out there smoking that water, huh?"

"Hell yeah, and trying to fuck everything moving!"

Me and Rocc head for the most part would be on the tier clowning. On the tier, every few days or so, getting our laugh on. When it's regular clowning and just talking about random shit of no significance, Breeze and Sugar Tank would chime in, cracking a few jokes here and there. As long as it wasn't about the set, homies, home girls, certain spots, events, or bitches, it was good. Otherwise, they were lost in translation. I was on the tier, telling Rocc Head about the Tuna Fights on Friday nights in Wayside. He was like, "What?" He fell out laughing. "Tuna Fights?"

"Yeah homie! Turned up non-affiliates, Tuna!" I was telling him how that activity was gang members and gang bangers Friday night entertainment.

Having non-affiliates fighting and betting on them with store items, meat logs, chips, soups, beans, sodas, etc. That shit was crazy as hell. The bunks would be moved and the two Tunas would get in the middle and go. There were a lot of good fights. I really had him laughing when I was telling him about a dude from East Coast who stuttered and were jacking Niggahs. They all fell out laughing. I even heard dudes laughing on the bottom tier. I was telling the homies how I was in a module on the 2000 floor and I was hearing someone coming up the tier stuttering. You couldn't really overstand what he was saying, but it sounded if he was hitting dudes up, "Wha wha where ya ya ya'll fr fr from?"

He stops in front of our cell. It was me, a couple of civilians, a couple of Hispanics, and a dude from a hustler clique. Hitting me up, one of the civilians up, just because he was black, and the hustler dude, "A a a a ho ho homie, wha wha where ya ya yall fr fr from?" The civilian said he didn't bang. I'm like, "Insane Crip!"

"Ra ra right! A a a a ho ho ho homie, wha wha where yu yu you fr fr from?"

He said something like, "6th Street Hustler." (SMH) I saw what was coming next.

"Sa sa sa six sta sta sta street hus hus hustler yu yu yu you sa sa sa say! Wha wha where dad a dats a a a at?" He told dude something, I'm in the back of the cell by the phone, watching and listening to this shit play out. A blind dude could see clearly where it's going though, but it's going to take this due a while to get there (SMH).

"Yu yu you ga ga ga got sta sta store?"

Ole Boy from Hustler was like, "Why?"

"Pa pa pa put it on on on da da da ba ba bars!"

"Niggah, you got me fucked up. I'm not putting shit on the bars!"

"Yu yu yu you na na na not go go gon pa pa pa put it it it on on da da da ba ba bars?"

Me, the civilians, and the Hispanics were looking at eachother like, "What the fuck!" We were just looking at those two at the bars, one on the inside and one on the outside.

"Hell nah I'm not putting shit on the bars!"

"O o o ok, I I I I'll ba ba ba be ba ba ba back wha wha wha wi wi wi with da da da ho ho homies!" He walked away from the cell, walking towards the front of the row, down the tier. After, I guess Ole Boy thought about it. He calls stutter box back. "Aye, aye, aye, homie! Aye, hold up. Let me holler at you!" We all look at eachother again. Ole Boy even looked at us. (SMH) Stutter box comes back. Ole Boy walked his bag to the bars, dumped his shit out of the bag on the floor, put the bag on the bars. Stutter box gets the bag and open it. Ole Boy started picking his stuff up from the floor and dripping it in the bag through the bars from inside of the cell.

Damn, that's all it took huh? We all started clowning that sucker! He could no longer use the phone, he had to sleep on the floor, and he had to keep the cell clean. He wasn't feeling the fact he was sleeping on the floor with Freeway Freddie. Freeway Freddie is a rat. Every rat in the county jail is Freeway Freddie, even the ones walking on two feet.

[I'm not making fun of anyone with a speech impediment. I'm making fun of the situation, telling the story. I have nothing against anyone with any type of handicap.]

The homies were crying they were laughing so hard and I was animated with it too, acting it out. Here comes Sugar Tank, "I wish a Niggah would!"

Rocc Head was like, "That Niggah was going to have to come in the cell and get that!"

I was like, "Hell yeah, he was going to have to come in and get it!"

Boo Dog and Treach moved into the building a couple of weeks after Me and Sugar Tank moved in. This was during Ramadan, which was what my cellie was participating in with Boo Dog. So they would go to the chapel every night for their services. One night, my cellie comes back from services and said Boo Dog said he was cool on the homies, fuck the homies, he's doing him and a bunch of other shit.

This was said a week prior to Boo Dog and Lil Treach moving into the building. So when they moved in the building and into our section right next door to us, to myself I'm like, "Damn my Niggah like that!" I hadn't met the homies, but had heard nothing but good things about them both on the lines from homies and other homies from other sets. After Sugar Tank leave away from the door and sit back on his bunk, "Psst!" I go to the door and see them coming up the stairs with their shit. I nod at them both, Lil Treach and Boo Dog, as they brought the last of their stuff upstairs. The next day we were having our building searched. We were strip searched and cuffed, then led to the buildings satellite kitchen, which weren't used.

None of the 180s satellite kitchens were ever used as far as inmates eating in them. You're cell fed or you're doing a drive by (food carts brought into your section and your cell door is opened and you walk to the carts and tables, grabbing your tray, your lunch, your milk, and your fruit). They'll pop you back out to return your tray to the cart and dump your trash, then it's right back to your cell. After the police take me and Sugar Tank to the satellite kitchen and we sat down, we were talking across the kitchen to other dudes at other tables.

The police bring the homies Boo Dog and Treach into the kitchen, sitting them on the other side of me and Sugar Tank at the next table. Boo

Dog was closest to me, so I spinned around in my stool to talk to him, after greeting both him and Treach. Sugar Tank was engaged in a conversation with someone at another table. I'm like, "Sup with the homie?"

"Same ole shit young!"

Then I'm like, "Yeah homie, I heard you were cool on homies. Ain't fucking with us and you're cool on banging."

The homie was like, "That's not what I said. I said I'm cool on Niggahs bullshit and bullshit homies. I'm not fucking with them!" Then he was like, "As far as me banging, I'm from Youngs first and foremost." He already figured out where it came from because he was in a whole different building and didn't program with us. The only person it could've come from was Sugar Tank because of services and Ramadan.

Sugar Tank was the only one who was around him because of Ramadan. They went to the chapel every night. Thus, it had to come from him. My thing was this, before I knew what the deal was, if you're not fucking with me, I'm straight with that. I didn't say anything to you when you and the homie were moving in the building because word was you weren't fucking with homies, and since you and Treach were Youngs and were cellies, I assumed he was on the same shit you were on, so I didn't say anything to him. But had I not addressed it, I would've found out that ya'll weren't on no bullshit.

The cold thing though, Sugar Tank started aggressively back peddling, "Oh, I misunderstood. I though this that and the third. I heard that wrong then." Me and Rocc Head looked at each other, then looked at Sugar Tank, shaking our heads like, "This Niggah here!" Wow! The Niggah was horse playing! Every time he would come back he would tell me and Rocc Head about something Boo Dog had said allegedly to other dudes about homies as to how he felt towards homies, which we found out was bullshit. Sometimes he would holler down the tier to Rocc Head and say some shit Boo Dog supposedly said, which wasn't sitting cool with me. This was going on before the homies moved in the building and on the tier next door to us.

It was just us four on the tier before Treach and Boo Dog came, Me, Sugar Tank, Rocc Head, and Breeze. I would have to tell Sugar Tank to get off of the tier with that (speaking on a homie over the tier for all to hear). Keep Long Beach biz Long Beach biz. Shit. I told him that wasn't cool and to knock it off and if he done it again we'd have to get down. One, you're speaking on a homie already, and two, you're putting Long

Beach business on the tier. That's no bueno! I had to get real aggressive. I hopped off of my bunk to stress my point of being serious with what I was telling him. "If you're tripping we can go ahead and just run that!" (If you're mad, we can fight now) Then we can hug it out on some homie shit! No love lost or no grudges!

After him and Boo Dog had their conversation, not long afterwards Boo Dog and Rocc Head were having a thing. They were having an issue about something. I didn't know, didn't care. Wasn't my business. It was homie business and it was between them. Whatever the issue was, they would figure it out. I personally don't get in between homies shit. Homies go through what they go through and then make up. Shit always blow over, now you have one of them feeling some type of way with you, feeling as though you chose a side, which is what I was trying to tell Sugar Tank. Don't get involved, stay out of their issue, it's not your business, it's between them.

So what if Rocc Head is saying shit. He's just venting and in his feelings at the moment. Don't comment on it. Just listen. Let him vent. He's venting. Let him vent! He's pistol hot with the homie right now. Key word stupid, homie, and a real one at that! Names out there, how about yours? Yeah, you're saying your names C Dog, but when homies hear that name, they're thinking Chris Gaither, or Junay, not Changa. He's just wanting to interject himself in their issue and wanting to speak on it. When Rocc Head would come to the cell and say something, here goes this Niggah right to the door. "Yeah big homie, fuck that Niggah. When you get his C.D.s to hold, just sell them to me. I'll buy them! (SMH) Boo Dogs a buster anyway!" I'm thinking to myself, you're playing yourself close. Rocc Head never disrespected the homie Boo Dog or called him out of his name.

He had major love and respect for Boo Dog. Obviously Sugar Tank couldn't see it though. He was seeing what he wanted to see. It was his narrative. Yeah, Rocc Head was venting, but venting out of frustration with whatever they had going on. I would hear him, but that's just it. I would hear him, but wouldn't comment. I'd just nod and be like, "Right, right, right . . . oh, ok, I hear you. I hear you. . . Right, I feel you. . . Right, right." That's all he would get from me. He saw and he knew I wasn't going to engage him no matter what he said or what he didn't say or how he said it. I'm not that guy homie. Who is? You're talking to the homie. One day we go to the yard. This is a few days after Rocc Head and Boo Dog had their talk or whatever. Boo Dog was coming from school or from a ducat, but he was way across the yard coming out of a building.

This dude Sugar Tanks talking to Rocc Head, "Here come ole buster ass Boo Dog (SMH)." He felt since Rocc Head and Boo Dog were at odds at the moment, he could basically say what he wanted to (SMH). I'm just looking at this dumb ass dude. He just doesn't get it. I can see that whole scenario playing out. Yeah, I could stop the train wreck, but he has to learn his lesson the hard way, since he wasn't taking heed to my wisdom and knowledge. I too am a real homie, and I know how real Insanes rock! Shit will blow up on you, Bloom Bloom Bloom Bloom, and homies are already looking at you suspect. You have no win. You should've stayed a shadow Niggah, someone who stays out of the way. It's ugly for you now though champ. You have no idea what's about to happen to your dumb ass! I tried to tell you.

The following yard, we're out there on the yard, we're just hanging out, doing what we do. The homie slid up on me, "Yeah, cuz, I'm going to fuck your cellie up first chance I get."

"Roger that, big fella!" I already figured that much out before he had approached me. I know homies. A couple of days later the police had snatched Rocc Head up for something and he never came back. I haven't seen Rocc Head since '05, but yeah, they just snatched him up. I couldn't begin to overstand that whole just come and snatch you up whole get down. Certain homies it happens to, older ones that's been around and have been active and documented. That's all I have on that, it's out of my lane. I can say though, it had nothing to do with Rocc Head and Boo Dog, or Boo Dog and Sugar Tank. There's nothing there to read into. No shenanigans involved. I guess Sugar Tank started feeling the pressure or that vibe of something being amiss and started missing the yard. He started coming up with reasons not to go to yard. When it was time for the yard, "Oh, I'm posted today. Oh, I got letters to catch up on. Oh, my leg hurt. Oh, damn, I have to take a shit (SMH)."

It was always something. When I would hit the yard solo, the homies would ask me where he was. I would be like, "He's in the cell, doing this that or the third." Boo Dog would just nod his head. I asked him straight up, "You want me to tell cuz to come outside so I can get some cell time?" He was like, "Nah, it's cool." Come store day though, he came outside to the yard to go to the store, and then went back inside on an in-line. The next day though he was back to the shenanigans. He didn't come out, but the following day he did. He fucked around and told Treach Boo Dog turned down his fade (turned down a fight) when he asked him for it. This Niggah's an idiot!

I didn't know stupid was that stupid. I knew he was stupid, but damn, how stupid could you really be? He was that stupid. Dudes and their horse playing (SMH)! Treach pulled up on me, "Guess what your cellie just told me, but I'm not going to tell Young?"

"What he tell you?"

"That Young turned down the fade with him when he called him out."

I was stunned. I couldn't believe this shit I was hearing. I'm like, "Whaaat!"

"I'm not going to tell Young though, he's going to trip!"

I'm looking at Treach like, "If you don't knock it off!" I knew the homie was going to pull up on his cellie, no doubt in my mind. My cellie ended up going in the building early on the in-line. Treach gave Boo Dog that heads up on what was said while they were on the basketball court. Boo Dog was pistol hot about the situation. "I'm fucking cuz up." Boy Blue (What up Catfish) had hit the yard and was cellies with Breeze. Ray Bone had popped up, but had transferred. He had came from the other yard, 4A, I think, like Rocc Head and Breeze. Boy Blue might've came from 4A too. Ray Bone was telling me about Jaquese, who had started going by Du'rocc now. I knew of Jaquese from the streets. He didn't gang bang or anything. I'd always seen him in the set with a ball, heading to King's Park. Him and one of Situation's in-laws baby daddy. He had gone down for smoking a homie, the homie (I.I.P.) Ippy, aka Infant Black.

A lot of homies were feeling some type of way about the situation, especially the Youngs, for the simple fact he was a civilian. He didn't bang, and the way the incident took place, homies really weren't feeling that. So, certain places he would land in the county, homies were tripping on him, even though Big Du'rocc told homies he's hands off. Fact remains, he's on the streets saying this, Niggahs are locked up with him and isn't hearing none of it. Overstanding is zero. I was in the county when homies were running him. He was fighting back to back to back to back. But yeah, Ray Bone was saying how he had got on him. I'm like, damn, he's in the pen still going through it!

Saddle Head popped up on the yard as well. Him and Ray Bone were in different buildings. At some point I'm thinking it'll die down, or stop, or he'll get tired and tap out. I haven't heard anything about him in at least ten or eleven years. I was thinking back to a day when me, Treach, Boo

Dog, and Rocc Head were on the tier, clowning and talking about the set, speaking on bitches, home girls, homies, and events. Thinking back to how Breeze or Sugar Tank couldn't add or elaborate to the festivities.

Us four were in sync, laughing and clowning, when Sugar Tank would try to jump in. He'd come with something way from left field. "Yeah, ya'll remember the radio station we had in the city on California and New York?" He caused an up roar! Radio station! New York and California! Radio station! Niggah, if you don't knock it the fuck off, pick it back up and knock it off again! Long Beach has never to my knowledge had a radio station and if there was one, it sure as hell wasn't on no New York and California. It's a Benkin's Storage Facility and has always been one since I could remember and I can remember back to the 70's, '75 on. I'd stayed on New York and California when I was 4 until around 7. To this very day, it's still Benkin's Storage Facility (SMH).

You couldn't have grown up on the East Side saying some dumb ass shit like that.

21

I just came back in from yard, working out with Snake, Vamp, and Big J Smash. We were all doing different routines, but the same routines, just at different times. I got my bird bath in and picked the pen back up. Before I had went out to the yard, I had called moms and we were chopping it up for a good minute. I was telling her how I had tried to call my Aunt Mart since the phone company, Global Tel-Link, were giving us free phone calls, but wouldn't anyone accept my call. I was feeling some type of way. I'm like damn, it's a free call and I wrote there explaining this and wouldn't anyone accept my call so I just stopped calling, fuck it! Moms was like, "That's why I don't call there. Someone's always on some bullshit and acting funny. I don't have time for it!"

"I was done after the second time!"

I just wrote my aunt and my cuzzo, explaining in full detail what the deal was just last week about the free calls due to the Corona Virus, how that the call was in fact free and how there's no such thing as a collect call anymore from prison or jail. Everything is prepaid, no money on the phone you're not getting through, period.

If you haven't hooked up your phone for calls by prepaying, it's not going to process the call and you'll never hear press 5. So, if you hear press 5 and you know you haven't put no money on your phone for someone to call you from jail or prison, you're not being charged. It's free (SMH). It wouldn't tell you to press 5, it would give you instructions on how to put loot on the phone. It'll tell you to stay on the line and they'll explain how it's done. That's the best way I can explain it to you. My point is though, if it's telling you to press 5 and you know you haven't went through the process of putting money on your phone, the call is free. She was telling me too about how she had to stop communicating with a so called family member.

They use to communicate frequently, until she tried to tell my mother, My Mother, some bullshit concerning me and her, giving me energy in my predicament (incarceration), which was crazy to me. It fucked me up. That was way out of left field. Just because you don't fuck with me, how are you going to tell the next person not to and my mother at that? You bullshit ass bitch! Cold thing about it, I've never said anything to her fucked up, never disrespected her or done anything to her, but it just showed me what her and her siblings and nephews and nieces felt about me. Trust, they feel the same way, weirdo ass people! I'm cool with all of you not fucking with me and have been and it's been 16 years. Been over it. I feel the same way you've been feeling about me, fuck you too, and the air you breathe, straight up! But this weirdo bitch had the nerve to tell moms "Keep your money to yourself. Why would you send your money to him. He should've stayed out here. Don't be doing nothing for him." Damn!

What the fuck I do to you or have ever done to you to feel this way towards me? Thing is, I've never tried communicating with you, never tried calling you, never tried writing you, never asked for your address or your number, nor have you offered it. So off top I knew how you and yours felt anyway, but for you to voice it you just confirmed what I've felt all along. But ain't nobody ask your punk ass for shit, funny acting ass bitch! That's my mutha fuckin mama. Worry about you and yours. Don't worry about me or what mine is doing for me! You're not doing shit for me! Who the fuck are you though to tell someone else not to do for someone else? If you really want to know the truth, silly bitch, I take care of myself for the most part and have for years! Anything I've had done was minimal, and not often. I've never been a needy Niggah or have just leaned hard on anyone. You better ask your brother, my Aunt, or whoever else about my steelo! I'm an in the mud type Niggah and get it how I live, off the mutha fucking land!

Don't concern yourself with me or about me. Do what you do best, leave me the fuck alone! Keep my name out of your mouth too, before I really get and be disrespectful and start hollering out disrespectful shit! So anyway, me and moms had a good conversation this morning. She told me she took care of that pen-pal shit for me. I asked her to. She sent the company that little loot, the form, and my add. I'm just shooting my shot and see what shit do. I'm just trying to find a cool friend. I'm cool on anything else. Too much of a headache (SMH). I just need a cool friend to communicate with on some cool intellectual shit.

I thought I'd see what it do! It's a new year. I'm fresh out of the sandbox from doing nine and a half months. It's about that time, especially being way out of the way in no man's land, High Desert. A Niggah might as well be on a rock, like Alcatraz. This is how it feels to be here, like you're on a rock, an island in the middle of nowhere. Look up High Desert on a map (Susanville). My cuzzo did. He was like, "Man, they have you in the middle of nowhere." Indeed they do, but yeah, the add will run for six months on the internet and I sent a captured moment. We'll see what happens. I'll fall back and just wait. Make no mistake, I tell no lies about my time, off the dribble. I let it be known. I have life. I don't have the energy for shenanigans. You deal with it or you don't. You have that choice and I won't lie, robbing them of that, though I'm a jacker.

I'm hopeful. My boy Vamp done it and hit already. She's already active and making it make sense. I need that on my line right now. Someone to communicate on another level with. Someone's that leveled up. What I like about the site though and the company, the females already know we're locked up coming in. So they know what it is from the gate. It's strictly for inmates and females who choose to appreciate putting pen to paper and enjoying the thrill of exchange. I'm basically looking for someone who doesn't mind the thrill of exchange by way of a dying art form with hopes of building a real friendship based on our efforts and energy. I believe in shaping friendships from a non-judgmental state. I also believe in chances, which is how my add came to exist. That and the fact of only tries beat failure.

As I've said all along, at the moment though, friendship is the only thing I'm emotionally equipped to handle, due to my current situation of confinement (life), but who knows what the future holds for me or my freedom. I define myself as a passionate and confident person when it comes to building the framework to a friendship. Though my views about love are vast, I'm mainly seeking friendship. My present situation has really given me more than enough time to do some soul searching regarding how much it means to have that female friend, especially now. I see I've robbed myself of the chance of finding that someone that could see pass my flaws. That's strong minded and on her grown woman friendship. But yeah, I had composed a brief combination of words to best describe myself and my desire for a loyal friend in this maze of unbalanced madness we call life. Inshallah, it'll happen.

I continued fucking with Sugar Tank, playing my Y.A. game with him. We were talking about homies. He could never add too or elaborate on anything. So, I just stopped talking to him about homies or the set shit. I really stopped when I had asked him about the home girl Big Skids and the home girls Jolly Rancher and Moon Beam (SMH). He was really entertaining it. Being in thought as if they really existed. "Did Jolly Rancher hang on Pine?" Wow! "I think Big Skids fucked with Ace!" (SMH) If you don't stop!

Ace can be any Ace. There are actually a few Aces. It's a common name in the set. "Moon Beam, she sounds familiar. I'd have to see her." I stopped messing with him though. It was just so easy to do. It was hard to resist. If I didn't know a homie or home girl, I would just say, "Nah." I'm over it. I might say, "I don't know cuz or I haven't heard of cuz." Especially with the set. We have a lot of homies. You're not going to know all of the homies. It's impossible, but you will know the ones that are active and who has names that are out there for the most part.

Also for the most part you should know the vast majority of homies in your generation or know of them, even if they weren't a part of your circle or your crowd. That's what I didn't overstand about him. We're only a year apart. We're supposed to be in the same generation. That was just crazy he didn't know any of the homies I'd spoke on and known individuals. The ones he acted like he knew, I knew he didn't know them. I knew because he wasn't around us, nor at any BG meeting. When I first got on the yard and in the building, the first homie I ran into was the homie Ronnie High Tower, who was a building porter. I hadn't seen him since '91 when we were in Old Folsom. He wasn't there that long after I'd gotten there. Then I ran into Baby Pep from 20's. He was straight though.

The homies had told me Big Nana from the set had just left there, going home. They were clowning him and calling him scandalous for taking his T.V., hot pot, clothes, C.D. player, C.D.s, clippers, soups, meat pouches, beans, and some rice to the house with him, talking about my kids can use that. Wow! Alright, kids. That's your story to tell. It's not mine. That was burnt out though. Real talk!

Who does that? You're going out there. You have homies who don't have shit and can't get shit based on having no means. Yet you're a homie going home and couldn't see them with it. That just says a lot about who you are as an individual and how you really feel about homies and this LBC shit. The two times I was fortunate to resurrect, I didn't leave with anything but memories, captured moments, and certain paper work. T.V.'s, hot pots, fans, tapes, C.D.'s, tape player, C.D. player, clippers, clothes, and food, left all of that shit when I paroled from Salina's Valley and then again when I done my violation and paroled from Ironwood. Yeah, I could see the homies with it, especially those with no dates and had life. It shows a lot about a person's character and who they are as an individual. Dudes like that will never have anything and will always have bad karma and he wondered why I felt the way I did. You don't give anyone shit or do shit for anyone, that's not being a homie. You don't treat a homie like a homie unless he's giving you something. You'll take but won't give. It's one sided with you. That's just keeping it a thousand (SMH).

I also ran into Sadiki who use to be from 20's but turned Muslim. I knew him way before he was Sadiki. We had had a run in, in the 80's. He popped at me when I was like 14 or 15. He didn't hit me though. I ran into him years later in the pen in Calipat. While he was on the weight bench doing his set, I had walked up behind him. He had three quarters in the air, "Sup Deon?" He finished his rep and got up. "You don't re-member me, huh?" He looked at me for a minute and couldn't place me, but was like, "Nah, but you have to know me. You know my first name." I told him who I was. He was like, "Nah, that wasn't me!"

I left it alone. A Niggah was a kid then when it happened. I brought it up to him again in Tehachapi, "Homie, you don't remember when you shot at me?"

"Why you keep saying that? I didn't shoot at you." To this day he'll say the same thing. I wouldn't bring it up now though. It was over 30 something years ago. He's a good dude and a solid dude. I've actually had conversations with him and he'd given me a lot of sound advice as far as pushing on these lines and dealing with homies. He was like, "Stay productive too and try to get back home. This shit (prison) is bullshit Tic." He even went as far as to say, "If you expect a situation to work out in a way that ultimately benefits you, be willing to invest a lot of effort and energy into it, even if you experience some lumps along the way." We'd tapped on a lot of different shit while I was there with him. I soaked it up like a sponge. I knew it was coming from a good place. He's genuinely a good dude, so it was all beneficial. Especially learning how to move on a vibe of a combination of what's seen, thought, learned, and felt. A lesson I've applied also that I'd gotten from him.

That was '08 when I'd saw him last. I still hear about him though. I had just heard about him recently before leaving Solano. He had given me more sound advice about the situation with the homies concerning the shit with the homie Boo Dog. So what happened with that was we were on the yard, me, Treach, Boo Dog, and a young dude from Sex Money Murder off of the north side of Long Beach named Cash, and Breeze. My cellie stays in the building. He didn't come out. They called a in-line and Boo Dog was like, "I'm going in cuz." and he bounces. It didn't dawn on me at first. Well right off, he was going in to get at my cellie dumb ass.

I'm sure Treach already knew the business and it was discussed between him and Dog as cellies do. We homies stay on the yard and chopped it up. I walk a few laps and then ended up on the basketball court, shooting the basketball around a little bit with Treach and Breeze on the court. It wasn't long after that, they were calling yard recall over the P.A. We all started walking towards our building. By the time I make it into our section, Breeze is behind me, all types of dudes are calling me from all over the section, loud, "Tic. . . Tic. . . Tic. . . Tic. . . Tic! Get the homie out! Get the homie out! Tic! Tic! Get the homie out!"

I'm looking around, "Get what homie out of where?"

"Tic! Get the homie Boo Dog out of your cell. He's in there trying to get out!"

As I go to my cell I pick my pace up, shooting up the stairs. Now I can see Boo Dog and hear him. He's inside of my cell and calling me. "Tic! Tic! Cuz, get me out!" I run up the stairs the rest of the way and get to my door. The homie had sat on the sink waiting for me. I stand in front of my cell and start waving my hands back and forth, calling the tower police, trying to get his attention and while he was distracted.

"Tower! Tower! Tower!" After about a couple of minutes he finally look in my direction and pops my door, then walks away from the control panel for a second. It was long enough for Boo Dog to come out of the cell. As the tower police steps back to the controls, he sees me and Boo Dog. I tell Boo Dog, "Let's just go downstairs and tell him you're having an asthma episode and you need to go outside and get some air." Just to be on the safe side, I had to come up with a ruse to throw off any suspicion, in case the police assumed anything. We get downstairs, I get Boo Dog by the arm and call up to the tower, "Tower!" The police comes to the window and looks down at us.

I'm like, "Aye, Tower, my homie is having asthma issues and needs to get some air. Can he go outside for a couple of minutes?"

The police was like, "Yeah, go ahead while I'm locking these guys up!"

"You straight Dog cuz?"

"I'm good cuz. I can manage. I just need a little air."

He heads out of the section and I shoot back upstairs to my cell. My door is partially closed. "Tower! Tower! Tower!" He looks over and sees me in front of my cell and opens my door. When I step in I'm like, "God damn, what the fuck happened up in this bitch?" I couldn't really see shit from outside of the cell because when Dog was sitting on the sink he was partially blocking my view from really seeing inside. It's not registering to me my cellies not in the cell. I'm just looking at the fucking mess, bloods everywhere on the floor, the walls, on the window, on the mattress, and on the bunk (SMH). It looked like some severe shit went on up in that mutha fucka! I'm like, damn! As I'm assessing shit I hear some muffled sounds in the cell.

I'm looking around, I'm still hearing it. I lift the mattress up off the floor. I'm still hearing it. I'm like, "Hell nah, I know this Niggah ain't up under this bunk!" I'm still hearing it. I bend down and look. That's exactly where he is, underneath the bunk. I don't know though. He's tied up and stuffed like a pig. He's still making the sounds. I can't see him really, just a part of his leg and a foot. One shoes off and a sock (SMH). "Get your ass from under that bunk Niggah. What the fuck!" I stood back up. I'm waiting for him to come out. I'm thinking he just crawled under there. I still don't see he's tied up.

"What the fuck you doing? Get out from under there and clean this shit up!" Now he's squirming around and making more sounds. I bend back down. That's when it hit me, this Niggahs tied the fuck up. He can't come from under there. I start moving shit around and then I saw he was tied up and tight too. I get under there, pulling him out, then standing back up, looking down at this pitiful ass Niggah (SMH). Pitiful ass Niggah and his eyes said a whole lot. I grab the razor. His eyes got big as fuck, especially after just suffering a traumatic situation. "Stop looking at me like that Niggah! I'm not about to do anything to you. Fall back!"

I started cutting him loose. "I told your stupid ass!" After I cut him loose I told him to clean the cell up and to get it done because it's about to be count in about thirty minutes or so. He was fucked up. The corner of his mouth was split and was bleeding bad. Where his eye brows are were swollen. He had big knots on his head and one eye was damn near closed. On some real shit, Sugar Tank looked like Martin on that episode on Martin when Martin fought Tommy Hitman Hearns. He was fucked over royally (SMH). He's moving around the cell all slow. I'm like, "You know what, get the fuck out of the way and get on your bunk."

He was trying to get his mattress up off the floor. I grabbed mine off of the top bunk and tossed it on the floor by the toilet where no blood was. I told him to put his on the top bunk because that's where he was now sleeping until we figure some shit out. He managed to get the mattress up there and climb up out of the way. I buss (clean) the cell down in ten to fifteen minutes. The homie had got back in the cell from outside. I hadn't noticed either, all of his shit was by the door, packed. I hadn't noticed either, Sugar Tanks head phones were around the homies neck when he left the cell. I hadn't noticed the cord on his T.V. was cut off either. I asked him what went on in the cell.

"Me and Boo Dog had a fight!"

"You and Boo Dog had a fight? You and Boo Dog had a fight? A fight?"

"He beat me up!"

"Oh, I see, because it don't look like ya'll had a fight. It looked one sided to me. What's going on with that shit by the door?" All his shit was packed, except his toothbrush, a soap he was using, and tooth paste he was using. His shower shoes were even packed.

"Boo Dogs taking my stuff!"

"Boo Dogs taking your stuff, or did you give Boo Dog your stuff?"

He thought about it and where I was going with the question. "I gave it to him!"

"So he didn't take it?"

"I gave it to him."

About fifteen minutes or so after the homie got back in his cell, he had called over through the vent, "Aye, BG!"

I get on the vent, "What's cracking cuz?"

"Aye, when you get a chance, slide that shit out for me. Whatever will come under the door. I'll get it when I come out for my shower. The rest I'll get later."

"For sho, I got you!"

"Aye, go ahead and get you some shit, but don't East Side me. I know how you homies get it."

"Aye bitch ass Niggah, tell the homie where you're from!"

I turn around to look at him. "I ain't from nowhere!"

"You ain't from nowhere?"

"Boo Dog told me I'm not from Insane no more."

I'm like, "Whaaat! Aye bitch ass Niggah, tell the homie your name!"

"Sugar Tank!"

"Sugar Whaaat?"

"Sugar Tank!"

"Wait, wait, wait, wait! Whaaat!" You could hear Boo Dog and Treach laughing. "Aye bitch ass Niggah, tell the homie what you deserve in yo mouth!"

"I deserve a dick in my mouth!"

"Wait, whaaat! You deserve what? What did you say you deserve? A dick in your mouth?"

"Yeah (SMH)!"

"Aye BG, check it out homie. This is the script. Cuz is gon slide the Youngs 16 a month and you 21 a month, so he's going to post up!"

"Where he gon post at? It won't be with me. He's out of here first chance."

"Aight trip. I'll come over there and you come with young."

"for sho!"

Sugar Tank going to say "You don't look at me differently do you?"

"Nah, we're good!"

He was like, "I want us to be straight still."

"We're good." We bullshitted for a minute, me, Treach and Boo Dog. After count I just watched T.V. and waited for chow. Sugar Tank was on his bunk, facing the wall (SMH). When chow time came I got the food. I asked him was he eating. "I'm good! That's all you!" I ate double cheese burger, double fries, two cakes, two issues of chili beans and Kool aid. I was straight. He couldn't eat if he wanted to. The next morning went kind of sideways. I forgot he was up on his bunk fucked up, so I didn't get right up, so he basically beat me getting up. When I woke up he was already awake and had his feet were hanging over the side of the bunk.

The tray slot opened and I jumped up and went to the door and got the trays. After the police left the homie hollered over, "Aye BG!"

"Yeah?"

"Aye was you up?"

"Yeah I was up. What up?"

"Did you hear what the police was saying?"

"Nah, I didn't hear shit. You heard something?"

"I think they said something about Sugar Tank. You sure you was up?"

"I was up." I was. I was just laying there and forgetting about Sugar Tank being fucked up. I'm just glad he didn't die from bleeding all night and I was stuck with a dead Niggah in the cell (SMH). After the police came and picked up the trays ad trash, they were looking funny. I knew something was up, because they didn't slide our lunches in the tray slot after getting the trays and our trash. They left.

Boo Dog hollered again, "Aye BG!"

"Aye!"

"I think they're on Sugar Tank!"

"I didn't hear anything."

"You sure?"

"Yeah!"

20 minutes or so later, the police came in the section, thick, a lot of them, right up the stairs and to our cell. "GEEETTT DOWWWN NOW! DO IT!" They had shields, batons, and spray at the ready. Me and Sugar Tank proned out on the floor. The cell door opened, we put our hands behind our back and were cuffed. As we were being walked out of the cell and down the stairs, the police started saying shit, "Awww, McClinton, I though you and Jones were cool. Why did you have to do him like that? That's fucked up!" I don't respond.

"That's fucked up of you McClinton. I though ya'll were boys. This how you do your boy?" I still don't respond. I just kept walking next to dumb ass and let them talk. They had a lot to say. I didn't say a word. As soon as we got to the sub-station area, they immediately put me in a holding cell and took my shoes. They took him directly to medical, in the back somewhere, down a long ass hallway. After they had me strip out, I was read my Miranda rights, the whole "you have the right to remain silent" thing, and left in the holding cell. After ten or twenty minutes of being in there, I hear the big door in the sub-station come open and close. Then you hear a holding cell door come open. I hear some talking but can't hear what was being said, then I hear the last name Lee. I'm like, "What the fuck!" to myself. It was Young Boo Dog. What is he doing in here? It's obvious Sugar Tank gave him up, because they already had me and I know I didn't do any talking. As far as they knew, they had their guy. It wasn't any need for them to even be on the homie unless Sugar Tank sent them. After they read Boo Dog his Miranda rights, a police came to my cell, "Aye, can you cell up with this guy Lee down here?"

"Hell yeah, why couldn't I? It's my homeboy!" We were took to the sandbox and put in the cell together. We talked about what had happened. He was like, he wouldn't have fucked him over like that if he had of apologized. "I was still going to fuck him up, but not as bad (SMH)." He basically brought that whole situation on himself, horse playing! I tried talking to him on several different occasions. He wasn't trying to hear or feel me. So the result of his actions were what they were. Hopefully though he learned his lesson. That whole situation could've been avoided had he not been trying to be who he wasn't.

We all have to look at our failures and own our side of the street. Simply put, he played with the game. IF you're going to play with the game, overstand and know the rules well, so if you do break them you can break them effectively. Do something once, it was a mistake, do something more than twice, it was a choice, a conscious choice. After a week in the sandbox, we go to committee. Me and Boo Dog are in the cages next to each other. Sugar Tank is in the cage about twenty feet away from us. We could see him and he could see us. After the police leave and leave us by ourselves, Boo Dog get at him.

"Aye, why did you tell them about me?"

". . . Tic, you straight!"

"Aye Niggah, what did you tell them?"

"Tic, you straight!"

"Yo bitch ass hear me talking to you!"

"Tic, you straight!"

Say no more, you already know what he did. He told on you straight up. He's ignoring you and telling me I'm straight. He never answers you. Boo Dog already had told me they'll be kicking me out back to the line, but they're going to make me ride it out for a minute because I didn't cooperate. Something I would never do, that's just not in me. They were on some bullshit too with me. "If you're in the cell, how you don't know what had happened to him. What if he had died?" I was just looking at them trying to play good cop bad cop. Didn't care either way.

"It was your responsibility to inform us so we could've got him medical treatment."

"Look, I didn't know he had a medical issue. When I came from yard he was on his bunk, facing the wall, under the blanket and his head was covered up. We both had life, sometimes when he's stressing that's how he deals with it and I don't fuck with him. I let him do him. What else can I tell you but that? I don't know anything, didn't hear anything, or see anything." It's not in my D.N.A. to be a snitch Niggah!

I'll get whupped on or die before I tell anything on the next dude That's no bueno and not going to happen. I hate snitches! I could never be one. That's just not how I'm built. The good squad tried to get at me on some sideways shit in Solano when I played ball on Oppie. "So who got the weight on the yard?"

I'm like, "Wow, really (to myself)?"

"Who got the phones?"

"I don't know. I don't fuck wit nothing or nobody. I'm out of the way."

"What happened with you and dude? Why did that situation go from zero to sixty?"

"A misoverstanding."

"It couldn't have been that much of a misunderstanding. You could've fought him, but you chose to use a weapon. Don't blow smoke up my ass McClinton. I rather you tell me you don't want to talk about it."

"I don't want to talk about it."

"I respect that. You can go. Have a good day sir."

They really thought they had one. They shot their shot and missed. I guess in their minds, checking ain't cheating. They're so use to mutha fuckas talking and cooperating, I fucked them up. Yeah, wrong guy! I got nothing for you, absolutely not! They even sent a Black one at me like that was going to seal the deal.

Ain't no horse playing over this way! I don't fuck around champ. I took my Black ass back to my cage. The police walking with me asked me what did they want. "I don't know. Whatever it was, they weren't getting it from me."

He was like, "That's right! You'll be surprised at who comes and talks." At the end of the day though, police use snitches. They don't like them or respect them rat bastards! They tell on them too, that part! I stayed in the sandbox with Boo Dog for about a month and some change before they let me out (SMH).

That was crazy. I didn't even have a 115. I was just there because they were in their feelings. Me and Boo Dog chilled and worked out. We stayed chopping it up about a lot of shit too. Him and Treach would boomerang kites to eachother through the mail. He would get them straight to the homie. Me and Boo Dog started writing and talking about getting into publishing books. We would talk about it every day and we had started writing. I started writing scripts, though my first being "Outtah Sight Outtah Mind". I just finished my last one, "Ponds", a few months ago. We would bounce ideas off of eachother about character development and building.

We also discussed how the market for West Coast writers were wide open and we should get into the urban novel lane. I told the homie, eventually I would, but I wanted to get at least ten scripts under my belt first and do a few street lits or prison lits, then get on my urban tip. You could hear and see the passion the homie had for writing and wanting to write novels. We talked every day about writing and we got in a few hours of writing every day. We would chop it up about the set, homies, bitches, kids, etc. You do a lot of that in the sandbox.

We would talk about his BM. I would talk about mine. One day we were talking about the home girl Baby Insane. I was like, "Cuz, I would fuck the shit out of Kelly. Kelly have a fat bubble ass, cool titties, and hips. Body nice as fuck!" The home girls right in all of the right places. She do Niggahs, but she fuck with bitches too. I had a cellie from Carver Park Compton Crip named Clebo. He knows her too and had told me a couple of stories about her and one of his homies she fucked with. She was like, "Maaan, they were fucking in the garage. You could hear them, but more so him than her. She had that Niggah oooh-ing and aaah-ing, groaning and some mo shit!"

Thing is, that's not the first time I've heard about her fuck game and her doing her do. I stayed across the street from her on the north side and would see her when I would go across the street and fuck with the big homie Cyco Mike from the set. They're related. I would see her sexy ass and would be like, "Damn!" She would be in some boxers and the way they would fit her you could see the shape and fatness of her ass, really see it.

I was telling Boo Dog about the home girl Baby Face. She smoked though she didn't really hang out. She stayed doing her thing with her other crowd. I was telling him how at the time I was fucking with my big homies niece, Miko. Me and Miko was serving at the Aloha Motel off of Long Beach BLVD and Columbia. That was our spot. It's the same one I caught Situation and her fake brother at trying to creep. I go upstairs about to go to me and Miko's room but ended up making a detour, going to Baby Face's room. She was in 16, me and Miko were in 21. Initially I went to go fuck with Baby Face's due, Mark. We weren't homies, we were just cool and he wasn't from the set.

I met Mark through I.C., but he wasn't fucking with Baby Face then, he was fucking with a bitch named Marlyn. Marlyn ended up going to jail, so he started fucking with Baby Face's thick ass. He was a yellow Niggah, pretty boy type Niggah, that smoked too, smoke one sell one. It was raining this morning. Baby Face's window was open. I call Mark's name. She was like, "Who is that?"

"It's Tic!"

"Marks not here, Tic!"

"Let me holler at you then."

She opens the door and lets me in. She was wearing a short ass robe that stopped just below her butt so you could see that dark under meat (skin under her butt cheeks). You could see her thick ass legs and her robe was fitting snug on her, hugging her body.

Baby Face was thick as fuck and had body, big ass titties too. She went and sat back down on her bed and her robe raised up so now I could see more of her thickness. I've always wanted to sex Baby Face and she knew it too with her chocolate ass. She would always wear tight shit to accent and compliment her frame, especially her ass and titties. I asked her if Miko was at the room. She told me yeah, she had just been over there about an hour ago. She also told me Mark and his boy Wayne had just left and wouldn't be back until later in the evening. They went to the county building to see what was going on with their loot. That's an all day process and they were both getting loot hustling. Wayne use to smoke, but stopped and started really eating. He started going by Quarter Piece from Insane. As I said about Mark, he was a smoke one sell one Niggah and he stayed fresh. Baby Face asked me if I had some work and could she hold something until Mark got back. "Yeah, I got something. This Dick. Fair exchange ain't no robbery. You know what's up. Just between us, we can look out for each other."

She was like, "Let me go pee."

Whaaat! She made her way to the bathroom. I've been drinking Yac and I'm coming down some off of a stick (sherm). I'm about to beat the pussy up like an old school champ, whaaat!

After she came out of the bathroom and walked back to the bed, on the side of it she dropped her robe, already naked. She pulled the sheets and blankets back. Talking about hard, it don't even give the word justice. I peeled out of my clothes, put my rubber on, and got in the bed with her. I got right on top of her and in between her legs. I had closed the window before she came out of the bathroom and put the chain on the door. The pussy was snug and warm too, "Unghh!" I had to push more than a few times to get in her. Between her legs were warm, her thick ass body was warm. We're going and she's working her hips, her ass, and her pussy. We're in sync.

I'm like, "Damn Face, yo pussy good as fuck!" I'm kind of raised up over her, looking down at her. Her eyes are closed, her heads turned to the side, mouth open, and she's moaning. Her titties are jumping, shaking, wiggling. She started cumming fast and asking me what was I doing to her, was I trying to make her leave her man. I made her cum a few times before I was able to. Remember, I have sherm and alcohol in my system. After that day, me and Baby Face had sex three or four more times. She would see me in traffic, "Tic, when are we going to fuck again?" She'll tell me where she'll be and I'll slide through and beat her shit up on G.P. (general principle). I didn't slide her nothing else. The last time we had sex was on the north side. She and Mark had a room at the Stallion Motel on Atlantic, across the street from Wayne's apartment building where Mark was staying off and on with Wayne and Wayne's wife, Ritha. I stayed down the street. I would hang out with Wayne's step son, Nu Nu from 20's. I was on my way to go smoke with him. I'm walking up the street by Party Time Liquor Store when I spot Mark walking across the street, going to Wayne's.

Baby Face was turning around, going back into the Motel. I push right up in there. Just as I got inside, she was just walking up the stairs. "Baby Face!" She turn around and see me with a big ass smile on her face. "I'm in room such and such, come back in 30 minutes." I leave and go across the street to Wayne's. I holler at Wayne and Mark. Ritha wasn't home and Nu Nu was on the phone. I put my fingers to my mouth, gesturing "Are we smoking?" He nodded yeah. Me and Nu Nu smoked a blunt of some gas.

By the time we were finished, Wayne and Mark left and were heading to the East Side. I told Nu Nu I'll be back later, and then I left. I went right across the street to the Motel to Baby Face's room. We had sex for about an hour or so and I bounced and went home. That was the last time I had sex with Baby Face or saw her. Me and Boo Dog were talking about how homies were suckers over bitches. We talked about my big homie having had an issue with Lil Papa from the set over this bitch that stayed by his moms house on Alamitos. My big homie was messing with her. Papa met her when he came to the Aloha to mess with me on some business. She had got a room at the Aloha and was trying to hustle, because whoever she was staying with on Alamitos, her moms, aunt, grandmother, whoever it was, had started tripping. She basically got at Miko to try and help her to get on her feet, so she could get her, her on spot for her and her baby. Miko was basically lacing her and showing her how to get loot, serve, and cut up work. Papa came through. He saw her in our room and started hollering at her. They ended up getting straight and whatnot. At this time, I messed with Papa tough, and I was getting work from him. Now, somehow, Lil Sugar Bear get wind of them (Papa and Ole Girl) chilling, and get in his feelings (SMH). Him and Papa have words to the point they're talking about playing ball.

I'm like, "Wow cuz, really?"

"That's my bitch. Cuz shouldn't be fucking with her!"

I tell Lil Sugar Bear, "I'm not getting in the middle of that. You're my big homie, but cuz is the homie too and I fuck with cuz! I'm not in it, so don't involve me." This shit happened again with a dude named Anamosity from 20's. They get into it behind some bitch. I met Anamosity one day. He tells me his name. He was more of a pimp Niggah than a 20 Crip. I tell him mine, "Lil Tic Loc from Insane Crip!" He was like, "Your big homie is Tic, the one who goes by Lil Sugar Bear sometimes?"

I'm like, "Yeah, what about him?"

He goes into how him and the homie are having issues behind a bitch, a hoe bitch at that! He was like, "I'm not trying to take it there, but I will on 20 Crip!"

I take offense to his slick ass mouth, "What you mean cuz?" I'm seconds from reaching for the 40. I started assessing my surroundings and saw it wasn't cool, so I stood down. If I would've whipped out, I was definitely pushing the play button, which takes me here against my butter judgement, I went against myself.

Chumlee be running around at work and he wasn't security conscious, which isn't cool, considering the type of environment we're in. High Desert is serious. It could go bad at the drop of a hat, just that quick, like this weather do. I put him on with a few simple words, "Don't be playing games or tripping for no reason, just because." Whip out, use it! No pump faking or horse playing, because at that point you've ventured into a whole different realm. It's serious now. Once you cock it, there is no un-cocking it. There's no taking that back. You have to go.

"Why did you say that?"

"You know why. You be on some bullshit!" I wanted him to just overstand what was going on and how he couldn't afford to drop the ball.

It took everything in me to go there, because the homies an unpredictable individual, you'll never know what he might do. It was a job, trying to keep him on track. To know him, you have to overstand my meaning. But yeah, me and Boo Dog would talk about a lot of shit. I learned a lot about the homie in that short period of time, being with him in the sandbox. We had a workout routine. We would do it early in the morning to get it out of the way. We would bird bath, then get into our writing and talk later. We messed with a lot of the same homies and we knew a lot of the same people, as we should.

We're East Side Long Beach Niggahs! Natives! We could actually chop it up about the set, about homies, and about bitches. Niggahs are official homies. That's my guy right there. He's a solid and real homie. I wouldn't see Young Boo Dog again until I ended up at Delano like three years later. Back briefly on the issue of pump faking, before I had gotten to Solano, it was an issue with a civilian named Rome that was pushing the city and pushing with the homies. This was my overstanding.

I had heard from other dudes outside of the car, Rome was pushing Long Beach and running with the homies through a civilian. They told me one day Rome had got into it with a Pissa. He whipped out on him and didn't use it. The issue was brought up to the homies about the incident on the yard with Rome. Rome claimed he had a pen and not a banger at the least he pump faked, acting as if he had something and using it in a threatening manner, but don't actually use it. That'll get you hurt. That was a DP'able offense. But the homies on the line at that time didn't do anything. They weren't trying to deal with the situation.

Them dealing with it was to say he's not pushing with the car. I was confused. I'm like, "Hold on though, he was pushing with the car or he wasn't?" From what I gather, dudes from other factions, Bloods, Crips, and Bay Areas, had the homies pressured up and were pressing the homies to get at Rome for jeopardizing everyone as a collective (Blacks). The homies kept saying Rome wasn't pushing with the homies like that, he's doing his own thing (SMH). So me being me, I needed clarification on what was what with him.

I needed to know if Rome was or wasn't pushing with the homies. I asked them, but was getting mixed answers. "Yeah", "No", "I don't know" (SMH). I go to Rome directly, "Aye Rome, what are you doing? Are you pushing with us, or are you doing you?" He flat out told me he's not pushing with the homies like that and he's doing him. It was clarification enough for me. He's doing him, we're not responsible for him, or his actions. He's not functioning with us. He was cool and all of that and was from the city, but it's a line in the sand, which was overstood by him. We weren't going to play games. He's pushing, but when something happens he's not, that was no bueno! One day he forgot his role and tried to listen in on some Long Beach business. We had an issue, so we were kind of in a group, like huddled up and Rome was right there. I politely asked him and respectfully, could he excuse himself, Long Beach business. Shit, it was, and he didn't have anything to do with it, so dismiss yourself. He was feeling some type of way about it and got at me later.

"That was fucked up how you just got at me like that."

What you mean? I was polite about it. I asked you. I could've just told you to beat it and fuck your feelings, but I came at you respectful and not sideways, could you excuse yourself, Long Beach business, that part!

22

I was tripping off of when we were on the slab yesterday working out and the Bay Areas were grouping up and having a discussion, which they'd been having the whole morning on the yard, damn near. They had been moving all around the yard and had found their way by where Me, Snake, Chumlee, J Smash, and Vamp once he came back from his medical ducat were, on the slab working out. I'd been watching them the whole time. They were like 40 plus feet away from us. Snake had started clowning with J Smash, looking at the Bay Areas and saying, "That's how you and your homies get it on the lower yard," and was laughing, "Yeah, that's ya'll like a mutha fucka!" Smash was like, "Hell yeah, that's me. That's how you get clarity. You have to talk shit out and put it on the table. How else are you going to have a overstanding if you don't talk it out."

If it's an issue, you have to meet it direct and head on. It's just the reality of it, or shit can go sideways and fast. I second that motion, adding, "If you don't talk, how can the issue get resolved? And if it's an issue it needs to be addressed." That's how it's supposed to be done, so there's no misoverstandings or miscommunication and everyone's on the same page, no ones in the dark. Snake also had brought up his hand was still hurting after that incident on the yard when him and his other homie had to get on Calbo some weeks ago. He had hit Calbo in the head because he was trying to find spots to hit him, since his defensive game was wicked.

They were getting at him, but not like they wanted to. Initially they got on him and got him good, but once he hit the ground, it wasn't no more spots to hit him. He did like a turtle and went into a shell, balled up. You were not getting no face. All you had action at was head, arms, and forearms. Yeah, he had a awesome defensive game. They couldn't get it, not how they had wanted to. That's when smash was like, "That's why I beat a Niggahs body up. Get them ribs and kidneys. He gon open up!"

Me and Chumlee hit the slab today by ourselves. It's Saturday. Normally it'll be a kick back day for me, on Sundays too. I won't work out on the weekends, but since I didn't work out yesterday because we were drinking, we chilled. Today was a makeup day. Tomorrow I'm not doing anything, except maybe get on a few dots and dashes and tap in. They'll be giving us weekend yard until this Corona Virus shit is over with. Everything that's going on around here right now as far as the program is abnormal. Nothing that's going on right now at High Desert is normal, that part!

I just talked to moms again. She told me she had just gotten a letter from Brody telling her he's in the sandbox. He had put someone on their back pockets (sleeeeeep)! He was like, "I tried moms. I was kicking back, trying to stay out of the way, but Niggah's wouldn't let me." I had told her the same shit when I went to the sandbox this last time. I was out of the way and doing me when I had to wake a Niggah's game up. She knows though, I don't fuck with people or look for drama. She also knows I don't run from it either. If it comes my way, I'll deal with it, lose, win, or draw.

I'm sure he just told her what he could, like me. You already know your mails being screened. No Deets. I don't speak on anything that's not already known and hit the yard TMZ. Tehachapi though was alright for the most part. I wasn't into much there. I wasn't into anything. I didn't really drink there, barely blew, nor did I hustle. I was literally out of the way. It seemed too my time there flew by and I was going to Calipat. After I left the sandbox and was sent to Behavior Management Unit, I stayed there a couple of weeks, then was sent back to the line.

I ended up getting Clebo from Carver for a cellie, who was my cellie when I left Tehachapi. me and Clebo were around the same age and he was a cool dude too. We would play dominoes, talk, and clown a lot. He was messing with some bitch from Long Beach. I didn't know her, but I had seen her before in traffic. She stayed in the set on 19th and King. Boy oh boy, did he have stories about her. Just thinking about some of them have me laughing, have my cellie looking over the side of his bunk, looking down at me, "What's so funny?"

"Oh, just tripping off of something (SMH)!"

He was a dirty dick Niggah too. He use to have me laughing about how he would fuck her in the ass and would pull out and his dick would be covered with chocolate and nugget. My side would hurt from laughing so hard (SMH). She was a nasty ass bitch. He was messing with a few bitches in the city. He was telling about one time he was in the city and some Enemigos (Longos) tried to get active on him and his homie. They had hit them up, "Aye fool, where ya'll from?"

"We're not from out here. We're from Compton!"

Then it was like, "Fuck Niggers!" They took it to some racial shit. I've ran into a few dudes that ran around in the city messing with bitches, coming across that similar type situation.

Not really overstanding the dynamics of the city with the racial shit. Hispanics in our city are racist as fuck. Crazy, but true. It went from gang shit to racial shit with them. For us, it remained on some gang shit, but we'll get our racial banter in too. Fair exchange is never a robbery though that's not our nature. We've never been a racist people. But yeah, Enemigos would get at these dudes initially thinking they're from the set (Insane), and when they tell them where they're from and they're not even from Long Beach, it's "Fuck Niggers!" I've heard instances where dudes got ball played on them. Also heard where it went bad on them, how Enemigo would press and trip after knowing the deal, found out the hard way. Come to Long Beach, know where you are, and what the deal is not being from the city.

I would tell dudes you have to be mindful of where you are in the city, because the Enemigos trip. They'll pull up on you and try to holler. They'll get at you in broad day light too. I was telling Clebo how I was at a music shop on Anaheim and King, getting some new speakers, a C.D. changer, and a bigger amp in my coupe. I was telling him how I had just been dropped off by a family member. Me, thinking I wouldn't be there long and my swoop was finished or damn near finished, I left the 40 in her swoop. As I'm walking towards the garage where my swoop is being worked on and I can see it and see the worker working on my shit, I saw a brown cutlass on Daytons in the parking lot next to the parking lot where I am. It's two Enemigos in the swoop. I made eye contact with one. I'm like, "Fuck!" I get to my swoop and lean over into the trunk, watching what the workers doing. At the same time, watching Enemigo from my peripheral vision.

The driver side door open and the driver gets out. I don't see anything in his hand. I'm like, cool, I'll beat his ass. I should've known better. They don't fight not no head up and if they act like they want to it's a thousand nearby. I raise all the way up and started walking out of the garage area towards him.

"Longo!"

"Insane Crip, fuck Chongo!"

"Fuck Bugs!"

He leans back, reaching behind his back. He whips out. I take off, "Bloom, Bloom, Bloom." He get off three times and miss. I break across King and go up Anaheim, making a left on Lewis. That happened like 11 in the morning.

Another day time shenanigan, I was at a family members house, the same one that had dropped me off at the music shop. Me and her had been chilling and smoking a couple of blunts. I had been drinking before I even got there. I'm leaving and as I'm walking up to my swoop, I stick my key into the door, and open it, shots start going off. "Bloom, Bloom." I duck. Swoop windows around me shatter, "Bloom, Bloom." My swoop get hit. This time I had that 40. It was under my seat, cocked and ready to go. "Bloom." My Doors open, so my window is shattered, glass going all over me. I could hear a female screaming, "They're killing him!" I never see anyone though.

The shots were coming from in between the houses in front of me. Swoops weren't parked up against the curb. They were parked at an angle, so my swoop was facing the houses directly. Not really expecting to his shit, I wanted to send a message. I raise my hand up and get back, "Bloom, Bloom, Bloom, Bloom. . . Bloom, Bloom!" The shooting stopped. I jumped in my shit and got on. That was like 8, 8:30 in the morning. You could hear the sirens, them boys, police, were on their way. Me and a homie went and got cracking that night. Clebo was like, "Yeah, they be tripping in the Beach!" Me and Clebo had started gambling with Dog from East Coast on baseball games. He was Twin's cellie at the time, from Q102. Normally that's not my thing, I'm not a gambler. I do enough gambling, being where I am and walking out of my cell every day.

I went through a phase, but just to make the games interesting, I would only bet on some gentlemen shit. Dollar bets, nothing serious. I was only betting because Clebo was betting on the games. I didn't even like baseball. Never have. I'm a football dude and the Indianapolis Colts are my squad. I'm a Raider fan as well, but that's the turf's squad. I've been a Colts fan since Peyton Manning came from Tennessee. I've remained a Colts fan and have stayed a Colts fan, even after he left the Colts and went to Denver Broncos (SMH). The Colts did my boy wrong and abandoned him.

Then we got Andrew Luck, who just retired last year. My teams in need of a quarterback. Ole boy we have right now sucks ass. Jacobie Brissette. Dude is trash! Boo, Boo! We need to get rid of dude and snatch up some of the talent that's coming out in the draft this season coming up. Brissette is not the guy. While we're betting with Dog, the wins and losses would go back and forth. He would win a lot of games, we would win a lot of games. We would win a lot of games, and it would cancel losses. We would bet a dollar on every game that weekend. Every week, we would bet the games we could or couldn't see. One week, it went bad for Clebo. He'd lost a lot of games that week and owed Dog. Dog would get at me, "Aye Tic, do your cellie got that loot to pay me?"

"As far as I know he do."

"Yeah, because I'm trying to get cashed out before we bet again."

Him and Clebo would start having side bars. Clebo told me he was going to pay Dog, but Dog needed to stop sweating him. He had him. He was going to pay him. Dog had got at me several times, "What's up with your cellie? He got me or what?" I'm like, "What did he tell you?" He really wanted to flight (attack) Dog, but I was like, "Stand down. That's not cool homie. You do owe him. How are you gon flight him?"

He really wanted to get on him. I had to really talk the homie down and tell him how that really wasn't cool. I guess Dog had pumped himself up to flight Clebo. From how the shit looked though, it looked like him and his cellie was going to try an jump him. It wasn't going to happen. It wasn't going to play out that way. I would've assisted my cellie. If anything, it was going to be head up. I peeped the whole move, how they were moving in the sections, as we were being released to yard. Dog kept looking at Twin, then at my cellie and looking around. The tower was releasing a few of us out of the section at a time. Somehow, Twin ended up going out with the group in front of us. I guess thinking Dog wasn't tripping since he hadn't made his move.

When the door closed and Twin looked back, he saw Dog still in the section with us. You saw the look, "Fuck" on his face, like he fucked up, confirming my suspicion. They were up to something. At that time, Dog aborted his mission, only to pull a stunt a few days later in the satellite kitchen. We were in the section waiting to go out to the yard. I don't remember where Twin was. We get into the satellite kitchen where we stripped out, ass booty naked, coming in from the yard and going out to the yard. I go in the kitchen first.

I'm at one table, Clebo at the table in the middle, then Dog get the table next to him. I'm at the table closest to the door we go out of going to the yard. Dogs on the opposite end. He's by the door we came into the satellite kitchen through, from the section. Police are standing in front of each table, two deep. Then you had other police just standing around, watching as they talked to each other. As soon as Clebo was getting ready to take off his boxers, "Bow!" Dog fired on him from the blind. He was damn near knocked out. Clebo kind of stumbled and fell, hitting his head on the table, "Bloop!" As he was trying to recover, he was trying to reach for Dog, but he don't it moving.

Clebo got a hand on his shirt, but before he could really do some harm, the police sprayed him and Dog up. I caught back splash. Clebo already couldn't see. He wore glasses and had token them off sitting them on the table. After they were cuffed and walked out of the kitchen and walked to the substation, they were there for hours. Dog never came back. Clebo did. He was pistol hot though. "Bullshit ass Niggah dope feined me in front of the police. Straight mark shit! If you wanted to get down, why take off on me with the police right there? Know why? Because you knew you had no win!" He was pacing the floor and looking at his eye. That mutha fucka was swollen. "Cuz almost knocked me out with his scary ass. I knew I should've just flighted that bullshit ass Niggah. Listening to you though Tic!"

He was looking at his eye in the mirror, "Look at this shit, cuz. Straight bullshit! This bitch ass Niggah!" He was hot about that shit for a few weeks. He was my cellie when I got the kite from the homies talking about "your name is in the air with some bullshit so come to the Jumma Islamic Services so we can holler". I had nothing to fear or worry about.

It's whatever. I know I didn't do anything. I'm going to stand fast in the face of adversity, regardless though, and I'm going unarmed. I'm not ducking or hiding form no Niggah! Whatever the issue is on the yard. One thing I do know, I'm always going to be on the right side of any issue. You only fear shit when you know you fucked up. I deal with all situations one way,, and that's the right way, head on. I push up, into the chapel, though still mindful of Niggahs and fuckery. Your mind always have two currents. It want to believe shit is straight, yet it has a self protective need to be suspicious of Niggahs. But you have to go far enough to allay my doubts though about your motives to the depths of your intentions. I'm very in tuned. Sometimes you have to stand, even when standings not easy. When it's all said and done, shits going to play out how it's going to play out. You just have to let it.

All you can do is your best with what's put before you. I'm always motivated though. That goes back to 20% being things that happens to us and 80% is how we respond to them. It's essential though to have a sense of what plays out well on your minds movie screen and what would and wouldn't translate into a real life situation. I was hot though and in my feelings about how they got at me on some bullshit like that, questioning my character, then turn around and tell me "We didn't believe the shit!" (SMH) Common sense though should've had a Niggah like, if that was in fact the case why didn't Boo Dog send word to Treach or Styme who were on the line? You know why he didn't? Because it wasn't true and manufactured, that's why! That would've been the first thing he done.

Second of all, we would've been cellies which we were the whole time I was back there with him. That clearly went over Niggah's heads. The homie Treach had got at him about it on paper, he never responded to it from my overstanding. First thing out of his mouth when I told him about it when I seen him in Delano, He was like, "That's bullshit!" I also told him too about me hollering at those who allegedly put that out there and how they said it wasn't them and put it on their turf.

It supposedly came from Big Lurch's cellie, Fo-Tay from some shit called No Love. He went home though. Boo Dog was like, "That was crazy BG, but you did the right thing, by addressing it once you got wind of it." That Part! It's crazy though how a dude will try to dirt you up on some straight fictitious shit. What's crazy though is how dudes will take it and run with it without facts, autobot. My whole thing was, when Ole Boy was there why didn't they tell me it was him who put that out there, whether they believed it or not? I felt they should've told me, because as far as other dudes knew, I knew and knew it was him who said it and had it out there, yet I'm just walking around there, walking around him, and not addressing it. Which is what I would've done and would've played ball, but you know what? Karma's a bitch.

What I do know, Niggah's cross paths like a intersection. You made that shit up and put a false narrative out there, and had dudes biting on it. That type of shit has serious consequences. It could've went sideways. Luckily though, homies knew my character and they didn't just react on what was said (SMH). But yeah, that Niggah straight horse played. These are the types of dudes you have running around these yards these days though, bullshit ass dudes. They need to be held accountable for their dirty games. If you play dirty, you deserve to be done dirty, especially when you're doing it to a good dude. Then this Sex Money Murder dude, Cash, had me hot as fuck. I wanted to beat his ass.

He tried to get at me about the situation, but on some soft shit. He tried easing into the situation. Dude, first off, you're not a factor. Second of all, I'm from insane. Third, fourth, and fifth, you have no input, no voice, or no opinion. It's an East Side matter, period. Not only that, but dude, you're a kid, fuck up out of here. If you're not a Insane or a 20, and it's a issue concerning me, I'm not trying to hear you or feel you about it. You were a young street punk. I don't know what possessed you twenty something years old to think you had anything to approach me about at thirty something. That's why I felt it was necessary to check you the way I did and told you to stay in your lane. You didn't even come straight with it. You beat around the bush about it. I couldn't respect it at all. Yeah, you tried to get at me, but you played it safe. You couldn't sell it. That was like '07-'08, twelve years ago. Nothing was ever brought up about it again. It was deaded, back then where it started at.

Bullshit should always be paused and frozen as a testament to being bullshit with no validity. Bullshit is never supposed to gain traction. If you're a real dude, you've been separating real from the fake from the beginning. Every situation I've learned from, it shows me who and what not to be. Even Clebo had tripped off of the bullshit, as far as the dudes that knew it was put out there, and didn't no one get at me that called themselves fucking with me. He was like, "Tic, Niggahs ain't cool. They fuck with you but couldn't tell you what was up and they probably was talking about you too all along." I wasn't messing with dudes the same no more and I looked at the differently as far as their conduct and character.

It showed major cracks and flaws in their moral and belief system (SMH). Those types of dudes are easily swayed and cant think for themselves, yet profess to be a real dude. A real dude would've been like, "Aye Tic, xyz is being said about you and since I fuck with you I'm letting you know the deal. That's not cool." That's a homie, or a dude that overstands how the game is played when it comes to this prison shit and him respecting the fact he mess with me and I shouldn't be kept in the blind on something so serious and has serious consequences, which would compel him to holler at me. That's just a real Niggah.

For instance, with the situation in Solano when I was in the sandbox, when I hollered at E.B.'s cellie in the cages at yard, he straight up said, "We didn't fuck with each other, but being as though I'm a real Niggah, this is what's being said about you." He let me know dudes were saying I was in the cell with a Wood in the sandbox. Yeah, that was out! All the way out! Then he told me about those dudes on the bullshit, saying I was trying to leave the yard and that was why I stabbed Oppie. He was like, "Yeah, that's what S.T. and Tall are putting out there and your other homies." True movements of bullshit dudes and autobots. I don't give a fuck what's going on, I'm not leaving no yard, no way, but the right way. On a adverse transfer or a regular transfer.

Either going to a 180 or a lower level and on my terms, not the next dudes. Here it is, a dude I didn't even mess with on the main-line kept it real and a thousand. He was like, "How can I say I'm a real Niggah and I'm communicating with you, but I can't tell you what was up." (SMH) I sat his mind on a course though when I painted the whole captured moment for him, as far as those dudes were concerned, with the shenanigans. He had a "ah ha" moment and began to see it from another perspective. Ok, I'm seeing the whole scene. It makes sense now that I'm hearing it from your side. What was being said didn't make sense or add up.

The real will always reveal itself, no matter how much you try to cover it up or come with the smoke and mirrors, as dirty intentions will be revealed. What's in the dark will always come to light, especially when it's dirty. Your bullshit will come to light. You're not that smart to cover shit up to where the real won't be exposed, too many holes. At the end of the day, I respect Ole Boys get down for keeping it clean with me and for keeping it clean with himself.

I just came back in from the yard. It's Sunday. Wasn't anything going on out there. I just posted up on the wall and observed the yard and chatted with a couple of people. It was cold and it was sprinkling outside. Earlier, before I went to the yard, I had written an introduction letter and sent it down the tier for my guy Lon to check out. He wrote me a response back on my rough draft, "Tic, I would suggest that you keep your conversation focused on initiating a friendship only, to plant the seed and provoke a response, because although you started it on that path, you went off course with looking for someone to call your own, and emotional intercourse with a woman's heart virginity." Then he was like, "That's too sexual and creepy. It will only attract someone who will be stuck on that page and run off anyone of substance."

I removed that part and came anew, however I am looking for that person that could be that loyal friend and who overstands loyalty and has substance, who does employ a want to have that friendship of substance and loyalty. Sometimes when I'm writing, I do get caught up in the moment, which comes very easy to me. I'll re-read something and then get a second opinion about it from someone I mess with and who's opinion I respect, because I know they're going to give it to me un-cut. Lons going to give it to you just like that, so now I'm cocked and loaded.

Yesterday it was sprinkling as well, and cold too. I just looked out of the window and from my peripheral vision I saw about eight deer that had came from the mountains and were on the other side of the electrical fence, walking and stopping to graze on the bushes and small grass. I like seeing animals in their natural element. Don't really get that on the norm. I sat at my desk and just watched them as they slowly made their way out of my view, going up the hill. I watched as they were going back towards the mountains, in the opposite direction, slowly ascending high and higher. I was wondering though if they were being tracked by a mountain lion or coyotes. You would think they wouldn't be that far behind. When I was in the sandbox in Solano, I use to watch the jack rabbits from my back window, watch them eating, humping, and chase eachother around. I use to see them in full sprint too, across the open field. They can move. They would run around on the yard too. You would see them all day around the prison, every day. When I first saw them I found it fascinating, but quickly got over it. After seeing them every day it became the norm.

I'd never saw animals on the yard outside of cats, birds (Pigeons were rare, but seagulls I'd seen a lot in different spots I'd been), and dogs.

You'd see the dogs when the goon squad brought them on the yard for the purpose of hitting cells. Tehachapi had rabbits. I used to watch them get chased down by coyotes. Every now and then one would get caught and that was his ass. I saw that in Solano where one of those big ass hawks would swoop down from the air and pluck one from off the ground. The hawk would take it up high and would drop it to the ground, then would swoop back down and get it, then would take it up on the roof top.

All you could see was flying fur. That shit was crazy, fur flying in the air and being caught by the slight breeze. This morning too, it's like four something, the night man just walked by, flashing his light into the cell, conducting his count and wellness check. He'll be by again at five something, unless that's it. He normally comes at 12:30, 2:20, and 5:00, then it'll be time to get up and get the day going, but shit, I'm already up. My mattress is rolled up, blankets folded, and I've already washed my face, brushed my teeth, and put my clothes on. I've always been an early riser. I'm usually up every morning around 4:30. I'm out though by 10:00 or 10:30 at night. I don't do no hanging out until the wee hours of the night. I take my ass to sleep. I'm cool on all of the late bird shit. I like my issue (my sleep). I don't like moving around tired and unfocused. I need all of my faculties on alert, high alert, especially around here.

It's going to be a bundled up morning, two pairs of socks, thermals, two beanies, two pair of gloves, my jacket, and boots. It's Monday, so it's a workout day. Still, it don't stop. We'll figure something to do. Plus, it's only an hour and we're back in the building. I think Lon has a couple of more weeks left on LOP (loss of privileges) before he can come back out and play with the rest of us. Yeah, for those observing the crew without Lon on the slab, they see it's can't stop, won't stop. We're still pushing on a daily. He's been getting his in, in the cell every morning. We finally had dayroom last night, after being fucked three times in a row without it and we came out late (SMH).

It was also a misoverstanding about to get ugly. Vamp was missing a C.D. It was on the Black's and Northerner's table, inside of a C.D. player, inside of a bag, which was tied with a knot. Someone went inside of the bag, untying the knot, and took the C.D. out of the C.D. player. So, it was a deliberate act when it was took. That was a suuuppppeeerrr no-no! Flag on the play! You will get maxed out (severely whupped if ball wasn't played on you) for stealing or picking up shit that doesn't belong to you. If it doesn't belong to you, leave it the fuck alone. No one likes a jail house thief, but play at your own risk. Don't get caught though. Just know though, if you do it and get caught up, that's a wrap Mr. Postman.

Vamp was feeling some type of way. Him and Snake, working in a collective effort, located the C.D. before the dayroom was over. It ended up being found in C-section. Snake came to our dayroom door, telling Vamp he located it. Vamp wanted to know who had it. Snake didn't want to tell him and bounced. Snake and Vamp are boys, so he'll tell him at some point in the game. A situation happened in Solano in regards to stealing. I was conflicted about the whole get down. The whole situation was really confusing to me in general. A porter, an older Black dude from the Bay named Manny, had cleaned out a cell that the police had just rolled up a Wood from.

They packed the Wood's property up after sending him to the sandbox, leaving little odds and ends in the cell they deemed trash to be thrown away, a couple batteries, wires, cable, pens, pencils, and a few other miscellaneous things. Manny wasn't the only one in the cell after the police had cleared it out and wanted it cleaned out by a porter. The cell had been officially cleared by the police. The Woods in the building came trying to make an issue, talking about some property was missing from their homie's property. It was like some shit came up missing out of the cell and they wanted it back.

No one came forward about anything, feeling as though they didn't take anything, everything left in the cell was trash. Manny however, not thinking or feeling he'd done anything wrong, told the Woods he had some rechargeable batteries he got from the cell that the police left behind after they packed up that property, telling him to clean out the cell. Other people had been in the cell before Manny got in there to clean it. By the time dayroom was released for the low side, which was my side of the building, the talk had already begun and had circulated that Manny stole, which I felt was some bullshit after I heard the script. Then, knowing what I knew about Manny and haters, so fuckery was at play. Dudes were looking for a reason to fuck over him. I saw some grouping up with a few Blacks and then I saw the Woods grouping up and talking. I go and inquire as to what was going on. I knew something was up. I was told Manny stole some batteries out of the Wood's cell and the Woods are tripping. They were making it seem like he went into a Wood's cell and stole them. They word played, making it seem one way, which wasn't the reality. I go and talk to Manny. As I said, he's an older Black dude, 50 plus, and I was seeing how he was being threw under the bus and threw to the wolves.

I saw he was trying to talk to a couple of people to get his side out there. Dudes weren't trying to hear him out. They were just nodding their heads, but wasn't fucking with him. He tells me the whole script and I'm like, "Ok." It didn't sound to me like he stole anything. He was like, "I'll give the batteries back. It's just two batteries." Then he asked me to go with him to go get at the Woods, because didn't anyone else want to. At the end of the day, it's a Black issue, regardless how it plays out. I push with him to the Wood's area in the dayroom to holler.

I'm the only one who would, so I'm the only one with him. He calls the Wood who's running the Woods in our building, "Aye B.D. (not his name)!" B.D. walked to where me and Manny were standing, him and a couple more woods came with him. I'm just standing there as Manny is talking to B.D., but I'm watching all three of them, really where their hands are. B.D. is listening to Manny, but was being dismissive about the situation, telling Manny it's up to his other homie and he needs to work it out with him. I asked Manny was he good, because we can bounce. I'm cool on this shit. We walked back to our area and side of the dayroom.

Later that day, during night dayroom, some young Bay Area dudes got on him and whupped him out. They fucked over Manny, beat the breaks off of him. He kept it a thousand. He didn't tell on no one. He just accepted his issue and was took out of the building (SMH). They put in him the sandbox and he was transferred. I'm still conflicted on that one. He didn't steal the batteries. Once the police pack the cell up, anything left is considered trash from my overstanding. He was told to clean the cell, which he'd done, and anything found he was supposed to technically throw away. Instead of throwing them away, he kept them. I've seen this type of shit go on, on numerous occasions when the police roll someone up. Porters are sent in the cell to clean it out and would keep stuff that was supposed to be thrown away.

That only says it was something bigger at play. I didn't overstand that one at all. If he was at fault, which I didn't see, it should've been because he went in the cell before a Wood was able to, or even a South Sider. He could've let a Wood porter or South Sider porter clean the cell out, because they fuck with the Woods, even though he was told to do it. That way it would've avoided any type of bullshit or foul play, which is what ended up happening, foul play which got him whupped. My boy, Rame was like, "Manny's stupid anyway for even saying he had the batteries. He shouldn't have said he had shit. It was trash!"

"Yeah, his bad!"

A lot of dudes were feeling some type of way about two 20 something year olds getting on Manny. I was even hot about the situation and how bad they don't the old man. They wouldn't have liked it very much if someone would've whupped their grandfather or pops out like that. That same Wood who were running the Woods in our building ended up going bad. He came to the sandbox while I was back there for something. He ended up in Quentin's sandbox where he got kicked out to their main-line and he stayed. A Wood I was messing with told me when we were in the cages talking, "Yeah, B.D. stayed on this line. That fucker is no good!" He came from Solano too. He went back to Solano after his sandbox time was up.

The snow stopped, but for how long? I know by the time we hit this yard, it'll crank back up. It's cold as fuck though. I have two to three years to be around here, doing this weather. This shit is not cool. Cold and snowing. I'm over it. I'm trying to stay out of the way to get up off of this island. High Desert is cold and it sucks! In the meantime, I'm going to get my winter gear up. Anything else is uncivilized, real talk.

Me and Chumlee were talking about Corcoran last night. He's still salty and not feeling his situation as to how he got here. He talks about it often. For the most part he's not feeling how he said the homies were getting at him, but ultimately how they got him off the yard, which he felt they were plotting to do all along. He was basically telling me they weren't feeling his program and stayed nitpicking about any and everything he done or said (SMH). "They sent D Deuce and Mo Tray at me!" D Deuce from 20's and Mo Tray from Babyz. He was telling me how it was telegraphed. "I saw it coming before it came by how they were moving and how the normalcy wasn't normal." Niggahs weren't doing what they normally did, which gave the play away and his perception was spot on.

All he heard was do ya'll shit and Mo Tray was trying to creep up slow and when he heard do ya'll shit, that's when Mo Tray took off on him. Then D Deuce came. Then they both got on him. He said it was a swing out until he hit the ground. He was like when the police got there they threw the smoke bombs and he tried to keep going, but backed up because of the smoke. The homies told him to just get down. Then he was like, when he was in the substation in the cage, BG and Baby Coop talked to him, telling him, "You know it wasn't personal. It was all business."

"All I got was a black eye and a small cut over my eyebrow."

I'm ready now to get to the yard though, to get my issue in and get back in the building, wash up, and get warm. We don't have showers today. It's not our dayroom, and I don't fuck with the police, so I won't ask for a shower. I'll just bird bath. I've been contemplating on writing a part 4 to "2nd Line". Snake has been on me about it. I told him though I only do that type of writing (entertainment) when I blowed or sipping. I really like being off trees though when I'm writing. It brings out my best shit. That's ducked off in the depths of my mental. I've started putting a story board together with a list of new characters.

That's about it and I gave it a title, "2nd Line Quattro – Blood of my Enemies". The story board is a drawn out process for me within itself, because I'll go through the last one, pulling certain things and events from it. Like how I'd done when I worked on part three, going and pulling things from "Prince Reigns" which is part two. Of everything Snake has read thus far, he said "2nd lines I, II, and III" is my best work, followed by "Outtah Sight-Outtah Mind". It's about prison life. Right now he's reading "Ponds", a story about an all Black special ops military unit. If I do "Quattro", it's a wrap for "Prince". If I were to venture into mafia stuff later, I'll come anew.

Right now I'm focused on this "Yard Life – Expose, Real Life Inside of Prison". I'm already being asked will I write another Yard Life. Maybe ten years from the time this one is published. I'm giving myself until 2024/2025 to have it done. I don't have anyone to help me get going, so I'll more than likely have to get myself going. Once I'm able to get to where I can get in a lane and do what I know how to do, to make it make sense. If that ends up being the case, I'll give myself a little more time. Can't go all gas, no break! Nothing is cracking here for me. I'll continue to stay out of the way. The bullshit that's surrounding the activities too, I'm really cool on. So to avoid the other bullshit that comes with being in a lane here, I'll just leave it alone and fall back until I'm where I can wiggle and do me. At the same time, I'm trying to be out of the way, suuuper trying to miss the radar.

I just want to be able to do me and fall the fuck back. Buss a few plays and handle what I need to handle to get where I'm trying to get. At the end of the day, no one is going to have me like I'm going to have myself.

That's what my mindset is and where it is. I just want to make it make sense and add up. The other day on the yard, I heard someone speaking on Lil Devil from Front Hood. I know him from Delano, when I was there from 2010-2014. In 2013 we were in the same building and in the same section.

At first we were ok and cordial, then we had a run in about some loot which was actually a misoverstanding on his homies part on the streets. That or some type of game was being played (SMH). One thing I don't do is play with Niggah's loot. I do a play with him and slide him the greenies. He slides them back an hour later with a kite, talking about the greenies weren't straight which I knew was bullshit. What type of game is this Niggah playing? His homie on the streets told him they weren't cool and of course he took his homie's word. Then he tried going left field with his words. I told homie to calm that noise down, he's not dealing with no buster. Though I knew the greenies were straight, I went and had them checked again.

After the greenies were checked again, they came back again, good! I took the greenies back to him with my own kite, sliding them both under his door, "Cuz, the greenies are straight!" and I kept it moving down the tier. I didn't speak to homie for a few weeks after that, feeling as though he was on some dirt bag shit and with foul play, so I just backed up off of him. We ended up chopping it up though much later and all was straight. He was like, his homie and his homie's girl had some shit going on. It was water under the bridge, but I got at homie on some real shit. "I don't play with Niggah's loot, period, for the simple fact I don't want a Niggah playing with mine, but as far as that other shit, that can't happen again. I didn't get at you or come at you sideways in no type of way."

We ended up being cool though and messing with eachother regularly. He was morning porter and would come by my cell every morning and we would hang out and chop it up. Sometimes we would blow. When he got a gadget, he would slide it while he was at work. About a month after our situation, I had ended up catching Valley Fever and almost dying. It was ugly. I was real fucked up. Valley Fever is no joke. It will take you down for the count. After I had gotten out of the hospital and had been back on the yard for a few weeks, still recovering, I had to go on that mission with the homie Tone on Shorty Mac. Three days after that, Devil had been at my cell fucking with me during the morning.

He had a medical ducat and left the building. Twenty or so minutes later of him being gone, the yard goes down. T.C., the homie from Acacia, had got on him inside of the holding cell at medical. T.C. had been around that mutha fucka, getting on shit (beating dudes up). He stayed fucking dudes over and so much so the police stayed talking about how he was around there fighting all the time. Good homie though. I was on my way to CTC to do my check up for my Valley Fever and had gotten on a van to be driven there and T.C. was on the van.

"What up cuz?"

"What that shit do?"

We were talking and he told me he heard about the shit with me and Tone with the homie and how they shot the block gun a few times. Then he was like, "Damn cuz, but ain't you sick? Didn't you just barely get back from the hospital?"

I was like, "Yeah, but my number was called."

He started telling me about the shit with Devil, "Yeah, homie had some shit going on. That's all I'll say bout that!"

23

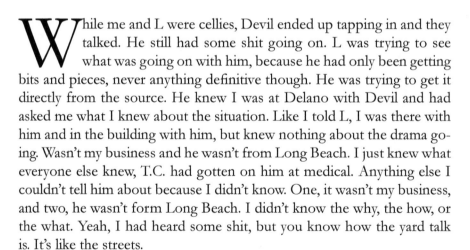

While me and L were cellies, Devil ended up tapping in and they talked. He still had some shit going on. L was trying to see what was going on with him, because he had only been getting bits and pieces, never anything definitive though. He was trying to get it directly from the source. He knew I was at Delano with Devil and had asked me what I knew about the situation. Like I told L, I was there with him and in the building with him, but knew nothing about the drama going. Wasn't my business and he wasn't from Long Beach. I just knew what everyone else knew, T.C. had gotten on him at medical. Anything else I couldn't tell him about because I didn't know. One, it wasn't my business, and two, he wasn't form Long Beach. I didn't know the why, the how, or the what. Yeah, I had heard some shit, but you know how the yard talk is. It's like the streets.

You have to take shit you hear with a grain of salt with so much foul play and dirt pool at work. It's always an under line. The surface shit don't always be what it appears to be. But yeah, just like the streets talk, the yards talk too. What I wasn't going to do though was repeat what I'd heard. No bueno! Anyway, for all I know, it could've been bullshit and

I wasn't going to be a contributor of it. Now, I could've said what the homie T.C. said, but I didn't. I left it where I heard it, on the van. L told Devil who his cellie was, and Devil told me, "What up!" I hit him back with "What up!" Him and L continued talking and I put my headphones on, banging that "Damn!" by Kendrick. After talking to the homie I don't think he gotten everything he was trying to get from the situation. L was like, a lot was unanswered, because a lot of evasiveness was going on and he vented his frustration. "I know this Niggah. I grew up with him. I know when he's shooting bullshit at me, and when he's keeping it clean." Like I told the homie though, you can't have irrational beliefs or expectations, real talk.

The reality may not be what you expected it to be, based on what your beliefs are, but as you said, you grew up with him and you know him. Today, my boy Spider, who's an Other, slid me his T.V. to watch until I get mine. The cold thing about it, he just went and got it today when we went to yard to get our packages. He gave it right to me. I took the plastic off of it and had to program it. It never made it to his cell. That was good looking out. He was like, "I fuck with you Tic. You're a good due and you're real. Just take care of my shit, homie."

"I gotchah!"

Snake was right there when he walked up to me and handed me the T.V. He told Spider that was a good look and that was what was up!

He told Snake he knew how it was to be without a T.V. He himself had someone else's T.V. before him and his cellie got theirs. They had a Northerner's T.C. that lived next door to me, which he gave back as soon as we walked in the building from yard and into our section. I'm hoping though I get my T.V. soon. I just received the notice, my appeal has made it to the second level coordinator. L hadn't heard of T.C. and was trying to find out who he was. He though he knew him. "He's from Acacia?"

"Yeah, he's dark complected, slim but cut up, and he has waves. Good Niggah though." Cuz be whupping Niggahs out, but he's straight. He doesn't be on no bullshit and he plays fair, My type of dude. It says a lot according to L or most dudes I fuck with. Let people tell it though, I don't like people, I got a bad wrap. Those outside of dudes I mess with say I'm funny acting, or I'm anti-social. No, I'm anti bullshit, anti bullshit Niggah, anti dirty politic Niggah, anti snitch Niggah, anti autobot, anti condone snitch Niggah, and anti extra'ed out Niggah! I keep my bullshit Niggah alarm activated, "Stay away! Stay away! Stay away!"

My moral compass works! I'm not fucking with you. Those are unde-sirables. I'm straight! I avoid those types to avoid any area of stagnation or stigma. No different than when I'm on the streets. I messed with certain homies and left the bullshit homies alone. Those I messed with I felt it was on some tight shit, to the point of me trusting them enough to put work in with or to do something around. I'm always cautious of who I mess with or socialize with. It's always said, birds of a feather flock together. True sentiment.

You're judged by the company you keep, period. Especially on the yard and trust you're being noticed. Police are watching you too, always, even when you think they aren't, they're on you. That's why you have to be mindful of your company. Today's the 7th. It's Chumlee's born day. I hooked him up some burritos. I got on his head this morning too, punched on him, Boom Bam! "Happy Born Day cuz!" He's running around at work right now. If he doesn't come across anything, he'll be sober living today. It's dryer than the Sahara Desert and has been (SMH). We've been sipping reggie though, a little bit. I don't celebrate born days anymore, but on my 50th, one last go around and I'm going B-I-G. That's next year. I'm talking about getting suuupppeeerrr white boy wasted! Just stay in the cell, lock myself in, and get it in. I'm talking reggie, white light-ning, and trees, starting at 4:30 A.M., like I've always done on my born days in prison, keeping it going all day. I wouldn't eat either while I got it cracking, just sipping and blowing. I'm already knowing I'll be parked right here in High Desert (SMH). I'll be prepared though, a couple of months ahead of time. I stay cocked and loaded like a 40 glock anytime I'm anticipating activities. If you stay ready, you don't have to get ready and I tried to told you! We had afternoon yard. The goon squad popped up in the building. Had dudes regrouping and pump faking. Any time they come around, a mutha fucka better be on his shit. They move, func-tion, and search differently than the regular police do. They credit card your shit.

They're coming all the way between your legs and up and they're running their hands around your waist. Simply put, they're extra'ed out with their searches. Those that have been searched by them know exactly what I mean. They're going that extra mile. That's what they're doing! On some real shit though, you're not trying to be on no IGI/goon squad radar. Once they're on you, it's a wrap. They'll stay pulling up on you. They'll hit your cell and take all of your paper work, looking for any signs of any type of activity, from drugs to gang affiliation and will put you in the sandbox pending investigation. Oh, and they'll have your paper work for weeks before you get it back. You're trying to stay out of their way. That's attention you don't want. They're primarily on dudes under paper work and drug and phone activity.

They don't fuck with light weight shit, but they'll look into you if your name keeps popping up on their desk. That puts you on their radar. I can say too, they're unpredictable, so you have to always be on point when they come around, even the regular police be on point. When I first got to Solano, goon squad would hit the building like 4:00 or 4:30 in the morning, but they always had specific targets.

They usually worked off a list. They work with rat bastards that feed them information and a lot of times their sources were reliable because they always get whatever it was they were told was there and their men. They function though a lot on information given by rat bastards, but yard police and building police will give them information based on shit they observe on the yard or in the building. What they did just yesterday when they hit our building, they went into every cell and ran the dogs through. They were looking for drugs and phones, which they'll do and have done on many yards I've been on. They'll just pop up and want to search. They'll come on integrity searches and they'll come on massive searches. Even then, they'll have their targets, but will do random searches.

Back to their unpredictability, they'll pop up on the yard and pick a group (Blacks, Whites, Others, or Hispanics) to search. They'll search their area and their persons, hope to catch you slipping. One time, I was on my way to work in the main kitchen in Delano. All of us that worked in the main kitchen ate early breakfast in the buildings satellite kitchen. After breakfast this particular day, we were walking out of the satellite kitchen, heading to the main kitchen, when 20 to 30 goon squads hit the yard, from the yards big doors. They were running with a lot of zip ties on them and in their hands, on the yard and yelling at us, "GEEETTT DOOOWWWN!"

As we were going down, we were approached by several goon squad and zip tied with our hands behind our backs, and was searched. Again, trying to catch you slipping. They had us down for about 35 minutes to 45 minutes on our stomachs and zip tied. It was uncomfortable as hell. After we were searched, the zip ties were cut off of us. They had them tight on our wrist. I guess in their mind, checking isn't cheating. We were allowed to continue to work. They didn't catch no one dirty. A few weeks later, they ran up on us again. This time they hit the main kitchen. They had us all on the back dock, searching us while some searched the whole kitchen. They had searched the vegetable room, the bakery, the distribution area, the kettle pot area, the scullery, the tool checkout room, and all of the freezers.

It was a random search supposedly, or the sgt. that worked in the main kitchen had them pull up by informing them that he'd gotten word it was a lot of activities going on back there as far as drugs being sold and used, along with dudes, several of them, being caught blowing trees in the different areas of the kitchen and being caught with drug paraphernalia. If it wasn't random, they were bound to come anyway, too much shit going on. We kept it blowed out! We blew in the bathroom and in the scullery, blowing smoke into the steam inside of the machine, then walked around eating up everything. It was munchy central, going from the distribution area eating cookies, chips, almonds, and gram crackers, to the kettles eating quesadillas and sandwiches, to the bakery eating cinnamon rolls or coffee cakes with milk, then to the grill having the homie S Bone hook up something.

That was damn near a daily occurrence and I would never eat dinner. I would be too full. I was basically good. We had yard this morning. Me, Chumlee, and Snake were on the slab, working out. Vamp was supposed to be working with Snake, but ended up coming a little later. He was telling Snake he didn't come right away because it was an issue going on. I asked him if it was a homie issue or a Black issue. He said it was a Black issue and was telling me, Chumlee, and Snake about it. We'll see how it plays out for sure. Right now it's a bunch of talk going on. Also, the claims are being investigated. It's always three versions.

At the end of the day it'll no doubt get figured out. If it comes back dude was in fact out of pocket, it'll have to be dealt with accordingly. The motions though have to be gone through first, in order to figure out what was what as far as the dynamics. That's a part of playing fair and not just acting without facts. Right or wrong, there are levels to this yard life, but it's not complicated. It only gets complicated when dudes don't play fair and complicate shit. You don't know what's going to happen though from day to day on the yard. It can go from cool, quiet, and straight, to someone's having ball played on him, someone's being two on one'ed or three on one'ed and whupped off the yard, to a simple fair one (head up fight). Can't forget about the spontaneous riot that can happen due to idiocacy. You never know. For the most part though you don't have to overstand the rules of engagement in this particular setting to be and remain actively vigilant in your push. It gets very hectic and fast at times. I was just looking outside of my cell door and saw someone talking to the police without someone else with them.

I was just telling Chumlee the same thing, you're never supposed to talk to the police without someone else being present. It alleviates speculation and talk, "Oh, what was he talking to the police about?" That type of interaction with the police is frowned upon. It just looks suspicious because no one knows what's being said. That's how speculation and insinuations start. But for all we know, you could be speaking on shit you shouldn't be, or just flat out telling. So, to avoid the talk or speculation or even the insinuations, always have someone with you to verify the context. If someone has an issue or if something were to come up later, you have someone to say "such and such didn't happen that way."

When you need to talk to the police, have someone with you. It's for your safety and it's to keep you on the right side of a potential situation. It leaves no room for the bullshit, real talk. It's no different than you putting a form in one of those boxes without letting anyone see it and read it before dropping it in. It's just you avoiding the bullshit. All it takes is for something to happen and there you go, "Well I saw such and such put something in the box yesterday and didn't nobody see what it was. Nobody saw it or read it." or it's "I saw such and such in the office talking to the police and it was just him. Nobody was with him. Don't know what they were talking about." or even, "Such and such was at the window talking to the police without nobody with him and he was talking low." You're just opening yourself up to the bullshit. Autobots will take it and run with it. Then you have dudes trying to put a jacket on you (saying you're snitching). That's not a jacket you'll want to rock. It's not fashionable. These autobots and bullshit dudes will put a jacket on you quick, so to avoid it, avoid putting yourself in that position. It's not even what they've seen, it's mostly what they've heard, "I heard such and such did this. I heard such and such did that." An autobot will take that "I heard" and run with it. It's enough for them.

Just follow the protocol. It's simple mathematics. To yet another point, certain jobs will get a jacket put on you. You'll definitely be put in the cross hairs of a scope, the scope of a fucked up situation. As with dudes who work in the sub-station, or working anywhere closely with the police. These dudes are continuously called a police or the police, walking around with that speculative cloud over their heads. That dark cloud just hovers. "He's the police, watch what you say to him or around him. He got to be the police!" It comes to he's the police.

Since you're working around the police and want to work around the police, you must want to be the police. You must be telling them shit or speaking on shit you shouldn't be. That's the speculation. We all know how dudes will feel just that comfortable to sit in an office with the police and have long drawn out conversations as if they're friends on the streets. The police will act like they're befriending, but it's merely a tactic to appear cool, to pump an individual for information under that guise of being cool. But the reality, they're trying to get information out of you. Everywhere I've been, as far as different yards, it's the same ole two step. Sub-station workers are always spoke on foully. They have to know it. "Those dudes working in the sub-station ain't cool. I don't fuck with the sub-station workers. They're working with the police. They telling this that and the third." Me personally, I'm cool on working in the sub-station or messing with the mac-rep shit. I'm cool on anything that could put me in a fucked up situation.

Not just that, but could possibly have that cloud hovering. Pushing on any yard and on any line, I'm avoiding all areas of stagnation, period. Let these other dudes horse play. I'm not going to be able to do it. That's out, all the way out! Yesterday I went out by myself and hit the slab. As I'm doing my workout, Snake and Squeek came walking up, because they only saw me on the slab working out by myself with no other Black nearby and I'm next to the South Siders. It's really a security risk, but I wasn't going to ask no one to come to the slab with me and a lot of these dudes I don't fuck with. I'm just cordial with them. Fucking with someone and being cordial are two different things.

"Aye Tic, where's your cellie?"

"He stayed in. He was tired!"

"We thought it was you over here by yourself, so we came to put us-alama on you (security)."

They started clowning him, talking about he wasn't tired, he just wanted to stay in and play with his dick. Like I told them, he could've stayed in. I didn't need him to babysit me. I've been walking these lines 16 years without one. A few people had asked me where he was because they didn't see him with me or see him on the yard. I told them he stayed. I didn't need him. He's his own man doing his own program.

As for me though, as long as that cell door opens for yard, I'm out of that cell. What the fuck you just want to sit in the cell for? To each his own. I can't do it though. I can't sit in the cell and to expect to know what's going on, especially nowadays. Dudes don't communicate. So, with that, if you want to know something, be where you can know. Something can happen on the yard, but as soon as you walk in the building, dudes are on the door, "What happened on the yard? Why did it go down?" If you were that concerned with the yard, should've been on the yard. I don't care what's going on or what isn't going on. I'm on the yard. My program is of a programmer. I program!

I program regardless. At the end of the day, I don't care how the next dude program, or do him. It doesn't affect me unless it does. On another note, on the political side of things, if something were to happen and you're in the cell when it does, that's on you, because someone is going to want to know why you weren't on the yard with the homie when xyz happened and it's only the two of you on the yard. That was a scenario that was brought up. I can't hold a dudes hand. He'll figure it out and I'm not watering anything down. Water id down, it becomes diluted, thus it's not effective. I'm putting it out there, un-cut. If a homie ask me what was the deal, this that and the third happen, period. I don't do feelings and I don't save dudes, especially when you're doing the wrong thing and knowing the ramifications. But the shit that kills me are the dudes who claim to be so level 4 and know how to program, know this, know that, and don't know shit.

Acting like you've been somewhere and knows the deal when clearly your actions and movements speak to the contrary, you're on a 4 yard, but your demonstration is level 1, level 2, or level 3. Nothing you do speak level 4. Since you know the deal, don't expect me to come to bat for you and speak on your behalf if you done some bullshit or some bullshit happened and you were on some other shit. If you're in the right though, I'm with you and for you, all the way. I'm an advocate. When I left the slab and I stepped over to the bars to do some bar work, they were occupied by a few Damus, J Smash, Nella, and Nightmare. Nella was on some funny shit. I was like, aight, he didn't respond. That's what's up. He won't ever have to worry about me ever speaking to him again as long as I'm on this yard. That's exactly why I don't even speak to most of these dudes from the get go. Wishy-washy, cool one day, the next they're on some other shit. I hate I even introduced myself to him.

I didn't speak to Nightmare, period. Snake and Squeek were having a friendly disagreement about a feast they'd had last year. Snake was telling Squeek he didn't remember having lamb fries at the feast. I'm laughing at them (SMH). Squeek kept telling Snake, "We had lamb fries at the feast!" Snake kept telling him, "I don't remember!"

Squeek hollered at the dude Nella, "Aye Nella, didn't we have lamb fries? Snakes saying we didn't have them." He made some comment and Snake was like, "Aye Squeek, don't put him in anything involving me. He's on some funny shit!"

That's when I told Snake about the interaction I'd just had with him before him and Squeek walked back up. They had left me walking back to the Black area, thinking I was heading in that direction. They assumed I meant I was heading there. I wasn't specific. I was like, "I'm going over here!" What I meant, over here, as in to the bars.

I told Snake dude didn't have to worry about it, because it'll never happen again. Snake said the same thing. We were like, "He must've got into it with a Crip or something earlier." It don't even matter. I'm good.

Of course, Squeek chimed in, "I didn't get that vibe from him. I was on some Islamic shit with him." Me and Snake are looking at him like, "Niggah please!"

"Plus he fuck with me. We go back 5 years. This that and the third, but you know, he's entitled to a bad day." Indeed he is. Have your bad days, but I'm good. I don't do the light switch shit. You're on, then you're off. As far as I'm concerned, we can keep it off on the dead homies! I didn't even complete all of my workout. I was like, "We can push!"

Snake was like, "Yeah, lets bounce. I'm not trying to be over here either!" Me, him, and Squeek walk off. Squeek was still saying something to Nella when me and Snake walked off ahead of him. "Why is Squeek still trying to talk to him? He sees he's on some funny shit (SMH)."

I had started talking to my Damu boy, P.F. damn near at the end of yard. We had gotten into some real deep conversations. It was actually the first time we'd really talked. We've had conversations, but not to this depth. He was telling me how he got to D-yard from C-yard. It was basically dirty shit and he was back doored, which led us to talking about how these dudes on the yards doing drugs and function with each other and their attitude being, if you're not using drugs too you're basically the odd man out. You're not on what they're on, so you're not with it. So, in order to be in, you have to be on drugs (SMH)!

Then since you're not on what they're on, it's a matter of time before the foul play come into play and they'll be trying to have you removed. It's a dirty game ya'll! He was telling me how a South Sider had played ball on him. I had been looking around the yard and just made a spontaneous comment about how many Hispanics (South Siders) were out there on the yard after they called yard recall, compared to the Blacks, due to them not coming to yard period, or due to them going in on in-line. P.F. was like, "Shit, if they wanted to, they could overrun us. It's not that many of us on the yard right now." Then he went into him being in the same type of situation where it wasn't that many Blacks on the yard and the South Siders took off on them and as a result he was played ball on and was stuck in the chest. We chopped it up for a cool minute and was touching on a lot of shit going on, on the yards. Turns out we have a lot of the same morals, values, and views when it comes to this prison shit, especially with the standing on the right side of right, being on the right side of a situation. Overstanding the rules and consequences of being on the wrong side of a situation.

Overall though, P.F. is a good guy and he's straight for sure. He knows his shit as it pertains to this unbalanced maze. He's a fair player. When it's all said and done, I salute! I just came from yard. It was a little cold out, but I was straight. I didn't bundle up either. I just had on my jacket, a beanie, and my gloves. I didn't do anything. It was Sunday. I just chilled and chopped it up with P.F. We were tripping off of the surroundings. It was a situation where a dude that wasn't cut was explaining a situation to someone who was cut and it wasn't an cut issue. Cut issues and non-cut issues are separate issues and doesn't have anything to do with each other. It was an instance where when I was in Solano a homie that was cut had drove up on the yard.

He basically gotten at by homies. Yeah, you're from the city, we love you and all that, but you can't speak on Long Beach issues or dictate anything to no homies. You can't be involved in no Long Beach matters or pow wows. Your loyalty and obligation are to those dudes. When I first started doing time in prison, I was told way back then not to get involved and not to fuck with dudes that was cut. Stay away from them. That's not for you. That's nothing but trouble. Do not get involved. I overstand now what I really didn't back then and what I really overstand is the structure. I get it, but it's not for me. The politics are for those who want to be politicians.

I'm not a politician. I've been informed somewhat as to how it functions, so I'm somewhat knowledgeable. At the end of the day though, the agendas are different. I did agree with how the homie was addressed though in regards to this Long Beach shit, as far as him not having a voice or input on what went on with the homies on the yard. I don't agree with cut homies having a say-so or influence over non-cut homies. We're not under what you're under or a part of. We don't have to listen to you, nor can you tell us anything. We don't fall under your rules or guide lines. We're strictly LBC Crips. We don't check in, report, or answer to you. You're just an homie. A homie with a overstanding in no fashion, shape, or form can we involve ourselves in your issues. Those aren't our issues, nor will we. Cut business is cut business.

In turn, we're also not going to involve you in ours in no fashion, shape, or form, based on the differences and we function. The homie however overstood and accepted it for what and as it was. He knew who and what he was loyal to, as well as obligated to. So, he kept his dealings with us to a minimum. He knew what it was and rightfully so. A good dude though for sure, and me and him have had several conversations. I just told the homie, no disrespect, but my issue is a non-cut issue, when I had one, and he respected that.

As far as that goes though, I didn't go to the homies if I had an issue with a dude. I dealt with my own shit without involving the homies. I only got at the homies after it was no longer an issue, which was rare anyway. I didn't have many personal issues or situations. Most of my issues, situations, or drama was set or city related. Homies into it with another car, or it's a DP and I have to get involved, which I have no problem with because it's what I signed up for.

But yeah, that'll be P.F.'s mind a long time, I'm sure on Dev's too. It's so much to be mindful of in this world we live in, from day to day. Can't take shit for granted, that's for sure. I had mentioned alienation, which isn't cool on no level. You can't alienate yourself from homies. You're only giving them a reason to trip or have your name in their mouth on some other shit. Them and the autobots, "Cuz don't fuck with the homies. Cuz is on some funny shit. What's up with cuz?" Then they'll start plotting and looking for a reason to vote you off the island and get you off of the yard. This isn't something I've heard that can happen. I've seen it. I was like, even if it's homies I don't like or feel, I'll still have a presence, tap in and be like, "Cuz, I'm over here though!"

It's nowhere in the code or rules you have to fuck with a homie. You're just obligated to ride with him. You don't have to be friends or socialize. It's keeping it cordial and being respectful, that's all it's about. I'll do it like the real politicians on the campaign trail, shake hands, dap, and keep it moving. I'm over here ya'll, he got the punch line, I got my game face on, my mindful face. In order to overstand what it is, you have to know what it is and move accordingly. It's nothing hard or complicated about navigation on these yards. It's simple mathematics, as I've said, and get no simpler. The main thing is you're being aware and being watchful. Know your lane. Never feel you're bigger than the car, or too big to be touched, because you're living in a false sense of security.

You're just one person and your shenanigans will get addressed when you're doing too much. It's always going to be individuals that'll want to give you a reality check. All it'll take is for one to set it in motion, "Cuz doing too much!" That's all it'll take, autobotism. Those four words puts it in motion. It'll be an easy sell for the rest of the homies to get on board. Everyone'll start bringing up incidents you've caused or were a part of, "Cuz thinks he's bigger than the homies. Cuz don't care about what the homies got going on. He don't care about putting everybody in harm's way." Now you're a liability. "Homie gots to go!" Yard down! "GEEETTT DOOOWWWN!" Horse playing! You also have to know when to keep relentless and when to show restraint. That's a big know. The yard will forge a Niggah into a structured Niggah, therefore he'll be able to navigate his way as it is for himself, as he want it to be and on his terms. It's imperative you know, get a bar.

Just pay attention! Homies will shake your hand while they're premeditating harm. Don't ever confuse that. It's not always what it seems. You better know your environment and have a feel for it. I know from experience. I shook a Niggah's hand, drunk with him, blew with him, all the while knowing once the yard open up, I'll be one of the homies participating in removing him off of the yard. Yard life is wicked and get real wicked. I'm like, it's fucked up, but it's the nature of the game.

The whole time I'm drinking and blowing with him, to myself I'm like, "Damn homie, you have no clue as to what's about to happen." He's clueless as hell. What I never get or overstand is how someone could be that clueless when you know you have a cloud looming over your head from some bullshit you've done somewhere else. You have to know shit follows you, yet you're laxed and comfortable. You have to know you have an issue coming at some point. To think otherwise, you're horse playing, homie. I don't know how dudes get lost in the translation. How could you (SMH)? You're supposed to always be at best leery of a situation, not laxed or comfortable to the point of feeling it's a deaded issue. It's not deaded.

A classic case of horse playing! Do overstand and as it's always sit, "It's not personal. It's business." It's never supposed to be personal. It should always be business, though for some it's personal. Those who choose to make it personal usually are on some side winder shit that has nothing to do with the underlying situation, nothing at all. They have a whole different agenda. I approach all situations as business. Nothing personal or ever personal. I'm just dealing with a situation. I'm not mentally or emotionally invested in it, just doing my part. Unless it's a personal issue, at which point it concerns me or my general safety or wellbeing. Then I'll deal with it accordingly.

Quick question, when you don't know who to trust, who do you trust? I don't see the yard (any yard) as the yard no longer. I just see the dark areas. I see having to question any and everything I feel is questionable, never losing sight or focus on this environment. Back to my point, if you see a situation with the potential of going sideways or crooked, abort. Give yourself the opportunity to run it back if you so choose to. You always have to give yourself action, self preservation.

To another point, never be the fool and never be afraid to be afraid. A fool is the only one who denies his fears, though Allah takes care of babies, old folks, and fools. Don't be that dude! Don't be the dude that has to learn a life lesson by a traumatic situation having to happen to you. Don't be that dude either. There are a lot of those types of dudes though, unfortunately, that don't believe fat meat is greasy, and it's greasy as fuck! I guess for some it has to happen, because they just don't get it and need that reality check. Some dudes are just into pain (SMH). No matter how much they see situations turn out bad or go sideways, they still choose to continue to horse play and self destruct, putting themselves in harm's way for no other reason than, "Can't no Niggah tell me shit. Nothing at all." Sometimes we can be our own worst enemy, thus deciding to make choices that are going to affect our push on the yard. Like that old saying goes, "You can lead a horse to water, but you can't make him drink." In essence, you can talk to a dude until you're grey in the face trying to lace them, but if they're not being receptive to it, they're just not trying to hear you. It's just that simple.

They just have to crash to get the message and overstanding, so be it. Crash if you must. If I'm getting at you and seeing you're not trying to hear me or feel what I'm saying, fuck it, do you. I'm done with it. Get your issue since that's what you seem to be looking for. A lack of self control and thought can and will cause you to crash to the point of no get back, ending your career, changing the whole dynamics of it, all because you chose to choose the latter, deciding not to take heed to it. As a homie though, an older homie, I've done my due diligence by showing you verbally, direction. Foreseeing the road you're on, trying to show you for the most part.

Once I'm in a position though and my hands are tied, they're tied. I can no longer be a voice or a supporter. I don't harbor or allow myself to be a shield, especially when you're in the wrong. You've made your bed. You have to lay in it! I don't condone tomfoolery, as I've reiterated. Don't be all in your feelings with me though. I didn't do it. That was all you. I'm not the one who has to compensate for a wrong decision. That's all you. Your conscious decision, and your choices. Blame yourself.

It's not on the homies, it's not on autobots, it's not on haters, and it's not on me. It's on you. No cut! You can hate or not feel the idea of absolute truth, but it is what it is, homie. It has to be recognized as such. It's not about trying to shift the weight. It's yours to carry. I wouldn't be able to stand on my beliefs, values, morals, principals, and my commitment of keeping it a thousand, my being real and true to it, if I was promoting the opposite. Like my guy Lon is always saying, "On the game!" What I promote comes from a place of good intentions, which is a quality that penetrates us and exceeds us on every side.

Those of us who advocate on the side of right, I'll always stand on that side, because it fuels my push. I've come to overstand the thing you think is important, become priority, and in turn, it determines how you map shit out and go about it, which you'll come to learn and overstand, walking these lines. The journey is also guided by allies around you, which you'll also come to learn and overstand. Trusting in what they do versus what they say. Be mindful. It's nothing else I can say to change that plain and simple fact. I've also come to appreciate how I'm wired, the way I'm supposed to be wired, the way that I'm wired and allowing my actions to show. I can conduct my push and on my terms, which is the way it should be in my mind.

Although we are who we are outwardly, our interactions with other people cause us to change inwardly. At some point, especially on these lines, you have to use that in terms of growth and awareness. Allow every experience to be a teachable moment, your teachable moment, because it contains growth. For me, it's not putting myself in a fucked up position, regardless of the individual, especially with a dude calling himself the homie. But just because a dude claims he's a homie, don't mean he is. Dudes are quick to claim homie, but will be quick to back bite you or plot against you. I've learned this first hand. That situation will never happen again that played out in Solano. Trials have a way of forcing you to re-think and reevaluate your push, as you're pushing. It has a way of having you focused as well. You always have to learn what you need to know. It's no getting around that, real talk though.

To another point, trials challenge us and change us for the better, for the most part. Question, do you find yourself reevaluating things you could've or should've done differently? I'm vigilant about my balance more so now than I've ever been, and it's due to my having a need for that different lens. For looking at things much differently in terms of my surroundings and those I choose to befriend and be loyal to, which aren't many. If tears hold value, I'll drop one for every lesson I've been taught as I've been navigating my way through this maze. It's been a ride thus far and I'm continuously learning shit. Just when you think you can't learn any more, you're hit with another lesson.

There's always a lesson to be learned, directly or indirectly, being on the line. Walking on these yards are lessons within themselves. I just talk-ed to moms last night at dayroom and she gave me some disturbing news. I was like, "Wow!" So yesterday I was called for a package. I'm thinking it was religious oil though, because I wasn't looking for a package. I had let Vamp get some oil in my name. When I got to the gym where packages were being handed out, they had a replacement T.V. for me for my T.V. being damaged, well, flat out broken. First off, it wasn't a fifteen inch RCA flat screen. They down sized me. Flag on the play! It was a thirteen inch flat screen, though still a RCA.

So that was discrepancy one. The second one, when I got back to the cell, turning it on, using the cable, I didn't get a picture nor could I program it, so it's useless. As I inspected it further, the T.V. was in poor condition. The back of it was cracked, the face of it was loose, and the stand isn't stable. It was someone else's T.V. that had been confiscated. The name had been scratched off and mine was added. Unacceptable. I tried to take it back to the gym, but wasn't allowed, so now I'm trying to get it back to R and R. They're still playing games. Why would they even give me a T.V. in that condition? So now I'm putting more paperwork in. This shit is crazy as fuck. It has been pretty quiet around here for the most part. Then it went bad yesterday for another Northerner succumbing to his injuries.

When it get real, it gets real. I'd met him and talked to him a couple of times. He appeared to be cool as fuck, and he only had ten months to the house (SMH). That takes me back to being in the cages in the sandbox when I was talking to E.B.'s cellie, which I'm just now remembering is T.O. He was saying how 20 Deee, S.T., and Tall were supposedly mad because I played ball on Opie and he was a few weeks to the house, which turned out to be a lie, but what was that supposed to mean to me? I didn't give a fuck. If you were hours away from being called to R and R, our issue will get resolved one way or another. Little that they all knew, if I wouldn't have got my greenies and he would've kept stringing me along until it was his day to go home, at breakfast I would've hung out by the handball court, security conscious, waiting on his damn ass, that part!

Though I took a loss on the greenies and didn't get my loot, he learned a valuable lesson. It wasn't a game. As for them saying I knew he was short to the house, so what! He wasn't thinking about that, playing with my greenies. Apparently he didn't care or wasn't tripping off of it, so who are you to? Everyone makes their own choices and have to live with them. As far as that goes though, dudes weren't really worried or concerned. They had an underlying motive for trying to make it seem like I was wrong for doing it knowing he was short. They didn't give a fuck about that. All smoke and mirrors. You're in a mindset, I couldn't move too. My thing is this, you're not home until you're home. You're still in play as long as you're on the yard. So basically, you can still be held accountable for shit you do. You're not exempt. Just like you're still technically obligated to participate in activities, short or not, unless the homies are like, "Fall back and go home." This is what we've signed up for, real talk! We know what it is. To think or suggest otherwise is horse playing, that part! It's like liquor, if you can't hold it, you better quit drinking. Sometimes the painful reality of life on the yard causes interruptions.

It's cruel that way and I'm being straighter than Indian hair. Protocols are protocols, rules are rules, and violations are violations. There are no in-betweens. There's no cut to that. Once the push begins, no one controls it, because its cause and effect, every day, all day. Tehachapi's program for the most part was alright.

It wasn't much really going on around there at that time while I was there. There were a few scrimmages though, and DP's. You're going to have those regardless and fights too are inevitable. I've had a few fights over the years, but not many, and they weren't premeditated. Head of the moment type shit. IF I'm going to premeditate some shit, it won't be a fight. It's too much energy being wasted on thinking about a fight. That's like when you're arguing with a dude, that's wasted energy. Why argue? If we have an issue, it's an issue. All of that other shit is drawing too much attention. We can void that and get to it!

24

I was also at Tehachapi with Lil Starchild from the set, though he stopped pushing in the sandbox. He didn't say though he was cool until after he was in the sandbox. He Basically was cool because he wasn't feeling the politics and being sent on a mission and it wasn't anything but a DP. It wasn't no ball playing. But damn, how do you expect not to get your hands dirty at all? If you're pushing with a car and you're a member, that comes with it. At some point, you will be called upon to participate in the activities and in some instances you have no choice, just based on being affiliated. You're involved, period. Yet you do though have a lot of dudes who are in that mind set as if they're exempt from having to participate in the activities, thinking they can just go through and represent without having to get dirty. That is not big brother, where you can just be a floater.

Real talk, it's not going to fly or you'll eventually be voted off of the island. I've been on yard where you couldn't be on it functioning with the homies if you weren't active or participating in the festivities. It was a rotation and when your number was called, you got cracking. That's how we functioned, period, point blank, and if you weren't with it, do it moving! For the simple fact, you're in the way, and just trying to do your time floating by. Being a floater wasn't going to cut it. You can benefit from what homies got going on, but you can't get involved? You can float that ass right up off of the yard.

On some real shit, I'm winding down. My whole 16 years have been active and I'm still pushing at 49. I'll be 50 next year. As long as it's in me and I'm physically able and capable, it is what it is, LBC. But when that time comes, I'll know. My body will tell me, "Aye Tic, sit your old ass down somewhere home. It's over. Fall back and it'll be on my terms." One thing is for certain, I'm not a floater, nor have I ever been, known fact. That's when I'll be ready to fully commit myself to Islam and be on my Deen. I'm not trying to be one of those dudes with one foot in and one foot out, and still running around talking about, "I'm a Muslim" but still hollering cuz/Blood and functioning with homies, engaging in all activities, still drinking, still blowing, still doing drugs and going on missions. Though I haven't been a practicing Muslim for years, I still don't eat pork. When someone tries to give it to me and I tell them I don't eat pork the first thing they'll say is, "Oh, you're a Muslim?"

"Yeah, I'm just not practicing right now. I'm doing me." Meaning I'm still blowing, drinking, and functioning with the homies. I overstand you can't do both. You're either or, a Muslim or a homie. Anything else you're horse playing. You can't serve two gods! Yet I see it all of the time and on every yard I've been on. Dudes are doing both. "Akh this, Akh that, cuz this, cuz that, Blood this, Blood that (SMH)!"

At the end of the day though, do you if that's what you're doing. I just can't do it. I'm not going to play with it. I'm on my Deen or I'm not. What resonate with me is me keeping it real with myself. So, as long as I'm still functioning with the homies, drinking, blowing, and doing me, it's no bueno! It's not an internal struggle. I can't have one foot on the yard with the homies and indulging in all of the festivities, but then my other foot is in the services in the chapel, trying to be on my Deen. It's not going to work, period. At some point, we'll all get to that point in our life, coming to that realization it's time to do something different, because I'm stuck in park.

Change will come in time and at its own page. It can't be forced, because it'll be quicker to fall back into that space. It can't be a have to, but a want to. Even a broke clock is right twice a day. Whenever the clock stops it'll be that time twice, morning and night. At which point I'll be living my version of it, being the better and best me I can be as I continue to navigate my way through this maze. We are all in conflict. We are all in contradiction, because that's what the world is. We always change as we always grow. It's the natural order of things. That doesn't mean you lose your integrity, your values, or your morals, not at all!

That doesn't mean either that you stop being a man. You're that first. That doesn't mean that I'll never be that turn the other check dude. Why? So you can sock (punch) the other side? That's out my guy, all the way out! Keeping it a thousand, I'm far off from love my enemy, bless those who curse me, and do good to those who hate me. Nah, I'm not there yet. I get Allah is behind the scenes and controls the scenes he stands behind. It'll be baby steps for me. As with being forgiving, that's far off too and won't come easy. Especially with those I feel that has turned on me and has turned their back on me, family especially. It'll be kind of hard for me to accept the fact you were anti me, and knowing you were basically saying fuck me.

Basically saying you could care less about my struggle or my well being. So for certain I'm on fuck you too! I'm a firm believer in fair exchange not being a robbery! Fuck you too, fuck your life, fuck what you stand for, fuck what you're going through, fuck your breath, and fuck any and everything you! Yeah, you're probably like, damn that's a bit extreme. When you're against me, I'm extreme! At the end of the day, how you got at me was extreme too. I'm not perfect. I just know how to manage my imperfections and by no means do I regret my past. I just regret the people I wasted it with. That's time and energy I'll never get back.

I have a lot of issues and unresolved issues to work through when it's all said and done. I also get the way I feel towards people isn't automatic consequences of what they've done or how they got at me, but the matter of what I've allowed myself to feel, which shouldn't have been anything at all. Not caring enough to feel anything towards them or their actions. Time and time again though I've been told if I feel I've misoverstood someone, ask them to clarify or restate their meaning or motive and not to give in to anger or give up out of frustration, because sometimes people don't state their position or directions clearly, so I'm hearing what I want to hear. At other times, I'm only hearing part of what has been said and it's usually the part that I don't like or want to believe. I can agree, but there's no mistaking actions. You can't mistake how a person moves, as far as a position being taken or how they act in general towards you. It's impossible to mistake. You can only take that one way and that's the right way. I said that because I was also told, "Maybe you read into something you saw and it really wasn't what you thought," and I might not of saw the situation for what it really was. Yeah, and Stevie Wonder ain't really blind. If you don't knock it off. It was exactly what it was and how I saw it to be.

At the end of the day, I accept it all for what and as it is, and I'm good with that. Clebo, L, and Lil Tray Deee asked me though what if they were to pop up out of the blue, trying to fuck with me, would I entertain it. I thought about it and that would be a hard no! Blood makes you related. Loyalty makes you family. All past relationships are deaded. They were fake, so called family especially, and all of that, it wasn't me. It was such and such. It's like this, if you fucking with them, you ducking with them. My past is in my rearview. However though, I'm working through past issues to be better with how I deal with situations and relationships moving forward.

Change always makes a big impact. It changes the dynamics and places you in a different space mentally, emotionally, and spiritually. I get when you're open to change, you're not boxed in. I'm a work in progress, forward progress. I was just the other day thinking about what a female I was corresponding with a couple of years ago said to me, when I was on the line and still at Solano. She was like, "If you don't change your thinking and allow yourself to forgive people and let shit go, you're going to end up by yourself. You're going to die in prison all alone." My response was, "Bitch, I don't give a fuck!" She was apparently under the impression just because I had life I wouldn't speak my mind or do or be me. Bitch had both life and bullshit fucked up! You do have those you deal with at times under that impression, if they're doing something for you they can just get at you any ole type of way or just do anything like it's cool and you'll be cool with it because you need them. That's all the way out! If you do or say something I'm not feeling, I'm going to let you know off top. I won't be biting my tongue, believe that! Though I'll be as respectful as I can be, but for certain you'll hear about it. My whole attitude with that is, don't get my situation or me confused, just because you're looking out you, have a pass to get at me sideways with your verbals or actions, that's no bueno!

Life or no life, you can rocks and cans! I don't need the drama or headaches. I'm dealing with enough. I'm dealing with a reality you can't begin to overstand. You're free. If I have to allow someone to get at me sideways, or get at me a certain way as to how they're trying to treat me in order for them to fuck with me, or do something for me, I'm good and will let them know just that and uncut, but respectfully. That's just something I can't or won't allow, regardless. That goes double for someone that's doing nothing for me or my struggle. I'm going to really let you know what time it is off the dribble.

You don't have no room or leg to stand on to get at me no type of way whatsoever. So you really need to stay in your lane (SMH). I see and hear all of the time how dudes let their wives, girls, family members, and their homies get at them sideways, just so they can keep getting whatever type of support and energy they're getting from them. They're cool with it as long as they're getting packages, going to canteen, able to call, able to get visits, get mail and captured moments. I'm not going to be able to do it. Fuck your packages, canteen, your visits, your mail, and your captured moments, or your lack thereof on all of the above. I'm not going to compromise my integrity in order to be fucked with. If I don't speak on it, I'm condoning it and allowing them to feel I'm down with it and I'm going to accept it, which I'm clearly not. I'm not that guy. It's just some shit I'm not accepting or are going to put up with, regardless of my situation. I wasn't going to accept it on the streets, so why would I now? For some punk ass pictures, money, mail, visits, or packages or a phone call! That goes back to dudes feeling a certain way about how their girls or wives are acting, by not doing what they're supposed to be doing and them not saying anything.

Not trying to rock the boat or upset them, feeling as though she'll leave or cut them off. The longer you don't say anything, the more shit they're going to pull and try to get away with. You have to let them know, "Just because I'm locked up don't mean I'm going to accept your bullshit, because you can go. I don't need you or your shenanigans." But what I do need is a piece of mind. If they're going to leave, they were going to leave anyway. At the end of the day, you no longer have an interest that's common. They're out there and you're in here. They're feeling some type of way and any little reason will be reason enough to free them of their conscious, justification for their actions.

In reality, you don't need justification, just beat it! I need to be stress and drama free, focusing on my surroundings. That's a distraction I really don't need and its anti-productive. It's anti-productive to my wellbeing and to my piece of mind. If it means I have to compromise that, I guess I'll be alone and will probably die that way, by myself. But you know what? I'm good with that though, and have come to terms with that long ago. I adjust. That's my reality.

A cruel fact of life is circumstance. The majority of circumstances dictate the course in life that we take and how we move. At the end of the day, I'm a firm believer. Part of defining who you are is making decisions about what you won't settle for or what you won't be and being vigilant, regardless of your circumstances or situation, especially under these circumstances of confinement. Every cellie I've had called me cold, based on my views and my feelings, saying they couldn't be like me, which is cool, because I couldn't accept what they're accepting. I couldn't be like them. From Clebo, Lil Tray Deee, L, to King, they felt I was hard in the paint, with no compassion or overstanding.

I feel them though. They're entitled to that. I found that all of the things we accept will be the things we regret when it's all said and done, in my mind. I'm not the dude I use to be. When you constantly go on the defensive and you're constantly telling yourself that people are on some other shit with you, you tend to act in ways that elicit negative type of responses. Really being reflective, sometimes you have to redefine your space and remove reminders of things or people that are anti what you're pushing. When the ground under your boots is shook, your perspective on things won't seem the same and that's just life.

Sometimes we're too clouded visually, and too engaged, so we sometimes often have trouble seeing shit as they are and for what they are, which you'll come to see in proper time. You have to go through the fire to come out refined, real talk! Get a bar. On that though, lastly, always retain independence and self possession, then you won't feel you have to compromise your integrity, because with or without someone, you're straight. You can stay blunt, stay in the paint, stay doing and being you and without having to play safe or watch your tongue if you're feeling some type of way, feel you have to. Some play on that. "He's not going to say this or that, or do this or that, because he needs me, however he needs me." (SMH) Aye, I've tried every conceivable alibi within the realm of reason to justify my actions and thought process .I'm moving and speaking based on experiences and not from an emotional space. My guy Lon has two more days left and he'll be off of his punishment. This morning though we have yard and he's trying to see if the building police will let him out so we can take a captured moment. Yeah, that was a negative on Lon being let out, but at the same time, they weren't even taking them. The sgt said next week, which is all good, because he'll be off by then.

These dudes had some bullshit going on though with this mac-rep shit, which I could really care less about. The mac-rep's cellie, Dre, got at me and Chumlee, asking us did we have issues with how his homies mac-repping, because it was being said someone in our section (B-section) had an issue and basically it was either me or Chumlee. I told Dre me and his cellie had already spoke on the issue I had about his mac-repping. As far as anything else, if I had an issue with a dude I know how to address it directly to them. I don't bite my tongue. From what I gather it's some other shit at play, back door politicking, which I found out.

Someone else wants Drake dethroned so there were a lot of discussions going on and a lot of grouping amongst the Damus and the Bay Areas, mainly just side bars. When I first hit the yard, I was seeing it, but wasn't paying no mind to it. I headed to the slab, which is what I do every day. Once Vamp finally made it to the slab where me and Snake were already working out, he briefly spoke on what was going on. I wasn't really interested in it, so I payed very little attention to what was being said. I caught bits and pieces. After we had finished working out and made it to our area by the tables, that's when Dre got at me and Chumlee.

Then he asked me could I get at his cellie about what I had said to him. That's when I told him me and Drake had had a conversation at my door already. My thing with him was basically this, when it's a Black issue and you're the mac-rep for the building, you should inform every Black in the building as to what's going on, since it'll affect them and not just assume everyone knows. You know as well as I do the games these dudes play with the different degrees of separation. For one, dudes be on that selective shit. "I'm only telling such and such and if I do that such and such will let these dudes know", or "I'll tell my homies and they'll tell whoever they fuck with, so and so forth." That ain't cool (SMH).

You know as well as I do how that's going to play out and to top it off, it's only 27 to 30 Blacks in this whole building, if that. It took three days after the fact for me to even hear it was an issue or a potential one. What type of shit is that? You best believe if the role was reversed and it was an issue with the other races, damn just the building knowing, the yard would know. They would communicate with their people. They're never left in the dark. Our people are burnt out with that look. He tells me though, "I assumed you knew." How could you assume that though when you didn't come to my door and let me know this? Secondly, when you hit our section, I don't even know you're in the section. You're in there to holler at who you're hollering at and you're out. It's not hard to tap in. It's not a lot of Blacks in each section. In my section, there are only three cells on top and three on the bottom.

How long would it have taken to tap in? At the end of the day, these dudes nowadays want and get that position to hang out. It's not about the people, yet that's the claim to get the position. "I'm for the people. I'm out here for ya'll!" Yeah, ok, out here for ya'll, I'm for the people. You can miss me with it. I know what the deal is. A bunch of ism. It appeared as though me or Chumlee were being used as the reason for Mad Face wanting to throw his hat into the ring for the mac-rep position, how I perceived it. How can one person feeling the current mac-rep is not doing his job warrant him being dethroned? It doesn't. It's a much bigger captured moment. "Oh, such and such said Drakes not mac-repping for the people. Let's all get behind that and get rid of him so such and such can be the mac-rep. But wait, do we have the votes?" Which brings me to the conversation I had with Squeek. No sooner than I walked away from Dre, I was walking towards Squeek and Snake, who had been chopping it up off to the side in a side bar.

As I'm approaching, Snakes walking off, "I'm cool on all of that. I don't want to talk about that shit. Fuck that shit!" He walks towards our building on his way inside. I was like, "What's up with Snake?" Squeek was like, "I was trying to ask him about what was going on with this mac-rep shit and he wasn't trying to talk to me about it." I asked Squeek what was it he was trying to know. He was basically like what was going on? I tell him about the conversation with Dre and how it was being put on me or Chumlee as to why it's even a question as to the job that's being done by Drake.

But then when I told him about Mad Face wanting to be the mac-rep, it all came into focus for him. That's when he was telling me about how the mac-rep position always been established as Crip or Blood in the building. If it wasn't a Crip, it was a Blood, no one else. The Bay wasn't even in the equation and up to this point the Damus didn't want the position, but all of a sudden they do and it's felt. Due I part because Chumlee don't want to pass for them. Then Squeek started breaking down the numbers. It's like six Damus, I think seven Bay Areas, so the Damus don't have the votes number wise, unless the Hoover homies give them their votes. It's eight of them. Vamp already said he wasn't giving his vote. I already know how Lon feels. Then that leaves me, Chumlee, Snake, and Squeek, four Crips. Squeek said he would take the job back if he had enough votes, but unfortunately it's not enough Crips to get him back in that spot. He was the mac-rep when I first got here, but was dethroned. The Bay Area's had three more numbers than us and one more than the Damus. Neither Crips nor Bloods can get that position without the Hoover homies votes at this point. Yeah, but don't make me or my cellies the reason for whatever ya'll got going on. Whether it was said it was him or me, we're only one person, our one vote won't help either party, because my vote isn't going to either.

Don't get it twisted though, Chumlee will pass for anyone. That's not an issue, but certain shit it's no bueno, and that's to avoid him from being put in the middle of some shenanigans, because dudes play games and do a bunch of weird shit. Dudes are real weirdos. Quick example, someone gave him something to take to another cell, "Aye, your homie said tuck this." They wouldn't take whatever it was, so he had to take it back, and mind you, the something was hot. So now you have him on the tier exposed with some hot shit. Now what if the police hit the section and see him on the tier and pull up on him? "Aye Brown, come here. What are you doing? What do you have?" You're in the cell, fuck him, it's on him. That's out! Because you Niggahs playing games. I told him to ban both of those cells and not to pass shit else for them. Have their homies pass for them.

Then it went somewhere else. The premeditated conversation went into play. So it was brought up too that shit, it could also be said that your cellie don't check in on the Blacks and he's the only Black porter out there in the section. Let me explain something though, a porter tapping in, it's a courtesy. When its all said and done homie, that's not their job to run around the building for you, me, or anyone else. Their job is to push a broom, mop the floor, wipe stuff down, and dump trash. Anything outside of their job description, it's because they want to do it. They don't have to. Now with that mac-rep situation, that's what you signed up for, to tap in and to check and see if a Black has an issue or a problem that needs to be addressed with the police or if he needs any type of form. It also entails him to keep the community informed of anything that's going on that can possibly affect them. That's just keeping it a thousand. That's not a porter's job. That argument you can save.

A courtesy is a courtesy, a job is a job. If you just want to get down to the essence of it all, yeah. Should he accommodate? He should, based on him being in the position he's in and he's out and about, where as you're not and you're in the cell needing assistance. But now if a dude just don't fuck with you, that's a whole different story. What's crazy, literally one minute ago as I'm writing, I had to stop and go to the door. It was Smash doing the votes for the mac-rep position. It's Drake, Mad Face, and Squeek. Me and Chumlee voted for Squeek based on, but we already know how it's going to play out. Either way, I don't care. I'm just supporting a Crip homie. He does tap in and he does push on issues. I'm good with that though.

I don't know what's going on. Dre, he just left the door, tapping in, as if he's a mac-rep, but then I see Drake in the section. Spoke too soon, Drake just left the door asking if I was good or if I needed something. I saw him running around in the section. When Dre had stopped at my door, a few minutes after Dre left my door, Drake pulled up. They had something going on. I guess at yard it'll be spoke on to some degree. So after yard, it was said Drake will remain the mac-rep. However, Hersh came and got at me and was like he had a long talk with Drake about my concerns.

Moving forward, after Drake was told that myself and Lon as older homies and active older homies were to be informed on issues and tapped in with on some security shit, that if he couldn't handle the task, he would be removed and replaced with someone who could and would. He also stressed that if either of us had an issue with his mac-repping to come and holler at him so we have an overstanding. If Hersh got at Lon, can't say, but I know he got at me, but our consensuses were the same for the most part. Fuck that mac-rep shit, but only outside of it's not affecting Blacks as a whole. Anything affecting me as a Black, I want to be informed, because it affects me.

At the end of the day, I want to know why I'm putting myself on the line and fucking my program off. I want to know what the issue is and who the issue with. Now for me to think or assume if it's with your homies you're going to come and tell me, I must still be on Sherm, because I wouldn't, but if it's racial for sure come and inform me. Hitting the play button isn't the issue. I just want to know the situation. I want to know the situation for what it is and as it is, based on my sacrifice I'm about to make. Yesterday me and Lon were speaking on how dudes be ear hustling, trying to listen to a conversation that doesn't concern them and don't know how to do it. If you're doing it, you're not supposed to be obvious about it. It should be done on the low.

It's an art to all of the madness. Chumlees just blatant with his ear hustling. He has no finesse about it. Dudes know he's listening to them or trying to, and just shake their heads and move away. Me and Lon catch him all the time doing it and we clown him about it. You would think he would've caught on by now, but he hasn't. That's a habit he needs to break. It's not a good one to have. Everything isn't meant for everyone to hear and know. It just isn't. It could easily put you in a fucked up situation, which is what I've always tried to convey to him.

Say for instance, something got out that shouldn't have. Fingers are pointed at you now. "Well when we were discussing the situation, he was standing right there next to us. It had to be him." but the cold thing about it, it didn't have to be you, but you made it you, wanting to be right there ear hustling (SMH). You made it easy for a mutha fucka to shift that weight in your direction, all because you wanted to be nosey. That's exactly what that is, being nosey, wanting to know shit that doesn't concern you in no fashion shape or form. You're just inviting drama to your space for no reason. If it's not your business and it doesn't concern you, push on. It's not affecting you, affecting the homies, or have no affect on your wellbeing or surroundings.

It's something behind that adage, mind your own, you'll live long. It's a true sentiment. You don't need to know everything and anything, nor should you want to. You don't know it, or didn't hear it, can't no one involve you in shit, period, if and when it goes sideways. I wasn't there, I wasn't around, I didn't see shit, or hear shit. That brings me to another instance when a few days back me and another Crip homie were speaking on how when homies are trying to show homies bad paperwork on other homies where they've told. If you get it and read it, you're obligated to do something to him if you ran across him for the simple fact you've read it.

We were speaking on basically how some homies refuse to read paperwork, not wanting to be involved or have to be involved, which will be because someone else can confirm that you've read it. "Yeah, homie such and such read it too. He knows." You no longer have deniability. You can no longer use, "I didn't read it. I didn't see it, not with my own eyes." I've ran across quite a few homies that's like, "Nah, I'm not trying to read a

Niggah's shit." due to what seeing it and reading it entails. It's been issues where dudes popped up and have been suspected of some telling, but wasn't any paperwork, just word of mouth. The thing is, you can't act on word of mouth alone. You need that black and white. You can't just rely on word of mouth. You don't know what's really at play, with so much dirty play going on. Someone could be horse playing and then you act. Now you're in a situation and have to answer for your actions. I get why, in that dudes be hesitant, not wanting shit to come back on them, because it will, thinking you were doing the right thing. It's a cold game.

So back to Chumlee, another race that he fucks with came and got at me about the ear hustling shit, which he claims he never does. Let him tell it though. Dude was like, "Look, I fuck with your cellie. He's my boy, but I don't want anything to happen to him. Not saying something is going to happen, but talk to him. A few people (his people, northerners) are saying he's being in business that doesn't concern him. When dudes are talking, he'll stand there trying to hear instead of walking away."

He was like, "I came to your door trying to talk to him, but he was like fuck that dude, this that and the other (which I heard him say)." However, the Northerner wasn't speaking on who Chumlee though he was speaking on, it was a completely different situation. Chumlee had so much shit going on, he was confusing situations. Come to find out, he'd been getting into a lot of little situations and here it is, I'm in the cell clueless. I don't know what's going on unless someone pull up on me as a courtesy, because they don't have to.

Just today I hollered at Drake. He pulled up on me. Him and Chumlee had something going on. I'm beginning to see a pattern with him, but it's always someone else doing something to him, then he'll come back with a completely different version of what actually happened. Tell me one thing when that's not the reality. Something far off from what he told me that happened, and he can't hold water. Drake was like, "He banged on me bruh. 20 Crip this, 20 Crip that, and I told him I don't gang bang. Why are you banging on me!" He was like, "Chumlee got mad and walked off because his cellie told him 'nevermind, my cellies here now' (meaning him)." Drake's cellie initially called Chumlee to their door. In the process of that, Drake popped up and his cellie told Chumlee it's cool now, my cellies here, I'll get him to do it. That's when Chumlee walked off talking shit. SO with that, Drake told him respectfully, "Well if you feel that way, don't come back to my door."

Then here comes, "Cuz, I don't give a fuck. This 20 Crip! This that and the third."

Then he tells me about an issue me and Chumlee had that was spoke on between him, Chumlee and Squeek. Squeek had told me, I just never brought it up. "Yeah, he was speaking on an issue you and him had in ya'll cell with me and Squeek and was on the tier with it loud. I had to tell him it's not my business and I walked away, but before I did I told him he shouldn't have ya'll business on the tier."

He told me himself he told Drake and Squeek about the situation, but down played it. He didn't tell me he'd done all of that animated shit and theatrics. I let it go though. That's just another one for the memory bank and another score. First and foremost, what go on in our cell isn't anyone's business, but that right there speaks volumes. Any time you bring something to his attention, someone else is the one, it's never him. Everyone's lying on him. It's their fault. I see it clearly now for what and as it is (SMH). At first I was like, "Yeah, I know how homies get down, so it's possible they were on some bullshit with him, had me fooled."

Nah, I see it, I'm getting it, up close and personal. My overstanding is never zero and bullshit ain't about nothing. I'm going to always call a ball a ball and a strike a strike. I'm going to have another long talk with the homie. After that, I'm done. I can't be babysitting no grown ass man or holding his hand. You'll have to learn the hard way continuously until you get it, since that appears to be the route you prefer. Do and be you! Lon got at you, I'm getting at you again, and technically we're both getting at him again for the third or fourth time. That shit gets old and fast. But yeah, I just told Drake not to fuck with him no more, to leave him alone to avoid the clashing, knowing how he is.

I had to tell Vamp that too. Him and Vamp are going through some shit because it stems from the back and forth. If you just cut it off it'll cease all of the bullshit. Just leave dude alone. A few days after the ear hustling situation, a whole different situation came about. Me and Lon had been trying to take a captured moment, but as always, some bullshit take place. So now it's supposed to be this upcoming Thursday or Friday. We'll see though. So this new situation was Chumlee playing with another race about his homie telling. He was passing our cell. He calls dude to our cell and not being mindful of his mouth or his words, "Aye, what's up with your boy telling? Saying my cellies A2B?" As soon as I heard it,

I'm like don't play with dude like that. I don't care how cool you think ya'll are.

I knew he was playing and not really thinking about what he was saying and how serious that was and could be (SMH). I knew it wasn't going to end there, especially with another race. He doesn't think, he just talks and says shit, but that's his mindset, and you have to overstand it. People aren't going to keep overlooking it and some aren't going to care and I've been told just that. He's a grown man and he's on a 180. I don't know how much longer it'll be before he crashes us or himself. I talk to him constantly. Lon talks to him constantly and he continues getting into shit. That situation almost blew up. Me and Lon were posted up, talking, when Vamp pull up on us, "Aye, your cellies running around talking about somebody telling. This was just brought to me. You need to get at him, because it's going to be an issue." I immediately call him, "Cuz, you running around here talking about somebody's telling?"

"I didn't say anything. I wasn't speaking on nobody!"

Then it was like, "I don't think they're trying to make an issue out of it, because they fuck with us, but your cellie better watch his mouth if he said it (SMH)."

He took that situation kind of serious apparently and rightfully so. You don't play like that and can't play like that. That's a serious accusation you can't play with. That'll get you hurt. He went and got at Ole Boy. He said that too and was like, "He was taken the wrong way." He was only clowning with him. Yeah, you'll probably have dudes like "Tics bias" but the fact is you don't have to take my word for it. At any time you can ask dudes on the outside looking in, especially in our building, how he push. I don't have to say anything. He's talked about and looked at in a certain way, but aye, he's cool with that. I already see though, we'll be splitting up. I don't program the way he programs, nor do I mess with his type of company, period. The next thing you know, dudes will be looking at me in a certain way for even being in the cell with him, seeing how he program and move.

I constantly hear, "I don't know how you do it. I would've been shook him!" Yeah, I see that happening though. Though normally he's not my type of dude to fuck with let alone live with, but I did anyway, because of history. Plus, I knew his moms. She's the G home girl from the set. The more I'm around him, the more I'm realizing we're not compatible on so many levels, and he's nosey as hell, too nosey for me. I never tripped off of it, outside of the cell, until it was brought to my attention and I started paying attention to him myself.

Just the other day at dayroom, I'm talking to Lon, Chumlee was behind me, supposedly talking to someone else, but he can't because he's too busy trying to see what me and Lon is talking about (SMH). He has that bad, then when you call him on it, "Oh, I wasn't trying to listen. I don't care what Niggahs got going on!" I can't tell! I knew a dude like that in Solano and he left the yard from being two on one'd for that very reason. He basically was where he shouldn't have been and when something happened it was able to be put on him. It had to be him. He's the only other person it could've heard it! Coincidence? Maybe, maybe not, but that's what he gets, always trying to hear and know shit. As he was getting whupped all he kept saying was "What I do? What I do? What I do?" If you don't know, you'll never know, or will never learn. But you know what? A hard head makes a soft ass. I'm a firm believer in that adage as well.

Switching lanes, it's already passed April. Knock on wood, my case hasn't been picked up. The incident was April 26th. It's now May 6th. I was told by a few homies that if they don't pick it up in the first y ear, usually they won't pick it up, though they have three years to pull up on me. I'm really not tripping off of it for the most part, especially the time part of it. What can they really do to me that hasn't already been done? The time won't matter anyway. I already have life.

The only thing it'll do as far as affecting me, is stagnating my program. As far as my comfortability, taking me out of my comfort zone for a minute, having to transpack my property, leaving my cell, having to take a long bus ride back to Solano and being there in the sandbox for a few weeks to a month. Then having to take another long bus ride back here to High Desert and be quarantined if this Corona Virus shits still going on before I can go back to a regular building. Then I'll have to wait to get my property back that's sitting in R and R.

That'll be the only inconvenience, me getting back to my program, getting back to comfortable. Wow, what's crazy, I just received a letter from some lawyers out of Fairfield, California, talking about their firm is representing me on my case. Fuuuck, they got me! So yeah, Solano County picked my case up. I'm scheduled for court June 5th for my arraignment. The waiting is over. I now know it's official. So, I'll see what's going on once I get down there. I'm just ready to be over with this whole situation. Yesterday Dre and Drake got on the weirdo from New Orleans in 115. He tried to play ball on them, but it didn't play out the way he anticipated. They whupped him out. He ended up going to C-yard. Dre and Drake came back to the yard. That was one of those situations where Ole Boy was a liability. He kept having issues with the Hispanics and he was getting into it with the police which could have an effect on the building based on how they get down. They'll fuck with the community in essence, saying as long as he's getting at us disrespectfully, we'll keep doing xyz until he's checked. Me and Chumlee just came back from 7 building from hollering at Get Drunk. Smash from Compton came to our building due to him saying the homie Get Drunk was drunk and tripping in his building and had gotten into it with another race. The Crips over there ain't feeling it. The police want him out of their building. The Crips want him out of the building too. Smash was like, being that me and Chumlee were Get Drunks direct homies from the city, he came to holler at us, because we needed to get at him and see what was up.

He told us he was going to go get at the police to see if we could go holler at Get Drunk. About thirty minutes later, our tower police popped me out. Chumlee was already out at work. We went and got at Get Drunk, telling him what was said. He was wondering why we were at his door and in his building, mind you at this time yard wasn't even out. It's early. He was like, the shit didn't happen how dudes were making it out to be. He told us to holler at the dude who he had supposedly disrespected and ask him did he get at him disrespectfully by calling him out of his name. After talking to the dude in front of Get Drunk's cell, it was basically a misoverstanding. They both felt disrespected by the other, by being loud with each other.

It wasn't a major issue to blow out of proportion. The dude homie assisted him during the conversation. The conclusion was they were just going to leave eachother alone if they couldn't be civil dealing with eachother. The situation was deaded right there. Me and Chumlee shook hands with them and we all parted ways. It wasn't any type of scene or loud talking. Everything was civil. We hollered at Get Drunk for a few minutes and we left 7-building.

From my assessment, dudes were putting more on the situation than actually was there. It was like some low key politic shit going on due to dudes not feeling Get Drunk. Me and Lon were bussing down on the slab when Vamp came to the slab where we were. A little while later, after we finished bussing down, we headed to the water fountain to get some water. While we were there at the water fountain getting water, two South Siders started squabbling up. The tower police started yelling, "GEEETTT DOOOWWWN!" The alarm was going off and police had started running from their buildings.

The yard went down, but the South Siders kept squabbling up. They fought until the police got to them, throwing smoke bombs, "Bloom, Bloom, Bloom!" After the yard had resumed and we got to our area, we heard a little more about the white boy situation that was on the lower yard. Initially I thought that situation was on our side of the yard. It was a white boy that was pushing Crip to our overstanding, but then he tried switching the play up in the middle of the play. Hold up, flag on the play. He was trying to push Crip, but then he wanted to run with the Woods (SMH).

He was got at, but a day later, lights out, playing with the game. Upon further looking into it, because dudes weren't really overstanding how that went down with the Woods and the white boy was pushing Crip. How was it that the Woods were able to even move on him, no questions asked and he was representing a faction? This was the question asked. Word was though the Woods did in fact get at dudes about dude first and from what was said, dudes were like, they're not accepting him, thus the woods had action.

We just left the dayroom and Lon was telling me about him coming back from committee and they had given him a SHU and the D.A. had picked up the banger case he caught right before I got on the yard. It should've been thrown out. He had no access to it, nor did he have the tools to get it, which had to be used to get it. Once it was retrieved, it was rusty and looked as if it had been there for years. Its ugly when you're Black.

I just received another letter from my lawyers telling me due to the Corona Virus my court date for June 5th has been pushed back, postponing until September 23rd, 2020.

25

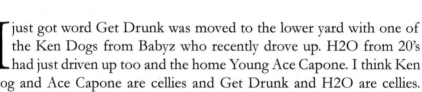

I just got word Get Drunk was moved to the lower yard with one of the Ken Dogs from Babyz who recently drove up. H2O from 20's had just driven up too and the home Young Ace Capone. I think Ken Dog and Ace Capone are cellies and Get Drunk and H2O are cellies. They're not in the same building. Get Drunk and H2O are in 3-building. Ace Capone and Ken Dog are in 2-building. Yeah, so I got word Get Drunk was moved to the lower yard on an emergency move, because he had another incident with another race in 7-building. Whatever the issue was, it wasn't anything serious or major. The issue was squashed from what Vamp told me. He'll keep me informed on situations due to him being out and about in traffic, which is a good look.

It's being said that Get Drunk is constantly having issues due to his drinking and not being able to hold his liquor. His drinking and not being able to hold it has came up on several different occasions and by several different individuals, even a few homies. It was believed that Get Drunks issues come about when he's drinking, which at the end of the day is going to cause a serious problem, which was stated. "He's going to be a problem for ya'll (LBC), and dudes are going to want to play ball if he's over there and has issues." The problem is clear and uncut. It's a little different on that side of the yard from what I can see, as far as politicking. You know how that goes, especially when it's a numbers game. Whoever has their numbers up, that's who feel they're the keepers.

So it's likely that if a situation comes up with Get Drunk and dudes feel he's putting Blacks at risk with his shenanigans, they're going to get at the homies to holler at Get Drunk, which is protocol. They can't just take that matter into their own hands. Off the dribble they have to let the homies deal with it. You have first action at whatever actions to be taken in regards to a homie being DP'ed for whatever reason. If it came to that point, it would get figured out amongst self. It's not anyone else's place to touch a dude from Long Beach. Yesterday a Hub and a Dub had gotten on a dude. He was a weirdo confused type. Hub and Dub got at him, asking him where he was from. Allegedly he first claimed he was from Long Beach, which was news to us. We never knew someone was in 5-building claiming they were from The Beach.

Not only that, but didn't anyone in 5-building let us know we had a homie over there so we could look into who dude was. As far as that goes, dude didn't make his presence known, not even sending word to us, trying to locate us. When you hit the line, it's the first thing you do is let Niggahs know where you're from so they can get word to homies so shit could get set in motion, mainly you getting in the cell with a homie if possible, or at least in the same building. That whole situation flashed me back to Solano with the young homie Nino. Him being on the line for a month before we knew he was on the line, on our yard mind you.

Didn't anyone tell us homies he was in 11-building, nor did he try and find out who was on the yard, and he had a homie in his building. I didn't overstand that whole situation. Anyway, it was confusion on his origin. First it was Long Beach, then it went to dude being from Vegas. It was said he was asked for his work by the Crips in his building. Anyone could've asked for it because he was a civilian. He never produced it and being that a month had passed, he was got at again about it and he was basically on some "fuck you Niggahs, I don't have to show you shit" type of shit. So the next day at yard, they got on him and got him up out of here! He had a whole month, but he never planned on showing dudes anything. His mind was pretty much set on I'm not showing you shit. Later that night another issue came about with a dude volunteering to go on a mission, but when the time came he didn't show up. So now he has an issue coming for flaking out and the cold thing about it, no one asked for his assistance from what was said.

He basically stepped up on his own, "I'm going with ya'll!" So for sure his assistance was accepted. "Ok, cool, that's what's up!" He left the yard on a in-line and went inside of the building, knowing he had volunteered to participate in the activities, which was not a good look. It just looked like dude was popping it. That got exposed when his homies were asked about his conduct, which came as a surprise to them, because from what his homies said, they didn't even know he had volunteered his services. He hadn't said anything to them about going on no mission, let alone with some Crips, which had his homies feeling some type of way. Then second, you didn't perform. You aborted the mission you volunteered for.

That's a no go. You have an issue coming and rightfully so. You were in violation twice. One, you didn't go, and two, you didn't let us know. It wasn't an issue of dude going with Crips on a mission, because from what I've come to know here that when it comes to civilians, it's an effort as far as the community is concerned (Crips, Bloods, Bays). When and if a civilian is out of pocket or is foul, whatever the case may be, it'll be a collaborative effort. Other than that, everyone governs their own. It's been real active as of late on both sides of the yard, upper and lower.

So as of today, we're on lock down due to too many violent incidents. That continues to happen and it's just July 12th, 2020. From what's being said, we'll be on lock down until they search, which should be over in like 14 days or so, but for sure they want those two weeks.

Well, we were finally searched yesterday. The water was turned off so the toilets wouldn't flush. The police came to our cell doors first and took our mattresses, then fifteen minutes later the police was at the cell door again. Me and Chumlee were stripped out one at a time, then we were let out of the cell. We didn't stay on our yard while the cells and building were being searched. We had to go to the lower yard until the search was completed. We were on the yard for a few hours. Once they had gotten back to our cells, we cleaned up, then put everything back in order.

Shortly after getting everything back in order, we took our showers. It's been eleven days now that we've been on this lock down. From what I just heard, we should be off tomorrow. We'll see. Nothing is guaranteed but uncertainty around here. An OG Hub had gotten into it with a Wood on the patio at pill call. I guess some words were exchanged and it got real disrespectful. The Wood he'd gotten into it with was willing to let it go, but another Wood was basically like, "Nah, someone need to holler at OG Hub." They felt he was out of pocket and should be hollered at. Word was sent to his homies. At that moment we were technically on lock down still, but officially off of the initial one. Then we had went on a modified lock down because of a fire that was going on near High Desert. (SMH) I was thinking two of the Hubs that move around would've popped up in our building to holler at OG. From what was said, OG disrespected that man and called him all out of his name. Crackers, honkeys, bitch ass, if you could think of it, he said it.

It was also said he's constantly getting into it with people and with the police. Basically, it had gotten to the point he'd been doing too much and old or not, the consensus is he needed to be DP'ed because as old as he is, he should've known better. He's too old for the shenanigans. 18 to 80, you will get DP'ed, beat the fuck up! Not what I've heard, but what I've seen. Someone did come and holler at OG Hub though, and then they left out of the section. OG Hub ended up being DP'ed. When I saw him at dayroom it didn't look like anything was really wrong with him, other than a Band-Aid by his right eye with a lump. He appeared to be straight though. He was back chilling in his spot in the dayroom, reading his book as if nothing ever happened. He accepted his issue like a champ and kept the line moving. Damn, July is already a wrap. It's the 31st (SMH).

So Vamp and Chumlee had a love/hate relationship going on. They messed with eachother and then they didn't. Vamp had pulled me to the side, "Aye Tic, let me holler at you." Then he called Chumlee, "Aye dough boy, check it out!" He was like, "Look, I called you Tic because I wanted to holler at dough boy and wanted you to be right here so you could witness what was being said and can't no misinterpretation come into play." Knowing how dudes like to play word games and twist words. Some dudes are good at what they do, real word smiths, and knows how to play the word game. He was like, "I don't want to make it seem like it's a issue. My homies are posted over there. It's just us."

Though T.C. was walking towards us (me, Vamp, and Chumlee), Vamp told him he got it, ain't nothing going on. We're just hollering. It ain't nothing. Vamp already told T.C. what was up. They talked before we even hit the yard. This was weeks back. Vamp was pistol hot and feeling some type of way because if someone were to ask Chumlee to pass something to Vamp, no matter who it is or whatever race it is, "I don't fuck with that Niggah." Vamp was like, "Cool. It is what it is, but check it out. You don't have to fuck with me or pass anything for me, but at the same time, you don't have to involve people or put them in our business. If somebody ask you to pass something, just tell them can they ask somebody else and leave it at that. All that other shit is bullshit."

At the conclusion of that conversation, at that point, it was supposed to be an overstanding. So I thought and so Vamp though. It appeared Chumlee got it and all was straighter than Indian hair. However, they still weren't messing with eachother. About two weeks ago their differences were put aside and it was cool. They were cordial. They had started to somewhat communicate and deal with eachother a little bit more each day. That shit don't last long at all. The other day, Vamp had him take a kite or a message to someone in A-section. When he came back, he told Vamp his baby mama got it, whatever he was referring to. So Vamp got at Chumlee on some "Look bro, I don't sex play with Niggahs. It's men in here. Ain't no man my baby mama." So Chumlee walk off mad and in his feelings, but he doesn't see what he done as wrong.

He pulls back up on Vamp and tells Vamp don't call him no more to pass shit for him. He's cool. Come on cuz, you went way left field and on some bullshit, but yet you're looking for me to side with you and be on your side condoning or supporting your shenanigans. That's no bueno! I don't support stupidity or shenanigans. He came to the cell and told me his version of what happened, which I knew was bullshit. I know how his mind works and operates, and how he operates he was like, "That's not sex playing huh?" Technically it is, because you're saying a dude is messing with another due, like on some homo shit.

We're in a man prison, all men. How is another man going to be another man's baby daddy or baby mama. By all rights if Vamp would've came out of the cell and fired his shit up, he would've been in the right. You don't get at dudes like that, cool or not. That's just a no-go with the sex play on any level. Especially if that's not ya'll relationship. I've been knowing Vamp since he was a puppy on the line trying to find his way. We've never went there. I've never got at him like that and he's never gotten at me like that. It's just some shit you don't do or you don't say. That's for sure one of them.

You have to always be mindful of things. You have to think. You done nothing wrong. He tripped on you though (SMH). Vamp basically told that man that no man was his baby mama and not to sex play him, period. That should've been it. So yesterday, Rat Tone had asked Chumlee to take something to Vamp, and again he goes into the "I don't fuck with that Niggah" song and dance. He had some other shit going on as well, knowing him. You k now it comes with the aggression. From what Rat Tone was saying, Chumlee got turned up for nothing. So we had yard. Rat Tone pulled me and Lon off to the side, filling us in on the situation with Chumlee, "Lets spin one on the track. I need to holler at ya'll!"

So we walked on the track doing the lap. He was basically on feeling disrespected by the aggression and the fact Chumlee can't be getting at him about none of his homies on some bullshit, or just speaking on them in a foul manner, which a dude get and overstand. He also said it wasn't the first time. It was the second and it can't be a third. He was like, "Niggahs need to watch their mouth." He was like the first time he got at him about Lon like that, he wanted Chumlee to take something to Lon or give Lon a message, and Chumlee hit him with the "I don't fuck with that Niggah this that and the third", which caught both me and Lon off guard. It was a blind side moment. We were like, "What the fuck!"

We just looked at eachother. It was a total surprise though. It must've been during the time Lon had briefly stopped fucking with him, putting him on a timeout. It happened twice, Lon having to back up off of him, because he doesn't know how to conduct himself, but at the end of the day, he fucked with me and tolerated him, because of me and him being my cellie. He hung out with us. He was given warning after warning to get his shit together and to stop with the shenanigans. It's not a good look. Now this last episode was a wrap. Dudes aren't messing with him as far as the Hoovers.

That's over with. It's not what you say but how you say shit and two, you don't speak on no dude about another due, about his homie. Who does that though, talking shit about a dudes homie to him like that's just acceptable? Nah, that's not ever cool! That would be no bueno! That shits just a no-go. That type of shit can go all types of sideways for you. What makes you think though rationally that you can just talk foul to a dude about his homie? Really though (SMH), how long you think you'll be allowed to do it before you either checked or got at? Like damn dude, that is my homie you're speaking on. How can you even be that comfortable to even get at a dude like that (SMH)?

I've seen him do it and just shook my head. This dudes lost and just don't get it. The more you talk to him, it's like the more he don't get it. He'll act like he does, but in reality it went above and over his head. After acting like he overstood, he reverts right back to his same ole program. Chumlee wasn't trying to feel it. Rat Tone was also like, when he told Chumlee he was going to let Vamp know what was up, here goes Chumlee, he was on some "so what" type shit basically, and Rat Tone told him to watch his mouth. The whole episode had started escalating. "I don't care about none of that you talking."

Vamp came and got at me and was pretty much like, "You need to get at your homie about him, because he'd going to have you caught up in his bullshit and Niggahs ain't trying to see that happen. You're a homie, a solid real homie, feel me." A few other Crip homies and other homies on the outside looking in, telling me not to allow dude to crash you, it'll happen, he has no sense. I'm got at all of the time. "That dudes going to crash you guys." I've told Chumlee this a thousand times, how you push can affect me and draw me into nonsense and bullshit. I can't have that.

I'm telling him constantly, do not draw me into no bullshit, especially being in the wrong and on the wrong side of it. How are you not only wrong, but drag a Niggah into it too? I've told him this over and over and over and over and over again! Do not put me in no bullshit, which he'll do and will drag me into. Off top and no matter what, I have to assist him, right or wrong, and deal with what needs to be dealt with later. If him and Vamp were to get down, it would draw me, because nine out of ten, if a dude see his homies fighting, they're getting involved. If he get down with a dude and his homies jump in on some "oh he's getting down with the homie" type shit, I would have to move, based on.

I can't just stand there and watch a Niggah from Long Beach get whupped out. That's a no-go. It's simply no bueno! I can't stand there and watch it play out like that. I'll have to get involved, whether I wanted to or not. He act like he overstand, but he can't. It's not really registering or computing in his mind, because if it was and it did, he wouldn't move the way that he does. At the end of the day, he's a grown as man. Yeah, he can do him, but its consequences that come with doing you when you're doing you reckless. It's not about just you. It never is.

You're just one dude out of many pushing this LBC. He stays having little confrontations and getting into it with different dudes because of his mouth. He doesn't know how to communicate and talk to people. He just goes left real quick with that tough man shit. It's his mouth though that's going to be the reason. Word was sent to the lower yard to the homies, however Young Ace had gotten word and was already on his way to the upper yard to holler. An incident with the Damus had jumped off on the yard and him and Chumlee was parked on the patio. Chumlee was coming from off of a ducat when he bumped into Ace on the patio. Chumlee told me that him and Ace spoke on the situation, which was cool.

Them having a conversation was cool, but I needed to know the other end of that conversation. I couldn't just accept or take his word at face value, knowing how he rocks. I needed Ace's version of the conversation. I sent a kite to the lower yard, per a request, telling Ace to try and get back to the patio so he could pull up on the yard, so we can get shit on the table, so it won't seem as though Niggahs are on some bull or I'm on some bullshit. Whether or not dudes know my get down and I'm not with bullshit, it'll always be at least the one who finds a reason to be with the bullshit and they know it's bullshit. So to kill all of that you talk to the involved parties, then come back and holler at me. Everybody can't be on no bullshit or playing games, especially knowing the history and the get down of the players, versus his.

That alone should tell it all, but let Chumlee tell it and he's the one being picked on. Niggahs are hating on him. Niggahs don't like him. It's never him. He never does anything wrong. It's always someone else doing, someone else's fault, never him, never his. Now it's like no Hoovers are fucking with him at all and the thing is, they all fucked with him. A couple of them fucked with him more than me. He fucked their relationship up. I told him to leave them alone. They're leaving you alone, you leave them alone. It's a wrap. It's too much drama, unnecessary drama. Lon has been straight on him for a minute.

So then comes Chumlee and his Jedi mind tricks he thinks he has going on. "So I can't work out with you no more?" Lon is my workout partner and has been my workout partner. "We can work out still. We'll work out in the cell." I'm not going to stop working out with my consistent partner. Lon is who I work out with on a daily and I fuck with him tough. That's not going to change. I already knew where his mind was going before he even got to it. "Oh, I see how it is. I knew you were on your Hoosane shit! (SMH)" Wow, really, my Hoosane shit huh? That's what you came up with with all of that brain storming? Me being on my Hoosane shit. That's what he got out of me continuing to work out and mess with Lon. But it was never a matter of a Hoosane when he was blowing with us, eating with us, sipping with us, and hanging out with us. I'm on my Hoosane shit, nah, I'm on my grown man shit, on my do me shit. A Hoosane doesn't have anything to do with anything. I'm not having issues, conflicts, or drama. Plus I'm not a fake dude, nor am I wishy-washy. I don't switch up on dudes I've created bonds with and mess with. I don't care who pulls up on a yard and we've known eachother from our sandbox days at the park. It could be Moses himself. My program will remain the same.

I'm suuuper not going to switch up on a dude for a bullshit ass one. I'm a man first, a dude can't and won't have me switching up on my dudes I fuck with. You can't dictate to me who or how I should conduct my relationships and you damn sure can't tell me who I can or can't mess with behind some cat shit, let alone behind a bullshit dude, that's out! If a dude can't see he's the problem, he'll forever remain clueless, until he gets that wakeup call he's looking for. It's there if you're looking hard enough. Someone will be your Huckleberry when it's all said and done. I'm for and about what's right.

I call a balls balls and strikes strikes. If you're wrong, that's what it is. I'm not suffering from autobotism. I know exactly what's going on. I don't side with wrong. I can't and don't condone it. I'm strictly real things and real situations. That's not what I'm about or who I am. It's not my nature to be that guy who's always with and about dirty pool. So hopefully the homie can get over here and we can all holler and come to some sort of resolution. I'm not about to keep dealing with the bullshit. It's becoming too much and a real headache (SMH). Come on now, when is enough, enough?

But back to the incident on the yard I was referring to yesterday that had parked the homie from making it on our yard. P.F. played ball on one of his homies. It lasted for a good while too before the police was aware of the get down. They tussled and then hit the ground. P.F. was doing his stuff the whole time they were scuffling to the point you could start seeing the blood from his various spots, in his back, the back of his head, his side, and his hand. Dude was trying to get a hold of P.F.'s hand, even grabbing his wrist. "GEEETTT DOOOWWWN!" The alarm goes off and the police started coming out of all of the buildings. Once they got closer to the incident, they threw a couple of smoke bombs, "Bloom, Bloom!"

They were on the ground already. They were tussling still. The yard had to get down. Yeah, it got really real and it don't get no realer than that! After the smoke cleared out, the ambulance pulled on the yard. They put P.F. in a wheelchair and wheeled him off of the yard. The other one took the ambulance ride after he was bandaged up with a head dressing. The yard was basically over at that point. The police had already called equipment recall.

So last night we had dayroom and I found out earlier in the day the Pomonas had got on the homie Suuuper Crip (Albu), on the yard. I knew the yard had went down. I just didn't know what the deal was. I knew though it wouldn't be long before word was out about what had happened. I heard our building tower police telling everyone to get down that were moving around in the building or moving around in the section. Mac-reps, porters, and dudes that are out suing the phone, which made me look out of my cell door, which I do anyways when I hear the section door open, "GEEETTT DOOOWWWN", or someone making a siren call, letting us know the police are in the section or building somewhere. What was crazy, I had just hollered at Albu the last time we were on the yard. He was telling me he was getting ready to shake this island (High Desert) and how he'd been out of the way. I hadn't seen him in a cool minute, because of how the yards are now being run due to the Corona Virus. The police threw the smoke bombs at them, "Bloom, Bloom, Bloom!" And from what was said, Albu's burnt out ass picked up a smoking bomb and threw it at one of his homies, and he tried to kick one while he was down (SMH).

We had yard today and I ran into Cavi and met his homie Rocket, who hadn't been on the yard long. Cavi told me, Lon, and a few other homies who weren't outside when the festivities took place what had happened. He told us it was him and his homie Rocket, who I'd just met, who had got on Albu. Cavi also let us read the 115 where it stated Albu picked up the bomb and threw it at Rocket. He was also the one Albu tried to put feet to too, but missed his target (SMH). It's been crazy as fuck around here lately. Last night OG Hub was fired on at pill call, but this time he tried to do his stuff with his cane and had a dude back peddling. He was not feeling being fired up. After the last time we had yard, we hadn't been outside for a minute because of the fires around here and due to the smoke situation and haze making the air quality fucked up, they'd been keeping us in.

Dayroom has been iffy at best. We've been on a modified program for the most part. We had it last night though. More bullshit surfaced with a dude in C-section. The word was dude came off of a 50-50 yard and dudes are on him about it. At first he was in the cell with a young Damu. His homies made him shake the spot ASAP. Then dude moved in the cell with a young Bay cat. Dude had been here though for a few weeks, thugging.

From what I saw, dude was programming, working out, and playing ball. I never talked to him though, but that's not really saying much because I don't talk to a lot of dudes. I'd see them and then don't. But yeah, I would just see him playing ball and hanging out, shooting the shit. Whatever though that had took place prior to word getting out about him coming from off of a 50-50 yard, who knows. I guess it reached the wrong ears and an issue was made of it and rightfully so. So of course politics were going to come into play, but being as though the word was out, the dynamics of the situation changed and the deck was flipped. At the end of the day, he was voted off of the island.

He had to go! His work had to have been read, so it was known already where he had come from. So I guess it was trying to be figured out and then you have that other side of the coin. You know it's a lot of dudes nowadays that has a different look on the 50-50 yards and how they view the whole situation. Some feel it's a way out for them to go home, so they'll choose that type of environment to program. It's either that, or be considered a program failure (SMH). Dudes know the consequences that come with that choice, if they don't they should. As of the past few years, 50-50 yards are no bueno, and for those that do go and then for some reason have their points back up and have to hit another 4 or 3 yard, it's going to be ugly.

50-50s aren't accepted on the main-line. Once they hit a yard and it's known that's where you came from, dudes aren't trying to hear it, but you would be amazed at how many actually feel it's bullshit. They don't want to be the one though speaking their mind and then made to feel some type of way. It's no different than those dudes who go EOP and think it's cool to be on that yard, the come back to the main-line. That's out, homies are tripping. EOP is basically a refuge and a route to take when you're trying to get away from some bullshit you gotten into and trying to duck off for a minute. That problem is still going to exist. It's just there's a delay on the response. From what I hear, the EOP yard is no different from a 50-50, because you're still programming with SNY's. It's basically a wrap for you, but those are politics that are being pushed. I know it's been that way for the Crips, Damus, and any other of the factions.

Hispanics, Woods, and Others, it's zero tolerance. Their people aren't getting any passes. You cross that bridge, there's no coming back over it.

It's a wrap. Messing with them, you're basically trying at your own risk. It's ugly though when you're exposed and you will be fucking with them. They're thorough. You're getting ran like you're trying to get a job for the national security in D.C. somewhere. They're running you, checking your paperwork and calling elsewhere to tap in on you, to be sure you don't slip through the crack and you came from where you claim to have come from. It's just business, nothing personal.

Chances are slim to none, you're getting pass. When dude in C-section was approached about the situation, he threw other dudes under the bus and exposed them too who had went undetected, or had they been? He gave them all up, "We all came from the same spot." He was on some shit like, "I'm not the only one. The other ones who came with me are on the other side (lower yard)." (SMH) At yard though the young Bay dude he had moved in the cell with ended up being one of the dudes on that DP. They really didn't do much to him. They punched on him a little bit, but then he balled up like a turtle.

They punched on him for a couple of minutes, and then the police finally got up on it, "GEEETTT DOOOWWWN!" The alarm goes off like clockwork, and the police run out of their buildings and on the yard from off of the patio and other yards. They both punched on him a couple of more times, then a smoke bomb was thrown, "Bloom!" They got off of him and scattered like roaches. The incident was wrapped up pretty quick. They were all cuffed and led off of the yard. The aggressors came back last night. The victim didn't. Either he's going to C-yard where OG Hub and Albu went, or he'll call it quits and tap out. Chances are though if he does end up going to C-yard, it's going to be a repeat and he knows it. If he didn't know then, he knows now, but with the variables at play, he'll take that walk of shame.

Today I moved cells and finally I moved from 216 with Chumlee to 211 by myself. There's nothing like being solo. It was basically that time for me to take that exit off of the ramp (SMH). I had to go. I hung in there as long as I could. I just couldn't do it no more. We're straight, considering what straight is nowadays. We're all straight as long as that common interest exists, though we're good. I couldn't take that ride again. A Niggah cool! I'm surprised though I lasted as long as I did. Technically I should've bounced.

We've never fought, but we've clashed a few times, but me being mindful of his short comings, I overlooked shit and let shit go. Under different circumstances we would've had issues. Outside of that though, he's a homie from the city, an East Side Niggah. On some real shit, I don't like living with homies from the city, because they feel privileged and you have to have a certain amount of patience and tolerance. You can't just take it there behind what dudes feel is bullshit. I mean you can, because you are men and if men have differences they settle them. If it can be talked out, it is what it is. Calmer heads has prevailed. Someone though is going to be in their feelings about it. I just had a conference call today with my attorney's investigator. He seemed pretty cool, real talkative guy, and he was hip. He was a white dude, but you could tell he grew up interacting with Blacks. He also listened to Black music. We talked for about thirty to thirty five minutes or so.

He was basically trying to get logged in with the situation and he was pretty much asking me if I had anything else other than what was in black and white to add to what was already in his report, which I didn't. He knew the deal and you could tell he's been around. Snitches get stitches. You're never supposed to tell on yourself. He even went in on how the police aren't cool and how they play dirty. Every now and then he would ask me was I sure we weren't being monitored because they couldn't do it. As far as I knew they weren't trying to listen to me and him.

He'd asked me how long I had, what city I was from, what was my controlling case, basic shit. He was asking me to put together a probation report. Once I told him I was from Long Beach he was telling me his son played football with Snoop Dogg's son, in Snoop's football league in Riverside County somewhere. He was telling me how cool Snoop and his son were. I really wasn't trying to hear his Snoop Dogg experience. Didn't care nothing about it. He told me my attorney should be contacting me before the 23rd to go over the logistics before we do the arraignment on video or whatever it is we're doing as it pertains to the proceedings.

So I should be having a conference call with her in a few days. Today's the 16th of September. My court appearance is on the 23rd. I'm just anticipating what's to come and trying to get it done and over with. I asked him though was it possible if I could do my sentencing on the video as well. He told me that it was possible, but it would pretty much be up to my attorney, however he doesn't see why it would be a problem if that was what I wanted to do. He was like, whatever I wanted to know or have questions about, ask her when we do the conference call.

I got the shock and surprise of the week yesterday. Of all the people I thought I would hear from was my daughter Tweet (SMH). Keeping it a thousand, I started not to respond to her. I felt compelled to give her a reality check, "You said you hated me." Which was the word I'd gotten, so why even bother writing me? It's been four years since I'd last heard from you. What could you really have to say to me? One thing's for certain, we're not doing the off and on shit like it's a light switch situation. Like you can just pop in and pop out like this shit is a game. Like you just know for sure every time you decide you want to be bothered with me I'll be there waiting. I'm not that guy. That doesn't work with me or fly with me. It's either you fuck with me or you don't, but all of that back and forth shit, I'm straight on it. I'd rather be left alone.

I basically told her though to do her out there and to live her best life. I really thought me and her was going to be close and have a bond on a different level with her being my baby girl and we'd connected, but the older she got, traits started appearing in her that wasn't a good look. So I basically can see her whole existence as far as who she is and I don't like what I see. I told her though not to concern or worry herself about me or my wellbeing. I was good. I also told her not to worry about writing anymore because I wasn't going to respond again. Letting her know too that the only reason she even got a response was because I didn't want to leave her wondering why I wasn't fucking with her, since she apparently felt there wasn't an issue between us, as if I was cool with her behavior in general towards me. The one who pulled up on her and tried to get and be involved as only I could, considering I had to set hers straight and put her mind and thoughts at east. Dealing with me, I'm not one you're use to dealing with. I'm on a different type of bird. Do I care if she wrote again? Nope! Do I care if she still hates me? Nope! Do I care if we have a relationship? Nope!

I'm good either way, but I can't lose a relationship I've never had. Out of sight, out of mind. Do I love her? I'll always love her, no doubt. That'll never change. But am I disappointed? Yup! Did she break my heart? Yup! I will say I did expect more from her, strength wise. Though overstand everyone can't be strong, or know how to be themselves, can't think or move without being told. From that assessment, I feel she's weak and broken. Anytime you can allow the next person to turn you against your parent, you're just weak, pathetic, and sorry. Who does that? Where's the loyalty? Where's the love? Where's the child/parent bond? I view that as her being compromised mentally and emotionally, but I tripped off of how easy it was for her to turn on me. You didn't even know me when I left to have an opinion of me, or have one on me. You were a baby.

Thus, your people put whatever thoughts you have about me in your head. Your mama, your ant Maxine, your uncle James, and whoever else on that side of your family, had something to say. I'm not feeling it, period, you're turning on me, but I can't do anything but accept it for what and as it is. That just makes us both mentally and emotionally unavailable and checked out. I respect it and accept it. I'm open minded to the things and situations I deem worthy of my energy and effort, however I feel I'm better off without her negative energy.

Shake Down and his homie Sheisty from 40's just got into it on the yard. A lot of us were standing around by the tables in our area, talking and watching the dice game that was going on. The mood changed just that quick. Dudes started looking around, which in turn caused me to look around. That's when I saw at my left the festivities were in motion. Then someone was like, "Niggahs is going to get cracked. Everybody's watching!" Shake Down and Sheisty were walking towards the gym wall, which is in the area furthest from the buildings. So basically, you had a few extra minutes to get it in before the police get to you.

However, that area is a death trap, especially in the event of a full blown riot and you were to get closed in, mainly between the gym and the back wall of 5-building's concrete yard. It'll go bad for you fast. They started fighting. It went kind of bad for Sheisty. Shake Down ended up on top of him. It was over pretty quick. The alarm goes off, "GEEETTT DOOOWWWN!" The police were all running from their buildings. After making it to where Shake Down and Sheisty were the smoke bomb was thrown, "Bloom!" After they separated, they were cuffed and taken off the yard.

It's been a lot of skirmishes and issues as of late, back to back instances. Like the other day when Manchester from 83 gangster (eight-tray) got into it with the homie June Bug from California Gardens, because him and another gangster homie got on an older gangster. From what was being said, everyone basically felt the same way, they were wrong for getting on the older homies. So with that, Manchester pulled up from off of the lower yard.

I was just called for my court video hearing a little while ago. It was scheduled for 9:30 A.M. but it didn't happen until like 10:45 A.M., at which time I was scheduled to make my next video appearance December 17th, my oldest daughter Solie's born day. I'm thinking my lawyer, Tiffany Evans, will get at me way before then to let me know if a deals on the table or if my next appearance will turn into a plea deal hearing at that point, which I'd be cool with.

We just went to the yard earlier. It was alright, considering the police came and snatched up Sheisty from out of C-section last night, after some days passed since he'd gotten into it with Shake Down, moving in with Squeek from 5-building. He had gotten the rewind button pressed on him.

So after the police reviewed the camera footage, they're saying they could see the homie put something into the trash can in the dayroom. Dudes were tripping off of how the police waited all that time to double back and snatch him up. Shit, it's what they do. Snake just left my door telling me Chumlee had sent him a kite saying whatever issue it was between them, he wanted to squash it. I read the kite. Chumlee brought it to me after he wrote it, so I was aware of the content and the nature in general. However, the kite wasn't taken seriously, because you can't take him seriously. Snake more so was like, as soon as you embrace him again, giving him another chance, he's right back with some shenanigans, repeating the same damn shit, lesson not learned from.

The basic consensus is dudes are just tired of the mood switches, the going back and forth with him and his general get down. The cycle got old and tired. He'll do some bullshit, we'll get at him about it, he'll seem like he get it, but then turn around and be right back on the same bullshit. Dudes told me flat out they're not fucking with him no more. They're cool on him, nor do they trust him, period, at all. For one, he talks too much and repeats everything he hears or knows and he's too nosey. When you call him on it, it's "Oh, I wasn't trying to listen" or "I wasn't trying to hear anything." (SMH) I've personally told him this on several occasions. I just gave up and stopped wasting my efforts or my energies. He just doesn't get it and won't ever get it. Something drastic or extreme will have to happen for him to really get it and overstand, personally. I'm not sure even then. Some people are just wired weird.

We just went to yard today. Damn, this month is moving quickly. It's already October 12th. The yard felt kind of weird. Something was cooking and it wasn't from the chow hall. Then I saw Vru off to the side by himself on some iso (isolation) type shit, and wasn't anyone really fucking with him or really trying to be around him. A tell tale sign that's saying whatever's going on, it's with you. I'm sure though he felt something was going on by how dudes were acting.

So I quickly figured it out. It's obvious now what's going on. I saw everything I needed to see to know what was going on. He had an issue of some sorts coming. K.B. and Fatal got on him, but right before it went in motion, Chumlee, in the blind again and as usual, was over there by the wall where Cru was sitting, talking to him. I had to pull him aside and lace his boots (tell him what was going on) and I needed to holler at him about some shit that happened at pill call last night. He had been trying to get some tape from the building police to put on his glasses where they were broken and cracked. The building police weren't fucking with him, no bueno on the tape, because he's a nuisance according to them and none of them like him because he's disrespectful and always cursing them out. I don't care either way, fuck the police, but don't disrespect them and in the same breath ask them for something (SMH).

So at pill call, he tried to get some at medical from one of the nurses at the medical window. A police that worked on the patio heard him asking for tape and was basically like, "Look, come in the office (which was actually the sub-station). I'll get you some because you haven't given me any type of problem." Now, without a thought or even an afterthought as to how that might be taken, never registered in his mind, he just bounced in there behind the police, like it was nothing. Mind you, he's in there by himself. That's a no-go. That's just not done. Someone is supposed to be with you when you're dealing with the police or talking to them. It's so it doesn't look weird or could be misconstrued as something it isn't. Autobots will have you, saying dudes saw you hand the police a kite, and they saw you whispering with the police. It could be an innocent act, but look where you are, but who's to say. Why even put yourself through that unnecessary drama? It's avoidable. At the end of the day you would want someone else present with you, just so it wouldn't look suspect, which he knows. It's not like he doesn't know this. It's not a good look.

26

I don't give a fuck! I don't give a fuck!" Same ole story. It's not the
police going to be DP'ed, that's your ride. What was supposed to
happen was him asking the police could he bring him the tape, because he couldn't go in there like that, or just asked could someone else
come with him, just that simple. The police know the implication game,
and probably wanted to see if he would actually go. He didn't do either.
He came to my door this morning, knowing it was brought to me, or it
would be by someone. So he thought he'd beat the traffic and give me
his version of what happened. His watered down version of what really
happened, leaving out he went into the sub-station by himself, gave me
a whole different version of the incident. He told me the Other, Spider,
who's Asian, was with him, making it appear as though Spider went with
him inside of the sub-station, which didn't happen.

Spider in fact came back from pill call and had gotten at a couple of
homies about it and was saying to them he had to get at Chumlee about
not going in the sub-station without anyone else present, because it's
not cool and didn't look right. He was told something he already knows
(SMH). We're on the yard and the Blacks were supposed to be playing

basketball with the Northerners, which had been planned a week prior, but all of a sudden the game was cancelled and the Blacks didn't get the memo. However saw what took place, but wasn't surprised. They were playing with the South Siders, instead. They've been playing sports with eachother on the yard as of late. I heard on C-yard it's normal for that to happen. At the end of the day, it was bound to happen, for them to start getting along more to where they started functioning and co-existing with eachother. It was going to happen sooner or later. I feel at some point, they'll come together as one. Times are different. Things are different. They're people, Hispanics, this is something I've been observing for several years, so it didn't come as a surprise or shock to me, nor to those I fuck with. I was just speaking on how when I was at Solano the Northerners came to the Blacks one day being that we shared a common space and asked could the South Siders come on our end of the yard and play handball with them.

That request had to be respectfully declined. It was like, that was a negative for the simple fact that it would be a breach of security. The South Siders were already on one end of the yard, so if a couple were to come and play handball that would bring more South Siders on our end of the yard. Those few that would come to play would bring more South Siders, as a means of their security, thus breaching ours. So the consensus was, "Look, you guys do ya'll. Play ya'll handball, but do it on their end of the yard, in their area. We don't need the breach. That's just a little too close for comfort for us as Blacks."

Just because ya'll cool and fuck with eachother doesn't make us cool or just that comfortable to have them in our area and in our space. Then the next thing you know, it's an ongoing situation until it becomes a norm. They'll be hanging out and wanting to post up or pull up whenever they felt like it. Yeah, they were in their feelings about our position and stance we took on it, but they had to respect it for what and as it was. If the role were in reverse of course they would've went the same route. It was a matter of security with us, plain and simple. Ya'll being cool with them and fucking with them has nothing to do with our relationship with them, not when it comes to security. A few dudes weren't feeling the brush off with the game. I felt them though. Dudes could've gotten a heads up from what was being voiced. It was like, we're doing this now, fuck telling ya'll anything. But to some, it put the question in the air, what is their position in terms of us being allies? How does that work and we share a space? It's like that uncertainty is at question. These questions should've been answered and an agreement came too, long ago. The question also was where do they really stand? If you have to ask, you have your answer. One thing that was agreed upon, which was not knowing, but it does set your wheels in motion. Have you tripping off of the overall dynamics of your surroundings, racially.

At the end of the day, I know what it is, overstand it, and accept it for what it is. It's only four Northerners in our section and we Blacks fuck with them daily. We hang out in the dayroom, we shoot the shit, we play board games, and we play dominoes. There are two on one side of the shower on the upper tier, and two on the other side of the shower on me and Lon's side. We have four South Siders on our side of the shower. The two cells are in between me and Lon's cell. Lon is in 214, South Siders are in 213 and 212. They're straight though. Bad Boy and Snaps are next to me in 212, and next to them in 213 are Toker and Crazy. I'm in 211. Me and Lon are in the cell solo, though conscious. The two Northerners are in 215.

One of them works in the kitchen and leaves like 4 something in the A.M. so he's basically by himself unless it's his cellies day off. My guy Lon waits for him and then they'll come on my end so we're all pushing together, or at least in close proximity, depending on how they decide to let out for chow. You never know how they'll open the cells, so you have to be on point regardless and mindful of what's going on around you. Being released for chow is never the same for the most part due in part to what police is working the tower in the building, whether it's break-fast or dinner time. That's your second or third watch tower police. A question was posed to me by a homie in another building after a couple of other questions to kind of get the overstanding of the surroundings. So the question was, if we're pushing with the Northerners at chow and something were to happen along racial lines, do I think they would get involved or would they stand by? If we're willing to go with them, would they go with us? With that, my thing was this, I'm like whatever the homies with I'm pushing with him. That's my every day guy. So off top, I'm going. Two, add my energy in any event. As to the questions, I don't have an answer to either question, nor did I give one.

Switching lanes, today is Lon's H Day, October 19th. Just a handful of us are putting something together and going to celebrate it with him. We'll be sipping on some lightning, hopefully blowing too. I think we're eating nachos or making burritos. I'm good with either. He doesn't fuck with many, just a few around here from what I see and know. The others are tolerated. These days have really been moving. It's the 31st of October now (SMH). All has been quiet, except for the other day Chumlee got into it with a young turned up dude from the Bay Area and was called out behind that same shit about telling other mutha fuckas who he don't fuck with, which is fine. You don't have to fuck with dudes. I'm the last one to trip off of someone else not fucking with someone. I don't fuck with dudes in general, very few.

However, an overstanding was reached as it pertained to the Hoovers and passing. Someone wanted him to pass a C.D. or something to Poke from Hoover (nine-foe). He was like, "I don't fuck with them Niggahs. My homies said for me to leave them alone." So he get at his coworker, a Northerner, to see if he would get the C.D. and take it to Poke. I assumed the Northerner done it, but word got back to Poke from the Bay dude, from what was brought to me (SMH). Poke get at Chumlee, not turned up, but on some calm shit, "We've already had this conversation." So I guess the Bay dude happen to walk up to the cell door while Chumlee and Poke were talking, because he was there to talk to his homie from the Bay who was in the cell with Chumlee. At that point and somewhere along the line, it went sideways, with Chumlee and the Bay dude, and words were exchanged. Then the C.D. situation was brought up. Then the Bay dude called him out, basically telling Chumlee they can get down at pill call. I get a kite from Chumlee giving me his version of events, which I knew would be watered down and far from what really took place.

So the next morning, when he came out for work, I get at him and asked him how it all came about. He was like, "It's good. It ain't nothing. It's been worked out. It's over with." I was like, "Nah." I was going to look into it myself for the simple fact I knew it was more to it. "You don't need to. It's good."

Right after he left, T.C. from Hoovers (Nine-Deuce) came and was giving me the script as to what went on at pill call. "Big Bro, he turned it down and the Bay Niggah was like, 'Tell my homies you don't want to get down!'" This was said in front of a lot of people, Others, Hispanics, and Blacks. What was just repeated, I had heard it from a couple of people the next day.

As the situation was being spoke on in different circles on the yard, he's clueless. This shit is all over the yard. I just told him, "Look, you running around here turning shit down (refusing to fight when someone wants to fight you). Stay off of my door and stop talking to me. I'm cool. I'm not fucking with you no more, period. It's always something going on with you, whether it was true or not, I'm still cool. It's too much drama with you. Every time I look around, it's a problem and it's never you. It's always someone else, never you." He tried getting loud as he do, "I ain't turned shit down. Mutha fuckas are lying! Watch when they call yard. We gon see!" I just told him, "Don't do nothing stupid. As a matter of a fact, go ahead and do you champ!" I got my package that morning too and ran into Young Ace in the gym. He was getting a package too. I put him up on the biz, if he wasn't already up on it. Shit travels fast, especially if it's some politics involved or can be involved. These dudes around here look for that type of shit, even when it has nothing to do with them or their homies. He wasn't aware, or at least it hadn't made it to his ears. He's like, "Don't say shit to cuz. He got a DP coming. I'm going to holler at Dog."

Ace ended up coming to the yard on our side. Him and Chumlee came through the yard door together. Me, Lon, Snake, Spooky from 9-0 (Nine-0) and Shakedown were on the concrete slab bussing down. Smash from Nutty was on the slab as well. He wasn't working out though. He was just talking and shooting the breeze. I leave from the slab to pull up on Ace and Chumlee. We hit the track. I'm basically listening to the conversation and commenting on certain shit I deemed worthy. The situation was being discussed, but nothing happened, because Ace gave his word to get on the yard, that he wasn't going to get into any trouble. He just needed to holler at a homie and he was gone, so he was granted access.

He hollered at Chumlee and let him know he came over to initially punch on him, but gave the police his word he wasn't over here to do anything, which surprised me. Chumlee didn't blow up and turn up like he normally does. Anyway, again he told Chumlee to stop getting into shit with Niggahs and having so many issues. Niggahs are really getting tired of his shit. "Get your shit together homie!" Dog ended up popping up on our yard shortly after Ace went back to the lower.

Chumlee left our yard with Ace and somehow came back to the yard with Dog. Before he left the yard and came back with Dog, he had been trying to talk to me, but I waved him off. I was done with the shenanigans. So when him and Dog came on the yard, I pulled up on them. We walked and talked. I really just listened and commented. That ended with Dog telling him he's moving in with him and to tell his cellie to find him another spot so he could move in. Mello, his cellie, was supposed to be moving out the cell with Chumlee anyway. He was just there temporarily. He just moved in with Chumlee because he was going through something and needed a spot until he got to where he wanted to be, which was another building. In that process though, a couple of things happened.

What killed Mello's move was Tiny Coo Coo from 20's hit the yard from C-yard. He was voted off of the island and was removed. So what he done was get off (attacked) on a South Sider on the patio, so the move was cancelled and we went on a temporary lockdown. The police later that night let a few Blacks (Crips) and a few South Siders go from building to building to holler at the people in the maze, being escorted in waist chains. I didn't see them though, until they made it to our building and in our section.

I saw Shake Down, J Smash, and Tank come in the section and were running around hollering at dudes. Shake Down saw me standing on my door and stopped. He let me know the biz though as far as what went down with Coo Coo and the fact that Coo Coo locked it up (went SNY), so we're supposed to be good tomorrow, because him being gone deaded the issue. However, later it was said that Coo Coo had came off of A or B-yard already and got sent to C-yard and homies over there got on him. Though it's said it's a deaded issue, don't mean it is. You know you have to stay on alert anyway with your antennas up, dealing with other races, especially South Siders.

It was a time you couldn't put a lot of stock in their word, because as soon as you were back lazed and comfortable, here they come. I asked Shake Down, "You do know I'm from The Beach, right?" He was like, "Yeah, that's why when I just saw you I stopped and hollered at you." So while Mello was waiting to move out of the cell with Chumlee, they were in the cell squabbling. Someone came and let me know what the deal was, then my boy Silent came and let me know what the deal was and what the deal was while he was at the door. Supposedly Chumlee stole something from him, but turned out he didn't. Damage was already done. But I had to send a onetime kite to the lower yard to let the homies know the biz.

Whether I did it or not, other dudes were. I done my due diligence. It was going to get them on the lower yard regardless. I just beat the traffic. Besides, I rather it came from me, so nothing was added or token from the situation (SMH). Just continuous problems with Chumlee. If it's not one thing, it's another. You can't talk to him. He's not trying to hear you.

You can basically talk until you're grey in the face. It just don't compute or register. That or he don't give a fuck, like he's always saying. Must be some truth to it, which you can't help but to believe.

As I'm at this desk writing at this very moment, T.C. just came to my door and told me H2O (Hard Dub) and Young Ace were on this side of the yard. He just walked away and before I could sit back down to resume my writing, the tower police in the building is yelling, "GEEETTT DOOOWWWN!" The alarm goes off. I'm standing at the door, looking into the hallway, trying to see something. I couldn't see much, but could hear the police yelling from the hallway, "Get the fuck down! Get the fuck down now!"

After that, you can smell the pepper spray waffling through the air into the cells. The smell has our section lit up right now. I'm still coughing. The chemicals are strong. The smell is strong. The skirmish ended in the hallway of our building and it started in front of our building. Our front door of our building was open when they got on him. They ended up inside and into the hallway by the building's sub-station. A couple of hours later, he popped back up and came to my door trying to talk to me. All I heard was, "The homies DP'ed me and Ace said he needs to holler at you." Which I kind of figured anyway, once I got the play by play on what transpired with the DP.

It's officially winter around here. It snowed hard last night. It was actually supposed to snow yesterday, but nothing happened (SMH). Damn weather people! When I got up this morning, it was colder than penguin nuts. You're probably thinking, how would I know that? It's because they drag on the snow and ice all day. I saw snow on the ground. Not a lot, but enough to cover everything up a couple of feet. I'm waiting for the yard. It's suspect at this point. It's a possibility we won't even get it. We haven't been going to the yard for the past several yards. Something always seem to happen or come up, short of staff, some type of half a day for training , something. Now I'm just hearing someone say the police are having a staff meeting and the yard is up in the air at this point, as I said.

So now it's 9:15 A.M. and they decided to call it after all. We went out and snow was all over the yard, but in spots. The suns been popping in and popping out, so it's been melting. It wasn't much from the get go. The mountains we could see far off from a distance were covered in snow, cold it was. We were definitely getting the cold air coming from those mountains. I went out in my big ass orange jacket, t-shirt, thermal top, sweat shirt, two beanies, thermal bottoms, state jeans, two pairs of socks, my cotton gloves that I covered with black rubber gloves I'd gotten from a porter, and my boots. I hit the yard suited and booted for the weather. As always, me and Lon waited for everyone to come out of the building, which we do every yard, so we can greet those we greet, and push to the slab to work out. We warmed up a little bit by doing some stretches and running in place, then we got going to stay warm. Just as we were getting into our workout routine, for some reason they up and call yard recall. Here we go, shenanigans! Yard was over, a wrap, pretty much.

So when I got back in the cell, I took a quick birdbath and then I washed my clothes. It's cold as hell in this cell right now. I had planned on writing a few dots and dashes, hitting up moms, who I started calling Church Lady, hitting up my son, who's in Corcoran State Prison/CSATF, Small Ace Capone, and then hitting up my Aunt Mart and my Cuzzo Nip, just to tap in, as I try to do as often as possible. It's good though at the end of the day to have some type of communication with the outside world, for the most part, to have that outside connection and energy. Nowadays you don't really get that. It's good though to have that different connection with someone outside of the prison walls, or have communication with someone other than those around you in the maze on a daily. You need that different mental state and release. For a lot of dudes, they don't get that, because they're left for dead. Bitches ran off, family ran off, homies ran off, kids aren't fucking with you, which is all based on the fact you're no longer any use to anyone. There's no longer an interest.

Then it goes to if you're out of sight, you're out of mind, until you aren't. One thing you'll learn quick is who was for you, with you, and about you, once you get behind these walls, but don't be in your feelings. Keep the line moving. Just recognize and overstand what it is. A lot of incarcerated males or females walking on prison yards choose not to have that outside communication or connection, because of the emotional and mental drama that follows. I truly get it and overstand it. Only those of us that are experiencing it or have experience it can really overstand it. Only then will you and can you overstand the emotional and mental psyche. A lot of us aren't mentally or emotionally equipped to deal with that and just choose to say, "Fuck it, I'm good!" It's basically minimized to be truthful and correct, though from my position the environment we're in requires a clear and focused head space, period, which is and can be dangerous at times. For the most part, it's dangerous.

Clouded thoughts have you vulnerable and are considered anti-productive in your navigation and movement on a prison yard. Flag on the
play! You need to be focused, alert, and aware at all times. You don't need
anything clouding choices or decisions, because your focus becomes
clouded, thus creating a liability and safety concern. That's what's going
on when you're arguing on the phone with a wife, a BM (baby mama),
or whoever. I can give a recent instance where I just heard my Brody is
going through some shit. He's locked up in Delano. His nephew, who
looked up to him since he was younger, just recently caught a case. I'm
assuming his first case. He's feeling like it's his fault though, because he's
not out there for him and to help guide him.

Moms was telling me she'd written him and was basically telling him
to pull himself together, because at this point in time there's nothing he
can do for his nephew while he's locked up and for him not to let the
devil use him by having him going off and getting himself caught up, and
for him to remain focused. From how she was explaining his dots and
dashes he wrote her, I can imagine just how worked up Brody was. I've
been his cellie for years. He can get distracted and frustrated, losing focus. So mom's was like, "Look, you can't let that get to you. You can't do
anything about it. Stay focused. Do what you have to do to come home.
Then tend to what you need to tend to. You can't do anything for anyone
where you are. You better use your head for more than a hat rack." Then
she was like, "If I didn't care about you as my son, I wouldn't be talking
to you. I wouldn't give a shit, but you have a wife out here, and a family.
You have to get yourself together, get a hold of yourself." Moms really
loves and cares about the homie. She was also telling me how he's just so
full of rage and hate right now, how upset and in his feelings about the
situation he's in, saying too she told him, "Revenge will get you locked
back up, or dead. Doing shit without thinking isn't the way to go, or the
route to go."

No, because you aren't thinking, you're just fired up and ready to go.
She was like, "I hope he doesn't do anything foolish. That's one of those
situations that'll easily have you not focused on your surroundings. That
and have you easily provoked to where you're getting into an altercation
or a situation that has nothing to do with the underlying cause. Whatever
the situation is, you're focus is no longer on your environment, no longer
on what's going on around you. You're caught up in that phone call or

that letter that pissed you off, which set a different course for you and put your mental and emotional state in another lane and space.

That's never a good thing, nor is it safe, but yeah, back to the point of arguing, or just going through the drama. You have those moments and times where you don't want to call or write anyone, knowing the possibility of your day being fucked up. Whether the responses are instant, or delayed, its like, "I'm cool on the game playing. I'm cool on the arguing. I'm cool on the lies. I'm cool on the disappointment. I'm cool on being frustrated. I'm just cool and suuuper cool on the mental and emotional shit that comes with it." This shit isn't drama and stress free. This shit is draining.

Me and my new cellie, New Year, an older Crip homie like myself from 40 Crip who just recently moved in, have already had this very conversation and at length. It's like, the same ole shit, different toilet. We overstand it based on firsthand knowledge and experience. Being locked up, at some point you're going to get a real bar of this reality. This is the reality, for what and as it is. These are realities that become lessons, teachable lessons, and reality checks. You really see who's who and what's what when it comes to those you were interacting with when you were on the streets. I get it and fully overstand the lack of not wanting to communicate or have that outside connection. It can be mentally frustrating and draining. When you get emotionally involved, you're going to get emotional, thus lose focus. I get it. Been there, still doing that.

However, I'm mindful and aware of that reality, especially with so much constantly going on around me. I know I can't allow myself to be side tracked or allow myself to lose focus and to lose focus on my present reality. These prison yards, these cells, the dog kennels, the autobots, dirty politics, and weirdos. I can't afford not to be mentally present, especially right here. I've been here a short time and have seen so much, even had learned a lot, which you can never do enough of regardless of your age. There's also that value in being receptive to it, but this is definitely not one of those places where you're walking around lost or with your head in the clouds. You'll lose it quick.

Though I'm going through different challenges and dealing with different situations I'm still navigating my way through, thus I'm able to sanetain (maintain) my focus with a clear head. Yeah, I'm going through something with my daughter, Tweet, but I'm not allowing it to obscure my mental vision. Same thing with Situation. What we're going through I'm not allowing it to obscure my vision. My court shit I'm presently going through, I'm not allowing that to be a distraction or obscurity as it pertains to my focus. On the surface though, being locked up, the outside world don't get, can't comprehend, can't grasp or overstand our mental and emotional challenges. It's, "They're okay. They're locked up. They don't need for anything. The state got them. They have no bills. They don't have to worry about food, clothing, or a roof over they're heads." I personally fell that's a copout so they won't have to be that energy dudes need. You know what else they don't get, can't comprehend, can't grasp or overstand? The obstacles, the trials, the tribulations, or challenges we have to deal with or are faced with. To them it's like, we don't have worries, we're not going through anything, we have it easy. Some feel too easy. If only they knew.

We have no cares. How can we? We're in prison. We shouldn't have any issues or concerns. We shouldn't be going through anything, again feeling like we don't have to pay for shit, we don't have to worry about eating, don't have to worry about a roof over our heads or worry about washing our clothes. Yeah, that all might be true, but to an extent, and at what cost? Yeah, we might not have the same worries, stress, or concerns, but you don't have to survive under these sometimes tense mental and emotional conditions. If you lose focus, oh well, no major consequences. If we lose focus, it could be the difference between life or death. Riddle me this, which would you choose?

Not only that, but they don't get the emotional and mental part of the shit we go through. How could they? It's a totally different world they don't get or overstand. We have to deal with all the different personalities have to deal with day in and day out, on top of the police, personalities, and drama, along with baggage and bullshit they bring to the job from home or the streets. Their different moods and bullshit, though they're not supposed to, they still do bring that shit in here, creating more bullshit. Whatever it is they have going on in their life, they want to fuck with us, being they're being fucked with, because of what they're going through. Keep your problems and drama at home. Come to work in a fucked up mood, because your bitch didn't give you none last night, or because she cheated and ain't shit, whatever the case might be. She might've left. That has nothing to do with us, yet we feel that struggle. This shits not drama, stress, or bullshit free. It's not the cake walk they think it is. This is me sharing my version of the realities, that reality in which we face. Just because we don't speak on it, don't mean it don't or doesn't exist. We just choose not to burden you or share certain shit, or the harsh realities. Case in point, here it is, I'm fighting a case, a serious one, but for all intended purposes, I've never shared that info with my Aunt Marty Lou. Why? Because she's going through enough in her personal life, and I know it wouldn't do anything but cause her to worry and cause her to really worry about me, because of how close we are.

She has her health to worry about and that would be selfish. Those that I wanted to know and felt should know, knows and knows to keep it from my aunt. I didn't tell her for a reason. She doesn't need that weighing on her. We're living this reality. It's our world. On another note, who wants to be on the phone or writing dots and dashes about this shit, what's going on in prison, or what's going on, on the yard? If I don't have to, I don't mention anything about a yard, or prison, or anything having to do with either, or the dudes I'm around. That space is reserved for more important things.

Like, how to try and get the fuck up out of prison, or how to get some energy. Dudes are really trying to miss talking about prison, a yard, or the dudes on it when we're on the phone or writing. It's the last thing we're trying to be on. We're trying to be as far as removed mentally and emotionally from here as we possibly can be. We need that release and that outlet, so no, we're not trying to be arguing, not trying to talk about prison shit, or trying to go through the bullshit. We're trying to be in a while different space.

However, I'm not the one to dwell on the darker side of being on the other end of a fucked up situation. I know what it entails. This was one of my motivations to write this book, to provide a glimpse with hopes of providing a better overstanding of the mindset. But yeah, this is my heartfelt reflection and overstanding, my rewind, my dark at times and deeply bruised psyche. Not meaning to be or to seem selfish. We do get you're out there going through whatever it is you're going through, maybe not to the full, only you know what that is exactly. At the same time, we can be that shoulder, ear, or outlet. We are mindful of the fact it's a struggle in general and acknowledge it. We're never blind to it. WE know life is hard. We know you're having to deal with shit and keeping a brave face, like all is good and well.

At the end of the day though, you're free and enjoying every day freedoms, enjoying even the simplest things in life. You have that freedom. You have your freedom to do as you please, when you please (get a bar), how you please. Freedoms we took for granted and clearly isn't your fault or on you. At the same time though, damn! More importantly, when you please, how bad can it really be? You have what we're trying to obtain once again. Any day of the week, I'll take what you're going through over what I'm going through.

Yeah, we get and overstand you didn't put us here, as we're so often reminded, especially when you're in your feelings about an issue, throw that out there quick! Even if you're just in general feeling some type of way about something, you don't and won't allow us to forget that fact. That's something that's always said, that sentiment is nothing new. It's not the first time it's said and definitely won't be the last. However, it wasn't an issue, or is never an issue, when we're out there with you and we're running around trying to make it add up, or make sense. Yet, the energy changes, but you were all for what a Niggah had going on and how he had it going on, as long as you were benefitting. You had no issue with us nor a problem with us running from the police, trying to get away from them, because we had that dope stack on us, or us trying to get away from the police because we have that pistol on us, on a mission, or coming from one, trying to get some loot. The energy is good as long as we were able to get them nails done for you, put that gas in your swoop, pay that payment, pay a bill, get you those kicks (shoes) you wanted, or get your hair braided. It wasn't an issue then. Where was this same energy?

It wasn't an issue when were were out there jacking (robbing) and you were able to keep smoking on that good ass weed and not smoking struggle (bullshit weed), able to drink on that good liquor and not that bullshit liquor, none of that Christian Bro's, EandJ, Paul Masson, or Taka Vodka. Not an issue then. Wasn't an issue when you were able to spend. It was all gravity (good) then. It only became a shift of energy or an issue after a dude was locked up. You couldn't wait to his a Niggah with, "Didn't nobody tell you to take your ass to jail. I didn't put you there!" Yeah, ok, all of that, but when are you going to come answer and stop using that bullshit? That's weak. It's a copout. It's old and you're just bullshit. You and I know what's going on!

To me, it's basically an excuse for you not to handle your wax (business). It's your way out of not being loyal, or a way to justify your bullshit and how you're conducting yourself. Your way of easing your mental as you're trying to justify it. I mean, if we're going to get to the root of all evil and keep it a thousand, getting down to the essence of what it really is, it boils down to L-O-Y-A-L-T-Y, which you don't know anything about. It takes loyalty to know loyalty. I bet I have you shook up right now and you in your head, huh? That concept and word is foreign to you, for the simple fact it's eluded you.

As I've said though, we get you're out there and are going through shit, but it's no reason to check out or leave a niggah for dead. It's life, and in life you go through shit, that's not lost on us. We acknowledge it and overstand it. That's one of the reasons we aren't trying to worry or stress you out no more than you probably are or trying to add our mental and emotional prison baggage on you. We're not trying to add to your financial struggles you may have or may be dealing with on some selfish shit. We're trying to keep our communications lighthearted when we communicate or attempt to, by no means though trying to downplay what you're going through.

I'm not calling you to argue or have a disagreement with you about anything, nor am I calling to be lied to either. I'm not calling you to have you pissed off or to be pissed off. I'm just trying to have a decent conversation, bullshit free. Trying to have that change of mental and emotional space. I'm not trying to be on or get on no negative shit. I get enough of that around here and just being locked up. Every time I call it's like, here we go again! (SMH) Bullshit! Why call? Why would I want to call? I'm not sending you dots and dashes to fuck the rest of your day up. In turn, I'm not trying to get one from you fucking mine up. Absolutely not! Then it's like, I heard this, that, or the other. Niggah, you ain't shit or the, all you're worried or concerned about is you, you don't care about what I'm going through!

This is the shit that's constantly shot at us. These are constant realities that'll take our focus off of the task at hand, our present reality. Whether it's this yard or the next yard, we might be on. Caught up in all of your rhetoric, nonsense, and bullshit. You were talking on the phone or in your dots and dashes. Have us mentally and emotionally off the mark. I'm sure, quite sure, in fact, you feel the same, "Why is he calling here or writing here with his bullshit? I'm trying to do this that and the other, or trying to handle this or that. He don't have no patience. He's always calling here talking shit!" That though only applies to her that's handling her wax and doing her part and being loyal. She overstands as long as she's doing you, she can do her. That don't or doesn't apply to you. That's not being loyal or handling your wax, not doing your part or not overstanding. Do you, but do me. Yet always have something to say or want to hear yourself talk. It's easy for us to have outside shit distract us, even when we're not trying to. It just has its way of fucking with us and weighing heavy on our minds.

That's why for me, I'm cool on all that drama and noise. Miss me with all of that. I can do without it, real talk. I'll just simplify it for you, if you're not for me, with me, or about me, you're against me and against my struggle, period, and I'm good. You can keep your distractions. I don't care about what you're doing, who you're doing it with. That doesn't concern me, really. Why you weren't home when I called? I couldn't get you or contact you for days. Why you haven't wrote? Why I didn't get those captured moments you claimed you were sending, yet I haven't got them.

You swear up and down you did though. Why I never got the energy or package you claimed to have sent? All distractions. That shit for some is super stressful. Why every time I call it's a different issue? Or every time you write it's a different issue? I'm straight as Indian hair. I'd rather just do my time by myself on some solo shit, if I have to deal with all of that, which is how a lot of us feel. Personally, I'd rather have that peace of mind, so I'm able to remain focused on the objective and can actually think. To be able to hear and see what I need to, when I need to, clear and uncut.

But yeah, we have to deal with the things as they are, not as we wish them to be. In addition, I think we can all agree that life is easier when you have a little support along the way. I've never refuted that fact. My overstanding and mindfulness is vast. You know what though, with all of my overstanding, mindfulness, and vastness, the one thing that I keep learning is that I don't know shit. It's so much more to learn, overstand, and be mindful of, especially being locked up and walking on these prison yards, where land is a testing ground and every step is a testament, a willingness, my "Aha" moment.

As I've said though, just when you think you've figured something out, thought you have or have seen it all, thought you've seen it all, really you haven't. It's more to be figured out and more to see. Shit is constantly changing with both relationships and interactions, dealing with those inside and outside. Two yet different entities, but so much similarities.

Speaking on outside, which was my last words, I had to park these dots and dashes, because I was interrupted by my cell door being opened.

I had to lean out of the door to ask the police why he had opened my door. He told me I had a phone conference to go to with my attorney.

I had been expecting her at some point to pull up on me. I'm barely getting back. I rushed, getting to where I had to be to take the call, and had to wait. The call was scheduled for 10:30 A.M. That's how it is though, with everything, you rush to wait. She finally get around to calling around 10:45. We were only going to have until 11:00 to talk. The longer it took her to call, the shorter the conversation would be, which is what the police had basically told one of my lawyer's staff at her office. At that point, she would have to reschedule. The police was getting frustrated. Like I said, she ended up calling at 10:45. We got right to it. She was saying she apologized for the delay, but she was running late because she was in court and had just gotten out of the courtroom. She went over everything with me in vast detail concerning the plea deal and what was said between her and the D.A. She was explaining what rights I had as it pertained to my taking the deal should I accept it and what rights I would be giving up. The deal on the table was three years. She went on to tell me she would be sending papers to me via mail concerning my plea to go over at length. Then for me to initial, date, sign, and send back to her. I again confirmed with her my next video hearing, which is still December 17th, 2020. It was actually my first time talking to her and hearing her voice. We've only communicated via mail. My first and only phone conference call was with her investigator, weeks earlier.

The conversation between us was smooth. She was real cool though. The conversation was very easy and not forced. We even shared a few laughs. I will admit, she sounded sexy as hell. Now back to my train of thought, change is what change is. You just have to adapt to it as it presents itself. When it comes to dealing with the outside and the inside, they coexist at the end of the day. You will no doubt find yourself shaking your head at the different challenges you face and are subjected to. It's a headache and can be overwhelming, can be consuming as well, if you allow it to be.

That's just it, you can't allow it to overwhelm of consume you. That overwhelming and consumption becomes stress. Sometimes it's better to admit defeat than push a pointless situation. Accept what is, let go of what was, and keep moving. You already know what it is, as far as the situation, why allow it to have you stuck or stagnated, having you off balance and unfocused? You can't let none of this shit consume your or dictate your security or your safety, especially with the shit that's actually going on around you. As of late, it's been plenty of activity. A lot of shit's been going on around me, directly and indirectly.

I was already speaking on earlier about how Chumlee had got DP'ed and how at the end of the day it wasn't a DP because one, when you were fired on in front of the building, the homies said you got in the wind, you broke and ran inside of the building into the hallway to where the sub-station was. At that point you could no longer be touched or got at. So after that whole incident and he stayed on the cage in the sub-station on the patio for an hour or so, if that long, he came back to the building like all was cool and it was dunzo. In his mind though, it was good, never factoring the fact of what really just happened, the gravity of it, the reality of it. You forgot about the fact that technically wasn't a DP. How could it be a DP? They really didn't do anything to you.

Everyone in A-section saw you and what happened. Ace didn't even get one off. It was like Go Go Gadget feet, don't fail me now! What you didn't realize though, now you turned the situation into a totally different situation entirely, making it worse. Now it's like a voted off the island situation. Dude has an issue coming, and as soon as possible. The bed was made, now it has to be layed in. Guess who it'll fall on. Me. It'll fall on me for the simple fact I'm on this side of the yard with you, so I have to participate in the removal, whether I want to or not. I'm from the city. I'm obligated.

So for a few days, kits were in flight, trying to figure out the best course of action to get the situation handled immediately. Though I'm an older homie, I'm still very much active, and mind you, I'm on this side of the yard by myself. Other than him, there are no other Long Beach Crips on this side of the yard. It's just us two and the situation is another DP, not a fight. A DP, a two on one, that's what the situation calls for, a two on one. So with me being the only Long Beach homie and it being hard at this particular time to get assistance from any homie from the city, because of the last incident, it wasn't going to be easy to get from the lower back to the upper. Word came back to me to look for outside assistance from a Crip homie outside of the city. It was a go on finding outside assistance. Though I wasn't really comfortable with going that route, I was like fuck it, it has to be handled. Basically though, it was a no go, because the consensus was it was LBC business at the end of the day, so another route had to be figured out. Personally, I feel Niggahs wasn't trying to fuck with it. Not so much because it was LBC business, but because I fuck with the Hoovers. A Crip could assist a Crip no matter where he's from and he's pushing C-R-I-P!

I get it, overstand it, and I'm cool with it. It is what it is. In the same breath, have that same energy when assistance is needed. Just know, it's not Long Beach business. Well let me say this, it's not Tic's from Long Beach business. However, another homie feel I can't speak for him. On some real shit though, I personally preferred it to remain LBC business, because though it was ok-ed for the assistance from an outside entity, it left room to be questioned and room from homies to feel a certain type of way.

It was room for uncertainty. It left a door wide open for blowback and room for the politicians to politic elsewhere. That's why you have to always be mindful of actions you take and how you move. The wrong action or move can always have consequences. Maybe not right at that present time, but later down that line. Yeah, what occurred may be good here at this spot, but frowned upon elsewhere. Then you'll have to answer to whatever it was that happened. To you, you made the right decision, but to the homies, it was a wrong decision.

27

One thing about prison life/yard life, shit follows you, good or bad. The bad spread quicker and much faster than the good, especially too with autobotism. So you would want to be on the right side of any situation like I've said, yeah it might've been cool here to get on him with another Crip homie that wasn't from Long Beach, but when that travels, it may be something different going on at the next spot, as far as someone feeling differently about the situation and want to take issue with what happened. It's going to need to be explained. This is merely a scenario, but at the end of the day, it's different rules and plays at play at different prisons and on different yards. Yeah, it's confusing, but you move accordingly and let shit play out as it may, however it play out.

These are questions that would've came about if it was an issue: How did that happen? Why did that happen? Who made that call? So you got on a homie with an outside Niggah and you thought that was going to be accepted? The questions would've went on and on and on. It had to really be justified. It had to really be overstood, and had to make sense to them. As soon as I would've landed somewhere else and happened to land on a yard where homies heard about it and inquired, anyone in their feelings and feeling some type of way about it might want to politic me. As I've stressed, yards are different. The dynamics of every yard is different as with who's on them. No yard is ever the same or move the same.

However, I'm a team player, win, lose, or draw when it comes to my LBC-ing. I approached a few Crip homies elsewhere and basically it was a no-go. If it had happened and another Crip homie would've went with me to handle it, so be it. It was handled, because I was the only Long Beach on this side of the yard, the only homie from the city. An older homie and assistance was needed, it wasn't a solo mission. It was a DP. It wasn't about him getting a head up fight (one on one). I would've and could've done that. The situation didn't warrant or required a one on one, it required and warranted foot-to-ass! Plain and simple, foot-to-ass ration. It was just way too much going on with you. You knew you had that coming. You should've just accepted your issue and kept the line moving. I was also told in a kite I got, no playing ball on him, just two on one him and send him on his way. He was not to be maxed out! Shit, I mean, I wasn't thinking about playing ball. Anyway, I'm presently dealing with an active in house case behind playing ball. So really, that was the last thing on my mind, but if it had to go that way, it had to go that way. I was going to move accordingly.

The bullshit was going on for days. It was frustrating. It was one of those ASAP situations. It was hard trying to get assistance at which point I'm like, fuck it, it's not gon happen. So I'm at the homies on a kite, "I'm on standby. Whenever a homie can make it over here to assist me, it's handled." Here don't anything too much get passed anyone. Cold thing about it, everyone for the most part felt or knew something was up and had to be, due to the events that took place previously with Chumlee. Some shit was heard, but a lot of what was heard was speculative. It was in the air though. Now with me trying to find assistance, I wasn't really trying to ask too many, because it could've easily got back to him.

It's always about not what you do, but how you do it, or go about it, without compromising the integrity of what you have going on. I'm trying to keep a Niggah sleep, dead to what's going on, giving up no indications of anything, not trying to expose myself as being one of the ones coming. So the thing is, I'm looking for assistance from a Crip homie to assist me, all while being mindful of who I got at and approached, and how I got at them. By no means was I trying to blow it up. It could've went one of a few ways. One, he could've chose to do something stupid, like take off on another race and kick off a riot between the Blacks and whoever, and leave the yard. Two, he could've snuck up on me somehow and tried to do something to me, which would've been unlikely. Three, he could've just avoided the whole situation all together by walking up to the police, telling them he couldn't be on the yard no longer. But just knowing him, that one wasn't going to happen. He was going how he went, or one of the other two ways. Nah, I couldn't see him walking up to the police, doing that, telling them, "Aye, I can't be here. I feel my life is in danger" and tapping out, choosing to leave on his own accord rather than deal with the issue. A lot of that though goes on dealing with this shit. Dudes rather take that trip to the dark side, taking that walk of shame, than deal with an issue, whatever it might be.

Some aren't made or built for this prison shit. Though they lived on the streets like they were and will be quick to say, fuck it I'm out, and tap out, go SNY. On the flip side, you'll have some that'll be like, fuck it, I'm not going out like that, and will keep going through whatever it is they're going through, no matter how many times they're played ball on, or have been two on one'ed, or three on one'ed, will keep coming back to the yard, to the point where the administration will step in, making that decision for you, giving you no choice in the matter.

The few options I gave an example of are basic options. Me, I'm not trying to give options or alternate routes. If you take a dudes choices or his options, you take them. So by me being mindful of that fact, I kept my asking for assistance to a minimum .Too much asking could backfire and blow shit up. It leaves too much room for it to be exposed. The more you ask, the more chances it is for it to reach who it's not meant to reach. It would be a matter of time. I've seen it happen multiple times. I know how it plays out. A few times I've seen it go sideways.

Then another variable, it's like you don't know who'll open a dudes eyes if he's asleep. It's hard to tell for simple fact it could be a dudes that know a situation, or have been made aware of it, yet still choosing to still fuck with the individual and continues to. How can you really trust that or trust them? They know what's going on, still talking to him and embracing him. For all I know, you could be feeding him info. What you heard, what you thought you heard, what you assume, or what you know, either way, how could you trust that? It's a double edged sword though, because it's like if a dudes switch up, that could be an alert to something being up. (SMH) What a tangled web. It's a lot to factor in, dealing with these types of matters.

Me being me though, and being around, and knowing what I know, knowing what I've learned and overstand, I watched him anyway. However, he kept his distance, which I was cool with. So we finally get back to the yard. I was pulled up on by someone with a message from the homies as to the situation. I'm like, "What's the word from over there?" He was like, "I'm on my way down there now to see for sure, but I think for sure somebody is coming to assist on that business." Me and Lon hit the slab to buss down, as we do every time we hit the yard. After we greeted those we greet, program as usual, and of course watch Chumlee and his movements.

Where he went and who he was talking to. What I did notice in my observation though, he kept his eyes in the direction of the yard door. Every time it opened, he was on it, watching for who walked though, which basically let me know he felt something, knew something, or was alerted by one of these dudes around here that he fuck with. If it wasn't a regular face that wasn't regularly on the yard, he locked in on them. He really watched and paid attention to them, gauging the temperature until he was satisfied enough to feel they weren't on this yard for him in no type of way.

Looking to see too if that person was coming to talk to me, I'll give him that, he was being cautious. He checked for stranger danger, and no doubt he watched for homies. Immediately, he would know something was up, especially if a homie popped up on the yard approaching me. What ended up happening though, he went back to the building for something. Don't know what for, but he comes back out dressed in his blues (state blue shirt, state blue jeans, and state boots). That's how you have to be dressed, in your blues, going on the patio. The police don't care though about you wearing your personal shoes on the patio. You have to have your blue shirt and blue jeans on, period.

He went through the yard door to the patio. A lot of us speculated where he was going, which we all ended up being wrong. What we didn't speculate on was him walking to the lower yard, thinking it was good. I still can't figure out what possessed him to go over there, or what made him. That's exactly what had happened. He went for whatever reason and Ace and Dog got on him immediately. The alarm goes off, police start running from the buildings heading to the lower yard. Our side of the yard is put down already, "GEEETTT DOOOWWWN!" The police working the yard tower is running on the cat walk above towards the lower yard, yelling, "GEEETTT DOOOWWWN!" As we're down on the yard, the yard doors open and we could see C-yard police running towards the lower yard.

We can hear three loud bangs, "Bloom, Bloom, Bloom" from the block gun going off, and the police still yelling, "GEEETTT DOOOW-WWN!" We can hear what's going on good, because the only thing that's separating the yards is a large wall that divides buildings 1, 2, 3, and 4 from 5, 6, 7, and 8. The police are cold though, knowing he just had an issue a few days go with the homies trying to get on him. They send him back to the yard. From what I've seen since I've been here, if you're two on one'ed, you're going to C-yard and the two are coming back to the yard. I guess they felt like, "Fuck it. We don't give a fuck. If you want to go back, go back!" Now, with the second situation happening and it getting handled, they actually contemplated on sending him back to the yard. This second go around, sending him back a second time, figuring again, "Fuck it, if he wants to go back send him back." They hadn't start-ed packing his shit and it was getting close to chow. Then I hear, "Aye Tic, you ain't gon like what you see in about 20 minutes!" Coming from down the tier, I already knew what they were speaking on. Chumlee is coming back (SMH). I'm like, this shit is crazy as fuck. This Niggah is coming back for another issue? He can't possibly think it's a deaded issue.

I'm thinking all of this to myself, but now I'm like, I know the issue still has to be addressed. He's been voted off of the island. He has to go, can't stay. So it's like, they send him back a third time, on him again. For certain they won't be sending him back a third time. No doubt in my mind, or no one else's. I don't care what he tries to convince them to let him back; it's not going to happen. They're not sending him back, because now they would be putting his life in jeopardy. What if he really gets hurt this time, after being sent back again (SMH).

Me and New Year both shook our heads and was like, "This shit is crazy. It's about to be six people getting 115's for the same situation." However, I guess someone saw the potential ramifications of it and fig-uring how it would be hard to justify or explain away sending him back again and again, he was attacked three times. How could it be justified or explained away? How could that be justified? What would be the reason? You know already he was attacked once, then twice, at which point he should have been removed. Seeing it's an apparent problem with him, a repeated problem, and he's the common denominator, yet you send him back a third time.

Something is really wrong with that captured moment. I mean, even Stevie Wonder could see it and he's blind. These are the types of dudes you'll deal with and come across. At some point, there's always one. So the young Damu homies Fatal and Ghost moved in his cell. He's officially gone this time (SMH). I'm assuming he's on C-yard and not in the sandbox. That's where they send dudes who get voted off of the island and two on one'ed off of D-yard, unless they go that other route, taking that walk of shame. I actually heard he got DP'ed because I didn't like him, not because of all the shit he had going on, but because I didn't like him. Wow!

"The old Niggah didn't like him, so he had him DP'ed." Really? Damn! I have that much influence or say so, to get a Niggah whupped out because I didn't like them. I didn't like him, but we were cellies for six months. I didn't like him, but a lot of issues I dealt with on my own and never took to the homies that he could've been DP'ed for. What these dudes don't know, a lot of shit was never brought up that could've been, as far as the homies. But that's how dudes are though, always looking to speak on shit or on issues that don't have anything to do with them. I can see you speaking on it though if you're invited. Outside of that, they're just basically concerning themselves with business not theirs.

Even if he involved you by speaking on it, which I'm sure he did and didn't give you the real on, he gave you a version that fit his narrative, gave you a bullshit version, and you took it and ran with it. Thus you formed an opinion of me that is utterly bullshit until you see it for what and as it is. That rock is in front of you. You'll kick it, but you know what though, you're basing your view of me on a bullshit narrative. But you want to know something else? Don't give a fuck! At the end of the day and in his words, "I don't give a fuck!" Really, I don't! For the simple fact I don't know you, don't fuck with you, don't deal with you, and don't care. We're not in eachother's space. I won't be losing any sleep over how you feel, what you feel, or what you think about me. Our worlds are worlds apart, my dude. Since you couldn't see my vision, I had to draw you a captured moment. Don't know you, and don't want to know you.

Switching lanes again, this morning me and New Year were chopping it up and I had him laughing, telling him stories about Situation. I had him shaking his head too. He really found it funny when I was telling him about the fight between McNeal and Situation, in the set on, the block.

I was also telling him how McNeal's mama, Yolanda, was trying to buss me out (tell on me) about me having sex with Mary, Situation's sister-in-law. Basically telling Situation while you're tripping with my daughter, you need to be tripping on that bitch standing next to you. She's fucking him too! I had him laughing too about the night Situation popped up out of nowhere when me and I.C., a homie at that time, went to the liquor store at like one something in the morning, last call for alcohol, and I had McNeal with me in my swoop and Situation ran up on us. She reached through the window and grabbed McNeal by her braids and was hitting her.

I even hit him with a few domestic instances. He was like, "I don't even see how you were dealing with Louie the 13th." A name he gave her from the stories about her. I was telling him too how she basically layed down on me and left me for dead. In my mind though, if you can just shake me, still in a Situationship, and have three kids and a possible with me, with little to no regard for love of loyalty, you weren't shit anyway. Love or loyalty never played a part in what we had, which was a Situationship. In my case though with Situation, I'll just say this, I was blindly loyal to a bitch that has no loyalty to nothing, to nobody, nobody at all. I overstand and get that the absence of a Niggah being locked up can force a bitch to survive and adapt, making her have to become independent and not be a dependant, but that don't mean you just up and shake with no regard or forget the struggles, the situationship you had, or how you were holding eachother down once upon a time. Sharing what you shared, all of that is out of the window and never meant shit, obviously. The struggle, nothing. What's crazy though, you could've been a good dude out there and handling your wax, taking care of what you needed to, though you ran the streets and stayed in them, never neglecting your household or her, doing what you were supposed to be doing as far as that goes. None of that seem to matter or played a factor, counting for nothing. The good shit is never factored in. That part is never factored in. It's just out of sight, out of mind.

Holding you down was never a part of the equation. You're no longer a part of the dynamic, which changed. Something you'll never know until that situation presents itself. When you're locked up, especially for a substantial amount of time, it's a wrap. She's out of there.

Me: "It's always about you, ain't it? It was about you when you shook and left me for dead and now it's about you since you're claiming to be in your feelings!"

Her: "No mutha fucka, it was about you, when you left me out here by myself, struggling. You left me lonely. I didn't leave you, Niggah, you left me. You left us!"

That's what it is when it's being justified. It's a typical response. Playing devil's advocate though, which I'll do at times, I can somewhat overstand her position. Regardless as to how I really feel about it, in which case you were doing the wrong thing and not handling your wax and just being on some suuuper scum bag shit with her. The thing is, do you but do her. Do what you're doing, but take care of home. How can you really expect her to hold you down or be there for you when you didn't hold her down or was there for her? That goes back to my saying, do you but do her. In turn, she's supposed to do the same, do her but do you. Fair exchange is never a robbery, not at all. That's how it's supposed to work, but it doesn't be the case. In most cases, because there's no loyalty on her part. My thing is too, with that, do you but do me, do you and don't let shit get back to me. I shouldn't hear about nothing you're doing, or who you're doing it with. Where's the loyalty? Where's the love? I've had this very conversation, play by play, with just about every cellie I've had from the County Jail to High Desert. How when you were out there with your birth and you were going through whatever it was you were going through, business was still being handled, regardless. That should outweigh anything you went through, in my mind.

So yeah, of course it's just natural to assume when you're up against it, she got you, and she's going to be there, she's going to hold you down, and have your back win, lose, or draw, just based on. Based on the bond, the struggle, the connection, and the fact you have kids, despite the pit falls and downs and ups. That's an average relationship out there. You're going to have issues and go through shit. It's a part of that maze we call life. It really fucks us up, dudes who are locked up, and has an effect on us when she doesn't respond the way we though she should've or would've. Basically, we're feeling like off top, off the dribble, we have that coming, which is clearly a false sense of both security and reality, a cold reality check on that ass.

A lot of the stories we tell each other and have told each other over the years about relationships and dealing with bitches are similar or the same, just told differently and the players are different. Similar or the same, all of the time, regardless of what it is, for the most part. It's pretty much the same T.V. show and story; it's just shown and told in a different way, but by a different dude. It's like, I saw this episode before. "It's the same shit I been through with my bitch", or "me and mine had that same shit going on". Don't forget about "that bitch been ran off"! That one and the "she layed down"! Same shit. We all have that in common.

Like the other day me and New Year were talking about how you run into these different younger dudes. It doesn't matter where they're from, Crip, Blood, Civilian, or Bay Area, how all of their stories are basically the same. "I had this many bitches, all of my bitches were bad (attractive). I didn't fuck with no ugly bitches. I had foreign cars out there. I had this that and the third out there. I was doing it like this. I was doing it like that. I was having major loot, moving big dope, and had big jewelry." This doesn't add up to me in any type of way.

If you had it like that, it would reflect that, but it reflects the opposite. It's your story; I'll let you tell it though. But one, you don't have a bitch now. Two, you don't have no food in your cell, none, period. Not even a top ramen noodle seasoning pack. You're living strictly off of the state, like most of these dudes. Three, you don't have a T.V., C.D. player, hot pot, or fan, no personal clothes, or shoes. Everything you own is state issued. Four, you don't go to canteen or get packages. Five, you don't get visits. Six, I don't ever see you on the phone and if I do, you're just continuously dialing number after number. If you don't knock it the fuck off!

You had all of this shit going on out there; you had all of these bitches, all of this loot, all these material things, doing all of these big things (SMH). In my mind though, what bitch in her right mind would shake a Niggah with all of this going on? If that was the case, and I do know what that looks like, you wouldn't be living like you are, or going through what you're going through. These are dudes that exist around here, in jail period. Me and New Year stay having good laughs. It's hilarious. Why would you need to be asking homies for shit? Asking anyone for anything? "Aye homie, you have a soup I can get? Aye homie, you have a shot of beans (what the fuck is a shot of beans)? Aye homie, you have a few chips? Aye homie, can I get such and such? Aye homie, aye homie, aye homie! Can I get? Do you have? How about can you get a hustle? I'm like 50 Cent." Damn homie, I thought you were the man, homie. What happened to you? You were out there doing all of this balling, yet here you are, asking homies or anyone else for shit (SMH). I know what that looks like too when a dude really was having it out there. That shit don't leave like that and the bitches either. Little that you know though, you're being clowned and talked about. You're being clowned, talked about, and laughed at. That's not even the half.

"Here comes this begging ass Niggah. Here comes this needy ass Niggah. This Niggahs a bum. Look at his bum ass. Broke bummy ass Niggah!" It goes on and on and on (SMH). You've done that to yourself though. They're going to be extra hard on you because of the shit you said you had, were having, and were doing out there, instead of keeping it real. Niggahs can respect that. If you don't have shit, you don't have shit, period. I'll tell a mutha fucka quick, "I ain't got shit, ain't had shit, and don't have a bitch. What I get outside of what moms or my cuzzo do, I hustle for it." That's my whole script. No big mystery, get a bar. I keep me a little food. I keep cosmetics to keep my hygiene right. I'm straight.

I don't have habits and I don't do debts. My main thing is, I don't go around asking anyone for anything and if I do need something I can always hit up my guy Lon. Outside of him, if I don't have it, I just don't have it. I'll wait until I can get it. That's just keeping it all the way a thousand with you. It makes you look like a bullshit dude and that's how you're seen. You'll get talked about without a doubt. Trust, you're being spoke on and talked about bad.

When you pull up, it's like, "What's up with the homie? What's up with my Niggah?" Before you pulled up though it was, "You know this bum ass Niggah such and such hit me up for a soup last night. . . He hit me up too for a shot of coffee. . . He's always begging!" If you're already with your homies or dudes you mess with, whoever it is you're with, it's, "Yeah homie, such and such." But let you walk off from them, now it's, "Bum ass, always begging. He's a cold bum. He don't have shit. He don't ever have shit. Hold up, here he comes. Talk baseball!" (SMH) That's one thing. It doesn't stop. It's relentless.

Dudes have always came to jail and be all they can be, young and old. It's not the exception, it's the norm. It's more of the younger ones now though. The older dudes kind of fell back on it. They knew it wasn't flying. "I had this. I had that. I was doing this. I was doing that." You weren't doing shit and didn't have shit. Knock it all the way off. Pac said it best, "You ain't got to lie to kick it!" IF you don't have shit, or didn't have shit, that's what it is and what it was. When you accept shit form homie and always needing something, yeah your homies, every time they look around they start looking at you a certain way and treating you a certain way. For sure start talking bad about you. That's going to happen. That's just what it is.

Pandora's box is open. Then the flip side of that, you have dudes that don't care and you can talk bad about them to their face and they don't give a damn! They'll still go cell to cell door asking for shit. Fuck what you think. A soup, a shot of coffee, some beans, a hand full of chips, it don't matter, it's "Aye, do you have, can I get?" You can talk about them until you're grey in the face. So what! No shame or self dignity, none, zero, zilch (SMH). Real live vermin.

You're going to be the ass butt of a lot of jokes, created ones and all. This is the type of shit we deal with. Dudes don't have anything better to do but talk about your ass all day. You're their entertainment until they find someone in a worse position than you're in, but you'll always be on their radar. "Broke ass Niggah, Bum ass Niggah!" You're not all the way off of the hook because that other dude is just another reminder of you. If you put yourself in that type of position or those type of positions, it is what it is. Then, if you do have a piece of a bitch and she's not doing too good and not doing anything for you or not much and you're running around talking about, "My bitch, my bitch, my bitch" these dudes are going to clown and talk about her too.

But I guess to you it's better than having no bitch at all. Yeah, she's getting clowned. "All she do is let this Niggah call. That's all she can afford with her broke ass. She's a bum too. A bum bitch. She's a bum bitch and he's a bum Niggah. Two bums. All he can do is call. He can't get nothing else. Why? Because she don't have shit with her broke dusty ass!" (SMH) Shots fired! Don't know nothing about her, just going by what they see. Him, running to the phone back and forth all day to talk to her, or him just speaking on her all the time but he doesn't have shit or gets very little.

Me and New Year even talked about how dudes have the nerve to be in their feelings with you, behind you wanting your loot that they owe you and probably been owing you the loot for the longest. Yet, they have an attitude, because you asked for it, like you don't have that right to ask for what's yours. Damn homie, I can't ask for what's mine? I've had this very scenario play out on a few occasions where this dude might've owed me or that dude might've owed me. The thing is, I've never sweated them about it, asked them for it continuously, "You got that for me? Aye, what's up with that? When are you gon have that for me?"

Every time I saw them, it was that, "Aye you got that?" I didn't do it, but it's what other dudes done. I guess it's contributed to them never having anything or not use to having anything. I don't know. For me though, when enough time has elapsed to where it's been so long that they've thought I forgot about it or hoped I did. Absolutely not. Just when you thought though I forgot, that's when I would ask you about it. Don't get it confused. I haven't. Not by a long shot. It just wasn't a priority for me at that time and I was on something else that I felt was more important. Now though, back to you, "Can I get my loot?" I mean, damn, it's been a minute since I'd asked you for it or about it. It's a month later. It's crazy as hell you have an attitude though. This again, is the type of shit you have to deal with, the type of characters. If you know you owe, pay the man. Stop trying to wait him out until you feel in your mind he forgot about it.

Nine out of ten, he hasn't. Trust me. But yeah, it's actually crazy how you have an attitude with me about what's mine (SMH). You're mad at me because I'm asking you about my loot. If you don't knock it off. Like, I'm getting at you wrong, or sideways, doing something to you, but wait, check me out. You have situations where dudes would actually want to fight you behind your loot. "You're sweating me too much. Let's get down. I don't like how you got at me. Let's get down. We can get down then." Look at how that sounds. You want to fight me because you owe me and don't want to pay me. In your mind though and in everyone else's, once we fight, the debt is paid. In your mind, and let me rephrase in everyone else's, in the minds of those you mess with feel that way, everyone don't feel that way. It goes back to my situation with Oppie and how he just fixed his mouth to tell me some shit like, "Yeah homie, I thought we were gon have to get down." Get down! So you can say since we got down I was paid. A no-go. Only in his mind though, that's what it was. That was the farthest thing from my mind, get down! I'm about to play ball! Get down! You sounded stupid as fuck! I'm going to fight you, but you owe me, that's out! Answer this riddle for me, Do we look like Jerry Cooney and Larry Holmes? Fighting for a purse? You're not Jerry Cooney and I'm damn sure not Larry Homes, not by a long shot!

You had me confused with someone else, all the way confused. "Yeah, ok, we gon fight." How did that work out for you though? No, how did that work out for you? That's what is wrong with these dudes, just feel they can just get at you a certain way, as if they won't get got at. Everyone's not with that shit. A fight isn't going to solve everything, or just because that's your mind state. While you're stuck on "fight, fight, fight", the next man's on "play ball, play ball, play ball" taking it way serious, much more serious than you. There's always a consequence for ones actions for certain, playing games.

Maybe if everyone had to pay one and was held to that standard shit wouldn't be as fucked up in prison as it is, because you would know and overstand you would be held accountable for your bullshit and your shenanigans will not be tolerated, period and is a no-go, and if you crossed that line you know what it is. You're not the exception and won't be the exception. You're not bigger than the cause or your car. You hear all the time how this die owe this dude, and hasn't paid him and has owed him for a while. It's just game after game, lie after lie, constant delays and stall tactics, bullshit after bullshit.

Patience at some point are going to wear thin and the situation has to come to an end, unless you just get so fed up you'll be like, "Fuck it. He can have it. It's small, I'm just not fucking with dude no more", which is what he was hoping for all along anyway. This dude got something from this dude, knowing he didn't have it to pay for it but accepted it anyway with hopes of coming across something to pay. That's called getting something on your ass, off the dribble, you have no means to pay for something you got but you're hoping you do some how some way. They have that bad too, with betting or gambling with dice or cards. Dudes are betting and gambling on their ass, knowing they don't have the loot to cover the loss but will still bet and still gamble literally that risk, like it's a game.

But it happens all day, every day dudes betting and gambling on their ass, don't have a dollar, hoping they come up (win) (SMH). It goes back to this dudes giving this dude bad greenies. Dudes will pass you some greenies quick as fuck and will sear up and down when they gave them to you, they were straight. But wait, they'll have the nerve to imply you must've done some bullshit or are playing games, one of the many tactics dudes come with "I know these numbers were right, I got those off of the phone from my bitch. She don't be playing those type of games. I got those numbers from moms." (SMH)

But yeah, dudes would actually pass you dead greenies, knowing they were already dead when they passed. That type of shit shouldn't be allowed to fly and shouldn't exist, but it does and why not? If they feel or know nothing is going to happen to them behind it, feel like they're not going to suffer no type of consequences, so fuck it, why not do it. No one's going to do nothing about it. I can do this or that, my homies ain't tripping. I can get this or that and if I don't pay I can just squabble a Niggah, debt paid! This is the mind set of these weirdos. "Yeah, I got you. Let me get this. Let me get that. Yeah shoot it, I'll pay you tomorrow. I'll pay you Friday." Tomorrow or Friday never comes. "I'll bet you 20 on the Raiders win, I'll bet you 15 the Lakers win", betting but don't have shit! Playing cards or shooting dice, knowing you don't have it to pay or gamble with. Yet you'll put yourself out there, like it's the thing to do (SMH).

Know why? Because he's not worried about his homies tripping on him. Eight out of ten, they're not tripping and won't trip unless it affects them or the program as a whole, or unless they're for the most part working out of that same kit, doing the same shit and are bullshit dudes themselves, and if you're tripping about your look, fuck it, squabble up on some real shit and real talk. The game would change if they knew those type of games or shenanigans wouldn't be tolerated by homies, righteous homies. If they didn't, they would and real quick having the slightest inclination that if I play games with this dude's loot he might play ball on me, plain and simple. They have no fear of being held to the fire, until that tone is set.

Once that tone is set and that bar is set, guarantee they'll set some act right, real quick because they'll know what comes with the games and the shenanigans, it's serious. Other races for the most part are held to the fire, but you do have those few that'll play with that fire and get burned. Their consequences are more severe, no games. You'll fuck around and get flat-lined being Hispanics, White, or an Other playing those type of games, and that's just real. They take shit a bit more serious and extreme, holding their people to a much higher standard. It's just what it is.

For one, if they owe you for anything, they're trying to keep it between the two of you, trying to keep the shit on the low (quiet). So they're not trying to pay you, technically South Siders or Whites weren't really suppose to deal with Blacks on any type of business, so they knew by dealing with Blacks they don't pay and it gets out. It's an issue, so it was really in their best interest to pay. However, if they don't and they're playing games and you turn them in (inform their people) they had problems. Over the years though, it's changed as far as their policy. It used to be if you turned them in they'd get whupped out (beat up) and still had to pay. Sometimes they would get ball played on them. Not so much as for the debt, in my mind, but because you were dealing with a Black and let your business get out there, being sloppy.

It's not what you do but how you do it. From that, it went to their people just flat out saying, "Stop dealing with our people, because we're tired of removing our people when you already knew you shouldn't have been doing business with them in the first place." So basically, "From now on, if you do do business with my people, that's on you!" With that it was you turn them in, they no longer owe you, they owe us. Now, how that works I have no clue.

But what I do know is this, you're no longer getting paid if you turn them in. That's over with, you play that game at your own risk. It's levels to this prison shit, to this yard shit, and should always be respected for what and as they are. Call a ball a ball and a strike a strike. Like, you can feed a dude, homie, or not a homie until he's full and he still want beef (looking for something to have issues with). Dudes you fuck with or homies in this instance are never satisfied. The more you look out (give them) the more they want.

If you're not looking out anymore, it's an issue in their feelings. They'll never be satisfied or content with what you do for them or how you help them, in terms of looking out. What's crazy though, you don't owe them shit, you're not obligated to do nothing for them at all. You're doing it or have done it because you're a homie or good dude that's done it from your heart and could see them with it. As far as homies go, the only thing I'm obligated to do is support them in some drama or conflict outside of the car, and they better hope they're in the right because they will be getting politicked. It's a dirty game.

You just opened a door believing it'll be appreciated and they'll take it and build on it. Absolutely not, it's the farthest thing from their mind. They figure, in their mind, they can keep coming back to you for shit. Nah, that's the case, they want you to keep on looking out for them. You can slide a dude something now if they choose to do the wrong thing with what you gave them, that's on them period. Only they know what their needs or habits are. I don't live in the cell with them. I don't know what they have or don't have. It's not my job to know, it's really not my concern, nor do I care. But if you chose to do the wrong thing and you knew you need shit and don't handle your wax, don't come back with your hands out like I'm just obligated to put something in it, because I'm not, been there done that.

I've done my part as a homie, being in a position to do it, which I never mind doing especially when it's a homie or a homie outside of the car. If I slid you something and you know you need deodorant, toothpaste, soap, lotion, grease, or whatever. Knowing you need shit on your shelf in your cell, and you choose to do the wrong thing, your bad. Then be like, "Aye homie, you have soup, some toothpaste. A few soups, a soap", that's no beuno! I looked out already, you chose to do the wrong shit whatever that was, knowing you needed shit. Priorities come first, period. You're supposed to handle your wax.

You get that shot though when you pull up on the yard, for the most part and you're a homie, especially if I got it to do. I'll do it because you just got on the yard and I wanted to see you get right until you got right. If I do it outside of you being a homie from the city, it was because I wanted to look out for you, just because. I might've saw you needed assistance and would appreciate it, that and being in the position to do it. It was an easy call, "Fuck it, let me look out", so I pulled up on you. It's just in my nature and charter.

If I'm in a position to help someone, I will. And I'm not looking for anything in return. It's out of the kindness of my heart. You owe me nothing. Just when you're in a position to help someone or look out, do it. Me personally, I'm not a selfish person anyway, nor have I ever been. On this note though, I do know though and overstand how easy and quick it is for dudes, especially in prison or jail, to misinterpret that. Then it's like they want to take your kindness, that kindness, for weakness or take you for being soft because you chose to look out for them, and that's just the type of person you are generally.

Feeling you're some type of sucker or mark, "We got one." It's like they'll keep coming and coming and coming, and the minute you don't have nothing for them their lips is poked out and they're with some shenanigans. All behind you choosing to look out for them on some homie shit like ,"Oh, he's done this and that. He'll keep doing it." Then it's like, "Hold up. Flag on the play," have to cut it off, I have nothing else for you. It's a wrap, I'm not giving you shit, it's over with. Cut them off. Then that's when the other shit come into play. Now they're plotting on you and politicking on you, looking for support from the autobots because you have nothing else for them; looking for anything to fit a narrative to fight you or two on one to remove you, just looking for a reason (SMH). I'= seen this done, time and time again. I get why dudes, homies included, don't even open that door because of what comes with it. So off the dribble, their attitude is like "I'm not giving you shit, I'm not giving a Niggah shit. For what, one they're not going to appreciate it, and two they're going to look into it for what it's not." You have dudes though, that are just not into the whole giving a Niggah anything, period. They've been through it and knows firsthand what follows. But too, they don't ask anyone for shit, for anything at all, and would rather go without then to ask for anything.

Not only they don't ask or give anyone shit, they don't expect shit from anyone because they're not giving anyone shit. The attitude is basically this, "You keep your shit. I'm going to keep mine. I have nothing for you, so don't ask". How can you be mad though? You can't be, you have to respect it for what and as it is. Me and New Year were already talking about something along these very lines and I brought up a kitty (where everyone who can afford to puts their items together and it's kept in a homie's cell for the less fortunate homies that pull up on the yard). It goes back to dudes not giving anyone anything, they're not contributing to it.

New Year was like, "A kitty, I haven't heard anything about a kitty in years, nothing. I thought that shit was dead!" He was like, "Dudes don't do those no more. Those been over and done with." Then I had to really dial it back. In thought he was absolutely correct, they have been nonexistent. If a dude get something now when he pull up (get on the yard) it's just a homie looking out for him, be it a Crip homie, a homie homie, a Damu homie, or Bay Area homie. It doesn't apply to other races, be it Wood, South Sider, Northerner, or Other. Due in part because they have kittys and keep kittys for their people. It's just how they pretty much function on a regular. But yeah, it was designed for homies just pulling up and haven't gotten their property yet, or just don't have anything at all and need assistance.

28

It was there for that reason. It was basically where you would have a homie or homies designated in a building to keep stuff in their cells for their homies. Those homies or that homie will pull up on you and ask you "Aye homie, what do you need, or are you straight (are you ok)? If you need anything, you let him know." I need x-y-z and you'll get it if it's in the kitty, but nine out of 10 it's there. When I first heard about a kitty was way back in the days in 91'. Where my overstanding was it was pretty much for homies that didn't have anything and didn't have no one on the streets looking out for them. So the homies would look out for them, but only with the things they needed not wanted, and the basic shit.

Soap to wash they ass, toothpaste to kill that hot ass breath, some lotion for the ash. You already know Niggahs get ashy as fuck! Some deodorant for them pits, and maybe some coffee. Outside of that, you had to figure it out, and at some point you had to figure it out how you were going to get your soap, toothpaste, lotion, deodorant, and coffee. They kitty wasn't there to take care of you. It was there to help you out until you got something going. That's it, that's all; either a hustle, a bitch, something, but to keep the kitty going everyone that gets stuff from it has to return it.

So that it's something there for the next homie(s) that pull up. It doesn't exist if nothing is being put back. That's just how that works. Like when I got here (High Desert) I didn't have my property when I landed on the yard and was put in the building. When I got in the cell it was with a young CriP homie from Watts. He was like, "Look, I have a soap for you, a toothpaste and a deodorant. It should hold you until your homie Mike from 20's come through. I'm pretty sure he's going to ask you what you need, because he knows you don't have your property and you're just pulling up", which is exactly what happened. Mike had actually made it to my cell an hour or so later, telling me he just heard I was in 6-Building and asked me what I needed. I let him know and the next time he was at my cell door he had it for me. It wasn't from a kitty, it was just a homie from the city pushing LBC looking out. What he gave me I slid back to the young homie from Watts. When I finally got my property I gave it back to Mike. He really wasn't trying to accept it back. He was like, "Just look out for the next homie who might not have anything, period." So to start a kitty it pretty much works like this. Every homie that's fortunate, fortunate to have someone on the streets taking care of them or might've left loot on the streets, whatever the case may be.

They're in a position to give, in a position to contribute something to the cause. They have it to do and don't mind doing it. So it's like maybe a couple of bars of soap from him and him, maybe a couple of toothpastes and deodorants from him and him, maybe some shower shoes and lotion from him and him, maybe some shampoo and grease from him and him. Possibly, a few homies might want to add some soups and coffee in it. Then lastly, you might have a homie or two who throws in writing material, a few tablets, pens, envelopes, and a couple books of stamp.

You maybe get a bunch of state envelops (indigent envelopes) homies might've accumulated them from indigent dudes who sold them to them. Shit, that's a hustle. Shit, if you're indigent and get those state envelops you can slang them (sell), ten for a hot ass dollar. At the end of the day, that's four soups. Amway you cut it it's a bar of soap, it's a roll-on deodorant. I'm just saying though, you don't have to worry about lotion now. They give you Thermaderm lotion if you're indigent. Toothpaste though, that's a different story, you'll have to give all twenty envelopes up. They'll give you twenty a month. But yeah, that's how your kitty is started and what it was intended for; how it functioned and how it was to keep functioning. It was there for temporary use. There too if you just didn't have anything.

No bitch, no family, no one on the streets tapping in or looking out for you. You just didn't have shit, or no way of getting shit. Which brings this to mind, for you not to have anyone looking out period, you must've set fire to bridges, or fucked over people out there doing and being you on whatever tip you were on. I'll give you a pass on bitches. We already know how they'll just bounce and leave a Niggah for dead based on. "Nobody though my Niggah, can't see you with nothing!" (SMH) That's just crazy as fuck. It was like at any time you're in a position to put something in the kitty you did it. As with all things, shit comes to an end. It's always going to be individual homies like, "Fuck that, I'm not gon keep putting shit in and no one else is. They have shit too".

Or the shit's constantly coming out of the kitty, but nothing is going back. Those two instances will kill kittys off quick. The same applies as far as kittys, when you're in the sandbox. In the sandbox it's like once you show your lock up order (the report that explains how you got in the sandbox) and it checks out, you'll pretty much get looked out for, with the basics, until you get your property within ten or so days. To my knowledge, there wasn't a kitty for the Blacks in the sandbox. It's just homies or other Blacks looking out and when you get your shit you shoot it back, so someone else can be looked out for when they pull up.

In the sandbox it'll be a homie just looking out, another Black just looking out, or even another race looking. But you always reach back (put back). What I've found in the sandbox though, other races will look out for you and a lot quicker at times than your own will, in some instances before your own will. They don't have a problem with it, as long as you're good. What they consider active in the sandbox. If you're active in the sandbox to them it's like we're all in it together; as with that being the consensus for all actives in the sandbox.

They, for the most part, just want to make sure you're not SNY or you're not in the sandbox for no bullshit (telling, tapping out, or jacking off to the free staff or police) to name a few instances. The kitty, however, on the mainline is pretty much a wrap. No one's trying to give anyone anything, period, point blank. Truly has a problem and an issue with it. The mindset is nothing good can come off it. It's like once you open that door, at some point bullshit's bound to follow. It never fails, dealing with the breed of dudes we're dealing within prison these days. These yards aren't the same as the 80's or 90's, and never will be again. I've seen it time and time again. I've experienced it a few times, and I continue to see it. You can't give nobody shit.

I continue to hear sentiment after sentiment, story after story of this same instance of how when you give someone something how you'll regret it later (SMH). So again, I overstand it on the different levels, for the most part and have to agree. Dudes aren't worthy. To an extent, I've become that way not wanting to give anyone anything because of how dudes are. They make you not want to by the shit they do. A few fuck it up for all, which is pretty much what happened. You can't do anything for anyone without them reading more into it, or they're just out to try and take advantage of your good nature.

"We're still cool, we're still straight. I deal with you. We talk the whole nine. I'm just not giving you shit!" It's nothing personal at all. Sometimes you do have to reset your trajectory in terms of attitude or thought process. Now it's like on the streets, how you circle the block before you park. You have to stay cautious, real talk (SMH). I'm constantly told you can't or you shouldn't put yourself out there like that, opening those types of doors with dudes. It'll go unappreciated, yet you were doing a good thing. It was with good intentions and nothing behind it, just you wanting to look out. As I've come to learn and overstand, it's wasted energy and a waste of time on a wasted cause. You can never give or do too

It's just too much like right being a good dude. You give the more they want, the more you do the more they want you to do I guess this is my attempt at trying to imprint the same advice I was given. At the end of the day though, god bless the child that has his own and can get it. He does give you that ability and know how. But yeah, it's like I don't do that, it's nothing against you I just don't give people shit. We're going to nip that right in the bud, so before you even ask you already know what it is. You know it's not going to happen. It's bad when you have to be that way but that's what it came to. You have to use your head over your heart. It's about self and self above all, anything outside of that is a misoversanding.

To look out now would be something very hard to do. It wouldn't come as easy as it once did and feeling as if nothing good can come from it, knowing nothing good can come from it. Dudes are poison and sour, always out to get something, fuck you over, or take advantage because they feel you have it like that. You exposed a little by the gesture and they assumed you had more than you really had. In all truth, you could've only had a little but was willing to share what you had. Damn shame, how they can take something good and taint it being thirsty and bullshit

But that's what they do, that's just how some dudes are bred and taught. It's too learned behavior. It's nothing for them to turn good dudes sour and it's crazy because these dudes are the majority. It used to be it was a few sour grapes that could turn the bunch bad. Now it's the bunch that's turning the few bad. I'm truly a firm believer of self preservation being one of the strongest motivations we have, which means to preserve self; self interest and do what it is we need to in order to achieve that.

A part of achieving that is being very mindful of who and what we're dealing with in our environment. It's definitely a science to how you deal with it. Once you overstand that then you can navigate your way through that maze known as yard life. Trust, it's complex to say the least and very contradictory. What's good for you though might not be good for me. I can do this a certain way but you can't. Situations can very much be the same but the results will play out very differently; a double standard indeed. A homie told another homie I can get away with shit you can't. Basically telling him I can do what I want to you but you can't do it to me. I can never say enough about dealing with prison, dealing with the different yards, and mind you again none are the same and function differently.

What goes on on this yard don't go on on the next yard, what's tolerated on this yard might not be tolerated on the next yard, so you're constantly having to adjust and re-adjust. The individuals will be different and move different and act different. You never know though, who's on the yard and how they function until you get on it. All you have to do anytime you pull up on a different yard though is observe and keep your ears open. Time reveals everything you need to know to make your adjustments accordingly. There's a lot of variables dealing with these different elements of the prison, the yard, and the individuals.

I can say this with strong conviction though and certainty, it's not about what you do but how you do what you do. It's definitely science to this madness. You move with the flow of traffic never against it, always with it but your way just mindful of your movement. What I mean by never move against the traffic, you never want to alienate yourself physically or by the things that come out of your mouth. Why? Because you'll make yourself a target for bullshit. You don't want to be the focus or need that attention. You open the door to bullshit. He don't want to be around the homies, you see how he stays away, you heard how he said such and such like he's better than us.

Now they're plotting on you and looking for a reason to DP you o have you DP'ed. You have to really be mindful. You have to pretty much make the alienation look like it's not your fault, if in fact that's what you're trying to do because you're not trying to be around the drama or not into what your homies are into. The reality of it is no one really mean you any good. They really could care less about you or what you're going through. They don't give a damn about your situation or your circumstances, and yeah it's always the closest ones to you that'll be the first to get you; looking to do you something at the slightest provocation. Here's a thought, all relations are made out of conveniences. As soon as our interest change the relationship change, trust and do believe the dynamics change.

It's the homie right now until something come up then they change on you. A dude can be on the yard with you for years and he'll be the one to DP you or be part of it; same shit, different stakes. There's nothing going on these yards or in these prison that's different than what's going on on the streets. It's just a different platform and space when something is at stake. It's the only difference, the stakes. On the streets you're dealing with material shit and finances, in here it's bullshit, soups, coffee, greenies, etc. depending on what the interest are. Today he's your friend, your homie, your boy, and your dog, tomorrow though he's your enemy or refuse someone something and they felt you were cool and see how they act towards you. It's never really the outsiders you have to be worried about.

You're not having issues or conflict with them like that if at all. It's those closest to you in your circle, the homie. It all stems from the homie who you're in relations with because of an interest and convenience. It's not the outsider you have to worry about, your interactions are limited. You know what the limits and boundaries are, where those lines are. I mean we all have dudes outside of our homies we fuck with and sometimes tough. Those outside relationships are at times better than relationships with a homie, different bond, different connection. There's no written or unwritten rule about exclusively dealing with the homies. Like I've told younger homies, just because a homie is a homie don't mean though you have to fuck with him do you. Can't anyone make you talk to another homie, hang out with him, or give him shit. That's your option at the end of the day. Your obligation is mainly to have his back and support him in the event of a situation and it's warranted. This is how I got the script when I first started my first prison term in '91. I was also told that if you don't want to live with a homie don't feel the need or obligation to, because you don't have to, sometimes it's best not to.

Just because you're homies or from the same city, same side of the block, or same set it doesn't mean you're compatible or will be. That doesn't automatically mean we're compatible based on us being from the same set, from the same block, from the same city. Doesn't mean shit and just because we're cool and hang out on the yard together doesn't just automatically make us compatible. You can be one way on the yard and totally different in the cell. You have a lot of dudes who will but who rather not live with a homie, because too living with a homie he feels privileged like there's no lines with what he can or can't do or what he can or can't have, playing the homie card. He's like in his mind "I'm the homie, I can do whatever I want. I can just go in the homie shit without asking. I can eat whatever, whenever. I can use whatever is his, we homies. He's not going to deny me shit, he's the homie".

Yeah when you live with homies they feel that type of privilege and feel they can't or shouldn't be denied based on being the homie. Then he might be a homie that's dirty and vermin. He don't and won't clean up behind himself, he don't wash his clothes, he's messy, he won't clean the cell, he barely takes showers and bird baths are out of the question. He'll come off the yard with his dirty yard clothes and hop on his bunk. So basically, be mindful of who you live with. It' is a small space, again just because our homies don't make you compatible. The dude you're with on the yard is not the same dude in the cell most of the time. Those are totally two different people. I've seen it and have experienced it, trust me I know firsthand. I'm not speaking on anything I have no knowledge of. Like you'll have cellies that fuck with the police, clown and joke with them, I don't. Outside of being cordial as to speaking when spoken to, I don't fuck with them. All of the clowning with them, that's not me. But yeah, dudes have two personalities and as different as night and day; cool on the yard but the most difficult person in the world to live within the cell, mood switches and all. Never saw those coming.

I don't like this, I don't like that, I don't do this this way, I don't do it that way. It's not the same person you fuck with on the yard. So back to the homies, the more of your homies there are the more chances of the bullshit to come into play internal and external. It'll always be something. It's a lot more personalities you're dealing with too. It's a lot more internal drama going on amongst each other and separation. Trust when I say something is always going on something is constantly going on. Even bullshit turn it on something when it's a lot of homies in the same space; a disaster waiting to happen indeed. On the internal this homie's fending with this homie, these homies don't really like these homies, these homies feel they're real homies, more official than those homies. These homies mad at this homie because he's not siding with them on an issue. These homies talk about these homies because they don't have anything. These homies feel this homie should be DP'ed because they don't like him so they're looking for a reason.

Then it's like these homies don't like you or aren't feeling you because you're not on the same shit they're on. These homies feel they're better than these homies, or it's I'm not fucking with this homie or these homies for this reason. It's just a bunch of bullshit every time you look around. With the external even more drama with it being a lot of homies. It get chaotic or let me just say it can get chaotic depending on the car. Every car don't function the same clearly and won't play that game or feed into it. What game? The numbers game, with the numbers you want to be the voice and the keeper. You do though have some homies, regardless of where they're from, demographic doesn't matter. If given the chance they'll flex their muscle and attempt to push their weight.

And let's call a ball a ball and a strike a strike. That includes talking to the police. Being able to move a certain way or do certain things, that's not a given. It's communication and overstanding amongst the powers that be and individuals within a group. The politics increase, the bullshit increase. It's like it's hard for them not to be in something or in the thick of it, because their presence has to be felt and their voice has to be heard. It's always a big production and it's like just based on the fact, the numbers are up. They feel they can press harder and be on some bully type shit and do whatever they feel like, feeling like they can get away with it.

Yeah you can for the time being but will most definitely pay for it later. Dudes don't always stay in comfort zones or remain with vast numbers. You always too pay for bullshit you do in the end. It doesn't matter who you are or who you think you are. That debt to karma will always get paid. One thing's for sure, she's going to get her issue. Whaaat!!! You do dirt, play dirty, dirt is coming back. It's how the ball bounces. Yeah, you can do what you do in the moment in that instance where you are. Just remember you won't always be there. At some point, you'll leave and go elsewhere and it'll come up. It always does.

It's just a whole different dynamic when the number game is being played and everyone around you can see it. It's no big mystery trying to press shorter cars, being quick to try to get on them, or trying to tell them how to DP their homie; the bully shit. Then it's like the attitude is fuck a diplomacy, let's do such and such because we can, we don't have to talk about nothing, what for, we don't have to this is just what we're doing. It's definitely a dirty game, some play fair and some don't. You see this a lot as I've said. It's not just with your own but with other factions too. But yeah, when it's a lot of you every time you look around it's an issue of some sort going on. If it's not internal it's external, at times both.

At times also a lot of the external is self-inflicted just because, or because of the numbers game. This is what you're dealing with when it's too many of you in the same space and at the same time, it gets ugly. Don't get me wrong though, or get it twisted. Every faction don't push or move like that, as far as on the numbers tip externally. So though it's bullshit and chaos for the most part with a lot of homies internally, a lot of it too be because the homie is bored and has nothing else better to do with himself, his time, or nothing going on, just miserable so he wants to make everyone else around him miserable. He has to keep something going on, especially amongst homies.

But yeah, chaos, that's the best way for me to explain it. Some people thrive on it, bullshit and dumb shit after bullshit and dumb shit, problem after problem. Little problems become big problems, little problems made into big problems and shit quickly escalates. Big problems don't always need a big response in my mind. Like little problems or issues don't need to turn into big problems or big issues, which is a quick way to get in a wreck. It's not just about you, your cause, or your agenda.

Yet, we're the homies but you don't' mind or have a problem putting us in harm's way. You don't give a fuck about getting us into a wreck or crashing us. It can be a instance where a homie doesn't let the rest of the homies know that he's about to take off on a dude, or play ball on him and he does it; which will be responded to quick. Not just that but he automatically draws the rest of the homies into id, period. That's just what it is, whether they want to be involved or not it's a collective. Though the homies know, it's a part of the game, they feel they're entitled to that heads up and rightfully so; so they can best prepare themselves for the situation and not be in the blind. They too overstand how spontaneity works, bam it's on! You fire a niggah shit up or play ball on him on the spot. At any rate, dudes are going to feel like it's an attack on their whole care and looked at as disrespect, period.

The mind set it's like how are you just going to take it upon yourself to attack our homie and the issue was never brought up or addressed. In all essence that's not yard or prison etiquette. You have to go through the channels, you can't just take off on someone. Well you're not supposed to. Technically, that's just not how it goes. I mean you can but expect what comes with that. You take off on or play ball on someone from another faction or race, automatically it's going to be a response from their collective. What would you do? How would you respond? What would your feelings be? No doubt, the conversation will be had after the fact if it's something to be conversed about.

Whether you're right or wrong and depending on the energy of the homies they're going to DP you for the blow back or feel pressured to and especially if you didn't go through the proper channels or hollered at them, you're going to get DP'ed. One because you didn't say anything to anyone and just moved, two because you didn't go through the proper channels, and three because you drew them into the bullshit. Fuck what the reason was, that's out of the window, it's irrelevant doesn't even matter. The reason holds no weight oh and don't let it be blow back. Then you leave and have to come back to the yard.

Come back to the yard after you go to the sandbox for however long. According to the homies you're still in debt, you have to pay your debt to the collective. Whether your homies want to or not, they'll be pressed too. To some it's complexed, to most it's simple math. But the thing is, it's like if you're not got on, then the collective can be got on for not getting on you. On the flip side, it depends on where you are and who's on the yard, what the dynamics are and what the outcome was of an incident, especially if there weren't any blow back for some reason or another and the incident was left as an isolated incident. It does happen.

Then in that instance, the dynamics are different and have changed. It might be left alone as far as with your homies and chalked up since their homies didn't respond for whatever reason and a discussion was had, homies aren't tripping. As far as homies are concerned though, okay, homies didn't clash with that other faction and no one got hurt collectively, they can let it go. Had they clashed though, had homies been hurt, that's a whole different ball game entirely and will be seen differently. Yeah, it's an issue. You do have problems, it's no getting around that champ. An instance that'll have homies crash or in a wreck and removed off of a yard as a collective is if you've created a Black issue and it's not dealt with internally, jeopardizing the community. It don't just affect the homies, but the Black population as a whole. Now you're affecting others outside of your car. That's no bueno! That can't happen and isn't tolerated no matter who you are or where you're from. It just can't happen.

All of the Blacks from everywhere will get on you and can and will be in the right. It'll be a collaborative effort and discussion. If the right decision isn't made, your whole car is voted off of the island. It's not a faction issue or a tribal issue, it's a Black issue and that outweighs the bullshit. Indeed, it's a quick way to get removed individually or collectively, getting into it with another race and it becomes an issue to the point it's an issue that the other race isn't trying to let go of it and is persistent with pressing it and the Black is In the wrong or out of pocket and it can potentially go somewhere else and the only way the issue can be resolved or squashed is if whoever the issue is initially behind or over that individual has to be DP'ed or removed depending on the situation or what's warranted. But it's either or, in order to keep the peace and the yard functioning. In any event, something has to be done. It can't just be swept under the rug or ignored. It has to be dealt with and confronted.

Amongst each other, Black on Black, it's an option depending on how severe the situation is. With another race it can play out the same way because there's always a bigger captured moment. There's always that question of is making an issue of something that's minor or not worth it really worth fucking off bigger captured moment, there's variables. Again, some things can be talked out and resolved that way using diplomacy instead of clashing but it's really because it's not in anyone's best interest. If in fact it's an issue that can potentially blow up the yard, cause a riot, and the individual or individuals aren't dealt with it'll no doubt become a bigger issue. The issue will escalate and become a racial issue, period.

Black versus Hispanics be it northern or southern Hispanics, Blacks versus Whites, Blacks versus Others; some will be emboldened to come like, "Look, this situation needs to be dealt with or it's going to be an issue" so with that warning, which is basically what it is "if you don't deal with the issue we'll deal with it our way". So before that happens or it comes to that, having the yard blown up and it escalates to a racial issue, the other factions will pull up on your car like, "Look, ya'll need to handle ya'll homies to kill the bullshit, because they're not trying to let it go and we don't need the yard blown up." Without directly saying it, it's an ultimatum.

Everyone concerned know what's being said without it being said. The language is universal when it comes to this maze, the yard. It's no secret, none at all, "He goes, they go, or you all go!" This is the way shit's been going since forever, you know what it is "Ya'll handle it or all of you get handled, period", no cut, that's just how the ball bounces, "Whaaat!" Get rid of your problem or it's going to be a bigger one. The one thing you can't do is jeopardize the whole community, putting them in harm's way behind a dude's stupidity or bad call. It's no doubt going to affect everyone, the yard and the community, because trust it'll be bally played and dudes will get hurt, some more serious than others. But they will get hurt, young and old. Any and everybody can get it and will get it. If it happens and you're on the yard, it's a possibility of you becoming a victim.

No matter if you done something, something was done to you though you might not of been seriously hurt point being harm was done. So yeah, with that your homies will pull up on you and ASAP. They have to, to resolve the issue or become victims themselves. Do you really think they're going to let that happen or transpire when it's way easier and less complicated to just remove you or whoever it is that needs to be removed? Do I really have to answer that question? That answer's been proven time and time again. That call is far too easy to make, you or them? Um... you!

It's always a bigger cause and no one's homies are above it or bigger than it. It's rules to this shit. Your homies aren't better than anyone else's, especially when it comes to this racial drama. Anything that's a racial factor or has a racial dynamic it's serious off the dribble and will be tooken serious because of the violence that ensues. Those of us that's been a part of racial drama knows that the drama doesn't end right away. It goes on and on at times until one side feels vindicated or satisfied. You can have one side feeling as though the other side is ahead on the score and don't want to feel one-upped so they'll want to keep it going to get even or feel even. At the end of the day, no one's trying to go through all of that especially if it can be avoided. It's a better option for everyone concerned, both sides trying to avoid the conflict if it can be avoided before it even starts or get to that point. Who wants war? Diplomacy will prevail and the issue will be resolved internally. Racial issues are always hot button issues. They aren't to be played with, period, or slept on, period, because they draw so many into it. Those are issues that are immediately dealt with. As an individual though, anytime it's an issue with another race all I can say is you better be on the right side of it because it's about to go bad for you, real bad.

If you're on the right side of it, it is what it is. Me personally, I've always told homies and tell homies always I don't care what the issue or situation is, be on the right side of it. Don't fall victim to the bullshit or autobotism, so that the homies that are politicians and into that realm can't politic you and ready to do something to you, which they have no problem doing; the jail politician or yard politician, whatever you want to call him. That's all he does, politic! He's always dealing with issues that's mainly involving his homies. He also deals with the outside factions when it involves issues with his homies or addressing them. All issues are brought to him to address or have addressed.

He'll be the one front and center, speaking on an issue. That's what he does. That's what he's into and that's what he's comfortable doing. I get and overstand someone has to be in that seagh though. He's going to be the one pressing for a DP if you're on the wrong side of a situation. He's the one who's going to be pressing for an issue to be resolved or to get resolved. Every car has a few, which sometimes lead to an internal power struggle because one of them or a couple of them wants to be head politician. Sometimes that draws homies into it and it causes separation, but for the most part the battle between them comes into play.

However everyone isn't fit for that role. You have good dudes with good and right intentions that are for maintaining a structure and not with the shenanigans. Then you have dirty ones that doesn't play fair or by the rules, he's in it for his-self. There's always a hidden agenda or motive, period, for how he moves and deals with things. He means you no good, or homies. Everything he stands for is bullshit. If he can cross you or have you in a fucked up situation, he will. He'll manufacture shit against you, he'll turn homies against you. He has no values or morals, a cold manipulator. Any and everything he can manipulate he will. Loyal he's not and should never be trusted. His whole movement consists of drama, he thrives on it.

Where drama isn't he creates it (SMH). He looks forward to waking up every day to do what he does on the yard. Again, some people thrive on bullshit and chaos and he's one. The dirty politician though always at some point meet their end, too caught up in their own hype and bullshit and don't see it coming. There always someone else who wants to be in that position, wanting that role and knows the game just a bit better and how to play it. Apparently so got you gone you were in the way and horse playing so yeah, if you're the problem it's an easy call; get rid of you problem is solved. That's the easiest shit in the world to do, remove you.

You put yourself in that position, so you have to deal with that. You as a part of a collective have to be very mindful of what you do and how you do it, especially when it affects more than you. It's not just about you, you as an individual don't matter, don't count when a bigger captured moment is factored in. You're disposable, expendable, you have other people and homies to consider to be factored in when you're on some bullshit. Your actions or foolishness just doesn't affect you, it affects me, it affects him, him, him and him too. It affects the whole community, the whole Black population with the racial shit.

Anything outside of you being mindful, having consideration for everyone else, you're being selfish and are basically saying fuck everyone else; making it about you and what you have going on. So yeah, you have to be removed, we don't need you around, you're a liability to us all. You're a disaster waiting to happen, off with your head. Shit, you don't care about my head, you don't care about a homie's head, or the next man's head as far as that goes. You don't even care about your own head, you couldn't possibly be and that makes you dangerous. So you're voted off the island, get up out of here. I've seen this instance play out time and time again on many of the yards I've been on, not just with my homies but with other factions too. No one is exempt.

There's always that one idiot! As you offer hear, you make your bed, you have to lay in I, especially in this maze of unbalanced madness. It's like determining the course of a bullet, is it fate or is it physics? You're playing with your survival, which is the first law of nature in the land of the beast next to self preservation. It goes to the question what do you do to a dude that threatens your survival, safety, or freedom? We make choices and conscious decisions to move left or right. We reap rewards or disasters of the choices and decisions we make, period.

With that you're living yard life. That means that you agree to live and move by the rules that govern the yard, thus you'll be held accountable for all actions, choices, or decisions that goes against what's been set forth. One thing though I can say about prison, the prison codes of today (2000's) doesn't mean the same as they once did; who different dynamic. The codes truly took on a whole different meaning and identity. You can't believe at of what you hear from these illusionists, dirty politicians and autobots, you never know when there's a motive behind something. The trust and loyalty is rare. You have to rewind your whole day, every conversation and every interaction you've had with people before you go to sleep at night. I know I do before I close my eyes for the night I rewind my whole day, playing everything back in my head, every conversation and every interaction I've had with individuals during the day. I leave nothing to chance, you can't, look where you are. Look at the type of dudes we're forced to deal with and be around on a daily. You're in prison and on a prison yard. Something might've gotten by you at that brief moment and went pass you, but when you're laying down about to go to sleep and you rerun the day you definitely catch what wasn't caught earlier. But yeah, for the most part I concern myself with issues that concern me, those I fuck with and my general well being. I don't care what the next man is doing, don't care what he have, what he don't have. What he's eating don't make me shit either way.

What you're doing don't affect me until it does. Otherwise I'm not affecting your program and you're not affecting mine in the slightest. I don't care if you don't like me or fuck with me, you know why? Because outside of just not giving a fuck I wasn't put on this earth to care about whether or not you feel I'm cool enough to fuck with. I'm in my own lane, which is where I stay and intend to stay. I'm comfortable being in it. I'm minding mine and not yours. I do me and mind my business, I deal with who I deal with and associate with. Outside of that I'm there when I need to be as part of the collective.

I'm not with all of the extras just because, nor am I with the nonsense. I'm not a politician. I leave that to those who're in that mode and who's into that. That's just not my lane, I'm good, that's not my look. It's never been me. The shit I was on I kind of out grew it. I will say this though and from my overstanding and experience you can change with the times and without compromising your integrity and morals. Dudes act like though it's a crime to evolve (SMH), going nowhere fast. Seems like the only way to navigate for some.

Being on the yard, it's nothing to dive into serious depths. It's there if that's what you're looking for and what floats your boat until it sinks. Waves has no mercy when the water's choppy. I don't see the yard any more as just the yard. I see the dark buildings. I can also tell you, you don't know what's going to happen from day to day on the yard. It can go from no drama, the yard being cool, no issues and quiet then change in an instance to someone having ball played on them, two on one'd, someone's going to the sandbox, not to mention a riot or melee could happen, out of nowhere the yard blows up. Sometimes shit just happens on the yard spontaneously. Boom it's on! It's happening and you respond accordingly, especially if it's directed towards you, or your race, or your homies. You just have to respond in that moment.

No time for planning or plotting, most of the time though shit's premeditated. The spontaneous activity is not as bad because too many aren't prepared for it. Maybe a handful are security conscious. A big maybe to truly be prepared for something and must actually expect it, but as the adage goes "if you stay ready you don't have to get ready". It's the premeditated activity though you have to concern yourself with and prepare yourself for, because you know what you're playing for and how shits being played. You know the stakes. You know what's going on and how it's coming, it's no puzzle. You might not know the when or where, you just know it's inevitable and it's in the air. You know the probability of it happening.

It really comes down to who's going to initiate it or fire the first shot. Nowadays, the police know too what's going on before it happens. It was already put in their ear "Aye, we need to take care of one of our own" for such and such reason or "Aye, we need to handle this to prevent that from happening: or whatever the situation is they're given heads up for the most part. I don't know when that became a part of the script, but it's the norm now. So the police are aware of a lot of things before hand, and allowing certain shit to take its course and play out for the greater cause, I assume. To them I'm also assuming it's basically a preventative measure. Allow this to prevent that, the goal being it's to keep the bigger bullshit down, controlling the chaos, gaining a better result. In this instance you can resist the bromide that everything happens for a reason. It's like they can go with the noise when it's on their terms and it's not imposed on them. I'm aware and overstand the rules of engagement in this particular setting. That's how I'm able to navigate my way through this maze. Most importantly, I'm receptive of and to the constant realities. As I've said, you're constantly coming to learn, know, and overstand different things being on the yard; teachable lessons, no doubt.

Like dealing with your emotions, our emotional states change. What our gut tells us, our gut is better at helping us in situations like determining whether we're in danger and it helps with identifying our preferences. It too helps ups make complex decisions and choices when we're clouded or have a lot going on and being overwhelmed with things, mainly choices. However, if the outcome of our choice will affect someone else it's not best to rely on our gut by itself. When should you though trust your gut? Pretty much you're supposed to trust it with the complex decisions.

If the stakes are high you have to try and think rationally. You're supposed to pay attention to your state of mind. Remember though off top that strong emotions can change your intuition, which we all have for the most part. If you're in your feelings, your gut will give you a different look than it normally would. That's why I've stressed you can't be clouded or distracted, especially with the things that are mainly out of your control. We really can't allow ourselves or afford ourselves to be clouded or distracted with the trivial shit that doesn't really matter.

What does matter is your focus on this present reality, this yard, this yard life, your world for the time being. You have a lot of dudes running around on these yards in denial and concerned about too many of the wrong things and with too many of the wrong things. What I can say though about denial, it's a funny thing. I've come to learn though you'll never know what it'll make a dude do or say (SMH), like with an instance of someone not having their homie around anymore to counter balance his tendency to gravitate towards bullshit or bullshit dudes. I'll add this before, I gain switch lanes, sometimes you wish you could take shit back but in yard life there's no rewind or un-kicking that rock you kicked.

You're turned on and if you don't follow suit or go along with whatever's going on right or wrong, they'll turn on you. This is the present climate. You have to remember the relationship is based on convenience anyway, so it's easy to turn on someone when it's in their best interest; turn or be turned on. It's a dirty game, a dirty game no doubt. Another type o individual you'll deal with and will come across is the one that wants any and everything he sees (SMH). You have a lot of these type running around. He'll see something and just because he visual sees it he'll ask for it or for some of it.

"Aye, can I get some of that. Can I have one of those. Can I get a little of it?" He wasn't thinking about it, nor was it at any point on his mind but as soon as he sees it he wants it. "Can I have, can I get" I used an example. Talking to New Year about how I had just got some oatmeal from Lon who had just dropped it off in front of my cell. Chumlee saw it there and he immediately asked for some it which I didn't mind it was nothing but if oatmeal had been on his mind or he wanted oatmeal he would've pulled up on me and asked me if I had any long before he saw it just sitting in front of my cell. Clearly he didn't want oatmeal until he saw oatmeal, which is the behavior of a lot of dudes and how they are.

He just couldn't see it sitting in front of my cell and not ask for none. That was too too much like right to see it and not ask for it. But you want to know what's real crazy, not one time since I was in the cell with him in all of the times he'd been to canteen he never bought oatmeal nor brought up buying oatmeal, not once. You have plenty of hims though. Those type are very common, like stuff but won't buy it only like it when someone else has it or buy it. You like oysters but won't buy them. You won't buy them, you won't be eating them. You drink coffee but won't buy none, or you drink coffee but buy the cheap shit but you want to drink Folgers, the next Niggah's Folgers.

You eat cheese crunchies but won't buy them. You better get your priorities straight. It's just crazy to me how these dudes' minds work. I'm going to buy what I want not what I like though, because I can get it from the next man or from my cellie. You have to make sacrifices if it's an either or choice. You get this but can't get that, you have to get what you like don't think you're going to buy what you wanted to and then think I'm going to give you something you could've bought but chose not to, you had enough. It didn't or doesn't matter if I had five or twenty, no! I bought what I bought because that's what I liked, that's what I wanted (SMH). Apparently I liked it, because I bought it, period point blank. You buy what you like.

The dudes that really kill me are the ones that see you come from canteen but will ask you "Aye you want to trade this for that". Dude, I just came from canteen, if I wanted that I could've just bought it. What I bought, I specifically wanted. I didn't buy it to trade it (SMH). Now what you would've been better off doing was asking me could I grab something for you specifically and you have such and such. Nine out of ten it would've been easier to switch something around not a problem, but you want to see me come back and then ask (SMH). But yeah, back to where I was, a lot of them though only like stuff when someone else buy it. I've had a couple of past cellies that were like that outside of Chumlee. But I wouldn't say anything until they went to canteen or got a package, to see if they bought the same shit they liked so much when I bought it. I couldn't wait to see, after the second package or second time going to the canteen. Once I still didn't see them buy any of the shit they liked so much when I bought it, I called them on it. I had to. I'm like looking at them pull shit out of their bags putting it away, never noticing the stuff they liked so much. "Damn my niggah, I thought those chorizo and beans went crazy (were really good)!" or hit them with the "I see, you didn't snatch up none of that bomb ass shredded beef. I could've swore you liked that, how off the chain you said it was!"

This niggah was sucking his teeth and picking shredded beef out of them talking about "Aye Tic, let me get one of your tooth picks my niggah. This shit's sticking all in my teeth" (SMH). Again, you use tooth-picks but won't buy them. They sell them in the canteen and you can get them the whole time, I'm saying, "I see you didn't snatch up none of that bomb ass shredded beef" I was hanging over the side of my bunk, looking down at him taking stuff out of his bags. Then came the reason why he didn't buy whatever it was I spoke on; oh I forgot, oh it wasn't oh my mind, or you should've reminded me. Whaaat!

From that point on the situation was different. I saw shit from a whole different perspective. Yeah, you're one of those dudes, the bullshit type looking to get over where ever he can. So I had to cut that short real shit, nah, we won't be shitting the same things, not unless you're buying it for yourself. Yeah, it's small, I totally agree but not when I see you're trying to take advantage of my kindness and coolness. I'm not no trick, sucker, or victim. You have me confused.

Like come on now, what type of shit are you on. I'm very versed in this maze. I can see through shit and read individuals. Once I see your type and you're one of those dudes I'll back up off of you and switch courses. The other night me and New Year were talking, which we're always doing, constantly doing about something or another. So I'm telling him more about McNeal, we were talking about females in general though. I was saying how I would be Skyping with her pretty much every day after she got off of work. We would Skype all the way, until she made it home. Then she would go in her room with me still on the phone and watching her. Then she would get naked after walking through the living room saying morning to everyone, me included.

They knew it was me on the phone. It was our daily thing. After she got naked, she would get her toy out and get in the bed, opening her legs, playing with herself for me; her way of sharing intimacy with me. That played out every morning. It was a every morning session. Her letting me watch her play with herself. I even told him about the time she had came home from work and was in the shower and had the phone positioned for me to watch her shower and play with herself. But while she was playing with herself her sister came knocking on the bathroom door, Shadeena was pregnant at the time. "Bitch, I gotta pee. Let me in!"

McNeal was like, "Bitch wait a minute." She was just about to have an orgasm. Again after she did, she got out of the shower, went and opened the door. "Damn bitch, what you in here doing?"

She rushed in the bathroom and pulled her pants down. I could hear her peeing. She just so happen to turn around and see McNeal's phone and how it was angled. She knew then what was going on. "Oooh bitch, you up here being nasty. I know what you in here doing! Nasty ass. You nasty too Tic!" I started laughing. Damn right, I was being nasty though. I'm in prison, I'm trying to see something; some tittles, some ass, and some pussy, and it's moving! New Year fell out laughing. Shit, it had been like eleven or twelve years since I'd seen a naked bitch, let alone one playing with herself for me. Whaaat! Hell yeah, I was looking and I thoroughly enjoyed the performance. I was glued to my gadget anytime she would do it for me. Whaaat! She was letting me watch her play with herself in the shower. She also done it for me in the car parked a couple of times. But yeah, these are the types of stories we'd tell each other. It's just a part of it, especially with cellies. You'd tell each other all times of stories. We don't just talk about prison shit or yard shit, really we're not trying to talk about that. We're living it and dealing with it daily.

We're talking about life, we bounce ideas or thoughts off of each other, talk about getting out. We talk about relationships, the good and the bad shit. We talk about bitches we've had sex with, how we had sex with them, how we met them. We talk about gang banging. We talk about homies, we talk about the set. We talk about how we're hustling or how we hustled and how things have changed. Every conversation or story can be learned. That's why you'll hear sometimes, dudes come out better criminals than when they went in, or he came out worse than when he went in. You pretty much talk about all types of shit.

A lot of my stories are funny too because I'm very animated when I'm telling a story, especially when I'm talking about females. I make faces, sounds, and crazy ass movements. I bring the situation to life, you can't help but to laugh at my theatrics. New Year was telling me I needed to have a podcast, just talking about my situation or as he dubbed her "Louie the 13th" from a lot of the antics and stunts I'd told him she had going on. I kept him laughing; he's always saying "that's funny". We've tapped on a few other things as well, which we do often. We start off talking about one thing and end up somewhere else, which is where most conversations go, like this book. Bounce from topic to topic. You'll start off talking about the yard and end up talking about TMZ and who was on it.

You never stay on topic they're always switching it up. It does make for good conversation though. We were talking about how you have dudes who will sell their personal stuff (property) because they want to get something they need or something they want and will. The need could be anything, running out of food, cosmetics, or whatever. It could be a debt they owe for something they'd gotten, could be for anything, or just something someone has and they want. So the conversation was like dudes will sell their shit if they needed or wanted something bad enough. I can agree to that, I've seen it, you do have those type. They'll sell their CDs, TV, CD player, hot pot, fan, shoes, whatever if it's going to get them what they need or want.

They have no problem liquidating a few things and without giving it a second thought, trust, there's always someone in the market for whatever it is you're selling. It may just be a hot commodity at that time. In any event, you won't have a problem getting it off depending on what it is you're trying to dump (get rid of), for the most part it'll get sold. I get too, to some everything has a price ad is for sell If someone need or want something bad enough. For me though, nothing that belongs to me is for sell for no reason, not happening. It'll just go without something before I start selling off my shit like a crack head, especially some shit my people spent their loot on. If it's something I got off of the land (the yard) it's a different story. I look at that like crack head shit, clucking (selling shit) you'll sell any and everything you have or get your hands on. I don't care what the reason is, I'm not going to be able to do it.

To me it's just not that serious, I don't have habits and I don't do debts. Outside of that, whatever it is I don't have I'll just wait until I can get it another way at another time. Sell my CD player, TV, CDs, hot pot, clothes, shoes, whatever, that's no bueno! It's not going to happen, not at all. I have a problem with clucking my shit off. I don't need anything bad enough to make me sell my shit or will want it bad enough. For those though that do and will cluck it off, I feel your struggle. Do what you do. I don't knock it if that's your thing. You have to do what's right for you. It's just not for me. I do though have an exception which is if I got it off of the land, it's for all intent and purposes of getting rid of it at some point. I'll sell it because that was my sole reason for buying whatever it was. I bought it to sell, it was an investment. I bought it dirt cheap to be sold off or possibly traded off at a later time if I needed to, or if it was a win-win for me. The outcome had to result in me making out on the sell or the trade. My yard version of stocks and bonds, buy low sell for more, or buy low and someone may come along wanting what you have and willing to make a trade with you for a greater value because what you have is of value to them.

With yard stocks and bonds it has to make sense or add up, period, for me to get rid of stock or bond. Then our conversation switched to how you have dudes that'll play this type of game with you where if they're selling something and you who too much interest in it, the games begin or the price goes up (SMH). Oh I don't know if I really want to sell it, I don't want to sell now, I'll let you know, let me think about it. They were asking for xyz, now it's xyz plus tuv then you just have to hit the delete button and be like you're cool. As soon as you show too much too much interest that's what's going to happen. Not with everyone though, just the bullshit dudes with the games and shenanigans.

Trying to up the ticket (price) on you, knowing you want it so basically you're willing to pay what he wants now. Seeing how bad you want it, now you're negotiating and he's constantly saying "Nah, what else you got? Throw this in or that in and we got a deal". You open that door of interest, too much interest, this is what you'll open yourself up to, shenanigans. I get flustered and frustrated quick, my patience isn't having none of it so I'm like, "You know what, I'm good!" I don't want it. I don't have time for all of that, that's too much wasted energy. Then the topic still within the same realm but went to how you have dudes with a little loot or fortunate, how they feel with them having loot, or being fortunate they can just buy any and everything they want, even people because they have loot or the means. I told New Year that's not necessarily the case because you can have all the loot in the world and your loot don't spend it's no good. You might as well have Mexico's money, Chinese's money, African money or Russian's money. You can have the loot and still can't get what it is you're trying to get from that person, that person just refuses to sell it to you. Someone can though, just not you. The message is "Your money don't mean shit, only to you, it does." You can't get every and anything you want, everything doesn't have a price tag, every person doesn't have a price whether you can afford it or them or not.

With me, it's not the case. I don't care what you have or how much of it you have, nothing of mine is for sell nor can I be bought, what you have don't move or impress me. I'll deny you, whether I'm selling something or not just because you asked me. If I was selling something just based on the fact you feel you can buy whatever it is I have and you want it. You can't afford my ticket, why? Because I don't have one and especially not for you. I'm not selling you anything nor can we work out any type of deals, that would be a no go! I have nothing for you. In your mind, you're the niggah. You're privileged, feel entitled and nobody will turn you down, you can buy or have anything you want, which is clearly not always the case.

There are a few of these type on every prison yard, I've ran across several. It doesn't matter if you have it to spend, your loot is no good here. Not just that type but anyone, for the most part, because I don't sell my shit whether I needed or wanted something or not. Mine is not for sell, don't ask, keep it moving. I had an instance though, where I have some art books that teaches you different drawing and shading techniques. I lent them to someone when he saw what I had, I saw his mind working. He didn't say anything right then, he immediately though was working out in his mind how he would get the books from me, not knowing it wasn't going to happen and he was going to get shut down. It didn't matter what the offer was on the fact I don't draw nor have any interest in it, but what I do do is trace patterns on card stock and color them, which I'm good at and cool with doing. I'm not an artist, far from it. As far as I go is tracing and coloring and making cards to send to my aunt, moms, or do as a hustle occasionally, which I haven't done in years. Dudes always buy those type of cards and I would charge two to three dollars for them depending on size. Saying all of that to say I don't draw, so there's really no reason for me to own them but I do.

Anyway they're not for sell, plus they're gifted to me by the homie Dirty Mike who went home last year which is another reason they're not for sell. I don't part with anything given to me by someone else. That's just not how I operate, so when he brought the books back I waited for his pitch which he shot, which fell on deaf ears. The first thing out of his mouth though, "You know you don't draw, Tic." Then he came with, "I'm not saying you need to sell them but", there's the but. I already knew what was coming next. "Do you want to sell them. You Know I draw, I could use them."

This, that, and the third, more reasons I should sell the books to him, I have this, I have that, I have the other meant nothing to me. It was wasted energy and wasted breath he could've used for breathing. "Nah homie, I don't sell my shit. I don't need anything, I'm not in need of anything."

"Well, if you do ever decide to sell them, let me know and I got you just let me know what you want."

I'm like, "I'll do that!" He'll be waiting on that "ever decide", it'll never come. He just assumed in his mind I could use the loot and I would just up and sell the books to him. That's all it was, an assumption, his bad though for assuming. If I have something to sell or have something I needed to sell I'll put it out there, let it be known. Aye I have such and such for sell and I want this, that, or the other for it.

If that was the case when I even spoke on having the books, knowing he draws, I would've said then, "Aye Gordo, I have these drawing books, I don't draw, I know you do though, I'll let you check them out. If you like them, I'm willing to sell them", but you asking me do I want to sell them, off the dribble, it's not bueno! You're shut down. Even if I thought about it, it was over you buried your action at them. Because now, I feel like you're implying something, implying I'm a bum, I'm broke, and I have to sell m shit, and you have what I need, want, or can use, like you're looking down on me or some shit. The reality of it though, you see what I want you to see, choose for you to see. At the end of the day, you don't know what I have or don't have in my cell, nor do you know what I'm doing or how I'm doing it.

You had me confused with that situation with Chumlee that night we were in the dayroom and you were there when the South Siders, PK and Lil Man, got at him asking him about some throwaways (warn out shoes) to turn in and they had looked straight down at his feet. Yeah, we know the implications there. You're wearing throwaways, they're right there on your feet where we're looking. Can we get those? Everyone right there started laughing. He got in his feelings, which evaporated when ten dollars were on the table. They only go for three to five dollars. Whaaat! I guess Gordo thought I was working out of that kit. "Uh… no!" Nah homie, not me.

It's not your business to know what's going on with me if I don't invite you. I don't put my business out there, dudes talk too much. You'll never know what I'm doing, how I'm doing it, or how I have what I have. As far as you know, I'm a bum and I'm broke. If that's your conclusion, so be it. I'm not going to correct you, I really don't care what you think and that's just in general. "I ain't got shit!" Maybe that'll keep you from asking for shit or keep the vultures away thinking I don't have shit. You can't get anything from someone who don't have anything. Dudes are nosey as fuck, always watching and looking to see what the next dude is doing or have going (SMH). Just so they can gossip and speak on you with the next niggah, watching to see what's coming in or out of your cell. They're worse than the old lady living on the block, peeping out of her blinds (SMH), "Don't watch me watch TV!" Back to how dudes talk too much, they do they talk and gossip like broads; always speaking on shit, whether it's about a person or about a situation. Especially the dudes that can't hold water, keeping something said to himself, you can tell him, "between me and you" keep it between me and you, it goes no further. All of that should've been implied when you said "between me and you" it means it stays between us, don't go running your mouth about what I'm about to tell you. Do not tell anyone, anyone period.

You would think though, you wouldn't have to say it, but you do at times, and to certain people "between me and you" mean just that, between me and you. That doesn't mean go tell the next person. You might as well not have said that at all. It basically fell on deaf ears. That shit went in one ear and out of the other. He's going to run his mouth, no doubt, whoever he tells is going to tell someone else, especially around here. Before you know it, it's all over the yard. He ran his mouth and whoever he told ran their mouth and I'm pretty sure he told him the same thing you told him "between me and you". You might as well have just said, "Between me, you, and everybody else".

In some instances it'll make it back to you. Whaaat! You know where it came from and who you told. He was the only person you told it to. It came from no one else, he's the culprit (SMH). He was the only person you told something to. You know where it came from, he'll swear up and down it wasn't him, he didn't say shit, he don't get down like that. It's crazy when you tell a dude something or anyone for that matter and the shit gets back to you. But yeah, it's hard as fuck for these dudes to keep shit to themselves. It's a damn shame. It's like they just have to run their mouth. Anything you speak on, it's at your own risk. You really have to be mindful of who you're telling something to, if and when you do. I don't care how many times you start off with "between me and you".

It's bad though when you tell someone something in confidence and it's boomeranged. You already know for a fact off the dribble, you have to cut him off. Just stop fucking with him like that because he can't be trusted and he can't hold water. How can you really deal with someone you can't trust? You don't, it's a wrap. When you suddenly park the relationship, you don't have to say why, he knows what it is. No explanation needed, nothing needs to be verbally communicated. My actions are going to show I'm not fucking with you no longer. If you don't want shit to get out, it's best you keep it to yourself. It's no different than when you're on the streets and you just finished having sex with your bitch and you're laying up in the bed talking. You don't pillow talk the business.

Why? Because you know like I do at some point your business will be the topic of a conversation to her friend or the next dude. She's going to run her mouth. I was in a situationship with situation. I didn't talk to her about shit. I didn't trust her like that. She wasn't to be trusted, period. It's no different though dealing with these dudes. There are a handful of dudes though that knows how to keep shit to themselves. Hear shit and don't hear them, respect between me and you for what and as it is. They do exist, they're rare and are the exception to the rule, but they exist.

Around here though (high desert) there are no secrets for the most part. If it's something to be spoke on, it's spoke on, and it spreads around the yard like a virus. It doesn't even have to be a serious issue and everyone knows it. It don't even have to be true or have no truth to it, it's just out there and dudes run with it like it's gospel (SMH). Autobots! The shit will be manufactured and dudes will still run with it, as I've expressed earlier in the book. Like with some politicians they're always looking to change the narrative to fit their objective, so they lie.

To be one you have to know how to manufacture bullshit, you have to know how to lie and manipulate, to make shit look good. For the most part, everything going on with them is a façade, nothing is real or what it seems. From what I've seen, you can be 18 to 80, you can get and will get it; wheelchair, cane, limping, don't give a fuck. You do anything not agreed with, you're gonna get it! But yeah, everyone knows everyone's business, some go out of their way to know something (SMH), want to know any and everything, dudes are nosey and watch everything around here, you don't always have to be told something to know something. You can be nosey, being nosey though can be a health hazard. Some dudes don't know how to even be nosey without appearing to be nosey, there's a method to any type of madness.

It's not what you do but how you do it, if that's your thing. I was told though, when I first got here, "Yeah homie, everyone around here knows everybody's business, there are no secrets at High Desert, you speak on something everybody's going to know" (SMH). All Niggahs do, ever do around here, is talk and gossip, talk about the next niggah, even talk about and badmouth their own homies. I'm listening to him, "Just fall back and watch, you'll see what I'm talking about. Don't trust none of these Niggah's homie, they're suuuper bullshit!", of course I logged in the advice. He's been here. It was sound advice, none the less it didn't take me long to weed out the bullshit dudes, how they move, how they speak, it all exposes itself. All you have to do is be patient.

Yeah, patience is a virtue, eyes and ears open, all you need to know will come to you. It'll surface, what's in the dark will reveal itself. Nothing valuable can be lost by being patient. There's nothing to lose but much to gain. The means justify the means. They talk, all you have to do is listen, which brings me to this point, you absolutely have to be mindful of what you say to or around dudes in general. I saw that first hand, how easy and quick shit can go bad, getting a dude caught up. You have to be mindful, point blank. You're talking bad about a dude to a dude he fuck with, socialize with, (SMH).

Whether he's on the street or on the yard, you're speaking foul about him to someone he fucks with. Whether you realize it or not, you've made an enemy. You never know who you're talking to, or who you're talking around. That's a quick way for shit to get repeated. You best believe it's going to get back to who you were speaking on, best believe it.

It works both ways, internally and externally, within your car, causing a disaster. Finding yourself politicked and DP'ed. You tell this dude something, not knowing if he deals with your homie or the other dude you're speaking on. You don't know if that dude deals with someone that deals with the dude you're speaking on, or your homie, you're just reckless with your mouth. That's the only way I can put it. You have a lot of that though, just quick to speak.

One thing you have to be mindful of and overstand, a lot of dudes are connected to different dudes some type of way you never know the relationships, you never know who socialize or deal with who. It's so many interactions and relationships, even unlikely ones come about. You can never say for certain who deals with who and who don't. Just because it's not visible don't make it nonexistent, you're just not privy to it. Bottom line, you don't know. You're on a yard and mind you the yard isn't that big, and it's like four buildings per yard, so there's interactions and communications constantly. There are various variables dealing with this yard life on the yard and how they function, and can function. I can't speak on enough how complex the yard is.

Everyone's not built or made for this shit. It's not for everyone. You have to shit or get off of the top. It's mentally, emotionally, and physically hazardous. Mindfulness plays a big part in your walk, and yeah one of the other things to be mindful of is being mindful of who it is you're talking to. It's really a way, an easy way, to find yourself twisted or crossed up in some bullshit, not knowing. You never know who you're talking to, who that person is talking to, or who he deals with. So, likely the chances of something getting back to someone you spoke on are high. The chances of it being repeated is high, especially if it was something negative. Oh and without a doubt, for effect, something's going to be added or took out. It's never going to be repeated the same way that it was told. It has to be verbal theatrics (word play). Must I repeat it again, it's levels to this yard life. However, your walk on the yard will never be the same as the next dude's, the shoes aren't the same size. The walk don't have to be difficult, size don't matter, it's about your choices, your decisions, your movements, and your mindfulness. Your walk is your walk, yours to walk, how you choose to walk it is your call.

I can't feel your pain or your struggle, nor can the next man. It all boils down to you being proactive in your walk as only you do and can. Set a standard and adhere to it. Do know though, what and who you're dealing with, for the most part. Also know what and who you're dealing with has nothing to do with truth or reason. These dudes aren't capable of it, aren't capable of either. This yard life is for those who want to be here. It's what I know to be true. They're cool with politicking and hanging on the yard, they're cool with keeping drama going on and feeding off of it, content with the life style and happy with it, content with being here in a mindset I could never move to. They'll also show you all of their cards at once, no challenge.

On some real shit, I don't care enough about any of them to dislike them. I just know who not to trust or befriend. Your walk is your walk. There's two ways though to navigate your walk, the easy route or the hard route. There's no middle route or middle ground. Make it light on yourself, my niggah, it's way deeper than what's going on on the surface, set up the overplay for the under play. With that, do the yard. Don't let the yard do you, let go of what in the great scheme of things don't really matter, people included, inside or outside. Like with you're going to shake a dude's hand or dap him, and neither match the smile, you can tell, he's not right. But hey, most of them aren't what they seem to be anyway. In this yard life, as with most things aren't what they seem to be. In this yard life, it's full of illusions and illusionists. I'll tell you what isn't an illusion, these younger dudes not having respect for older homies. Every time you look around it's a situation going on. The younger dudes feeling like the older homies are washed up and all of the fight in them left, feeling like also they have an easy win (SMH) some may've lost a step but not all of us, I'm very much still an active old niggah. I just see the shit that's going on around me and just shake my head. I'm like, this shit is crazy and it's actually flying, older homies being DP'ed and two on one'd by these young dudes. They have no problem with it either.

But yeah, you have to learn how to think your way through and work around certain situations and people, to achieve the result you want, navigation, especially knowing when dudes have more opportunity. They tend to turn up and act on that opportunity, again it's never about what you do but how you do what you do. Me, I pride myself on being genuine, one way, and structured; mindful of knowing to every move you have to have a smart reaction, period. Dudes are not playing fair, to know this is to overstand what's going on; knowing what I know, knowing what I've come to overstand, that vibe and that combination of what I've seen, thought, learned and felt.

Being able to differentiate between real and real bullshit, this is based on us living in a world where everything is for the most part controlled and manufactured. In here we only have a past and a future, get a bar. The present is just another yesterday that'll never matter to nobody but us, on this note though, I don't care who we are when we look at the reality of our push (walk) on these yards and look at who we are in the eye, humility supposed to follow. We might act out of ego or even pride but even as we act we know we're nothing special. We know we have our issues, our flaws, our drama, and our baggage. We know that at times we're hypocrites. As we know that often enough we try to be something or someone other than we actually are. We also know for a fact that we're no one to judge or shouldn't be judging when we're not living right. We're no better than the next man, we all have what? Issues, flaws, drama, and baggage in our space, we can't throw rocks, bricks, or stones, shit, we can't even kick a can. He who's without sin, issues, flaws, drama, or baggage cast the first rock, brick, or stone, or kick that can. We criticize, dislike, and despise, we know we shouldn't be judging anyone else because at the end of the day if we were to be judged by some of the same standards that we use, shit, we'll find ourselves condemned, and that's calling a ball a ball and a strike a strike.

This is what plays out on my mind's movie screen and what translate into reality. One thing's for certain though, if you're wearing a mask on the yard you won't and can't hide behind it forever. One thing about a mask you'll come to know, it's always one that's going to give you away and expose you. Be who you are, play your position and your role. That's some of the soundest advice I can give to any young homie, Crip, Blood, Bay Area, or civilian. Anything outside of that would be a misoverstanding. However and with that advice is this, you can learn a lot about yards and individuals on them if you're patient enough to observe. You have to exercise patience, with patience comes the overstanding of twenty percent being the things that happen to us and the other eighty percent are how we respond to them. It goes back to navigation, navigation is everything.

Yesterday, me and New Year, I believe it was yesterday, had gotten into dealing with people on the streets. Specifically, how they will tend to pop in and pop out. Pop in and Pop out after years of not fucking with you, no connection, communication, or contact of any kind, zero communication, zero contact, dead air. I was telling him about how a family member had just popped up recently, just before he'd moved in and I hadn't heard from them in years, a decade plus. It was out of the blue and unexpected. She pulled up on me. I just one day get a dot and dashes like, "Hey, how are you, this, that and the third". I thought it was moms, my son, or my cuzzo, Nip. It was neither, I entertained it though. I had already decided to send everyone's mail back, return to sender outside of those three, which I went against and will never happen again. Just know any mail in the future will be returned, return to sender, thank you Kemaijaye for reminding me how bullshit so-called family are, good looking out! So anyway, I told New Year how I got the song and dance from her bullshit ass. Here's my number, it didn't work, I love you, I miss you, I'm working, if you need anything get at me. I responded to her but never even commented on her telling me if I needed something to get at her, why? Because for one, I knew it was just smoke (talk).

I knew it was just her making conversation, I didn't take her serious, I knew it had no substance behind it. That and the fact she only said it because she felt obligated to say it, felt obligated to put it in the air which she shouldn't have. In my opinion and experience, it's common practice, everyone does it. It means nothing. The intent off the dribble is bullshit clearly. It's only mere words being expressed, the gesture and reach is empty. Nor did I mention the captured moments she claimed she would be sending. Why? Again, it was just smoke. If the intent was there captured moments would've came with the dots and dashes, not I'll send you some (SMH). I knew it was more conversation without substance and her feeling like it was something she felt she needed to say.

I bit though, entertained her and responded, never got a reply. I never got a response from my reply to her, again dead air. Never, so I'm like, "Ok, I recognize!" After a few weeks, damn near a month, I'm like, I'm about to hit her up, pull up on her. I wrote her and was like, "What was your reason for even writing me, I don't get it. You already weren't fucking with me (communicating with me) what was the point?" I don't get it, and didn't get it, what was the reason? Oh and mind you, I tried the number she sent me too and it didn't work. I tried it several times but to no avail. I was never able to connect, not once. I never got through (SMH) I tried more than a few times. My whole attitude to that first was bitch never again! You'll never get that action again! For the simple fact you could've just left me the fuck alone, like you've been doing. I was good, been good! You should've left me buried, like the rest of the so-called family I hadn't heard from in over a decade! But yeah, as a matter of a fact you can bury me again and don't ever dig me up, and for the rest don't even try digging me up. I'm not fucking with you, period! Keep me out of sight out of mind, and keep that same energy towards me. KTSE (keep the same energy) trust mine won't change, believe it!

So New Year was like, "It was basically curiosity that had her pulling up. That was the motive and nothing else, it was strictly curiosity. It was no more than not hearing from me in years and curiosity got the best of her." Thus, I briefly crossed her mind, but only out of curiosity, but that's it. He basically was like, I read too much into it. It wasn't out of love for me, loving me, concern for me, or concern for my well being for that matter or even missing me. None of those played a factor in why she pulled up on you or reached out. It was strictly curiosity, nothing more nothing less.

Don't give a damn about me clearly, it was evident. It didn't have anything to do with love for me, concern, or missing me. He was like, "That's what they do on the streets though, they get curious and when curiosity get the better of them they have to react, thus they'll tap in and then tap back out. But for sure, they'll pull up in that moment." It made perfect sense and makes perfect sense. That's basically what she'd done, tapped in and then tapped out once I responded to her and she felt she got what she needed from me she was good. It was back to program as usual. Her pulling up on me had nothing to do about nothing, nothing to do with sending a niggah no energy, communication, love or concern, all of that was irrelevant. It was clearly her bullshit ass being curious and wondering what I've been up to over the years and who I've been in communication with (SMH).

You were better off leaving shit as it was instead of getting me in my feelings. Now I see you for what as you really are, a bullshit ass bitch! When I last saw you, you were a kid so my thoughts about you were different, but you brought me from the illusion of you to reality and the reality is you suck and now you're dead to me. So yeah, she put a whole lot of energy into her curiosity. She went out of her way to seek me out too. I'm assuming it was through Inmate Locater, the site you can go on to find any inmates location in the California Department of Corrections (CDC). It had to be how she found me because no one had my current whereabouts, outside of the four I communicate with and she doesn't fuck with them.

She couldn't have gotten it from those I haven't been in communication with, outside of moms, my Aunt Mart, my son, or my cuzzo Nip. I've been off of the radar and doing a SHU program (segregated housing unit program). My son though, I just started communicating with him. Who I'd found through my counselor when I heard he was locked up and doing time in Corcoran. Outside of them, no one had my location, but it wasn't like they couldn't have gotten it. They could've gotten it the same way the bullshit bitch got it, didn't want it but will be quick to say "oh I never had your information" or "no one would give it to me", save that shit for someone who's trying to hear it!

I've been here since January 6th. I don't where else she could've gotten my location from, like I'd said she doesn't fuck with any of the people I'm in communication with nor do they fuck with her; so she couldn't have gotten it from anywhere else but there. Not only that but those I communicate with don't and wouldn't pass my information to anyone. If anything, they would let me know if someone was trying to holler, which I'd refuse, I'm good on all of that! You would definitely have to find your own route to holler if you're that adamant about contacting me.

So she had to get it by tapping into the site. He was also saying how those people out there aren't concerned about us in here, family etc. We're locked up, no longer a part of that society and dynamic, a non-entity. We're no use to them or what they have going on. This I've never been lost to. We can't help their cause or contribute to it. They're worried about what's going on with them in their world. Fuck you! You're not in that equation, you're out of sight, out of mind, dead and buried. Facts are they are, as those dynamics show them to be. You can close your eyes to the things you don't want to see but reality is what it is. They're not fucking with you. When you have and overstand that reality, you're no longer boxed in.

Accepting that reality for what and as it is, is your reality. That took me back to some dots and dashes I just received from my son a couple of daces ago. Just out of curiosity, I had to ask him had he heard from his brother Craig, my second oldest son, or their mother. He was basically like, "Nah pops, I don't hear from either of them. They don't write me, or check up on me", verbatim (SMH). He was like, "I only deal with them when I'm out there with them, otherwise it's not beuno!" Yeah, typical, out of sight, out of mind shit; as was suspected but checking is never cheating.

In my mind though, for some reason it, it played out much differently. I really don't see how though, knowing what it is and what I know to be true. In here, raw and uncut, we're no longer factors nor do we matter or count, which is shown time and time again by their actions towards us when it's all said and done. It's universal; you don't have to go through it to overstand it. Just as yard life is universal you don't have to be on the yard to overstand what's going on, on the yard. It's just the reality of it when you're locked up. It's easy to close the door on what was, comes easy as breathing, because the interest and dynamics of the relationship has changed, whether dealing with homies, family (so-called), and bitches.

Same thing on the yard, the interest and dynamics change, the relationship change. Its how things move, they're temporary anyway. It's good until it's not. You'll, no doubt, see the real come to light. It's good until something comes up, you'll no doubt see the real. How you choose to deal with it, you choose to deal with it trying to make sense of it all. Me personally, I'm good with how it all played out but I accept it for what and as it is. Outside of those I communicate and deal with, the rest can keep me buried, leave me buried. I'm cool without being dug up, let me rest in peace! As I've been doing and without you, amongst the worms and maggots. I've accepted the reality, my reality of doing and being me, as only I do and as only I can.

I don't have any problem with not being fucked with, believe me, I don't. As I've said and have stressed, continue doing and being you and living your life as you've been. I'm no doubt going to do the same. For the record though, your curiosity is an illusion. One I can do without, but don't let it bother you. My solution or remedy for that is to no longer accept mail from anyone I haven't been communicating with. All mail, moving forward, will be refused and sent back. I'm not accepting it, period. Now their buried and I've really given them an excuse. Run with it! He's not accepting communication from anyone. Yeah, that part! I'm no longer entertaining their curiosity. Whaaat! It's a done deal.

Sometimes you have to redefine your space and position and move into the passing lane. Every lane though isn't a passing lane. I don't seek anyone out in no fashion, shape, or form. It was never had to find Tic, if that's truly your intent, trying to have a relationship, to be a presence or to have one. I was never hard to find. I've been where I've been for 17 years. You can't go far enough, to alley my doubts about your motive or intent. I will say trials and disappointments does test one's character and strengthen it.

Playing devil's advocate, can I really hold you accountable when I don't know you? Really, I don't, we're strangers. You're actually a stranger, and we are strangers to each other. I don't know you, you don't know me, it has been 17 years. So being strangers, why would you want to communicate with me or fuck with me? Let alone give me a time of day. Someone told me my view was distorted, but you know what, I've never given it much thought. As it pertains to how I see yard life or situations outside of it, I navigate as I do and keep moving. My approach to dealing with either is just that, my approach as far as I'm concerned.

Intelligence and tact will sustain you but panic diplomacy will fuck over you. Most importantly, you have to know the difference between reality and fiction, and fiction has to be credible. Do know this as well, anytime you step out of your element, shits going to go crooked or sideways. This prison shit, this yard life shit, it's not a game with the cards facing down (get a bar). It's a harsh and cruel existence on many levels. You get no mercy, don't care who you are, don't care about your economical or social status, don't care about your politics, who you know, or where you're from. It's everything to defend, even more to lose, in a crowded world such as this. An atmosphere of a routine life on the yard conform to the moods, adapt to the navigation, and play along with whatever's sent your way.

I feel, again, it's not what you do but how you do it. I know you've probably noticed how there hadn't been much talk about the yard since speaking on the incident with Chumlee. Since then though, we've been shut down and on modified lockdown due to the pandemic. Covid-19 hit our yard. They brought a bunch of infected inmates from off of B yard and placed them on our yard quarantining them, clearing out two buildings, 7 and 8, putting those inmates removed in different buildings. That's how New Year became my cellie, he was in 8-building. They put inmates in 5-building, sent some to C-yard and sent some to the lower yard. There's been no outside movement, no yard, no medical (came to building unless priority), no canteen or no packages.

No phone calls, nothing, shutdown! Then things eased up to where we're now getting phone calls. One cell at a time allowed out, we're getting showers every other day, it started off every other three days. Still no yard though, medical's till coming into the building. They started canteen too, bagging and dragging it, canteen being brought directly to the building, inmates come out of their cells and walk to the rotunda/hallway to sign for it. That stopped and now supposedly it's back, a go. It's been like three weeks now, since those sick inmates landed on our yard. It's been an outbreak, a boom in cases. It's hit several inmates in our building and in our section. Inshallah, God willing, it doesn't get me.

More and more inmates on the yard including the police are getting infected. As of the other day, they made 1-building on the lower yard a quarantine building, so now 7, 8, and 1-building are quarantine buildings for infected inmates (SMH) but you better believe if we weren't on lockdown something would be going on. It's daily life and existence. Not to say anything isn't going on, because kites are being flown throughout individual buildings internally, from section to section, no doubt. Now depending on how serious things are, you could see the effect once the yards opens back up and it's fully functioning. It wouldn't be the yard if it didn't.

This Covid-19 has shook this yard up, this yard and every other yard with a spike in cases. Before they brought those infected inmates to our yard we had no cases, non period. Watching the news in the earlier stages and days, Lassen County, which is the county High Desert is in (Susanville), were showing zero cases for months, while surrounding counties were going up in cases daily. Lassen stayed zero for awhile, month after month. Then a case or two popped up. Now at this current time, it's 300 plus cases and those numbers are being added because of the cases here at High Desert.

Due in part because High Desert is part of Lassen County though, these inmates aren't a part of the community. They're a part of a prison population that's in Susanville, which in turn makes them a part of the community. For a while they had nurses coming around the building doing temperature checks. It went from once a day to twice a day, once in the morning to once at night. It went from that to zero. We haven't seen those nurses now for like five days and counting. Since being on lockdown we've been tested twice. In my mind though, why would you bring those out break monkeys to another yard where there were no infections when you could've removed those uninfected and sent them somewhere else and kept it contained to that one location, but in my mind though.

From my overstanding, it all stemmed from San Quentin having a lot of cases and the order was for them to release or remove them, inmate population, from the prison. Basically shut it down. We know that wasn't happening. The staff there too were getting infected. Of course they weren't going to release anyone, so what did they do? Just moved inmates around the system (CDCR) to other prisons, which basically created another problem that didn't fix the problem, it just added to it. But in my mind, only in my mind though, I didn't see a solution but a temporarily one, which in the end will have done more harm than good. In theory it was a good idea, only in theory though in my mind.

Somewhere between supposed to and want to exist, again in my mind. A few days ago I received the plea forms via legal mail from lawyer, Tiffany, to go over initial sign, date, and put in traffic (mail them back). I got it done, read what I needed to read, initialed it where I needed to, signed and dated everything, and sent it back that same day I got them, they were back in traffic that night. Now, all I'm waiting for is the conference call we should be having before my actual court date via video. With everything currently going on and how things are playing out around here, it's hard to say what's going to take place.

Things are constantly changing on a daily basis and from one thing to the next. This can happen but that can't happen, this can go on but that can't go on. Then it's like this, this is allowed but this isn't! Everything up in the air and is being played by ear from what I'm seeing and hearing. That's CDCR anyway, unpredictability, it's the norm on the regular. You learn to adapt and just move with the flow of traffic. What else can you really do? Ask yourself this too, what aspect of a situation do you have control over when it comes to CDCR? You have none, what's going on will go on, period.

If they say there's no yard today, there's no yard today. You can bitch and complain all you want, that's just facts. That applies to anything else they so no to. Cry and bitch all you want, it changes nothing, especially the facts. If they say today you can have something but tomorrow you can't, that's just what it is. They can care less about your crying and bitching. The general consensus is "So what, deal with it!" What else can you do but deal with it? All of that, what they can and can't do, let me say this, they're going to do what they want to do at the end of the day. As they'll tell you, "If you don't like it, write it up!" or the classic, "Put it on paper!" (602 inmate complaint form), and depending on how it's written or what the contents are it may disappear.

It may get thrown away, it may get lost in between channels or levels. There's all type of variables that may play out with a 602, again no control, facts. I may have the conference call, I may not, at this point who's to say. It's out of my control. I have like 14 days though, before my court date. Even with the shit going on, on the streets with the pandemic my court dates could possibly be pushed back. It may not even happen. That's a possibility, as with CDCR saying it has to be pushed back and rescheduled because they don't want inmates out at this time due to the rapid cases of Covid-19. Who's to say how it's going to play out. It's a guessing game. I'm cocked and loaded though, ready to go, I'm just ready to get this case wrapped up. I'm just so over it. It's time to be done with it. I honestly didn't think they would pick it up based on my having a life already. It did come as a surprise and a shock that they would even waste their energy or time on it, especially with my time that I have. I'm a lifer already, damn! What more can you really do to me though? Add a couple of more years to my sentence or three.

Apparently though, they felt it was worth their energy and time. The time I already have didn't matter, obviously. Tiffany said the same thing, "With all of the time you have, I don't see why they would've even bothered." Facts remain they did bother and booked me. Solano County picks up everything from what I'm seeing and your current time doesn't matter, not even considered a factor. Nor does it play a deciding factor in prosecuting the case. Basically, they just want the conviction whether they get a plea or if you decide to fight it out with them and go to trial. If I felt I had win I would've took it to trial and fought it, but it was too much stacked against me. I wasn't going to waste my time and energy on a lost cause. There were multiple witnesses, they had surveillance footage (cameras were on the yard), and they had the weapon. To think I could win that fight I had to be mentally challenged or crazy as hell.

I would've had to have been on dope and dynamite to think I would beat that case. I had little to nothing going in my favor and everything going against me. "Nah, I wasn't even going to horse play or play that game!" I just decided to take my lumps and accept my L (loss). Sometimes it is what it is, you have to accept your L's and move on. They do happen, and they will happen. You can only do what's right for you and what's in your best interest. It's no different than knowing which bridge to cross or which one to burn. It's your decision, and if you're good with it and can live with it, so be it. Who am I to say otherwise? I'm good though, with every choice and decision I make, as it regards me and my walk on the line. The one's I've made are the ones I was sure I could live with.

From who I've aligned myself with to how I walk and move on these yards to how I program, I feel I've done it and do it effectively. I pretty much stay away from the bullshit and the bullshit dudes. Whatever drama comes my way I deal with it as I deal with any and everything else, one way and that's the right way. If it can be helped, I try not to draw anyone else in, but sometimes that choice isn't yours to make. The circumstances can play a role in the outcome; yard life is funny that way. For the most part I'm out of the way, because I'm allergic to the feathers of most of the bird-ass Niggahs walking around. But yeah, what you know is different from what you know, and the latter comes only from the lessons painful or otherwise. Being on any yard you're no doubt faced with many choices and many decisions that has to be made at some point, and often times we tend to mess with the individuals we mess with who can help us stay focused and make the right ones.

But shit, even they need somebody to mess with because try as we might, it's impossible for any of imperfect individuals to have a perfect perspective. None of us really have all of the answers. Sometimes the reality of yard life interrupts, causes interruptions, so the checks and balances are very necessary. Sometimes we're going to feel like, in these battles, we're losing on most fronts based on the family discord, setbacks, yard drama, and the like. It's just the reality we're faced with. It's a new era, a new breed and different mindsets. Fucked up situations can put a pessimistic spin on the way we look at shit. As far as our view and view those we're interacting with, regardless of the level of interaction. Yeah, you're going to be in your feelings. You're going to be disappointed.

You're going to be lied to; games are going to be played. You're going to have frustrations. There's going to be confrontation and disagreements, it's facts. Now, how you choose to deal and cope, it's entirely up to you. It's rooted in your decisions and choices you make as it pertains to your navigation. It's your dynamic to change, that's the take away and what should resonate, regardless of the complexity and we know yard life is complex as with the different relationships we have with those, both inside and out. The aspects might change, but not the essence. I'm still the same dude, I just have a different mentality. A lot of my values, morals, standards, and principles are the same. It's just my mentality is different. So my case is completed. I'm just waiting for my paper work from proceedings, which I still haven't received yet. It was done 12/17/2020, but here it is 1/14/2021. I'm getting a letter from the county of Solano

Probation Department telling me that I was to be advised, that based upon a change in law pursuant to Proposition 63 all persons convicted of felonies and qualifying misdemeanors are now required to compete the Prohibited Persons Relinquishment Forms (PPRF's).

Advising whether I own or possess any registered fire arms, ammunition, or ammunition feeding devices, and based upon my qualifying conviction in my case, I was being sent these PPRF forms for me to complete and highlighted the sections I'll need to complete. I'm like whaaat! This is is stupid. Why would you send me some shit like this and I have life. Not only that, where the hell am I going to get some damn guns and bullets from (SMH). Me and Lon and a dude we call the Black Captain Jack Sparrow were speaking on 2Pac's music on the yard today. I was telling them the only Pac music I fuck with is Makaveli, All Eyes On Me, Me Against The World, Strictly 4 My Niggaz, Thug Life, and 2Pacalypse Now.

All of that other bullshit after his death Deathrow Records and his moms put out, I was straight on it. I couldn't and wouldn't support it. They just threw shit together and had a lot of his enemies on tracks with him, Niggahs we know had he been alive he wouldn't fucked with them. I'm an avid Pac fan. I wouldn't and couldn't support anything put out there after his death, it was a money grab. It wasn't about the music or preserving his legacy, for them it was all about the loot. They put out music wasn't meant to be released. He would've released it himself long ago in my opinion if he intended on putting it out.

Best of 2Pact part 1-Thug, ah nope! Best of 2Pac part 2-Life, ah nope! Better Dayz, ah nope! 2Pac Greatest Hits, nope! Loyal To The Game, ah nope! Pac's Life, nope! Ru Still Down, nope! Rose That Grew From Concrete, nope! Until The End Of Time, ah nope! And anything else that was put out after he died, ah nope! We even got into who we thought Pac would've done music with or fucked with had he still been alive today. I was debatable, but off the dribble I'm like he wouldn't have fucked with Bad Boy, nobody out of that camp, Jarule, or Murder Inc, Dr Dre, or nobody out of his Aftermath Camp, Jay-z and Nas. He still would've been shitting on them and Mobb Deep, Deathrow would've been in his rear view.

I think He would've messed with T.I. and BG, BG after Cashmoney). I don't think he would've messed with Cashmoney or No Limit. I want to say he would've messed with Jeezy and maybe a few other dudes, but outside of the he wouldn't been on dudes. The Black Captain Jack Sparrow didn't agree. But then too you have to think a lot of dudes wouldn't existed while he was alive, especially those who imitated him when he died. It made a lane for dudes to pass in. Today Ace Capone made it to our side of the yard since an incident happened with him. He had been hit with a tray and had a cut over his right eye, which he showed me. A Damu had dope fiend him, hit him from the blind. He told me his cut was leaking, bleeding pretty bad. He had went to the sand box and stayed for four days, then came back to the yard.

The day it happened our program was shut down for the remainder of the day. Later that night, J Smash had came through and hollered at me and Lon letting us know what had happened. Smash was like, "Yeah homie, I had to come and do my due diligence, based on." The issue was over at that point so it was said, but based on the dynamics of the situation being Crip and Blood you still had to be aware and alert. Just it being a Crip and Blood issue, it could've easily went sideways and blew the yard up. The homie came himself though, as I was saying and pretty much gave me the whole script. He was like, "The shits squashed, but I wanted you to hear it from me."

I asked him what happened, basically he was like, "Dude was on some P.C. shit and he ain't worth wrecking homies (Crips) over", which he was told by other Crip homies, dude isn't worth blowing up the program. Then we switched lanes about him doing some self reflecting as far as him and his program, realizing he needed to make some changes. He realized he was fucking up and needed to get his shit together, also recognizing the fact he's not perfect like none of us are and he's still learning though. He's been down ten years. Me and the homie chopped it up for a cool minute before he had to go back to the lower yard. It was actually the second time me and the homie really had a chance to talk, he's a good guy. He just has to figure some things out as he's still navigating his way through this life.

Right after he left the yard, I made my way back to the Black area. Later that night there was an issue in 5-building, where Crip homies had to get on one of their homies for disrespecting the South Siders; well a South Sider which wasn't the first time so I guess it came to that point where it has to be dealt with. So to avoid a bigger problem it was. What the disrespect was it depends on who you hear it from, but at the end of the day it was crazy because homie was suuuper short to the house (SMH). Yeah, that's just crazy to me, short to the house, found yourself getting DP'ed and then sent to C-yard where everything is sent after getting whupped off this yard. Some dudes just don't get it and won't get it (SMH).

Something just happened, we're on lock down. It happened on C-yard. We got up this morning and it was like we might be on lock down but it's undecided at this point, but we're being cell fed. Whatever went down it had to be serious. The police are being tight lipped, so I knew it was something racial off the dribble. I asked the police was it short of staff. I used that because that had been going on as of late. For some reason we're not getting yard and it's because we're short of staff. That's their go to excuse when we're getting fucked out of our program "Short of staff!" The police was too quick with his answer, "Yeah!". . . Um . . . No! I knew for sure it was something going on at that point. That "Yeah" was the throw off, only I wasn't thrown off.

So when we finally hi the yard you could feel the tension in the air, and you could tell by the movements and actions of everyone. Me and Lon stuck to our program, greeted everyone and headed to the slab but we're on alert as always and aware of our surroundings. It was whatever. We find out it was in fact some racial shit that had went down on C-yard. A South Sider had hung the phone up on a Black and the Black handled his business taking flight. The shit went ugly after that. Not only was it just four Blacks in the dayroom but they were flighted by the Rainbow Coalition: the South Siders, the Northerners, and the Whites. In all of my years of doing time, this was unheard of and definitely a new twist of events. That incident alone opened my eyes to a lot.

The issue was spoken on and the consensus was that it happened on that yard, let it stay on that yard. It's not even summer yet. It's only May and it got active in 5-building, a four on four melee between the Crips and Bay Area happened, so of course we're on lockdown. There's no movement and no activity of no kind at the moment and we were cell fed for breakfast. It happened last night at dayroom. As of right now, no one knows what actually happened. We just know we're on lock down. We'll know soon enough though; know, not know, dudes are on point. Yeah, shit's starting to heat up and summer isn't even here. Our Building ended up going to the yard and though tension was in the air, didn't anything happen. You could feel the tension when it's all said and done. It didn't happen in our building anyway.

The police basically done a temperature check, but the temperature check was with the wrong building. It should've been with 5-building if any checking was going on. Where it happened at, it didn't happen in 6. Word was though, it was behind the damn phone, that was the gist of it. Somebody was on somebody else's phone time (SMH). A couple of weeks after that happened, it was something else. It went quiet for a minute, and then the dayroom goes down due to an alarm in another building. I'm in the cell, we (top tier) didn't have dayroom, of course though I looked out of my cell door. A couple of hours later, after the program was over, the building police comes to my door asking me was it cool for Peacock to move in with me. I'm like, without hesitation, "Yeah for sho, it's cool!" The move was put in around 8 something at night. The police brought his name and picture tag putting it on the wall by the door. He still hadn't came though. Then 9 rolls around, I get at the police like, "What's up with the move?" They told me not to worry about it, he wasn't coming. Why? Couldn't say, didn't know, that was on a Friday. The police locked us down Saturday and Sunday, behind the incident with the homie. Come to find out though Monday, it was Ace and another young homie who had gotten into it, but Ace had also gotten into a situation with the police supposedly swinging on them. It was all type of shit being said, clarity was never gotten as to the incident.

We hadn't had yard so I couldn't get the full script and what I was getting came from dudes other than homies. I needed to get it from homies. Just as we were about to get yard the following day another incident happens (SMH) I'm like, "Damn, I'm not ever going to get to see what went on with the homie Ace." We go on lock down on another Friday night. The alarm goes off, again I'm in the cell. It isn't top tier day room. "GEEETTTT DOOOWWWN!" I go to the cell door and look out. I see the homie Poke sitting on the bench and a few South Siders sitting at their table. I look into the rotunda and could see a lot of police running Towards C-Section. A few seconds later, I could see some scuffling and fast movement, but couldn't see who the scuffling was with. From the legs though, it appeared to be a Hispanics or light complected Black. Come to find out though, it was a Black. He had gotten into it with our building police, which drew in a couple of other Blacks. All behind a phone call a dude wasn't even suppose to get, being as though he was A2-B. Dudes lost a lot of shit from that search, behind that foolishness

You think that was crazy, they doubled back on us and searched the building. Again, we never made it off of the lock own. I was sitting in the cell laughing at these dudes crying and whining about the lockdown and asking the police every other day if not every day, "When are we coming off, how much longer is it going to be?" I even heard the police pass my cell saying how dudes couldn't handle this little bullshit lockdown and how it wasn't nothing. I totally agree. I wasn't nothing and bullshit! I can recall a time (90's) where we were going six, seven, and eight month lock downs easy, come off for a month and go right back on for another six to eight months, the longest was a year. No canteen, no packages, no nothing! They've changed the rules since those days, now it's 10 to 14 days at a time. This generation isn't equipped, can't do cell time. The walls start closing in on them and talking to them (SMH). That's why it was changed. It became a mental health concern. You're even allowed T.V.'s and radios in the sandbox. That was not happening in the 90's, you better grab a book to read, write a letter, or work out and lay your ass down somewhere and that was that. So yeah, after being solo for months, I finally get a homie from the set, Lil Crip Cal from Babyz.

Come to find out, he's two of my childhood friends' son, Baldie's and Casta's, which came as a surprise. I never even knew they liked each other. We all grew up around each other and played together as kids. He lived around the corner on Lemon across the street from Kings Park and she stayed next door to me. Remember, I hung out with her older brothers Punkin and William. Cal has features of his pops but look more like his mama's side. To me he looks more like his mama and his Uncle William. Since we've been cellies we've been chopping it up. He's filled me in on a lot that has been going on with homies and with what's been going on in the L.A. County Jail for the past six years.

He was pretty much telling me how the county has changed a lot, even with the relationship with the Hispanics, which I couldn't believe. Hanging out together, eating together, gambling together, yeah a lot has changed. On the gang scale though, he was telling me how the Brick Boys and 80's were running with the Neighborhoods, and how a lot of shenanigans were going on. The 20's were participating as well with the shenanigans; though he was trying to keep shit strictly LBV. It was ugly, ball was being played. He was telling me he played ball and ball was played on him.

He came a few days before his born day and we got it in (celebrated it). We ate, me, him and Lon had some reggie and blew. Yeah, had the homie hugging that toilet, had his young ass White boy wasted. A born day he'll never forget. He came with a lot of time (life) and with a little points, his whole thing is to try and lay low so e can get off of this island. It can happen, depending on how you program. It's not hard to stay out of the way if you're a stay out of the way type dude. For the most part, we're all trying to get off of this island. High Desert is not cool. It's fucked up and nothing is going on here. There's no programs, no jobs, you're just here. Idle time on your hands is a setup to fail, you'll never leave here. It's how it's designed. With that, forgive me for my brash delivery but I'm just remembering vividly!

I feel I've shamed enough about yard life, as only I could and hopefully without depreciating the value. As it's been said, why decorate an expensive watch with cloudy diamonds (bullshit). It's already expensive, why over do it. Those will only what? Depreciate the value. I truly hope though you've enjoyed this journey thoroughly that I've took you on with me and hopefully my reach exceeded my grasp, exceeded my grasp as I've navigated you through the maze and depths of my thoughts. For it was my intent to bring about something natural and sudden to you, to help you overstand yard life for what and as it is, through my lenses.

The lens for looking at things in terms of my surroundings and as thorough as I could possibly be; I know there's a deep curiosity that exist in the civilian world, so I had to make an attempt to satisfy that curiosity and thirst for knowledge and overstanding as only I could make that attempt as vivid, gritty, and raw as I could, as uncut as I could. My attitude from the onset was if I'm going to give it to you I'm going to give it to you. I couldn't see doing it any other way, or giving it to you any other way. This, in my opinion, is where you're going to get the best version of that, hands down.

I had to hold you down (give it to you real), and in my way I didn't want you to have to decipher anything for the most part. I know how some things can be translated. I wanted to give you a real look, a clear look, a real feel of what is was to be on a yard, walking on the main line and dealing with the many obstacles and different challenges that we're faced with even with the yard life being filled with inconveniences and plans being constantly stagnated by forces beyond our control; how these checks and balances came into play. No matter what, I believe in good, I believe in bad, I believe in ups and downs, right and wrong.

It was very important for me to know that there was room for everything, as I'm living under distressing times. Though the state of yard life has me setting the timer of my temperament, navigating through the maze, my goal was to do this well and as long as it was done well I know I've fulfilled my objective, which was to have you feel it and overstand it. I want to you thank and appreciate you whole heartedly for your energy and support. Thank you for allowing me to share with you these in depth paragraphs, introducing you to yard life, which derived from my walk that I'm still currently walking with my life sentence, that I did my best to compose with these various combinations of words to describe it extensively. I also want to thank you for choosing "Yard Life" as your guide to get knowledge and better overstanding of that in which you sought, in terms of information as it pertains to this maze of unbalanced madness we call "Yard Life".

Lastly, thank you for your time and patience it took for you to get through these pages to acknowledge this invitation of enlightenment put to paper.

Sincerely,

"SoDo"

In Closing

You know who you are, there's no need for you to respond to my thoughts or feelings towards you, because I have no plans or desire to communicate with you by no means. So with that you can keep it moving and continue doing and being you, your best you! I truly wish you all the best and a happy and progressive life.

Be on the lookout for the following projects:

"Feelin Some Type of Way" and "Yard Life (Expose Real Life Inside of Prison) Second revised Edition"
I grabbed a pad and pen, scribbled a few lines about life in prison, walking on different yards, where stories get twisted. . .
Politics in full effect, homies is witching, conversating with the wrong man, sparks attention, the transition. . .
See where the odds land, testing heat in the kitchen. It's making no sense, still screaming in prison. . .
Killing his lungs and kidneys, moving on convicts, dudes is shifty. Fuck friends, my enemies get me. . .
Drama spread like cancer, walks is iffy, life fans. Imagination on fifty, such a calamity, homies is drifting. . .
Fitting dudes with jackets, minds fried to crispy, mama said he would panic, falling short of a witness. . .
Separating, the real from the fake, putting effort on distance, for the sake, of conversating, lines and visions. . .
"I.I.P." (Insanes In Peace)
Big Touche, Big Ant Dog, Lil Bullet, Baby Bullet, Big Nick Dog, Tiny Tic, Big Sinbad, the home girl Reppy, Big Fruity, Big Ace Capone, and the rest of the homies that left the set and the city way too soon... 3's!!!

OUTRODUCTION

Salutes

In conclusion, I salute everyone who's walked these lines (yards) past and present, especially on these level 4 yards and continue to do so with morals and values and who refuse to compromise them on their integrity. I salute those who keep it and kept it shitty, but fair and not succumbing to the pressures of peers and their dirty play, overstanding the dynamics of this walk, taking a position and standing firmly by it. I salute those for not condoning the bad conduct or being a contributor of it, yet embracing all that's threw at you or have been thrown at you, never folding or faltering; for being outspoken when you needed to be in your push for the truth of a situation, moving on that very vibe of a combination of seen, thought, learned or felt which propels you, for not being a victim of autobotism, for remaining vigilant and relentless as you navigate your way through the maze as we know it to be. In this yard life, I salute you!

I salute you for overstanding how not to alienate yourself with words that's anti-productive to your agenda and being mindful of the struggles and being fully engaged, lastly for being selfless and stepping up when sacrifices is needed, doing it without thought or a thought to pass the buck. We like noise though, when it's on our term and when it's imposed on us. I appreciate your time, energy, and patience. You've took venturing into my "Yard Life" journey and as it is with me, allowing me to illuminate and expose my space. As I've reflected coming as easily to me as it had based on my intent on being what it was, being just enough to keep shit interesting, varying the formula as I journeyed into the opulence of my thoughts. I salute you. I graciously salute you for your support both inside and outside supporters. I had to send my salutes, best wishes, and prayers.

Prayer

Allah, I ask that you cover me, my loved ones, my other, my father, my kids, my aunt Martha, my uncle Johnny (RIP), my cousins Chris Sr., and my supporters with your blood and armor. Shield and protect us all from evil and danger that lurks as we sleep, so that in your blessings and through your blessings, we see and live yet another day in your world. In your name I offer this prayer.

Amen!

I enjoyed writing about life, sharing the stories and experiences as they are and were with me during the many phases. That hopefully brought satisfaction to you, the reader. For me, it's a channel of expression. If I got a point across that makes/made one person rethink the wrong move they might've decided to make, then me writing this book has served its purpose and paid off. To you who gave me feedback, cheered me on, and supported the struggle, many salutes! Be on the lookout for the revised and second expanded edition.